W9-AKY-789

Dictionary of Central Asian Islamic Terms

Allen J. Frank
Jahangir Mamatov

Dictionary of Central Asian Islamic Terms

Allen J. Frank
Jahangir Mamatov

2002
Dunwoody Press

Dictionary of Central Asian Islamic Terms

All inquiries should be directed to:
Dunwoody Press
6564 Loisdale Ct, Suite 800
Springfield, VA 22150
USA

ISBN: 1-881265-88-9
Library of Congress Catalog Card Number: 2002111215
Printed and Bound in the United States of America

Table of Contents

Acknowledgments I

Introduction III

What is an Islamic term? IV

Sources V

Central Asia VI

Sources (graphic and audio) VII

General Sources: VII
Bashkir Sources: VII
Karakalpak Sources: VII
Kazakh Sources: VII
Kyrgyz Sources: VIII
Tajik Sources: VIII
Tatar Sources: VIII
Turkmen Sources: IX
Uyghur Sources: IX
Uzbek Sources: IX

Abbreviations X

Indexes:

Pronunciation i
Arabic xxi
Bashkir xli
Karakalpak li
Kazakh lxvii
Kyrgyz lxxix
Tajik lxxxix
Tatar cvii
Turkmen cxxv
Uyghur cxxxv
Uzbek cxlix
Uzbek Latin clxix
Subjects clxxxix

The Dictionary 1

Acknowledgments

The authors wish to thank the staff of McNeil Technologies, in Hyattsville, Maryland, for their enthusiastic support over the course of this project, particularly Dr. Elizabeth Bergman, Tom Creamer, Alan Downing, Aung Kyaw Oo, Zeeya Pashtoon, Stephen Poulos, and Mustafa Sayd.

Allen J. Frank
Jahangir Mamatov
Hyattsville, Maryland
August, 2002

Introduction

This dictionary owes its existence to several features evident in the development of Central Asian languages over the course of the twentieth century. The first feature is the development of vernacular "national" languages, to a large degree created by Soviet academic establishments both in the ethnic republics and in Moscow. Beginning in the 1920's these formalized vernacular languages, declared to exist for each of the titular ethnic republics, supplanted existing and more or less standardized classical languages of Islamic scholarship and discourse, namely, Persian, Arabic, and Turki, also known as Chaghatay. As Soviet lexicographers codified and established languages for the respective Central Asian republics, they not only formalized literary norms in grammar and lexicons, but also consciously excluded vocabulary believed to be obsolete or irrelevant.

Thus, another feature of Soviet Central Asian lexicography was the minimal inclusion of Islamic terminology in these dictionaries, which form the lexicographic foundation for all modern Central Asian languages. As a result of Soviet ideological dogma, the bulk of Islamic terms were excluded from these dictionaries, and those that were included were often labeled "obsolete" or were given erroneous or misleading definitions. Most dictionaries of the Central Asian languages produced in the West have themselves in large part been translations of earlier Russian or monolingual dictionaries, and for various reasons have offered little in the way of an expanded treatment of Islamic terms.

It should be added that the modern Uyghur literary language evolved under very similar circumstances, albeit under the aegis of the Chinese Communist Party, which differed little from the Communist Party of the Soviet Union in its evaluation of religion and its general lexicographic approaches to documenting "minority" languages. As a result, the standardization of the modern Uyghur literary language followed largely the same patterns as the Soviet Central Asian languages.

Since the collapse of the Soviet Union, Islamic institutions and Islamic discourse have been reestablishing themselves throughout the Muslim regions of the former Soviet Union. Both Westerners seeking to read Central Asian Islamic texts, as well as Central Asians themselves, are lacking basic lexicographic resources to define an important body of vocabulary that is at best poorly documented in existing dictionaries. Thus, at a minimum, it is hoped this dictionary can serve as a supplement to the existing lexicographic corpus.

What is an Islamic term?

Identifying and documenting Islamic terminology is admittedly a subjective, and even prescriptive, task. Nevertheless, some explanation is in order as to the criteria by which Islamic terminology was identified, selected, and included in this dictionary. The authors first of all determined that words simply borrowed from Arabic, or in the case of the Turkic languages, from Persian as well, were not necessarily Islamic terms. Rather, terms relating specifically to Islamic concepts, Islamic ritual and law, technical terms relating to hadith, hajj, philosophy, Sufism, hagiolatry, and pilgrimage, as well as proper nouns relating to the names and epithets of God and the prophets, those relating to specific religious locales central to the Islamic faith as a whole, and the names of the suras of the Qur'an, were the central features of the Islamic terminology the authors sought to document. The authors expressly refrained from an encyclopedic approach, thereby avoiding very extensive definitions and leaving out the bulk of names and locales relating to Islamic history following the rule of the first four Caliphs. Readers who require a more detailed discussion of a given term can consult an encyclopedia, such as the various editions of the Encyclopedia of Islam. In short, the compilers did not seek to use Central Asian Islamic terminology to exclusively define what is Islamic, but rather sought to *inclusively* determine what *can* be considered Islamic terminology in the Central Asian languages.

Another principle underlying the documentation of Islamic terms is the emphasis on a common and shared Islamic vocabulary among the modern Central Asian languages. To be sure, the Islamic vocabulary of each Central Asian language is a unique phenomenon, and it is hoped this dictionary encourages the examination of Islamic terminology on a regional level as well as for each language individually, both historically and in terms of current usage. While the structure of this dictionary documents the semantic variance of some specific terms across region, nevertheless, it is hoped that this dictionary can at least partially establish the survival of a common Islamic vocabulary among Central Asians through the Soviet era. As a result, each entry appears in a classical Arabic-script spelling (as it would appear in Chaghatay or Persian), a standard romanized transcription (without diacritics), and a common definition. The cognate forms (or occasionally the semantic equivalents) in the modern languages appear underneath, with accompanying variants in the common definitions where applicable.

Sources

The dictionary is based entirely on verifiable sources. The authors expressly avoided "reconstructing" terms, and only included vernacular forms that appeared in graphic or audio texts or that could be corroborated by native speakers. Native speakers were extensively consulted for Uzbek, Tajik, Karakalpak, and Uyghur terms. In addition to the admittedly inadequate Soviet dictionaries—although the treatment of Islamic terms in Soviet dictionaries varies widely by language and deserves a study in its own right—the authors made use of a large body of published materials. This included popular Islamic dictionaries, educational literature about Islam, hagiographic pamphlets, calendar books, explanations of Islamic legal principles, and collections of legends concerning prophets. Another important source was vernacular translations of the Qur'an. The authors had access to complete Uzbek, Tajik, Kazakh, and Uyghur translations of the Qur'an. The authors also made use of literature produced by Uzbek and Tajik Islamic opposition groups, including leaflets and press releases, but also audio cassettes of sermons and recordings of press interviews. While the corpus of materials was far from exhaustive, given the volume of Islamic publishing in Central Asia, the authors are confident it is a sufficiently representative corpus. Nevertheless, the sources for some languages remain better than others as the volume (and availability) of religious publishing varies widely among the nine vernacular languages covered in this dictionary.

The user should be made aware that the Islamic terminology, as it appears in the sources, displays a great variety of spellings and even semantic values. The absence of most Islamic terms in Soviet-era dictionaries makes such a situation inevitable. However, it is also important to realize that the educational levels of the authors of these Islamic texts vary widely as well. Some are well-educated Islamic scholars who are conversant both in the Islamic terminology and may or may not be equally at ease in their vernacular literary languages. Others have no Islamic education at all or are the exclusive product of the Soviet education system. Indeed, many "specialists" on Islam who have emerged since 1990 had in Soviet times been "specialists" on Scientific Atheism and the authors of anti-religious treatises, in which understanding the fine points of Islamic religious practice or terminology was, to say the least, not required. The immediate result, then, is a wide variation in spellings and, occasionally, in definitions as well.

Central Asia

A note is also in order regarding the definition of Central Asia. In defining this region the authors have in mind the accepted scholarly definition of Islamic Central Asia as a specific and unified historical and cultural region within the Islamic world at large. This region comprises the republics of Tajikistan, Uzbekistan, Kyrgyzstan, Kazakhstan, and Turkmenistan, plus the Xinjiang-Uyghur Autonomous Region of the People's Republic of China. Linguistically it comprises the respective titular literary languages of these republics, namely: Tajik, Uzbek, Kyrgyz, Kazakh, and Turkmen, as well as Karakalpak, the titular literary language of the Karakalpak Autonomous Republic in northwestern Uzbekistan.

Tatar and Bashkir have also been added to this dictionary, two languages spoken by Muslim nationalities residing in the Volga-Ural region of Russia, centered in the republics of Tatarstan and Bashkortostan. While the Volga-Ural region is itself a specific historical and cultural region within the Islamic world and is not, strictly speaking, part of Central Asia, these languages were included because of the Volga-Ural region's close ethnic, historical, and religious connections with Central Asia. As a particular region of the Islamic world, the Volga-Ural region's religious bonds with Central Asia are closer than with any other part of the Islamic world, and the development of virtually every aspect of Islamic culture in the Volga-Ural region, especially before 1917, can be directly linked to Central Asian models and institutions. Furthermore, since the mid 1980's Islamic publishing has been especially intense in the Tatar language throughout Russia.

Sources (graphic and audio)

General Sources:

Akhmet'ianov, R. G. *Obshchaia leksika dukhovnoi kul'tury narodov Srednego Povolzh'ia* (Moscow, 1981).

Budagov, Lazar. *Sravnitel'nyi slovar' turetsko-tatarskikh narcheii* I-II (St. Petersburg, 1869–1871).

Clauson, Sir Gerard. *An Etymological Dictionary of Pre-Thirteenth Century Turkish* (Oxford, 1972).

Cowan, L. J. M. (ed.). *The Hans Wehr Dictionary of Modern Written Arabic*, 3rd ed. (Ithaca, New York, 1976).

Hughes, Thomas Patrick. *Dictionary of Islam* (Chicago, 1994) [1st ed. 1887].

Netton, Ian Richard. *A Popular Dictionary of Islam* (Richmond, 1997).

Radlov, V. V. *Opyt slovaria tiurkskikh narechii* I-IV (St. Petersburg, 1893–1911).

Redhouse Turkish-English Dictionary, 3rd ed. (Istanbul, 1979).

Redhouse, Sir James W. A. *Turkish and English Lexicon* (Beirut, 1987) [1st ed. 1890].

Steingass, F. *A Comprehensive Persian-English Dictionary* (Beirut, 1975) [1st ed. 1892].

Superanskaia, A.V. *Spravochnik lichnykh imen narodov RSFSR*, 3rd ed. (Moscow, 1987).

Bashkir Sources:

Adhnagholov, R. Gh. *Bashqort teleneng orfografiya hüdhlege* (Ufa, 1998).

Bashkirsko-russkii slovar' (Moscow, 1958).

Bashkirsko-russkii slovar' (Moscow, 1996).

Bashqort teleneng hüdhlege I-II (Moscow, 1993).

Russko-Bashkirskii slovar' (Moscow, 1964).

Samsitova, L. Kh. *Realii bashkirskoi kul'tury* (Ufa, 1999).

Karakalpak Sources:

Baskakov, N. A. (ed.). *Karakalpaksko-russkii slovar'* (Moscow, 1958).

Qaraqalpaq tilining tüsindirme sözdigi I-IV (Nukus, 1986–1991).

Kazakh Sources:

Arïstanbab (Almaty, 1992).

Bekmukhametov, E. B. *Qazaq tilindegi arab-parsï sözderi* (Alma-Ata, 1977).

Bektaev, Qaldïbay (ed.). *Ülken qazaqsha-orïssha, orïssha-qazaqsha sözdik* (Almaty, 1999).

Ghuzïkhan, Aqpanbek. *Qazaqtardïng dünietanïmï*, (Almaty, 1993).

Ïsqaqov, A. (ed.). *Abay tili sözdigi* (Alma-Ata, 1968).

Krippes, Karl. *Kazakh (Qazaq)-English Dictionary* (Kensington, Maryland, 1994).

Makhmudov, Kh. and G. Musabaev. *Kazakhsko-russkii slovar'* (Alma-Ata, 1988).

Nurghaliev, R. N. (ed.). *Islam entsiklopediya* (Almaty, 1995).

Oraza Ait (pamphlet).

Qazaq tilining orfografiq sözdigi (Alma-Ata, 1988).

Qazaq tilining orfografiyalïq sözdigi (Almaty, 2001).

Qazaq tilining tüsindirme sözdigi I-X (Alma-Ata 1974–1986).

Qazaq tilining tüsindirme sözdigi I-X (Urumchi, 1989–1991).

Quran Kärim: Qazaqsha maghïna zhäne tüsinigi (Madina, 1991 AH).

Qurban Ait (pamphlet).

Russko-Kazakhskii slovar' (Moscow, 1954).

Russko-kazakhskii slovar' I-II (Alma-Ata, 1978–1981).

Tileuberdi, Nusipbay (ed.). *Qazaq tilining sözdigi* (Almaty, 2000).
Tutïbayev, Q. and O. Zholdïbayev. *Islam: qïsqacha angïqtamalïq* (Alma-Ata, 1998).
Zharmukhamedulï, Mukhamedrakhïm. *Qozha Akhmet Iasawi zhäne Türkistan* (Almaty, 1999).

Kyrgyz Sources:

Abdïllayev, E. et al. (eds.). *'Manas' eposunun sözdügü* (Bishkek, 1995).
Iudakhin K. K. (ed.). *Kirgizsko-russkii slovar'* (Moscow, 1965).
———. *Russko-kirguzskii slovar'* (Moscow, 1957).
Karasaev, Kh. K. *Orfografiyalïq sözdük* (Frunze, 1983).
———. *Özdöshtürülgön sözdör: sözdük* (Frunze, 1986).
Krippes, Karl. *Kyrgyz-English Dictionary* (Kensington, Maryland, 1998).
Maanaev, E. *Ateizm boyuncha terminderdin oruscha-qïrghïzcha sözdügü* (Frunze, 1969).
Urstanbekov, B. U. and T. K. Choroev. *Qïrghïz tarikhï: qïsqacha entsiklopediyalïq sözdük* (Frunze, 1990).

Tajik Sources:

Farhangi zaboni tojiki I-II (Moscow, 1969).
Odobi tahoratu namoz (Dushanbe, 1992).
Qur'oni Majid (Tehran, 1371).
Russko-Tadzhikskii slovar' (Moscow-Stalinabad, 1949).
Russko-tadzhikskii slovar' (Moscow, 1985).
Tadzhiksko-russkii slovar' (Moscow, 1954).

Tatar Sources:

Akhïrzaman (Kazan, n.d.).
Ghahednamä doghasï vä Doghai-khäbib kitabï (Kazan, 1998).
Ghaniev, F. A. *Tatarcha-ruscha süzlek*, 2nd ed. (Kazan, 1995).
Ghafurov, Mäjit. *Khäzräte räsülullah sallallahu ghaläyhi väsälläm vä dürt khälifä* (Ufa, 1991).
Imamov, Rail. *Khötbälär, väghazlär* (Kazan, 1995).
Idel buyïnda sufichïlïq: tarikhï häm üzenchileklare (Kazan, 2000).
"Iman shartï." *Idel* 12 (1990).
Khätem khuja häm dogha i khätem (Kazan, 1996).
Khabibullin, Z. I. *Namaz* (Moscow, n.d.).
Mäkhmütov, M. I. (ed.). *Gharäpchä-tatarcha-ruscha alïnmalar süzlege* I-II, 2nd ed. (Kazan, 1993).
Mäülüd (Kazan, n.d.).
Miras (Kazan 1991–1996).
Möslimi. *Tävarikhï bolghariya (Bolghar tarikhï)* (Kazan, 1999).
Nabiev, R. A. (ed.). *Tatarstan respublikasï: vöjdan irege häm dini berläshmälär* (Kazan, 2001).
Näsïykhäte-s-salikhin yaki izgelärneng näsïykhätläre (Kazan, 1996).
Nasïyrov, Räüf. *Zäynulla ishan* (Kazan, 2000).
Qadïyri, Zakir. *Khatïn-qïz mäs'äläse* (Ufa, 1991).
Qïsqacha din beleme turïnda ruscha häm tatarcha beleshmä-süzlek (Kazan, 2000).
Russko-Tatarskii slovar' I-IV (Kazan, 1955–1959).
Russko-tatarskii slovar' (Moscow, 1991).
Shäfighïy, Zahid (ed.). *Islam: beleshmä-süzlek*, 3rd edition (Kazan, 1993).
Shifalï doghalar (isme äghzam doghasï, Allah Täghaläneng meng dä ber iseme) (Kazan, 1996).
Sibghatullina, Älfinä. *Ilahi ghashïyqlar yulïnnan* (Kazan, 1999).
Tatar möselman kalendare 1994 (Kazan, 1993).

Tatar möselman kalendare 1997 (Kazan, 1996).
Tatar möselman kalendare 2002 (Kazan, 2001).
Tatar teleneng anglatmalï süzlege I-III (Kazan, 1977–1981).
Tatarsko-russkii slovar' (Moscow, 1966).
Yakhin, Farit (ed.). *Islam dine nigezläre* (Kazan, 1997).
———. *Päyghambärlär tarikhï* (Kazan, 1992).
Zäynullin, J. G. *Shärïq alïnmalar süzlege* (Kazan, 1994).

Turkmen Sources:

Abdïyev, Shöhrat. *Köneurgench rovayatlarï* (Ashgabat, 1993).
Ata Akhun. *Musulmanlar üchin esasï ve tiz övrenmeli meselelering yïgïndïsï*, Galkan Hoja oglï and Bars Hojagulïyev eds. (Ashgabat, 1997).
Atamämmedov, N. V. (ed.). *Pïgamberler, dört charïyarlar, perishdeler (Ashkhabad,* 1991).
Bayramsähedov, N. *Ïslam: gïsga sözlük* (Ashgabat, 1994).
Begjanov, Amantagan. *Ärsarïbaba ve ärsarïlar* (Ashgabat, 1993).
Bol'shoi Russko-turkmenskii slovar' I-II (Moscow, 1986–1987).
Durdïmämmedov, A. *Cheshmeler* (Ashgabat, 1989).
Frank, Allen J. and Jeren Touch-Werner. *Turkmen-English Dictionary* (Kensington, Maryland, 1999).
Hanov, Sapargeldi (ed.). *Üch pïgamber* (Ashgabat, 1992).
Niyazi, A. *Musulman bayramchïlïklar* (Ashgabat, 1993).
Öräev, Arazbay. *Ïrïmlar* (Ashgabat, 1993).
Orazgulï Murmämmet (ed.). *Mulla Töre Ahunïng risalasï* (Ashgabat, 1993).
Rozïyev, J. and M. Mektasov. *Novruz* (Charjew, 1994).
Russko-Turkmenskii slovar' (Moscow, 1956).
Tächmïradov, T. and A. K. Gurbanova. *Türkmen adam atlarïnïng spravochnigi* (Ashkhabad, 1988).
Turkmensko-russkii slovar' (Moscow, 1968).
Türkmen dilining sözligi (Ashgabat, 1962).
Veyisov, B. (ed.). *Türkmen dilining orfografik sözlügi* (Ashkhabad, 1989).

Uyghur Sources:

Ghulam Ghopuri, Muhämmät Tursun Ibrahimi, and Khoja Äkhmät Yünüs (eds.). *Uyghur Kilassik Ädibiyatidin Qisqichä Sözlük* (Urumchi, 1986).
Nadzhip, E. N. *Uigursko-Russkii slovar'* (Moscow, 1968).
Schwarz, Henry. *Uyghur-English Dictionary* (Bellingham, Washington, 1992).
Shahidi, Burhan. *Uyghurcha-Khänsucha-Ruscha Lughat* (Peking, 1953).
Qur'an Kärim: Uyghurchä tärjimisi (Madina: 1413 AH).
Türkchä-uyghurchä lughät (Urumchi, 1989).
Uigursko-russkii slovar' (Alma-Ata, 1961).
Uyghur tilining izahliq lughiti I-III (Urumchi, 1990–1992)

Uzbek Sources:

Abduvali Qori. *Va'zlar* (18 audio cassettes of sermons) (1993).
Abu Muhammad Mahbubiy. *Dalilul khoyrot (yakhshiliklarga boshlovchi)* (Ferghana, 1996).
Akobirov, S. F. and G. N. Mikhailov (eds.). *Uzbeksko-russkii slovar'* (Tashkent, 1988).
Kamol, Muhammad. *Musulmon ayollarga maslahatlar* (Tashkent, 2000).
Komilov, Najmiddin. *Najmiddin Kubro* (Tashkent, 1995).
———. *Tasavvuf: birinchi kitob* (Tashkent, 1996).
Lapasov, J. *Mumtoz adabiy asarlar öquv lughati* (Tashkent, 1994).

Mansur, Alouddin (ed.). *Qur'oni Karim: Özbekcha izohli tarjima* (Tashkent, 1992).
Möminov, Ashirbek (ed.). *Yassaviy nasabnomasi va Amir Timur* (Tashkent, 1996).
Muhammad, Jahongir. *99 nur yoki allohning 99 nomi va 99 karomati* (Istanbul, 1996).
Narziqulov, Ahmad. *Dehqon taqvimi* (Tashkent, 1991).
Olimkhon, Amir Sayyid. *Bukhoro khalqining hasrati tarikhi* (Tashkent, 1991).
Özbek tilining ilohli lughati I-II (Moscow, 1981).
Rushdiy, Muhammad Siddiq. *Avliyolar sultoni, Turonlik valiylar* (Tashkent, 1995).
Russko-Uzbekskii slovar' (Moscow, 1954).
Sadriddin Salim Bukhoriy. *Tabarrik ziyoratgohlar* (Tashkent, 1993).
Said Azim Muhammad Ali. *Imom Bukhoriy Ta'rifi* (Tashkent, 1997)
Shamsiev, Porso and S. Ibrohimov (eds.). *Navoiy asarlari lughati* (Tashkent, 1972).
Turon, Usmon. *Turkiy khalqlar mafkurasi* (Tashkent, 1995).
Usmonov, M. A. (ed.). *Islom Spravochnik*, 3d ed. (Tashkent, 1989).
Valikhöjaev, Boturkhon. *Khoja Ahror tarikhi* (Tashkent, 1994).
Recordings of BBC and Voice of America interviews with members of the Uzbekistani Islamic Opposition (1999–2002).

Abbreviations

adj.	adjective
adv.	adverb
BAS	Bashkir
esp.	especially
intj.	interjection
KAR	Karakalpak
KAZ	Kazakh
KYR	Kyrgyz
lit.	literally
n.	noun
np.	noun phrase
pn.	proper noun
TAJ	Tajik
TAT	Tatar
TUR	Turkmen
UYG	Uyghur
UZB	Uzbek
v.	verb

Pronunciation Index

abad ابد
'Abasa عبس
'abd عبد
abdal[1] ابدال
abdal[2] ابدال
abdal[3] ابدال
abdast آبدست
abdasta آبدسته
abdastkhana آدستخانه
'Abdullah[1] عبدالله
'Abdullah[2] عبدالله
ab-i hayat آب حيات
ab-i Zamzam آب زمزم
'abid عابد
'abida عابده
abida آبيده
'abir عبير
abiz آبض
abjad ابجد
abrar ابرار
abu ابو
Abu Bakr ابو بكر
Abu Hanifa ابو حنيفه
abvab al-Qur'an ابواب القرآن
'Ad عاد
adab ادب
'adalat عدالت
Adam آدم
'adat عادات
'adavat عداوة
'adil عادل
'Adiyat عاديات
'adl عدل
'Adl, al- العادل
'adn عدن
Aflatun افلاطون
afsana افسانه
afsun افسون
aftada افتاده
'Afuv, al- العفو
afyun افيون
ahad آحد
Ahad, al- الاحد
ahbab احباب
'ahd عهد
ahkam احكام
ahl al-vilayat اهل الولايت
ahl-i dil اهل دل
ahl-i Islam اهل اسلام
ahl-i kitab اهل كتاب
ahl-i qalam اهل قلم
ahl-i ra'y اهل رأى
ahl-i salib اهل صليب
ahl-i sunna اهل سنّه
ahl-i tariqat اهل طريقت
ahl-i zimmat اهل زمّة
ahliyyat-i ada اهليّت ادا
ahliyyat-i vujub اهليّت وجوب
Ahmad احمد
Ahqaf احقاف
ahrar احرار
Ahzab احزاب
'A'isha عائشه
ajal اجل
'ajam عجم
ajnabi اجنابى
ajr اجر
akbar
akhbar اخبار
akhi اخى
Akhir, al- الآخر
akhir zaman آخر زمان
akhirat آخرت
akhirat batqaghi آخرت باطقاغى
akhiravi آخراوى
akhlaq اخلاق
akhun آخون
akhund آخوند
akmal اكمل
akram اكرم
A'la اعلى
a'lam اعلم
'alam[1] عالم
'alam[2] علم
'alamat علامت
'Alaq علق
'alaviyat علويات
'alayhi al-salam عليه السلام
'alaykim al-salam و عليكم السلام
al-hamdulillahi rabbi'l-'alamin الحمد لله رب العالمين
al-hamdullilah الحمدلله
'Ali على
al-i aba آل ابا
'Ali, al- العلى
Al-i Imran آل عمران
alif lam mim ا ل م
'alim عالم
'Alim, al- العليم
Allah الله
Allah hu الله هو
Allah ta'ala الله تعالى
Allah ya Allah الله يا الله
allahi billahi الله با لله
Allahu akbar الله اكبر
Allahu a'lam bi'l-savab الله أعلم بالصواب
Allahu 'Alimun الله عالم
Allahu Bashirun الله بشير
Allahu Sami'un الله سميع
allahyar الله يار
'Allam al-ghuyub علّام الغيوب
'allama علّامه
Alyasa' اليسع
a'ma اعما
'amal عمل
'amama عمامه
amanat امانات
'amd
amin[1] آمين
Amin[2] امين
amir امير
Amir al-mu'minin امير المؤمنين
amir al-muslimun امير المسلمون
amir al-umara امير الامرا
amlak املاك
amniyat امنيت
amr امر
amr-i Ma'ruf امر معروف
ana al-haqq انا الحقّ
An'am انعام
anbar[1] عنبر
anbar[2] عنبر
anbiya[1] انبياء
Anbiya[2] انبياء
andarun اندرون
Anfal انفال
anjuman انجمن
'Ankabut عنكبوت
'Anqa عنقا
ansar انصار
anvar انوار
'aqibat عاقبت

ʿaqida عقیده
ʿaqiqa عقیقه
ʿaqliyat عقلیات
ʿAqrab عقرب
aqraba اقربا
aʿraf[1] اعراف
Aʿraf[2] اعراف
ʿarafa عرفة
ʿArafat عرفات
ʿArasat عرصات
ʿarif عارف
arkan ارکان
ʿarsh عرش
ʿarsh-i aʿla عرش اعلا
ʿarsh-i kursi عرش کرسی
arvah ارواح
ʿasa عصا
Asad اسد
Asadullah اسدالله
asar اثر
asarat اسارت
asfal al-safilin اسفل السافلین
ashab اصحاب
ashab al-rass
ashab-i Badr اصحاب بدر
ashab-i jannat اصحاب جنّت
ashab-i kahf اصحاب کهف
ashab-i kiram اصحاب کرام
ʿashiq عاشق
ashir عاشر
ashraf اشرف
ashrat-i saʿat اشرط ساعت
ʿAshura[1] عاشورا
ʿashura[2] عاشورا
ʿasi عاصی
asir اسیر
asitana آستانه
asma al-husna اسما الحسنه
asman اسمان
ʿasr[1] عصر
ʿAsr[2] عصر
assalamu ʿalaykum السلام علیکم
astaghfirullah استغفرالله
astana
atash آتش
atashparast آتشپرست
ʿattar عطّار
aʿuzu billah اعوذ بالله
aʿuzu billahi min al-shaytani al-rajim اعوذ بالله من الشیطان الرجیم
avlad اولاد
avliya[1] اولیا
avliya[2] اولیا
avliyazada اولیا زاده
ʿavrat عورت
Avval, al- الاوّل
ayan ایان
ayat آیت
ayat al-kursi آیت الکرسی
ayat al-muhkamat آیت المحکمت
ayat al-mutashabihat آیت المتشبهت
ayat-i karima آیت کریمه
ayatullah ایت الله
ʿayn
Ayyub ایّوب
ʿaza عزا
azab عذاب
ʿazab al-kabir عذاب الکبیر
ʿazab-i qabr عذاب قبر
aʿzam[1] اعظم
Aʿzam[2] اعظم
azan اذان
azar آزار
ʿazayimkhan عزائم خوان
ʿAzazil عزازیل
ʿAzim, al- العظیم
ʿaziz[1] عزیز
ʿaziz[2] عزیز
ʿAziz, al- العزیز
ʿAzraʾil عزرائل
ʿAzza va Jalla عزوجل
bab باب
bachcha بچّه
bachchabaz بچّه باز
bachchabazi بچّه بازی
badal بدل
badal-i askari بدل عسکری
badal-i naqdi بدل نقدی
badal-i shakhsi بدل شخصی
bad-duʿa بددعا
Badiʿ, al- البدیع
Badr بدر
Baʿis, al- الباعث
baj باج
bakhshi بخشی
bakhshish بخشیش
bakht بخت
bakira باکره
Balad بلد
balaghat بلاغت
baligh بالغ
bamdad بامداد
banda بنده
bang بنگ
bani hashimi بنی هاشمی
bani Islam بنی اسلام
bani Isra'il[1] بنی اسرائیل
Bani Isra'il[2] بنی اسرائیل
baqa[1] بقا
baqa[2] بقا
Baqara بقره
baqi باقی
Baqi, al- الباقی
bara'at[1] برائت
Bara'at[2] برائت
barakat برکت
barakullah بارك الله
barat برات
barhaq برحق
Bari, al- الباری
barq برق
Barr, al- البرّ
bashariyat بشریت
Bashir بشیر
basir بصیر
Basir, al- البصیر
Basit, al- الباسط
Batha بطحه
batil باطل
batin باطن
Batin, al- الباطن
bavar باور
bayʿat بیعت
bayram بیرام
bayt بیت
bayt al-ahzan بیت الاحزان
Bayt al-ʿatiq, al- البیت العطیق
bayt al-mal بیت المال
Bayt al-muqaddas بیت المقدس
Baytullah بیت الله
Bayyina بیّنه
baz gasht باز گشت
bi diyanat بی دیانت

bi gunah بی گناه
bi iman بی ایمان
bi namaz بی نماز
bi taharat بی طهارت
bibi بی بی، بیبی
Bibi Maryam
bid'at بدعت
bid'at-i hasana بدعت حسنه
bid'at-i sayyi'a بدعت سیئه
bihablillah بحبل الله
bihisht بهشت
bihukmillah بحکم الله
Bilal بلال
billahi با لله
Bilqis بلقیس
biradar برادر
bisat بساط
bismillah بسم الله
bismillah al-Rahman al-Rahim
بسم الله الرحمن الرحیم
buhtan بهتان
Buraq براق
Buruj بروج
but بت
butkhana بت خانه
butparast بت پرست
buzurg بزرگ
chadra چادره
Chahar yar چهار یار
chalma چالما
childan چلدان
chilla[1] چلّه
chilla[2] چلّه
chillakhana[1] چلّه خانه
chillakhana[2] چلّه خانه
chillayasin چلّه یاسن
chiltan چلتن
Dabba دابّه
dafn دفن
dahir
dahr دهر
dahri دهری
dahr-i dun دهر دون
dahriya دهریه
Dajjal دجّال
dalil دلیل
dalil-i 'aqli دلیل عقلی
dalil-i naqli دلیل نقلی
dalil-i shar'i دلیل شرعی
Dalv دلو
damulla داملّا
danishmand دانشمند
dar al-aman دار الآمان
dar al-baqa دارالبقا
dar al-fana دارالفنا
dar al-ghurur دارالغرور
dar al-harb دار الحرب
dar al-havadis دار الحوادث
dar al-huffaz دار الحفّاظ
dar al-Islam دار الاسلام
dar al-qasas دار القصاص
dar al-qaza دار القضا
dar al-salam دارالسلام
dar al-sulh دار الصلح
dar al-surur دار السرور
darayn دارین
dargah درگاه
darra درّه
darskhana درسخانه
darvish درویش
dastar دستار
dastarkhan دسترخان
dastshuy دست شوئی
Da'ud داود
da'va[1] دعوا، دعوی
da'va[2] دعوا، دعوی
da'vat دعوت
davir دور
didar دیدار
din دین
dindar دیندار
dini دینی
din-i samavi دین سماوی
div دیو
divan دیوان
divana دیوانه
diyanat دیانت
diyanatkar دیانتکار
diyat دیة
du'a[1] دعا
du'a[2] دعا
du'a[3] دعا
du'adar دعادار
du'agu دعاگو
du'akhvan دعاخوان
du'a-yi qunut دعای قنوت
du'a-yi salam دعاء سلام
dubba دبّه
Duha
Dukhan[1] دخان
dukhan[2] دخان
Duldul دلدل
dunya دنیا
dunyavi دنیاوی
durud درود
durus دروس
durust درست
dust دوست
Duzakh دوزخ
duzakhi دوزخی
fahisha فاحشه
fahsh فحش
fa'iz فائض
fajir فاجر
Fajr فجر
fal فال
falak[1] فلك
falak[2] فلك
falaq[1] فلق
Falaq[2] فلق
falbin فالبین
falgu فالگو
falnama فالنامه
falsafa فلسفه
fana فنا
fani فانی
fann فنّ
faqahat فقاهت
faqih فقیه
faqir[1] فقیر
faqir[2] فقیر
faqr فقر
fara'iz[1] فرائض
fara'iz[2] فرائض
farid فرید
farid al-'asr فریدالعصر
farishta فرشته
farsakh فرسخ
faruq فاروق
faryad فریاد
farz فرض
farz-i 'ayn فرض عین
farz-i da'im فرض دائم
farz-i kifaya فرض کفایه

farz-i muvaqqat فرض موقّت
fasad فساد
fasiq فاسق
Fath فتح
Fath-i Makka فتح مكّه
fatiha[1] فاتحه
fatiha[2] فاتحه
Fatiha[3] فاتحه
Fatiha, al- الفاتحه
fatihagu فاتحه گو
Fatima فاطمه
Fatir[1] فاطر
fatir[2] فاطر
Fattah, al- الفتّاح
fatva فتوى
faylasuf فيلسوف
fazil فاضل
fazl فضل
fida فدا
fida'i فدائى
fidakyar فداكار
fidya فديه
fikrat فكرت
Fil فيل
fiqh فقه
Fira'un فرعون
Firdaus فردوس
firqa فرقه
fisq فسق
fitna فتنه
fitr[1] فطر
fitr[2] فطر
fitra فطره
fitrat فطرة
Furqan[1] فرقان
Furqan[2] فرقان
Fussilat فصّلت
futuvat فتوت
fuzala فضلا
Ghaffar, al- الغفّار
ghafil
Ghafir غافر
ghaflat[1] غفلت
ghaflat[2] غفلت
Ghafur, al- الغفور
ghaliz
Ghambar غامبر
ghamm[1] غمّ
ghamm[2] غمّ
Ghani, al- الغنى
ghanimat غنيمت
gharib[1] غريب
gharib[2] غريب
ghasb غصب
Ghashiya غاشيه
ghasl غسل
ghassal غسّال
Ghavs al-A'zam غوث الاعظم
ghayb
ghayr-i din غير دين
ghayr-i mashru' غير مشروع
ghayr-i misr غير مصر
ghayr-i mu'akkad قير مؤكّد
ghayr-i shar'i غير شرع
Ghayya غيّا
ghaza غزا
ghazab غضب
ghazavat غزوات
ghazi غازى
ghilman غلمان
ghul غل
ghurbat غربت
ghusl غسل
ghuslkhana غسلخانه
gumbaz گنبذ
gunah گناه
gunahkar گناهكار
gur گور
guristan گورستان
gurkhana گورخانه
habash حبش
Habashistan حبشستان
Habib حبيب
Habibullah حبيب الله
Habil هابيل
hadd حدّ
hadd-i qazf حدّ قذف
hadd-i shurb حدّ شرب
hadd-i sirkat حدّ سركة
hadd-i zakr
hadd-i zina حدّ زنا
Hadi, al- الهادى
Hadid حديد
hadis حديث
hadis-i arba'in حديث اربعين
hadis-i qudsi حديث قدسى
hafiz حافظ
Hafiz, al-[1] الحافظ
Hafiz, al-[2] الحفيظ
haft-i yak هفتيك
Hajar هاجر
hajar-i asvad حجر اسود
hajj[1] حجّ
Hajj[2] حجّ
hajj badal حجّ بدل
hajji حاجّى
hajjikhana حاجّى خانه
Hakam, al- الحكم
hakim حكيم
Hakim, al- الحكيم
hal حال
halal حلال
halif حليف
halim حليم
Halim, al- الحليم
halimkhana حليمخانه
hall حلّ
halqa[1] حلقه
halqa[2] حلقه
Hamal حمل
Haman همان
Hamid, al- الحميد
hamila حامله
hamiladar حامله دار
Hanafi حنفى
Hanafiya حنفيه
Hanbali حنبلى
Hanbaliya حنبليه
hanif[1] حنيف
hanif[2] حنيف
haqiqat حقيقة
haqq[1] حقّ
Haqq[2] حقّ
Haqq, al- الحقّ
haqq al-yaqin حقّ اليقين
Haqq Rasul حقّ رسول
Haqq Ta'ala حقّ تعالى
Haqqa حاقّه
haqqullah حقّ الله
haram[1] حرام
haram[2] حرم
haram qat'i حرم قطعى
haram zanni حرم ظنّى
Haramayn حرمين

haramzada حرامزاده
harif du'a حریف دعا
harim حریم
Harun هارون
Harut va Marut هاروت و ماروت
hasan[1] حسن
hasan[2] حسن
Hasan[3] حسن
hasana
hashr[1] حشر
Hashr[2] حشر
hasht-i yak هشت یاك
Hasib, al- الحسیب
hattat حطّاط
Hava هوا
havajim هواجم
havajis هواجس
havala هوالة
havari حواری
haviya هاویة
havl هول
hay ya hu حی یا هو
hayan حیاً
hayat-i abadiya حیات ابدیه
Haydar حیدر
Hayy, al- الحیّ
hayz حیض
hazrat حضرت
hiba هبه
Hibatullah هبة الله
hidayat هدایت
hijab حجاب
Hijr حجر
hijra هجره
hijri هجری
hijriya هجریه
hikmat حکمت
hilal هلال
hila-yi shar'i حیلهء شرعی
hiliya-yi sharif حلیهء شریف
hilya حلیه
hilya-yi sa'adat حلیهء سعادت
himmat همّة
hirz حرز
hiss حسّ
hiss-i batin حسّ باطن
hiss-i zahiri حسّ ظاهری
hizb[1] حزب
hizb[2] حزب
hizb al-shaytan حزب الشیطان
Hu هو
hubb حبّ
Hud[1] هود
Hud[2] هود
hudud حدود
hujra حجره
Hujurat حجرات
hukm حکم
hukm-i samad حکم صمد
hukumat حکومت
hulla حلّه
hulul حلول
Humaza همزه
hur حور
huri حوری
hurr حرّ
Husayn حسین
husn حسن
husn-i adab حسن ادب
husn-i akhlaq حسن اخلاق
husn-i khat حسن خط
husn-i tarbiya حسن تربیه
Hut حوت
i'ana اعانة
'ibadat[1] عبادت
'ibadat[2] عبادات
'ibadatgah عبادتگاه
'ibadatkhana عبادتخانه
ibaha اباحه
Iblis ابلیس
Ibrahim[1] ابراهیم
Ibrahim[2] ابراهیم
'ibrani عبرانی
'id عید
'Id al-Azha عید الاضحی
'Id al-Fitr عید الفطر
i'dam اعدام
'iddat عدّة
Idris ادریس
'iffat عفّت
'ifrit عفریت
ifta افتا
iftar افطار
iftitah افتتاح
ihdad احداد
ihram احرام
ihsan[1] احسان
ihsan[2] احسان
ihsar احصار
ihtida اهتدا
ihtijab احتجاب
ihtilam احتلام
ihzar احضار
ijab ایجاب
ijabat اجابت
ijazat اجازة
ijazatnama اجازة نامه
ijma' اجماع
ijma'-i ummat اجماع امّة
ijtihad اجتهاد
ikhlas[1] اخلاص
Ikhlas[2] اخلاص
ikhtilaf اختلاف
ikhvan اخوان
ilah اله
ilaha الهه
ilahi[1] الهی
ilahi[2] الهی
ilahi[3] الهی
ilahiyat الهیات
ilahiyun الهیون
ilhad الحاد
ilham الهام
illa-billah الاّ بالله
'illat علّة
'ilm[1] علم
'ilm[2] علم
'ilm al-'aqa'id علم العقائد
'ilm-i hal[1] علم حال
'ilm-i hal[2] علم حال
'ilm-i qal علم قال
iltija التجا
Ilyas الیاس
imam[1] امام
imam[2] امام
imam[3] امام
imam[4] امام
imam al-qiblatayn امام القبلتین
imamat[1] امامت
imamat[2] امامت
Imam-i A'zam امام اعظام
iman[1] ایمان
iman[2] ایمان
imarat امارت

ʿImran[1] عمران
ʿImran[2] عمران
inabat انابة
Infitar انفطار
Injil اينجيل
injizab انجذاب
inna aʿtaynaka al-kavsara انّا اعطينك الكوثر
insaf انصاف
Insan انسان
insan-i kamil انسان كامل
insha'allah انشاء الله
Inshiqaq انشقاق
Inshirah انشراح
ins-jins انس جنس
intiha انتها
intikhab انتخاب
intiqam انتقام
inzal انزال
ʿiqab عقاب
iqamat اقامت
iqrar[1] اقرار
iqrar[2] اقرار
iqtida اقتدا
irada[1] اراده
irada[2] اراده
irada[3] اراده
irada-yi la yazal ارادهءلايزال
irim اريم
irshad ارشاد
irshadnama ارشادنامه
irtidad ارتداد
ʿIsa عيسى
Isagujikhvan ايساغوجى خوان
ʿIsaparast عسى پرست
ʿIsavi عيسوى
ʿIsaviyat عيسويت
ishan ايشان
ishanzada ايشان زاده
Ishaq اسحاق
isharat اشارة
ʿishq عشق
ishrak اشراك
ishraq اشراق
Iskandar اسكندر
Islam اسلام
islamiyat اسلاميت
Ismaʿil اسماعيل
ʿismat عصمة
ʿismatullah عصمة الله
ism-i aʿzam اسم اعظام
isnad اسناد
isqat اسقاط
Isra اسرا
israf اسراف
Israfil اسرافيل
Isra'il اسرائيل
istibdad استبداد
istibra استبرا
istidlali iman استدلالى ايمان
istiʿfar استعفار
istighfar استغفار
istihaza استحاضه
istihsan استحسان
istikhara استخاره
istilahat اصطلاحات
istinja استنجا
istinshaq استنشاق
istiqamat استقامة
istiqbal استقبال
istishhad استشهاد
istislah استسلاح
istisna استثنا
istisqa استسقا
ʿisyan عصيان
ʿisyankar عصيانكار
itaʿat اطاعت
iʿtikaf اعتكاف
iʿtikafkhana اعتكافخانه
iʿtimad اعتماد
iʿtiqad اعتقاد
iʿtiqadat اعتقادات
itlaq اطلاق
itmam اتمام
ittihad[1] اتّحاد
ittihad[2] اتّحاد
izar ازار
izdivaj ازدواج
izn اذن
ʿizzat عزّة
Jabbar, al- الجبّار
jabr جبر
Jabra'il جبرائيل
Jadi جدى
jadid جديد
jadu جادو
jadugar جادوگر
jadugu جادو گو
jafa جفا
Jahannam جهنّم
jahili جاهلى
jahiliyat جاهليت
jahim جحيم
jahl جهل
jahr جهر
ja'iz جائز
Jalil, al- الجليل
Jalla Jalaluh جلّ جلاله
jallad جلّاد
jalsa جلسه
jamʿ al-jamʿ جمع الجمع
jamaʿat[1] جماعت
jamaʿat[2] جماعت
jamiʿ جامع
Jamiʿ, al- الجامع
Jamra جمره
jan جان
janab جناب
Janab-i haqq جناب حقّ
janaza[1] جنازه
janaza[2] جنازه
janda جنده
Jannat جنّت
Jannat al-ʿAdn جنّت العدن
Jannat al-Firdaus جنّت الفردوس
Jannat al-Khuld جنّت الخلد
Jannat al-Ma'va جنّت المأوى
Jannat al-Naʿim جنّت النعيم
jarima جريمه
jasad
Jasiya جاثيه
javabnama جوابنامه
Javza جوزا
jaynamaz جانماز
jaza جزا
jazb جذب
jazba جذبه
Jibril جبريل
Jibt جبت
jihad جهاد
jihad-i akbar جهاد اكبر
jihad-i asghar جهاد اصغر
jilva-yi rabbaniya جلوهء ربايّة
jinayat جنايت

jinaza
jinn[1] جنّ
Jinn[2] جنّ
Jirjis جرجس
jizya جزيه
juda جدا
Judi جودى
jughrafiya جغرافيا
juhud جهود
jum'a[1] جمعه
jum'a[2] جمعه
Jum'a[3] جمعه
Jumada al-akhira جمادى الآخره
Jumada al-ula جمادى الاولا
jumalik جمعه لك
jumla جمله
junub جنب
junun[1] جنون
junun[2] جنون
jurh جرح
juz'[1] جزء
juz'[2] جزء
juz'[3] جزء
juz'[4] جزء
Ka'ba كعبه
Ka'batullah كعبة الله
Kabir, al- الكبير
kabira كبيره
kafalat كفالت
kaffarat كفّارت
kafil كفيل
kafir كافر
kafiristan كافرستان
Kafirun كافرون
kafn كفن
Kahf كهف
kahin كاهن
ka'inat كائنات
kajraftar كج رفتار
kalam كلام
Kalam-i Sharif كلام شريف
Kalamullah كلام الله
kalima كليمه
kalimagu كلمه گو
kalimatullah كليمة الله
kalima-yi shahadat كليمهء شهادت
kalimullah كليم الله
kalisa كليسه
kanisa كنيسه
kaniz كنز
karam كرم
karamat كرامت
Karbala كربلا
Kardigar كردگار
Karim, al- الكريم
kashish كشيش
kashishkhana كشيشخانه
kashkul كشكول
katib كاتب
kavnayn كونين
Kavsar[1] كوثر
Kavsar[2] كوثر
khabar خبر
khabar-i vahid خبر واحد
Khabir, al- الخبير
khach خاچ
khachparast خاچپرست
Khadija
khafif
khalaqa خلقه
khalfa[1] خلفه
khalfa[2] خلفه
khalifa[1] خليفه
khalifa[2] خليفه
Khalilullah خليل الله
Khaliq, al- الخالق
Khallaq خلّاق
khalvat خلوت
khalvat dar anjuman خلوت در انجمن
khalvatgah خلوتگاه
khamr خمر
khanaqa خانقا
kharaj خراج
khata خطا
Khatam al-anbiyah خاتم الانبيا
Khatam al-nabiyin خاتم النبين
khatib خطيب
khatim[1] خاتم
khatim[2] خاتم
khatm[1] ختم
khatm[2] ختم
khat-mahr خط مهر
khatm-i khvajagan ختم خواجه گان
khatm-i kutub ختم كتب
khatm-i suluk ختم سلوك
khatna ختنه
khavarij خوارج
khavf خوف
Khaybar خيبر
khayr[1] خير
khayr[2] خير
khayr-sadaqa خير صدقه
khilafat[1] خلافت
khilafat[2] خلافت
khilafat[3] خلافت
khilaf-i shar' خلاف شرع
khilkhana خلخانه
khilqat خلقت
khilvat خلوت
khirqa[1] خرقه
khirqa[2] خرقه
khirqa push خرقه پوش
khirqa-yi sa'adat خرقهء سعادت
khirqa-yi sharif خرقهء شريف
khitan ختان
Khizr خضر
Khuda خدا
khudaguy خداگو
khudajuy خداجوى
khudaparast خداپرست
khudatars خداترس
Khudavand خداوند
khudavanda خداونده
khuday خداى
khudaygu خداى گو
khudayi خدائى
khudaykhana خدايخانه
khuftan
khul' خلع
Khulafa-yi rashidin خلفاى راشدين
Khuld خلد
khulq
khums خمس
khunsa خنثى
khurafat خرافات
khurma خرما
khush dar dam خوش در دم
khutba خطبه
khvaja[1] خواجه
khvaja[2] خواجه
khvajazada خواجه زاده
kifaya كفايه
kiramin katibin كرام كاتيبين

kitab كتاب
kuffar كفّار
kufr كفر
kufran كفران
kulah كلاه، كله
kursi كرسى
la havla لا حول
la ilaha illa allah va muhammadun rasulullah لا اله الا الله و محمد رصول لله
La makan لا مكان
labbay لبّى
labbayka لبّيك
lafzan va maʻnan لفظاً و معناً
lafz-i kufr لفظ كفر
Lahab لهب
lahid[1] لحد
lahid[2] لحد
laʻin لعين
laʻnat لعنت
lashkar-i Islam لشكر اسلام
Lat لات
Latif, al- اللطيف
lavh لوح
lavh al-mahfuz, al- اللوح المحفوظ
Layl ليل
Laylat al-Qadr ليلة القدر
laza لظى
lifafa لفافه
lillah لله
Luqman[1] لقمان
Luqman[2] لقمان
Lut لوط
ma favq al-tabiʻat مافوق الطبيعت
maʻad معاد
Maʻarij معارج
maʻasi معاصى
maʻaz allah معاذ الله
ma'b مآب
maʻbad معبد
maʻbud[1] معبود
maʻbud[2] معبود
maddah مدّاح
maddiyun مادّيون
madfan مدفن
madhiya مدحيه
Madina مدينه
Madina-yi munavvara مدينهء منوّره
madini مدنى
madrasa مدرسه
maghasil مغاسل
maghfirat مغفرت
maghlub مغلوب
maghrib مغرب
mahafatullah محافت الله
mahalla محلّه
maharim[1] محارم
maharim[2] محارم
mahbus محبوس
Mahdi مهدى
mahfil محفل
mahkam محكم
mahkama محكمه
mahkama-yi kubra محكمهء كبره
mahkum محكوم
mahparast ماه پرست
mahr[1] مهر
mahr[2] مهر
mahram محرم
mahrum محروم
mahshar محشر
mahshargah محشر گاه
mahsi محسى
Ma'ida مائده
Majid, al- المجيد
majlis مجلس
majnun[1] مجنون
majnun[2] مجنون
majus مجوس
majusi مجوسى
majusiyat مجوسيت
majzub مجذوب
makhdum مخدوم
makhluq مخلوق
makhluqat مخلوقات
Makka مكّه
Makka al-mukarrama مكّه المكرّمه
Makkatullah مكّة الله
makki مكّى
makruh مكروه
makruh tahrima مكروه تحريمى
makruh tanzih مكروه تنزيه
maktab مكتب
mal مال
mala'ika ملائكه
malak ملك
malakut ملكوت
malakutiyat ملكوتية
Malik[1] مالك
malik[2] ملك
Malik, al- الملك
Malik al-Mulk مالك الملك
Maliki مالكى
Malikiya مالكيه
maliyat ماليت
Malʻun[1] ملعون
malʻun[2] ملعون
mamat ممات
mamluk مملوك
ma'mur مأمور
maʻnan معناً
manaqib مناقب
manaqibnama مناقبنامه
manara مناره
manasik مناسك
Manat منات
maʻnavi معنوى
maʻnaviya معنويه
manfur منفور
manhi منهى
maniʻ منيع
Maniʻ, al- المانع
mankuha منكوحه
mansak منسك
manshur منشور
mantiq منطق
mantiqi منطقى
manzur منذور
maqam مقام
Maqam-i Ibrahim مقام ابراهيم
maqbara[1] مقبره
maqbara[2] مقبره
maqsura مقصوره
maqtuʻ مقطوع
maqtul مقتول
maʻraka معركه
marasim مراسم
mardud مردود
marfuʻ مرفوع
marfuʻ hukman مرفوع حكماً
marfuʻ sarihan مرفوع صريحاً
marhamat مرحمت
marhum مرحوم

ma'rifat[1] معرفت
ma'rifat[2] معرفت
marsiya مرثيه
ma'ruf معروف
Marva مروه
Maryam[1] مريم
Maryam[2] مريم
Masad مسد
mas'ala مسئله
masbuq مسبوق
mashaallah ما شا الله
mashayikh مشايخ
mashhad مشهد
mashhadi مشهدى
mashhur مشهور
mashkuk مشكوك
mashrab مشرب
mashru' مشروع
mashvarat مشورت
Masih[1] مسيح
masih[2] مسيح
masihi مسيحى
masjid مسجد
Masjid al-Aqsa, al- المسجد الاقسا
Masjid al-Haram, al- المسجد الحرام
mast مست
ma'sum معصوم
matam ماتم
matamzada ماتمزاده
Matin, al- المتين
matruka متروكه
Ma'un ماعون
mavhum موهوم
mavhumat موهومات
mav'iza موعظه
mavjud موجود
mavjudat موجودات
Mavla[1] مولا
mavla[2] مولى
mavlana مولانا
mavlavi مولوى
Mavlid[1] مولد
mavlid[2] مولد
mavliyat ماوليت
mavqi' موقع
mavquf موقوف
mavzu' موضوع
ma'yub معيوب
mayyit ميّت
mazalim مظالم
mazar مزار
mazaristan مزارستان
mazarkarda مزاركرده
mazhab[1] مذهب
mazhab[2] مذهب
mazlum مظلوم
mazmaza مضمضه
maznib مذنب
ma'zun مأذون
ma'zur معذور
mihrab محراب
Mika'il ميكائل، ميكال
milad ميلاد
miladi ميلادى
milk ملك
Mina منى
minbar منبر
Miqat ميقات
mir مير
mi'raj معراج
mi'rajiya معراجيّه
mi'rajnama معراجنامه
miras ميراث
miraskhur ميراث خور
mirghazab مير غضب
mirza ميرزا
misaq ميثاق
miskin مسكين
misr[1] مصر
Misr[2] مصر
misvak[1] مسواك
misvak[2] مسواك
mizan[1] ميزان
mizan[2] ميزان
Mizan[3] مزان
mizana مئذنة، ميذنة
mu'abbir معبّر
Mu'akhkhir, al- المؤخّر
mu'akkad مؤكّد
mu'akkada
mu'akkal مؤكّل
mu'allif مؤلّف
mu'allim معلّم
mu'amalat معاملات
mu'arrikh مؤرّخ
Mu'avvizatan معوّذتان
Mu'avvizatayn معوّذتين
mu'azzin مؤذّن
mubah مباح
mubahasa مباحثه
mubarak مبارك
mubaraza مبارزه
mubariz مبارز
mubashir مباشر
mubashshir مبشّر
mubassir مبصّر
Mubdi', al- المبدع
mubham مبهم
mudafa'a مدافعه
mudallas مدلّس
mudarris مدرّس
Muddassir مدثّر
mudrik مدرك
mufassal مفصّل
mufassir مفسّر
mufsid[1] مفسد
mufsid[2] مفسد
mufti مفتى
muftir مفتر
Mughni, al- المغنى
muhabbat محبّت
muhaddis محدّث
muhajarat مهاجرت
muhajir مهاجر
muhajirin مهاجرين
muhakama محاكمه
muhallil محلّل
Muhammad[1] محمّد
Muhammad[2] محمّد
muhammadi[1] محمّدى
muhammadi[2] محمّدى
muhaqqiq محقّق
muharaba محاربه
muharram[1] محرّم
Muharram[2] محرّم
muharramat محرّمات
muhasara محاصره
Muhaymin, al- المهيمن
muhibb محبّ
Muhsi, al- المحصى
muhsin محسن
muhtadi مهتدى
muhtasib[1] محتسب
muhtasib[2] محتسب

muhtazir محتضر
Muhyi, al- المحيی
mu'id معيد
Mu'id, al- المعيد
Mu'izz, al- المعزّ
Mujadala مجادله
mujahid مجاهد
mujahida[1] مجاهده
mujahida[2] مجاهده
mujassam مجسّم
mujavir مجاور
mujda مجده
Mujib, al- المجيب
Mujid, al- الموجد
mu'jiza[1] معجزة
Mu'jiza[2] معجزة
mujtahid[1] مجتهد
mujtahid[2] مجتهد
mukafat مكفاة
mukallaf مكلّف
mukammal مكمّل
mukarram مكرّم
mukarrir مكرّر
mukashifa مكاشفه
mukatib مكاتب
mukhaddara مخدّرة
mukhalifat lil-havadis مخالفة للحواديث
mukhasamat مخاصمات
mukhlis مخلص
mukhtariyat مختاريت
mukhtasar مختصر
mulazim ملازم
mulhaq ملحق
mulhid ملحد
mulk[1] ملك
Mulk[2] ملك
mulk-amlak ملك املاك
mulla ملّا
mullabachcha ملّابچّه
mu'min[1] مؤمن
Mu'min[2] مؤمن
Mu'min, al- المؤمن
mu'mina مؤمنه
Mu'minin مؤمنين
Mumit, al- المميت
Mumtahana ممتحنه
munafiq منافق
Munafiqun منافقون
munajat[1] مناجات
munajat[2] مناجات
munajatkhana مناجاتخانه
munajjim منجّم
munakahat مناكحات
munavvar منوّر
munazara مناظرة
munazzal منزّل
munkar منكر
Munkar va Nakir منكر و نكير
munkir
munsalik منسلك
Muntaqim, al- المنتقم
muqaddas مقدّس
Muqaddim, al- المقدّم
muqallid مقلّد
muqarrab مقرّب
muqavala مقاوله
muqim مقم
Muqit, al- المقيت
Muqsit, al- المقسط
Muqtadir, al- المقتدر
murafa'a مرافعه
murahaqa مراهقة
muraqaba مراقبه
murda مرده
murdakhana مرده خانه
murdar مردار
murdashuy مرده شوی
murid مريد
mursal[1] مرسل
mursal[2] مرسل
Mursalat مرسلات
mursalin مرسلين
murshid مرشد
murshid-i afaq مرشد آفاق
murtadd مرتدّ
Murtaza مرتضى
Musa موسى
musab مثاب
musadara مصادره
musafaha مصافحه
musafir مسافر
musalaha مصالحه
musalla[1] مصلّى
musalla[2] مصلّى
musalli مصلّى
musavi[1] موسوى
musavi[2] موسوى
Musavvir, al- المصوّر
musbat مثبت
mushaf مصحف
mushahida مشاهده
mushkilkushad مشكلكشاد
mushrik مشرك
musibat مصيبت
muslim مسلم
muslima مسلمه
muslimin مسلمين
musnad مسند
mustabidd مستبدّ
Mustafa مصطفى
mustahabb مستحبّ
mustajab مستجاب
mustakrah مستكره
mustashrik مستشريق
musulman مسلمان
muta'abbid متعبّد
Muta'ali, al- المتعالي
muta'assib متعصّب
mu'tabar معتبر
mutadayyin متديّن
Mutaffifin مطفّفين
mutahhar مطهّر
Mutakabbir, al- المتكبّر
mutakallim متكلّم
mutala'a مطالعة
mu'tamir معتمر
mutanassir متنصّر
mutasavvif متصوّف
mutashayyikh متشيّخ
mutavalli متولّى
mutavalliyat متولّيت
mutavarri' متورّع
mutavatir متواتر
mutlaq مطلق
muttasil متّصل
muvahhid موحّد
muvaqqat
muzaffar مظفّر
Muzdalifa مزدلفه
Muzill, al- المذلّ
Muzzammil مزمّل
Naba نبا
nabi نبى

nabi'ullah نبی الله
nabuvat نبوت
nafaqa نفقه
nafas نفس
Nafi', al- النافع
nafila نافله
nafl نفل
nafs[1] نفس
nafs[2] نفس
nahalal نا حلال
nahaq نا حق
nahi نهی
Nahl نحل
nahs نحس
nahu نحو
na'ib نائب
Na'im[1] نعیم
na'im[2] نعیم
najas نجس
najasat نجاست
najasat ghaliz نجاسط غلیظ
najasat khafif نجاست خفیف
najat نجات
najis نجس
Najm نجم
namahram نا محرم
namashru' نامشروع
namaz نماز
namazgah نمازگاه
namazgu نماز گو
namazkhan نمازخوان
Naml نمل
napak[1] نا پاك
napak[2] نا پاك
naqib نقیب
naqis ناقص
naqliya نقلیه
narava ناروا
Nas ناس
nasab نسب
nasabnama نسبنامه
nasara نصارا
na'sh[1] نعش
na'sh[2] نعش
nashar'i ناشرعی
nasib نصیب
nasiba نصیبه
nasihat نصیحت
nasl نسل
Nasr نصر
nasrani نصرانی
nasraniyat نصرانیت
nasta'liq نستعلیق
nasuh نصوح
nasut ناسوت
na't نعت
na't-i sharif نعت شریف
na'uzu billahi نعوذ بلله
navkar نوکر
Navruz نوروز
nayran نیران
nazahat نزاهت
nazar[1] نظر
nazar[2] نظر
nazar bar qadam نظر بر قدم
Nazi'at نزعت
nazil نازل
nazr[1] نذر
nazr[2] نذر
nifas نفاس
nigah dasht نگاه داشت
nihrir نحریر
nikah نکاح
ni'mat نعمت
Nisa نسا
nisab نصاب
nisar نثار
nishalla نشتاله
nishallafurush نشتاله فروش
niyat نیت
niyaz نیاز
nizam نظام
nubuvvat نبوّت
Nuh[1] نوح
Nuh[2] نوح
Numrud نمرود
nur[1] نور
Nur[2] نور
Nur, al- النور
nur-i 'arshullah نور عرش الله
nushur نشور
nusrat نصرت
nutq نطق
pak پاك
para پاره
paranja پرنجه
pari پری
parikhan پری خوان
parikhani پری خوانی
parsa پارسا
Parvardigar پروردگار
payam پیام
paygham پیغم
payghambar پیغمبر
pir پیر
pir-i mughan پیر موغان
pishqadam پیشقدم
prighuvur پریغور ، پریغوور
pul-i sirat پل صراط
purtaqsir پرتقصیر
put پت
putkhana پتخانه
putparast پتپرست
qabahat قباحت
qabih قبیح
Qabil قابیل
qabila قبیله
Qabiz, al- القابض
qabr قبر
qabristan قبرستان
qa'da قعده
qadam قدم
qadamgah قدمگاه
qadamjay قدمجای
qadar قدر
Qadim, al- القدیم
qadimi قدیمی
Qadir, al- القدیر
Qadr[1] قدر
qadr[2] قدر
Qaf[1] قاف
Qaf[2] قاف
Qahhar, al- القهّار
Qahr, al- القاهر
qa'ida قاعده
qal قال
qalam[1] قلم
qalam[2] قلم
Qalam[3] قلم
qalandar قلندر
qalandarkhana قلندرخانه
qalb قلب
Qamar قمر
qamat قامت

qamis قميص
qana'at قناعت
qanun قانون
qari قارئ
Qari'a قارعه
qarikhana قاری‌خانه
qarz قرض
qasam قسم
qasas[1] قصاص
Qasas[2] قصص
qasd قصد
qasis قسيس
qat'i
qat'iyat قتعيت
qatl قتل
qatl 'amd قتل عمد
qatl sabab قتل سبب
qatl shubha 'amd قتل شبه عمد
qavam قوام
Qavi, al- القوى
qavm قوم
Qavs قوس
Qayyum, al- القيّوم
qaza قضا
qaza-yi mu'allaq قضاى معلّق
qazi قاضى
qazikhana قاضى‌خانه
qazizada قاضى‌زاده
qibla قبله
qiblagah قبله گاه
qiblanama قبله نامه
qidam قدم
qimar قمار
qira'at قرائت
qira'atkhana قرائت‌خانه
qiran قران
qisas قصاص
qisas al-anbiya قصص الانبيا
qismat قسمت
qisvat قسوة
Qitmir قطمير
qiyam قيام
qiyam binafsihi قيام بنفسه
qiyamat[1] قيامت
Qiyamat[2] قيامت
qiyamat qa'im قيامت‌قائم
qiyas قياس
qiyas-i fuqaha قياس فقها

qubba قبّه
Qubbat al-Islam قبّة الاسلام
qubur قبور
quddus قدّوس
Quddus, al- القدّوس
qudrat قدرت
quds قدس
Quds, al- القدس
qudsi قدسى
qudsiyat قدسيت
qul hu allah ahad قل هو الله احد
qunut قنوت
Qur'an قرآن
Qur'an khatima قرآن خاتمه
Qur'an-i 'Azim قرآن عظيم
Qur'an-i Karim قرآن كريم
Qur'an-i Majid قرآن مجيد
qur'ankhana قرآنخانه
Quraysh[1] قريش
Quraysh[2] قريش
qurb قرب
qurban قربان
Qurban Bayrami قربان بيرامى
qurra قرّا
qusuf قصوف
qutb قطب
Rabb ربّ
Rabb al-'alamayn ربّ العلمين
Rabb al-Falak ربّ الفلك
Rabbana ربّنا
rabbani ربّانى
Rabbi ربّى
Rabi' al-akhir ربيع الآخر
Rabi' al-avval ربيع الاوّل
rabita رابطه
Ra'd رعد
radd ردّ
Rafi', al- الرافع
ragha'ib رغائب
rahban رهبان
rahbaniyat رهبانيت
rahib راهب
rahil رحل
rahim رحيم
Rahim, al- الرحيم
rahm رحم
Rahman رحمن
Rahman, al- الرحمن

rahmani رحمنى
rahmat رحمت
rahmati رحمتى
ra'i رأى
ra'is[1] رئيس
ra'is[2] رئيس
raja رجا
Rajab رجب
rajim رجيم
rajm رجم
rak'at ركعت
Ramazan رمضان
ramazaniya رمضانيّه
rammal رمّال
Raqib, al- الرقيب
raqs رقص
Rashid, al- الرشيد
rasm-rusum رسم رسوم
Rass رسّ
rasul رسول
rasulana رسولانه
Rasulullah رسول الله
Rauf, al- الروف
rava روا
ravi راوى
Ravza روضه
Ravza-yi mutahhar روضهء متهّر
razi allahu 'anhu رضى الله عنه
Razzaq, al- الرزّاق
ri'aya رعايه
riba ربا
rida[1] ردا
rida[2] ردا
rijal-i ghayb رجال غيب
rind رند
risala رساله
risalat رسالت
rishvat رشوت
rivayat روايت
riya ريا
riyakar رياكار
riyazat رياضت
riza[1] رضا
riza[2] رضا
rizq رزق
Rizvan رضوان
rizvanullah 'alayhi[2] رضوان الله عليه

rububiyat ربوبيت
ruh[1] روح
Ruh[2] روح
Ruh al-Amin روح الامين
Ruh al-Quddus روح القدّوس
ruhani روحانى
ruhaniyat روحانيت
ruhi روحى
Ruhullah روح الله
rukhsat رخصت
rukhsatnama رخصتنامه
ruku‘ ركوع
Rum[1] روم
Rum[2] روم
rutba رتبه
ruza روزه
ruz-i ‘arafat روز عرفات
ruz-i jaza روز جزا
sa‘at ساعة
Saba سبا
sabab
sabi’ صابئ
sab‘i samavat سبع سموات
sabir صابر
sabr[1] صبر
sabr[2] صبر
Sabur, al- الصبور
Sad ص
sadaqa صدقه
sadr[1] صدر
sadr[2] صدر
saf صاف
Safa صفا ، الصفا
safa’il سفائل
safaliyat سفليات
Safar صفر
safar dar vatan سفر در وطن
Saff صفّ
Saffat صفّت
safi’ullah صفى الله
saghir صغير
sahaba صحابه
sahabi صحابى
sahar سحر
sahib-i karamat صاحب كرامت
sahifa صحيفه
sahih صحيح
sahir ساحر
sahv سهو
sa‘i سعى
sa‘ir سعير
sajda[1] سجده
Sajda[2] سجده
sajdagah سجده گاه
sajda-yi tilavat سجدهء تلاوت
sakhavat سخاوت
salaf سلف
salaf-i salihin سلف صالحين
salam سلام
Salam, al- السلام
salam ‘alaykum سلام عليكم
salat صلات
salat al-‘asr صلات العصر
salat al-fajr صلات الفجر
salat al-hajat صلات الحاجت
salat al-‘idayn صلات العيدين
salat al-‘isha صلات العشا
salat al-ishraq صلات الاشراق
salat al-istikhara صلات الاستخاره
salat al-istisqa صلات الاستسقا
salat al-janaza صلات الجنازه
salat al-jum‘a صلات الجمعه
salat al-khavf صلات الخوف
salat al-khusuf صلات الخسوف
salat al-maghrib صلات المغرب
salat al-mariz صلات المريض
salat al-musafir صلات المسافر
salat al-qusuf صلات القصوف
salat al-ragha’ib صلات الرغايب
salat al-safar صلات السفر
salat al-subh صلات الصبح
salat al-tahajjud صلات التهجّد
salat al-taravih صلات التراويح
salat al-tasbih صلات التسبيح
salat al-vitr صلات الوتر
salat al-zuha صلات الضحا
salat al-zuhr صلات الظهر
salavat صلوات
salavat-i nafila صلوات نافله
salb صلب
salib صليب
salibiya سليبيه
salibiyun صليبيون
salih[1] صالح
Salih[2] صالح
salla سلّه
salla allahi ‘alayhu va sallam صلّى الله عليه و سلّم
Salsabil سلسبيل
sama سما
sama‘[1] سماع
sama‘[2] سماع
Samad, al- الصمد
samavi سماوى
sami‘ سميع
Sami‘, al- السميع
Samud ثمود
sana[1] سنه
sana[2] ثنا
sanam صنم
sana-yi hijriyya سنهء هجريّه
sana-yi miladiyya سنهء ميلاديّه
sana-yi qamariyya سنهء قمريّه
sana-yi shamsiyya سنهء شمسيّه
saqafat ثقافت
Saqar سقر
Sara ساره
sar-ab سر آب، سراب
Saratan سرطان
sarf صرف
sarraf صرّاف
Satir, al- الساتر
Sattar, al- الستّار
Sattar al-‘uyub ستّار العيوب
savab[1] ثواب
savab[2] صواب
savab[3] صواب
savma‘a صومعه
Savr ثور
sayyi’a سيئه
sayyid سيّد
sazayi سزايى
Sha‘ban شعبان
shab-i barat شب برات
shafa‘at شفاعت
Shafi‘i[1] شفعى
Shafi‘i[2] شفعى
Shafi‘iya شافعيه
shagird شاگرد
shahadat[1] شهادت
shahadat[2] شهادت
Shah-i mardan شاه مردان
shahid[1] شاهد
shahid[2] شهيد

Shahid, al- الشاهد
shahr-i ramazan شهر رمضان
shahvat شهوت
shajara شجره
shak شك
shakk شكّ
shakkak شكّاك
shaklik
Shakur, al- الشكور
sham' شمع
shama'il شمائل
shama'il-i sharifa شمائل شريفه
sham'dan شمعدان
Shams شمس
shar' شرع
sharab شراب
shar'an شرعاً
shar'i شرعى
shari'at شريعت
sharif شريف
sharifa شريفه
sharik شريك
sharr شرّ
shavq شوق
Shavval شوّال
shaykh شيخ
shaykh al-islam[1] شيخ الاسلام
shaykh al-islam[2] شيخ الاسلام
Shaytan شيطان
shaytan al-'ayn شيطان العين
shaytanat شيطنت
shifa شفاء
shi'i شيعى
shirk شرك
Shis شيث
Shu'ara شعرا
Shu'ayb شعيب
shubha شبه
shuhrat شهرت
shukr شكر
shura [1] شورا
Shura[2] شورا
shu'ur شعور
shuzuz شذوز
sibghat صبغة
sibghatullah صبغة الله
sidaq[1] صداق
sidaq[2] صداق
siddiq صدّيق
Sidrat al-muntaha سدرة المنتهى
sihirbaz سحرباز
sihr سحر
sihri سحرى
sijjil سجّيل
silah سلاح
silsila[1] سلسله
silsila[2] سلسله
silsilanama سلسله نامه
Simurgh سيمرغ
sirat[1] سيرة
Sirat[2] صراط
siyar al-nabi سيرالنبى
subha سبحه
subhan سبحان
subhanahu va ta'ala سبحانه و تعالى
subhanaka سبحانك
subhanallah سبحان الله
subutiya ثبوتيه
sud سود
sudkhur سودخوار
sudur صدور
sufi[1] صوفى
sufi[2] صوفى
suftajah سفتجه
suhuf صحف
sui qasd سؤ قصد
sujud سجود
sukra سكره
sukut سكوت
Sulayman سليمان
sulh صلح
sultan سلطان
suluk سلوك
sunan سنن
Sunbula
sunna سنّه
sunnat[1]
sunnat[2]
sunnat ghayr-i mu'akkada سنّت غيرى مؤكّده
sunnat mu'akkada سنّه مؤكّده
sunni سنّى
sur صور
sura سوره
surat صورت
surnay سورناى
sutra ستره
Ta ha تا ها
ta'abbud[1] تعبّد
ta'abbud[2] تعبّد
ta'akhir تأخر
ta'ala تعالى
ta'am طعام
ta'assub تعصّب
ta'at طاعت
ta'at-'ibadat طاعت عبادت
ta'avvuz تعوّذ
taba'-i tabi'in تبع تابعين
tabarak تبارك
tabarruk تبرّك
Tabbat تبّت
tabi' تابع
tabi'at طبيعت
tabib طبيب
tabi'in تابعين
tabi'iyun طبيعيون
ta'bir تعبير
ta'birnama تعبيرنامه
tablighat تبليغات
tabrik تبريك
tabut تابوت
tadayyun[1] تديّن
tadayyun[2] تديّن
tadfin تدفين
ta'dil تعديل
ta'dil-i arkan تعديل اركان
tadlis تدليس
tafrid تفريد
tafsir تفسير
Taghabun تغابن
tahajjud تهجّد
tahammul تحمّل
taharat طهارت
taharatkhana طهارتخانه
tahir طاهر
tahiyat تحيات
tahiyat, at- التحيات
tahlil تهليل
tahmid تحميد
tahqiqi iman تحقيقى ايمان
tahrif تحريف
tahrim[1] تحريم
Tahrim[2] تحريم

tahrimi تحریمی
tahrir تحریر
ta'ib تائب
ta'ifa طائفه
tajalli تجلّی
tajvid تجوید
Takasur تکاثر
takbir تکبیر
takbir al-tahrima تکبیر التحریمه
takfin تکفین
takfir تکفیر
takhrij تخریج
ta'kid تأکید
takiya تکیه
taklif تکلیف
takrir تکریر
takvin تکوین
Takvir تکویر
takya تکیه
talaq[1] طلاق
Talaq[2] طلاق
talaq khat طلاق خط
talaqnama طلاقنامه
tali' طالع
talib طالب
ta'lim تعلیم
ta'limat تعلیمات
talqin[1] تلقین
talqin[2] تلقین
talqin[3] تلقین
talvasa تلواسه
tamattu' تمتّع
tamjid تمجید
Tamuq تاموغ، تاموق
tanakuh تناکح
tanassur تنصّر
tanasukh تناسخ
tanavvu' تنوّع
Tangri تنگری
tankih تنکیح
tansir تنصیر
tanzih[1] تنزیه
tanzih[2] تنزیه
taqaddus تقدّس
taqdir تقدیر
taqdir تقدیر
taqdis[1] تقدیس
taqdis[2] تقدیس
taqi تقی
taqiya طقیه
taqiyyat تقیّت
taqlid[1] تقلید
taqlid[2] تقلید
taqsir تقصیر
taqva تقوی
taqvadar تقوی دار
taqvim تقویم
taraka ترکه
taravih تراویح
tarbiya تربیه
targhib ترغیب
targhibat ترغیبات
tarikh[1] تاریخ
tarikh[2] تاریخ
Tariq طاریق
tariqat[1] طریقت
tariqat[2] طریقت
tark-i dunya ترك دنیا
tarsa ترسا
tasadduq تصدّق
tasattur تستّر
tasavvuf تصوّف
tasbih تسبیح
tashahhud تشهّد
tashayyu' تشیّع
tashbih تشبیه
tashir تسحیر
tashnab تشناب
tashri'[1] تشریع
tashri'[2] تشریع
tashriq تشریق
taslim[1] تسلیم
taslim[2] تسلیم
Tasnim تسنیم
tasvib تثویب
tatavvu' تطوّع
tatliq تطلیق
tavaf[1] طواف
tavaf[2] طواف
tavaf-i nafila طواف نافله
tavaf-i qudum طواف قدوم
tavaf-i sadr طواف صدر
tavaf-i ziyarat طواف زیارت
tavahhum توهّم
tavajjuh توجّه
tavakkul[1] توکّل
tavakkul[2] توکّل
tavaqquf توقّف
tavarikh تواریخ
tavarruq تورّق
tavazi' تواضع
tavba[1] توبه
tavba[2] توبه
Tavba[3] توبه
tavba-tazarru توبه تضرّع
tavfiq توفیق
tavhid[1] توحید
tavhid[2] توحید
ta'viz[1] تعویذ
ta'viz[2] تعویذ
tavq طوق
Tavrat تورات
tavsif توصیف
tavsim توسیم
Tavvab, al- التوّاب
tayammum تیمّم
tayyiba[1] طیّبة
tayyiba[2] طیّبة
tazahhud تزهّد
tazavij تزوج
ta'zim تعظیم
ta'zir تعزیر
ta'ziya تعزیه
tazkirat al-avliya تذکرة الاولیه
tazkiya تزکیه
tibb طبّ
tijarat تجارت
tilavat تلاوت
tilmiz تیلمذ
tilsim[1] طلسم
tilsim[2] طلسم
tilsim[3] طلسم
Tin تین
Tuba طوبی
tufan طوفان
tugh[1] طوغ، توغ
tugh[2] طوغ، توغ
tumar طومار
Tur طور
turba تربه
udum
Ughan اوغان
Ujmakh اوجماخ
ukaz اوکاز، اوقاز

ukhravi اخروی
ʿulama علما
ʿUmar عمر
umara امرا
Umm al-kitab امّ‌الكتاب
Umm al-mu'minin امّ المؤمنين
ummat امّت
ummi امّی
umm-i valad امّ ولد
ʿumr عمر
ʿumra عمره
uns انس
unsur عنصر
ʿuqba عقبى
ʿuqubat[1] عقوبت
ʿuqubat[2] عقوبت
ʿuqubat[3] عقوبات
ʿurf عرف
ʿurf fasid عرف فاسد
ʿurf sahih عرف صحيح
ʿushr عشر
ʿUsman عثمان
ustabika اوسته بيكه
ustad استاد
ustaz استاذ
usul[1] اصول
usul[2] اصول
usul-i jadid اصول جديد
usul-i khamsa اصول خمسه
usul-i qadim اصول قديم
ʿuzlat عزلت
ʿuzr[1] عذر
ʿuzr[2] عذر
vabal وبال
vaʿda وعده
Vadud, al- الودود
vafa وفاء
vafat وفات
vahdaniyat وحدانيت
vahdat-i vujud وحدت وجوب
Vahhab, al- الوهّاب
Vahhabiya وهّابيه
vahi وحی
Vahid, al- الواحد
vahshat وحشت
vahshiyana وحشيانه
vaʿiz واعظ
vajd وجد
vajh وجه
vajib واجب
vajib al-vujud واجب الوجود
Vajid, al- الواجد
vakalat وكالت
vakil وكيل
Vakil, al- الوكيل
vali ولی
vali ahd ولی عهد
Vali, al- الولی
vali niʿmat ولی نعمت
vallahu aʿlam والله اعلم
vallahu aʿlam bil-savab و الله اعلم بالصواب
vaqf وقف
vaqfa وقفه
Vaqiʿa واقعه
vaqif[1] واقف
vaqif[2] واقف
varaʿ[1] ورع
varaʿ[2] ورع
varaqa ورقه
varasat وراثت
varis وارث
Varis, al- الوارث
vasan وثن
vasani وثنی
Vasiʿ, al- الواسع
vasiqa وثيقه
vasiyat وصيت
vasiyatnama وصيتنامه
vasl وصل
vasvas وسواس
vasvasa وسوسه
vatan وطن
Vays al-Qarani ويس القرانی
vaʿz وعظ
vazifa وظيفه
vazir وزير
vijdan وجدان
vildan ولدان
viqar وقار
virasat
vird[1] ورد
vird[2] ورد
virsa ورثه
vitr وتر
vujud وجود
vuquf وقوف
vuquf-i ʿadadi وقوف عددی
vuquf-i qalbi وقوف قلبی
vuquf-i zaman وقوف زمان
vuzu' وضوء
ya allah يا الله
ya pirim يا پيرم
ya rabbi يا ربّی
ya ramazan يا رمضان
Ya Sin يسن
yad dasht ياد داشت
yad kard ياد كرد
Yafis يافث
yahu ياهو
yahud يهود
yahudi يهودی
Yahya يحی
Ya'juj va Ma'juj يأجوج و مأجوج
Yaʿqub يعقوب
yar يار
Yaratqan ياراتقان
yarhamukallah يرحمك الله
Yar-i Ghar يارغار
yarullah يارالله
Yasuʿ يسوع
yatim يتيم
Yazdan يزدان
yighi ييغی
Yunus[1] يونس
Yunus[2] يونس
Yushaʿ يوشع
Yusuf[1] يوسف
Yusuf[2] يوسف
zabiha ذبيحه
zabt ضبط
Zabur زبور
zafar ظفر
zahadat زهادت
zahid زاهد
zahir ظاهر
zaʿif ضعيف
zaʿifa ضعيفه
Zakariya زكريا
zakat[1] زكات
zakat[2] زكات
zakat al-fitr زكات الفطر
zalalat ذلالت
zalim ظالم

Zamzam زمزم
zamzami زمزمی
zanb ذنب
zanni
Zaqqum زقّوم
zar zaman زار زمان
Zariyat ذریت
Zarr, al- الضارّ
zarurat ضرورت
Zat-i kibriya ذات کبریا
Zat-i pak ذات پاك
zaval زوال
zaviya زاویه
zidd ضدّ
zifaf زفاف
zikr ذکر
zikrchi ذکرچی
zikr-i jahr ذکر جهر
zikr-i khafi ذکر خفی
zikrkhana ذکرخانه
zillat
Zilzal زلزال
zimmi ذمّی
zina زنا
zinakar زناکار
zindan زندان
zindiq زندیق
ziya' ضیاء
ziyarat زیارت
ziyaratchi زیارتچی
ziyaratgah زیارتگاه
ziyaratkhana زیارتخانه
zubani زبانی
Zuha ضحی
zuhd[1] زهد
zuhd[2] زهد
zuhr ظهر
Zukhruf زخرف
Zu'l-fiqar ذوالفقار
Zu'l-hijja ذوالحجّه
Zu'l-ihsan ذو الاحسان
Zu'l-jalal va'l-ikram ذو الجلال و الاکرام
zu'l-janahayn ذوالجناحین
Zu'l-Kifl ذو الکفل
zulm ظلم
zulmat[1] ظلمت
zulmat[2] ظلمت
Zu'l-qa'da ذوالقعده
Zu'l-Qarnayn ذولقرنین
zulum ظلوم
Zumar زمر
zunnar زنّار

Arabic Script Index

ibaha اباحه
abjad ابجد
ab-i hayat آب حيات
abad ابد
abdal[1] ابدال
abdal[2] ابدال
abdal[3] ابدال
abdast آبدست
abdasta آبدسته
abrar ابرار
Ibrahim[1] ابراهيم
Ibrahim[2] ابراهيم
ab-i Zamzam آب زمزم
abiz آبض
Iblis ابليس
abu ابو
abvab al-Qur'an ابواب القرآن
Abu Bakr ابو بكر
Abu Hanifa ابو حنيفه
abida آبيده
ittihad[1] اتّحاد
ittihad[2] اتّحاد
atash آتش
atashparast آتشپرست
itmam اتمام
asar اثر
ijabat اجابت
ijazat اجازة
ijazatnama اجازة نامه
ijtihad اجتهاد
ajr اجر
ajal اجل
ijma‘ اجماع
ijma‘-i ummat اجماع امّة
ajnabi اجنابى
ahbab احباب
ihtijab احتجاب
ihtilam احتلام
ahad آحد
ihdad احداد
ahrar احرار
ihram احرام
Ahzab احزاب
ihsan[1] احسان
ihsan[2] احسان
ihsar احصار
ihzar احضار
Ahqaf احقاف
ahkam احكام
Ahmad احمد
akhbar اخبار
ikhtilaf اختلاف
akhiravi آخراوى
akhirat آخرت
akhirat batqaghi آخرت باطقاغى
akhir zaman آخر زمان
ukhravi اخروى
ikhlas[1] اخلاص
Ikhlas[2] اخلاص
akhlaq اخلاق
ikhvan اخوان
akhun آخون
akhund آخوند
akhi اخى
adab ادب
Idris ادريس
abdastkhana آدستخانه
Adam آدم
azan اذان
izn اذن
irada[1] اراده
irada[2] اراده
irada[3] اراده
irada-yi la yazal ارادهٔ لايزال
irtidad ارتداد
irshad ارشاد
irshadnama ارشادنامه
arkan اركان
arvah ارواح
irim اريم
azar آزار
izar ازار
izdivaj ازدواج
asarat اسارت
ustad استاد
ustaz استاذ
asitana آستانه
istibdad استبداد
istibra استبرا
istisna استثنا
istihaza استحاضه
istihsan استحسان
istikhara استخاره
istidlali iman استدلالى ايمان
istisqa استسقا
istislah استسلاح
istishhad استشهاد
isti‘far استعفار
istighfar استغفار
astaghfirullah استغفرالله
istiqamat استقامة
istiqbal استقبال
istinja استنجا
istinshaq استنشاق
Ishaq اسحاق
Asad اسد
Asadullah اسدالله
Isra اسرا
israf اسراف
Israfil اسرافيل
Isra'il اسرائيل
asfal al-safilin اسفل السافلين
isqat اسقاط
Iskandar اسكندر
Islam اسلام
islamiyat اسلاميت
asma al-husna اسما الحسنه
ism-i a‘zam اسم اعظام
Isma‘il اسماعيل
asman اسمان
isnad اسناد
asir اسير
isharat اشارة
ishraq اشراق
ishrak اشراك
ashrat-i sa‘at اشرط ساعت
ashraf اشرف
ashab اصحاب
ashab-i Badr اصحاب بدر
ashab-i jannat اصحاب جنّت
ashab-i kiram اصحاب كرام
ashab-i kahf اصحاب كهف

istilahat اصطلاحات
usul[1] اصول
usul[2] اصول
usul-i jadid اصول جديد
usul-i khamsa اصول خمسه
usul-i qadim اصول قديم
itaʿat اطاعت
itlaq اطلاق
iʿana اعانة
iʿtiqad اعتقاد
iʿtiqadat اعتقادات
iʿtikaf اعتكاف
iʿtikafkhana اعتكافخانه
iʿtimad اعتماد
iʿdam اعدام
aʿraf[1] اعراف
Aʿraf[2] اعراف
aʿzam[1] اعظم
Aʿzam[2] اعظم
aʿlam اعلم
Aʿla اعلى
aʿma اعما
aʿuzu billah اعوذ بالله
aʿuzu billahi min al-shaytani al-rajim اعوذ بالله من الشيطان الرجيم
ifta افتا
aftada افتاده
iftitah افتتاح
afsana افسانه
afsun افسون
iftar افطار
Aflatun افلاطون
afyun افيون
iqamat اقامت
iqtida اقتدا
iqrar[1] اقرار
iqrar[2] اقرار
aqraba اقربا
akram اكرم
akmal اكمل
al-i aba آل ابا
illa-billah الاّ بالله
Ahad, al- الاحد
Akhir, al- الآخر
Avval, al- الاوّل
Bari, al- البارى
Basit, al- الباسط
Batin, al- الباطن
Baʿis, al- الباعث
Baqi, al- الباقى
Badiʿ, al- البديع
Barr, al- البرّ
Basir, al- البصير
Bayt al-ʿatiq, al- البيت العطيق
iltija التجا
tahiyat, at- التحيات
Tavvab, al- التوّاب
Jamiʿ, al- الجامع
Jabbar, al- الجبّار
Jalil, al- الجليل
ilhad الحاد
Hafiz, al-[1] الحافظ
Hasib, al- الحسيب
Hafiz, al-[2] الحفيظ
Haqq, al- الحقّ
Hakam, al- الحكم
Hakim, al- الحكيم
Halim, al- الحليم
al-hamdullilah الحمدلله
al-hamdulillahi rabbi'l-ʿalamin الحمد لله رب العالمين
Hamid, al- الحميد
Hayy, al- الحىّ
Khaliq, al- الخالق
Khabir, al- الخبير
Rafiʿ, al- الرافع
Rahman, al- الرحمن
Rahim, al- الرحيم
Razzaq, al- الرزّاق
Rashid, al- الرشيد
Raqib, al- الرقيب
Rauf, al- الروف
Satir, al- الساتر
Sattar, al- الستّار
Salam, al- السلام
assalamu ʿalaykum السلام عليكم
Samiʿ, al- السميع
Shahid, al- الشاهد
Shakur, al- الشكور
Sabur, al- الصبور
Samad, al- الصمد
Zarr, al- الضارّ
ʿAdl, al- العادل
ʿAziz, al- العزيز
ʿAzim, al- العظيم
ʿAfuv, al- العفو
ʿAlim, al- العليم
ʿAli, al- العلى
Al-i Imran آل عمران
Ghaffar, al- الغفّار
Ghafur, al- الغفور
Ghani, al- الغنى
Fatiha, al- الفاتحه
Fattah, al- الفتّاح
Qabiz, al- القابض
Qahr, al- القاهر
Quds, al- القدس
Quddus, al- القدّوس
Qadir, al- القدير
Qadim, al- القديم
Qahhar, al- القهّار
Qavi, al- القوى
Qayyum, al- القيّوم
Kabir, al- الكبير
Karim, al- الكريم
Latif, al- اللطيف
Allah الله
Allahu aʿlam biʿl-savab الله أعلم بالصواب
Allahu akbar الله اكبر
allahi billahi الله با لله
Allahu Bashirun الله بشير
Allah taʿala الله تعالى
Allahu Samiʿun الله سميع
Allahu ʿAlimun الله عالم
Allah hu الله هو
Allah ya Allah الله يا الله
allahyar الله يار
lavh al-mahfuz, al- اللوح المحفوظ
alif lam mim ا ل م
Maniʿ, al- المانع
Mubdiʿ, al- المبدع

Muta'ali, al- المتعالی
Mutakabbir, al- المتکبّر
Matin, al- المتین
Mujib, al- المجیب
Majid, al- المجید
Muhsi, al- المحصی
Muhyi, al- المحیی
Muzill, al- المذلّ
Masjid al-Aqsa, al- المسجد الاقسا
Masjid al-Haram, al- المسجد الحرام
Musavvir, al- المصوّر
Mu'izz, al- المعزّ
Mu'id, al- المعید
Mughni, al- المغنی
Muqtadir, al- المقتدر
Muqaddim, al- المقدّم
Muqsit, al- المقسط
Muqit, al- المقیت
Malik, al- الملك
Mumit, al- الممیت
Muntaqim, al- المنتقم
Muhaymin, al- المهیمن
Mujid, al- الموجد
Mu'akhkhir, al- المؤخّر
Mu'min, al- المؤمن
Nafi', al- النافع
Nur, al- النور
ilah اله
Hadi, al- الهادی
ilham الهام
ilaha الهه
ilahiyat الهیات
ilahiyun الهیون
ilahi[1] الهی
ilahi[2] الهی
ilahi[3] الهی
Vajid, al- الواجد
Vahid, al- الواحد
Varis, al- الوارث
Vasi', al- الواسع
Vadud, al- الودود
Vakil, al- الوکیل
Vali, al- الولی
Vahhab, al- الوهّاب

Ilyas الیاس
Alyasa' الیسع
imarat امارت
Umm al-kitab امّ‌الکتاب
Umm al-mu'minin امّ المؤمنین
imam[1] امام
imam[2] امام
imam[3] امام
imam[4] امام
Imam-i A'zam امام اعظام
imam al-qiblatayn امام القبلتین
imamat[1] امامت
imamat[2] امامت
amanat امانات
ummat امّت
amr امر
umara امرا
amr-i Ma'ruf امر معروف
amlak املاك
amniyat امنیت
umm-i valad امّ ولد
amir امیر
amir al-umara امیر الامرا
amir al-muslimun امیر المسلمون
Amir al-mu'minin امیر المؤمنین
amin[1] آمین
Amin[2] امین
ummi امّی
inna a'taynaka al-kavsara انّا اعطینك الکوثر
ana al-haqq انا الحقّ
inabat انابة
anbiya[1] انبیاء
Anbiya[2] انبیاء
intikhab انتخاب
intiqam انتقام
intiha انتها
injizab انجذاب
anjuman انجمن
andarun اندرون
inzal انزال
uns انس
Insan انسان
insan-i kamil انسان کامل

ins-jins انس جنس
insha'allah انشاء الله
Inshirah انشراح
Inshiqaq انشقاق
ansar انصار
insaf انصاف
An'am انعام
Anfal انفال
Infitar انفطار
anvar انوار
ihtida اهتدا
ahl-i Islam اهل اسلام
ahl al-vilayat اهل الولایت
ahl-i dil اهل دل
ahl-i ra'y اهل رأی
ahl-i zimmat اهل زمّة
ahl-i sunna اهل سنّه
ahl-i salib اهل صلیب
ahl-i tariqat اهل طریقت
ahl-i qalam اهل قلم
ahl-i kitab اهل کتاب
ahliyyat-i ada اهلیّت ادا
ahliyyat-i vujub اهلیّت وجوب
Ujmakh اوجماخ
ustabika اوسته بیکه
Ughan اوغان
ukaz اوکاز، اوقاز
avlad اولاد
avliya[1] اولیا
avliya[2] اولیا
avliyazada اولیا زاده
ayan ایان
ayat آیت
ayat al-kursi آیت الکرسی
ayatullah ایت الله
ayat al-mutashabihat آیت المتشبهت
ayat al-muhkamat آیت المحکمت
ayat-i karima آیت کریمه
ijab ایجاب
Isagujikhvan ایساغوجی خوان
ishan ایشان
ishanzada ایشان زاده
iman[1] ایمان
iman[2] ایمان

Injil اینجیل
Ayyub ایّوب
bab باب
baj باج
barakullah بارك الله
baz gasht باز گشت
batil باطل
batin باطن
baqi باقی
bakira باكره
baligh بالغ
billahi با لله
bamdad بامداد
bavar باور
but بت
butparast بت پرست
butkhana بت خانه
bachcha بچّه
bachchabaz بچّه باز
bihablillah بحبل الله
bihukmillah بحکم الله
bakht بخت
bakhshish بخشیش
bakhshi بخشی
bachchabazi بخّه بازی
bad-duʿa بددعا
Badr بدر
bidʿat بدعت
bidʿat-i hasana بدعت حسنه
bidʿat-i sayyi'a بدعت سیئه
badal بدل
badal-i shakhsi بدل شخصی
badal-i askari بدل عسکری
badal-i naqdi بدل نقدی
barat برات
biradar برادر
Buraq براق
bara'at[1] برائت
Bara'at[2] برائت
barhaq برحق
barq برق
barakat برکت
Buruj بروج
buzurg بزرگ
bisat بساط
bismillah بسم الله
bismillah al-Rahman al-Rahim بسم الله الرحمن الرحيم
bashariyat بشریت
Bashir بشیر
basir بصیر
Batha بطحه
baqa[1] بقا
baqa[2] بقا
Baqara بقره
balaghat بلاغت
Bilal بلال
Balad بلد
Bilqis بلقیس
banda بنده
bang بنگ
bani Isra'il[1] بنی اسرائیل
Bani Isra'il[2] بنی اسرائیل
bani Islam بنی اسلام
bani hashimi بنی هاشمی
buhtan بهتان
bihisht بهشت
bayt بیت
bayt al-ahzan بیت الاحزان
Baytullah بیت الله
bayt al-mal بیت المال
Bayt al-muqaddas بیت المقدس
bayram بیرام
bayʿat بیعت
Bayyina بیّنه
bi iman بی ایمان
bibi بی بی، بیبی
bi diyanat بی دیانت
bi taharat بی طهارت
bi gunah بی گناه
bi namaz بی نماز
parsa پارسا
para پاره
pak پاك
put پت
putparast پتپرست
putkhana پتخانه
purtaqsir پرتقصیر
paranja پرنجه
Parvardigar پروردکار
prighuvur پریغور، پریغوور
pari پری
parikhan پری خوان
parikhani پری خوانی
pul-i sirat پل صراط
payam پیام
pir پیر
pir-i mughan پیر موغان
pishqadam پیشقدم
paygham پیغم
payghambar پیغمبر
tabiʿ تابع
tabiʿin تابعین
tabut تابوت
ta'akhir تأخر
tarikh[1] تاریخ
tarikh[2] تاریخ
ta'kid تأکید
Tamuq تاموق، تاموغ
Ta ha تا ها
ta'ib تائب
tabarak تبارك
Tabbat تبّت
tabarruk تبرّك
tabrik تبریك
tabaʿ-i tabiʿin تبع تابعین
tablighat تبلیغات
tasvib تثویب
tijarat تجارت
tajalli تجلّی
tajvid تجوید
tahrir تحریر
tahrif تحریف
tahrim[1] تحریم
Tahrim[2] تحریم
tahrimi تحریمی
tahqiqi iman تحقیقی ایمان
tahammul تحمّل
tahmid تحمید
tahiyat تحیات
takhrij تخریج
tadfin تدفین

tadlis تدليس
tadayyun[1] تديّن
tadayyun[2] تديّن
tazkirat al-avliya تذكرة الاوليه
taravih تراويح
turba تربه
tarbiya تربيه
tarsa ترسا
targhib ترغيب
targhibat ترغيبات
tark-i dunya ترك دنيا
taraka تركه
tazkiya تزكيه
tazahhud تزهّد
tazavij تزوج
tasbih تسبيح
tasattur تستّر
tashir تسحير
taslim[1] تسليم
taslim[2] تسليم
Tasnim تسنيم
tashbih تشبيه
tashri‘[1] تشريع
tashri‘[2] تشريع
tashriq تشريق
tashnab تشناب
tashahhud تشهّد
tashayyu‘ تشيّع
tasadduq تصدّق
tasavvuf تصوّف
tatliq تطليق
tatavvu‘ تطوّع
ta‘ala تعالى
ta‘abbud[1] تعبّد
ta‘abbud[2] تعبّد
ta‘bir تعبير
ta‘birnama تعبيرنامه
ta‘dil تعديل
ta‘dil-i arkan تعديل اركان
ta‘zir تعزير
ta‘ziya تعزيه
ta‘assub تعصّب
ta‘zim تعظيم
ta‘lim تعليم
ta‘limat تعليمات
ta‘avvuz تعوّذ
ta‘viz[1] تعويذ
ta‘viz[2] تعويذ
Taghabun تغابن
tafrid تفريد
tafsir تفسير
taqaddus تقدّس
taqdir تقدير
taqdir تقدير
taqdis[1] تقديس
taqdis[2] تقديس
taqsir تقصير
taqlid[1] تقليد
taqlid[2] تقليد
taqvim تقويم
taqva تقوى
taqvadar تقوى دار
taqiyyat تقيّت
taqi تقى
Takasur تكاثر
takbir تكبير
takbir al-tahrima تكبير التحريمه
takrir تكرير
takfir تكفير
takfin تكفين
taklif تكليف
Takvir تكوير
takvin تكوين
takiya تكيه
takya تكيه
tilavat تلاوت
talqin[1] تلقين
talqin[2] تلقين
talqin[3] تلقين
talvasa تلواسه
tamattu‘ تمتّع
tamjid تمجيد
tanasukh تناسخ
tanakuh تناكح
tanzih[1] تنزيه
tanzih[2] تنزيه
tanassur تنصّر
tansir تنصير
Tangri تنکری
tankih تنكيح
tanavvu‘ تنوّع
tahajjud تهجّد
tahlil تهليل
tavarikh تواريخ
tavazi‘ تواضع
tavba[1] توبه
tavba[2] توبه
Tavba[3] توبه
tavba-tazarru توبه تضرّع
tavajjuh توجّه
tavhid[1] توحيد
tavhid[2] توحيد
Tavrat تورات
tavarruq تورّق
tavsim توسيم
tavsif توصيف
tavfiq توفيق
tavaqquf توقّف
tavakkul[1] توكّل
tavakkul[2] توكّل
tavahhum توهّم
tilmiz تيلمذ
tayammum تيمّم
Tin تين
subutiya ثبوتيه
saqafat ثقافت
Samud ثمود
sana[2] ثنا
savab[1] ثواب
Savr ثور
Jasiya جاثيه
jadu جادو
jadugar جادوگر
jadugu جادو گو
jami‘ جامع
jan جان
jaynamaz جانماز
jahiliyat جاهليت
jahili جاهلى
ja’iz جائز
Jibt جبت
jabr جبر

Jabra'il جبرائیل
Jibril جبریل
jahim جحیم
juda جدا
jadid جدید
Jadi جدی
jazb جذب
jazba جذبه
Jirjis جرجس
jurh جرح
jarima جریمه
juz'[1] جزء
juz'[2] جزء
juz'[3] جزء
juz'[4] جزء
jaza جزا
jizya جزیه
jughrafiya جغرافیا
jafa جفا
jallad جلّاد
Jalla Jalaluh جلّ جلاله
jalsa جلسه
jilva-yi rabbaniya جلوهء ربانیّة
Jumada al-akhira جمادی الآخره
Jumada al-ula جمادی الاولا
jama'at[1] جماعت
jama'at[2] جماعت
Jamra جمره
jam' al-jam' جمع الجمع
jum'a[1] جمعه
jum'a[2] جمعه
Jum'a[3] جمعه
jumalik جمعه لك
jumla جمله
jinn[1] جنّ
Jinn[2] جنّ
janab جناب
Janab-i haqq جناب حقّ
janaza[1] جنازه
janaza[2] جنازه
jinayat جنایت
junub جنب
Jannat جنّت
Jannat al-Khuld جنّت الخلد
Jannat al-'Adn جنّت العدن
Jannat al-Firdaus جنّت الفردوس
Jannat al-Ma'va جنّت المأوی
Jannat al-Na'im جنّت النعیم
janda جنده
junun[1] جنون
junun[2] جنون
jihad جهاد
jihad-i asghar جهاد اصغر
jihad-i akbar جهاد اکبر
jahr جهر
jahl جهل
Jahannam جهنّم
juhud جهود
javabnama جوابنامه
Judi جودی
Javza جوزا
hayat-i abadiya حیات ابدیه
chadra چادره
chalma چالما
chiltan چلتن
childan چلدان
chilla[1] چلّه
chilla[2] چلّه
chillakhana[1] چلّه خانه
chillakhana[2] چلّه خانه
chillayasin چلّه یاسن
Chahar yar چهار یار
hajji حاجّی
hajjikhana حاجّی خانه
hafiz حافظ
Haqqa حاقّه
hal حال
hamila حامله
hamiladar حامله دار
hubb حبّ
habash حبش
Habashistan حبشستان
Habib حبیب
Habibullah حبیب الله
hajj[1] حجّ
Hajj[2] حجّ
hijab حجاب
hajj badal حجّ بدل
Hijr حجر
Hujurat حجرات
hajar-i asvad حجر اسود
hujra حجره
hadd حدّ
hadd-i zina حدّ زنا
hadd-i sirkat حدّ سرکة
hadd-i shurb حدّ شرب
hadd-i qazf حدّ قذف
hudud حدود
hadis حدیث
hadis-i arba'in حدیث اربعین
hadis-i qudsi حدیث قدسی
Hadid حدید
hurr حرّ
haram[1] حرام
haramzada حرامزاده
hirz حرز
haram[2] حرم
haram zanni حرم ظنّی
haram qat'i حرم قطعی
Haramayn حرمین
harif du'a حریف دعا
harim حریم
hizb[1] حزب
hizb[2] حزب
hizb al-shaytan حزب الشیطان
hiss حسّ
hiss-i batin حسّ باطن
hiss-i zahiri حسّ ظاهری
hasan[1] حسن
hasan[2] حسن
Hasan[3] حسن
husn حسن
husn-i akhlaq حسن اخلاق
husn-i adab حسن ادب
husn-i tarbiya حسن تربیه
husn-i khat حسن خط
Husayn حسین
hashr[1] حشر
Hashr[2] حشر
hazrat حضرت
hattat حطّاط
haqq[1] حقّ

Haqq[2] حقّ
haqqullah حقّ الله
haqq al-yaqin حقّ اليقين
Haqq Ta'ala حقّ تعالى
Haqq Rasul حقّ رسول
haqiqat حقيقة
hukm حكم
hikmat حكمت
hukm-i samad حكم صمد
hukumat حكومت
hakim حكيم
hall حلّ
halal حلال
halqa[1] حلقه
halqa[2] حلقه
hulla حلّه
hulul حلول
halif حليف
halim حليم
halimkhana حليمخانه
hilya حليه
hilya-yi sa'adat حليهء سعادت
hiliya-yi sharif حليهء شريف
Hamal حمل
Hanbaliya حنبليه
Hanbali حنبلى
Hanafiya حنفيه
Hanafi حنفى
hanif[1] حنيف
hanif[2] حنيف
havari حوارى
Hut حوت
hayan حياً
Haydar حيدر
hayz حيض
hila-yi shar'i حيلهء شرعى
hay ya hu حى يا هو
khatim[1] خاتم
khatim[2] خاتم
Khatam al-anbiyah خاتم الانبيا
Khatam al-nabiyin خاتم النبين
khach خاچ
khachparast خاچپرست
khanaqa خانقا

khabar خبر
khabar-i vahid خبر واحد
khitan ختان
khatm[1] ختم
khatm[2] ختم
khatm-i khvajagan ختم خواجه گان
khatm-i suluk ختم سلوك
khatm-i kutub ختم كتب
khatna ختنه
Khuda خدا
khudaparast خداپرست
khudatars خداترس
khudajuy خداجوى
khudaguy خداگو
Khudavand خداوند
khudavanda خداونده
khudaykhana خدايخانه
khuday خداى
khudaygu خداى گو
khudayi خدائى
kharaj خراج
khurafat خرافات
khirqa[1] خرقه
khirqa[2] خرقه
khirqa push خرقه پوش
khirqa-yi sa'adat خرقهء سعادت
khirqa-yi sharif خرقهء شريف
khurma خرما
Khizr خضر
khata خطا
khutba خطبه
khat-mahr خط مهر
khatib خطيب
khilafat[1] خلافت
khilafat[2] خلافت
khilafat[3] خلافت
khilaf-i shar' خلاف شرع
Khallaq خلّاق
khilkhana خلخانه
Khuld خلد
khul' خلع
Khulafa-yi rashidin خلفاى راشدين
khalfa[1] خلفه
khalfa[2] خلفه

khilqat خلقت
khalaqa خلقه
khalvat خلوت
khilvat خلوت
khalvat dar anjuman خلوت در انجمن
khalvatgah خلوتگاه
khalifa[1] خليفه
khalifa[2] خليفه
Khalilullah خليل الله
khamr خمر
khums خمس
khunsa خنثى
khvaja[1] خواجه
khvaja[2] خواجه
khvajazada خواجه زاده
khavarij خوارج
hur خور
huri خورى
khush dar dam خوش در دم
khavf خوف
Khaybar خيبر
khayr[1] خير
khayr[2] خير
khayr-sadaqa خير صدقه
Dabba دابّه
dar al-Islam دار الاسلام
dar al-aman دار الآمان
dar al-baqa دارالبقا
dar al-harb دار الحرب
dar al-havadis دار الحوادث
dar al-huffaz دار الحفّاظ
dar al-surur دار السرور
dar al-salam دارالسلام
dar al-sulh دار الصلح
dar al-ghurur دارالغرور
dar al-fana دارالفنا
dar al-qasas دار القصاص
dar al-qaza دار القضا
darayn دارين
damulla داملّا
danishmand دانشمند
Da'ud داود
dubba دبّه
Dajjal دجّال

Dukhan[1] دخان
dukhan[2] دخان
durust درست
darskhana درسخانه
dargah درگاه
darra درّه
durud درود
durus دروس
darvish درویش
dastar دستار
dastarkhan دسترخان
dastshuy دست شوئی
du‘a[1] دعا
du‘a[2] دعا
du‘a[3] دعا
du‘akhvan دعاخوان
du‘adar دعادار
du‘a-yi salam دعاء سلام
du‘agu دعاگو
du‘a-yi qunut دعای قنوت
da‘va[1] دعوا ، دعوی
da‘va[2] دعوا ، دعوی
da‘vat دعوت
dafn دفن
Duldul دلدل
Dalv دلو
dalil دلیل
dalil-i shar‘i دلیل شرعی
dalil-i ‘aqli دلیل عقلی
dalil-i naqli دلیل نقلی
dunya دنیا
dunyavi دنیاوی
dahr دهر
dahr-i dun دهر دون
dahriya دهریه
dahri دهری
davir دور
Duzakh دوزخ
duzakhi دوزخی
dust دوست
diyanat دیانت
diyanatkar دیانتکار
diyat دیة
didar دیدار

din دین
dindar دیندار
din-i samavi دین سماوی
dini دینی
div دیو
divan دیوان
divana دیوانه
Zat-i pak ذات پاك
Zat-i kibriya ذات کبریا
zabiha ذبیحه
Zariyat ذریت
zikr ذکر
zikr-i jahr ذکر جهر
zikrchi ذکرچی
zikrkhana ذکرخانه
zikr-i khafi ذکر خفی
zalalat ذلالت
zimmi ذمّی
zanb ذنب
Zu’l-ihsan ذو الاحسان
Zu’l-jalal va’l-ikram ذو الجلال و الاکرام
zu’l-janahayn ذوالجناحین
Zu’l-hijja ذوالحجّه
Zu’l-fiqar ذوالفقار
Zu’l-qa‘da ذوالقعده
Zu’l-Kifl ذو الکفل
Zu’l-Qarnayn ذولقرنین
rabita رابطه
rahib راهب
ravi راوی
ra’i رأی
Rabb ربّ
riba ربا
Rabb al-‘alamayn ربّ العلمین
Rabb al-Falak ربّ الفلك
rabbani ربّانی
Rabbana ربّنا
rububiyat ربوبیت
Rabi‘ al-akhir ربیع الآخر
Rabi‘ al-avval ربیع الاوّل
Rabbi ربّی
rutba رتبه
raja رجا

rijal-i ghayb رجال غیب
Rajab رجب
rajm رجم
rajim رجیم
rahil رحل
rahm رحم
rahmat رحمت
rahmati رحمتی
Rahman رحمن
rahmani رحمنی
rahim رحیم
rukhsat رخصت
rukhsatnama رخصتنامه
radd ردّ
rida[1] ردا
rida[2] ردا
rizq رزق
Rass رسّ
risalat رسالت
risala رساله
rasm-rusum رسم رسوم
rasul رسول
Rasulullah رسول الله
rasulana رسولانه
rishvat رشوت
riza[1] رضا
riza[2] رضا
Rizvan رضوان
rizvanullah ‘alayhi[2] رضوان الله علیه
razi allahu ‘anhu رضی الله عنه
ri‘aya رعایه
Ra‘d رعد
ragha’ib رغائب
raqs رقص
rak‘at رکعت
ruku‘ رکوع
rammal رمّال
Ramazan رمضان
ramazaniya رمضانیّه
rind رند
rahban رهبان
rahbaniyat رهبانیت
rava روا
rivayat روایت

ruh[1] روح
Ruh[2] روح
Ruh al-Amin روح الامين
Ruh al-Quddus روح القدّوس
Ruhullah روح الله
ruhaniyat روحانيت
ruhani روحانى
ruhi روحى
ruz-i jaza روز جزا
ruz-i ʿarafat روز عرفات
ruza روزه
Ravza روضه
Ravza-yi mutahhar روضهء متهّر
Rum[1] روم
Rum[2] روم
riya ريا
riyazat رياضت
riyakar رياكار
ra'is[1] رئيس
ra'is[2] رئيس
zar zaman زار زمان
zahid زاهد
zaviya زاويه
zubani زبانى
Zabur زبور
Zukhruf زخرف
zifaf زفاف
Zaqqum زقّوم
zakat[1] زكات
zakat[2] زكات
zakat al-fitr زكات الفطر
Zakariya زكريا
Zilzal زلزال
Zumar زمر
Zamzam زمزم
zamzami زمزمى
zina زنا
zunnar زنّار
zinakar زناكار
zindan زندان
zindiq زنديق
zahadat زهادت
zuhd[1] زهد
zuhd[2] زهد

zaval زوال
ziyarat زيارت
ziyaratchi زيارتچى
ziyaratkhana زيارتخانه
ziyaratgah زيارتگاه
sahir ساحر
Sara ساره
saʿat ساعة
Saba سبا
subhan سبحان
subhanallah سبحان الله
subhanaka سبحانك
subhanahu va ta'ala سبحانه و تعالى
subha سبحه
sabʿi samavat سبع سموات
Sattar al-ʿuyub ستّار العيوب
sutra ستره
sajda[1] سجده
Sajda[2] سجده
sajda-yi tilavat سجدهء تلاوت
sajdagah سجده گاه
sujud سجود
sijjil سجّيل
sahar سحر
sihr سحر
sihirbaz سحرباز
sihri سحرى
sakhavat سخاوت
Sidrat al-muntaha سدرة المنتهى
siddiq سدّيق
sar-ab سر آب، سراب
Saratan سرطان
sazayi سزايى
saʿir سعير
saʿi سعى
safa'il سفائل
suftajah سفتجه
safar dar vatan سفر در وطن
safaliyat سفليات
Saqar سقر
sukra سكره
sukut سكوت
silah سلاح
salam سلام

salam ʿalaykum سلام عليكم
Salsabil سلسبيل
silsila[1] سلسله
silsila[2] سلسله
silsilanama سلسله نامه
sultan سلطان
salaf سلف
salaf-i salihin سلف صالحين
salla سلّه
suluk سلوك
salibiya سليبيه
Sulayman سليمان
sama سما
samaʿ[1] سماع
samaʿ[2] سماع
samavi سماوى
samiʿ سميع
sunnat ghayr-i mu'akkada سنّت غيرى مؤكّده
sunan سنن
sana[1] سنه
sunna سنّه
sana-yi shamsiyya سنهء شمسيّه
sana-yi qamariyya سنهء قمريّه
sunnat mu'akkada سنّه مؤكّده
sana-yi miladiyya سنهء ميلاديّه
sana-yi hijriyya سنهء هجريّه
sunni سنّى
sahv سهو
sud سود
sudkhur سودخوار
surnay سورناى
sura سوره
sui qasd سؤ قصد
sayyid سيّد
siyar al-nabi سيرالنبى
sirat[1] سيرة
Simurgh سيمرغ
sayyi'a سيئه
Shafiʿiya شافعيه
shagird شاگرد
shahid[1] شاهد
Shah-i mardan شاه مردان
shab-i barat شب‌برات

shubha شبه
shajara شجره
shuzuz شذوز
sharr شرّ
sharab شراب
shar‘ شرع
shar‘an شرعاً
shar‘i شرعی
shirk شرك
shari‘at شريعت
sharif شريف
sharifa شريفه
sharik شريك
Sha‘ban شعبان
Shu‘ara شعرا
shu‘ur شعور
Shu‘ayb شعيب
shifa شفاء
shafa‘at شفاعت
Shafi‘i[1] شفعی
Shafi‘i[2] شفعی
shak شك
shakk شكّ
shakkak شكّاك
shukr شكر
shama’il شمائل
shama’il-i sharifa شمائل شريفه
Shams شمس
sham‘ شمع
sham‘dan شمعدان
shahadat[1] شهادت
shahadat[2] شهادت
shuhrat شهرت
shahr-i ramazan شهر رمضان
shahvat شهوت
shahid[2] شهيد
Shavval شوّال
shura [1] شورا
Shura[2] شورا
shavq شوق
Shis شيث
shaykh شيخ
shaykh al-islam[1] شيخ الاسلام
shaykh al-islam[2] شيخ الاسلام

Shaytan شيطان
shaytan al-‘ayn شيطان العين
shaytanat شيطنت
shi‘i شيعی
Sad ص
sabir صابر
sabi’ صابئ
sahib-i karamat صاحب كرامت
saf صاف
salih[1] صالح
Salih[2] صالح
sabr[1] صبر
sabr[2] صبر
sibghat صبغة
sibghatullah صبغة الله
sahaba صحابه
sahabi صحابی
suhuf صحف
sahih صحيح
sahifa صحيفه
sidaq[1] صداق
sidaq[2] صداق
sadr[1] صدر
sadr[2] صدر
sadaqa صدقه
sudur صدور
Sirat[2] صراط
sarraf صرّاف
sarf صرف
saghir صغير
Saff صفّ
Safa صفا ، الصفا
Saffat صفّت
Safar صفر
safi’ullah صفی الله
salat صلات
salat al-istikhara صلات الاستخاره
salat al-istisqa صلات الاستسقا
salat al-ishraq صلات الاشراق
salat al-taravih صلات التراويح
salat al-tasbih صلات التسبيح
salat al-tahajjud صلات التهجّد
salat al-jum‘a صلات الجمعه
salat al-janaza صلات الجنازه

salat al-hajat صلات الحاجت
salat al-khusuf صلات الخسوف
salat al-khavf صلات الخوف
salat al-ragha’ib صلات الرغايب
salat al-safar صلات السفر
salat al-subh صلات الصبح
salat al-zuha صلات الضحا
salat al-zuhr صلات الظهر
salat al-‘isha صلات العشا
salat al-‘asr صلات العصر
salat al-‘idayn صلات العيدين
salat al-fajr صلات الفجر
salat al-qusuf صلات القصوف
salat al-mariz صلات المريض
salat al-musafir صلات المسافر
salat al-maghrib صلات المغرب
salat al-vitr صلات الوتر
salb صلب
sulh صلح
salavat صلوات
salavat-i nafila صلوات نافله
salib صليب
salibiyun صليبيون
salla allahi ‘alayhu va sallam صلّى الله عليه و سلّم
sanam صنم
savab[2] صواب
savab[3] صواب
sur صور
surat صورت
sufi[1] صوفی
sufi[2] صوفی
savma‘a صومعه
zabt ضبط
Zuha ضحی
zidd ضدّ
zarurat ضرورت
za‘if ضعيف
za‘ifa ضعيفه
ziya’ ضياء
Tariq طاريق
ta‘at طاعت
ta‘at-‘ibadat طاعت عبادت
talib طالب

tali' طالع
tahir طاهر
ta'ifa طائفه
tibb طبّ
tabib طبيب
tabi'at طبيعت
tabi'iyun طبيعيون
tariqat[1] طريقت
tariqat[2] طريقت
ta'am طعام
taqiya طقيه
talaq[1] طلاق
Talaq[2] طلاق
talaq khat طلاق خط
talaqnama طلاقنامه
tilsim[1] طلسم
tilsim[2] طلسم
tilsim[3] طلسم
taharat طهارت
taharatkhana طهارتخانه
tavaf[1] طواف
tavaf[2] طواف
tavaf-i ziyarat طواف زيارت
tavaf-i sadr طواف صدر
tavaf-i qudum طواف قدوم
tavaf-i nafila طواف نافله
Tuba طوبى
Tur طور
tugh[1] طوغ، توغ
tugh[2] طوغ، توغ
tufan طوفان
tavq طوق
tumar طومار
tayyiba[1] طيّبة
tayyiba[2] طيّبة
zalim ظالم
zahir ظاهر
zafar ظفر
zulm ظلم
zulmat[1] ظلمت
zulmat[2] ظلمت
zulum ظلوم
zuhr ظهر
'abid عابد
'abida عابده
'Ad عاد
'adat عادات
'adil عادل
'Adiyat عاديات
'arif عارف
ashir عاشر
'ashiq عاشق
'ashura[2] عاشورا
'Ashura[1] عاشورا
'asi عاصى
'aqibat عاقبت
'alam[1] عالم
'alim عالم
'A'isha عائشه
'ibadat[2] عبادات
'ibadat[1] عبادت
'ibadatkhana عبادتخانه
'ibadatgah عبادتگاه
'abd عبد
'Abdullah[1] عبدالله
'Abdullah[2] عبدالله
'ibrani عبرانى
'Abasa عبس
'abir عبير
'Usman عثمان
'ajam عجم
'adalat عدالت
'adavat عداوة
'iddat عدّة
'adl عدل
'adn عدن
azab عذاب
'azab al-kabir عذاب الكبير
'azab-i qabr عذاب قبر
'uzr[1] عذر
'uzr[2] عذر
'arsh عرش
'arsh-i a'la عرش اعلا
'arsh-i kursi عرش كرسى
'Arasat عرصات
'urf عرف
'Arafat عرفات
'arafa عرفة
'urf sahih عرف صحيح
'urf fasid عرف فاسد
'aza عزا
'Azazil عزازيل
'azayimkhan عزائم خوان
'izzat عزّة
'Azra'il عزرائل
'uzlat عزلت
'Azza va Jalla عزوجل
'aziz[1] عزيز
'aziz[2] عزيز
'Isaparast عسى پرست
'ushr عشر
'ishq عشق
'asa عصا
'asr[1] عصر
'Asr[2] عصر
'ismat عصمة
'ismatullah عصمة الله
'isyan عصيان
'isyankar عصيانكار
'attar عطّار
'iffat عفّت
'ifrit عفريت
'iqab عقاب
'uqba عقبى
'Aqrab عقرب
'aqliyat عقليات
'uqubat[3] عقوبات
'uqubat[1] عقوبت
'uqubat[2] عقوبت
'aqida عقيده
'aqiqa عقيقه
'Allam al-ghuyub علّام الغيوب
'alamat علامت
'allama علّامه
'illat علّة
'Alaq علق
'alam[2] علم
'ilm[1] علم
'ilm[2] علم
'ulama علما
'ilm al-'aqa'id علم العقائد
'ilm-i hal[1] علم حال

farz-i da'im فرض دائم
farz-i ʻayn فرض عين
farz-i kifaya فرض کفایه
farz-i muvaqqat فرض موقّت
Fira'un فرعون
Furqan[1] فرقان
Furqan[2] فرقان
firqa فرقه
faryad فریاد
farid فرید
farid al-ʻasr فريدالعصر
fasad فساد
fisq فسق
Fussilat فصّلت
fazl فضل
fuzala فضلا
fitr[1] فطر
fitr[2] فطر
fitrat فطرة
fitra فطره
faqahat فقاهت
faqr فقر
fiqh فقه
faqir[1] فقير
faqir[2] فقير
faqih فقيه
fikrat فکرت
falsafa فلسفه
falaq[1] فلق
Falaq[2] فلق
falak[1] فلك
falak[2] فلك
fann فنّ
fana فنا
Fil فيل
faylasuf فيلسوف
Qabil قابيل
Qariʻa قارعه
qarikhana قاری خانه
qari قارئ
qazi قاضی
qazikhana قاضی خانه
qazizada قاضی زاده
qaʻida قاعده
ghamm[1] غمّ
ghamm[2] غمّ
ghanimat غنيمت
Ghavs al-Aʻzam غوث الاعظم
Ghayya غيّا
ghayr-i din غير دين
ghayr-i sharʻi غير شرع
ghayr-i mashruʻ غير مشروع
ghayr-i misr غير مصر
fatiha[1] فاتحه
fatiha[2] فاتحه
Fatiha[3] فاتحه
fatihagu فاتحه گو
fajir فاجر
fahisha فاحشه
faruq فاروق
fasiq فاسق
fazil فاضل
Fatir[1] فاطر
fatir[2] فاطر
Fatima فاطمه
fal فال
falbin فالبين
falgu فالگو
falnama فالنامه
fani فانی
fa'iz فائض
Fath فتح
Fath-i Makka فتح مکّه
fitna فتنه
futuvat فتوت
fatva فتوی
Fajr فجر
fahsh فحش
fida فدا
fidakyar فداکار
fida'i فدائی
fidya فديه
fara'iz[1] فرائض
fara'iz[2] فرائض
Firdaus فردوس
farsakh فرسخ
farishta فرشته
farz فرض
ʻilm-i hal[2] علم حال
ʻilm-i qal علم قال
ʻalaviyat علويات
ʻalayhi al-salam عليه السلام
ʻAli على
ʻamama عمامه
ʻUmar عمر
ʻumr عمر
ʻImran[1] عمران
ʻImran[2] عمران
ʻumra عمره
ʻamal عمل
anbar[1] عنبر
anbar[2] عنبر
unsur عنصر
ʻAnqa عنقا
ʻAnkabut عنكبوت
ʻahd عهد
ʻavrat عورت
ʻid عيد
ʻId al-Azha عيد الاضحى
ʻId al-Fitr عيد الفطر
ʻIsaviyat عيسويت
ʻIsavi عيسوی
ʻIsa عيسى
ghazi غازی
Ghashiya غاشيه
Ghafir غافر
Ghambar غامبر
ghurbat غربت
gharib[1] غريب
gharib[2] غريب
ghaza غزا
ghazavat غزوات
ghassal غسّال
ghasl غسل
ghusl غسل
ghuslkhana غسلخانه
ghasb غصب
ghazab غضب
ghaflat[1] غفلت
ghaflat[2] غفلت
ghul غل
ghilman غلمان

Qaf[1] قاف
Qaf[2] قاف
qal قال
qamat قامت
qanun قانون
qabahat قباحت
Qubbat al-Islam قبّة الاسلام
qabr قبر
qabristan قبرستان
qibla قبله
qiblagah قبله گاه
qiblanama قبله نامه
qubba قبّه
qubur قبور
qabih قبيح
qabila قبيله
qat‘iyat قتعيت
qatl قتل
qatl sabab قتل سبب
qatl shubha ‘amd قتل شبه عمد
qatl ‘amd قتل عمد
qadar قدر
Qadr[1] قدر
qadr [2] قدر
qudrat قدرت
quds قدس
qudsiyat قدسيت
qudsi قدسى
qadam قدم
qidam قدم
qadamjay قدمجاى
qadamgah قدمگاه
quddus قدّوس
qadimi قديمى
qurra قرّا
qiran قران
Qur’an قرآن
Qur’an khatima قرآن خاتمه
qur’ankhana قرآنخانه
Qur’an-i ‘Azim قرآن عظيم
Qur’an-i Karim قرآن كريم
Qur’an-i Majid قرآن مجيد
qira’at قرائت
qira’atkhana قرائتخانه
qurb قرب
qurban قربان
Qurban Bayrami قربان بيرامى
qarz قرض
Quraysh[1] قريش
Quraysh[2] قريش
qasam قسم
qismat قسمت
qisvat قسوة
qasis قسيس
qasas[1] قصاص
qisas قصاص
qasd قصد
Qasas[2] قصص
qisas al-anbiya قصص الانبيا
qusuf قصوف
qaza قضا
qaza-yi mu‘allaq قضاى معلّق
qutb قطب
Qitmir قطمير
qa‘da قعده
qalb قلب
qalam[1] قلم
qalam[2] قلم
Qalam[3] قلم
qalandar قلندر
qalandarkhana قلندرخانه
qul hu allah ahad قل هو الله احد
qimar قمار
Qamar قمر
qamis قميص
qana‘at قناعت
qunut قنوت
qavam قوام
Qavs قوس
qavm قوم
qiyas قياس
qiyas-i fuqaha قياس فقها
qiyam قيام
qiyam binafsihi قيام بنفسه
qiyamat[1] قيامت
Qiyamat[2] قيامت
qiyamat qa’im قيامت قائم
ghayr-i mu’akkad قير مؤكّد
katib كاتب
Kafirun كارفون
kafir كافر
kafiristan كافرستان
kahin كاهن
ka’inat كائنات
kabira كبيره
kitab كتاب
kajraftar كج رفتار
karamat كرامت
kiramin katibin كرام كاتبين
Karbala كربلا
Kardigar كردگار
kursi كرسى
karam كرم
kashkul كشكول
kashish كشيش
kashishkhana كشيشخانه
Ka‘batullah كعبة الله
Ka‘ba كعبه
kuffar كفّار
kaffarat كفّارت
kafalat كفالت
kifaya كفايه
kufr كفر
kufran كفران
kafn كفن
kafil كفيل
kalam كلام
Kalamullah كلام الله
Kalam-i Sharif كلام شريف
kulah كلاه، كله
kalimagu كلمه گو
kalisa كليسه
kalimullah كليم الله
kalimatullah كليمة الله
kalima كليمه
kalima-yi shahadat كليمهٔشهادت
kaniz كنز
kanisa كنيسه
Kahf كهف
Kavsar[1] كوثر
Kavsar[2] كوثر
kavnayn كونين

gunah گناه
gunahkar گناهکار
gumbaz گنبذ
gur گور
gurkhana گورخانه
guristan گورستان
la ilaha illa allah va muhammadun rasulullah لا اله الا الله و محمد رصول لله
Lat لات
la havla لا حول
La makan لا مکان
labbayka لبّیك
labbay لبّی
lahid[1] لحد
lahid[2] لحد
lashkar-i Islam لشکر اسلام
laza لظی
la‘in لعن
la‘nat لعنت
lifafa لفافه
lafzan va ma‘nan لفظاً و معناً
lafz-i kufr لفظ کفر
Luqman[1] لقمان
Luqman[2] لقمان
lillah لله
Lahab لهب
lavh لوح
Lut لوط
Layl لیل
Laylat al-Qadr لیلة القدر
ma’b مآب
matam ماتم
matamzada ماتمزاده
maddiyun مادّیون
ma’zun مأذون
mashaallah ما شا الله
Ma‘un ماعون
ma favq al-tabi‘at مافوق الطبیعت
mal مال
Malik[1] مالك
Malik al-Mulk مالك الملك
Malikiya مالکیه
Maliki مالکی
maliyat مالیت
ma’mur مأمور
mahparast ماه پرست
mavliyat ماولیت
Ma’ida مائده
mubah مباح
mubahasa مباحثه
mubariz مبارز
mubaraza مبارزه
mubarak مبارك
mubashir مباشر
mubashshir مبشّر
mubassir مبصّر
mubham مبهم
mutadayyin متدیّن
matruka متروکه
mutashayyikh متشیّخ
muttasil متّصل
mutasavvif متصوّف
muta‘abbid متعبّد
muta‘assib متعصّب
mutakallim متکلّم
mutanassir متنصّر
mutavatir متواتر
mutavarri‘ متورّع
mutavalliyat متولّیت
mutavalli متولّی
musab مثاب
musbat مثبت
Mujadala مجادله
mujahid مجاهد
mujahida[1] مجاهده
mujahida[2] مجاهده
mujavir مجاور
mujtahid[1] مجتهد
mujtahid[2] مجتهد
mujda مجده
majzub مجذوب
mujassam مجسّم
majlis مجلس
majnun[1] مجنون
majnun[2] مجنون
majus مجوس
majusiyat مجوسیت
majusi مجوسی
muharaba محاربه
maharim[1] محارم
maharim[2] محارم
muhasara محاصره
mahafatullah محافت الله
muhakama محاکمه
muhibb محبّ
muhabbat محبّت
mahbus محبوس
muhtasib[1] محتسب
muhtasib[2] محتسب
muhtazir محتضر
muhaddis محدّث
mihrab محراب
mahram محرم
muharram[1] محرّم
Muharram[2] محرّم
muharramat محرّمات
mahrum محروم
muhsin محسن
mahsi محسی
mahshar محشر
mahshargah محشر گاه
mahfil محفل
muhaqqiq محقّق
mahkam محکم
mahkama محکمه
mahkama-yi kubra محکمهء کبره
mahkum محکوم
muhallil محلّل
mahalla محلّه
Muhammad[1] محمّد
Muhammad[2] محمّد
muhammadi[1] محمّدی
muhammadi[2] محمّدی
mukhasamat مخاصمات
mukhalifat lil-havadis مخالفة للحوادیث
mukhtariyat مختاریت
mukhtasar مختصر
mukhaddara مخدّرة
makhdum مخدوم
mukhlis مخلص
makhluq مخلوق

makhluqat مخلوقات
maddah مدّاح
mudafa‘a مدافعه
Muddassir مدّثّر
madhiya مدحيه
mudarris مدرّس
madrasa مدرسه
mudrik مدرك
madfan مدفن
mudallas مدلّس
madini مدنى
Madina مدينه
Madina-yi munavvara مدينهٔ منوّره
maznib مذنب
mazhab[1] مذهب
mazhab[2] مذهب
marasim مراسم
murafa‘a مرافعه
muraqaba مراقبه
murahaqa مراهقة
murtadd مرتدّ
Murtaza مرتضى
marsiya مرثيه
marhamat مرحمت
marhum مرحوم
murdar مردار
murda مرده
murdakhana مرده خانه
murdashuy مرده شوى
mardud مردود
mursal[1] مرسل
mursal[2] مرسل
Mursalat مرسلات
mursalin مرسلين
murshid مرشد
murshid-i afaq مرشد آفاق
marfu‘ مرفوع
marfu‘ hukman مرفوع حكماً
marfu‘ sarihan مرفوع صريحاً
Marva مروه
murid مريد
Maryam[1] مريم
Maryam[2] مريم
mazar مزار
mazaristan مزارستان
mazarkarda مزاركرده
Mizan[3] مزان
Muzdalifa مزدلفه
Muzzammil مزّمّل
musafir مسافر
masbuq مسبوق
mast مست
mustabidd مستبدّ
mustajab مستجاب
mustahabb مستحبّ
mustashrik مستشريق
mustakrah مستكره
masjid مسجد
Masad مسد
miskin مسكين
muslim مسلم
musulman مسلمان
muslima مسلمه
muslimin مسلمين
musnad مسند
misvak[1] مسواك
misvak[2] مسواك
Masih[1] مسيح
masih[2] مسيح
masihi مسيحى
mas’ala مسئله
mushahida مشاهده
mashayikh مشايخ
mashrab مشرب
mushrik مشرك
mashru‘ مشروع
mushkilkushad مشكلكشاد
mashkuk مشكوك
mashhad مشهد
mashhadi مشهدى
mashhur مشهور
mashvarat مشورت
musadara مصادره
musafaha مصافحه
musalaha مصالحه
mushaf مصحف
misr[1] مصر
Misr[2] مصر
Mustafa مصطفى
musalla[1] مصلّى
musalla[2] مصلّى
musalli مصلّى
musibat مصيبت
mazmaza مضمضه
mutala‘a مطالعة
Mutaffifin مطفّفين
mutlaq مطلق
mutahhar مطهّر
mazalim مظالم
muzaffar مظفّر
mazlum مظلوم
ma‘ad معاد
ma‘az allah معاذ الله
Ma‘arij معارج
ma‘asi معاصى
mu‘amalat معاملات
ma‘bad معبد
mu‘abbir معبّر
ma‘bud[1] معبود
ma‘bud[2] معبود
mu‘tabar معتبر
mu‘tamir معتمر
mu‘jiza[1] معجزة
Mu‘jiza[2] معجزة
ma‘zur معذور
mi‘raj معراج
mi‘rajnama معراجنامه
mi‘rajiya معراجيّه
ma‘rifat[1] معرفت
ma‘rifat[2] معرفت
ma‘raka معركه
ma‘ruf معروف
ma‘sum معصوم
mu‘allim معلّم
ma‘nan معناً
ma‘naviya معنويه
ma‘navi معنوى
Mu‘avvizatan معوّذتان
Mu‘avvizatayn معوّذتين
mu‘id معيد
ma‘yub معيوب
maghasil مغاسل

maghrib مغرب
maghfirat مغفرت
maghlub مغلوب
muftir مفتر
mufti مفتى
mufsid[1] مفسد
mufsid[2] مفسد
mufassir مفسّر
mufassal مفصّل
maqam مقام
Maqam-i Ibrahim مقام ابراهيم
muqavala مقاوله
maqbara[1] مقبره
maqbara[2] مقبره
maqtul مقتول
muqaddas مقدّس
muqarrab مقرّب
maqsura مقصوره
maqtu' مقطوع
muqallid مقلّد
muqim مقم
mukatib مكاتب
mukashifa مكاشفه
Makkatullah مكّة الله
maktab مكتب
mukarrir مكرّر
mukarram مكرّم
makruh مكروه
makruh tahrima مكروه تحريمى
makruh tanzih مكروه تنزيه
mukafat مكفاة
mukallaf مكلّف
mukammal مكمّل
Makka مكّه
Makka al-mukarrama مكّه المكرّمه
makki مكّى
mulla ملّا
mullabachcha ملّابچّه
mulazim ملازم
mala'ika ملائكه
mulhid ملحد
mulhaq ملحق
Mal'un[1] ملعون
mal'un[2] ملعون

malak ملك
malik[2] ملك
milk ملك
mulk[1] ملك
Mulk[2] ملك
mulk-amlak ملك املاك
malakut ملكوت
malakutiyat ملكوتية
mamat ممات
Mumtahana ممتحنه
mamluk مملوك
Manat منات
munajat[1] مناجات
munajat[2] مناجات
munajatkhana مناجاتخانه
manara مناره
manasik مناسك
munazara مناظرة
munafiq منافق
Munafiqun منافقون
manaqib مناقب
manaqibnama مناقبنامه
munakahat مناكحات
minbar منبر
munajjim منجّم
manzur منذور
munazzal منزّل
mansak منسك
munsalik منسلك
manshur منشور
mantiq منطق
mantiqi منطقى
manfur منفور
munkar منكر
Munkar va Nakir منكر و نكير
mankuha منكوحه
manhi منهى
munavvar منوّر
mani' منيع
Mina منى
muhajir مهاجر
muhajarat مهاجرت
muhajirin مهاجرين
muhtadi مهتدى

Mahdi مهدى
mahr[1] مهر
mahr[2] مهر
mavjud موجود
mavjudat موجودات
muvahhid موحّد
mu'azzin مؤذّن
mu'arrikh مؤرّخ
musavi[1] موسوى
Musa موسى
mavzu' موضوع
mav'iza موعظه
mavqi' موقع
mavquf موقوف
mu'akkad مؤكّد
mu'akkal مؤكّل
Mavla[1] مولا
mavlana مولانا
Mavlid[1] مولد
mavlid[2] مولد
mu'allif مؤلّف
mavlavi مولوى
mavla[2] مولى
mu'min[1] مؤمن
Mu'min[2] مؤمن
mu'mina مؤمنه
Mu'minin مؤمنين
mavhum موهوم
mavhumat موهومات
mayyit ميّت
misaq ميثاق
mir مير
miras ميراث
miraskhur ميراث خور
mirza ميرزا
mirghazab مير غضب
mizan[1] ميزان
mizan[2] ميزان
Miqat ميقات
Mika'il ميكائل، ميكال
milad ميلاد
miladi ميلادى
mizana مئذنة، ميذنة
napak[1] نا پاك

napak[2] نا پاك
nahaq نا حق
nahalal نا حلال
narava ناروا
nazil نازل
Nas ناس
nasut ناسوت
nashar'i ناشرعی
nafila نافله
naqis ناقص
namahram نا محرم
namashru' نامشروع
na'ib نائب
Naba نبا
nabuvat نبوت
nubuvvat نبوّت
nabi نبی
nabi'ullah نبی الله
nisar نثار
najat نجات
najasat نجاست
najasat khafif نجاست خفيف
najasat ghaliz نجاسط غليظ
najas نجس
najis نجس
Najm نجم
nihrir نحرير
nahs نحس
Nahl نحل
nahu نحو
nazr[1] نذر
nazr[2] نذر
nazahat نزاهت
Nazi'at نزعت
Nisa نسا
nasab نسب
nasabnama نسبنامه
nasta'liq نستعليق
nasl نسل
nishalla نشتاله
nishallafurush نشتاله فروش
nushur نشور
nisab نصاب
nasara نصارا
Nasr نصر
nasraniyat نصرانيت
nasrani نصرانی
nusrat نصرت
nasuh نصوح
nasib نصيب
nasiba نصيبه
nasihat نصيحت
nutq نطق
nizam نظام
nazar[1] نظر
nazar[2] نظر
nazar bar qadam نظر بر قدم
na't نعت
na't-i sharif نعت شريف
na'sh[1] نعش
na'sh[2] نعش
ni'mat نعمت
na'uzu billahi نعوذ بلله
Na'im[1] نعيم
na'im[2] نعيم
nifas نفاس
nafas نفس
nafs[1] نفس
nafs[2] نفس
nafaqa نفقه
nafl نفل
naqliya نقليه
naqib نقيب
nikah نكاح
nigah dasht نگاه داشت
namaz نماز
namazkhan نمازخوان
namazgah نمازگاه
namazgu نماز گو
Numrud نمرود
Naml نمل
nahi نهی
Nuh[1] نوح
Nuh[2] نوح
nur[1] نور
Nur[2] نور
nur-i 'arshullah نور عرش الله
Navruz نوروز
navkar نوكر
niyaz نياز
niyat نيت
nayran نيران
Habil هابيل
Hajar هاجر
Harut va Marut هاروت و ماروت
Harun هارون
haviya هاوية
Hibatullah هبة الله
hiba هبه
hijra هجره
hijriya هجريه
hijri هجری
hidayat هدايت
hasht-i yak هشت ياك
haft-i yak هفتيك
hilal هلال
Haman همان
himmat همّة
Humaza همزه
Hu هو
Hava هوا
havajis هواجس
havajim هواجم
havala هوالة
Hud[1] هود
Hud[2] هود
havl هول
vajib واجب
vajib al-vujud واجب الوجود
varis وارث
va'iz واعظ
Vaqi'a واقعه
vaqif[1] واقف
vaqif[2] واقف
vallahu a'lam والله اعلم
vallahu a'lam bil-savab و الله اعلم بالصواب
vabal وبال
vitr وتر
vasan وثن
vasani وثنی
vasiqa وثيقه

vajd وجد
vijdan وجدان
vajh وجه
vujud وجود
vahdaniyat وحدانیت
vahdat-i vujud وحدت وجوب
vahshat وحشت
vahshiyana وحشیانه
vahi وحی
varasat وراثت
virsa ورثه
vird[1] ورد
vird[2] ورد
vara'[1] ورع
vara'[2] ورع
varaqa ورقه
vazir وزیر
vasvas وسواس
vasvasa وسوسه
vasl وصل
vasiyat وصیت
vasiyatnama وصیتنامه
vuzu' وضوء
vatan وطن
vazifa وظیفه
va'da وعده
va'z وعظ
'alaykim al-salam و علیکم السلام
vafa وفاء
vafat وفات
viqar وقار
vaqf وقف
vaqfa وقفه
vuquf وقوف
vuquf-i zaman وقوف زمان
vuquf-i 'adadi وقوف عددی
vuquf-i qalbi وقوف قلبی
vakalat وکالت
vakil وکیل
vildan ولدان
vali ولی
vali ahd ولی عهد
vali ni'mat ولیٔ نعمت
Vahhabiya وهّابیه

Vays al-Qarani ویس القرانی
ya allah یا الله
ya pirim یا پیرم
Ya'juj va Ma'juj یأجوج و مأجوج
yad dasht یاد داشت
yad kard یاد کرد
yar یار
Yaratqan یاراتقان
yarullah یارالله
ya rabbi یا ربّی
Yar-i Ghar یارغار
ya ramazan یا رمضان
Yafis یافث
yahu یاهو
yatim یتیم
Yahya یحی
yarhamukallah یرحمك الله
Yazdan یزدان
Ya Sin یسن
Yasu' یسوع
Ya'qub یعقوب
yahud یهود
yahudi یهودی
Yusuf[1] یوسف
Yusuf[2] یوسف
Yusha' یوشع
Yunus[1] یونس
Yunus[2] یونس
yighi ییغی

Bashkir Index

абелхаят ab-i hayat
абыз abiz
абыз hafiz
аҙан azan
Айдар Haydar
аҡшам намаҙы salat al-maghrib
Алла Allah
алла мәхлуғы makhluq
Алла тәғәлә Allah ta'ala
аллаһы әкбәр Allahu akbar
амин amin[1]
Асадулла Asadullah
асман asman
астәнә asitana
ахун akhund
ахыр заман akhir zaman
ахыры заман akhir zaman
аят ayat
баб bab
байрәм bayram
баҡый baqi
балиғ baligh
бата fatiha[1]
бата fatiha[2]
батыл batil
бетеү tumar
бидғәт bid'at
Билал Bilal
билләһи billahi
билләһи-вәлләһи billahi
бисмилла bismillah
бисә bisat
Бораҡ Buraq
бот but
бот put
бут but
буты but
бәддоға bad-du'a
бәдәл badal
бәдәл хаж hajj badal
бәйғәмбәр payghambar
бәйғәт bay'at
бәйтулла Baytullah
бәлиғ baligh
бәндә banda
бәндәл милад milad
бәни исраил bani Isra'il[1]
Бәрат shab-i barat
Бәрат кисәһе shab-i barat
бәрей pari
бәрәкалла barakullah
бәрәкәт barakat
бәхет bakht
важиб vajib
вазифа vazifa
ваҡыф vaqf
Варис Varis, al-
вариҫ varis
васил vasl
васият vasiyat
васыят vasiyat
васыятнамә vasiyatnama
ватан vatan
вафа vafa
вафат vafat
Вахит Vahid, al-
Ваһап Vahhab, al-
вилдан vildan
вирд vird[1]
вирд vird[2]
вөжүд vujud
выждан vijdan
вәғәҙә va'da
вәғәз va'z
вәғәләйкүм 'alaykim al-salam
вәғәләйкүм әссәләм 'alaykim al-salam
вәжип vajib
вәжһе vajh
вәзир vazir
Вәкил Vakil, al-
вәкил vakil
вәкәләт vakalat
вәкиф vaqif[1]
Вәли Vali, al-
вәли vali
вәсүәсә vasvasa
вәхи vahi
Вәхид Vahid, al-
Вәхит Vahid, al-
вәхшәт vahshat
гөҙөр 'uzr[1]
гөмбәҙ gumbaz
гөнаһ gunah
гөнаһкар gunahkar
гөсөлхана ghuslkhana
гүр gur
гүрстан guristan
гәйет намаҙы salat al-'idayn
ғабид 'abid
Ғазазил 'Azazil
ғазап azab
ғази ghazi
Ғазраил 'Azra'il
Ғайса 'Isa
Ғали 'Ali
ғалим 'alim
ғаләм 'alam[1]
ғареш 'arsh
ғаса 'asa
ғаси 'asi
ғасыр 'asr[1]
ғафил ghafil
Ғафир Ghafir
ғибәҙәт 'ibadat[1]
ғибәҙәт йорто 'ibadatkhana
ғибәҙәтхана 'ibadatkhana
ғиззәт 'izzat
ғилем 'ilm[1]
ғилман ghilman
Ғимран 'Imran[1]
Ғимран 'Imran[2]
ғифрит 'ifrit
ғишыҡ 'ishq
ғоҡба 'uqba
Ғосман 'Usman
ғөләмә 'ulama
ғөрөф 'urf
ғөсөл ghusl
ғөшөр 'ushr
Ғумер 'Umar
ғүмер 'umr
ғәбит 'abd
ғәҙел 'adil
ғәҙел 'adl
ғәҙәләт 'adalat
ғәҙәт 'adat
ғәзиз 'aziz[1]
Ғәзим 'Azim, al-
ғәйеп ирәндәр rijal-i ghayb
ғәйет 'id
Ғәйсә 'Isa
Ғәйшә 'A'isha

ғәкидә ʿaqida
Ғәкрәп ʿAqrab
ғәлиәссәләм ʿalayhi al-salam
ғәләйһессәләм ʿalayhi al-salam
ғәм ghamm[1]
Ғәмбәр Ghambar
ғәмбәр anbar[1]
ғәмәл ʿamal
Ғәни Ghani, al-
ғәнимәт ghanimat
ғәрип gharib[1]
ғәрше көрси ʿarsh-i kursi
ғәрәсәт ʿArasat
ғәрәфә ʿarafa
ғәрәфә көн ʿarafa
Ғәрәфәт ʿArafat
ғәүрәт ʿavrat
ғәфләт ghaflat[1]
Ғәфү ʿAfuv, al-
Ғәффар Ghaffar, al-
дамолла damulla
данишмән danishmand
дарелхәреб dar al-harb
Дауыт Da'ud
дин din
диндар dindar
дини dini
диуан divan
диуана divana
диянәт diyanat
доға duʿa[1]
доғаи сәләм duʿa-yi salam
Дозах Duzakh
донъя dunya
донъяуи dunyavi
Дөлдөл Duldul
дөрөҫ durust
дуҫ dust
дәғүә daʿva[1]
дәғүә daʿva[2]
Дәжжәл Dajjal
дәлил dalil
Дәлү Dalv
дәргәһ dargah
дәресхана darskhana
дәрүиш darvish
дәстәрхан dastarkhan
дәфен dafn
дәһри dahri
ен jinn[1]
енәйәт jinayat
Жабраил Jabra'il
жаһил jahili
жаһилиә jahiliyat
жиназа janaza[2]
жиһат jihad
Жөмадиәлахыр Jumada al-akhira
Жөмадиәләүүәл Jumada al-ula
Жәббар Jabbar, al-
Жәди Jadi
жәлләд jallad
жәмәғәт jamaʿat[1]
жәмәғәт jamaʿat[2]
Жәннәт Jannat
Жәүзә Javza
закат zakat[1]
Заҡым Zaqqum
залим zalim
заман ахыры akhir zaman
зарурат zarurat
заһир zahir
зекер zikr
зина zina
зиндан zindan
зиндиҡ zindiq
зифаф zifaf
зобаный zubani
золмәт zulmat[1]
золом zulm
Зөлйәләл Zu'l-jalal va'l-ikram
Зөлҡарнай Zu'l-Qarnayn
Зөлҡәғиҙә Zu'l-qaʿda
Зөлҡәрнай Zu'l-Qarnayn
зөлмәт zulmat[1]
Зөлфәҡәр Zu'l-fiqar
Зөлхизә Zu'l-hijja
зыя ziya'
зыярат ziyarat
Зәбур Zabur
зәҡат zakat[1]
Зәҡҡум Zaqqum
зәмзәм Zamzam
Зәмзәм һыуы ab-i Zamzam
зәуал zaval
Иблис Iblis
Ибраһим Ibrahim[1]
иғанә iʿana
иғдам iʿdam
иғтиҡад iʿtiqad
иғәнә iʿana
иғәнәт iʿana
Идрис Idris
иҙен izn
Иҙрис Idris
ижазәт ijazat
ижап ijab
ижап-ҡабул ijab
ижтиһад ijtihad
изге avliya[1]
изге vali
икенде намаҙы salat al-ʿasr
иҡамат iqamat
иҡрар iqrar[1]
илаһ ilah
илаһи ilahi[1]
илаһи ilahi[3]
илаһым ilahi[2]
илаһә ilaha
илһам ilham
Ильяс Ilyas
имам imam[1]
имам imam[2]
имамат imamat[1]
имамат imamat[2]
иман iman[1]
иман iman[2]
Инжил Injil
инсаф insaf
интиҡам intiqam
интиһа intiha
иншалла insha'allah
иртәнге намаҙ salat al-subh
иртәнге намаҙы salat al-fajr
иршад irshad
Искәндәр Iskandar
исҡат isqat
Ислам Islam
исламиат islamiyat
Исмағил Ismaʿil
иснад isnad
исраф israf
Исрафил Israfil
истибдад istibdad

истибра istibra
истиғфар istighfar
истиғфар isti'far
истиҡамат istiqamat
истиҡбал istiqbal
истилах istilahat
истисҡа istisqa
истихара istikhara
истихара salat al-istikhara
Исхаҡ Ishaq
итлаҡ itlaq
иттиһад ittihad[1]
иттиһад ittihad[2]
итәғә ita'at
итәғәт ita'at
ифтар iftar
ихлас ikhlas[1]
ихсан ihsan[1]
ихтилаф ikhtilaf
ихуан ikhvan
ишан ishan
ишраҡ ishraq
ишраҡ salat al-ishraq
йома jum'a[1]
йома jum'a[2]
Йомадилахыр Jumada al-akhira
Йомадиләүүәл Jumada al-ula
йома намаҙы jum'a[1]
йома намаҙы salat al-jum'a
Йосоп Yusuf[1]
Йософ Yusuf[1]
йөмлә jumla
йыназа janaza[2]
йыназа janaza[1]
йыназа намаҙы salat al-janaza
йыһат jihad
йә аллам ya allah
йәбер jabr
йәдит jadid
йәдитселек usul-i jadid
Йәлил Jalil, al-
йәлләт jallad
йәмәғәт jama'at[1]
йәмәғәт jama'at[2]
йән jan
Йәннәт Jannat
йәр yar
йә рабби ya rabbi
йәсиғ намаҙы salat al-'isha
йәтим yatim
йәһел jahl
йәһүд yahud
йәһүди yahudi
Йәһәннәм Jahannam
Йәьжүж вә Мәьжүж Ya'juj va Ma'juj
Йәьжүж-Мәьжүж Ya'juj va Ma'juj
кафыр kafir
киске намаҙ salat al-maghrib
китап kitab
кифая kifaya
көмбәҙ gumbaz
көрси kursi
көфөр kufr
көффар kuffar
Кәбир Kabir, al-
кәлам kalam
кәлимә kalima
кәлисә kalisa
Кәрим Karim, al-
кәрәм karam
кәрәмәт karamat
кәтмән 'ushr
Кәүсәр Kavsar[1]
кәфаләт kafalat
кәфарәт kaffarat
кәфен kafn
кәфил kafil
кәшәнә turba
ҡабер qabr
ҡағиҙа qa'ida
Ҡадир Qadir, al-
ҡаза qaza
ҡазый qazi
ҡамәт qamat
ҡанун qanun
ҡара таш hajar-i asvad
ҡарыз qarz
ҡарый qari
Ҡаф тауы Qaf[2]
ҡибла qibla
ҡибланма qiblanama
ҡираәт qira'at
ҡираәтхана qira'atkhana
ҡисас qisas
ҡисмәт qismat
ҡиәмәт qiyamat[1]
ҡиәмәт көнө qiyamat[1]
ҡиәмәт ҡайымы qiyamat qa'im
ҡоббә qubba
ҡодес quds
ҡомар qimar
Ҡорбан Qurban Bayrami
Ҡорбан 'Id al-Azha
ҡорбан qurban
Ҡорбан байрамы Qurban Bayrami
Ҡорбан байрамы 'Id al-Azha
Ҡорбан ғәйете 'Id al-Azha
ҡотоп qutb
Ҡөддөс Quddus, al-
ҡөддөс quddus
ҡөдси qudsi
ҡөдсиәт qudsiyat
ҡөҙрәт qudrat
ҡөлһыуалла qul hu allah ahad
Ҡөрьән Qur'an
ҡыбла qibla
ҡыям qiyam
ҡыяс qiyas
ҡәбилә qabila
ҡәбих qabih
ҡәбәхәт qabahat
Ҡәғбә Ka'ba
ҡәғбә ташы hajar-i asvad
Ҡәғбәтулла Ka'batullah
ҡәдәм qadam
ҡәҙер Qadr[1]
ҡәҙими qadimi
ҡәҙимсе qadimi
ҡәҙимселек usul-i qadim
Ҡәҙыр төн Laylat al-Qadr
ҡәҙәр qadar
ҡәлб qalb
ҡәләм qalam[1]
ҡәнәғәт qana'at
ҡәтел qatl
ҡәүем qavm
Ҡәүес Qavs
Ҡәүи Qavi, al-
Ҡәһһар Qahhar, al-
Латиф Latif, al-
Лоҡман Luqman[1]

ләбәйкә labbayka
ләгин la'in
ләғин shaytan al-'ayn
ләғнәт la'nat
лә илаһи илла алла la ilaha illa allah va muhammadun rasulullah
ләүх lavh
ләүх әл-мәхфүз lavh al-mahfuz, al-
ләхет lahid[1]
ләхет lahid[2]
ләхәүлә la havla
лә хәүлә la havla
мағбүд ma'bud[2]
маҙар mazar
маҡам maqam
мал mal
Малик Malik[1]
Малик Malik, al-
малик malik[2]
манара manara
мантик mantiq
мантиксы mantiqi
матәм matam
машалла mashaallah
миғраж mi'raj
миғраж көнө mi'raj
миҙам көнө mizan[2]
Мизан Mizan[3]
мизан көнө mizan[2]
милад milad
миләди miladi
милек milk
мир mir
мираҫ miras
мирза mirza
мисүәк misvak[1]
мисүәк misvak[2]
михраб mihrab
михрап mihrab
Мортаза Murtaza
мосаләхә musalaha
Мосауир Musavvir, al-
мосафир musafir
мосибәт musibat
мосолман musulman
Мостафа Mustafa
мосхәф mushaf
мотлаҡ mutlaq
мохтариәт mukhtariyat
мохтасар mukhtasar
мөбариҙ mubariz
мөбассир mubassir
мөбах mubah
мөбһәм mubham
мөбәрәк mubarak
мөғаббир mu'abbir
мөғжизә mu'jiza[1]
мөғәллим mu'allim
мөдәррис mudarris
мөжтаһид mujtahid[1]
мөжәссәм mujassam
мөжәһид mujahid
мөкәммәл mukammal
мөкәрәм mukarram
мөҡәддәс muqaddas
мөнафиҡ munafiq
мөнбәр minbar
мөнкир munkir
Мөнкир вә Нәнкир Munkar va Nakir
мөнкәр munkar
мөнәжжим munajjim
мөнәжәт munajat[1]
мөнәжәт munajat[2]
мөнәүүәр munavvar
мөрит murid
мөрсәлин mursalin
мөртәт murtadd
мөршид murshid
мөршит murshid
мөслим muslim
мөслимә muslima
мөстәбид mustabidd
мөтәғәссиб muta'assib
мөтәүәлли mutavalli
мөүәррих mu'arrikh
мөүәххит muvahhid
мөфти mufti
мөфтөй mufti
мөфәссир mufassir
мөхакәмә muhakama
мөхсин muhsin
мөхтәсиб muhtasib[1]
мөхәббәт muhabbat
Мөхәммәт Muhammad[1]
мөхәррәм Muharram[2]
мөһажир muhajir
мөшрик mushrik
мөьмин mu'min[1]
мөәллиф mu'allif
мулла mulla
Муса Musa
мырҙа mirza
мәғаз алла ma'az allah
мәғаси ma'asi
мәғбүд ma'bud[1]
мәғбәд ma'bad
мәғлүб maghlub
мәғрип maghrib
мәғрифәт ma'rifat[1]
мәғруф ma'ruf
мәғсүм ma'sum
мәғъюб ma'yub
Мәҙинә Madina
мәҙрәсә madrasa
мәҙхиә madhiya
мәҙхиәсе maddah
мәҙһәп mazhab[1]
мәҙһәп mazhab[2]
Мәжит Majid, al-
мәжлес majlis
мәжнүн majnun[1]
мәжүс majus
мәжүси majusi
мәжүсилек majusiyat
мәзин mu'azzin
мәйет mayyit
Мәккә Makka
мәкруһ makruh
мәктәп maktab
мәҡбәрә maqbara[1]
мәлаик mala'ika
мәлғүн Mal'un[1]
мәлғүн mal'un[2]
мәләк malak
мәләкүт malakut
мәмлүк mamluk
мәнзур manzur
мәнфүр manfur
мәншүр manshur
мәрасим marasim
Мәрйәм Ана Maryam[1]

мәрçиә marsiya
мәрхүм marhum
мәрхәмәт marhamat
мәсет masjid
мәсих masih[2]
мәсьәлә mas'ala
мәтрукә matruka
мәүжүд mavjud
мәүжүдәт mavjudat
мәүҡиғ mavqi'
мәүлит бәйрамы Mavlid[1]
мәүлә Mavla[1]
мәүлә mavla[2]
мәхбүс mahbus
мәхзүм makhdum
мәхкүм mahkum
мәхкәмә mahkama
мәхлуҡ makhluq
мәхрүм mahrum
мәхшәр mahshar
мәхшәр көнө qiyamat[1]
мәхәллә mahalla
Мәһди Mahdi
Мәһҙи Mahdi
мәһәр mahr[2]
назар nazar[1]
назар nazar[2]
наиб na'ib
наҡыç naqis
намаҙ namaz
намаҙлыҡ jaynamaz
насип nasib
нафел намаҙы salavat-i nafila
нахаҡ nahaq
ниғмәт ni'mat
низам nizam
никах nikah
ниәт niyat
нияз niyaz
Ноҡ Nuh[1]
носрат nusrat
нотоҡ nutq
нөгөр navkar
нөгәр navkar
Нур Nur, al-
нур nur[1]
Нух Nuh[1]
нүкәр navkar
нәби nabi
нәбүәт nabuvat
нәҙер nazr[1]
нәжес najis
нәжәт najat
нәсихәт nasihat
нәсәп nasab
нәçел nasl
нәүкәр navkar
Нәүруз Navruz
нәфел nafl
нәфес nafs[1]
нәфес nafs[2]
нәфәкә nafaqa
нәхес nahs
нәхеү nahu
нәһи nahi
ожмах Ujmakh
Озмах Ujmakh
остаҙ ustad
остаҙ ustaz
оçтабикә ustabika
охрауи ukhravi
өйлә намаҙы salat al-zuhr
өммәт ummat
пак pak
пара para
пир pir
пишҡәдәм pishqadam
приговор prighuvur
пәйғәмбәр payghambar
пәрей pari
пәрәнжә paranja
рабби Rabb
рабби Rabbi
раббы Rabb
Раббы әл-ғаләмин Rabb al-'alamayn
Раббы әл-фәләк Rabb al-Falak
рабиғылахыр Rabi' al-akhir
рабиғыләссани Rabi' al-akhir
рабиғыләүүәл Rabi' al-avval
радд radd
рай ra'i
рамаҙан Ramazan
рамаҙан шәриф Ramazan
Рауза Ravza
рауи ravi
Рахман Rahman, al-
риғәйә ri'aya
риғәйәт ri'aya
риза riza[1]
Ризуан Rizvan
ризыҡ rizq
рисаләт risalat
рисәлә risala
риүәйәт rivayat
ришүәт rishvat
риязәт riyazat
рөҡүғ ruku'
рөтбә rutba
рөхсәт rukhsat
рөхсәтнамә rukhsatnama
рух ruh[1]
рухани ruhani
рухи ruhi
рыя riya
рәд radd
рәжа raja
рәжем rajm
рәжәп Rajab
Рәзәҡ Razzaq, al-
рәис ra'is[1]
Рәҡип Raqib, al-
рәҡәғәт rak'at
рәсүл rasul
Рәсүле алла Rasulullah
рәуа rava
Рәхим Rahim, al-
рәхим rahim
рәхмәт rahmat
Рәшит Rashid, al-
сабыр sabir
саҙаҡа sadaqa
салауат salavat
салиҡ salih[1]
Салих Salih[2]
салла аллаһө ғалиһө вә сәлләм salla allahi 'alayhu va sallam
Самат Samad, al-
санам sanam
Саратан Saratan
сарыф sarf
сауап savab[2]
саф saf
сахир sahir

сахих sahih
сижжил sijjil
силсилә silsila[1]
силсилә silsila[2]
сират sirat[1]
Сират күпере Sirat[2]
ситдиҡ siddiq
сихри sihri
сихыр sihr
собхан subhan
собхан алла subhanallah
солох sulh
солтан sultan
сөлүк suluk
Сөләйман Sulayman
Сөләймән Sulayman
Сөмбәлә Sunbula
Сөнбәлә Sunbula
сөнни sunni
сөннәт sunna
сөннәт sunnat[1]
сөннәт sunnat[2]
суфый sufi[1]
суфый sufi[2]
суфыйлыҡ tasavvuf
сүрә sura
сүрәт surat
сыхырсы sihirbaz
сәғи sa‘i
сәждә sajda[1]
сәйет sayyid
сәҡар Saqar
сәллә salla
Сәлсәбил Salsabil
Сәләм Salam, al-
сәләм salam
сәма sama
сәмауи samavi
сәнә sana[1]
Сәүер Savr
сәфәр Safar
сәфәр намаҙы salat al-safar
сәхифә sahifa
сәхәбә sahaba
сәхәр sahar
табиб tabib
табиғ tabi‘
табип tabib
табут tabut
тағат ta‘at
талаҡ talaq[1]
талаҡ ҡағыҙы talaq khat
талаҡ хаты talaq khat
талиғ tali‘
талип talib
Тамуҡ Tamuq
тариҡ tariqat[1]
тариҡ tariqat[2]
тарих tarikh[1]
тарихсы mu’arrikh
Таурат Tavrat
тижарәт tijarat
торба turba
төрбә turba
туфан tufan
тәбғи табиғин taba‘-i tabi‘in
тәбиғин tabi‘in
тәбиғәт tabi‘at
тәбәррек tabarruk
тәбәрәк сүрәһе tabarak
тәғбир ta‘bir
тәғбирнамә ta‘birnama
тәғзим ta‘zim
тәғзир ta‘zir
тәғзиә ta‘ziya
тәғлим ta‘lim
тәғлимәт ta‘limat
тәғәла ta‘ala
тәғәм ta‘am
тәғәссөб ta‘assub
тәжүит tajvid
тәзәүүеж tazavij
тәифә ta’ifa
тәйәммөм tayammum
тәкбир takbir
тәклиф taklif
тәҡдир taqdir
тәҡдир taqdir
тәҡлид taqlid[1]
тәҡсир taqsir
тәҡүә taqva
тәлкин talqin[1]
тәлкин talqin[2]
тәлкин talqin[3]
Тәңре Tangri
тәрбиә tarbiya
тәрүәх taravih
тәрәүех taravih
тәсаууыф tasavvuf
тәсбих tasbih
тәслим taslim[1]
тәуарих tavarikh
тәуаф tavaf[1]
тәуаф tavaf[2]
тәүбә tavba[1]
Тәүрат Tavrat
тәүсиф tavsif
тәүфиҡ tavfiq
тәүәжжеһ tavajjuh
тәүәккәл tavakkul[1]
тәфрит tafrid
тәфсир tafsir
тәхрир tahrir
тәһлил tahlil
тәһәжжед tahajjud
тәһәрәт taharat
тәшбиһ tashbih
Уған Ughan
указ ukaz
Ураҙа ‘Id al-Fitr
ураҙа ruza
Ураҙа ғәйете ‘Id al-Fitr
үләкһә murdar
фазыл fazil
фаҡир faqir[1]
фаҡир faqir[2]
фал fal
фалнама falnama
фараиз fara’iz[1]
фарыз farz
фасиҡ fasiq
Фатима Fatima
фатиха fatiha[1]
фатиха fatiha[2]
фидаи fida’i
фидия fidya
фиҙа fida
фикһе fiqh
Фирғәүен Fira‘un
Фирҙәүес Jannat al-Firdaus
фирҙәүес Firdaus
фирҡа firqa
фытыр fitr[1]
Фытыр бәйрамы ‘Id al-Fitr

фытыр саҙаҡаһы fitr[2]
фәйләсуф faylasuf
фәкр faqr
фәлсәфә falsafa
фәләк falak[1]
фәләк falak[2]
фән fann
фәна fana
фәрештә farishta
фәрьяд faryad
фәсад fasad
фәтүә fatva
фәхеш fahsh
фәхишә fahisha
Хабибулла Habibullah
хаж hajj[1]
хажи hajji
хажый hajji
хаҡ Haqq[2]
хаҡ haqq[1]
Хаҡ тәғәлә Haqq Ta'ala
ханаҡа khanaqa
хата khata
хатим khatim[2]
хатип khatib
хач khach
хижаб hijab
хикмәт hikmat
хилҡәт khilqat
хилүәт khalvat
хилүәт khilvat
хираж kharaj
Хоҙа Khuda
Хоҙай khuday
Хоҙаүәндә khudavanda
хөжрә hujra
хөкөм hukm
хөкөмәт hukumat
хөрмә khurma
хөрәфәт khurafat
Хөсәйен Husayn
хөтбә khutba
хужа khvaja[2]
хур hur
хур ҡыҙы hur
Хут Hut
Хызыр Khizr
Хәбибулла Habibullah
хәбәш habash
хәдис hadis
хәҙрәт hazrat
хәҙрәте рәсүл rasul
хәер-саҙаҡа khayr-sadaqa
хәйез hayz
хәйер khayr[1]
хәйер khayr[2]
Хәким Hakim, al-
хәҡиҡәт haqiqat
хәл hal
хәлифә khalifa[1]
хәлифә khalifa[2]
хәлфә khalfa[1]
хәләл halal
хәмер khamr
Хәмид Hamid, al-
Хәмәл Hamal
хәниф hanif[1]
хәниф hanif[2]
хәрәм haram[1]
хәрәм һарайы harim
Хәсән Hasan[3]
хәсән hasan[1]
хәтем khatim[1]
Хәүзе Кәүсәр Kavsar[1]
хәшер hashr[1]
һади Hadi, al-
һажер Hajar
һалат salat
һарун Harun
һауа Hava
һауап savab[2]
һидайәт hidayat
һижри hijri
һижрә hijra
һижрәт hijra
һүрәт surat
һәфтиәк haft-i yak
Шағбан Sha'ban
шайтан Shaytan
шарап sharab
шариф sharif
Шаһит Shahid, al-
шаһит shahid[1]
шифа shifa
шөбһа shubha
шөкөр shukr
шөхрәт shuhrat
шура shura [1]
шәжәрә shajara
шәйех shaykh
шәкерт shagird
Шәкүр Shakur, al-
шәм sham'
шәрғе shar'
шәрғи shar'i
шәриғәт shari'at
шәрр sharr
шәүеҡ shavq
Шәүүәл Shavval
шәфәғәт shafa'at
шәһәҙәт shahadat[1]
шәһит shahid[2]
шәһүәт shahvat
ырым irim
ысул usul[1]
ысул usul[2]
ысулы йәдит usul-i jadid
әбжәт abjad
әбрәр abrar
Әбү abu
Әбүбәкер Ситдик Abu Bakr
әбәд abad
Әғзәм A'zam[2]
әғзәм a'zam[1]
әғраф a'raf[1]
Әҙәм Adam
әҙәп adab
әжәл ajal
әлғаязы билләһи a'uzu billah
әлиф alif lam mim
әлмисаҡ misaq
әлхәмделилла al-hamdullilah
әмир amir
әмират imarat
әнбия anbiya[1]
әнүәр anvar
әруах arvah
әрәпә 'arafa
әсир asir
әсман asman
әссәләмәғәләйкүм assalamu 'alaykum
әстәғәфирулла astaghfirullah
әсхаб ashab

Әсәд Asad
әүлиә avliya[1]
әүләд avlad
әфтиәк haft-i yak
әхирәт akhirat
әхкәм ahkam
әхләҡ akhlaq
Әхмәд Ahmad
әһле Ислам ahl-i Islam
әһле ҡәләм ahl-i qalam
Я алла Allah ya Allah
Ябраил Jabra'il
яза jaza
Яҡуп Ya'qub
ямиғ jami'
я рабби Rabbi
я рабби ya rabbi
ярабби ya rabbi
яраббым ya rabbi
ярулла yarullah
Ясин Ya Sin
ястү намаҙы salat al-'isha
яуаплама javabnama
Яхыя Yahya
яһил jahili

Karakalpak Index

абат abad
абд ‘abd
абдал abdal[1]
абдәст abdast
абдәсте abdasta
абдәстехана abdastkhana
Абдулла ‘Abdullah[1]
Абдылла ‘Abdullah[1]
абжат abjad
Абу abu
абыдә abida
Абызәмзәм ab-i Zamzam
абы Кәўсар Kavsar[1]
абыр ‘abir
абыт ‘abid
абытә ‘abida
абыҳәят ab-i hayat
ағзам a‘zam[1]
Адам әлеусәләм Adam
адан ‘adn
адаўат ‘adavat
аза janaza[2]
аза ‘aza
азан azan
азап ‘uqubat[2]
азап azab
азап ‘azab al-kabir
азапул қәбир ‘azab-i qabr
азрет hazrat
Айдар Haydar
айт ‘id
Айша ‘A’isha
Айып Ayyub
ақибат ‘aqibat
ақидә ‘aqida
Ақмет Ahmad
ақпар akhbar
ақрап ‘Aqrab
ақрар ahrar
ақун akhund
Ақыр Akhir, al-
ақырат akhirat
ақырзаман akhir zaman
Алақ суўреси ‘Alaq
алейким-у-салам ‘alaykim al-salam
Ал-қәрия суўреси Qari‘a
Алла Allah
аллаакбар Allahu akbar
Алла Алим Allahu ‘Alimun
Алла-Алла! Allah ya Allah
аллабәрекелла barakullah
Алла Бәшир Allahu Bashirun
Алла билла allahi billahi
Аллакбар Allahu akbar
Алла мукәпати mukafat
Алла Сәми Allahu Sami‘un
Алла тағала Allah ta‘ala
Алла тала Allah ta‘ala
аллатала Allah ta‘ala
Алла тәала Allah ta‘ala
Аллаў! Allah hu
аллаяр allahyar
аллияр allahyar
аллыяр allahyar
алым ‘alim
аманат amanat
Аннәс суўреси Nas
Арапат күн ruz-i ‘arafat
арўақ arvah
аса ‘asa
Асан Hasan[3]
асан hasan[1]
асед Asad
аседулла Asadullah
асерет asarat
асман asman
аспан asman
аспан sama
аспаний samavi
аср ‘asr[1]
Аср суўреси ‘Asr[2]
ассалаўма әлейкум salam ‘alaykum
астапыралла astaghfirullah
аттар ‘attar
ахун akhund
ашыў jahl
аян ayan
аят ayat
аяталла ayatullah
Әбәсә суўреси ‘Abasa
әбд ‘abd
әбдәл abdal[2]
әбдәл abdal[3]
Әбдулле ‘Abdullah[1]
Әбдулле ‘Abdullah[2]
Әбизәмзәм ab-i Zamzam
әбрар abrar
Әбу abu
Әбу Бакр Abu Bakr
Әбу Қанифа Imam-i A‘zam
Әбу Қанифе Abu Hanifa
Әбүўбәкир Abu Bakr
әврат ‘avrat
әгузибиллә a‘uzu billah
Әд ‘Ad
әдалат ‘adalat
Әд-Дар Zarr, al-
әдеп adab
әдет ‘adat
әдил ‘adil
Әдил ‘Adl, al-
әдл ‘adl
әдыл ‘adil
Әдыят суўреси ‘Adiyat
әжел ajal
әжем ‘ajam
әжнебы ajnabi
әжр ajr
Әзазил ‘Azazil
Әзем A‘zam[2]
әзиз ‘aziz[1]
Әзийз ‘Aziz, al-
әзийз ‘aziz[1]
Әзим ‘Azim, al-
Әзиреил ‘Azra’il
әкибәт ‘uqba
әкрем akram
әкреб ‘Aqrab
әләўмет ummat
әлем ka’inat
әлем ‘alam[1]
Әли ‘Ali
Әли Имран суўреси Al-i Imran
Әлий ‘Ali
Әлий ‘Ali, al-
Әлим ‘Alim, al-
әлим ‘alim
әлимсақ misaq
әлип alif lam mim
әлламе ‘allama
әлмысак misaq

әлҳәмдиллила al-hamdullilah
Әлҳәмдиллилау реббил аламин al-hamdulillahi rabbi'l-ʿalamin
әлҳәмдулла al-hamdullilah
Әляса Alyasaʿ
әмел ʿamal
әмийин amin[1]
әмин Amin[2]
әмин amin[1]
әмир amir
әмирәт imarat
әмирул мүмин Amir al-mu'minin
әмирул-үмера amir al-umara
әмлак amlak
әмниет amniyat
әмр amr
әмри меруп amr-i Maʿruf
әнбер anbar[1]
әнбия anbiya[1]
Әнбия сүўреси Anbiya[2]
әнел-ҳақ ana al-haqq
әнжумен anjuman
Әнкәбут сүўреси ʿAnkabut
әнқә ʿAnqa
Әнпал сүўреси Anfal
әнсар ansar
әнўәр anvar
Әнъәм сүўреси Anʿam
Әпиў ʿAfuv, al-
Әплатун Aflatun
әпсана afsana
әпсын afsun
әптийәк haft-i yak
әптүйек haft-i yak
Әрапат ʿArafat
әрапә ʿarafa
әресат ʿArasat
әрип ʿarif
әркан arkan
әрўақ arvah
әрш ʿarsh
әршала ʿarsh-i aʿla
Әсен Hasan[3]
әсет Asad
әсир asir
әстапыралла astaghfirullah
әсҳаб ashab
әсҳабул жәннат ashab-i jannat
әтешпәрест atashparast
әттәхият tahiyat, at-
Әузибилле мынешетан режым aʿuzu billahi min al-shaytani al-rajim
Әўел Avval, al-
әўлад avlad
әўлийе avliya[1]
әўлийе avliya[2]
әўлийезадә avliyazada
әўмийин amin[1]
әхбаб ahbab
Әҳед Ahad, al-
Әҳзап сүўреси Ahzab
Әхқәф сүўреси Ahqaf
әхлақ akhlaq
әҳли Ислам ahl-i Islam
әҳли китап ahl-i kitab
әҳли қәлем ahl-i qalam
әҳли рәй ahl-i ra'y
әҳли селиб ahl-i salib
әҳли сунна ahl-i sunna
әҳли тәриқет ahl-i tariqat
әшреп ashraf
әшура ʿAshura[1]
әъләм aʿlam
әъраф aʿraf[1]
Әъраф сүўреси Aʿraf[2]
Әьла сүўреси Aʿla
баж baj
байрам bayram
байт bayt
Байтул әтиқ Bayt al-ʿatiq, al-
байтуләҳзан bayt al-ahzan
байтулкәрамат Bayt al-muqaddas
байтулла Baytullah
байтулмал bayt al-mal
Байыс Baʿis, al-
бакира bakira
бақсы bakhshi
Бақый Baqi, al-
бақый baqi
бақыт bakht
бал fal
бамдат намазы bamdad
бани Ислам bani Islam
бани Исраил bani Isra'il[1]
банги bang
бап bab
батыл batil
бахыт bakht
баччә bachcha
баччебәз bachchabaz
баччебәзлиқ bachchabazi
бәддиўа bad-duʿa
бәдел badal
Бәдр Badr
Бәдый Badiʿ, al-
Бәййина сүўреси Bayyina
бәқә baqa[1]
Бәқәре сүўреси Baqara
бәлагат balaghat
Бәләд сүўреси Balad
бәнде banda
бәрат barat
Бәрәт shab-i barat
бәрекелла barakullah
бәрекет barakat
Бәрр Barr, al-
бәрҳақ barhaq
Бәсит Basit, al-
Бәсыр Basir, al-
Бәтин Batin, al-
бәтин batin
Бәтхә Batha
бәшериет bashariyat
бәят bayʿat
бейиш bihisht
бенде banda
берекет barakat
бет перде hijab
бигуна bi gunah
бидәт bidʿat
бидәт bidʿat-i hasana
бидиянет bi diyanat
бий raqs
бийби bibi
Бийбимерям Maryam[1]
бийгүна bi gunah
бийдәрет bi taharat
бийиман bi iman
Билал Bilal
биллаў billahi
бинамаз bi namaz

бисат bisat
бисмилла bismillah
бисмилла ирахма ниррахим bismillah al-Rahman al-Rahim
бисмиллахир рахманыр рәйим bismillah al-Rahman al-Rahim
бихишт bihisht
бузурук buzurg
Бурақ Buraq
Буруж сүўреси Buruj
бут but
бут put
бутқана butkhana
бутқана putkhana
бутпәрәст putparast
бутпәрест butparast
бутхана butkhana
вүжүт vujud
география jughrafiya
гөр gur
гөристан guristan
гөрыстән guristan
гүмбез gumbaz
гүна gunah
гүнакар gunahkar
гүнәкәр gunahkar
гүўа shahid[1]
ғаза qaza
ғаза ghaza
ғазабат ghazavat
ғазап ghazab
ғазий ghazi
ғайры мәшру ghayr-i mashru'
ғайып ерен rijal-i ghayb
ғам ghamm[1]
Ғамбәр Ghambar
ғаплат ghaflat[1]
ғапләт ghaflat[1]
Ғаппар Ghaffar, al-
ғапыл ghafil
ғәйрыдин ghayr-i din
ғәйры шарий ghayr-i shar'i
Ғәний Ghani, al-
ғәнийбет ghanimat
ғәпил ghafil
Ғәпыр Ghafur, al-
Ғәпыр сүўреси Ghafir
ғәрип gharib[1]
Ғәшия сүўреси Ghashiya
ғилмән ghilman
ғусыл ghusl
ғусылхана ghuslkhana
далп Dalv
дамулла damulla
данишпан danishmand
дастурқан dastarkhan
даў da'va[1]
даў da'va[2]
дәлил dalil
дәлилы ақылынан dalil-i 'aqli
дәлилы нәқылынан dalil-i naqli
дәлилы шәрият dalil-i shar'i
дәлүў Dalv
дәпн dafn
дәрга dargah
дәргаҳ dargah
дәрет taharat
дәретхана taharatkhana
дәрре darra
дәрүламан dar al-aman
дәрүларшыллық dar al-ghurur
дәрүлбәқа dar al-baqa
дәрүлислам dar al-Islam
дәрүлқәза dar al-qaza
дәрүлқәсас dar al-qasas
дәрүлсәлем dar al-salam
дәрүлсулух dar al-sulh
дәрүлсурур dar al-surur
дәрүлфәна dar al-fana
дәрүлхәрб dar al-harb
дәрүлхәўадис dar al-havadis
дәрүлхуппаз dar al-huffaz
дәрўиш darvish
дәрысхана darskhana
дәстурхан dastarkhan
дәў div
дәўән divan
дәўәна divana
дәўәт da'vat
дәўир davir
дәўмет buhtan
Дәўуд Da'ud
дервиш darvish
дийәнәт diyanat
дийәнәткар diyanatkar
дийўана divana
дин din
дини dini
диншил dindar
Дозақ Duzakh
дозақи duzakhi
дос dust
дуббә dubba
дуға du'a[1]
дуға du'a[2]
дуға du'a[3]
дурыс durust
дуўа du'a[1]
дуўа du'a[2]
дуўа du'a[3]
дуўагөй du'agu
дуўадар du'adar
дуўаисәлам du'a-yi salam
дуўахан jadugar
дуўахан du'akhvan
дуўаши du'agu
дуўаши du'akhvan
Духан сүўреси Dukhan[1]
Дүлдүл Duldul
дүнья dunya
дүньяўи dunyavi
ежтыҳәт ijtihad
етеги келиў hayz
Жабрайыл Jabra'il
жадигөй jadugu
жадүгар jadugu
жаза jaza
жайнамаз jaynamaz
Жақып Ya'qub
Жалил Jalil, al-
жаллат jallad
жалса jalsa
жамаат jama'at[1]
Жамра Jamra
жан jan
жаназа janaza[1]
жаназа janaza[2]
жанап janab
жанапи Ҳақ Janab-i haqq
жан дос dust
жаныў janab
жапа jafa
Жаппар Jabbar, al-
жарамазан ya ramazan

Жаратқан Yaratqan
жасат jasad
жаўапнама javabnama
жаўза Javza
жахыл jahl
жахылият jahiliyat
жәбирлеў ʻuqubat[2]
жәди jadu
жәдигар jadugar
жәдигөй jadugu
жәдий Jadi
жәдит jadid
жәлеп fahisha
жәллат jallad
жәмәат jamaʻat[1]
Жәмий Jamiʻ, al-
жәмийет jamaʻat[2]
жәмы jamiʻ
жәнде janda
Жәннет Jannat
Жәннетул Пирдаўс Jannat al-Firdaus
Жәсия сүўреси Jasiya
жәўзә Javza
Жәҳәннем Jahannam
жәхыл jahili
жебир jabr
жедди Jadi
жетим saghir
жетим yatim
жигер irada[3]
жин jinn[1]
жиназа janaza[1]
жинаят jinayat
Жин сүўреси Jinn[2]
жөҳит juhud
жөхит yahud
жуғрәпия jughrafiya
жуда juda
жукли hamiladar
жума jumʻa[1]
жума jumʻa[2]
Жумадиүләўәл Jumada al-ula
Жумадул-аўўал Jumada al-ula
Жумадул-ахир Jumada al-akhira
жумалиқ jumalik
жума намаз salat al-jumʻa
Жума сүўреси Jumʻa[3]
Жумәдиүссәни Jumada al-akhira
жумлә jumla
Жүнис Yunus[1]
Жүнис сүўреси Yunus[2]
Жүсип Yusuf[1]
Жүсип сүўреси Yusuf[2]
жын jinn[1]
жыназа janaza[1]
жыназа намаз salat al-janaza
жыҳад jihad
зайып zaʻifa
закат zakat[1]
закон qanun
залым zalim
заўза Javza
зәкат zakat[1]
зәкәт zakat[1]
Зәлзәла сүўреси Zilzal
Зәмзәм Zamzam
Зәмзәм абы ab-i Zamzam
Зәмзәм суўы ab-i Zamzam
зәрурият zarurat
зәўәл zaval
зикир zikr
зикирбант zikrchi
зикирхана zikrkhana
зикирши zikrchi
зикри хупи zikr-i khafi
зина zina
зинакор zinakar
зинахор zinakar
зиндан zindan
зулмат zulmat[1]
Зулпықар Zu'l-fiqar
зулым zulm
Зумәр сүўреси Zumar
Зухруф сүўреси Zukhruf
зүлқәдә Zu'l-qaʻda
зүлхиже Zu'l-hijja
зыт zidd
зыярат ziyarat
зыяратхана ziyaratkhana
зыяратшы ziyaratchi
ибадат ʻibadat[1]
ибадатгаҳ ʻibadatgah
ибадатхана ʻibadatkhana
Ибирайым Ibrahim[1]
идәм iʻdam
иддә ʻiddat
иззет ʻizzat
изн izn
ийжабат ijabat
ийжазат ijazat
ийжазатнаме ijazatnama
ийжап ijab
иймам imam[1]
иймам imam[2]
иймам imam[3]
иймам imam[4]
иймамат imamat[1]
иймамат imamat[2]
ийман iman[1]
ийман iman[2]
Ийса ʻIsa
ийсави ʻIsavi
ийсавият ʻIsaviyat
Ийсақ Ishaq
ийсапәрест ʻIsaparast
ийшан ishan
иқрар iqrar[1]
иқрар iqrar[2]
илаҳ ilah
илаҳа ilaha
илаҳи ilahi[3]
илаҳий ilahi[1]
илаҳий ilahi[2]
илаҳиун ilahiyun
илаҳият ilahiyat
илим ʻilm[1]
илимқал ʻilm-i qal
илимҳал ʻilm-i hal[1]
илимҳал ʻilm-i hal[2]
Илияс Ilyas
илла-биллә illa-billah
илтийжа iltija
илҳам ilham
илҳәм ilham
Имран ʻImran[1]
Имран ʻImran[2]
Инжил Injil
инис-жинис ins-jins
Инсан сүўреси Insan
инсап insaf
интиқам intiqam
иншалла insha'allah
Иншиқақ сүўреси Inshiqaq

иприт ʿifrit
иптар iftar
ираде irada[3]
ирик dukhan[2]
ирим irim
иршат irshad
иршатнама irshadnama
исён ʿisyan
исёнкәр ʿisyankar
Искендер Iskandar
Ислам Islam
исламият islamiyat
Ислам ләшкерләри lashkar-i Islam
Исмайыл Ismaʿil
иснад isnad
Исрапил Israfil
исрәп israf
Исрә суўреси Isra
истибдәд istibdad
истиқбал istiqbal
истиләҳат istilahat
истинжа istinja
истисна istisna
итәат itaʿat
итиқат iʿtiqad
итмам itmam
иттиҳад ittihad[1]
иттиҳад ittihad[2]
ихлас ikhlas[1]
ихрам ihram
иҳсан ihsan[1]
иҳсан ihsan[2]
ихтижаб ihtijab
ишиқ ʿishq
Каба Kaʿba
Каўсар суўреси Kavsar[2]
Кәба Kaʿba
Кәбатулла Kaʿbatullah
Кәбуд Qabiz, al-
Кәбыр Kabir, al-
кәбыр kabira
кәдер qadar
кәлам kalam
кәлами Шарип Kalam-i Sharif
кәламулла Kalamullah
кәлийма kalima
кәлимагөй kalimagu
кәлимаи шаҳәдат kalima-yi shahadat
кәлимә kalima
кәниз kaniz
кәнизек kaniz
кәпил kafalat
кәпил kafil
кәпин kafn
кәпир kafir
кәпиристан kafiristan
Кәпирун суўреси Kafirun
кәппарат kaffarat
кәрам karam
кәрамат karamat
Кәрбалә Karbala
Кәрим Karim, al-
Кәўсар Kavsar[1]
кәхин kahin
кебин kafn
кепил kafil
кепин kafn
китап kitab
класс darskhana
кудайи khudayi
Кудайўан Khudavand
кулах kulah
куппар kuffar
купран kufran
купур kufr
курапәт khurafat
курсы kursi
қабат hamiladar
қабих qabih
Қабыл Qabil
Қавий Qavi, al-
қағыйда qaʿida
қадимшилик usul-i qadim
Қадр суўреси Qadr[1]
қадым Qadim, al-
қадыми qadimi
қаза qaza
қазы qazi
қазызәдә qazizada
қазыхана qazikhana
қайир khayr[1]
қайир-садақа khayr-sadaqa
Қайийм Qayyum, al-
қайырқом himmat
қайыр-садақа khayr-sadaqa
қалп qalb
Қалық Khaliq, al-
қалын sidaq[1]
қалынлиқ sidaq[1]
қамар жыл sana-yi qamariyya
қамария жыл sana-yi qamariyya
Қамәр суўреси Qamar
қамр khamr
қанапий Hanafi
Қанапия Hanafiya
Қанафия Hanafiya
қанип hanif[1]
қанип hanif[2]
қарамат karamat
қарғыс laʿin
қарж kharaj
қары qari
қарыз qarz
қарый qari
қарыханә qarikhana
қасәм qasam
қасәс qasas[1]
қасәс qisas
Қасәс суўреси Qasas[2]
қасыт qasd
қатип khatib
қатл qatl
Қатыйша Khadija
қатым khatim[2]
қатым khatm[1]
қатым khatm[2]
қаўым qavm
қаўыс Qavs
Қахп суўреси Kahf
Қаххәр Qahhar, al-
қаҳыр Qahr, al-
қаыдә qaʿida
қәбахәат qabahat
қәбийле qabila
қәбир qabr
қәбирстан qabristan
қәбристан qabristan
қәдем qadam
қәдемгөх qadamgah
қәдемжөй qadamjay
Қәдир Qadir, al-
қәдир ақшамы Laylat al-Qadr

қәдир түн Laylat al-Qadr
қәләм qalam[2]
қәләм qalam[1]
қәлем qalam[2]
Қәлем суўреси Qalam[3]
қәлендер qalandar
қәлендерхана qalandarkhana
қәлендерханә qalandarkhana
қәмәт qamat
қәнун qanun
қәтам khatim[1]
қәте khata
қәтип katib
қәўим qavm
Қәф суўреси Qaf[1]
Қәф таға Qaf[2]
Қәҳәр Qahhar, al-
қимәр qimar
қиплә qibla
қипләгә qiblagah
қипләнамә qiblanama
қиран qiran
қирәет qira'at
қисмәт qismat
Қитмир Qitmir
қиямәт qiyamat[1]
қиямәт қәйим qiyamat qa'im
Қиямәт суўреси Qiyamat[2]
қияс qiyas
қожа khvaja[1]
қозғалан ʻisyan
қорғай mudafaʻa
қубба qubba
Қуббатул Ислам Qubbat al-Islam
Қудай Khuda
Қудай khuday
қудайгөй khudaguy
қудайгөй khudaygu
қудайжөй khudajuy
қудайихана khudaykhana
қудайпәрест khudaparast
қудайсыз ghayr-i din
қудайсыз dahri
қудайсызлар dahriya
Қудайўандә khudavanda
Қуддус Quddus, al-
қуддус quddus
Қуддуси Шарип Quds, al-
қудирет qudrat
қудрәт qudrat
қудс quds
қудс qudsi
қулхиаллаахад qul hu allah ahad
қуптан salat al-ʻisha
қуптан khuftan
Қуран Qur'an
Қурани Азийм Qur'an-i ʻAzim
Қурани қатим Qur'an khatima
Қуран Кәрим Qur'an-i Karim
Қуранханә qur'ankhana
қурәйиш Quraysh[1]
Қурәйиш суўреси Quraysh[2]
қурбан ʻId al-Azha
қурбан qurban
Қурбан айти Qurban Bayrami
қурбан айты ʻId al-Azha
қурбанлиқ qurban
қурбан ҳайт ʻId al-Azha
қурма khurma
қурмә khurma
қутбә khutba
Қыдыр Khizr
Қызыр Khizr
қыраат qira'at
қысўа qisvat
қыямат qiyamat[1]
қыяс qiyas
Лайил суўреси Layl
лайн laʻin
Латип Latif, al-
Латманат Lat
Латманат Manat
ләббай labbay
ләббайка labbayka
ләббәй labbay
ләйләтулқәдир Laylat al-Qadr
ләлатулқедр Laylat al-Qadr
ләхад lahid[1]
ләхад lahid[2]
Луқман Luqman[1]
Луқман суўреси Luqman[2]
Лут Lut
Мааириж суўреси Maʻarij
мағрип maghrib
маддах maddah
маддылиқ maddiyun
мажилис majlis
мазар maqbara[1]
мазар maqbara[2]
мазар mazar
мазарстан mazaristan
мақам maqam
Мақамбет Muhammad[1]
мақлуқ makhluq
мақлуқат makhluqat
мақсым makhdum
мал mal
малақ malak
Малийк Malik, al-
малийк malik[2]
малсыз gharib[1]
манзур manzur
марапат maʻrifat[1]
мариз намаз salat al-mariz
марҳум marhum
Масад суўреси Masad
масайиқ mashayikh
масәк mansak
матам janaza[2]
матам matam
матамзада matamzada
маҳр mahr[2]
маҳрәм maharim[1]
маҳрәм maharim[2]
маҳрум mahrum
маҳшер mahshar
маҳшер mahshargah
маҳшер күни mahshar
мәғлуп maghlub
мәғси mahsi
мәджус majus
мәджус majusi
мәджусия majusiyat
Мәдийна Madina
Мәдина Madina
мәжилис majlis
мәжнүн majnun[2]
мәзин mu'azzin
мәзлум mazalim
мәзлум mazlum
мәзҳәп mazhab[1]
мәзхеп mazhab[2]
Мәида суўреси Ma'ida

мәйит mayyit
мәкируў makruh
Мәкке Makka
Мәкке пәтхи Fath-i Makka
Мәккетуллла Makkatullah
мәкруў makruh
мәктеп maktab
мақәм maqam
мәқпират maghfirat
мәқшер mahshar
мәлғият maliyat
мәлғүн mal‘un[2]
Мәлийк Malik[1]
Мәлики Maliki
мәликия Malikiya
мәлун Mal‘un[1]
мәлүн mal‘un[2]
мәмат mamat
Мәмбет Muhammad[1]
мәмур ma’mur
мәнгилик baqa[1]
мәнпур manfur
мәнтиқ mantiq
мәнтиқий mantiqi
мәрака ma‘raka
мәрасим marasim
Мәрва Marva
мәрем mahram
мәрипат ma‘rifat[1]
Мәриям сүўреси Maryam[2]
мәрсия marsiya
мәрҳәмат marhamat
Мәрьям Maryam[1]
мәс mast
мәсәла mas’ala
мәсиўек misvak[1]
мәсиўек misvak[2]
Мәсих Masih[1]
мәсих masih[2]
мәсихи masihi
Мәуўн сүўреси Ma‘un
мәўжуд mavjud
мәўжудат mavjudat
мәўла Mavla[1]
мәўла mavla[2]
мәўлана mavlana
мәўлаўи mavlavi
мәўлит Mavlid[1]
мәўлит mavlid[2]
мәўхум mavhum
мәҳәлле mahalla
мәҳбус mahbus
Мәҳди Mahdi
мәҳкәм mahkam
мәҳкәма mahkama
мәҳкум mahkum
мәҳпәрәст mahparast
мәҳр mahr[1]
мәҳрем mahram
мәшҳад mashhad
мәшҳур mashhur
мәшру mashru‘
медресе madrasa
мереке bayram
Метин Matin, al-
мешит jami‘
мешит masjid
мешит Ақса Masjid al-Aqsa, al-
мешиткәўим qavm
мешит Харам Masjid al-Haram, al-
мизән mizan[1]
мийзан Mizan[3]
мийзан mizan[2]
мийзана mizana
мийрас miras
мийрасхор miraskhur
Микәйыл Mika’il
милат жыл sana-yi miladiyya
милəд milad
миләди miladi
минара manara
минәжат munajat[1]
минәжат munajat[2]
минәжатхана munajatkhana
минбер minbar
мираж mi‘raj
миражия mi‘rajiya
миражнәма mi‘rajnama
мирза mirza
мискин miskin
Миср Misr[2]
миср misr[1]
мисўәк misvak[1]
мисўәк misvak[2]
михрап mihrab
молла mulla
мубәриза mubaraza
мубәх mubah
мубәхиса mubahasa
мубҳәм mubham
мувәққат farz-i muvaqqat
муғаллим mu‘allim
муғбәриз mubariz
муғбәшыр mubashir
муғбәшыр mubashshir
мудәррис mudarris
мудрик mudrik
Мужәдала сүўреси Mujadala
мужәҳид mujahid
муждә mujda
Мужип Mujib, al-
музаппар muzaffar
Музәммил сүўреси Muzzammil
Муздәлип Muzdalifa
Музил Muzill, al-
мукәлләп mukallaf
мукәррем mukarram
мукәммәл mukammal
муқаллит muqallid
Муқамбет Muhammad[1]
Муқамбет сүўреси Muhammad[2]
муқәддәс muqaddas
муләзим mulazim
мулк milk
мулки амләк mulk-amlak
Мумин Mu’min, al-
мумин mu’min[1]
Муминун сүўреси Mu’minin
Мумтахана сүўреси Mumtahana
муназәра munazara
мунапиқ munafiq
Мунапиқиун сүўреси Munafiqun
мунәжжым munajjim
мунәўўер munavvar
мункәр munkar
муптыр muftir
мурда murda
мурсал mursal[1]
мурсалин mursalin
муртад murtadd
муршит murshid
Муса Musa
мусадәра musadara

мусаўи musavi[1]
мусәпир намаз salat al-musafir
Мусәўўыр Musavvir, al-
мусбәт musbat
мусибәт musibat
муслыма muslima
муслымун muslimin
Мустафа Mustafa
мустәбит mustabidd
мустәжәб mustajab
мусылман muslim
мусылман musulman
мусырман musulman
мусырман muslim
мутавәли mutavalli
мутасаўўип mutasavvif
Мутаффипин сүўреси Mutaffifin
мутаххәр mutahhar
муташайих mutashayyikh
мутәкәллим mutakallim
Мутәкәппир Mutakabbir, al-
Мутәли Muta'ali, al-
мутәссип muta'assib
мутәўллият mutavalliyat
мутләқ mutlaq
муттәсил muttasil
муфәссәл mufassal
муҳаббат muhabbat
муҳәдийс muhaddis
муҳәжир muhajir
муҳәжир muhajirin
муҳәжирәт muhajarat
муҳәкәмә muhakama
мухтәсиб muhtasib[1]
мухтәсиб muhtasib[2]
мушрик mushrik
мүәзин mu'azzin
мүбәрек mubarak
мүдәрис mudarris
Мүддассир сүўреси Muddassir
мүлик mulk[1]
мүлк mulk[1]
Мүлк сүўреси Mulk[2]
мүнәўар munavvar
Мүнкәр-Нәкир Munkar va Nakir
мүнкир munkir
мүпти mufti
мүрид murid
мүсәпир musafir
Мүхаррәм Muharram[2]
Мүхәррәм Muharram[2]
Мына Mina
мыр mir
Мыртаза Murtaza
Мәний Mani', al-
набиўәт nabuvat
нажәс najis
найб na'ib
найып na'ib
нақлия naqliya
намаз namaz
намаз salat
намазгөй namazgu
намазгөҳ namazgah
намаздигер salat al-'asr
намаздыгер salat al-'asr
намазхан namazkhan
намазшам salat al-maghrib
намәҳрәм namahram
Намл сүўреси Naml
напс nafs[1]
напс nafs[2]
насәрә nasara
насрани nasrani
насраният nasraniyat
Наср сүўреси Nasr
Наўруз Navruz
наҳақ nahaq
Нахл сүўреси Nahl
нәәш na'sh[1]
нәәш na'sh[2]
Нәбә сүўреси Naba
нәби nabi
нәбиалла nabi'ullah
нәбий nabi
нәвкер navkar
нәжас najasat
нәжас najas
нәжасәт najasat
нәжат najat
нәзар nazar[1]
нәзар nazar[2]
нәзил nazil
нәзир nazr[1]
нәзр nazr[2]
нәиб na'ib
нәим Na'im[1]
нәим na'im[2]
нәқип naqib
нәлет la'nat
нәмашру namashru'
Нәмруд Numrud
нәпак napak[1]
нәпак napak[2]
нәпақа nafaqa
нәпес nafas
Нәпий Nafi', al-
нәпилә nafl
нәпилә намаз nafila
нәсап nasab
нәсапнамә nasabnama
нәсийҳат nasihat
нәсил nasl
нәсип nasib
нәсихат nasihat
нәсият nasihat
нәхақ nahaq
нәхалал nahalal
нәхс nahs
нәшари nashar'i
неке nikah
несийбе nasiba
несип nasib
неше afyun
ниғмет ni'mat
ниет niyat
низам nizam
нийет niyat
Нимрут Numrud
нисап nisab
Нисә сүўреси Nisa
нияз niyaz
нөкер navkar
Нур Nur, al-
нур nur[1]
нури аршиалла nur-i 'arshullah
Нур сүўреси Nur[2]
нусрет nusrat
нутиқ nutq
Нух Nuh[1]
Нух сүўреси Nuh[2]
нызам nizam
нызам qanun

озр ʻuzr[1]
ойын raqs
Омар ʻUmar
омр ʻumr
ораза ruza
Ораза ҳайт ʻId al-Fitr
Осман ʻUsman
Оспан ʻUsman
өкибәт ʻuqubat[1]
өкибәт ʻuqubat[2]
өлик jasad
өлик murda
өликсе murdar
өтиниў ʻuzr[2]
өш intiqam
пазыл fazil
пазыл fazl
пайғамбар payghambar
пайғәм paygham
пақыр faqir[2]
пал fal
палбын falbin
палнама falnama
палшы falgu
пара para
паранжи paranja
парзайн farz-i ʻayn
парзы кипая farz-i kifaya
парияд faryad
парыз fara'iz[1]
парыз fara'iz[2]
парыз farz
пасәд fasad
пасық fasiq
Паттах Fattah, al-
патўә fatva
Патыйма Fatima
Патых сүўреси Fath
пахыр aftada
пәис fa'iz
пәк pak
пәкыр faqr
пәқих faqih
пәқыр faqir[2]
пәқыр faqir[1]
пәлақ falaq[1]
Пәлақ сүўреси Falaq[2]
пәләк falak[1]
пәләк falak[2]
пәмдет намаз salat al-fajr
пәмдет намаз salat al-subh
пән fann
пәнә fana
пәний fani
пәра para
пәренже paranja
пәрид farid
пәрийшта farishta
пәриште mala'ika
пәрияд faryad
пәрух faruq
пәряд faryad
пәтия fatiha[1]
пәтия fatiha[2]
пәтиягөй fatihagu
Пәтия сүўреси Fatiha[3]
пәтўа fatva
пәтўә fatva
Пәтыр сүўреси Fatir[1]
пәҳишә fahisha
пәхыш fahsh
пери pari
перихан parikhan
периште farishta
перўардигар Parvardigar
пешқәдәм pishqadam
пида fida
пидакер fidakyar
пидә fida
пидәи fida'i
пикх fiqh
пир pir
пирадер biradar
Пирғаўын Firaʻun
пирдаўс Firdaus
пирқә firqa
пирмуған pir-i mughan
питир fitr[1]
питир fitr[2]
питнә fitna
пузалә fuzala
пулсират pul-i sirat
Пурқән Furqan[1]
Пурқән сүўреси Furqan[2]
Пуссиләт сүўреси Fussilat
пыдия fidya
Пыл сүўреси Fil
рабб Rabb
Раббанә Rabbana
Рабби Rabbi
Раббил әламин Rabb al-ʻalamayn
Рабиўул аввәл Rabiʻ al-avval
рабиўул ақыр Rabiʻ al-akhir
рағәйип ragha'ib
Разақ Razzaq, al-
райыс ra'is[1]
райыс ra'is[2]
Рамазан Ramazan
Рамазан байрамы ʻId al-Fitr
рамазан пытыри zakat al-fitr
Расулалла Rasulullah
Рахман Rahman, al-
Рахман сүўреси Rahman
рахмет rahmat
рахметли rahmati
Раъд сүўреси Raʻd
Рәбийүләўәл Rabiʻ al-avval
рәбийүссәни Rabiʻ al-akhir
рәбита rabita
Рәвза Ravza
рәжап Rajab
рәжәп Rajab
рәжм rajm
рәжым rajim
Рәйим Rahim, al-
рәйим rahim
рәйис ra'is[1]
рәкет rakʻat
Рәқип Raqib, al-
Рәпи Rafiʻ, al-
рәсим rasm-rusum
Рәсул Haqq Rasul
рәсул rasul
Рәсулалла Rasulullah
рәсүўл rasul
Рәсүўлалла Rasulullah
Рәуп Rauf, al-
рәўият rivayat
рәҳим rahim
рәхип rahib
рәҳмәт rahmat
Рәшит Rashid, al-
ривәят rivayat

риза riza[1]
Ризвэн Rizvan
ризиқ rizq
рисале risala
риязат riyazat
Рум Rum[1]
Рум суўреси Rum[2]
рутбэ rutba
руўза ruza
руўх ruh[1]
руўхий ruhi
руўхсат rukhsat
руўхый ruhi
рух ruh[1]
рухани ruhani
руханий ruhani
руханият ruhaniyat
рухсат rukhsat
рухсат етиў ijazat
рухсэт rukhsat
рухсэтнэма rukhsatnama
руҳый ruhi
саат sa'at
сабақхана darskhana
Сабэ суўреси Saba
сағат sa'at
сағир saghir
садаға sadaqa
садақа sadaqa
сажда sujud
сазэйи sazayi
сайит sayyid
салам salam
салап salaf
салаўат salavat
салаўмэлейкум salam 'alaykum
салип salb
Самут Samud
сап saf
Сапа Safa
сапар Safar
сапар намазы salat al-safar
Сара Sara
Саратан Saratan
Саратэн Saratan
Саттэр Sattar, al-
саўап savab[2]
саўэп savab[1]
саўэп savab[2]
саўэп savab[3]
Саўр Savr
Саф суўреси Saff
саҳаба sahaba
сахэба sahaba
сахэват sakhavat
Сэбр Sabur, al-
сэбр sabir
сэбр sabi'
сэбр sabr[1]
сэбр sabr[2]
сэдэқе sadaqa
Сэд суўреси Sad
сэжде sajda[1]
сэждегах sajdagah
Сэжде суўреси Sajda[2]
сэзим hiss
Сэлем Salam, al-
сэлем assalamu 'alaykum
сэлем salam
сэлем алейкум salam 'alaykum
Сэлих Salih[2]
сэлих salih[1]
сэлле dastar
сэлле salla
сэлле 'amama
Сэмат Samad, al-
сэмэўи дин din-i samavi
Сэми Sami', al-
сэнам sanam
сэпэр Safar
Сэп суўреси Saff
Сэўир Savr
сейит sayyid
сема sama'[1]
силэх silah
силсилэ silsila[1]
Сират Sirat[2]
сопы sufi[1]
сопы sufi[2]
сөз nutq
судхүр sud
судхүр sudkhur
сукут sukut
сулих sulh
султэн sultan
сунбулэ Sunbula
сунна sunna
суннизм sunni
суннит sunni
супы sufi[1]
суўпы sufi[1]
суўре sura
сүбхэн subhan
сүбхэналла subhanallah
сүбхэнэка subhanaka
сүбхэнэтала subhanahu va ta'ala
Сүлэйман Sulayman
сүнбиле Sunbula
сүннет sunna
сүннет sunnat[1]
сүннет sunnat[2]
сүре sura
сүтхор sudkhur
сыйқыр sihr
сыйқырлы sihri
табэрак tabarak
табынун tabi'in
табыныў 'ibadat[1]
табыт tabut
табыун tabi'iyun
Тағэбун суўреси Taghabun
тағзым ta'zim
такбир takbir
такбир takbir al-tahrima
такпин takfin
такрим tahrim[1]
такримий tahrimi
Такрим суўреси Tahrim[2]
Такўир суўреси Takvir
тақсыр taqsir
тақўа taqva
тақыўа taqva
тақыя taqiya
тала ta'ala
талақ talaq[1]
талэқ talaq[1]
талэқнэме talaqnama
Талэқ суўреси Talaq[2]
талэқхат talaq khat
тамақ ta'am
тапсир tafsir
тарэвих намаз taravih
тарийх tarikh[1]
тарийх tarikh[2]

тарийхшы mu'arrikh
тасаттық tasadduq
тасаўўуп tasavvuf
таўап tavaf[1]
таўап tavaf[2]
таўәзы tavazi'
таўәрих tavarikh
таўқ tavq
таўпиқ tavfiq
Таўрәт Tavrat
таўхид tavhid[1]
Таха суўреси Ta ha
тәала ta'ala
тәат ta'at
тәат-ибадат ta'at-'ibadat
тәәббут ta'abbud[2]
Тәббәт Tabbat
тәбе tabi'
тәберик tabarruk
тәберик tabrik
тәбийғат tabi'at
тәбият tabi'at
тәблиғат tablighat
тәғдир taqdir
тәғдир taqdir
тәжалли tajalli
Тәжжал Dajjal
тәйиб ta'ib
Тәкәсур суўреси Takasur
тәкит ta'kid
тәкия takiya
тәкия takya
тәклип taklif
тәқия taqiya
тәқлит taqlid[1]
тәқўа taqva
тәқўәдәр taqvadar
тәле tali'
тәлим ta'lim
тәлимат ta'limat
тәлип talib
тәлқин talqin[1]
тәлқин talqin[2]
тәлқин talqin[3]
тәлўәса talvasa
тәмәки dukhan[2]
тәнассыр tanassur
Тәнир Tangri
Тәнри Tangri
тәпсир tafsir
тәрәўих намаз salat al-taravih
тәрбия tarbiya
тәрғибәт targhibat
тәрийқа tariqat[1]
тәриқә tariqat[2]
тәриқәт tariqat[1]
Тәриқ суўреси Tariq
тәркдунья tark-i dunya
тәсби tasbih
тәсир tashir
тәслим taslim[1]
тәслим taslim[2]
тәўәжжух tavajjuh
тәўап tavaf[2]
тәўәккәл tavakkul[1]
тәўбә tavba[1]
тәўбе tavba[1]
тәўбе tavba[2]
тәўбе ету tavba-tazarru
Тәўбе суўреси Tavba[3]
тәўекел tavakkul[1]
тәўип tabib
тәҳарәтхана taharatkhana
тәҳарет taharat
тәхир tahir
тәхия tahiyat
тәхлил tahlil
тәхриж takhrij
тәхрип tahrif
тәхрир tahrir
тәшбих tashbih
теберик tabarruk
тийпе ta'ifa
тилсим tilsim[1]
тилсим tilsim[2]
тилсим tilsim[3]
тоба tavba[1]
толық mufassal
тор hijab
түс намз salat al-zuhr
узләт 'uzlat
улама 'ulama
умбәт ummat
умрә 'umra
унсур unsur
урип 'urf
урықсат rukhsat
Усен Husayn
устаз ustaz
устәз ustad
устәз ustaz
усыл usul[1]
усыл usul[2]
усылжадит usul-i jadid
ушр 'ushr
үрп 'urf
үрп-әдет rasm-rusum
ўадә va'da
ўаж vajh
Ўажит Vajid, al-
ўаз va'z
Ўаз-зәрият суўреси Zariyat
Ўаз-зуха суўреси Zuha
ўакәләт vakalat
ўақыф vaqf
Ўақыя суўреси Vaqi'a
Ўал-мурсаләт суўреси Mursalat
Ўан-нажм суўреси Najm
Ўан-нәзиәт суўреси Nazi'at
ўапа vafa
ўапә vafa
ўапәт vafat
Ўа-саппәт суўреси Saffat
ўатан vatan
Ўат-тийин суўреси Tin
Ўат-Тур суўреси Tur
Ўахап Vahhab, al-
ўахапизим Vahhabiya
Ўахит Vahid, al-
Ўаш-шамс суўреси Shams
ўәғз va'z
ўәде va'da
ўәде 'ahd
ўәжип vajib
ўәкил vakil
ўәлий vali
ўәсият vasiyat
ўитр намаз salat al-vitr
фарьяд faryad
Фәжр суўреси Fajr
фери pari
фида fida
философ faylasuf
философия falsafa

хабар akhbar
хабар khabar
Ҳабыл Habil
ҳадал halal
хадал halal
ҳадд hadd
Ҳадид сүўреси Hadid
ҳаж hajj[1]
Ҳажар Hajar
ҳаж бәдәл hajj badal
ҳаж намаз salat al-hajat
Ҳаж сүўреси Hajj[2]
ҳажы hajji
хажыхана hajjikhana
ҳазирет hazrat
ҳайт bayram
ҳайт ʿid
ҳайт намаз salat al-ʿidayn
хайыр khayr[1]
Ҳақ Haqq[2]
Ҳақ Haqq, al-
ҳақ haqq[1]
ҳаққулла haqqullah
Ҳақ тала Haqq Taʿala
ҳақыйқат haqiqat
ҳал hal
ҳалақа khalaqa
халийфа khalifa[1]
халиф halif
халиф khalfa[2]
халифа khilafat[1]
халифатлық khilafat[2]
халифатлық khilafat[3]
ҳалл hall
халфа khalfa[1]
халфе khalfa[1]
Ҳалық Khaliq, al-
ҳамилә hamila
ханақа khanaqa
ҳанбалий Hanbali
Ҳанбалия Hanbaliya
ҳарам haram[1]
ҳарам muharram[1]
ҳарамзада haramzada
Харун Harun
ҳаса ʿasa
хатиб khatib
ҳаўия haviya
ҳашр hashr[1]
Ҳашр сүўреси Hashr[2]
Хәбар Khabir, al-
ҳәбаш habash
Ҳәбашистән Habashistan
ҳәбиб Habib
Ҳәбийбулла Habibullah
ҳәвале havala
Ҳәдий Hadi, al-
ҳәдийс hadis
ҳәйыз hayz
Ҳәким Hakim, al-
ҳәким hakim
Ҳәққа сүўреси Haqqa
Ҳәлиқ Khaliq, al-
Хәлилулла Khalilullah
Ҳәлим Halim, al-
хәлип khalifa[1]
хәлип khalifa[2]
Хәлләқ Khallaq
ҳәмал Hamal
ҳәмәл Hamal
Хәмийт Hamid, al-
Ҳәпиз Hafiz, al-[2]
ҳәпиз hafiz
Ҳәпит Hafiz, al-[1]
ҳәптияк haft-i yak
ҳәрем haram[1]
ҳәрем haram[2]
ҳәрем harim
ҳәреми haramzada
ҳәрипдуўа harif duʿa
ҳәттат hattat
Ҳәўа Hava
хәч khach
хәчпәрэст khachparast
ҳәштыяк hasht-i yak
Хедийша Khadija
хиджаб hijab
хиджре hijra
хиджрия hijri
хижре hijriya
хижри жыл sana-yi hijriyya
Ҳижр сүўреси Hijr
хизб hizb[1]
хизб hizb[2]
ҳизбу шайтан hizb al-shaytan
ҳикмет hikmat
ҳилал hilal
хилўәт khalvat
хилўәтга khalvatgah
химмәт himmat
ҳис hiss
хожа khvaja[1]
хожа khvaja[2]
хожазада khvajazada
ҳор hur
Худ Hud[1]
Худ Hud[2]
худуд hudud
ҳужрә hujra
Хужурәт сүўреси Hujurat
Хумаза сүўреси Humaza
хуптән намаз salat al-ʿisha
хурапет khurafat
хурма khurma
ҳусн husn
ҳусни әдап husn-i adab
ҳусни әхлақ husn-i akhlaq
ҳусни тәрбие husn-i tarbiya
ҳусни хат husn-i khat
ҳут Hut
хутбә khutba
ҳүким hukm
ҳүкимет hukumat
ҳүкми Сәмат hukm-i samad
ҳүр hur
шадыр chadra
Шаймәрдән Shah-i mardan
шайтан Shaytan
шайтанат shaytanat
шақырыў daʿvat
шам shamʿ
шамадан shamʿdan
шамс жыл sana-yi shamsiyya
шапаат shafaʿat
шарап sharab
шарәп sharab
Шарх сүўреси Inshirah
Шаўўал Shavval
шаҳәдет shahadat[1]
шаҳәдет shahadat[2]
шахид shahid[2]
Шахмардан Shah-i mardan
Шәбан Shaʿban
Шәбән Shaʿban

шәжире shajara
шәйих shaykh
шәйихул ислам shaykh al-islam[1]
шәйихул ислам shaykh al-islam[2]
шәк shak
шәк shakk
Шәкир Shakur, al-
шәкирт shagird
шәккәк shakkak
шәклиқ shaklik
шәлме chalma
шәм sham‘
шәпи Shafi‘i[1]
шәпи Shafi‘i[2]
шәпилық Shafi‘iya
шәр shar‘
шәрән shar‘an
шәрий shar‘i
шәрип sharif
шәрипа sharifa
шәрият shari‘at
шәряр Chahar yar
Шәўәл Shavval
шәхит Shahid, al-
шәхит shahid[1]
шежәрә shajara
шейит shahid[2]
шейих shaykh
шейихул-ислам shaykh al-islam[1]
шерик sharik
шиит shi‘i
шилде chilla[1]
шилде chilla[2]
шилде chillakhana[2]
шилдехана chillakhana[1]
шилле chilla[1]
шилле chilla[2]
шилясын chillayasin
шипа shifa
ширик shirk
ширкеў kalisa
Шуайип Shu‘ayb
шубҳә shubha
Шуғара сүўреси Shu‘ara
шукур shukr
шурә shura [1]
Шурә сүўреси Shura[2]
шүкир shukr
шылдан childan
шылтан chiltan
шылым dukhan[2]
Ыблыс Iblis
Ыбрайым Ibrahim[1]
Ыбрайым мәқәмы Maqam-i Ibrahim
Ыбрайым сүўреси Ibrahim[2]
ыбрани ‘ibrani
Ыдрыс Idris
ылайық mu‘tabar
Ынпитар сүўреси Infitar
Ысқақ Ishaq
Ысмайыл Isma‘il
Ыхлас сүўреси Ikhlas[2]
ыштарап jarima
Юсип Yusuf[1]
Юсуп Yusuf[1]
Яқып Ya‘qub
яр yar
ярамазан ya ramazan
ярамазан shahr-i ramazan
Яратқан Yaratqan
Ясин сүўреси Ya Sin

Kazakh Index

абд ‘abd
абжәд abjad
абыз abiz
абыз hafiz
Ағла сүресі A‘la
ағраф a‘raf[1]
Ағраф сүресі A‘raf[2]
ағузү білла a‘uzu billah
ағузы a‘uzu billah
адал halal
Адам Ата Adam
Адамата Adam
ажал ajal
аза ‘aza
азаб ал-қабр ‘azab-i qabr
азан azan
азаншы mu’azzin
азап azab
Айдар Haydar
айт ‘id
Айша ‘A’isha
Айып Ayyub
акида ‘aqida
ақ haqq[1]
ақиқат haqiqat
ақирет akhirat
ақпар akhbar
ақшам намазы salat al-maghrib
ақы haqq[1]
ақын akhund
ақырет akhirat
ақырет күні akhirat
ақырзаман akhir zaman
алдияр allahyar
Алла Allah
Алла-акпар Allahu akbar
Алла тағала Allah ta‘ala
аллаһу-акбар Allahu akbar
аллаһу-әкбәр Allahu akbar
ал-Маруа Marva
ансар ansar
ант ‘ahd
арам haram[1]
арамза haramzada
арамзада haramzada
арапа күні ‘arafa
арафа күні ‘arafa
Арафат ‘Arafat
ар-Рахим Rahim, al-
ар-Рахман Rahman, al-
аруақ arvah
аса ‘asa
Асад Asad
аса-муса ‘asa
аспан asman
ассалату salat
ассалаумағалайкум assalamu ‘alaykum
ас-Сафа Safa
асхаб ashab
асхаб әл-кахф ashab-i kahf
асхабу-л-жаннә ashab-i jannat
асхап ashab
ауыз ашар iftar
ахар akhirat
ахбар akhbar
ахд ‘ahd
Ахзап сүресі Ahzab
ахирет akhirat
ахкам ahkam
Ахқаф сүресі Ahqaf
ахлақ akhlaq
ахл ал-сунна ahl-i sunna
Ахмәд Ahmad
ахун akhund
аhл әл-кітаб ahl-i kitab
ашура ‘Ashura[1]
аят ayat
аятолла ayatullah
аятүл-күрси ayat al-kursi
әбжет abjad
Әбу abu
Әбу Бакр Abu Bakr
Әбу Бакір Abu Bakr
әдет ‘adat
әділ ‘adil
әділет ‘adalat
Әзәзіл ‘Azazil
әзиз ‘aziz[1]
Әзірейіл ‘Azra’il
әзірет hazrat
Әзірет Әлі ‘Ali
Әйуп Ayyub
әл-ансар ansar
әл-асма әл-хусна asma al-husna
әл-Әзиз ‘Aziz, al-
әл-Бари Bari, al-
әл-Бурақ Buraq
әлейкүмүссәлем ‘alaykim al-salam
әлем ‘alam[1]
әлем ‘alam[2]
әлеумет ummat
әл-Жаббар Jabbar, al-
Әли Ғымран сүресі Al-i Imran
әл-Илаh ilah
әл-Қаййум Qayyum, al-
әл-Құддыс Quddus, al-
әл-Мәлік Malik, al-
әлмисақ misaq
әл-Мумин Mu’min, al-
әл-Мутакаббир Mutakabbir, al-
әл-Мухаймин Muhaymin, al-
әл-Мұсаввир Musavvir, al-
әл-хажж hajj[1]
әл-Хайи Hayy, al-
әл-Халиқ Khaliq, al-
Әлі ‘Ali
Әлясағ Alyasa‘
әмір amir
әнбие anbiya[1]
Әнбия сүресі Anbiya[2]
Әнғам сүресі An‘am
Әнфал сүресі Anfal
әптиек haft-i yak
әс-Салам Salam, al-
әт-тәхият tahiyat, at-
әулет avlad
әулие avliya[1]
әхлақ akhlaq
әhли кітап ahl-i kitab
әhли тариқат ahl-i tariqat
баб bab
байа bay‘at
байрам bayram
бақа baqa[1]
Бақара сүресі Baqara
бақи baqi
бақсы bakhshi
бақыт bakht
бал fal
балгөй falgu
балдама falnama

бану Исраил bani Isra'il[1]
Басар Basir, al-
Бата Fatiha[3]
бата fatiha[1]
бата fatiha[2]
Батима Fatima
батыл batil
Бәййіна сүресі Bayyina
Бәлад сүресі Balad
бәнде banda
бәни Исраил bani Isra'il[1]
Бәни Ісраил сүресі Bani Isra'il[2]
Бәра-ат сүресі Bara'at[2]
бәрекелде barakullah
бәтуа fatva
Бәшир Bashir
бейкүнә bi gunah
бейіт bayt
бенде banda
Берат кеші shab-i barat
берекет barakat
бесін намазы salat al-zuhr
бигүнә bi gunah
бикүнә bi gunah
Билқис Bilqis
Бисмиллаһир рахманир рахим bismillah al-Rahman al-Rahim
бойтұмар tumar
Бурақ Buraq
Бұруж сүресі Buruj
бұт but
Былқыс Bilqis
бісмилла bismillah
бісміллаһір-Рахманір-Рахим bismillah al-Rahman al-Rahim
бісміллә bismillah
гази ghazi
ганима ghanimat
гөрхана gurkhana
Ғабәсә сүресі 'Abasa
ғабд 'abd
Ғад 'Ad
ғадет 'adat
ғадл 'adl
ғадн 'adn
ғадын 'adn
ғадын жаннаты Jannat al-'Adn
ғаділ 'adil
Ғадят сүресі 'Adiyat
ғажем 'ajam
ғазабат ghazavat
Ғазазыл 'Azazil
ғазап azab
ғазауат ghazavat
Ғазезіл 'Azazil
Ғазиз 'Aziz, al-
ғазиз 'aziz[1]
Ғазим 'Azim, al-
ғайрі мү'аккад ghayr-i mu'akkad
Ғайса 'Isa
ғайыперен rijal-i ghayb
ғақибат 'aqibat
ғақлия 'aqliyat
Ғақраб 'Aqrab
Ғалақ сүресі 'Alaq
ғалам 'alam[1]
ғалаһиссаләм 'alayhi al-salam
ғаләйһиссәләм 'alayhi al-salam
Ғали 'Ali, al-
Ғалим 'Alim, al-
ғаллама 'allama
ғалым 'alim
ғамал 'amal
Ғани Ghani, al-
ғанимат ghanimat
Ғанкәбұт сүресі 'Ankabut
Ғарапат 'Arafat
Ғарасат 'Arasat
Ғарасат мейданы 'Arasat
ғарыш 'arsh
ғаси 'asi
Ғасыр сүресі 'Asr[2]
Ғаусыл Ағзам Ghavs al-A'zam
ғафлет ghaflat[1]
ғафлет ghaflat[2]
Ғафұр Ghafur, al-
Ғаффар Ghaffar, al-
Ғафыр сүресі Ghafir
ғафіл ghafil
Ғашия сүресі Ghashiya
ғибадат 'ibadat[1]
ғибадатхана 'ibadatkhana
ғиддат 'iddat
ғилман ghilman
Ғиса 'Isa
ғумыр 'umr
ғурып 'urf
ғұзыр 'uzr[1]
ғұлама 'ulama
ғұмра 'umra
ғұсыл ghusl
ғыззет 'izzat
ғылым 'ilm[1]
ғылым 'ilm[2]
ғылымхал 'ilm-i hal[1]
дағуа da'va[1]
дамолла damulla
данышпан danishmand
дар ал-ислам dar al-Islam
дар ал-харб dar al-harb
дар ас-сулх dar al-sulh
дастарқан dastarkhan
дау da'va[1]
Дауыт Da'ud
Дауіт Da'ud
Даһыр сүресі dahir
дәлү Dalv
дәрет taharat
дәрет алу taharat
дәретхана taharatkhana
дәруіш darvish
дәрілхараб dar al-harb
дәрісхана darskhana
дәуір davir
диуана divana
Дозақ Duzakh
дос dust
дуа du'a[2]
дуа du'a[3]
дұға du'a[1]
дұғагой du'agu
дұғагөй du'agu
дұғакөй du'agu
дұрыс durust
Дұхан сүресі Dukhan[1]
Дүлдүл Duldul
дүние dunya
дүния dunya
дүнияуи dunyavi
дін din
діндар dindar
діни dini
ежтиһат ijtihad

екінді намазы salat al-ʿasr
екінті намазы salat al-ʿasr
екі Харам Haramayn
ережеп Rajab
Жабрил Jabra'il
жады jadu
жаза jaza
жазу адамдары ahl-i kitab
жайнамаз jaynamaz
Жақия Yahya
жақұт yahud
Жақып Yaʿqub
жамағат jamaʿat[1]
жамағат jamaʿat[2]
Жамра Jamra
жан jan
жаназа janaza[1]
жаназа janaza[2]
жаназа намазы janaza[2]
Жаннат Jannat
жарамазан shahr-i ramazan
жарамазан ya ramazan
жарапазан shahr-i ramazan
жарапазан ya ramazan
Жаратушы Yaratqan
Жасия сүресі Jasiya
Жасын Ya Sin
Жаһаннам Jahannam
жаһил jahili
жаһилийа jahiliyat
жаһилия jahiliyat
жаһыл jahl
жаһіл jahili
жашыйық намазы salat al-ʿisha
Жәди Jadi
жәдит jadid
жәдитші jadid
жәдитшілдік usul-i jadid
Жәннәт Jannat
Жебрәйіл Jabra'il
Жебірейіл Jabra'il
жетім yatim
Жибрил Jibril
жизья jizya
жихад jihad
жиһат jihad
жолаушының намазы salat al-safar
Жуди тауы Judi
Жунус Yunus[1]
жұма jumʿa[1]
жұма jumʿa[1]
жұма jumʿa[2]
Жұмақ Ujmakh
Жұма сүресі Jumʿa[3]
Жүніс Yunus[1]
Жүсіп Yusuf[1]
Жыбт Jibt
жын jinn[1]
Жын сүресі Jinn[2]
Забур Zabur
завия zaviya
Заққұм Zaqqum
залалат zalalat
залым zalim
заман ақыр akhir zaman
зар заман zar zaman
Зауза Javza
захид zahid
заһид zahid
Зәкәрия Zakariya
зәлім zalim
Зәмзәм Zamzam
Зәмзем Zamzam
Зәрят сүресі Zariyat
зекет zakat[1]
зимдер zimmi
зина zina
зинақор zinakar
зинақорлық zina
зират ziyarat
зиратшы ziyaratchi
зиярат ziyarat
Зу-л-кифл Zu'l-Kifl
Зу-л-хиджжа Zu'l-hijja
зухд zuhd[1]
зухд zuhd[2]
Зұлқарнайын Zu'l-Qarnayn
Зұлпықар Zu'l-fiqar
зұлым zulm
зұлым zulum
зұлымдық zulm
зұха salat al-zuha
Зұха сүресі Zuha
Зұхрұф сүресі Zukhruf
Зүлкәфил Zu'l-Kifl
Зүмәр сүресі Zumar
зікір zikr
Зілзал сүресі Zilzal
Зілхажжа Zu'l-hijja
Ибраһим Ibrahim[1]
иғтиқад iʿtiqad
иғтиқат iʿtiqad
Ид әл-Адха ʿId al-Azha
Идрис Idris
Иерусалим Quds, al-
изар izar
иқамет iqamat
илаһи ilahi[1]
илаһи ilahi[2]
илаһи ilahi[3]
имам imam[1]
имам imam[2]
имам imam[3]
имам imam[4]
имама ʿamama
Имам Ағзам Imam-i Aʿzam
имамат imamat[1]
имамат imamat[2]
иман iman[1]
иман iman[2]
Имран ʿImran[2]
иншалла insha'allah
ираде irada[1]
Иса ʿIsa
Ислам Islam
Исмаил Ismaʿil
иснад isnad
Исраил Isra'il
Исрафил Israfil
истинжа istinja
истисқа istisqa
истислах istislah
истихсан istihsan
Исхақ Ishaq
итикад iʿtiqad
иттихад ittihad[1]
иттихад ittihad[2]
ифрит ʿifrit
ихван ikhvan
ихрам ihram
ишан ishan
ишара isharat
Йа син Ya Sin

кабира kabira
кабих qabih
Каґба Ka'ba
калам kalam
Камар сүресі Qamar
Каусар Kavsar[1]
кахин kahin
кәким hakim
кәләм kalam
кәппарат kaffarat
кәпір kafir
Кәусар Kavsar[1]
Кәусәр сүресі Kavsar[2]
Кәфирұн сүресі Kafirun
кәффәрат kaffarat
кәфір kafir
кебін kafn
Кербала Karbala
керемет karamat
кесене turba
Кеусер Kavsar[1]
кефил kafil
Кеһф сүресі Kahf
көр gur
күмбез gumbaz
күнә gunah
күнәкар gunahkar
күпір kufr
күпірлик kufr
күфір kufr
кінә gunah
кіпая kifaya
кітап kitab
кіфая kifaya
Қабыл Qabil
қабыр qabr
қабір qabr
қағида qa'ida
қади qazi
қадими qadimi
Қадиша Khadija
қадыми qadimi
Қадыр Khizr
қадыр кеші Laylat al-Qadr
Қадыр сүресі Qadr[1]
қадімшілдік usul-i qadim
қажы hajj[1]
қажы hajji
қажылық hajj[1]
қаза qaza
қазы qazi
қазірет hazrat
Қайиұм Qayyum, al-
қайыр khayr[1]
қайыр khayr[2]
қайыр-садақа khayr-sadaqa
қақ haqq[1]
қал qal
қалам kalam
қалам qalam[2]
Қалам сүресі Qalam[3]
қалың мал sidaq[1]
қамис qamis
қара тас hajar-i asvad
қари qari
Қариға сүресі Qari'a
Қасас сүресі Qasas[2]
қате khata
Қаус Qavs
Қаф сүресі Qaf[1]
қәлам qalam[1]
қийас qiyas
қира'әт qira'at
қирağа qira'at
қирағат qira'at
қисуа qisvat
қиямет qiyamat[1]
қиямет күні qiyamat[1]
Қиямет сүресі Qiyamat[2]
қожа khvaja[1]
қожа khvaja[2]
Қорбан айты Qurban Bayrami
Қорбан мейрамы Qurban Bayrami
құдірет qudrat
құбыла qibla
құбыланама qiblanama
Құдай khuday
Құдайы khuday
құдайы khudayi
құжыра hujra
құнұт qunut
Құрайш сүресі Quraysh[2]
құрайыш Quraysh[1]
Құран Qur'an
Құран-Кәрім Qur'an-i Karim
Құр'аны Кәрим Qur'an-i Karim
құрбан qurban
Құрбан айт 'Id al-Azha
құрман qurban
Құт Hud[1]
құтб qutb
құтба khutba
қыдем qidam
Қыдыр Khizr
Қызыр Khizr
қыран qiran
қырық шілтен chiltan
қысас qisas
қыям qiyam
қыям бі-нәфсіһі qiyam binafsihi
қыяс qiyas
лағнат la'nat
лағынат la'nat
лағынет la'nat
лақат lahid[2]
Ләйіл сүресі Layl
Ләһеп сүресі Lahab
лифафа lifafa
Лұқман Luqman[1]
Лұқман сүресі Luqman[2]
Лұқпан Luqman[1]
Лұт Lut
Мағарыж сүресі Ma'arij
мағрифат ma'rifat[1]
мағруф ma'ruf
Мағұн сүресі Ma'un
мағфире maghfirat
мазалим mazalim
мазар mazar
мазлұм mazlum
мазһаб mazhab[1]
майрам bayram
мақам maqam
мақсура maqsura
малакут malakut
малғун Mal'un[1]
малғун mal'un[2]
маликтік мазхаб Malikiya
мантық mantiq
Марв Marva
марқұм marhum
махлұқ makhluq
махр mahr[2]

махшар mahshar
машайих mashayikh
машайық mashayikh
машхад mashhad
Мәди Mahdi
мәжуси majusi
мәжүс majus
мәжіліс majlis
Мәида сүресі Ma'ida
мәйте murdar
мәйіт mayyit
мәкрук makruh
мәкрүк makruh
мәкрүһ makruh
мәлғүн Mal'un[1]
Мәлік Malik[1]
Мәлікші Maliki
Мәриям Maryam[1]
мәрхамет marhamat
Мәсәд сүресі Masad
Мәсих Masih[1]
мәсих masih[2]
Мәуа жаннаты Jannat al-Ma'va
мәужуд mavjud
мәуліт Mavlid[1]
Мәһди Mahdi
мәһір mahr[2]
мерғаж mi'raj
Медине Madina
медресе madrasa
Медіне Madina
медінелік madini
мейір mahr[1]
мейірім mahr[1]
Мекке Makka
меккелік makki
мектеп maktab
Мерям сүресі Maryam[2]
мешит masjid
Мизан Mizan[3]
мийрас miras
мийрасхор miraskhur
Микаил Mika'il
Микал Mika'il
Микәйіл Mika'il
милад milad
милк milk
Мина Mina
мираж mi'raj
Михаил Mika'il
михраб mihrab
молда mulla
муаззин mu'azzin
муәзин mu'azzin
мубах mubah
мударис mudarris
муджтахит mujtahid[1]
мужжағид mujtahid[1]
Муздалиф Muzdalifa
Муздәлипа Muzdalifa
мумин mu'min[1]
мутакаллим mutakallim
муфсит mufsid[1]
муфти mufti
муъмін mu'min[1]
мұғалім mu'allim
мұғжиза mu'jiza[1]
Мұззәмміл сүресі Muzzammil
Мұминүн сүресі Mu'minin
мұнапық munafiq
мұнара manara
мұнафиқ munafiq
Мұса Musa
Мұстапа Mustafa
Мұстафа Mustafa
мұсылман musulman
мұтакаллим mutakallim
Мұтаффифун сүресі Mutaffifin
мұфассал mufassal
мұхаддис muhaddis
мұхаджир muhajirin
мұхакама muhakama
Мұхаммед Muhammad[1]
Мұхаммед сүресі Muhammad[2]
Мұхаррам Muharram[2]
мұхраб mihrab
мұхтасиб muhtasib[1]
мұхтасиб muhtasib[2]
Мұһаррам Muharram[2]
мү'әккад mu'akkad
мүбарак mubarak
Мүддәссір сүресі Muddassir
мүджиза mu'jiza[1]
Мүжадәлә сүресі Mujadala
мүжтаһід mujtahid[1]
мүлік mulk[1]
Мүлік сүресі Mulk[2]
Мүмтахина сүресі Mumtahana
мү'мін mu'min[1]
Мүмін сүресі Mu'min[2]
Мүнафиқун сүресі Munafiqun
Мүңкір мен Нәңкір Munkar va Nakir
мүпсіт mufsid[1]
мүрде murda
мүрид murid
Мүрсәлат сүресі Mursalat
мүсалла musalla[1]
мүсәпір musafir
мүслим muslim
мүслім muslim
мүстахап mustahabb
мүфти mufti
мүшрік mushrik
Мысыр Misr[2]
мінажат munajat[1]
мінажатхана munajatkhana
мінбар minbar
мінбе minbar
мір amir
міршіт murshid
місуак misvak[1]
місуак misvak[2]
Нағым жаннаты Jannat al-Na'im
нажес najis
нажес najis
нажіс najis
назар nazar[1]
назар nazar[2]
нақлия naqliya
нақып naqib
намаз namaz
намаздық jaynamaz
насабнама nasabnama
насара nasara
Насиғат сүресі Nazi'at
насихат nasihat
насрани nasrani
Нас сүресі Nas
насут nasut
Насыр сүресі Nasr
Наурыз Navruz
Нахыл сүресі Nahl

Нәбә сүресі Naba
нәби nabi
нәзр nazr[2]
нәзір nazr[1]
нәлет la'nat
Нәміл сүресі Naml
нәпсі nafs[2]
нәпіл nafl
нәпіл намазы salavat-i nafila
нәсіл nasl
нәфақа nafaqa
нәфс nafs[2]
неғмат ni'mat
Нежім сүресі Najm
неке nikah
ниғмәт ni'mat
ниет niyat
низам nizam
Ниса сүресі Nisa
нифас nifas
нөкер navkar
Һуһ Nuh[1]
нұр nur[1]
Нұр сүресі Nur[2]
нұсрат nusrat
Нұх Nuh[1]
Нұх сүресі Nuh[2]
нығмат ni'mat
нысап insaf
нысап nisab
Омар 'Umar
опа vafa
ораза ruza
Ораза айты 'Id al-Fitr
ораза айы Ramazan
оразаның бітірі zakat al-fitr
Осман 'Usman
Оспан 'Usman
отан vatan
Өкіл Vakil, al-
өкіл vakil
өкім hukm
өкімет hukumat
өлексе murdar
өмір 'umr
өсиет vasiyat
өсиет-нама vasiyatnama
пазыл fazl
пайғамбар payghambar
пак pak
пақыр faqir[1]
памдат намазы salat al-fajr
памдат намазы salat al-subh
пара para
параз farz
парыз farz
пасық fasiq
Патиха Fatiha[3]
патиха fatiha[2]
пән fann
пәренже paranja
пәруардигәр Parvardigar
пәтуа fatva
пенде banda
Перғауын Fira'un
пері pari
періште farishta
пида fida
пұт put
Пырақ Buraq
Пырғғауын Fira'un
підия fidya
пір pir
пірәдар biradar
пісміллә bismillah
пітіне fitna
пітір fitr[1]
пітір fitr[2]
рабб Rabb
Раббы Rabbi
рабита rabita
Рағыд сүресі Ra'd
раджм rajm
рай ra'i
райыс ra'is[1]
райыс ra'is[2]
ракат rak'at
рақмет rahmat
рақым rahim
рақым rahm
рақыс raqs
рамазан Ramazan
рауаят rivayat
рахим rahim
Рахман сүресі Rahman
рахмат rahmat
рахмет rahmat
рахым rahim
рахым rahm
рәсул rasul
Ребиғул-ақыр Rabi' al-akhir
Ребиғул-әууәл Rabi' al-avval
реғайып ragha'ib
риба riba
рида rida[1]
риза riza[1]
рисалат risalat
рисале risala
рух ruh[1]
рухани ruhani
рұқсат rukhsat
Рұм Rum[1]
Рұм сүресі Rum[2]
рұх ruh[1]
Рұх Ruh al-Amin
рукұғ ruku'
рукүғ ruku'
рыздық rizq
рызық rizq
рікғат rak'at
саби sabi'
сабыр sabir
садақа sadaqa
Сад сүресі Sad
сажде sajda[1]
сайид sayyid
сайтан Shaytan
салат salat
салауат salavat
Салих Salih[2]
салих salih[1]
сама sama'[1]
сама sama'[2]
Сапа Safa
сапар Safar
сапар намазы salat al-safar
Саратан Saratan
сауап savab[2]
сауап savab[3]
саф saf
Сафа Safa
Саф сүресі Saff
Саффат сүресі Saffat
сахаба sahaba

сахипа sahifa
сахих sahih
Сәбә сүресі Saba
сәжда sajda[1]
сәжде sajda[1]
Сәжде сүресі Sajda[2]
сәлде salla
сәлем salam
Сәлсәбил Salsabil
сәмиғ sami'
Сәмут Samud
Сәмүд Samud
Сәуір Savr
сәһу sahv
сейіт sayyid
семағ sama'[1]
Семіғ Sami', al-
сиқыр sihr
сиқыршы sahir
силсила silsila[1]
силсила silsila[2]
сира sirat[1]
Сират Sirat[2]
сопы sufi[1]
сопы sufi[2]
судур sudur
сунна sunna
сунна sunnat[1]
суннит sunni
сунниттер ahl-i sunna
суре sura
сурет surat
сұбхан subhan
сұлтан sultan
сұр sur
сұхұф suhuf
сүбхан subhan
сүбханәкә subhanaka
сүжұд sujud
Сүлейман Sulayman
Сүлеймен патша Sulayman
Сүмбіле Sunbula
сүндет sunnat[2]
сүннәт sunna
сүннәт sunnat[1]
сүре sura
сықыршылық sihr
сыхр sihr
табиғат tabi'at
табыт tabut
таваккул tavakkul[1]
Тағабұн сүресі Taghabun
тағала ta'ala
тағат ta'at
тағат-ғибадат ta'at-'ibadat
тағдыр taqdir
тағзым ta'zim
тағлим ta'lim
таджвид tajvid
Тажал Dajjal
тазкират әл-әулие tazkirat al-avliya
тайпа ta'ifa
тайфа ta'ifa
такбир takbir
тақия taqiya
тақият tahiyat, at-
тақлид taqlid[1]
тақрим tahrim[1]
тақсыр taqsir
тақуа taqva
тақуім taqvim
талақ talaq[1]
Талақ сүресі Talaq[2]
талақ хат talaq khat
талиб talib
Тамұқ Tamuq
танасух tanasukh
танзих tanzih[1]
таң намазы salat al-fajr
таң намазы salat al-subh
таравих taravih
тарауық taravih
тариқа tariqat[1]
тариқа tariqat[2]
тариқат tariqat[1]
тариқат tariqat[2]
тарих tarikh[1]
тарихшы mu'arrikh
Тарық сүресі Tariq
тасаввуф tasavvuf
тасаттық tasadduq
тасбық tasbih
таспен ату rajm
тауап tavaf[1]
тауап tavaf[2]
тауап ету tavaf[1]
тауап ету tavaf[2]
тауаф tavaf[2]
Таурат Tavrat
таухид tavhid[1]
тахажжұд tahajjud
тахрим tahrim[1]
Тахрим сүресі Tahrim[2]
Таһа сүресі Ta ha
ташбих tashbih
тәбәрік tabarruk
Тәббет Tabbat
тәберік tabarruk
Тәкәсүр сүресі Takasur
тәкия takiya
тәклиф taklif
тәкпір takbir
тәқлид taqlid[1]
тәлім ta'lim
тәмәттұғ tamattu'
Тәңір Tangri
тәпсир tafsir
тәрбие tarbiya
тәркдуния tark-i dunya
тәсбих tasbih
тәслім taslim[1]
Тәсним Tasnim
тәуап tavaf[1]
тәуап tavaf[2]
тәуәккүл tavakkul[1]
тәубә tavba[2]
тәубе tavba[1]
Тәубе сүресі Tavba[3]
тәуеккел tavakkul[1]
тәуеп ету tavaf[1]
тәуеп ету tavaf[2]
тәуіп tabib
тәфсир тәпсір tafsir
тәшәһһүд tashahhud
тәшрық tashriq
тәяммүм tayammum
тәям соғу tayammum
Текуир сүресі Takvir
темекі dukhan[2]
тесхир tashir
тилауәт сәждесі sajda-yi tilavat
Тин сүресі Tin
Тозақ Duzakh

тозақы duzakhi
тұмар tumar
Тұр сүресі Tur
тылсым tilsim[1]
тылсым tilsim[2]
тылсым tilsim[3]
уағалайкүмүссәләм ʻalaykim al-salam
уағыз vaʻz
уағыздаушы vaʻiz
уажіп vajib
Уақиға сүресі Vaqiʻa
уақиф vaqf
уара varaʻ[2]
уахданиет vahdaniyat
уахи vahi
уаххабит Vahhabiya
уаһһабшы Vahhabiya
уәде vaʻda
уәли vali
уәсуәсә vasvasa
уерд vird[1]
уерд vird[2]
умма ummat
умра ʻumra
усул usul[1]
ушр ʻushr
уітір vitr
ұждан vijdan
Ұжмақ Ujmakh
Ұжмақ Ujmakh
ұжуд vujud
ұжым ijmaʻ
ұстаз ustad
ұстаз ustaz
Ұшпақ Ujmakh
үкім ʻiqab
үкімет hukumat
үмбет ummat
үммет ummat
үшір ʻushr
факих faqih
Фалақ сүресі Falaq[2]
фани fani
фасат fasad
фасық fasiq
Фатах сүресі Fath
Фатима Fatima
фатиха fatiha[2]
Фатиха сүресі Fatiha[3]
фатуа fatva
Фатыр сүресі Fatir[1]
Фәжір сүресі Fajr
фәлсәпа falsafa
Перғауын Firaʻun
фидаи fida'i
фикх fiqh
фирка firqa
Фуркан Furqan[1]
Фұрқан Furqan[1]
Фұрқан сүресі Furqan[2]
Фұссилат сүресі Fussilat
фырдаус Firdaus
фытрат fitrat
фідие fidya
Філ сүресі Fil
Фірдауыс жаннаты Jannat al-Firdaus
фітне fitna
хабар khabar
Хабир Khabir, al-
Хабыл Habil
хадд hadd
Хаджар Hajar
Хадид сүресі Hadid
хадис hadis
хаж hajj[1]
Хаж сүресі Hajj[2]
хажы hajj[1]
хажы hajji
хазірет hazrat
Хайбар Khaybar
хайыз hayz
хакім hakim
хақ haqq[1]
Хақ Haqq[2]
Хақ Haqq, al-
Хаққа сүресі Haqqa
хал hal
халал halal
Халил Алла Khalilullah
халим halim
халимхана halimkhana
халифа khalifa[1]
халифа khalifa[2]
халифат khilafat[1]
халифат khilafat[2]
халифат khilafat[3]
халуа khalvat
халфе khalfa[1]
Халық Khaliq, al-
Хамал Hamal
ханака khanaqa
ханафит Hanafi
Ханафиттік мазхаб Hanafiya
ханбалдық Hanbali
ханбалит Hanbali
ханбалшы Hanbali
ханіф hanif[2]
харам haram[1]
Харун Harun
Харут-Марут Harut va Marut
Хасан Hasan[3]
хасан hasan[1]
хатиб khatib
хатым khatm[1]
Хауа Hava
Хауаана Hava
хауари havari
хашыр hashr[1]
Хашыр сүресі Hashr[2]
хиджаб hijab
хиджра hijriya
хижра hijriya
хикмат hikmat
хикмет hikmat
хилофат khilafat[2]
хирқа khirqa[1]
хожа khvaja[1]
хор hur
Худ Hud[1]
хумс khums
Хууа Hu
Хұжрат сүресі Hujurat
Хұсайын Husayn
Хұт Hut
хұтба khutba
хұтпа khutba
хүкім hukm
Хыдыр Khizr
Хыжыр сүресі Hijr
хырқа khirqa[2]
хікмет hikmat
һаман Haman

һарұн Harun
һидайәт hidayat
һуд Hud[1]
һұд сүресі Hud[2]
һұмәзә сүресі Humaza
чадра chadra
Шағбан Sha'ban
шадыра chadra
шайқы shaykh
Шаймерден Shah-i mardan
шайтан Shaytan
шалма chalma
шариға shari'at
шариғат shari'at
шариф sharif
шарр sharr
Шарх сүресі Inshirah
шафағат shafa'at
шафиғалық мазхаб Shafi'iya
шафии Shafi'iya
шафиит Shafi'i[2]
шахид shahid[2]
шахид shahid[1]
Шәкүр Shakur, al-
шәкірт shagird
Шәміс сүресі Shams
Шәуүал Shavval
шежіре shajara
шейт shahid[2]
шейх shaykh
шейхы әл-ислам shaykh al-islam[1]
шейіт shi'i
шерк shirk
шерік sharik
шеһит shahid[2]
шиашы shi'i
шиит shi'i
шипа shifa
ширк shirk
Шис Shis
шоқыну tanassur
Шуайб Shu'ayb
Шуғайб Shu'ayb
Шұғайып Shu'ayb
Шұғара сүресі Shu'ara
Шұра сүресі Shura[2]
шүкір shukr
шілде chilla[2]
шілдехана chillakhana[2]
Ыбылыс Iblis
Ыбырайым Ibrahim[1]
ығтикәф i'tikaf
Ыдріс Idris
Ыдырыс Idris
ыждағат ijtihad
ықылас ikhlas[1]
ынсап insaf
Ынфитар сүресі Infitar
ырза riza[1]
ырым irim
Ысқақ Ishaq
Ысмағил Isma'il
Ысмайыл Isma'il
Ысхақ Ishaq
ысырап israf
Ыхлас сүресі Ikhlas[2]
ыхрам ihram
Ібраһим Ibrahim[1]
Ібраһим сүресі Ibrahim[2]
Ібіліс Iblis
іжтиһат ijtihad
ізін izn
Ілияс Ilyas
ілхад ilhad
ілхам ilham
ілім 'ilm[1]
Ілияс Ilyas
інжил Injil
інжіл Injil
інзәл inzal
Інсан сүресі Insan
Іншиқақ сүресі Inshiqaq
Іскендір Iskandar
Ісмағил Isma'il
Ісра сүресі Isra
Ісрафил Israfil
істібра istibra
істіғфар istighfar
істінжа istinja
іфтитах iftitah
іфтітаһ iftitah
іһтида ihtida
ішрак ishrak
Юныс Yunus[1]
Юныс сүресі Yunus[2]
Юсып Yusuf[1]
Юсып сүресі Yusuf[2]
Юсыф Yusuf[1]
Яғқұп Ya'qub
Яжуж-Мажуж Ya'juj va Ma'juj
Яжұж-Мажұж Ya'juj va Ma'juj
ясту намазы salat al-'isha
Ясін сүресі Ya Sin
Яхя Yahya
яһуд yahud
яһуди yahudi
яһудилік yahudi

Kyrgyz Index

аалам ʻalam[1]
аалим ʻalim
Аалы ʻAli
аалым ʻalim
абжат abjad
абзи Көвсар Kavsar[1]
абид ʻabid
Абу abu
Абубакир Abu Bakr
Абубакр Abu Bakr
Абу Замзам Zamzam
абузамзам суусу ab-i Zamzam
абыз Көөсар Kavsar[1]
абырак arvah
авлад avlad
Агзам Aʻzam[2]
агзам aʻzam[1]
агузу aʻuzu billah
агузу биллаахи aʻuzu billah
адал halal
Адам Adam
адат ʻadat
адел ʻadil
адеп adab
адил ʻadil
адилат ʻadalat
адыс hadis
ажал ajal
ажы hajj[1]
ажы hajji
ажы бедел hajj badal
аза ʻaza
Азазил ʻAzazil
азан azan
азанкеш mu'azzin
азап azab
Азезил ʻAzazil
азиз ʻaziz[1]
Азирейил ʻAzra'il
азирет hazrat
Азирет Аалы ʻAli
Азирети Жусуп Yusuf[1]
Азым ʻAzim, al-
Айдар Haydar
айт ʻid
Ак Haqq[2]
ак haqq[1]
акбар Allahu akbar
акпар Allahu akbar
Ак Расул Haqq Rasul
акрет akhirat
Ак Таала Haqq Taʻala
акун akhund
акыйкат haqiqat
акын akhund
акырет akhirat
акыр заман akhir zaman
ал hal
ал hall
Алда Allah
алда-жалда Allah ya Allah
Алда Таала Allah taʻala
алдаяр allahyar
алдоо акпар Allahu akbar
алдо уй ilahi[1]
алейкиме салам ʻalaykim al-salam
алейки-салам ʻalaykim al-salam
алейкүм-ассалам ʻalaykim al-salam
алей салам ʻalayhi al-salam
алейсалам ʻalayhi al-salam
алик ʻalayhi al-salam
алкамду лиила al-hamdullilah
Алла Allah
аллаяр allahyar
Алло Allah
алло акпар Allahu akbar
алмустак misaq
алооки акбар Allahu akbar
алхамдуллила алхамду лилла al-hamdullilah
алым ʻalim
амал ʻamal
аманат amanat
амин amin[1]
амир amir
амыр amir
анбия anbiya[1]
анвар anvar
ант ʻahd
аптиек haft-i yak
аптээк haft-i yak
апыз abiz
апыз hafiz
Аразат ʻArasat
арам haram[1]
арамза haramzada
арамзаада haramzada
аранзаа haramzada
арапа ʻarafa
Арасат ʻArasat
арбак arvah
арш ʻarsh
арши агла ʻarsh-i aʻla
арып дуба harif duʻa
арыш-корш ʻarsh-i kursi
аса ʻasa
асаб ashab
асабул жаннат ashab-i jannat
аса-муса ʻasa
Асан Hasan[3]
асман asman
Асрейил ʻAzra'il
ассалам алейкоом assalamu ʻalaykum
ассалам алейкүм assalamu ʻalaykum
ассалам алйким assalamu ʻalaykum
ассалоому алейкум assalamu ʻalaykum
ассалообу жаназа janaza[2]
астакпурулда astaghfirullah
астакпырылда astaghfirullah
астапурулда astaghfirullah
астахбурулла astaghfirullah
атсалоому алейкүм assalamu ʻalaykum
ат-Таура Tavrat
ахлак akhlaq
ахун akhund
ашура ʻAshura[1]
аят ayat
багымдат salat al-fajr
багымдат salat al-subh
багымдат намаз salat al-fajr
бадал badal
байгамбар payghambar
байрам bayram
бак bakht
бакт bakht
бакты bakht

бакшы bakhshi
бакы baqi
бакыр faqir[1]
бакыр faqir[2]
бакыт bakht
бал fal
балчы falgu
Бани Ысрайыл bani Isra'il[1]
Бани Ысырайыл bani Isra'il[1]
бапа vafa
барайыз fara'iz[2]
баракат barakat
баракелде barakullah
баракелди barakullah
баранжы paranja
барбардигер Parvardigar
барз farz
барыз farz
Бата Fatiha[3]
бата fatiha[1]
бата fatiha[2]
батакөй fatihagu
батуба fatva
батыба fatva
батыл batil
батын batin
бейгүнөө bi gunah
бейит bayt
бейиш bihisht
бейкүнөө bi gunah
бейнамаз bi namaz
бейт bayt
бенде banda
бербердигер Parvardigar
береке barakat
берекет barakat
бери pari
периште farishta
бешим salat al-zuhr
бидия fidya
бир pir
бисмилла bismillah
бистымылда bismillah
битир fitr[1]
битир fitr[2]
Бурак Buraq
Бурак Ат Buraq
бурана manara
бусулман musulman
бусурман musulman
бут put
бут but
буткана butkhana
буткана putkhana
бутпарас butparast
бутпарас putparast
Бүбү Мариям Maryam[1]
бысмылда bismillah
бысмыллаи-ррахманы ррахым bismillah al-Rahman al-Rahim
важип vajib
вакуп vaqf
вакф vaqf
валекиме салам 'alaykim al-salam
газават ghazavat
гөр gur
даарат taharat
дааратканa taharatkhana
Дажаал Dajjal
дамбылда damulla
дамылда damulla
данышман danishmand
дарвиш darvish
дарвыш darvish
даргөй dargah
дарыскана darskhana
дасторкон dastarkhan
Даут Da'ud
депкир takbir
дербиш darvish
дервиш darvish
дигер salat al-'asr
дийвана divana
дин din
диндар dindar
диний dini
диникайыр ghayr-i din
доо da'va[1]
дос dust
дөө div
Дөөтү Da'ud
дуба du'a[1]
дуба du'a[2]
дуба du'a[3]
дубагөй du'agu
дубай салам du'a-yi salam
дубайы салам du'a-yi salam
дубакөй du'agu
дубана divana
дува du'a[1]
дува du'a[2]
дува du'a[3]
дувакөй du'agu
дувана divana
дуга du'a[1]
дуга du'a[2]
дуга du'a[3]
дугадар du'adar
дугай салам du'a-yi salam
Дулдул Duldul
думана divana
дурус durust
дүйнө dunya
дүнүйө dunya
жаа алда ya allah
жаал jahili
жаалы jahili
Жааннам Jahannam
Жаасын Ya Sin
жадит jadid
жаду jadu
жадугөй jadugu
жады jadu
жадыгер jadugar
жадыгөй jadugu
жадыкөй jadugu
Жажуш-мажуш Ya'juj va Ma'juj
жайбаракат barakat
жайнамаз jaynamaz
жайыл jahili
Жакып Ya'qub
жамаат jama'at[1]
жамаат jama'at[2]
жамагат jama'at[1]
жан jan
жаназа janaza[1]
Жаннат Jannat
Жапар Jabbar, al-
Жапас Yafis
Жапес Yafis
Жапет Yafis
жа пирим ya pirim
жар yar

жарамазан Ramazan
жарамазан shahr-i ramazan
жарамазан ya ramazan
Жараткан Yaratqan
Жафет Yafis
Жаханнам Jahannam
Жебирейил Jabra'il
Жебреил Jabra'il
жетим yatim
Жибирейил Jabra'il
жин jinn[1]
жөөт yahud
жума jum'a[2]
жума намаз jum'a[1]
Жунус Yunus[1]
Жусуп Yusuf[1]
жүүт yahud
Забур Zabur
зайыр zahir
закет zakat[1]
залим zalim
Замзам Zamzam
замзам суусу ab-i Zamzam
зар заман zar zaman
зекет zakat[1]
зикир zikr
зина zina
зиярат ziyarat
Зулжалал Zu'l-jalal va'l-ikram
Зулкарнайн Zu'l-Qarnayn
Зулпукор Zu'l-fiqar
зулум zulm
зулум zulum
зыйкыр sihr
зына zina
зындан zindan
зыярат ziyarat
зыяратчы ziyaratchi
ибадат 'ibadat[1]
ибадаткана 'ibadatkhana
Ибилис Iblis
Идирис Idris
ижаза ijazat
ижарат hijra
ижират hijra
икмет hikmat
икрар iqrar[1]
илдалда la ilaha illa allah va muhammadun rasulullah
илим 'ilm[1]
Илияс Ilyas
иллалда la ilaha illa allah va muhammadun rasulullah
илхам ilham
имам imam[1]
имам imam[2]
имам imam[3]
имам imam[4]
Имам Агзам Imam-i A'zam
Инжил Injil
инна а тайна inna a'taynaka al-kavsara
иншаалла insha'allah
иншахалла insha'allah
ирекет rak'at
ирсаалы risala
Иса 'Isa
Искендер Iskandar
Ислам Islam
исми агзам ism-i a'zam
испарас 'Isaparast
Исрафил Israfil
итихад ittihad[2]
ифрит 'ifrit
Кааба Ka'ba
каада qa'ida
каапыр kafir
кабарлар akhbar
кабарыж khavarij
кабыр qabr
Кава Ka'ba
кадими qadimi
Кадыр Qadir, al-
кадыр Qadr[1]
Кадыр Ак Qadir, al-
кадыр ак Qadr[1]
Кадыр алла Qadir, al-
кадыр алла Qadr[1]
кадыр түн Laylat al-Qadr
каза qaza
казат ghazavat
казатчы ghazi
казы ghazi
казы qazi
казый qazi
Кайбар Khaybar
кайберен rijal-i ghayb
кайрыдин ghayr-i din
кайыз hayz
кайып эр rijal-i ghayb
кайып эрен rijal-i ghayb
кайыр khayr[1]
кайыр khayr[2]
Калам Qalam[3]
калам qalam[1]
Калем Qalam[3]
калем qalam[2]
календер qalandar
календеркана qalandarkhana
калпа khalfa[1]
Калык Khaliq, al-
калыпа khalifa[1]
калыпа khalifa[2]
Камбар Ghambar
Камбар Ата Ghambar
канимет ghanimat
капсылазам Ghavs al-A'zam
Кап тоо Qaf[2]
капыз hafiz
капыр kafir
кара дин ghayr-i din
карам haram[1]
кара таш hajar-i asvad
Карун Harun
кары qari
Карымбай Harun
Карынбай Harun
карыя qari
ката khata
катым khatm[1]
Кеаба Ka'ba
келем kalam
келеме шарып Kalam-i Sharif
Келе молдо Kalamullah
келем шарып Kalam-i Sharif
келме kalima
келмекөй kalimagu
келме шаадат kalima-yi shahadat
кеперет kaffarat
кепин kafn
Кербала Karbala
керемет karamat
китеп kitab

кожо khvaja[1]
кожо khvaja[2]
коом qavm
коомат qamat
Коосул аазам Ghavs al-A'zam
Көйкап тоо Qaf[2]
Көөсөр Kavsar[1]
көр gur
көр азабы 'azab-i qabr
көркана gurkhana
көрсү kursi
көрүстөн guristan
Кудаа Khuda
Кудай khuday
кудайкөй khudaygu
кудайы khudayi
кудрет qudrat
кудурет qudrat
кулкулдабат qul hu allah ahad
кунут qunut
купа qubba
куптан намазы salat al-'isha
Куран Qur'an
куранкана qur'ankhana
Куран катма Qur'an khatima
курбан qurban
курман qurban
Курман айт Qurban Bayrami
Курман айт 'Id al-Azha
кусул ghusl
кусулдаарат ghusl
кутпа khutba
кутпа дубасы khutba
күмбөз gumbaz
күнө gunah
күнөө gunah
күнөөкөр gunahkar
күпүр kufr
кыбла qibla
кыбыла qibla
Кыдыр Khizr
Кызыр Khizr
Кызыр-Илияс Ilyas
кыраат qira'at
кырк чилтен chiltan
кыямат qiyamat[1]
кыямат кайым qiyamat qa'im
лаанат la'nat
лаат Lat
лаббай labbay
лаббайка labbayka
лавих lavh
лаилахаилалла la ilaha illa allah va muhammadun rasulullah
ла илахи иллалла Мухаммед Расул Алла la ilaha illa allah va muhammadun rasulullah
лайым ilahi[1]
лапайка labbayka
лат Lat
Лат-Манат Manat
лахат lahid[1]
лоух махфуз lavh al-mahfuz, al-
ляббай labbay
Маади Mahdi
маала mahalla
маарек mubarak
магрифат ma'rifat[1]
магрыбыт ma'rifat[1]
мажилис majlis
мажус majus
мажусу majusi
мазап mazhab[1]
мазап mazhab[2]
мазар mazar
мазаркерде mazarkarda
мазин mu'azzin
майрам bayram
макирөө makruh
Маккатулла Makkatullah
маклукат makhluqat
макрам muharram[1]
макрөө makruh
макүр makruh
макүрөө makruh
макшар mahshar
малгун Mal'un[1]
Малик Malik[1]
Манат Manat
марифат ma'rifat[1]
маркабат marhamat
маркамат marhamat
маркум marhum
маркун marhum
махшар mahshar
махшар майдан. машыр mahshar
машаалла mashaallah
машайык mashayikh
машар mahshar
машат mashhad
машаяк mashayikh
Медина Madina
медиресе madrasa
медресе madrasa
мейир mahr[1]
мейит mayyit
Меке Makka
Мекейил Mika'il
мекирик makruh
мекирин makruh
мектеп maktab
мечит masjid
минбар minbar
мирас miras
мисбек misvak[1]
мисбек misvak[2]
мисибек misvak[1]
мисибек misvak[2]
Мисир Misr[2]
мискин miskin
михрап mihrab
можур muhajir
молдо mulla
молла mulla
молло mulla
момун mu'min[1]
моолут Mavlid[1]
мөтабар mu'tabar
мубайрек mubarak
мубакил mu'akkal
мубарек mubarak
муварек mubarak
мугалим mu'allim
мударис mudarris
мужтаид mujtahid[1]
мужтахит mujtahid[1]
мукаддас muqaddas
мукам maqam
Мукамбет Muhammad[1]
мукараб muqarrab
мукарап muqarrab
мукил mu'akkal
мукиреб muqarrab
муктасар mukhtasar

мунажаат munajat[1]
мунажат munajat[1]
мунапык munafiq
мунар manara
мунара manara
мупту mufti
мурас miras
мурдар murdar
мурид murid
мурут murid
Муса Musa
мусап mazhab[1]
мусап mazhab[2]
мусапыр musafir
муслим muslim
Мустапа Mustafa
мустахаб mustahabb
мусулман musulman
мусурман musulman
мутабар mu'tabar
Мухаммед Muhammad[1]
мүлк milk
мүлк mulk[1]
мүлүк mulk[1]
Мүнкүр-Накир Munkar va Nakir
Мүнкүр-Нанкир Munkar va Nakir
мүрдө murda
мүртөс murtadd
мырдар murdar
мээр mahr[1]
наалат la'nat
набий nabi
назар nazar[1]
назир nazr[2]
назр nazr[2]
назыр nazr[2]
намаз namaz
намазгер salat al-'asr
намазгөй namazgu
намаздигер salat al-'asr
намазшам salat al-maghrib
напака nafaqa
напил nafl
напил намаз salavat-i nafila
насаат nasihat
насил nasl
насип nasib
насият nasihat
насталик nasta'liq
насып nasib
насыят nasihat
ниет niyat
нике nikah
нифас nifas
нишалла insha'allah
нияз niyaz
Нооруз Navruz
нөкөр navkar
нур hur
нур huri
нур nur[1]
нургунча hur
нургунча huri
Нух Nuh[1]
ныяз niyaz
нээт niyat
нээти казат ghazavat
Обо эне Hava
обурак arvah
овлад avlad
Ойсул Ата Vays al-Qarani
Олдо Allah
олдо-бүлдө allahi billahi
олдо үй Allah hu
олуя avliya[1]
олуя заада avliyazada
Омейил Mika'il
омийин amin[1]
Омор 'Umar
оолат avlad
оомийин amin[1]
оомийн amin[1]
опаа vafa
орозо ruza
орозо айы Ramazan
орой ruh[1]
Оруздама Navruz
Осмон 'Usman
осуят vasiyat
отан vatan
ошур 'ushr
Өкил Vakil, al-
өкил vakil
өкмөт hukumat
Өкүл Vakil, al-
өкүл vakil
өкүм hukm
өкүмөт hukumat
өмүр 'umr
пайгамбар payghambar
пак pak
пал fal
паранжы paranja
парз farz
парыз farz
пенде banda
пербердигер Parvardigar
пери pari
перипте farishta
пида fida
пидия fidya
пир pir
питир fitr[1]
питир fitr[2]
пут put
рабаят rivayat
рабби Rabbi
раис ra'is[1]
райис ra'is[1]
райым rahm
ракмат rahmat
ракым rahm
рамазан Ramazan
расул rasul
Расулулла Rasulullah
рахмат rahmat
рекет rak'at
риваят rivayat
рисала risala
руксат rukhsat
рух ruh[1]
Рух Аллах Ruhullah
руханий ruhani
рухий ruhi
рүкү ruku'
сааба sahaba
сабыр sabr[2]
садага sadaqa
садага-кайыр khayr-sadaqa
садака sadaqa
сажда sajda[1]
сажыда sajda[1]
сакаба sadaqa

сакаба sahaba
сакабат sakhavat
салабат salavat
салават salavat
салам salam
салам алейкум assalamu ʻalaykum
салам-дуба duʻa-yi salam
Салейли галейхи вассалам salla allahi ʻalayhu va sallam
салоом алейкум assalamu ʻalaykum
салоом алеки assalamu ʻalaykum
сана sana[1]
санжыра shajara
сап saf
сапар Safar
сапар намазы salat al-safar
сежде sajda[1]
сейде sajda[1]
сейит sayyid
секет zakat[1]
селде salla
собоп savab[2]
собоп savab[3]
солтон sultan
cooп savab[3]
сопу sufi[1]
сопу sufi[2]
сөннөт sunna
сөннөт sunnat[1]
сөрөө sura
ссоп savab[2]
субханалла subhanallah
Сулайман Sulayman
султан sultan
Султан Вайис Гарани Vays al-Qarani
суннет sunna
суннет sunnat[2]
сурайыл surnay
сүннөт sunna
сүннөт sunnat[2]
сүрнөт sunna
сүрнөт sunnat[2]
сүрө sura
сүрөт surat
сүт sud
сүткер sudkhur
сүткор sudkhur
сүткөр sudkhur
сыйкыр sihr
сыйкырчы sihirbaz
Сырат көпүрөө Sirat[2]
сээр sihr
таазим taʻzim
Таала taʻala
таалим taʻlim
таалым taʻlim
таат taʻat
табарик tabarruk
табийет tabiʻat
табип tabib
табият tabiʻat
табыйгат tabiʻat
табып tabib
табыпчы tabib
табыт tabut
тагдыр taqdir
Тажаал Dajjal
тажия taʻziya
тазия taʻziya
тайпа ta'ifa
таква taqva
такдыр taqdir
таксыр taqsir
такыба taqva
такыбаа taqva
такыя taqiya
талак talaq[1]
талак кат talaq khat
таңгы макшар mahshar
таңды макшар mahshar
тапсир tafsir
тараба taravih
тарабих taravih
тарбия tarbiya
тарийка tariqat[1]
тарийка tariqat[2]
тарих tarikh[1]
тарки дүйнө tark-i dunya
тарса tarsa
тарых tarikh[1]
тарыхат tariqat[1]
тарыхат tariqat[2]
тарыхчы mu'arrikh
таслим taslim[1]
таспи tasbih
тасторкон dastarkhan
ташбыйкат tablighat
текпир takbir
Теңир Tangri
теспе tasbih
тилсим tilsim[1]
тилсим tilsim[2]
тилсим tilsim[3]
тобо tavba[1]
тобокел tavakkul[1]
тобоп tavaf[1]
тобоп tavaf[2]
Тозок Duzakh
тозоку duzakhi
тооп tavaf[1]
тооп tavaf[2]
Тоорат Tavrat
топу dubba
төрт мукиреб muqarrab
төрт чарыяр Chahar yar
тумар tumar
убажип vajib
убал vabal
увакып vaqf
уждан vijdan
Ужмак Ujmakh
улама ʻulama
улуксат rukhsat
Умай эне Hava
ур hur
ур huri
урп ʻurf
урук ruh[1]
уруксат rukhsat
устаз ustaz
устат ustad
усул usul[1]
усул жадит usul-i jadid
усул кадим usul-i qadim
Учмак Ujmakh
үжүрө hujra
үммөт ummat
үмөт ummat
Үнкүр-Нанкир Munkar va Nakir
үрөй ruh[1]
үрп ʻurf

үрүкү ruku'
Үт Hut
үү Hu
үшүр 'ushr
Фараон Fira'un
фарыз farz
Фатима Fatima
фитне fitna
хазрет hazrat
Хак Haqq[2]
Халил Аллах Khalilullah
халиф khalifa[1]
халиф khalifa[2]
хафыз hafiz
чадыра chadra
чажыра shajara
чалма chalma
чалыяр Chahar yar
чарыяр Chahar yar
чаряр Chahar yar
чежире shajara
чилде chilla[2]
чилтен chiltan
шаадат shahadat[1]
Шаймерден Shah-i mardan
шайтан Shaytan
шайхул ислам shaykh al-islam[1]
шайык shaykh
шайых-ул-ислам shaykh al-islam[1]
шак shak
шакирт shagird
шам намаз salat al-maghrib
шараат shari'at
шарип sharif
шарып sharif
шарыят shari'at
шежире shajara
шейит shahid[2]
шейит shi'i
шекирт shagird
шекит shagird
шерик sharik
Ыбрайым Ibrahim[1]
ыйбадат 'ibadat[1]
ыйбадаткана 'ibadatkhana
ыймам imam[1]
ыймам imam[2]
ыймам imam[3]
ыймам imam[4]
ыйман iman[1]
ыйык avliya[1]
ылаайым ilahi[2]
ылаанат la'nat
ылаббай labbay
ылаббайка labbayka
ылайым ilahi[1]
ылайым ilahi[2]
Ыланат Manat
ыланат Lat
ыман iman[1]
ынсап insaf
ыптар iftar
ырайым rahm
ыракмат rahmat
ырамазан Ramazan
ырасул rasul
Ыслам Islam
ыстыкпар isti'far
Ысырапыл Israfil
ышкы 'ishq
элдияр allahyar
эшен ishan

Tajik Index

абад abad
абд ‘abd
абдал abdal[1]
абдал abdal[2]
абдалон abdal[3]
Абдулло ‘Abdullah[1]
Абдулло ‘Abdullah[2]
абир ‘abir
абобил қуръон abvab al-Qur’an
аброр abrar
Абу abu
Абу Бакр Abu Bakr
Абу Ҳанифа Abu Hanifa
Абу Ҳанифа Imam-i A‘zam
абчад abjad
Аввал Avval, al-
авлиё avliya[1]
авлиё avliya[2]
авлиёзода avliyazada
авлод avlad
аврат ‘avrat
Авфу ‘Afuv, al-
Ад ‘Ad
адаб adab
адан ‘adn
Ад-Дорр Zarr, al-
адл ‘adl
адоват ‘adavat
адолат ‘adalat
аён ayan
Аззау Ҷалла ‘Azza va Jalla
Азиз ‘Aziz, al-
азиз ‘aziz[1]
Азим ‘Azim, al-
азо ‘aza
азоб azab
азоби кабир ‘azab al-kabir
азоби қабр ‘azab-i qabr
Азозил ‘Azazil
азоимхон ‘azayimkhan
азон azan
Азроил ‘Azra’il
азҳоби Бадр ashab-i Badr
акром akram
алайҳисалом ‘alayhi al-salam
Али ибн Толиб ‘Ali
Алийоса Alyasa‘
алиф лом мим alif lam mim
аллаёр allahyar
Аллам ал ғаюб ‘Allam al-ghuyub
Аллаҳи биллаҳ allahi billahi
аллома ‘allama
Аллоҳ ё Аллоҳ Allah ya Allah
Аллоҳу! Allah hu
Аллоҳу Акбар Allahu akbar
Аллоҳу Баширун Allahu Bashirun
Аллоҳу Олимун Allahu ‘Alimun
Аллоҳу Самиун Allahu Sami‘un
Аллоҳу тавалло Allah ta‘ala
алмисоқ misaq
аломат ‘alamat
ал Фотиҳа! Fatiha, al-
алҳамдулилло al-hamdullilah
Алҳамдуллилоҳу раббил оламин al-hamdulillahi rabbi'l-‘alamin
амал ‘amal
амир amir
амир ал муслимун amir al-muslimun
амир ал умаро amir al-umara
амират imarat
амирул мумин Amir al-mu’minin
амлок amlak
аммома ‘amama
амн amniyat
амният amniyat
амо a‘ma
амр amr
амри маъруф amr-i Ma‘ruf
анал-хақ ana al-haqq
анбар anbar[1]
анбиё anbiya[1]
анбор anbar[2]
анвор anvar
андарун andarun
андоза hadd
ансор ansar
анқо ‘Anqa
анҷуман anjuman
арасот ‘Arasat
арафа ‘arafa
арвоҳ arvah
аркон arkan
Арофат ‘Arafat
арш ‘arsh
аршӣ аъло ‘arsh-i a‘la
аршӣ курси ‘arsh-i kursi
Асад Asad
асадулоҳ Asadullah
асир asir
асо ‘asa
асорат asarat
аср ‘asr[1]
ассалому алайкум assalamu ‘alaykum
ассалому алайкум salam ‘alaykum
астағфируллоҳ astaghfirullah
асфалуссофилин asfal al-safilin
асҳоб ashab
асҳоби киром ashab-i kiram
асҳобил кахф ashab-i kahf
асҳоби расс Rass
асҳоби ҷаннат ashab-i jannat
аттаҳият tahiyat, at-
аттор ‘attar
аузи биллоҳи a‘uzu billah
Аузи биллоҳи минашайтони раҷим a‘uzu billahi min al-shaytani al-rajim
Афлотун Aflatun
афсона afsana
афсун afsun
афтода aftada
афьюн afyun
ахбор akhbar
ахлоқ akhlaq
ашраф ashraf
ашура ‘ashura[2]
ашура ‘Ashura[1]
Аъзам A‘zam[2]
аъзам a‘zam[1]
аълам a‘lam
аълам ‘alam[2]
аъраф a‘raf[1]
Аюб Ayyub
ақида ‘aqida
ақиқа ‘aqiqa
ақлият ‘aqliyat

Акраб ʿAqrab
акрабо aqraba
Ахад Ahad, al-
ахбоб ahbab
ахд ʿahd
ахком ahkam
ахлал вилоят ahl al-vilayat
ахли дил ahl-i dil
ахли зиммат ahl-i zimmat
ахли Китоб ahl-i kitab
ахли рай ahl-i ra'y
ахли салиб ahl-i salib
ахли Сунна ahl-i sunna
ахли тарикат ahl-i tariqat
ахлияти адо ahliyyat-i ada
ахлияти вучуб ahliyyat-i vujub
ахли калам ahl-i qalam
Ахмад Ahmad
ахрор ahrar
ачал ajal
ачам ʿajam
ачли Ислом ahl-i Islam
ачнабӣ ajnabi
ачр ajr
бадал badal
бадали асакарӣ badal-i askari
бадали накдӣ badal-i naqdi
бадали шахсӣ badal-i shakhsi
бадали хач hajj badal
баддуо bad-duʿa
Бадр Badr
Бадӣ Badiʿ, al-
байрам bayram
байт bayt
Байтул атик Bayt al-ʿatiq, al-
байтулахзон bayt al-ahzan
Байтуллох Baytullah
байтулмол bayt al-mal
Байтулмукаддас Bayt al-muqaddas
балоғат balaghat
банг bang
банда banda
бани Ислом bani Islam
Бани Исроил Bani Isra'il[2]
бани Исроил bani Isra'il[1]
баракалло barakullah
баракат barakat
барак barhaq
бароат bara'at[1]
供бародар biradar
барот barat
Барр Barr, al-
барки саодат barq
Басир Basir, al-
Батхо Batha
бахт bakht
бахшиш bakhshish
бахшӣ bakhshi
бачча bachcha
баччабоз bachchabaz
баччабозӣ bachchabazi
башарият bashariyat
баят bayʿat
бако baqa[1]
бако baqa[2]
бегунох bi gunah
бедиёнат bi diyanat
бедин dahri
беимон bi iman
бенамоз bi namaz
бетахорат bi taharat
биби bibi
бибӣ Марям Maryam[1]
бидъа bidʿat
бидъа bidʿat-i hasana
бидъат bidʿat
бидъат bidʿat-i hasana
биллах illa-billah
биллахи billahi
Билол Bilal
Билкийс Bilqis
бисмилло bismillah
бисмуллоху Рахмону Рахим bismillah al-Rahman al-Rahim
бисот bisat
бихалфа khalfa[2]
бихабиллах bihablillah
бихишт bihisht
боб bab
бовар bavar
бозгашт baz gasht
Боис Baʿis, al-
бокира bakira
Борӣ Bari, al-
Босит Basit, al-
ботил batil
Ботин Batin, al-
ботин batin
Бокӣ Baqi, al-
бокӣ baqi
боч baj
бузург buzurg
Бурок Buraq
бут but
бутпараст butparast
бутхона butkhana
бухтон buhtan
ва алайкум ассалом ʿalaykim al-salam
вабол vabal
вазир vazir
вазифа vazifa
Вакил Vakil, al-
вакил vakil
ваколат vakalat
валиахд vali ahd
валинеъмат vali niʿmat
валлохи аълам vallahu aʿlam
валлохи аълам vallahu aʿlam bil-savab
Валӣ Vali, al-
валӣ vali
варасат varasat
варъ varaʿ[1]
варака varaqa
васаваса vasvasa
васан vasan
васанӣ vasani
васвос vasvas
васият vasiyat
васиятнома vasiyatnama
васика vasiqa
васл vasl
ватан vatan
вафо vafa
вафот vafat
вахий vahi
ваъда vaʿda
ваъз vaʿz
вакф vaqf
вакфа vaqfa
вахданият vahdaniyat
вахдат vahdat-i vujud

Вахоб Vahhab, al-
вахобизм Vahhabiya
вахшат vahshat
вахшиёна vahshiyana
вач vajh
вачд vajd
вилдан vildan
вирд vird[1]
вирд vird[2]
вирса virsa
витр vitr
виқор viqar
вичдон vijdan
воиз va'iz
Ворис Varis, al-
ворис varis
восил vasl
Восӣ Vasi', al-
воқиф vaqif[1]
воқиф vaqif[2]
Вохид Vahid, al-
вочиб vajib
Вочид Vajid, al-
Вудуд Vadud, al-
вузу vuzu'
вуқу vuquf
вучуд vujud
гиръя yighi
гумбаз gumbaz
гунох gunah
гунохкор gunahkar
гӯр gur
гӯристон guristan
давр davir
Далв Dalv
далил dalil
далили ақлӣ dalil-i 'aqli
далили наклӣ dalil-i naqli
далили шаръӣ dalil-i shar'i
дарача hadd
дарвеш darvish
даргох dargah
дарра darra
дарсхона darskhana
дастор dastar
дастурхон dastarkhan
дастшӯяк dastshuy
дафн dafn
Даъбба Dabba
даъват da'vat
даъво da'va[2]
дахр dahr
дахри дун dahr-i dun
дахрӣ dahri
дахрӣхо dahriya
Даччол Dajjal
дев div
девон divan
девона divana
дидор didar
диёнат diyanat
диёнаткор diyanatkar
дин din
диндор dindar
дини самовӣ din-i samavi
динӣ dini
добба Dabba
Довуд Da'ud
домулло damulla
донишманд danishmand
дорилсурур dar al-surur
доруламон dar al-aman
дорулбақо dar al-baqa
дорулислом dar al-Islam
дорулсалом dar al-salam
дорул сулх dar al-sulh
дорулуффоз dar al-huffaz
дорулфано dar al-fana
дорулғурур dar al-ghurur
дорулқазо dar al-qaza
дорулқарор dar al-qasas
дорулхаводис dar al-havadis
дорулхарб dar al-harb
дубба dubba
Дулдул Duldul
дуньё dunya
дуньёвӣ dunyavi
дуо du'a[1]
дуо du'a[2]
дуо du'a[3]
дуогӯй du'agu
дуодор du'adar
дуоисалом du'a-yi salam
дуохон du'akhvan
дуруст durust
духан dukhan[2]
Дӯзах Duzakh
дӯзахӣ duzakhi
дӯст dust
етим yatim
ёддошт yad dasht
ёд кард yad kard
ё Оллох! ya allah
ё пирим ya pirim
ёр yar
ё Рабби! ya rabbi
ё Рамазон ya ramazan
ёриаллох yarullah
Ёқуб Ya'qub
Ёху yahu
забиха zabiha
забт zabt
Забур Zabur
завия zaviya
завол zaval
заифа za'ifa
Закариё Zakariya
закот zakat[1]
закотал фитр zakat al-fitr
залолат zalalat
Замзам Zamzam
замзамӣ zamzami
занб zanb
зарзамон zar zaman
зарурият zarurat
заъфар zafar
Заққум Zaqqum
захадат zahadat
зидд zidd
зиё ziya'
зиёрат ziyarat
зиёратгох ziyaratgah
зиёратхона ziyaratkhana
зикр zikr
зикри хуфӣ zikr-i khafi
зикри чахр zikr-i jahr
зикрхона zikrkhana
Зилқаъда Zu'l-qa'da
Зилчалол Zu'l-jalal va'l-ikram
зиммӣ zimmi
зиндиқ zindiq
зиндон zindan
зино zina
зинокор zinakar

золим zalim
Зотй пок Zat-i pak
зоҳид zahid
зоҳир zahir
Зулиҳсон Zu'l-ihsan
зулм zulm
зулм zulum
зулмат zulmat[1]
зулфиқор Zu'l-fiqar
Зулқарнайн Zu'l-Qarnayn
Зулқаъда Zu'l-qa'da
Зул Қуфл Zu'l-Kifl
Зулҳаҷҷа Zu'l-hijja
Зулҳиҷҷа Zu'l-hijja
зулҷанаҳайн zu'l-janahayn
зуннор zunnar
зуфаф zifaf
зухр zuhr
зӯҳд zuhd[1]
Иблис Iblis
ибодат 'ibadat[1]
ибодатгоҳ 'ibadatgah
ибодатхона 'ibadatkhana
ибоҳа ibaha
иброний 'ibrani
Иброҳим Ibrahim[1]
ид 'id
Идал Адха 'Id al-Azha
Идал Фитр 'Id al-Fitr
идда 'iddat
иддат 'iddat
иди Рамазон 'Id al-Fitr
Иди Қурбон 'Id al-Azha
Идрис Idris
издивоҷ izdivaj
иззат 'izzat
изн izn
изор izar
ийди Қурбон Qurban Bayrami
Илёс Ilyas
иллоҳиун ilahiyun
илм 'ilm[1]
илми ҳол 'ilm-i hal[1]
илоҳ ilah
илоҳа ilaha
илоҳи ilahi[1]
илоҳиёт ilahiyat
илоҳӣ ilahi[2]
илоҳӣ ilahi[3]
илтиҷо iltija
илҳад ilhad
илҳом ilham
имом imam[1]
имом imam[2]
имом imam[3]
имом imam[4]
имомал қиблатайн imam al-qiblatayn
имомат imamat[1]
имомат imamat[2]
имон iman[1]
имон iman[2]
Имрон 'Imran[1]
Имрон 'Imran[2]
инзал inzal
Инна аттайнака алкавсара inna a'taynaka al-kavsara
иноба inabat
инсони комил insan-i kamil
инсоф insaf
инс-ҷинс ins-jins
интихоб intikhab
интиқом intiqam
интиҳо intiha
иншооллоҳ insha'allah
инҷизоб injizab
Инҷил Injil
ионат i'ana
ирим irim
ирода irada[1]
ирода irada[3]
иродаи лайазал irada-yi la yazal
иртидод irtidad
иршод irshad
иршоднома irshadnama
исён 'isyan
исёнгар 'isyankar
Искандар Iskandar
Ислом Islam
исломият islamiyat
исмат 'ismat
исматилло 'ismatullah
исми аъзам ism-i a'zam
Исмоил Isma'il
иснод isnad
Исо 'Isa
исовият 'Isaviyat
исовӣ 'Isavi
исопараст 'Isaparast
Исоқ Ishaq
Исроил Isra'il
исроф israf
Исрофил Israfil
истибдод istibdad
истилоҳот istilahat
истиншоқ istinshaq
истинҷо istinja
истисло istislah
истисно istisna
истисшод istishhad
истисқо istisqa
истифор isti'far
истихсон istihsan
истиғфор istighfar
истиқбол istiqbal
истиқома istiqamat
истиҳоза istihaza
истиҳора istikhara
исқот isqat
итиқоф i'tikaf
итлоқ itlaq
итмом itmam
итоат ita'at
иттиҳод ittihad[1]
иттиҳод ittihad[2]
ифрит 'ifrit
ифта ifta
ифтитоҳ iftitah
ифтор iftar
иффат 'iffat
ихван ikhvan
ихзор ihzar
ихлос ikhlas[1]
ихтилоф ikhtilaf
ишорат isharat
ишорати қиёмат ashrat-i sa'at
ишрак ishrak
ишрок ishraq
ишқ 'ishq
иъдом i'dam
иқаб 'iqab
иқомат iqamat
иқрор iqrar[1]
иқрор iqrar[2]

иқтидо iqtida
иҳдод ihdad
иҳсан ihsan[2]
иҳсор ihsar
иҳтилам ihtilam
иҳтиҷоб ihtijab
иҷмо ijma'
иҷоб ijab
иҷобат ijabat
иҷозат ijazat
иҷозатнома ijazatnama
иҷтиҳод ijtihad
Кабир Kabir, al-
кабира kabira
Кавсар Kavsar[1]
кадар qadar
каламулло Kalamullah
калима kalima
калимаи шаҳодат kalima-yi shahadat
калиматуллло kalimatullah
калимулло kalimullah
калисиё kalisa
калисо kalisa
калисьё kalisa
калом kalam
каломи Шариф Kalam-i Sharif
каниз kaniz
каниса kanisa
карам karam
Карбало Karbala
Карим Karim, al-
каромот karamat
кафан kafn
кафил kafil
кафилӣ kafalat
кафорат kaffarat
кашиш kashish
кашишхона kashishkhana
кашкӯл kashkul
Каъба Ka'ba
Каъбаи мукаррам mukarram
каъбапӯш qisvat
Каъбатулло Ka'batullah
каҷрафтор kajraftar
кироммн котибун kiramin katibin
китоб kitab
кифоя kifaya
Кобуд Qabiz, al-
коинот ka'inat
комил akmal
котиб katib
кофир kafir
кофиристон kafiristan
коҳин kahin
кула kulah
кулоҳ kulah
курсӣ kursi
куфр kufr
куфрон kufran
куффор kuffar
кӯҳи Муздалиф Muzdalifa
кӯҳи Қоф Qaf[2]
лабайка labbayka
лаббай labbay
лаббайк labbayka
лавхал маҳфуз lavh al-mahfuz, al-
лавҳ lavh
лазо laza
лаин la'in
лайлатул қадр Laylat al-Qadr
Латиф Latif, al-
лафзи куфур lafz-i kufr
Лашкари Ислом lashkar-i Islam
лаънат la'nat
лаҳад lahid[1]
лаҳад lahid[2]
лиллоҳ lillah
лифафа lifafa
ло илоҳо иллоллоҳ Муҳаммадин расулиллоҳ la ilaha illa allah va muhammadun rasulullah
ломакон La makan
лот Lat
Лут Lut
Луқмон Luqman[1]
мааъд ma'ad
мавзу mavzu'
мавлавӣ mavlavi
мавлид Mavlid[1]
мавлид mavlid[2]
мавло Mavla[1]
мавло mavla[2]
мавлоно mavlana
мавлуд Mavlid[1]
мавъиза mav'iza
мавқеъ mavqi'
мавҳум mavhum
мавҳумот mavhumat
мавҷуд mavjud
мавҷудот mavjudat
маддоҳ maddah
Мадина Madina
Мадинаи мунаввир Madina-yi munavvara
мадраса madrasa
мадфан madfan
мадҳия madhiya
мазлум mazlum
мазнуб maznib
мазор mazar
мазористон mazaristan
мазоркарда mazarkarda
мазҳаб mazhab[1]
мазҳаб mazhab[2]
майит mayyit
Макка Makka
Маккатулло Makkatullah
маккӣ makki
макруҳ makruh
мактаб maktab
малак malak
Малик Malik[1]
Малик Malik, al-
малик malik[2]
малоик mala'ika
малоика mala'ika
малоикот malakut
малъун mal'un[2]
мамлук mamluk
мамот mamat
манзур manzur
манкуҳа mankuha
Манот Manat
мансак mansak
мантиқ mantiq
мантиқӣ mantiqi
манфур manfur
манҳи manhi
маоб ma'b
маозоллоҳ ma'az allah

маосил maghasil
маосӣ ma'asi
Марва Marva
мардуд mardud
маросим marasim
марсия marsiya
марсият marsiya
марҳамат marhamat
марҳум marhum
масали mas'ala
масбук masbuq
Масиҳ Masih[1]
масиҳ masih[2]
масиҳи masihi
масси mahsi
маст mast
масҷид masjid
масҷиди Ақсо Masjid al-Aqsa, al-
Масҷиди Харам Masjid al-Haram, al-
матрука matruka
мафавқал табиат ma favq al-tabi'at
махдум makhdum
махлукот makhluqat
махлуқ makhluq
машоварат mashvarat
машойих mashayikh
машраб mashrab
машруҳ mashru'
машҳад mashhad
машҳадӣ mashhadi
маъбад ma'bad
маъбуд ma'bud[1]
маъбуд ma'bud[2]
маъзун ma'zun
маълун Mal'un[1]
маъмур ma'mur
маънавӣ ma'navi
маърака ma'raka
маърифат ma'rifat[1]
маърифат ma'rifat[2]
маъруф ma'ruf
маъсум ma'sum
маъюб ma'yub
мағлуб maghlub
мағриб maghrib
мағфират maghfirat
мақбара maqbara[1]
мақбара maqbara[2]
мақом maqam
мақоми Ибройим Maqam-i Ibrahim
мақсура maqsura
мақтул maqtul
маҳалла mahalla
маҳафатулла mahafatullah
маҳбус mahbus
Маҳди Mahdi
маҳкам mahkam
маҳкама mahkama
маҳкум mahkum
маҳр mahr[1]
маҳр mahr[2]
маҳрам maharim[1]
маҳрам maharim[2]
маҳрам mahram
маҳрум mahrum
маҳфил mahfil
маҳшар mahshar
маҳшаргоҳ mahshargah
маҷзуб majzub
Маҷид Majid, al-
маҷлис majlis
маҷнун majnun[1]
маҷнун majnun[2]
маҷус majus
маҷусият majusiyat
маҷусӣ majusi
мерос miras
меросхӯр miraskhur
Метин Matin, al-
меъроҷ mi'raj
меъроҷия mi'rajiya
меъроҷнома mi'rajnama
меҳроб mihrab
мизан mizan[2]
мизана mizana
Мизон Mizan[3]
мизон mizan[1]
Микаил Mika'il
милод milad
милодӣ miladi
Мина Mina
минбар minbar
минора manara
мир mir
мирзо mirza
мириғазаб mirghazab
мисвок misvak[1]
мисвок misvak[2]
мискин miskin
Миср Misr[2]
миср misr[1]
моддӣ maddiyun
мол mal
Моликия Malikiya
Моликулмулк Malik al-Mulk
Моликӣ Maliki
молият maliyat
момои Бараҳна Hava
Монӣ Mani', al-
мотам matam
мотамзада matamzada
мохпарастӣ mahparast
мошолло mashaallah
муаззин mu'azzin
муаллим mu'allim
муаллиф mu'allif
муаррих mu'arrikh
муаққад mu'akkad
мубассир mubassir
Мубдӣ Mubdi', al-
муборак mubarak
мубориз mubariz
мубориза mubaraza
мубошир mubashir
мубошшир mubashshir
мубоҳ mubah
мубоҳиса mubahasa
мубҳам mubham
муваҳҳид muvahhid
мудаллас mudallas
мударрис mudarris
мудофиа mudafa'a
мудрик mudrik
музаффар muzaffar
Музил Muzill, al-
мукаллаф mukallaf
мукаммал mukammal
мукаррам mukarram
мукаррир mukarrir
мукофоти Худой mukafat

мулк milk
мулк mulk[1]
мулки амлок mulk-amlak
мулла mulla
муллобачча mullabachcha
мулозим mulazim
мулҳақ mulhaq
мулҳид mulhid
Мумин Mu'min, al-
Мумит Mumit, al-
мунаввар munavvar
муназзал munazzal
мунақиб manaqib
мунаҷҷим munajjim
мункар munkar
Мункар-Накир Munkar va Nakir
мункиршавӣ munkir
мунозара munazara
мунофиқ munafiq
муноҷат munajat[1]
муноҷат munajat[2]
Мунтақим Muntaqim, al-
муомалат mu'amalat
Муоъххир Mu'akhkhir, al-
мурда murda
мурдахона murdakhana
мурдашӯй murdashuy
мурдор murdar
мурид murid
мурофаъ murafa'a
муроқиба muraqaba
мурохақа murahaqa
мурсал mursal[1]
мурсалин mursalin
муртад murtadd
Муртазо Murtaza
муршид murshid
мусаб musab
Мусаввир Musavvir, al-
мусалла musalla[1]
мусалла musalla[2]
мусалли musalli
мусбат musbat
мусибат musibat
муслима muslima
муслимин muslimin
Мусо Musa
мусовӣ musavi[1]
мусодира musadara
мусолиҳа musalaha
мусофаҳа musafaha
мусофир musafir
мустабид mustabidd
Мустафо Mustafa
мустаприк mustashrik
мустаҳобб mustahabb
мустаҷоб mustajab
мусулмон muslim
мусулмон musulman
мутаассиб muta'assib
мутаваллият mutavalliyat
мутаваллӣ mutavalli
мутадаййин mutadayyin
Мутакаббир Mutakabbir, al-
мутакаллим mutakallim
Мутаолӣ Muta'ali, al-
мутасаввиф mutasavvif
муташайх mutashayyikh
мутаъббид muta'abbid
мутаҳҳар mutahhar
мутлақ mutlaq
мутолиа mutala'a
муфассал mufassal
муфассир mufassir
муфсид mufsid[1]
муфсит mufsid[1]
муфтир muftir
муфтӣ mufti
мухаддарат mukhaddara
Мухаймин Muhaymin, al-
мухлис mukhlis
мухосамат mukhasamat
Мухсӣ Muhsi, al-
мухтасар mukhtasar
мухторият mukhtariyat
Мухӣ Muhyi, al-
мушкилкушо mushkilkushad
мушоҳида mushahida
мушрик mushrik
Муъид Mu'id, al-
Муъиз Mu'izz, al-
муъиз mu'id
муътамир mu'tamir
Муғнӣ Mughni, al-
муқавала muqavala
муқаддас muqaddas
Муқаддим Muqaddim, al-
муқаллид muqallid
муқарраб muqarrab
Муқит Muqit, al-
Муқсит Muqsit, al-
Муқтадир Muqtadir, al-
муҳаббат muhabbat
муҳаддис muhaddis
муҳаллил muhallil
Муҳаммад Muhammad[1]
муҳаммадӣ muhammadi[1]
муҳаммадӣ muhammadi[2]
Муҳаррам Muharram[2]
муҳаррамат muharramat
муҳиб muhibb
муҳокама muhakama
муҳориба muharaba
муҳосира muhasara
муҳоҷир muhajir
муҳоҷират muhajarat
муҳоҷирун muhajirin
муҳсин muhsin
муҳтадӣ muhtadi
муҳтасиб muhtasib[1]
муҳтасиб muhtasib[2]
муҷавир mujavir
муҷассам mujassam
муҷда mujda
муҷдаҳид mujtahid[2]
Муҷиб Mujib, al-
муҷоҳид mujahid
муҷтаҳид mujtahid[1]
мӯсовӣ musavi[2]
мӯъмин mu'min[1]
мӯъмина mu'mina
мӯътабар mu'tabar
мӯъҷиза mu'jiza[1]
нааш na'sh[1]
нааш na'sh[2]
набивот nabuvat
набиулло nabi'ullah
набӣ nabi
навкар navkar
Наврӯз Navruz
назар nazar[1]
назар nazar[2]
назоҳат nazahat
назр nazr[1]

назр nazr[2]
наим Na'im[1]
наим na'im[2]
найрон nayran
намоз salat
намоз namaz
намозгоҳ namazgah
намозгӯ namazgu
намози бомдод salat al-fajr
намози бомдод bamdad
намози бомдод salat al-subh
намози витр salat al-vitr
намози дигар salat al-'asr
намози зуҳр salat al-zuhr
намози ийд salat al-'idayn
намози истисқо salat al-istisqa
намози истиҳора salat al-istikhara
намози ишроқ salat al-ishraq
намози мариз salat al-mariz
намози мағриб salat al-maghrib
намози мусофир salat al-musafir
намози нофила nafila
намози пешин salat al-zuhr
намози рағойиб salat al-ragha'ib
намози сафар salat al-safar
намози субҳ salat al-subh
намози субҳ salat al-fajr
намози таровеҳ taravih
намози тарових salat al-taravih
намози таҳаҷҷуд salat al-tahajjud
намози хауф salat al-khavf
намози хусуф salat al-khusuf
намози хуфтон salat al-'isha
намози част salat al-zuha
намози шом salat al-maghrib
намози қусуф salat al-qusuf
намози ҳаҷ salat al-hajat
намози ҷаноза salat al-janaza
намози ҷумъа salat al-jum'a
намозхон namazkhan
Намруд Numrud
насаб nasab
насабнома nasabnama
насиб nasib
насиба nasiba
насил nasl
насиҳат nasihat
насоро nasara
насронийт nasraniyat
насронӣ nasrani
настаълиқ nasta'liq
насу nasut
насух nasuh
нафас nafas
нафақа nafaqa
нафс nafs[1]
нафс nafs[2]
нақиб naqib
нақлия naqliya
нақс naqis
наҳс nahs
наҳу nahu
наҷас najas
наҷис najis
наҷот najat
неъмат ni'mat
ниёз niyaz
низом nizam
никоҳ nikah
нисаб nisab
нисор nisar
нифос nifas
нишалло nishalla
нишаллофурӯш nishallafurush
ният niyat
ниҳрир nihrir
нозил nazil
ноиб na'ib
номашру namashru'
номаҳрам namahram
нопок napak[1]
нопок napak[2]
нофил nafl
Нофӣ Nafi', al-
ношаръӣ nashar'i
ноҳалол nahalal
ноҳақ nahaq
нубувват nubuvvat
Нумруд Numrud
Нур Nur, al-
нур nur[1]
нури аршулло nur-i 'arshullah
нусрат nusrat
нутқ nutq
нушур nushur
Нуҳ Nuh[1]
обдаст abdast
обдаста abdasta
обид 'abid
обида abida
обида 'abida
оби Замзам ab-i Zamzam
оби ҳаёт ab-i hayat
Одам Adam
одат 'adat
Одил 'Adl, al-
одил 'adil
Оиша 'A'isha
олам 'alam[1]
Олим 'Alim, al-
олим 'alim
Олӣ 'Ali, al-
Оллоҳ Allah
Оллоҳу Акбар Allahu akbar
олӣабо al-i aba
омин Amin[2]
омин amin[1]
ориф 'arif
осмон asman
оташ atash
оташпараст atashparast
офтоба abdasta
Охир Akhir, al-
охират akhirat
охирзамон akhir zaman
охун akhund
охунд akhund
ошиқ 'ashiq
оя ayat
оятул курси ayat al-kursi
оятулло ayatullah
оятул муташабиҳот ayat al-mutashabihat
оятул мухкамат ayat al-muhkamat
оқибат 'aqibat
оқибат 'uqba
Оҷмах Ujmakh
паём payam
пайғамбар payghambar
пайғом paygham
парвардигор Parvardigar

парихон parikhan
парихони parikhani
парӣ pari
пешқадам pishqadam
пир pir
пири муғон pir-i mughan
пок pak
порсо parsa
пули Сирот Sirat[2]
пули сирот pul-i sirat
пут put
путпараст putparast
путхона putkhana
рабб Rabb
Раббано Rabbana
Рабби Rabbi
Раббил оламин Rabb al-ʿalamayn
Раббил Фалак Rabb al-Falak
раббонӣ rabbani
рабеулаввал Rabiʿ al-avval
рабеулохир Rabiʿ al-akhir
Равза Ravza
раво rava
Раззоқ Razzaq, al-
разиаллоҳу анҳу razi allahu ʿanhu
раис ra'is[1]
раис ra'is[2]
ракъат rakʿat
рамазон Ramazan
раммол rammal
расм-русум rasm-rusum
расул rasul
расулона rasulana
Расулуллоҳ Rasulullah
Рауф Rauf, al-
рахил rahil
Рашид Rashid, al-
раъй ra'i
рағойиб ragha'ib
рақс raqs
раҳбон rahban
раҳбония rahbaniyat
Раҳим Rahim, al-
раҳим rahim
раҳм rahm
раҳмат rahmat
раҳматӣ rahmati
Раҳмон Rahman, al-
раҳмонӣ rahmani
раҷаб Rajab
раҷим rajim
раҷм rajm
рибо riba
ривоят rivayat
ридо rida[1]
ридо rida[2]
риё riya
риёзат riyazat
риёкор riyakar
Ризвон Rizvan
ризвонулоҳу алайҳи rizvanullah ʿalayhi[2]
ризо riza[1]
ризқ rizq
ринд rind
риоя riʿaya
рисола risala
рисолат risalat
ришват rishvat
риҷоал ғайб rijal-i ghayb
робита rabita
ровӣ ravi
Рофӣ Rafiʿ, al-
Роқиб Raqib, al-
роҳиб rahib
рубобият rububiyat
руку rukuʿ
Рум Rum[1]
рутба rutba
рухсат rukhsat
рухсатнома rukhsatnama
руҳ ruh[1]
руҳий ruhi
руҳоният ruhaniyat
руҳонӣ ruhani
Руҳул Амин Ruh al-Amin
Руҳуллоҳ Ruhullah
Рӯза ʿId al-Fitr
рӯза ruza
рӯзи Арафат ruz-i ʿarafat
рӯзи шак shak
рӯзи ҷазо ruz-i jaza
Сабр Sabur, al-
сабр sabr[1]
савмаъ savmaʿa
савоб savab[1]
савоб savab[2]
савоб savab[3]
Савр Savr
садақа sadaqa
садр sadr[1]
садр sadr[2]
сайид sayyid
сайийийа sayyi'a
салавот salavat
салаф salaf
салафи солиҳин salaf-i salihin
салиб salb
салиб salib
салибиун salibiyun
салла dastar
салла salla
Саллаллоҳу алайҳи васаллам salla allahi ʿalayhu va sallam
саловати нофила salavat-i nafila
Салом Salam, al-
салом assalamu ʿalaykum
салом salam
салот salat
Салсабил Salsabil
Самад Samad, al-
само sama
само samaʿ[1]
само samaʿ[2]
самовӣ samavi
Самуд Samud
Самӣ Samiʿ, al-
сана sana[1]
санаи милодия sana-yi miladiyya
санаи шамсия sana-yi shamsiyya
санаи қамария sana-yi qamariyya
санаи ҳиҷрия sana-yi hijriyya
санам sanam
сано sana[2]
Сара Sara
Саратон Saratan
сар об sar-ab
сарроф sarraf
сарф sarf
Саттор Sattar, al-

Сафа Safa
сафар Safar
сафийилло safi'ullah
сафойл safa'il
сахир sahir
саховат sakhavat
саъӣ sa'i
сағир saghir
сақар Saqar
саҳар sahar
саҳв sahv
саҳифа sahifa
саҳих sahih
саҳоба sahaba
саҷда sajda[1]
саҷда sujud
саҷдагоҳ sajdagah
сеҳр sihr
сеҳрбоз sihirbaz
сеҳрий sihri
сибғатилло sibghatullah
сиддиқ siddiq
Сидратал мунтаҳа Sidrat al-muntaha
сиёр ал набӣ siyar al-nabi
силоҳ silah
силсила silsila[1]
силсила silsila[2]
силсиланома silsilanama
симурғ Simurgh
сираи Зориёт Zariyat
Сирот Sirat[2]
сирот sirat[1]
сиҷҷил sijjil
соат sa'at
собир sabir
сойир sa'ir
Солеҳ Salih[2]
солеҳ salih[1]
соф saf
соҳиби каромат sahib-i karamat
субҳа subha
субҳон subhan
субҳонака subhanaka
субҳоно атаалло subhanahu va ta'ala
субҳоноллоҳ subhanallah
судур sudur
судхӯр sudkhur
судхӯри sud
суиқасд sui qasd
сукут sukut
Сулаймон Sulayman
султон sultan
сулук suluk
сулҳ sulh
Сунбула Sunbula
суннат sunna
суннат sunnat[1]
суннат sunnat[2]
суннӣ sunni
сур sur
сура sura
сураи Абас 'Abasa
сураи Алақ 'Alaq
сураи Анбиё Anbiya[2]
сураи Анкабут 'Ankabut
сураи Анфол Anfal
сураи Анъом An'am
сураи Аср 'Asr[2]
сураи Аъло A'la
сураи Аъроф A'raf[2]
сураи Аҳзоб Ahzab
сураи Аҳқоф Ahqaf
сураи Байинна Bayyina
сураи Балад Balad
сураи Бароат Bara'at[2]
сураи Бақара Baqara
сураи Буруҷ Buruj
сураи Воқеъа Vaqi'a
сураи Даҳр dahir
сураи Духон Dukhan[1]
сураи Ёсин Ya Sin
сураи Зилзол Zilzal
сураи Зумар Zumar
сураи Зухруф Zukhruf
сураи Зуҳо Zuha
сураи Иброҳим Ibrahim[2]
сураи Инсон Insan
сураи Инфитор Infitar
сураи Инширох Inshirah
сураи Иншиқоқ Inshiqaq
сураи Исуро Isra
сураи Ихлос Ikhlas[2]
сураи Кавсар Kavsar[2]
сураи Каҳф Kahf
сураи Кофурун Kafirun
сураи Лайл Layl
сураи Лаҳаб Lahab
сураи Луқмон Luqman[2]
сураи Марям Maryam[2]
сураи Масад Masad
сураи Маъориҷ Ma'arij
сураи Моида Ma'ida
сураи Моъун Ma'un
сураи Мудассир Muddassir
сураи Музаммил Muzzammil
сураи Мулк Mulk[2]
сураи Мумтаҳана Mumtahana
сураи Мунофиқун Munafiqun
сураи Мурсалот Mursalat
сураи Мутаффифин Mutaffifin
сураи Муҳаммад Muhammad[2]
сураи Муҷодала Mujadala
сураи Мӯмин Mu'min[2]
сураи Мӯмин Ghafir
сураи Мӯъминун Mu'minin
сураи Набо Naba
сураи Намл Naml
сураи Наср Nasr
сураи Наҳул Nahl
сураи Наҷм Najm
сураи Нисо Nisa
сураи Нозиъот Nazi'at
сураи Нос Nas
сураи Нур Nur[2]
сураи Нуҳ Nuh[2]
сураи Одиёт 'Adiyat
сураи Оли Имрон Al-i Imran
сураи Рахмон Rahman
сураи Раъд Ra'd
сураи Рум Rum[2]
сураи Сабо Saba
сураи Саф Saff
сураи Саҷда Sajda[2]
сураи Сод Sad
сураи Соффот Saffat
сураи Тавба Tavba[3]
сураи Таквир Takvir
сураи Такосур Takasur
сураи Талоқ Talaq[2]
сураи Тағобун Taghabun
сураи Таҳрим Tahrim[2]
сураи Тин Tin

сураи Торик̧ Tariq
сураи Тоҳо Ta ha
сураи Тур Tur
сураи Фалак̧ Falaq[2]
сураи Фатҳ Fath
сураи Фаҷр Fajr
сураи Фил Fil
сураи Фотир Fatir[1]
сураи Фотиҳа Fatiha[3]
сураи Фурқон Furqan[2]
сураи Фуссилат Fussilat
сураи Хумиза Humaza
сураи Шамс Shams
сураи Шуъаро Shu'ara
сураи Шӯро Shura[2]
сураи Юнус Yunus[2]
сураи Юсуф Yusuf[2]
сураи Ғошия Ghashiya
сураи Қадр Qadr[1]
сураи Қалам Qalam[3]
сураи Қамар Qamar
сураи Қиёмат Qiyamat[2]
сураи Қисас Qasas[2]
сураи Қориъа Qari'a
сураи Қоф Qaf[1]
сураи Қурайш Quraysh[2]
сураи Ҳадид Hadid
сураи Ҳашр Hashr[2]
сураи Ҳаҷ Hajj[2]
сураи Ҳиҷр Hijr
сураи Ҳоққа Haqqa
сураи Ҳуд Hud[2]
сураи Ҳуҷурот Hujurat
сураи Ҷин Jinn[2]
сураи Ҷосия Jasiya
Сураи ҷумъа Jum'a[3]
сурат surat
сурной surnay
суфтаҷо suftajah
суҳаф suhuf
суҳуф suhuf
сӯфӣ sufi[1]
сӯфӣ sufi[2]
тааббуд ta'abbud[2]
таавиз ta'avvuz
таассуб ta'assub
табаррук tabarruk
табауттобеъин taba'-i tabi'in
табиат tabi'at
табиб tabib
табииюн tabi'iyun
таблиғот tablighat
табозӯъ tavazi'
таборак tabarak
таваккал tavakkul[1]
таваррук̧ tavarruq
тавақкуф tavaqquf
таваҳҳум tavahhum
таваҷҷӯҳ tavajjuh
тавба tavba[1]
тавба-тазаррӯ tavba-tazarru
Таввоб Tavvab, al-
таворих tavarikh
тавоф tavaf[1]
тавоф tavaf[2]
тавофи зиёрат tavaf-i ziyarat
тавофи нофила tavaf-i nafila
тавофи садр tavaf-i sadr
тавофи қудум tavaf-i qudum
Таврот Tavrat
тавсим tavsim
тавсиф tavsif
тавфик̧ tavfiq
тавк̧ tavq
тавқи бандагӣ tavq
тавҳид tavhid[1]
тадайин tadayyun[2]
тадаюн tadayyun[1]
тадлис tadlis
тадфин tadfin
тазахуд tazahhud
тазвиҷ tazavij
тазкия tazkiya
таййиба tayyiba[1]
таййиба tayyiba[2]
такбир takbir
такбир takbir al-tahrima
такия takya
таклиф taklif
такфин takfin
такфир takfir
такъя takiya
такя takya
талвоса talvasa
талок̧ talaq[1]
талоқхат talaq khat
талоқхат talaqnama
талқин talqin[1]
талқин talqin[2]
талқин talqin[3]
таматтуъ tamattu'
тамоки dukhan[2]
тамҷид tamjid
танаввӯъ tanavvu'
танассир tanassur
танассух tanasukh
Тангрӣ Tangri
танзиҳ tanzih[1]
танзиҳ tanzih[2]
таоло ta'ala
таом ta'am
тарака taraka
тарбия tarbiya
тарих tarikh[2]
тарик̧ tariqat[1]
тарик̧ tariqat[2]
тарикат tariqat[1]
тарикат tariqat[2]
тарки дунё tark-i dunya
тарс khavf
тарсо tarsa
тарғиб targhib
тарғибот targhibat
тасаввуф tasavvuf
тасаддик̧ tasadduq
тасбеҳ subha
тасбеҳ tasbih
тасвиб tasvib
тасир tashir
таслим taslim[1]
таслим taslim[2]
Тасним Tasnim
татавву tatavvu'
тафрид tafrid
тафсир tafsir
тахаммул tahammul
тахрим tahrim[1]
тахримӣ tahrimi
ташахудд tashahhud
ташбеҳ tashbih
ташноб tashnab
ташриғ tashri'[1]
ташриғ tashri'[2]
ташрик̧ tashriq

таъбир ta'bir
таъбирнома ta'birnama
таъвиз ta'viz[1]
таъвиз ta'viz[2]
таъдили аркон ta'dil-i arkan
таъзим ta'zim
таъзир ta'zir
таъзия ta'ziya
таъкид ta'kid
таълим ta'lim
таълимот ta'limat
таъоми саҳарӣ sahar
таърих tarikh[1]
таяммум tayammum
тақаддис taqaddus
тақвим taqvim
тақво taqva
тақводор taqvadar
тақдир taqdir
тақдир taqdir
тақдис taqdis[1]
тақдис taqdis[2]
тақий taqi
тақия taqiya
тақлид taqlid[1]
тақлид taqlid[2]
тақсир taqsir
таҳаҷҷуд tahajjud
таҳия tahiyat
таҳлил tahlil
таҳмуд tahmid
таҳорат taharat
таҳоратхона taharatkhana
таҳрир tahrir
таҳриф tahrif
таҳриҷ takhrij
таҷалли tajalli
таҷвид tajvid
тибб tibb
тилмиз tilmiz
тиловат tilavat
тирмизак tilmiz
тиҷорат tijarat
тоат ta'at
тоат-ибодат ta'at-'ibadat
тобеъ tabi'
тобеъи табиин taba'-i tabi'in
тобут tabut
тобъеин tabi'in
тоиб ta'ib
тоифа ta'ifa
толеъ tali'
толиб talib
тоҳир tahir
Туба Tuba
тумор tumar
турбат turba
тӯфон tufan
Увайс ал-Қаранӣ Vays al-Qarani
удум udum
узлат 'uzlat
узр 'uzr[1]
узр 'uzr[2]
уламо 'ulama
Умар 'Umar
умаро umara
Уммалмӯмин Umm al-mu'minin
уммат ummat
умми ummi
умр 'umr
умра 'umra
унсур unsur
урф 'urf
Усмон 'Usman
устод ustad
устоз ustaz
усул usul[1]
усул usul[2]
усули хамса usul-i khamsa
усули қадим usul-i qadim
усули ҷадид usul-i jadid
ушр 'ushr
уқибат 'uqubat[1]
уқубат 'uqubat[2]
фазл fazl
файласуф faylasuf
фақиҳ faqih
фалак falak[1]
фалак falak[2]
фалақ falaq[1]
фалсафа falsafa
фан fann
фано fana
паранҷи paranja
фарёд faryad
фарз farz
фарзайн farz-i 'ayn
фарзи кифоят farz-i kifaya
фарзи муваққат farz-i muvaqqat
фарид farid
фаридал аср farid al-'asr
фаришта farishta
фароиз fara'iz[1]
фароиз fara'iz[2]
фарсанг farsakh
фарсах farsakh
фасл bab
фасод fasad
фасх fisq
фатво fatva
фатр fatir[2]
Фаттоҳ Fattah, al-
Фатҳи Макка Fath-i Makka
фақир faqir[1]
фақоҳат faqahat
фақр faqir[2]
фақр faqr
фаҳш fahsh
фидо fida
фидой fida'i
фидокор fidakyar
фидья fidya
фирдавс Firdaus
Фиръавн Fira'un
фирқа firqa
фитна fitna
фитр fitr[1]
фитр fitr[2]
фитра fitra
фитрат fitrat
фитри закот zakat al-fitr
фиқеҳ fiqh
фозил fazil
фоиз fa'iz
фол fal
фолбин falbin
фолгӯ falgu
фолнома falnama
фонӣ fani
форуқ faruq
фосиқ fasiq
Фотима Fatima
фотиҳа fatiha[1]
фотиҳа fatiha[2]

фотиҳагӯ fatihagu
фоҳиша fahisha
фоҷир fajir
фузало fuzala
Фурқон Furqan[1]
Хабар Khabir, al-
хабар khabar
хабари воҳид khabar-i vahid
Хабашистон Habashistan
хавориҷ khavarij
хавф khavf
хадди зино hadd-i zina
хадди сиркат hadd-i sirkat
Хадиҷа Khadija
хаират khayr[1]
Хайбар Khaybar
хайир khayr[2]
хайр khayr[1]
хайр-садақа khayr-sadaqa
халват khalvat
Халилулло Khalilullah
халифа khilafat[1]
халифа khalifa[1]
халифа khalifa[2]
халифат khilafat[2]
халифат khilafat[3]
халфа khalfa[1]
хамир khamr
хараҷ kharaj
хароҷ kharaj
хатиб khatib
хатим khatim[2]
хати маҳр khat-mahr
хатм khatm[1]
хатми сулук khatm-i suluk
хатми Қуръон khatm[2]
хатми қутб khatm-i kutub
хатна khatna
хато khata
хилват khilvat
хилватгоҳ khalvatgah
хилватнишин khalvatgah
хилватсарой khalvatgah
хилватхона khalvatgah
хилофа khilafat[1]
Хилофатул Рашиддин Khulafa-yi rashidin
хилофи шаръӣ khilaf-i sharʿ
хилқат khilqat
хироҷ kharaj
хирқа khirqa[1]
хирқа khirqa[2]
хирқаи саодат khirqa-yi saʿadat
хирқаи шариф khirqa-yi sharif
хирқапӯш khirqa push
хитон khitan
хонақаҳ khanaqa
хонақоҳ khanaqa
хориҷӣ khavarij
хотам khatim[1]
хоч khach
хочпараст khachparast
Худо Khuda
Худованд Khudavand
Худовандо khudavanda
худогӯй khudaguy
худогӯй khudaygu
Худой khuday
худойи khudayi
худойихона khudaykhana
худонотарс khudatars
худопараст khudaparast
худоҷӯй khudajuy
Хулд Khuld
хулқ khulq
хумс khums
хунасо khunsa
хунсо khunsa
хурмо khurma
хурофот khurafat
хутба khutba
хутбат khutba
хутбахон khatib
хуфтон khuftan
хӯҷа khvaja[1]
хӯҷа khvaja[2]
хӯҷаи Хизр Khizr
чалма chalma
чаҳорёр Chahar yar
чилдон childan
чилла chilla[1]
чилла chilla[2]
чиллаёсин chillayasin
чиллахона chillakhana[1]
чиллахона chillakhana[2]
чилтан chiltan
чодар paranja
чодра chadra
чорёр Chahar yar
Шаввол Shavval
шайтанат shaytanat
шайтон Shaytan
шайтонлайин shaytan al-ʿayn
шайх shaykh
шайхул ислом shaykh al-islam[1]
шайхул ислом shaykh al-islam[2]
шак shakk
шаккок shakkak
шамоил shama'il
шамоили шариф shama'il-i sharifa
шамъ shamʿ
шамъдон shamʿdan
шамъчароғ shamʿ
шариат shariʿat
шарик sharik
шариф sharif
шарифа sharifa
шароб sharab
шарр sharr
шаръ sharʿ
шаръан sharʿan
шаръӣ sharʿi
шафоат shafaʿat
Шаъби барот shab-i barat
Шаъбон Shaʿban
шаҳид shahid[2]
шаҳодат shahadat[1]
шаҳодат shahadat[2]
шаҳри Рамазон shahr-i ramazan
шаҷара shajara
шеа shiʿi
шиа shiʿi
ширк shirk
шифо shifa
шогирд shagird
Шокир Shakur, al-
шофия Shafiʿiya
Шофӣ Shafiʿi[1]
шофӣ Shafiʿi[2]
Шоҳид Shahid, al-
шоҳид shahid[1]
Шоҳмардон Shah-i mardan
Шуайб Shuʿayb

шубҳа shubha
шукр shukr
шуур shuʿur
шӯро shura [1]
шӯҳрат shuhrat
эзор izar
эсма ул ҳусна asma al-husna
эшон ishan
эшонзода ishanzada
эътимод iʿtimad
эътиқод iʿtiqad
эҳром ihram
эҳсон ihsan[1]
эҳтидоъ ihtida
Юнус Yunus[1]
Юсуф Yusuf[1]
Юшо Yushaʿ
Яздон Yazdan
ярҳамукалло yarhamukallah
ятим yatim
Яъҷуҷу Маъҷуҷ Ya'juj va Ma'juj
Яҳё Yahya
яҳуд yahud
яҳудӣ yahudi
Ғавс ал Аъзам Ghavs al-Aʿzam
ғазаб ghazab
ғазв ghaza
ғазва ghaza
ғазва ghazavat
ғазо ghaza
ғаййа Ghayya
ғайр динӣ ghayr-i din
ғайридин ghayr-i din
ғайри муъаккат ghayr-i mu'akkad
ғайр машруҳ ghayr-i mashruʿ
ғайр шарӣ ghayr-i sharʿi
ғам ghamm[1]
ғам ghamm[2]
Ғамбар Ghambar
ғанимат ghanimat
Ғанӣ Ghani, al-
ғариб gharib[1]
ғасб ghasb
ғасл ghasl
ғассол ghassal
ғафлат ghaflat[1]
ғафлат ghaflat[2]
Ғафур Ghafur, al-
Ғаффор Ghaffar, al-
ғилмон ghilman
ғозӣ ghazi
ғофил ghafil
ғулл ghul
ғулом mamluk
ғурбат ghurbat
ғусл ghusl
қабила qabila
қабиҳ qabih
қабоҳат qabahat
қабр qabr
қабристон qabristan
қавм qavm
қавом qavam
қавс Qavs
қадам qadam
қадамгоҳ qadamgah
қадамҷой qadamjay
қадим Qadim, al-
қадимӣ qadimi
қазо qaza
қазову муаллақ qaza-yi muʿallaq
қал qal
қалам qalam[1]
қалам qalam[2]
қаландар qalandar
қаландархона qalandarkhana
қалб qalb
қамис qamis
қаноат qanaʿat
қарз qarz
қасам qasam
қасд qasd
қасис qasis
қасос qasas[1]
қасос qisas
қатл qatl
қатъият qatʿiyat
қаъда qaʿda
Қаюм Qayyum, al-
қаҳр Qahr, al-
Қаҳҳор Qahhar, al-
қибла qibla
қиблагоҳ qiblagah
қибланамо qiblanama
қиём qiyam
қиёмат qiyamat[1]
қиёмат қойим qiyamat qa'im
қиёс qiyas
қимор qimar
қироат qira'at
қироати қурро qurra
қироатхона qira'atkhana
қирон qiran
қисмат qismat
Қитмир Qitmir
Қобил Qabil
Қовӣ Qavi, al-
Қодир Qadir, al-
қози qazi
қозизода qazizada
қозихона qazikhana
қоида qaʿida
қомат qamat
қонун qanun
қорихона qarikhana
қорӣ qari
қубба qubba
Қуббатул Ислом Qubbat al-Islam
қубур qubur
қуддус quddus
Қуддус Quddus, al-
Қуддус Quds, al-
қудрат qudrat
қудс quds
қудсият qudsiyat
қудсӣ qudsi
қулҳи Аллоҳу Аҳад qul hu allah ahad
қунут qunut
қурайш Quraysh[1]
қурбонӣ qurban
Қуръон Qur'an
Қуръони Азим Qur'an-i ʿAzim
Қуръони Карим Qur'an-i Karim
Қуръони Маҷид Qur'an-i Majid
Қуръони хотима Qur'an khatima
қуръон хона qur'ankhana
қусуф qusuf
қутб qutb

кутуб qutb
ҳабаш habash
Ҳабиб Habib
Ҳабиби Оллоҳ Habibullah
Ҳабил Habil
ҳави havl
ҳавия haviya
ҳавола havala
ҳавориён havari
ҳавоҷим havajim
ҳавоҷис havajis
ҳад hadd
ҳадди закр hadd-i zakr
ҳадди шароб hadd-i shurb
ҳадди қазф hadd-i qazf
ҳадис hadis
ҳаёти абадия hayat-i abadiya
ҳаёҳу hay ya hu
ҳазрат hazrat
Ҳазрат Али ‘Ali
ҳазрати Муҳаммад Muhammad[1]
Ҳай Hayy, al-
Ҳайдар Haydar
ҳайз hayz
Ҳакам Hakam, al-
ҳаким hakim
Ҳаким Hakim, al-
ҳалим halim
Ҳалим Halim, al-
ҳалиса halim
ҳалисахона halimkhana
ҳалиф halif
ҳалл hall
Ҳаллоқ Khallaq
ҳалол halal
ҳалқа halqa[1]
ҳамал Hamal
Ҳамид Hamid, al-
Ҳанафия Hanafiya
ҳанафӣ Hanafi
Ҳанбалия Hanbaliya
ҳанбалӣ Hanbali
ҳаниф hanif[1]
ҳаниф hanif[2]
ҳарам haram[2]
ҳарам harim
ҳариф дуо harif du‘a
ҳаром haram[1]
ҳаром muharram[1]
ҳаромзода haramzada
ҳарому занний haram zanni
ҳарому қатъӣ haram qat‘i
Ҳарун Harun
Ҳарут ва Марут Harut va Marut
ҳасан hasan[1]
Ҳасан Hasan[3]
ҳаттот hattat
Ҳафиз Hafiz, al-[2]
ҳафтияк haft-i yak
ҳашр hashr[1]
ҳашргоҳ mahshargah
ҳаштьяк hasht-i yak
ҳақ haqq[1]
Ҳақ Haqq[2]
Ҳақ Haqq, al-
ҳақиқат haqiqat
Ҳақ Расул Haqq Rasul
Ҳақ таолло Haqq Ta‘ala
ҳаққуллоҳ haqqullah
ҳаққул яқин haqq al-yaqin
ҳаҷарул асвад hajar-i asvad
ҳаҷҷ hajj[1]
Ҳибатулло Hibatullah
ҳибаҳ hiba
ҳидоят hidayat
ҳизб hizb[1]
ҳизб hizb[2]
ҳизбу шайтон hizb al-shaytan
ҳикмат hikmat
ҳилаи шарӣ hila-yi shar‘i
ҳилол hilal
ҳиммат himmat
ҳирз hirz
ҳирзи амон hirz
ҳирзи ҷон hirz
ҳис hiss
ҳисси ботиний hiss-i batin
ҳисси зоҳири hiss-i zahiri
ҳиҷоб hijab
ҳиҷра hijra
ҳиҷрат hijra
ҳиҷрия hijriya
ҳиҷрӣ hijri
Ҳодӣ Hadi, al-
ҳол hal
ҳолимхона halimkhana
Ҳолиқ Khaliq, al-
ҳомила hamila
ҳомиладор hamiladar
Ҳомон Haman
Ҳосиб Hasib, al-
Ҳотамул Анбиё Khatam al-anbiyah
Ҳотамул набиун Khatam al-nabiyin
Ҳофид Hafiz, al-[1]
ҳофиз hafiz
ҳоҷари асвад hajar-i asvad
ҳоҷи hajji
ҳу Hu
Ҳуд Hud[1]
ҳудуд hudud
ҳукм hukm
ҳукми Самад hukm-i samad
ҳукумат hukumat
ҳул khul‘
ҳулла hulla
ҳулул hulul
ҳур hur
ҳури huri
Ҳусайн Husayn
ҳусн husn
ҳусни адаб husn-i adab
ҳусни ахлоқ husn-i akhlaq
ҳусни тарбия husn-i tarbiya
ҳусни хат husn-i khat
ҳут Hut
ҳуҷра hujra
Ҷаббор Jabbar, al-
ҷабр jabr
Ҷаброил Jabra’il
ҷавзо Javza
ҷадид jadid
ҷадӣ Jadi
ҷазб jazb
ҷазбаъ jazba
ҷазо jaza
Ҷалил Jalil, al-
ҷаллод jallad
ҷалса jalsa
ҷамоа jama‘at[1]
ҷамоат jama‘at[2]
Ҷамра Jamra
ҷамулҷамъ jam‘ al-jam‘

Ҷамӣ Jami‘, al-
Ҷаннат Jannat
Ҷаннату Адн Jannat al-‘Adn
Ҷаннатул маъво Jannat al-Ma’va
Ҷаннатул Фирдавс Jannat al-Firdaus
Ҷаннатул хулд Jannat al-Khuld
Ҷаннатун наъим Jannat al-Na‘im
ҷаноб janab
ҷаноби Ҳаққ Janab-i haqq
ҷаноза janaza[1]
ҷаноза janaza[2]
ҷарима jarima
ҷасад jasad
ҷафо jafa
Ҷаҳаннам Jahannam
ҷаҳл jahl
ҷаҳм jahim
ҷаҳр jahr
ҷизя jizya
ҷилваи раббонӣ jilva-yi rabbaniya
ҷин jinn[1]
ҷиноят jinayat
Ҷирҷис Jirjis
ҷиҳод jihad
ҷиҳоди акбар jihad-i akbar
ҷиҳоди асгар jihad-i asghar
ҷоду jadu
ҷодугар jadugar
ҷодугар jadugu
ҷойинамоз jaynamaz
ҷомеъ jami‘
ҷон jan
ҷоҳили jahili
ҷоҳилият jahiliyat
ҷудо juda
Ҷудӣ Judi
ҷуз juz’[1]
ҷуз juz’[2]
ҷуз juz’[3]
ҷуз juz’[4]
ҷузъя jizya
Ҷумадалаввал Jumada al-ula
Ҷумадалохир Jumada al-akhira
ҷумла jumla
ҷумъа jum‘a[1]
ҷумъа jum‘a[2]
ҷунун junun[1]
ҷунун junun[2]
ҷуҳуд juhud

Tatar Index

абдаллар abdal[3]
абдэст abdast
абдэстханэ abdastkhana
абелхэят ab-i hayat
абыз abiz
авыз ачу iftar
Адэм Adam
Адэм ата Adam
азан azan
азанчы mu'azzin
азар azar
Айдар Haydar
алиhэ ilaha
Алла Allah
Аллатэгалэ Allah ta'ala
Аллаh Allah
Аллаh тэгалэ Allah ta'ala
аллаhу экбэр Allahu akbar
амийн amin[1]
амин Amin[2]
амин amin[1]
ант 'ahd
ар-Рэхман Rahman, al-
аситанэ asitana
астэнэ asitana
атэш atash
атэшпэрэст atashparast
ахи akhi
ахирэт akhirat
ахирэт күлмэге akhirat batqaghi
ахун akhund
ахунд akhund
ахшам намазы salat al-maghrib
ахыр заман akhir zaman
аятелкөрси ayat al-kursi
аятулла ayatullah
аять ayat
баб bab
бавэр bavar
бакый baqi
балиг baligh
Бари Bari, al-
барэкэаллаh barakullah
Басыйр Basir, al-
батыйль batil
батыйн batin
бажҗ baj
биби bibi
бигать bay'at
бигөнаh bi gunah
бидгать bid'at
бидгать сэййиъэh bid'at-i sayyi'a
бидгать хэсэнэ bid'at-i hasana
бидиянэт bi diyanat
Билкыйс Bilqis
биллаhи billahi
бисмиллаh bismillah
Бисмиллэhир-рахмэнир-рахим bismillah al-Rahman al-Rahim
бихэблиллаh bihablillah
бихөкмиллаh bihukmillah
биhишт bihisht
Борак Buraq
бот but
ботпэрэст butparast
ботханэ butkhana
Бурак Buraq
бяз гэшт baz gasht
бэддога bad-du'a
бэдэл badal
бэйгать bay'at
бэйрам bayram
бэйт bayt
Бэйтел Кодес Bayt al-muqaddas
бэйтелмал bayt al-mal
Бэйтелмөкаддэс Bayt al-muqaddas
Бэйтулла Baytullah
Бэйтүлмөкаддэс Bayt al-muqaddas
бэка baqa[1]
бэка baqa[2]
Бэкара сүрэсе Baqara
бэндэ banda
бэни Ислам bani Islam
Бэни-Исраил bani Isra'il[1]
Бэни-Исраил сүрэсе Bani Isra'il[2]
Бэрат shab-i barat
бэраэт bara'at[1]
Бэраэт кичэсе shab-i barat
бэрык barq
бэрэкэт barakat
бэсар basir
бэсыйр basir
бэтын batin
бэхт bakht
бэхшиш bakhshish
бэччэ bachcha
бэччэбазлык bachchabazi
Бэшир Bashir
бэшэрият bashariyat
бөhтан buhtan
вагыйз va'iz
вазыйфэ vazifa
Вакыйга сүрэсе Vaqi'a
вакыйф vaqif[1]
вакыйф vaqif[2]
валлаhе эгълэм vallahu a'lam
валлаhе эгълэм биссэваб vallahu a'lam bil-savab
Варис Varis, al-
варис varis
васыл vasl
васыять vasiyat
васыятьнамэ vasiyatnama
ватан vatan
вафа vafa
вафат vafat
Вахид Vahid, al-
вахшиянэ vahshiyana
важҗиб vajib
важҗибэл вуҗүд vajib al-vujud
Ваhаб Vahhab, al-
Ваhап Vahhab, al-
ваhhабизм Vahhabiya
ваhhабилар Vahhabiya
вилдан vildan
вирасэт varasat
вирд vird[1]
вирд vird[2]
вирсэ virsa
витер vitr
виждан vijdan
вукуфи адэди vuquf-i 'adadi
вукуфи заман vuquf-i zaman
вукуфи кальби vuquf-i qalbi
вэбал vabal
вэгазь va'z
вэгъдэ va'da
Вэддухэ сүрэсе Zuha
вэзир vazir

Вәйселкарани Vays al-Qarani
Вәкил Vakil, al-
вәкил vakil
вәкыф vaqf
вәкяләт vakalat
Вәли Vali, al-
вәли vali
вәли гаһед vali ahd
вәли нигъмәт vali niʿmat
вәрасәт varasat
вәрәгъ varaʿ[1]
вәрәка varaqa
вәсвәсә vasvasa
вәсика vasiqa
вәсән vasan
вәсәни vasani
вәхданиять vahdaniyat
вәхи vahi
Вәхид Vahid, al-
вәхшәт vahshat
вәҗип vajib
вәҗһе vajh
вәһһабичылык Vahhabiya
вөзуэ vuzu'
вөкуф vuquf
вөждан vijdan
Габдулла ʿAbdullah[1]
Габдулла ʿAbdullah[2]
габед ʿabd
габид ʿabid
Гад ʿAd
гадавәт ʿadavat
гадаләт ʿadalat
гадел ʿadl
гаден ʿadn
гадил ʿadil
гадәт ʿadat
Гает ʿId al-Fitr
гает ʿid
газа ghaza
газават ghazavat
Газазил ʿAzazil
газап azab
Газзә вә Җәллә ʿAzza va Jalla
газиз ʿaziz[1]
газиз ʿaziz[2]
Газраил ʿAzra'il
газый ghazi
Газыйм ʿAzim, al-
газәват ghazavat
гайб ирәннәр rijal-i ghayb
гайд ʿid
Гайдел-корбан ʿId al-Azha
гайдел мәүлид Mavlid[1]
Гайдел-фитыр ʿId al-Fitr
Гайдел әдха ʿId al-Azha
Гайде фитыр ʿId al-Fitr
Гайде әзхия ʿId al-Azha
Гайсә ʿIsa
Гайшә ʿA'isha
гаклыять ʿaqliyat
Гакрәб ʿAqrab
гакыйбәт ʿaqibat
гакыйдә ʿaqida
гакыйка корбаны ʿaqiqa
Гали ʿAli
Галим ʿAlim, al-
галим ʿalim
Галлямелгоюб ʿAllam al-ghuyub
галлямә ʿallama
галямәт ʿalamat
галәвият ʿalaviyat
галәйһиссәлам ʿalayhi al-salam
галәм ʿalam[1]
гамамә ʿamama
гамь ghamm[1]
гамь ghamm[2]
гамәл ʿamal
ганбәр anbar[1]
ганимәт ghanimat
ганка ʿAnqa
гареш ʿarsh
гариб gharib[2]
гариф ʿarif
гарше көрси ʿarsh-i kursi
гарше әгъля ʿarsh-i aʿla
гарәсат ʿArasat
Гарәсат мәйданы ʿArasat
гарәфә ʿarafa
гарәфә көне ruz-i ʿarafat
Гарәфәт ʿArafat
гаса ʿasa
гасб ghasb
гасый ʿasi
гасыр ʿasr[1]
гасыр сүрәсе ʿAsr[2]
гаурәт ʿavrat
Гаус Ghavs al-Aʿzam
гафил ghafil
гафләт ghaflat[1]
гафләт ghaflat[2]
Гафу ʿAfuv, al-
гашикъ ʿashiq
гашир ashir
гашура ʿAshura[1]
гашурә ʿAshura[1]
гашыйк ʿashiq
гаҗәм ʿajam
гаһед ʿahd
гозер ʿuzr[1]
гозләт ʿuzlat
гокба ʿuqba
гокубә ʿuqubat[3]
гокубәт ʿuqubat[1]
гол ghul
голяма ʿulama
гомер ʿumr
горбәт ghurbat
гореф ʿurf
гореф сахих ʿurf sahih
гореф фәсид ʿurf fasid
госел ghusl
горелханә ghuslkhana
Госман ʿUsman
гошер ʿushr
гыйбадат ʿibadat[2]
гыйбадәт ʿibadat[1]
гыйбадәтханә ʿibadatkhana
гыйбрани ʿibrani
гыйддәт ʿiddat
гыйддәт чоры ʿiddat
гыйззәт ʿizzat
Гыйзраил ʿAzra'il
гыйкаб ʿiqab
гыйлем ʿilm[1]
гыйлем ʿilm[2]
гыйлләт ʿillat
гыйлме хал ʿilm-i hal[2]
гыйлмүс сарф sarf
гыйльман ghilman
Гыймран сүрәсе Al-i Imran
гыйсави ʿIsavi
гыйсавиять ʿIsaviyat

гыйсмәт ʿismat
гыйсъян ʿisyan
Гыйсә ʿIsa
гыйфрит ʿifrit
гыйффәт ʿiffat
гыйшык ʿishq
гәрш ʿarsh
гөмбәз gumbaz
гөмрә ʿumra
гөнаһ gunah
гөнаһкяр gunahkar
гүр gur
гүрестан guristan
гүрстан guristan
даббә Dabba
Давыт Da'ud
дамелля damulla
данишмәнд danishmand
дарелбәка dar al-baqa
дарелфәна dar al-fana
дарелхәреб dar al-harb
дарәйн darayn
дау daʿva[1]
Дауд Da'ud
ден din
диван divan
дивана divana
дидар didar
дин din
диндар dindar
дини dini
дисбе tasbih
диянәт diyanat
диянәткяр diyanatkar
дияри золмәт zulmat[2]
диять diyat
дога duʿa[1]
дога duʿa[2]
доха намазы salat al-zuha
Дохә Zuha
Дузәх Duzakh
дус dust
дуст dust
Духан сүрәсе Dukhan[1]
дәвер davir
дәгъва daʿva[1]
дәгъвәт daʿvat
дәлил dalil
дәлил гакъли dalil-i ʿaqli
дәлиле гакыли dalil-i ʿaqli
дәлиле нәкъли dalil-i naqli
дәлил нәкъли dalil-i naqli
дәлил шәргый dalil-i sharʿi
Дәлү Dalv
дәрвиш darvish
дәргяһ dargah
дәресханә darskhana
дәстәрхан dastarkhan
дәфен dafn
Дәҗҗал Dajjal
дәһер dahr
дәһри dahri
Дөлдөл Duldul
дөнья dunya
дөньяви dunyavi
дөрес durust
дөрест durust
дөхан dukhan[2]
Жәбраил Jabra'il
забыт zabt
завия zaviya
Заккум Zaqqum
залим zalim
заләләт zalalat
зарурәт zarurat
зате пакь Zat-i pak
зафәр zafar
заһид zahid
заһир zahir
зикер zikr
зикр zikr
зикре хәфи zikr-i khafi
зикре җәһри zikr-i jahr
зикре һафи zikr-i khafi
Зилкагдә Zu'l-qaʿda
Зилхиҗҗә Zu'l-hijja
зимми zimmi
зина zina
зинакяр zinakar
зиндан zindan
зиндикъ zindiq
зират ziyarat
зифаф zifaf
зиярәт ziyarat
зиярәтгяһ ziyaratgah
зобани zubani
золмәт zulmat[1]
золым zulm
зольмәт zulmat[1]
зоха намазы salat al-zuha
Зоха сүрәсе Zuha
зоһер zuhr
зулзилә сүрәсе Zilzal
Зумр сүрәсе Zumar
зыйдд zidd
зыя ziya'
зәбихә zabiha
Зәбур Zabur
зәвал zaval
зәгыйф zaʿif
зәгыйфә zaʿifa
Зәкъкум Zaqqum
зәкят zakat[1]
Зәкәрия Zakariya
зәляләт zalalat
Зәмзәм Zamzam
зәмзәми zamzami
Зәмзәм суы ab-i Zamzam
зәнб zanb
Зәхрәф сүрәсе Zukhruf
зәһадәт zahadat
Зөлкагдә Zu'l-qaʿda
Зөлкарнәен Zu'l-Qarnayn
Зөлфикар Zu'l-fiqar
Зөлфөкар Zu'l-fiqar
Зөлхиҗҗә Zu'l-hijja
Зөлҗәлал Zu'l-jalal va'l-ikram
зөлҗәнахәен zu'l-janahayn
зөннар zunnar
зөфаф zifaf
зөхед zuhd[1]
зөхед zuhd[2]
зөһд zuhd[1]
зөһд zuhd[2]
зөһед zuhd[1]
зөһед zuhd[2]
ибахә ibaha
Иблис Iblis
Ибраһим Ibrahim[1]
Ибраһим сүрәсе Ibrahim[2]
Ибраһим Хәлил Ibrahim[1]
иганә iʿana
иганәт iʿana
игъдам iʿdam

игътикад i'tiqad
игътикадат i'tiqadat
игътикяф i'tikaf
игътимад i'timad
Идрис Idris
изар izar
изге avliya[1]
изге vali
издиваҗ izdivaj
изен izn
икамәт iqamat
икенде намазы salat al-'asr
икърар iqrar[1]
икътидаэ iqtida
илаһ ilah
илаһи ilahi[1]
илаһи ilahi[2]
илаһи ilahi[3]
илаһиун ilahiyun
илаһият ilahiyat
илаһә ilaha
илтиҗа iltija
Ильяс Ilyas
илһам ilham
имам imam[1]
имам imam[2]
имам imam[3]
имам imam[4]
имамәт imamat[1]
имамәт imamat[2]
имамү кыйблатәйн imam al-qiblatayn
иман iman[1]
иман iman[2]
инабәт inabat
инзал inzal
инсан-уль камил insan-i kamil
инсаф insaf
интикам intiqam
интихаб intikhab
инша алла insha'allah
Иншикак Inshiqaq
иншираx сүрәсе Inshirah
Инҗил Injil
ирадә irada[1]
ирадә irada[2]
ирадә irada[3]
ирадәи ля язаль irada-yi la yazal
иртидад irtidad
иртәнге намаз salat al-fajr
иртәнге намаз salat al-subh
иршад irshad
иршаднамә irshadnama
исагуҗихан Isagujikhvan
искат isqat
Искәндәр Iskandar
Ислам Islam
ислямиять islamiyat
Исмәгыйл Isma'il
иснад isnad
Исраи Isra
исраф israf
Исрафил Israfil
Исраэ Isra
истибдад istibdad
истибра istibra
истигъфар istighfar
истигъфар isti'far
истидлали иман istidlali iman
истидляли иман istidlali iman
истикамәт istiqamat
истикъбаль istiqbal
истинҗа istinja
истиска istisqa
истиска намазы salat al-istisqa
истихазә istihaza
истихара istikhara
истихара намазы salat al-istikhara
истихарә istikhara
истихсан istihsan
истишхад istishhad
Исхак Ishaq
итагать ita'at
итлак itlaq
итмам itmam
иттихад ittihad[1]
иттихад ittihad[2]
ифта ifta
ифтар iftar
ифтар мәҗлесе iftar
ифтитах iftitah
ихван ikhvan
Ихлас сүрәсе Ikhlas[2]
ихляс Ikhlas[1]
ихрам ihram
ихсан ihsan[1]
ихтиляф ikhtilaf
ихтиҗаб ihtijab
ишан ishan
ишарәт isharat
ишракъ ishraq
ишракъ намазы salat al-ishraq
ишрәк ishrak
иҗабәт ijabat
иҗазә ijazat
иҗазәт ijazat
иҗазәтнамә ijazatnama
иҗмаг ijma'
иҗтиһад ijtihad
иһтида ihtida
йад дәшт yad dasht
йад кәрд yad kard
йа рабби ya rabbi
Йасин Ya Sin
Йасуг Yasu'
Йаһу yahu
Йосыф Yusuf[1]
Йосыф сүрәсе Yusuf[2]
Йәздан Yazdan
йәрхәмүкә yarhamukallah
йәсигъ намазы salat al-'isha
йәстү намазы salat al-'isha
кабахәт qabahat
кабер qabr
кабер газабы 'azab-i qabr
каберстан qabristan
Кабиз Qabiz, al-
Кабил Qabil
кабилә qabila
кабих qabih
кабәхәт qabahat
Кави Qavi, al-
Кавәс Qavs
кагадә qa'da
кагъдә qa'da
кагыйдә qa'ida
кадер кичәси Laylat al-Qadr
Кадер сүрәсе Qadr[1]
кади qazi
Кадим Qadim, al-
кадими qadimi
кадимчелек usul-i qadim

Кадир Qadir, al-
кадəм qadam
кадəр qadar
каза qaza
казый qazi
кальб qalb
калəм qalam[2]
Калəм сүрəсе Qalam[3]
калəндəр qalandar
камис qamis
Камəр сүрəсе Qamar
камəт qamat
канагать qana'at
канун qanun
кара таш hajar-i asvad
караташ hajar-i asvad
карз qarz
кари qari
Каригаh сүрəсе Qari'a
кариэ qari
касд qasd
касис qasis
касəм qasam
кател qatl
каум qavm
Каф сүрəсе Qaf[1]
кирамен кятибин kiramin katibin
кисвə qisvat
кисвəт əл-Кəъбə qisvat
китап kitab
кифая kifaya
Калəме Шəриф Kalam-i Sharif
коббə qubba
кобур qubur
Коддус Quddus, al-
коддус quddus
кодес quds
кодрəт qudrat
кодси qudsi
кодсиять qudsiyat
колhуаллаh qul hu allah ahad
Колhуаллаh сүрəсе Ikhlas[2]
конут qunut
корб qurb
корбан qurban
Корбан бəйрəме Qurban Bayrami
Корбан бəйрəме 'Id al-Azha
Корбан гаете 'Id al-Azha
корра qurra
Коръан Qur'an
Коръане Кəрим Qur'an-i Karim
Коръəн-Кəрим Qur'an-i Karim
Коръəн-Мəҗид Qur'an-i Majid
коръəнхафиз hafiz
Корьəн-Газим Qur'an-i 'Azim
Корьəн-Газыйм Qur'an-i 'Azim
косуф qusuf
косуф намазы salat al-qusuf
котып qutb
Куббəтүл ислами Qubbat al-Islam
кунут qunut
кыйам бинəфсиниhи qiyam binafsihi
кыйасе фөкаhа qiyas-i fuqaha
кыйбла qibla
кыйбланамə qiblanama
кыйдəм qidam
кыйраьəт qira'at
кыйраəт qira'at
кыйраəтханə qira'atkhana
кыйсас qisas
кыйсва qisvat
кыйсмəт qismat
кыйссасел-əнбия qisas al-anbiya
кырыклар chiltan
кырык хəдис hadis-i arba'in
кыям qiyam
кыямəт qiyamat[1]
кыямəт көне qiyamat[1]
Кыямəт сүрəсе Qiyamat[2]
кыяс qiyas
кяинат ka'inat
кятиб katib
кяфир kafir
кяфирстан kafiristan
кяhин kahin
Кəбир Kabir, al-
кəбирə kabira
Кəгъбə Ka'ba
Кəгъбəтулла Ka'batullah
кəлимə kalima
кəлимəи шəhəдəт kalima-yi shahadat
кəлисə kalisa
кəлям kalam
Кəляме шəриф Kalam-i Sharif
Кəлямулла Kalamullah
кəнисə kanisa
кəрамəт karamat
Кəрдигяр Kardigar
Кəрим Karim, al-
кəрəм karam
кəфалəт kafalat
кəфен kafn
кəфил kafil
Кəфирун сүрəсе Kafirun
кəффарəт kaffarat
кəшиш kashish
кəшишханə kashishkhana
кəүнəен kavnayn
Кəүсəр Kavsar[1]
Кəүсəр сүрəсе Kavsar[2]
Кəhф сүрəсе Kahf
Кəhəф сүрəсе Kahf
Көрьəни-Кəрим Qur'an-i Karim
көрəйш Quraysh[1]
Көрəйш сүрəсе Quraysh[2]
көфер kufr
көферлек kufr
көфран kufran
көффар kuffar
Күдс Quds, al-
лиллаh lillah
лифафə lifafa
Лут Lut
ля мəкян La makan
ля хəүлə la havla
лəгнəт la'nat
лəгын la'in
Лəел сүрəсе Layl
лə илəhə иллал-лаh Мөхəммəдин Рəсүллүла la ilaha illa allah va muhammadun rasulullah
лəйлəт əл-кадр Laylat al-Qadr
Лəтыйф Latif, al-
лəфзан вə мəгънан lafzan va ma'nan
лəфзы көфер lafz-i kufr
лəхед lahid[1]

ләхед lahid[2]
ләхет lahid[2]
ләүх lavh
ләүхел-мәхфуз lavh al-mahfuz, al-
ләүхелмәхфуз lavh al-mahfuz, al-
маддиюн maddiyun
Маидә сүрәсе Ma'ida
мал mal
Малик Malik[1]
Малик Malik, al-
малик malik[2]
Малики Maliki
манара manara
Манигъ Mani', al-
мантыйк mantiq
матәм matam
матәмзадә matamzada
ма фәвыкыттабигать ma favq al-tabi'at
машалла mashaallah
мескен miskin
мигъраҗ mi'raj
мигъраҗия mi'rajiya
мигъраҗнамә mi'rajnama
Мизан Mizan[3]
мизан mizan[1]
Микаил Mika'il
микат Miqat
милек milk
миляд milad
миляди miladi
Мина Mina
минбәр minbar
мир mir
мирас miras
мирас хор miraskhur
мирза mirza
мисак misaq
мисвәк misvak[1]
мисвәк misvak[2]
мискин miskin
Мисыр Misr[2]
мисыр misr[1]
михраб mihrab
мовәххид muvahhid
Могни Mughni, al-
Могҗиза Mu'jiza[2]
могҗиза mu'jiza[1]
мозаффар muzaffar
Моктадир Muqtadir, al-
мокыйм muqim
молла mulla
монафикъ munafiq
моракабә muraqaba
морафәга murafa'a
мосалла musalla[1]
мосалла musalla[2]
мосалли musalli
мосаләхә musalaha
Мосаувир Musavvir, al-
мосафәхә musafaha
Мостафа Mustafa
Мосхәф mushaf
Мосхәф Шәриф mushaf
мосыйбәт musibat
мотаһһәр mutahhar
мотлак mutlaq
мофтыйр muftir
мохтазир muhtazir
мохтариять mukhtariyat
мулла mulla
муракабә muraqaba
Муса Musa
мусави musavi[1]
Муҗид Mujid, al-
мәаб ma'b
мәгад ma'ad
мәгаз алла ma'az allah
мәгасил maghasil
мәгасый ma'asi
мәгриб maghrib
мәгъбәд ma'bad
мәгъбүд ma'bud[1]
мәгъбүд ma'bud[2]
мәгъзүр ma'zur
мәгълүб maghlub
мәгънан ma'nan
мәгънәви ma'navi
мәгънәвия ma'naviya
мәгърифәт ma'rifat[1]
мәгърифәт ma'rifat[2]
мәгърәкә ma'raka
мәгъсум ma'sum
мәгъфирәт maghfirat
мәгъюб ma'yub
Мәгүзәтәйн Mu'avvizatayn
мәддах maddah
Мәдинаи мүнәүвәрә Madina-yi munavvara
Мәдини madini
Мәдинә Madina
Мәдинәнеке madini
мәдрәсә madrasa
мәдфән madfan
мәдхия madhiya
мәет mayyit
мәзар mazar
мәзарстан mazaristan
мәзлум mazlum
мәзмәзә mazmaza
мәзһәб mazhab[1]
мәзһәб mazhab[2]
мәкам maqam
мәкаме Ибраһим Maqam-i Ibrahim
Мәкки makki
Мәккә Makka
Мәккә ал-мөкәррәмә Makka al-mukarrama
Мәккәи Мөкәррәмә mukarram
Мәккәнеке makki
мәкруһ makruh
мәктәп maktab
мәкъбәрә maqbara[1]
мәкъбәрә maqbara[2]
мәкъсурә maqsura
мәкътуг maqtu'
мәкътүл maqtul
мәлгун Mal'un[1]
мәлгун mal'un[2]
мәлгунь Mal'un[1]
мәляикә mala'ika
мәләк malak
мәләкүт malakut
мәләкүтиять malakutiyat
мәмат mamat
мәмлүк mamluk
мәнакыйб manaqib
мәнакыйбнамә manaqibnama
мәнасик manasik
Мәнат Manat
мәнзур manzur
мәнкүхә mankuha

мантыйкый mantiqi
манфур manfur
маншүр manshur
манһи manhi
марасим marasim
Марва Marva
Марва тауы Marva
мардүд mardud
Марйам Maryam[2]
марсия marsiya
марфугъ marfu'
мархамат marhamat
мархүм marhum
Марьям Maryam[1]
Марьям сүрәсе Maryam[2]
масбук masbuq
Масих Masih[1]
масих masih[2]
масихи masihi
маст mast
масьәлә mas'ala
масҗед masjid
масҗид masjid
Масҗиделхарам Masjid al-Haram, al-
Масҗидел Әкъса Masjid al-Aqsa, al-
Масҗиде харам Masjid al-Haram, al-
Матин Matin, al-
матрүка matruka
махарим maharim[1]
махарим maharim[2]
махафатуллаh mahafatullah
махбус mahbus
махдүм makhdum
махкамә mahkama
махкүм mahkum
махлук makhluq
махлукат makhluqat
махрам mahram
мәхфил mahfil
махшар mahshar
мәхәббәт muhabbat
мәхәллә mahalla
мәчет masjid
мәшаих mashayikh
мәшкүк mashkuk
мәшруг mashru'
мәшрәб mashrab
мәшхәд mashhad
мәшә алла mashaallah
мәшһүр mashhur
мәәзүн ma'zun
мәәмүр ma'mur
мәүгазә mav'iza
мәүзугъ mavzu'
мәүкуф mavquf
мәүкыйг mavqi'
мәүла Mavla[1]
мәүла mavla[2]
мәүлид Mavlid[1]
мәүлид mavlid[2]
мәүләви mavlavi
мәүләна mavlana
мәүлүд Mavlid[1]
мәүҗүд mavjud
мәүҗүдат mavjudat
мәүһүм mavhum
мәүһүмат mavhumat
мәҗзүб majzub
Мәҗид Majid, al-
мәҗлес majlis
мәҗлис majlis
мәҗнүн majnun[1]
мәҗнүн majnun[2]
мәҗүс majus
мәҗүси majusi
мәҗүсиять majusiyat
Мәһди Mahdi
мәһпәрәст mahparast
мәһәр mahr[2]
мөбариз mubariz
мөбарәзә mubaraza
мөбарәк mubarak
мөбассыйр mubassir
мөбах mubah
мөбахәсә mubahasa
мөбашир mubashir
Мөбдигъ Mubdi', al-
мөбәшшир mubashshir
мөбһәм mubham
мөгаббир mu'abbir
мөгаллим mu'allim
мөгамәлә mu'amalat
мөдафәга mudafa'a
мөдәррис mudarris
Мөздәлифә Muzdalifa
мөзниб maznib
мөкаддәс muqaddas
мөкаррәб muqarrab
мөкяфәт mukafat
мөкяшәфә mukashifa
мөкәлләф mukallaf
мөкәммәл mukammal
мөкәррир mukarrir
мөкәррәм mukarram
мөлек mulk[1]
Мөлек сүрәсе Mulk[2]
мөлкәт mulk-amlak
мөлля mulla
мөлхак mulhaq
мөлхид mulhid
мөлязим mulazim
мөнакәхә munakahat
мөнаҗат munajat[1]
мөнаҗат munajat[2]
Мөнкир-Нәкир Munkar va Nakir
Мөнкир һәм Нәкир Munkar va Nakir
мөнкәр munkar
мөнсәлик munsalik
Мөнтәкыйм Muntaqim, al-
мөнәззәл munazzal
мөнәүвәр munavvar
мөнәҗҗим munajjim
мөрдар murdar
мөрид murid
мөрсәл mursal[1]
мөрсәл mursal[2]
Мөрсәлат сүрәсе Mursalat
мөртәд murtadd
мөршид murshid
мөсаб musab
мөсадәрә musadara
мөсафир musafir
мөсбәт musbat
мөселман musulman
мөслим muslim
мөслимин muslimin
мөслимә muslima
мөснәд musnad
мөстахәб mustahabb
мөстәбид mustabidd

мөстәкрәh mustakrah
мөстәҗаб mustajab
мөтасаувыф mutasavvif
мөтассил muttasil
мөтәватир mutavatir
мөтәвәлли mutavalli
мөтәвәллият mutavalliyat
мөтәвәрриг mutavarriʿ
мөтәгаббид mutaʿabbid
Мөтәгали Mutaʿali, al-
мөтәгассыйб mutaʿassib
мөтәдәйин mutadayyin
Мөтәкәббир Mutakabbir, al-
мөтәкәллим mutakallim
мөтәнассыйр mutanassir
мөтәшәйех mutashayyikh
мөфассал mufassal
мөфсид mufsid[1]
мөфсид mufsid[2]
мөфти mufti
мөфәссир mufassir
мөхакәмә muhakama
мөхалифәтүн лилхәвадис mukhalifat lil-havadis
мөхарәбә muharaba
мөхасарә muhasara
мөхсин muhsin
мөхтәзыйр muhtazir
мөхтәсиб muhtasib[1]
мөхтәсиб muhtasib[2]
мөхәкъкыйк muhaqqiq
мөхәллил muhallil
мөхәммәди muhammadi[1]
мөхәммәди muhammadi[2]
Мөхәммәт Muhammad[1]
Мөхәммәт сүрәсе Muhammad[2]
Мөхәррәм Muharram[2]
мөхәррәм muharram[1]
мөшрик mushrik
мөъмин mu'min[1]
мөъәккәт mu'akkad
мөәззин mu'azzin
мөәмин mu'min[1]
Мөәминнәр сүрәсе Mu'minin
мөәккәд mu'akkad
мөәллиф mu'allif
мөәррих mu'arrikh
Мөәххәр Mu'akhkhir, al-
мөҗавир mujavir
мөҗаhид mujahid
Мөҗиб Mujib, al-
мөҗтәhид mujtahid[1]
мөҗтәhит mujtahid[1]
мөҗәссәм mujassam
мөhаҗир muhajir
мөhаҗирин muhajirin
мөhаҗәрәт muhajarat
мөhтәди muhtadi
Мүзәммил сүрәсе Muzzammil
назар бер кадәм nazar bar qadam
назил nazil
наиб na'ib
накыйс naqis
намаз namaz
намазлык jaynamaz
намәхрәм namahram
намәшруг namashruʿ
напакь napak[1]
напакь napak[2]
нарәва narava
Нас сүрәсе Nas
насут nasut
насыйхәт nasihat
Нафигъ Nafiʿ, al-
нафилә nafila
нахак nahaq
нахәлял nahalal
нигъмәт niʿmat
нигяh дәшт nigah dasht
низам nizam
никах nikah
никях nikah
нисаб nisab
нисар nisar
Ниса сүрәсе Nisa
Нисаэ сүрәсе Nisa
нифас nifas
нихрир nihrir
нияз niyaz
ният niyat
носрәт nusrat
нотык nutq
Нур Nur, al-
нур nur[1]
нуре гаршеллаh nur-i ʿarshullah
Нур сүрәсе Nur[2]
Нух Nuh[1]
Нух сүрәсе Nuh[2]
нәби nabi
нәбиулла nabi'ullah
нәбүвәт nabuvat
нәгузе биллаhи naʿuzu billahi
нәгъти шәриф naʿt-i sharif
нәгыйм Naʿim[1]
нәгыйм naʿim[2]
нәгыть naʿt
нәгыш naʿsh[1]
нәгыш naʿsh[2]
нәзар nazar[1]
нәзар nazar[2]
нәзаhәт nazahat
нәзер nazr[1]
нәзер nazr[2]
нәйран nayran
нәкълият naqliya
нәкыйб naqib
Нәмел сүрәсе Naml
Нәмруд Numrud
нәсара nasara
нәсел nasl
нәсрани nasrani
нәсраниять nasraniyat
нәсыйб nasib
Нәсыр сүрәсе Nasr
нәсәб nasab
нәфел nafl
нәфес nafs[1]
нәфес nafs[2]
нәфилә намазы salavat-i nafila
нәфәка nafaqa
нәфәс nafas
Нәхел сүрәсе Nahl
нәхү nahu
Нәүруз Navruz
Нәүрүз Navruz
нәҗасәт najasat
нәҗасәт гализ najasat ghaliz
нәҗасәт хәфиф najasat khafif
нәҗат najat
Нәҗем сүрәсе Najm
нәҗес najis
нәhи nahi
нөбөввәт nubuvvat

нөбүвәт nubuvvat
остабикә ustabika
остад ustad
остаз ustaz
осул usul[1]
осуле кадим usul-i qadim
осуле җәдид usul-i jadid
охрави ukhravi
Оҗмах Jannat
Оҗмах Ujmakh
пакь pak
парса parsa
парә para
пигамбәр payghambar
пир pir
пишкадәм pishqadam
пот put
потпәрәст putparast
потханә putkhana
приговор prighuvur
пәйгам paygham
пәйгамбәр payghambar
пәрвәрдикяр Parvardigar
пәри pari
пәрәнҗә paranja
пәям payam
пөртакъсыйр purtaqsir
Раббе Rabb
Рабби Rabbi
Раббәна Rabbana
рабигылахыр Rabiʿ al-akhir
рабигыләүвәл Rabiʿ al-avval
рабита rabita
рави ravi
разы Аллаһу ганһе razi allahu ʿanhu
раи ra'i
рамазан Ramazan
Рамазан гаете ʿId al-Fitr
рамазания ramazaniya
Расүлүллаһ Rasulullah
рахим rahim
раһиб rahib
риба riba
риваять rivayat
ригая riʿaya
ригаять riʿaya
рида rida[2]
ридвану аллаһу галәйһи rizvanullah ʿalayhi[2]
риза riza[1]
риза riza[2]
Ризван Rizvan
ризык rizq
рисалә risala
рисаләт risalat
ришвәт rishvat
рия riya
риязәт riyazat
риякяр riyakar
риҗале гайб rijal-i ghayb
риҗалел-гаиб rijal-i ghayb
рузә ruza
рукугы rukuʿ
Рум Rum[1]
Рум сүрәсе Rum[2]
Рух Ruh[2]
рух ruh[1]
рухани ruhani
руханиять ruhaniyat
рухи ruhi
Рухулла Ruhullah
Рухыл-Әмин Ruh al-Amin
рәббәни rabbani
рәва rava
Рәгаиб ragha'ib
Рәгаиб кичәсе ragha'ib
рәгаиб намазы salat al-ragha'ib
Рәгыд сүрәсе Raʿd
Рәззак Razzaq, al-
рәис ra'is[1]
Рәкыйб Raqib, al-
рәкыс raqs
рәкәгать rakʿat
рәсүл rasul
Рәсүлулла Rasulullah
Рәуза Ravza
рәхем rahm
рәхмани rahmani
Рәхман сүрәсе Rahman
рәхмәт rahmat
Рәшид Rashid, al-
Рәүзаи мотаһһәр Ravza-yi mutahhar
Рәүзә Ravza
Рәүф Rauf, al-
рәҗем rajm
рәҗим rajim
рәҗәб Rajab
рәһбан rahban
рәһбаниять rahbaniyat
рөбүбиять rububiyat
рөкүгъ rukuʿ
рөтбә rutba
рөхсәт rukhsat
рөхсәтнамә rukhsatnama
сабах намазы salat al-fajr
сабах намазы salat al-subh
сабидар sabi'
сабир sabir
сабиэ sabi'
сабыр sabr[1]
сабыр sabr[2]
саваб savab[3]
Сад Sad
садака sadaqa
садыр sadr[1]
салават salavat
салаваты нафилә salavat-i nafila
салат salat
салеб salb
салиб salib
салибиюн salibiyun
Салих Salih[2]
салих salih[1]
Салләллаһү галәйһи вәсәлләм salla allahi ʿalayhu va sallam
саләт salat
саләт әт-тәсбих salat al-tasbih
Самәд Samad, al-
санәм sanam
Сара Sara
Саратан Saratan
сарраф sarraf
сарф sarf
сарыф sarf
Сатир Satir, al-
саф saf
Сафа тауы Safa
Саф сүрәсе Saff
Саффа Safa
Саффа тауы Safa
Саффат сүрәсе Saffat
сахабә sahaba

сахибе кәрамәт sahib-i karamat
сахир sahir
сахифә sahifa
сахих sahih
Сидрәтелмөнтәһа Sidrat al-muntaha
сийәр ән-нәби siyar al-nabi
силах silah
силсилә silsila[1]
силсилә silsila[2]
силсилә намә silsilanama
Сират күпере Sirat[2]
сирә sirat[1]
сирәт sirat[1]
сирәтен-нәби sirat[1]
сихер sihr
сихерче sihirbaz
сихри sihri
сихыр sihr
сихырбаз sihirbaz
сияреннәби siyar al-nabi
сиҗҗил sijjil
содур sudur
солтан sultan
солых sulh
соумәга savmaʻa
сохоф suhuf
субутия subutiya
сур sur
сурәт surat
суфи sufi[1]
суфи sufi[2]
суфичылык tasavvuf
сыйбгать sibghat
сыйдак sidaq[1]
сыйдак sidaq[2]
сыйддикъ siddiq
Сыйрат Sirat[2]
Сыйрат күпере Sirat[2]
сәбгы сәмәват sabʻi samavat
сәваб savab[1]
сәваб savab[2]
Сәвер Savr
сәгый saʻi
сәгыйр saʻir
сәдака sadaqa
сәед sayyid
сәйид sayyid
сәйииъәһ sayyi’a
Сәкарь Saqar
сәлам salam
сәлибия salibiya
сәллә salla
Сәлсәбил Salsabil
Сәлям Salam, al-
сәләф salaf
сәләфе салихин salaf-i salihin
сәма sama
сәмави samavi
Сәмигъ Samiʻ, al-
сәмигъ samiʻ
Сәмуд Samud
Сәмүт Samud
сәна sana[2]
сәнә sana[1]
сәнәи камәрия sana-yi qamariyya
сәнәи миладия sana-yi miladiyya
сәнәи шәмсия sana-yi shamsiyya
сәнәи һиҗрия sana-yi hijriyya
сәраб sar-ab
Сәттар Sattar, al-
сәфәлият safaliyat
сәфәр Safar
сәфәр дәр ватан safar dar vatan
сәфәр намазы salat al-musafir
сәфәр намазы salat al-safar
сәхабә sahaba
сәхавәт sakhavat
сәхифә sahifa
сәхих sahih
сәхәр sahar
сәхәр намазы salat al-fajr
Сәҗдә Sajda[2]
сәҗдә sajda[1]
сәҗдәи тилавәт sajda-yi tilavat
сәһив sahv
сәһү sahv
сөбхан subhan
сөбхан алла subhanallah
сөбханәкә subhanaka
сөкүт sukut
Сөләйман Sulayman
сөлүк suluk
Сөнбелә Sunbula
сөнни sunni
сөннә sunna
сөннәт sunna
сөннәт sunnat[1]
сөннәт sunnat[2]
сөннәт гайре мөвәкдә sunnat ghayr-i mu’akkada
сөннәт мөвәкдә sunnat mu’akkada
сөннәтче бабай abdal[2]
сөтрә sutra
сөҗуд sujud
сүрә sura
Сүрәтүл-дөхан Dukhan[1]
Сүрәтүл-исраэ Isra
Сүрәтүл-кадри Qadr[1]
табиб tabib
табигъ tabiʻ
табигыйн tabiʻin
табигыят tabiʻat
табут tabut
тагать taʻat
таифә ta’ifa
такбир тәшрыйк tashriq
такыя taqiya
талак talaq[1]
Талак сүрәсе Talaq[2]
талиб talib
талигъ taliʻ
тарикать tariqat[1]
тарикать tariqat[2]
Тарик сүрәсе Tariq
тарих tarikh[1]
тарих tarikh[2]
тарихчы mu’arrikh
татликъ tatliq
таук tavq
таһарәт taharat
таһир tahir
Таһә сүрәсе Ta ha
тилавәт tilavat
тилмиз tilmiz
тиҗарәт tijarat
Туба Tuba
туфан tufan
тыйбб tibb
тәбарәк tabarak

тәбгы табигыйн tabaʿ-i tabiʿin
тәблигат tablighat
тәбрик tabrik
тәбәррек tabarruk
тәвазыг tavaziʿ
тәвазыйг tavaziʿ
тәварих tavarikh
тәваф tavaf[1]
тәваф tavaf[2]
тәвсим tavsim
тәвәккел tavakkul[1]
тәвәкъкыф tavaqquf
тәвәррүк tavarruq
тәвәҗҗеһ tavajjuh
тәвәһһем tavahhum
тәгаббед taʿabbud[1]
тәгаввез taʿavvuz
тәгалә taʿala
тәгам taʿam
тәгассыб taʿassub
тәгъбир taʿbir
тәгъбирнамә taʿbirnama
тәгъвиз taʿviz[1]
тәгъвиз taʿviz[2]
тәгъдил taʿdil
тәгъзир taʿzir
тәгъзия taʿziya
тәгълим taʿlim
тәгълимат taʿlimat
тәдфин tadfin
тәдәйен tadayyun[1]
тәдәйен tadayyun[2]
тәзкирәтел-әүлия tazkirat al-avliya
тәзкия tazkiya
тәзәүвеҗ tazavij
тәзәһһед tazahhud
тәйәммүм tayammum
тәкаддес taqaddus
тәкбир takbir
тәкбир takbir al-tahrima
тәкбир әйтү takbir al-tahrima
тәквин takvin
тәкия takiya
тәклиф taklif
тәкфин takfin
тәкфир takfir
тәкъва taqva
тәкъвим taqvim
тәкъдир taqdir
тәкъдис taqdis[1]
тәкъдис taqdis[2]
тәкълид taqlid[1]
тәкъсыйр taqsir
тәкый taqi
тәлкыйн talqin[1]
тәлкыйн talqin[2]
тәлкыйн talqin[3]
Тәмуг Tamuq
Тәмугъ Tamuq
тәмәке dukhan[2]
тәмәттег tamattuʿ
тәмҗид tamjid
тәнакех tanakuh
тәнасых tanasukh
тәнзиэ tanzih[1]
тәнзиһ tanzih[2]
тәнких tankih
тәнсыйр tansir
тәнәссыр tanassur
тәнәүвыг tanavvuʿ
тәравих taravih
тәравих намазы salat al-taravih
тәрбия tarbiya
тәргыйб targhib
тәрса tarsa
тәсаувыф tasavvuf
тәсбих tasbih
тәсбих намазы salat al-tasbih
тәслим taslim[1]
тәссадык tasadduq
тәсхир tashir
тәсәттер tasattur
тәуваф tavaf[1]
Тәурат Tavrat
тәфрид tafrid
тәфсир tafsir
тәхиййәт tahiyat, at-
тәхкыйкый иман tahqiqi iman
тәхмид tahmid
тәхрим tahrim[1]
тәхрими tahrimi
Тәхрим сүрәсе Tahrim[2]
тәхрир tahrir
тәхриф tahrif
тәхриҗ takhrij
тәхәммел tahammul
тәшбиһ tashbih
тәшригъ tashriʿ[1]
тәшригъ tashriʿ[2]
тәшрик tashriq
тәшрикъ tashriq
тәшәйегъ tashayyuʿ
тәшәһһөд tashahhud
тәяммәм tayammum
тәәхир ta’akhir
тәүбә tavba[1]
Тәүбә сүрәсе Tavba[3]
тәүбә-тәзәррыг tavba-tazarru
Тәүваб Tavvab, al-
Тәүрат Tavrat
тәүсыйф tavsif
тәүфыйк tavfiq
тәүхид tavhid[1]
тәүхид tavhid[2]
тәҗвид tajvid
тәҗәлла tajalli
тәҗәлли tajalli
Тәңре Tangri
тәһийәтүл-мәчет tahiyat
тәһлил tahlil
тәһәҗҗид tahajjud
тәһәҗҗуд tahajjud
тәһәҗҗуд намазы salat al-tahajjud
тәһәҗҗүд tahajjud
төрбә turba
указ ukaz
ураза ruza
Ураза бәйрәме ʿId al-Fitr
фазыйл fazil
фазыл fazl
фаиз fa’iz
фал fal
фалчы falgu
фани fani
фарук faruq
фарыз farz
фарыз гаен farz-i ʿayn
фарыз гайн farz-i ʿayn
фарыз даим farz-i da’im
фарыз кифая farz-i kifaya
фарыз мүвәккать farz-i muvaqqat

фасик fasiq
фасикъ fasiq
фасыйк fasiq
Фатир сурәсе Fatir[1]
фатиха Fatiha[3]
фатиха fatiha[1]
фатиха fatiha[2]
Фатиха сурәсе Fatiha[3]
Фатыймә Fatima
фатыйр fatir[2]
фахишә fahisha
фаҗир fajir
фетнә fitna
фида fida
фидаи fida'i
фидакяр fidakyar
фидия fidya
фикъһе fiqh
фикыһ fiqh
Фиргавен Fira'un
Фирдавес Jannat al-Firdaus
фирдәвес Firdaus
фирка firqa
фисык fisq
фитнә fitna
фитра садакасы fitra
фитрәт fitrat
фитыр fitr[1]
фитыр fitr[2]
Фитыр гаете 'Id al-Fitr
фитыр садакасы fitr[2]
фозала fuzala
Форкан Furqan[1]
Фуркан Furqan[1]
Фуссыйләт сурәсе Fussilat
фәйләсуф faylasuf
фәкаһәт faqahat
фәкыйр faqir[1]
фәкыйр faqir[2]
фәкыйһ faqih
фәкыр faqr
Фәлакъ сурәсе Falaq[2]
фәлсәфә falsafa
фәләк falak[1]
фәләк falak[2]
фән fann
фәна fana
фәраиз fara'iz[1]
фәраиз fara'iz[2]
фәрештә farishta
фәрид farid
фәриделгасыр farid al-'asr
фәрсәх farsakh
фәрьяд faryad
фәсад fasad
фәтва fatva
Фәтех Мәккә Fath-i Makka
Фәтхе Мәккә Fath-i Makka
фәхеш fahsh
фәҗер сурәсе Fajr
Фөркан Furqan[1]
фөрьяд faryad
Хава Hava
хадисе шәриф hadis
Хак Haqq[2]
хак haqq[1]
Хак тәгала Haqq Ta'ala
хакыйкать haqiqat
Халикъ Khaliq, al-
халка halqa[1]
хамилә hamila
ханәка khanaqa
хата khata
хатиб khatib
хатим khatim[1]
хатим khatim[2]
Хатәменнәбини Khatam al-nabiyin
Хафиз Hafiz, al-[1]
хафиз hafiz
хач khach
Хаҗ Hajj[2]
хаҗ hajj[1]
хаҗи hajji
хаҗәт намазы salat al-hajat
хизеб hizb[1]
хизеб hizb[2]
Хизыр Khizr
хикмәт hikmat
хилафе шәрыг khilaf-i shar'
хилафәт khilafat[1]
хилафәт khilafat[2]
хилафәт khilafat[3]
хилйә hilya
хилйәи сәгадәт hilya-yi sa'adat
хилйәи шәриф hiliya-yi sharif
хилка halqa[1]
хилкате галәм khilqat
хилкать khilqat
хирз hirz
хирка khirqa[1]
хиркапуш khirqa push
хирка пуш khirqa push
хиссе батыйн hiss-i batin
хиссе заһири hiss-i zahiri
хитан khitan
хиҗаб hijab
Хода Khuda
ходаи khudayi
Ходай khuday
Хозыр Khizr
Холд Khuld
хомес khums
хонса khunsa
хонәса khunsa
хорафат khurafat
хосуф намазы salat al-khusuf
хотбә khutba
хур hur
хури huri
Хут Hut
хуш дәр дәм khush dar dam
хуҗа khvaja[2]
Хәбиб Habib
Хәбир Khabir, al-
хәбәр khabar
Хәбәш Habashistan
хәбәш habash
Хәбәшстан Habashistan
хәвари havari
хәвариҗ khavarij
хәдд hadd
Хәдид сурәсе Hadid
хәдис hadis
хәдиси әрбагыйн hadis-i arba'in
хәез hayz
хәер khayr[1]
хәер khayr[2]
хәер-садака khayr-sadaqa
хәзрәт hazrat
Хәй Hayy, al-
хәйан hayan
Хәйдәр Haydar
хәйз hayz

Хәййү Hayy, al-
хәким hakim
хәкъ haqq[1]
хәкыйкать haqiqat
хәл hall
хәл hal
хәлвәт khalvat
хәлвәт khilvat
хәлвәтгяһ khalvatgah
хәлвәт дәр әнҗән khalvat dar anjuman
хәлифа khalifa[2]
хәлифә khalifa[1]
хәлл hall
Хәллякъ Khallaq
хәлфә khalfa[1]
хәлял halal
хәләл halal
хәмеде лилляһ al-hamdullilah
хәмер khamr
Хәмәл Hamal
Хәнбәли Hanbaliya
хәнбәли Hanbali
хәниф hanif[1]
хәниф hanif[2]
Хәнәфи Hanafiya
хәнәфи Hanafi
хәрам haram[1]
хәрамзадә haramzada
хәрим harim
хәрәм haram[2]
хәрәм занни haram zanni
хәрәм катгый haram qat'i
Хәрәмәен Haramayn
Хәсән Hasan[3]
хәсән hasan[1]
хәсән hasan[2]
хәтем хуҗа khatm-i khvajagan
хәтме көтиб khatm-i kutub
хәтме сөлүк khatm-i suluk
хәттат hattat
Хәува Hava
хәшер hashr[1]
Хәшер сүрәсе Hashr[2]
хәят әбәдия hayat-i abadiya
хәүф намазы salat al-khavf
хәҗәре әсвәд hajar-i asvad
хөб hubb
хөдүд hudud
Хөзер Khizr
хөкем hukm
хөкеме самәд hukm-i samad
хөкүмәт hukumat
хөллә hulla
Хөләфаи рашидин Khulafa-yi rashidin
хөрмә khurma
хөсен husn
хөсне тәрбия husn-i tarbiya
хөсне хат husn-i khat
хөсне әдәб husn-i adab
хөсне әхлак husn-i akhlaq
хөтбә khutba
хөҗрә hujra
чадра chadra
чалма chalma
чилләханә chillakhana[2]
чиркәү kalisa
чукыныру tanassur
чәр яр Chahar yar
чәһар яр Chahar yar
чәһәр яр Chahar yar
Шафиг Shafi'i[1]
Шафигый Shafi'i[2]
шафигый Shafi'iya
Шаһит Shahid, al-
шаһит shahid[1]
шаһәдәт shahadat[1]
шаһәдәт shahadat[2]
шигый shi'i
шик shakk
ширек shirk
Шис Shis
шифа shifa
Шогаип Shu'ayb
шура shura [1]
Шура сүрәсе Shura[2]
Шәгбан Sha'ban
шәех shaykh
шәйтан Shaytan
шәйтанәт shaytanat
шәйхелислам shaykh al-islam[1]
шәйхелислам shaykh al-islam[2]
шәк shakk
шәкерт shagird
Шәкүр Shakur, al-
шәмаил shama'il
шәмгъ sham'
шәмгыдан sham'dan
шәмес сүрәсе Shams
шәр sharr
шәраб sharab
шәрган shar'an
шәргъ shar'
шәригать shari'at
шәрик sharik
шәриф sharif
шәрр sharr
шәфагәт shafa'at
шәүк shavq
Шәүәл Shavval
шәҗәрә shajara
шәһадәт shahadat[1]
шәһадәт shahadat[2]
шәһвәт shahvat
шәһит shahid[2]
шөбһә shubha
Шөгарә сүрәсе Shu'ara
шөгур shu'ur
шөкер shukr
шөһрәт shuhrat
Юныс Yunus[1]
Юныс сүрәсе Yunus[2]
Язьдан Yazdan
Якуп Ya'qub
яр yar
ярабби ya rabbi
Яргар Yar-i Ghar
Ясин Ya Sin
ясту намазы salat al-'isha
ятим yatim
Яфес Yafis
яхшы avliya[1]
Яхъя Yahya
Яэҗүҗ вә Мәэҗүҗ Ya'juj va Ma'juj
Яһу yahu
яһүд yahud
яһүди yahudi
әбдал abdal[1]
әбрар abrar
Әбу abu
Әбу Бәкер Abu Bakr
әбъдәст abdast

əбъдəстханə abdastkhana
əбəд abad
Əбү Хəнифə Abu Hanifa
əгузе биллаhи a'uzu billah
Əгъзам A'zam[2]
əгъзам a'zam[1]
Əгъла сүрəсе A'la
əгълəм a'lam
əгъраф a'raf[1]
Əгъраф сүрəсе A'raf[2]
Əгүзү биллəhи минəш-шəйтанир-рəҗим a'uzu billahi min al-shaytani al-rajim
əдəб adab
Əдəм Adam
Əйүп Ayyub
əкмал akmal
əкрəм akram
əкъриба aqraba
əлбəйтүл гатикъ Bayt al-'atiq, al-
Əл-Ихлас сүрəсе Ikhlas[2]
əл-Кадыйр Qadir, al-
əл-Кодес Quds, al-
Əл-Маидə сүрəсе Ma'ida
əлмөhаҗир muhajirin
əлхəмде лилля al-hamdullilah
əлхəмдүллилаh al-hamdullilah
əлхəмдүллилаh раббелгалəмийн al-hamdulillahi rabbi'l-'alamin
Əлхəм сүрəсе Fatiha[3]
Əл-əгъраф сүрəсе A'raf[2]
əлəм 'alam[2]
Əл-Əнгам сүрəсе An'am
əманəт amanat
əмарəт imarat
əмин Amin[2]
əмин amin[1]
əминият amniyat
əмир amir
Əмирел-мөэминин Amir al-mu'minin
əмляк amlak
əнбия anbiya[1]
Əнбия сүрəсе Anbiya[2]
əнвəр anvar
Əнгəм сүрəсе An'am
əндəрун andarun
əн-Нас сүрəсе Nas
əнсар ansar
əнҗемəн anjuman
əрвəх arvah
əркян arkan
Əррагд сүрəсе Ra'd
əсарəт asarat
əсир asir
əсман asman
əссəламе галəйкем assalamu 'alaykum
əстəгъфируллаh astaghfirullah
əсфалессафилин asfal al-safilin
əсхаб ashab
əсхабе кəhəф ashab-i kahf
Əсəд Asad
Əсəдулла Asadullah
əсəр asar
əттəслиму taslim[2]
əттəхиййəт tahiyat, at-
əт-тəхият tahiyat, at-
əттəхият tahiyat, at-
Əфлəтун Aflatun
əфсанə afsana
əфсун afsun
əхбаб ahbab
əхбар akhbar
əхи akhi
əхкям ahkam
əхлакъ akhlaq
Əхмəд Ahmad
əхрар ahrar
əхыйрави akhiravi
əүлия avliya[1]
əүляд avlad
əҗер ajr
əҗмəгу өммəт ijma'-i ummat
əҗəл ajal
əhле Ислам ahl-i Islam
əhле Китап ahl-i kitab
əhлел-виляят ahl al-vilayat
əhле салиб ahl-i salib
əhлес-сөннə ahl-i sunna
əhле сөннəт ahl-i sunna
өйлə намазы salat al-zuhr
Өммелкитаб Umm al-kitab
Өммелмүъминин Umm al-mu'minin
өммəт ummat
өмрə 'umra
өмəра umara
өстад ustad
өстаз ustaz
үлəксə murdar
җаду jadu
җаиз ja'iz
җамигъ jami'
җан jan
җаhили jahili
җаhилиять jahiliyat
җен jinn[1]
җеназа janaza[2]
җеназа намазы janaza[2]
Җен сүрəсе Jinn[2]
Җибрил Jibril
җизия jizya
җин jinn[1]
җинаять jinayat
җиhад jihad
җомга jum'a[1]
җомга jum'a[2]
Җəббар Jabbar, al-
җəбер jabr
Җəди Jadi
җəдид jadid
җəдидчелек usul-i jadid
җəза jaza
җəзаэ jaza
җəзеб jazb
җəзия jizya
Җəлил Jalil, al-
җəлляд jallad
Җəллə Җəлəлуh Jalla Jalaluh
җəлсə jalsa
җəмагать jama'at[1]
җəмагать jama'at[2]
җəмəгать jama'at[1]
җəмəгать jama'at[2]
җəнаб janab
Җəнабе хак Janab-i haqq
Җəнаби хак Janab-i haqq
җəназа janaza[1]
җəназа janaza[2]
Җəннəт Jannat
җəримə jarima
җəфа jafa

җәхим jahim
Җәүза Javza
җәһр jahr
Җәһәннәм Jahannam
җөда juda
җөзэ juz'[1]
җөзэ juz'[2]
җөзэ juz'[4]
Җөмадиәлахир Jumada al-akhira
Җөмадиәләүвәл Jumada al-ula
җөнүн junun[1]
җөнүн junun[2]
җөһүд juhud
һабыл Habil
һавия haviya
һади Hadi, al-
һарун Harun
һарут вә Марут Harut va Marut
һаҗәр Hajar
һибә hiba
һибәтулла Hibatullah
һидая hidayat
һидаят hidayat
һилял hilal
һиммәт himmat
һиҗри hijri
һиҗрия hijriya
һиҗрәт hijra
һу Hu
һуд Hud[1]
һуүә Hu
һәвел havl
һәфтеяк haft-i yak
һәүл havl

Turkmen Index

абд ʿabd
Абдылла ʿAbdullah[1]
Абдылла ʿAbdullah[2]
Абу abu
Абу Бекир Abu Bakr
Абу земзем Zamzam
Абыл Habil
агзачар iftar
агшам намазы salat al-maghrib
Ад ʿAd
Адам Adam
Адам ата Adam
Адамата Adam
адат ʿadat
ад-Дарр Zarr, al-
ажал ajal
аза ʿaza
Азазыл ʿAzazil
азан azan
азанчы mu'azzin
азап azab
азап ал-кабр ʿazab-i qabr
азап ал-кебир ʿazab al-kabir
айжын jinn[1]
Айша ʿA'isha
айыд ʿid
акыда ʿaqida
ал-Аввал Avval, al-
ал-Адл ʿAdl, al-
ал-Азым ʿAzim, al-
ал-Алим ʿAlim, al-
ал-Алы ʿAli, al-
ал-арвах arvah
ал-Афу ʿAfuv, al-
ал-Ахад Ahad, al-
ал-Ахир Akhir, al-
ал-Бады Badiʿ, al-
ал-Баис Baʿis, al-
ал-Баки Baqi, al-
ал-Бари Bari, al-
ал-Барр Barr, al-
ал-Басид Basit, al-
ал-Басир Basir, al-
ал-Батин Batin, al-
ал-Вадуд Vadud, al-
ал-Важыд Vajid, al-
ал-Вали Vali, al-
ал-Варис Varis, al-
ал-Васи Vasiʿ, al-
ал-Ваххап Vahhab, al-
ал-Векил Vakil, al-
ал-Ганы Ghani, al-
ал-Гафур Ghafur, al-
ал-Гаффар Ghaffar, al-
алейхис салам ʿalayhi al-salam
алейхэссалам ʿalayhi al-salam
ал-Жамы Jamiʿ, al-
ал-Желил Jalil, al-
ал-Жепбар Jabbar, al-
ал-Кабид Qabiz, al-
ал-Кабир Kabir, al-
ал-Кавп Qavi, al-
ал-Кадир Qadir, al-
ал-Каййум Qayyum, al-
ал-Каххар Qahhar, al-
ал-Керим Karim, al-
ал-Куддус Quddus, al-
Алла Allah
Аллатагала Allah taʿala
Алла тагала Allah taʿala
ал-Латиф Latif, al-
аллаху акбер Allahu akbar
аллаху экбер Allahu akbar
Аллахы аглам бес соваб Allahu aʿlam biʿl-savab
ал-Мани Maniʿ, al-
ал-Матин Matin, al-
ал-Межит Majid, al-
ал-Мубтди Mubdiʿ, al-
ал-Мувахир Mu'akhkhir, al-
ал-Мувид Muʿid, al-
ал-Мугни Mughni, al-
ал-Мужиб Mujib, al-
ал-Музилл Muzill, al-
ал-Муизз Muʿizz, al-
ал-Мукаддим Muqaddim, al-
ал-Мукит Muqit, al-
ал-Муксит Muqsit, al-
ал-Муктадир Muqtadir, al-
ал-Мумин Mu'min, al-
ал-Мумит Mumit, al-
ал-Мунтаким Muntaqim, al-
ал-Мусаввир Musavvir, al-
ал-Мутавали Mutaʿali, al-
ал-Мутакаббир Mutakabbir, al-
ал-Мухаймин Muhaymin, al-
ал-Мухйи Muhyi, al-
ал-Мухси Muhsi, al-
ал-Мәлик Malik, al-
ал-Рахым Rahim, al-
ал-Салам Salam, al-
ал-Фаттах Fattah, al-
ал-Хабир Khabir, al-
ал-Хади Hadi, al-
ал-Хайй Hayy, al-
ал-Хак Haqq, al-
ал-Хакам Hakam, al-
ал-Хаким Hakim, al-
ал-Халим Halim, al-
ал-Халык Khaliq, al-
алхамдиллила al-hamdullilah
ал-Хамыт Hamid, al-
ал-Хасиб Hasib, al-
ал-Хафид Hafiz, al-[1]
ал-Хафиз Hafiz, al-[2]
Алы ʿAli
алым ʿalim
ал-Эзиз ʿAziz, al-
аманат amanat
амр amir
анна jumʿa[2]
ан-Нафи Nafiʿ, al-
ан-Нур Nur, al-
ансар ansar
ант ʿahd
арафа ʿarafa
Арафат ʿArafat
ар-Равуф Rauf, al-
ар-Раззак Razzaq, al-
ар-Ракып Raqib, al-
ар-Рафи Rafiʿ, al-
ар-Рахман Rahman, al-
ар-Рашид Rashid, al-
арш ʿarsh
арыш ʿarsh
асман asman
ас-Сабур Sabur, al-
ас-Самад Samad, al-
ас-Сами Samiʿ, al-
асхаб ashab
асхаб ал-кахф ashab-i kahf
асхап ashab
аташ берес atashparast

ат-Таввап Tavvab, al-
ахбар akhbar
ахлак akhlaq
ахл ал-китап ahl-i kitab
ахун akhund
ахырет akhirat
ахырзаман akhir zaman
ахырзамана akhir zaman
ашура ʻAshura[1]
аш-Шакур Shakur, al-
аш-Шахид Shahid, al-
Ашыр Muharram[2]
аят ayat
аятолла ayatullah
Баба Гаммар Ghambar
багт bakht
багшы bakhshi
Байрам Shavval
байрам bayram
бакы baqi
балагат balaghat
балыг baligh
барака barakat
батыл batil
бейтил мал bayt al-mal
Бейтулмукаддес Bayt al-muqaddas
бенде banda
Бени исраил bani Isra'il[1]
бени хашымы bani hashimi
берекелла barakullah
берекет barakat
бехишт bihisht
бигүнә bi gunah
бисимилла bismillah
бисмилла bismillah
Бисмиллахыр рахманыр рахым bismillah al-Rahman al-Rahim
биссимилла bismillah
бут but
бутпараз butparast
бутхана butkhana
бүренҗек paranja
Былкыс Bilqis
Бырак Buraq
вагыз vaʻiz
вагыз vaʻz
важып vajib
вакф vaqf
вакыф vaqf
варыс varis
ватан vatan
ваххабийлер Vahhabiya
векил vakil
вели vali
вепат vafat
весиет vasiyat
весъет vasiyat
витир vitr
витир намазы salat al-vitr
вукуф vuquf
вүтир vitr
вүтир намазы salat al-vitr
выждан vijdan
габрыстан qabristan
габрыстанлык qabristan
габыр qabr
гадыр гиҗеси Laylat al-Qadr
газават ghazavat
гази ghazi
газы ghazi
гайры мусур ghayr-i misr
галам qalam[2]
галандар qalandar
галың sidaq[1]
ганымат ghanimat
гара даш hajar-i asvad
гөр gur
гудрат qudrat
Гурбан Zu'l-hijja
гурбан qurban
Гурбан байрамы ʻId al-Azha
Гурбан байрамы Qurban Bayrami
Гурхан Qur'an
гусул ghusl
гүммез gumbaz
гүнә gunah
гүнәкәр gunahkar
гүнәли gunahkar
дава daʻva[1]
Давут Da'ud
даң намазы salat al-fajr
даң намазы salat al-subh
дар ал-сулх dar al-sulh
дар ал-харб dar al-harb
дар ал-ыслам dar al-Islam
дервүш darvish
дергәх dargah
дессерхан dastarkhan
Дечҗал Dajjal
дивана divana
диет diyat
дин din
диндар dindar
дини dini
диянат diyanat
Довзах Duzakh
довзахы duzakhi
дога duʻa[1]
дога duʻa[2]
дога duʻa[3]
догагөй duʻagu
догаи кунут duʻa-yi qunut
дога-төвир takbir
дост dust
дөв div
дөртчарыяр Chahar yar
дуруд durud
Дүлдүл Duldul
дүнйә dunya
дүнйәви dunyavi
дүнъе dunya
дүнъеви dunyavi
дүрс durust
дүрст durust
Еке-тәк Ahad, al-
еке-тәк tavhid[1]
еке-тәк vahdaniyat
ерхемукаллах yarhamukallah
есир asir
етим yatim
еходы yahudi
җады jadu
җадыгөй jadugu
җайыз ja'iz
җами jamiʻ
җан jan
Җаналгыч ʻAzra'il
Җебрайыл Jabra'il
җезит jadid
җемагат jamaʻat[1]
җенаб janab
Җенаб-и хакк Janab-i haqq

женаят jinayat
Женнет Jannat
жериме jarima
жизья jizya
Жиржис Jirjis
жихад jihad
жуграфия jughrafiya
жума jum'a[1]
жума jum'a[2]
жума jum'a[1]
Жумадилахыр Jumada al-akhira
Жумадиловвал Jumada al-ula
жума метжиди jami'
жумга намазы jum'a[1]
жунун junun[1]
жүнүб junub
жүнүп junub
жын jinn[1]
жыназа janaza[1]
жыназа janaza[2]
жыназа намазы janaza[2]
жыхад jihad
жәзитчилик usul-i jadid
жәр zikr-i jahr
Жәхеннем Jahannam
жәхер zikr-i jahr
завия zaviya
залым zalim
захид zahid
зебаих zabiha
Зебур Zabur
зекат zakat[1]
зекат zakat[2]
зекат ал-питре zakat al-fitr
Зекеря Zakariya
Зем-Зем Zamzam
Земзем чешмеси Zamzam
Зул жалал ва-л-Икрам Zu'l-jalal va'l-ikram
зулум zulm
Зулькаъда Zu'l-qa'da
Зульхичже Zu'l-hijja
зухт zuhd[1]
Зүлкаада Zu'l-qa'da
Зүлпикәр Zu'l-fiqar
Зүлхичже Zu'l-hijja
зүмми zimmi
зыкыр zikr
зына zina
зынахор zinakar
зыярат ziyarat
зыяратчы ziyaratchi
зәкир zikr
Иблис Iblis
ид 'id
Ид ал-адха 'Id al-Azha
Ид ал-фитр 'Id al-Fitr
Идрис Idris
ижма ijma'
иҗтихат ijtihad
икинди намазы salat al-'asr
иман iman[1]
иман iman[2]
Инжил Injil
Иса 'Isa
исайы 'Isavi
Исгендер Iskandar
иснат isnad
истыхаза istihaza
Исхак Ishaq
ифтар iftar
ифтитах төвири iftitah
ихван ikhvan
ихрам ihram
ишан ishan
Кабыл Qabil
каза qaza
казы qazi
камары йыл sana-yi qamariyya
канун qanun
капыр kafir
Карун Harun
кары qari
катыл qatl
катыл амыд qatl 'amd
катыл себәб qatl sabab
катыл шубхе амыд qatl shubha 'amd
кахин kahin
келам kalam
келамулла Kalamullah
келамчы mutakallim
келамылла Kalamullah
келеме шахадат kalima-yi shahadat
кепен kafn
керамат karamat
кефарат kaffarat
кефен kafn
килисе kalisa
китап kitab
кифая kifaya
кияс qiyas
Куддус Quds, al-
Кудс Quds, al-
кунут qunut
курайыш Quraysh[1]
Куран Qur'an
курейиш Quraysh[1]
Куръан Qur'an
кутб qutb
кыбла qibla
кыбланама qiblanama
кыраат qira'at
кырагат qira'at
кысас qisas
кыям qiyam
кыямат qiyamat[1]
кыямат гүни qiyamat[1]
Кәбе Ka'ba
кәфир kafir
Кәъбе Ka'ba
кяфир kafir
лагнат la'nat
лахат lahid[1]
лейлят ал-кадр Laylat al-Qadr
лифафа lifafa
Лукман Luqman[1]
лукма Хеким Luqman[1]
Лут Lut
лә иляха иллелах Мухаммедүр ресулуллах la ilaha illa allah va muhammadun rasulullah
Лэйлят ал-бараа shab-i barat
ләш murdar
ляббейка labbayka
мавлид Mavlid[1]
магзур ma'zur
магшар mahshar
мазар mazar
мазарыстан mazaristan
мазарыстанлык mazaristan
мал mal
марифет ma'rifat[1]

матам matam
маулид Mavlid[1]
махр mahr[2]
Медине Madina
медресе madrasa
межлис majlis
межнун majnun[2]
мезхеп mazhab[1]
мезхеп mazhab[2]
мейит mayyit
Мекге Makka
мекру makruh
мекру тахрымы makruh tahrima
мекру тәнзих makruh tanzih
мектеп maktab
мелгун Mal'un[1]
мелек malak
меммер minbar
менхи manhi
меныг mani'
Мерет Sha'ban
мерхемет marhamat
Меръем Maryam[1]
месвах misvak[1]
месвах misvak[2]
меселе mas'ala
месжид masjid
месих masih[2]
мессеп mazhab[1]
мессеп mazhab[2]
мест mast
метжит masjid
мешкук mashkuk
мешхеди mashhadi
миграж mi'raj
Микайыл Mika'il
милад milad
милады miladi
Мина Mina
минара manara
мираж mi'raj
мирас miras
мисгин miskin
молла mulla
мөвлит Mavlid[1]
мөмин mu'min[1]
мубах mubah
мугаллим mu'allim
мугжуза mu'jiza[1]
мужахид mujahid
мужтахид mujtahid[1]
Муздалиф дагы Muzdalifa
мукаддес muqaddas
мукатеб mukatib
мукым muqim
мукәтеб mukatib
мунажат munajat[1]
мунафык munafiq
муртад murtadd
Муртаза Murtaza
Муса Musa
мусайы musavi[1]
Мустафа Mustafa
мустахаб mustahabb
мустахап mustahabb
мусулман musulman
мусур misr[1]
мусыр misr[1]
мутакаллим mutakallim
мутлак mutlaq
муттасыл muttasil
муфсид mufsid[1]
муфсит mufsid[1]
мухаббет muhabbat
мухажир muhajir
мухажир muhajirin
Мухаммат Muhammad[1]
Мухаррам Muharram[2]
мухтазар muhtazir
муэззин mu'azzin
муәккет mu'akkad
мүжевир mujavir
мүжевүр mujavir
мүлк mulk[1]
мүмин mu'min[1]
мүнбер minbar
Мүңкүр ве Некир Munkar va Nakir
мүрит murid
мүртөз murtadd
мүршит murshid
Мүсүр Misr[2]
мүфти mufti
мүшриклик shirk
мүъмүн mu'min[1]
мүъүззен mu'azzin
Мыкайыл Mika'il
мәлик malik[2]
Мәлик ал-Мүлк Malik al-Mulk
мәхелле mahalla
Мәхеррем Muharram[2]
мәхеррем 'Ashura[1]
мәхр mahr[2]
мәхраб mihrab
мәхрап mihrab
мәхрем mahram
назыл nazil
найып na'ib
намаз namaz
намазгәх namazgah
намаз дийгер salat al-'asr
намазлык jaynamaz
намаз хуфтан salat al-'isha
намаз шам salat al-maghrib
неби nabi
нежис najis
незир nazr[2]
Немрут Numrud
непес nafas
несил nasl
несип nasib
несихат nasihat
нефас nifas
нефил nafila
ниет niyat
ника nikah
Новруз Navruz
нөкер navkar
нур nur[1]
Нух Nuh[1]
ныяз niyaz
нәмәхрем namahram
оврат 'avrat
Омар 'Umar
оразa ruza
Ораза байрамы 'Id al-Fitr
Осман 'Usman
өвлат avlad
өвлүйә avliya[1]
өвләт avlad
өйле намазы salat al-zuhr
өмүр 'umr
пазыл fazil
пазыл fazl

пакыр faqir[1]
пал fal
палчы falgu
парз farz
парз кефая farz-i kifaya
пата fatiha[2]
патер fatir[2]
Патма Fatima
патыха fatiha[2]
пахыр faqir[1]
пейда fida
пейшин намазы salat al-zuhr
Пелек Allah
пелек falak[1]
пелек falak[2]
пелсепе falsafa
перенжи paranja
пери pari
перишде farishta
пир pir
питива fatva
питне fitna
питре fitr[1]
питре fitr[2]
пүренжек paranja
пыгамбер payghambar
Пыргаун Fira'un
равы ravi
ражм rajm
рахмет rahmat
рахым rahm
Реб Rabb
ребигиловвал Rabi' al-avval
ребигилсани Rabi' al-akhir
режеп Rajab
рекагат rak'at
рекуг ruku'
ремезан Ramazan
ресул rasul
Ресулуллах Rasulullah
рехим rahim
риба riba
Ридван Rizvan
рисала risala
роваят rivayat
ругсат rukhsat
ругсатнаме rukhsatnama
Рум Rum[1]
рух ruh[1]
руханы ruhani
рухы ruhi
рүкү ruku'
сабыр sabir
садака sadaqa
салават salavat
салавмалейким assalamu 'alaykum
Салых Salih[2]
салых salih[1]
салят salat
сапар Safar
Сара Sara
Саттар Sattar, al-
Саттарул уюб Sattar al-'uyub
Сафа дагы Safa
сахаба sahaba
сахават sakhavat
сежде sajda[1]
сеждэи тилеват sajda-yi tilavat
сеждети тилеват sajda-yi tilavat
сейит sayyid
семави samavi
Семут Samud
сене sana[1]
сира sirat[1]
согап savab[2]
солтан sultan
сопучылык tasavvuf
сопы sufi[1]
сопы sufi[2]
субхан Алла subhanallah
сураи Аграф A'raf[2]
сураи Алак 'Alaq
сураи Бени исраил Bani Isra'il[2]
сураи Вен нежим Najm
сураи Меръем Maryam[2]
сураи Нахыл Nahl
сураи Немл Naml
сураи Рагт Ra'd
сураи Сат Sad
сураи Сежде Sajda[2]
сураи Фуркан Furqan[2]
сураи Хаж Hajj[2]
сураи Ыкра 'Alaq
сурат surat
сурнай surnay
суура sura
сужүт sujud
сүйтхор sudkhur
сүйтхорлык sud
Сүлейман Sulayman
сүнне sunna
сүннет sunna
сүннет sunnat[1]
сүннет sunnat[2]
сүнни sunni
сүңни sunni
сүре sura
сүрэт sura
Сырат Sirat[2]
Сырат көпрүси Sirat[2]
Сырат көпрүси pul-i sirat
сэхив sahv
сэхув sahv
табыт tabut
таваф tavaf[1]
таваф tavaf[2]
тавах tavaf[1]
тагалла ta'ala
тагат ta'at
тагсыр taqsir
тайпа ta'ifa
такбир takbir
таква taqva
такдыр taqdir
такид ta'kid
талак talaq[1]
талып talib
танасух tanasukh
Таңры Tangri
тарава намазы taravih
тарыкат tariqat[1]
тарыкат tariqat[2]
тарых tarikh[1]
тахара taharat
тахя taqiya
тебиб tabib
тебигат tabi'at
тейим tayammum
текбир takbir
текбир тахрыма takbir al-tahrima
текке takiya
теммэки dukhan[2]

тербие tarbiya
тереке taraka
теркидүнйәлик tark-i dunya
тесби tasbih
тесбих salat al-tasbih
тесеттур tasattur
тефсир tafsir
техеҗҗуд намазы tahajjud
тешеххуд tashahhud
тилеват tilavat
тоба tavba[1]
товаккуф tavaqquf
төвир takbir
Төврат Tavrat
тумар tumar
тупан tufan
тылавет tilavat
тәрет taharat
тәхәрет taharat
тәъәхыр ta'akhir
тәьәхир ta'akhir
узур ʻuzr[1]
улама ʻulama
умма ummat
умра ʻumra
урп ʻurf
уссат ustad
уссат ustaz
усул usul[1]
үмивелед umm-i valad
үшүр ʻushr
факих faqih
факыр faqir[1]
фарз farz
фасд fasad
Фатыха сүреси Fatiha[3]
феряд faryad
фетва fatva
фидъе fidya
фикх fiqh
Фираун Firaʻun
фитре fitr[1]
фитре fitra
хабарлар akhbar
Хабыбылла Habibullah
хадд hadd
хадыс hadis
хаҗ hajj[1]
Хаҗар Hajar
хаҗы hajji
Хайдар Haydar
хайыз hayz
хайыр khayr[1]
хайыр khayr[2]
Хак Haqq[2]
хак haqq[1]
Хакк Haqq[2]
Хактагала Haqq Taʻala
хакыкат haqiqat
хал hal
халал halal
халиф khalifa[1]
халиф khalifa[2]
Халылылла Khalilullah
халыфат khilafat[1]
халыфат khilafat[2]
ханака khanaqa
Ханафи Hanafiya
ханафи Hanafi
Ханбали Hanbaliya
ханбали Hanbali
хапыз hafiz
харам haram[1]
харам haram[2]
харамзада haramzada
харем harim
Хартечҗал Dajjal
Харун Harun
харыҗы khavarij
хаса ʻasa
Хасан Hasan[3]
хата khata
Хатыҗа Khadija
хатым khatim[2]
хатып khatib
хач hajj[1]
хач khach
хачпараз khachparast
хачпараст khachparast
хезрет hazrat
хеким hakim
хиҗри hijri
хиҗрия hijriya
хикмет hikmat
Хов Hava
Хов Эне Hava
хоҗа khvaja[1]
хоҗа khvaja[2]
хөкүм hukm
хөкүмет hukumat
Худай khuday
хурма khurma
Хут Hud[1]
хутба khutba
хүҗре hujra
хүйр hur
Хүсейин Husayn
хүшүр ʻushr
Хыдыр Khizr
хыҗап hijab
хылаф khilaf-i sharʻ
хырка khirqa[1]
хырка khirqa[2]
чадра chadra
чалма chalma
чарыяр Chahar yar
чиле chilla[2]
чокундырмаклык tanassur
Шаввал Shavval
Шагбан Shaʻban
Шаймердан Shah-i mardan
шайы shiʻi
шафи Shafiʻi[2]
шафи Shafiʻiya
шафыгы мезхеби Shafiʻiya
шахадат shahadat[1]
шахадат shahadat[2]
шеҗере shajara
Шейс Shis
шейтан Shaytan
шейх shaykh
шек shakk
шергы sharʻi
шеригат shariʻat
шерип sharif
шехит shiʻi
шехит shahid[2]
ширк shirk
Шугайп Shuʻayb
шүбхе shubha
шых shaykh
шәгирт shagird
шәрик sharik
шәхвет shahvat

ыбадат 'ibadat[1]
ыбадатхана 'ibadatkhana
Ыбрайым Ibrahim[1]
ыгтыкат i'tiqad
ылах ilah
ылахы ilahi[1]
ылхам ilham
ылым 'ilm[1]
Ыляс Ilyas
ымам imam[1]
ымам imam[2]
ымам imam[3]
ымам imam[4]
ыммат ummat
ынсап insaf
ырым irim
Ыслам Islam
Ысмайыл Isma'il
ыфрит 'ifrit
ыхлас ikhlas[1]
ыхрам ihram
ыхтылам ihtilam
ышк 'ishq
эдеп adab
эжаза ijazat
эзиз 'aziz[1]
Эзрайыл 'Azra'il
Эйюп Ayyub
Элиеса Alyasa'
элхамдү лилләхи реббил әлеминә al-hamdulillahi rabbi'l-'alamin
эмир amir
эмирлик imarat
эмир эл-мөмин Amir al-mu'minin
эншалла insha'allah
эртир намазы salat al-fajr
эртир намазы salat al-subh
Эседулла Asadullah
Эсрафыл Israfil
эттехиат tahiyat, at-
Әжит-Мәжит Ya'juj va Ma'juj
әлем 'alam[1]
әмин Amin[2]
әмин amin[1]
әузу билләхи минеш шейтаныр ражым a'uzu billahi min al-shaytani al-rajim
Юнус Yunus[1]
Юсуп Yusuf[1]
Юшаг Yusha'
Якуп Ya'qub
яр yar
ярамазан ya ramazan
яссы намазы salat al-'isha
Ясын Ya Sin
Яфес Yafis
Яфет Yafis
яхуди yahud
яхуди yahudi
Яхя Yahya

Uyghur Index

abad abad
Abäsa süräsi ‘Abasa
abdal abdal[1]
abdal abdal[2]
Abdalla ‘Abdullah[1]
Abdalla ‘Abdullah[2]
abdasta abdasta
abdäst abdast
abdästkhanä abdastkhana
abid ‘abid
abidä abida
abidä ‘abida
abihayat ab-i hayat
abir ‘abir
Abizamzam ab-i Zamzam
abjad abjad
abrar abrar
Abu abu
Abu Bekr Abu Bakr
Abu Hanipa Abu Hanifa
abu hayat ab-i hayat
Ad ‘Ad
adalät ‘adalat
adäb adab
Adämata Adam
adät ‘adat
adävät ‘adavat
Adil ‘Adl, al-
adil ‘adil
Ahäd Ahad, al-
Ahqäp süräsi Ahqaf
ahrär ahrar
Ahzäb süräsi Ahzab
ajr ajr
akhirät akhirat
akhir zaman akhir zaman
akhun akhund
A’la süräsi A‘la
Al-Azim ‘Azim, al-
aläm ‘alam[1]
a’läm a‘lam
alim ‘alim
alip alif lam mim
Alla Allah
allahi ta’ala Allah ta‘ala
allahu äkbär Allahu akbar
allahuäkbär Allahu akbar
allämä ‘allama
amäl ‘amal
amin Amin[2]
amin amin[1]
amläk amlak
An’äm süräsi An‘am
Annäs süräsi Nas
Anpol süräsi Anfal
ansär ansar
aptädä aftada
aptuwa dastshuy
Arapat ‘Arafat
A’räp A‘raf[2]
Asadulla Asadullah
asärät asarat
ashir ashir
asi ‘asi
asman asman
atäshpäräs atashparast
atäshpäräst atashparast
attär ‘attar
auzibilla a‘uzu billah
Auzibillahu minäshaytani räjiym a‘uzu billahi min al-shaytani al-rajim
awrät ‘avrat
Awwal Avval, al-
ayät ayat
Ayüp Ayyub
aza ‘aza
azap azab
äbd ‘abd
äbdäst abdast
Äd ‘Ad
ädl ‘adl
ähbäb ahbab
ähd ‘ahd
ähkäm ahkam
ähli Islam ahl-i Islam
ähli kitap ahl-i kitab
ähli qäläm ahl-i qalam
ähli räy ahl-i ra'y
ähli salib ahl-i salib
ählisälip salibiyun
ähli täriqat ahl-i tariqat
äjal ajal
äjäl ajal
äjäm ‘ajam
äjnabi ajnabi
äjnibi ajnabi
äkhlaq akhlaq
Äkhmät Ahmad
äkmäl akmal
äkräm akram
äläm ‘alam[2]
äläyhissalam ‘alayhi al-salam
ämäl ‘amal
ämir amir
ämirul möminin Amir al-mu’minin
ämirulmu’minin Amir al-mu’minin
ämniyät amniyat
ämr amr
ämri märüp amr-i Ma‘ruf
änäl haq ana al-haqq
änbär anbar[1]
änbiya anbiya[1]
änjumän anjuman
Änkabut süräsi ‘Ankabut
änwär anvar
äpsana afsana
äpsanä afsana
äpsun afsun
äqibat ‘aqibat
äqidä ‘aqida
äqiqä ‘aqiqa
Äqrap ‘Aqrab
äräpä ‘arafa
äripä ruz-i ‘arafat
äripä ‘arafa
ärkän arkan
ärpat ‘arafa
ärsh ‘arsh
ärsh-äla ‘arsh-i a‘la
ärshi a’la ‘arsh-i a‘la
ärwah arvah
ärway arvah
äsäd Asad
äshabi kähäf ashab-i kahf
äshaburräs Rass
äshap ashab
äshräp ashraf
Äshur Muharram[2]
äshurä ‘Ashura[1]
äshurä ‘ashura[2]

Äshurä bayrimi ʻAshura[1]
äsir asir
äsr ʻasr[1]
Äsr süräsi ʻAsr[2]
ästaghpurulla astaghfirullah
äwläd avlad
äwliya avliya[1]
äwliya avliya[2]
äwliyaliq avliya[2]
äyän ayan
äzan azan
Äzäm Aʻzam[2]
äzäm aʻzam[1]
äzän azan
äzäp azab
äzgü vali
Äziz ʻAziz, al-
äziz ʻaziz[1]
Äzra'il ʻAzra'il
bab bab
Badi Badiʻ, al-
Badr Badr
Bais Baʻis, al-
baj baj
bakhshi bakhshi
bakira bakira
Balad süräsi Balad
balagat balaghat
baligh baligh
bamdat bamdad
bamdat salat al-fajr
bamdat namizi bamdad
bamdat namizi salat al-fajr
bani Isra'il bani Isra'il[1]
Baqi Baqi, al-
baqi baqi
baqt bakht
Bara'ät shab-i barat
bara'ät bara'at[1]
Barat Shaʻban
barhaq barhaq
Barr Barr, al-
Basir Basir, al-
Bathä Batha
batil batil
Batin Batin, al-
batin batin
bawär bavar
bayät bayʻat
bayram bayram
bayt bayt
baytul ähzän bayt al-ahzan
Baytulla Baytullah
baytulmal bayt al-mal
Baytul muqaddas Bayt al-muqaddas
Bayyina süräsi Bayyina
bädäl badal
bäddua bad-duʻa
bäkhit bakht
Bäkkä Makka
bändä banda
bäng bang
bäqä baqa[1]
bäräkällä barakullah
bäräkät barakat
bärät barat
bäshäriyät bashariyat
Bäsit Basit, al-
Bäytulmuqäddäs Bayt al-muqaddas
bid'at bidʻat-i hasana
bid'ati säyyi bidʻat-i sayyi'a
bid'ät bidʻat
bidyänät bi diyanat
biguna bi gunah
Bilal Bilal
billahi billahi
Bilqis Bilqis
binamaz bi namaz
birädär biradar
bisat bisat
bismilla bismillah
bismillahir Rähmanir Rähim bismillah al-Rahman al-Rahim
biyish bihisht
buräq Buraq
Burj süräsi Buruj
but but
butkhana butkhana
butpäräs butparast
büzrük buzurg
chadir chadra
chalma chalma
charyar Chahar yar
childän childan
chillä chilla[1]
chillä chilla[2]
chilläkhana chillakhana[2]
chiltan chiltan
chilyasin chillayasin
chong tärät ghusl
damolla damulla
dapn dafn
dargäh dargah
Darr Zarr, al-
darulbaqa dar al-baqa
darulpäna dar al-fana
das dastshuy
dastikhan dastarkhan
Dawud Da'ud
Dawut Da'ud
dähri dahri
dährilik dahriya
Däjjäl Dajjal
dälil dalil
dänishpand danishmand
därilharp dar al-harb
däril häwädis dar al-havadis
däril huppäz dar al-huffaz
däril islam dar al-Islam
däril sulh dar al-sulh
däris surur dar al-surur
därrä darra
därskhana darskhana
därulbäqä dar al-baqa
därulghürür dar al-ghurur
därulpanä dar al-fana
därulqäsäs dar al-qasas
därulqäzä dar al-qaza
därussalam dar al-salam
därwish darvish
dästar dastarkhan
dästar dastar
däwä daʻva[1]
däwä daʻva[2]
däwät daʻvat
delil dalil
delu Dalv
dew div
digär salat al-ʻasr
din din
dindar dindar
dini dini

diwan divan
diwanä divana
diyänät diyanat
diyänätchi diyanatkar
doppa dubba
dost dust
Dozaq Duzakh
dozaqi duzakhi
du'a du'a[1]
du'a du'a[2]
du'a du'a[3]
du'adär du'adar
du'agoy du'agu
du'akhan du'akhvan
du'ayisalam du'a-yi salam
dubbä dubba
dukhän dukhan[2]
Dukhän süräsi Dukhan[1]
Duldul Duldul
dunya dunya
dunyawiy dunyavi
durus durust
ehram ihram
ehsan ihsan[1]
ehtilam ihtilam
elip alif lam mim
etikap i'tikaf
etikapkhana i'tikafkhana
etimät i'timad
etiqad i'tiqad
etiqat i'tiqad
Fajr süräsi Fajr
Ghambar Ghambar
ghanimät ghanimat
Ghaniy Ghani, al-
ghapil ghafil
Ghappar Ghaffar, al-
Ghapur Ghafur, al-
gharip gharib[1]
ghashura 'Ashura[1]
Ghavsal A'zam Ghavs al-A'zam
ghayrimashrü ghayr-i mashru'
ghayrishar'iy ghayr-i shar'i
ghazab ghazab
ghazavät ghazavat
ghazi ghazi
ghäm ghamm[1]
Ghäpir süräsi Ghafir
Ghäplät ghaflat[1]
ghässäl ghassal
ghäyridin ghayr-i din
ghäyridiniy ghayr-i din
ghäyri muäqqäd ghayr-i mu'akkad
ghäzäp ghazab
ghäzi ghazi
ghilman ghilman
ghoja khvaja[1]
ghoja khvaja[2]
ghul ghul
ghusl ghusl
ghuslkhana ghuslkhana
gor gur
goristan guristan
gör gur
göristan qabristan
görüstan guristan
guna gunah
gunah gunah
gunakar gunahkar
gümbäz gumbaz
Habibullah Habibullah
Habil Habil
haiz hayz
haj hajj[1]
Hajär Hajar
haj badal hajj badal
haji hajji
Hakam Hakam, al-
Hakim Hakim, al-
hakim hakim
hal hal
halal halal
hall hall
halqa halqa[1]
Haman Haman
Hamid Hamid, al-
hamilä hamila
hamilidar hamiladar
hanapi Hanafi
Hanapiya Hanafiya
hanbaliy Hanbali
Hanbaliya Hanbaliya
hanip hanif[1]
Hapiz Hafiz, al-[2]
hapiz hafiz
haptiyak haft-i yak
Haqqa süräsi Haqqa
haram haram[1]
haram haram[2]
haram muharram[1]
haramzadä haramzada
harip du'a harif du'a
harpa 'arafa
Harun Harun
Harut-Marut Harut va Marut
Harut wä Marut Harut va Marut
Hasan Hasan[3]
hasan hasan[1]
hashir hashr[1]
Hashr süräsi Hashr[2]
hashtiyak hasht-i yak
Hawa Hava
hawalä havala
Hawashstan Habashistan
Haydar Haydar
Hayy Hayy, al-
haza 'aza
häbäsh habash
Häbäshistan Habashistan
Häbib Habib
hädd hadd
Hädid süräsi Hadid
hädis hadis
Hädiy Hadi, al-
häj hajj[1]
Häjar Hajar
häjari-äsväd hajar-i asvad
Häj süräsi Hajj[2]
Hälim Halim, al-
hälim halim
hälimkhana halimkhana
Hämäl Hamal
hämiläliq hamiladar
häq haqq[1]
Häq Haqq, al-
häqiqät haqiqat
Häqq Haqq[2]
häqq haqq[1]
Häq Rasul Haqq Rasul
Häq ta'ala Haqq Ta'ala
häräm harim

Häsib Hasib, al-
häwari havari
häwariyun havari
häwl havl
häzrät hazrat
heyit ʿid
heyt ʿid
Hibatulla Hibatullah
hibäh hiba
hidäyät hidayat
hijab hijab
hijrä hijra
hijrät hijra
hijriyä hijri
hijriyä hijriya
hikmät hikmat
hiläl hilal
himmät himmat
his hiss
hiyläi shä'ri hila-yi sharʿi
hizp hizb[1]
hizp hizb[2]
hökmu Samat hukm-i samad
höküm hukm
hökümа payghambar
hökümät hukumat
hör hur
hör-päri huri
hör qizi huri
Hösain Husayn
hösün husn
hösünu adäb husn-i adab
hösünu ahläq husn-i akhlaq
hösünu khät husn-i khat
Hud Hud[1]
Hud Hud[2]
hudud hudud
hujra hujra
Hujurät süräsi Hujurat
Humäzä süräsi Humaza
Hut Hut
i'anä iʿana
ibadät ʿibadat[1]
ibadätgah ʿibadatgah
ibadätkhana ʿibadatkhana
ibähä ibaha
Iblis Iblis
Ibrahim Ibrahim[1]
Ibrahim süräsi Ibrahim[2]
ibräniy ʿibrani
idda ʿiddat
iddät ʿiddat
Idris Idris
ihsän ihsan[2]
ijab ijab
ijabät ijabat
ijazat ijazat
ijazätnama ijazatnama
ijmä ijmaʿ
ijtihäd ijtihad
ijtihät ijtihad
ikhlas ikhlas[1]
Ikhlas süräsi Ikhlas[2]
ikhtilaf ikhtilaf
ikhvan ikhvan
ikki häräm Haramayn
ilah ilah
ilaha ilaha
ilahi ilahi[1]
ilahiy ilahi[2]
ilahiy ilahi[3]
ilahiyät ilahiyat
ilham ilham
ilhäd ilhad
ilimhal ʿilm-i hal[2]
ilimihal ʿilm-i hal[1]
ilimqal ʿilm-i qal
ilm ʿilm[1]
iltija iltija
Ilyas Ilyas
Ilyäsä' Alyasaʿ
imam imam[1]
imam imam[2]
imam imam[3]
imam imam[4]
imamat imamat[1]
imamat imamat[2]
imam A'zam Imam-i Aʿzam
iman iman[1]
iman iman[2]
Imran ʿImran[1]
Imran ʿImran[2]
Imrän Al-i Imran
Injil Injil
Inpitar süräsi Infitar
Insan süräsi Insan
insap insaf
insha'alla insha'allah
inshalla insha'allah
Inshiqäq süräsi Inshiqaq
insi-jins ins-jins
ins-jins ins-jins
intihä intiha
intiqam intiqam
inzal inzal
ipar ʿabir
ippät ʿiffat
iprit ʿifrit
ipta ifta
iptar iftar
iptitäh iftitah
iqämät iqamat
iqrar iqrar[1]
iqrar iqrar[2]
iradä irada[1]
irädä irada[3]
irim irim
irshat irshad
irshatnama irshadnama
Isa ʿIsa
Isapäräs ʿIsaparast
Isaq Ishaq
isawi ʿIsavi
isawiyat ʿIsaviyat
ishan ishan
Ishaq Ishaq
ishän ishan
ishq ʿishq
ishräk ishrak
ishräq ishraq
isiwi ʿIsavi
Iskändär Iskandar
Islam Islam
islamiyät islamiyat
Isma'il Ismaʿil
isnäd isnad
isqät isqat
Isra'il Isra'il
israp israf
Israpil Israfil
Isrä süräsi Isra
istibat istibdad
istibdäd istibdad
istighpär istighfar

istinja istinja
istipär isti'far
istiqamät istiqamat
istiqbal istiqbal
istisna istisna
ita'ät ita'at
izzät 'izzat
jadu jadu
jaduchi jadugu
jadugär jadugar
jadugär jadugu
jahalät jahili
jahalätlik jahiliyat
jahm jahim
jama'ä jama'at[1]
jama'ät jama'at[2]
jan jan
jarimanä jarima
Jawza Javza
jaynamaz jaynamaz
Jäbra'il Jabra'il
jädit jadid
jäditlik usul-i jadid
Jähännäm Jahannam
jähl jahl
jällat jallad
jändä janda
Jännät Jannat
Jäppär Jabbar, al-
jäsät jasad
Jedi Jadi
Jibri'il Jabra'il
jin jinn[1]
jinayät jinayat
jinaza janaza[1]
jinaza janaza[2]
johut juhud
Joza Javza
jughrapiya jughrafiya
Jumadil-akhir Jumada al-akhira
Jumadil-äwwäl Jumada al-ula
jumä jum'a[1]
jumä jum'a[2]
Jüdi teghi Judi
jümä jum'a[1]
kahin kahin
kapan kafn
kapir kafir
karamät karamat
Käbä Ka'ba
Käbud Qabiz, al-
Käwsar Kavsar[1]
Kewus Qavs
khaniqa khanaqa
khata khata
khawarich khavarij
khawarish khavarij
khälipä khilafat[1]
khälipä khilafat[2]
khälipä khilafat[3]
khälpä khalfa[1]
khälpä khalfa[2]
khälpä khalifa[1]
khälpä khalifa[2]
khälpät khalfa[1]
khätib khatib
khätma khatm[2]
khätmä khatim[2]
khätmä khatm[1]
khätmä Quran khatm[2]
khätmä sülük khatm-i suluk
khätnä khatna
khättat hattat
Khäybär Khaybar
khäyr khayr[1]
khäyr khayr[2]
khäyr-sädiqä khayr-sadaqa
Khelilulla Khalilullah
khilätgoh khalvatgah
khilwät khalvat
khimir khamr
khoja khvaja[1]
khoja khvaja[2]
khojä khvaja[1]
khorma khurma
Khuda Khuda
khudagöy khudaguy
khudagöy khudaygu
khudajöy khudajuy
khudapäräs khudaparast
khudatärs khudatars
Khudawänd Khudavand
Khudawändä khudavanda
Khuday khuday
khudayi khudayi
khums khums
khuptän khuftan
khuptän salat al-'isha
khurapat khurafat
khutbä khutba
kilisä kalisa
kipayä kifaya
kipin kafn
kitap kitab
kupar kuffar
kuparät kaffarat
kupran kufran
kupur kafir
kupur kufr
kupuristan kafiristan
kupurluq kuffar
läbbaykä labbayka
lähät lahid[1]
lähät lahid[2]
lä'in la'in
lä'nat la'nat
länät la'nat
Lokhmen Luqman[1]
Loqman Luqman[1]
Loqman Häkim Luqman[1]
Lut Lut
machit masjid
madda maddah
maddah maddah
maddiliq maddiyun
Madina Madina
maktap maktab
mal mal
mala'ika mala'ika
malak malak
malakiyat malakut
Manat Manat
ma'rup ma'ruf
Marwa Marva
Masad süräsi Masad
masha'alla mashaallah
mashayikh mashayikh
mashhad mashhad
mashparat mashvarat
mashru mashru'
ma'sum ma'sum
matäm matam
matämlik matamzada

mazar mazar
mazaristan mazaristan
mä'bud ma'bud[2]
mädhiya madhiya
mädris madrasa
mädrisä madrasa
mäghlub maghlub
mäghpirät maghfirat
mäghrib maghrib
mähällä mahalla
mähbus mahbus
mähdum makhdum
mähkäm mahkam
mähkimä mahkama
mähkum mahkum
mähluq makhluq
Mähmät Muhammad[1]
mähpil mahfil
mähr mahr[1]
mähr mahr[2]
mähräm maharim[1]
mähräm maharim[2]
mähräm mahram
mährämkhana harim
mährum mahrum
mähshär mahshar
mähshärgah mahshargah
Mäjit Majid, al-
mäjlis majlis
mäjus majus
mäjusi majusi
mäjusiy majusi
mäjusiyät majusiyat
Mäkkä Makka
Mäkkä mukärrämä Makka al-mukarrama
Mäkkä mükärrämä mukarram
Mäkkä pathi Fath-i Makka
Mäkkätulla Makkatullah
mäkru makruh
mäkruh makruh
Mälik Malik[1]
Mälik Malik, al-
mälik malik[2]
Mälikul-Mulk Malik al-Mulk
mäliyät maliyat
Mäl'un Mal'un[1]
mäl'un mal'un[2]
mämluk mamluk
Mäniy Mani', al-
mänkuha mankuha
mänpur manfur
mäntiq mantiq
mäntiqiy mantiqi
mäqbärä maqbara[1]
mäqbärä maqbara[2]
märhämät marhamat
märhum marhum
märipät ma'rifat[1]
märsiya marsiya
Märwä Marva
Märyäm Maryam[1]
mäsilä mas'ala
Mäsjidi Äqsa Masjid al-Aqsa, al-
Mäsjidi häram Masjid al-Haram, al-
mä'sum ma'sum
mätäm matam
Mä'uwn süräsi Ma'un
mävlänä mavlana
mäwhüm mavhum
mäwjud mavjud
mäwjudat mavjudat
mäwjudiyät mavjudat
mäwjut mavjud
mäwlä Mavla[1]
mäwlä mavla[2]
mäwlud Mavlid[1]
mäwlut Mavlid[1]
mäyräm bayram
mäzhäp mazhab[1]
mäzhäp mazhab[2]
mäzin mu'azzin
mäzlum mazlum
mehir mahr[1]
mehrap mihrab
Metin Matin, al-
meyit mayyit
michit masjid
mihrab mihrab
Mika'il Mika'il
Mikäil Mika'il
milad milad
miladi miladi
Mina Mina
minara manara
minbar minbar
mir mir
miraj mi'raj
miras miras
miraskhor miraskhur
miräj mi'raj
mirghazap mirghazab
mirza mirza
mirzä mirza
Misir Misr[2]
misir misr[1]
miskin miskin
miswak misvak[1]
miswak misvak[2]
Mizan Mizan[3]
mizänä mizana
molla mulla
möjizä mu'jiza[1]
Mömin Mu'min, al-
mömin mu'min[1]
Möminin süräsi Mu'minin
mu'allip mu'allif
mu'amilä mu'amalat
Muähhir Mu'akhkhir, al-
mu'äkkäl mu'akkal
mu'ällim mu'allim
mubahisä mubahasa
mubaräk mubarak
mubarizä mubaraza
mubashir mubashir
mubäriz mubariz
Mubdiy Mubdi', al-
mubhäm mubham
mudapiä mudafa'a
mudärris mudarris
Muddässir süräsi Muddassir
mufti mufti
Mughniy Mughni, al-
muhajir muhajir
muhajirät muhajarat
muhajirun muhajirin
muhakimä muhakama
muhariba muharaba
muhasira muhasara
Muhaymin Muhaymin, al-
muhäbbät muhabbat
muhäddis muhaddis

Muhämmät Muhammad[1]
muhämmäti muhammadi[1]
muhämmäti muhammadi[2]
Muhärräm Muharram[2]
Muhiy Muhyi, al-
Muhsiy Muhsi, al-
Muid Mu'id, al-
Muiz Mu'izz, al-
Mujädälä süräsi Mujadala
mujässäm mujassam
Mujib Mujib, al-
mukapat mukafat
mukämäl mukammal
mukärräm mukarram
mukärrir mukarrir
mukhlis mukhlis
mukhtariyät mukhtariyat
mukhtasär mukhtasar
mulazim mulazim
mulik-ämläk mulk-amlak
Mulik süräsi Mulk[2]
Mumiyt Mumit, al-
Mumtahana süräsi Mumtahana
munajat munajat[1]
munajat munajat[2]
munajathana munajatkhana
munapiq munafiq
Munapiqun süräsi Munafiqun
munar manara
munäjjim munajjim
munärä manara
munbar minbar
munbär minbar
munkir munkar
munkir munkir
Munkir- Näkir Munkar va Nakir
Muntaqiym Muntaqim, al-
mupässäl mufassal
mupti mufti
Muqaddim Muqaddim, al-
muqam maqam
muqäddäs muqaddas
Muqit Muqit, al-
Muqsit Muqsit, al-
Muqtadir Muqtadir, al-
muraqabä muraqaba
murasim marasim
murda murda
murdär murdar
murit murid
murshit murshid
Murtaza Murtaza
murtäd murtadd
Musa Musa
musadira musadara
musadirä musadara
musapir musafir
musawi musavi[1]
Musawwir Musavvir, al-
musälähä musalaha
mushrik mushrik
musibät musibat
muslim muslim
mustajäb mustajab
Mustapa Mustafa
mustäbit mustabidd
musulman musulman
Mutaäli Muta'ali, al-
mu'tabär mu'tabar
mutä'assip muta'assib
mutä'ässip muta'assib
Mutäkäbbir Mutakabbir, al-
mutälää mutala'a
Mutäppipun süräsi Mutaffifin
mutiwälli mutavalli
mutiwälliyät mutavalliyat
mutläq mutlaq
Muzammil süräsi Muzzammil
muzäppär muzaffar
Muzil Muzill, al-
mülük milk
mülük mulk[1]
münäwwär munavvar
müräpä murafa'a
Nabää süräsi Naba
nahäq nahaq
Nahl süräsi Nahl
najas najas
najat najat
namaz namaz
namaz salat
namaz bamdat bamdad
namaz bamdat salat al-fajr
namaz digär salat al-'asr
namazgah namazgah
namazgo namazgu
namazkhan namazkhan
namaz khuptan khuftan
namaz khuptän salat al-'isha
namaz peshin salat al-zuhr
namaz sham salat al-maghrib
namähräm namahram
Naml süräsi Naml
Namrut Numrud
napak napak[1]
napak napak[2]
napaqa nafaqa
nasap nasab
nashar'iy nashar'i
Nasr süräsi Nasr
nawkar navkar
näbi nabi
näbiulla nabi'ullah
näib na'ib
näim Na'im[1]
näim na'im[2]
Näpi Nafi', al-
näpil nafl
näpilä nafila
näps nafs[1]
näps nafs[2]
näsara nasara
näsara nasrani
näsara nasraniyat
näsibä nasiba
näsihät nasihat
näsip nasib
Näwbahar Navruz
näzir nazr[2]
näzr nazr[2]
näzr nazr[1]
nijis najis
nika nikah
nikah nikah
nisär nisar
Nisä süräsi Nisa
niyat niyat
niyät niyat
nizam nizam
Nuh Nuh[1]

Nuh süräsi Nuh[2]
Nur Nur, al-
nur nur[1]
Nur süräsi Nur[2]
ölima ʻulama
ömür ʻumr
örp ʻurf
öshrä ʻushr
pahisha fahisha
pahsh fahsh
pak pak
pal fal
palaq falaq[1]
Palaq süräsi Falaq[2]
paläk falak[1]
paläk falak[2]
palnamä falnama
paqir faqir[1]
paqir faqir[2]
paqir faqr
parä para
parid farid
paridal asr farid al-ʻasr
paryäd faryad
Patihä Fatiha[3]
patihä fatiha[1]
patihä fatiha[2]
Patima Fatima
pazil fazil
pazil fazl
päiz fa'iz
päjir fajir
päläk falak[2]
pälsäpä falsafa
pän fann
pänä fana
päni fani
päqih faqih
päränjä paranja
päri pari
pärishtä farishta
pärsäkh farsakh
pärüq faruq
pärwärdigar Parvardigar
pärz fara'iz[1]
pärz fara'iz[2]
pärz farz
pärzi ayn farz-i ʻayn
pärzi kipäyä farz-i kifaya
päsat fasad
päsiq fasiq
pätä fatiha[1]
pätiwa fatva
Pätkh süräsi Fath
Pättäh Fattah, al-
pätwa fatva
päyghämbär payghambar
päylasup faylasuf
perishtä farishta
peshin namaz salat al-zuhr
pida fida
pidakar fidakyar
pidayi fida'i
pidya fidya
pilsirat pul-i sirat
Pil süräsi Fil
pir pir
Pir'äwn Firaʻun
pirdäws Firdaus
piri pari
pirikhon parikhan
pirikhonluq parikhani
pirqa firqa
pisq fisq
pitir fitr[1]
pitir fitr[2]
pitir sadiqisi zakat al-fitr
pitnä fitna
Purqän Furqan[1]
Purqän süräsi Furqan[2]
putuwat futuvat
Qabil Qabil
qabilä qabila
Qadir Qadir, al-
qadir Laylat al-Qadr
qadir kechisi Laylat al-Qadr
qa'idä qaʻida
qalam qalam[1]
Qalam süräsi Qalam[3]
Qamar süräsi Qamar
qanun qanun
qari qari
qarikhana qarikhana
Qarun Harun
qawristan qabristan
Qaws Qavs
qazi qazi
qazikhana qazikhana
qazizada qazizada
qäbilä qabila
qäbr qabr
qädäm qadam
qädämgah qadamgah
qädämjay qadamjay
Qädir süräsi Qadr[1]
Qähhär Qahhar, al-
qäländär qalandar
qäländärkhana qalandarkhana
qälb qalb
qänäät qanaʻat
Qäp süräsi Qaf[1]
Qäriya süräsi Qariʻa
qärz qarz
qäsäm qasam
qäst qasd
qäwrä qabr
qiblä qibla
qiblänama qiblanama
qibligah qiblagah
qimär qimar
qira'at qira'at
qira'atkhana qira'atkhana
qisas qasas[1]
qisas qisas
qismät qismat
qissasul-änbiya qisas al-anbiya
qiwla qibla
qiyam qiyam
qiyamät qiyamat[1]
qiyas qiyas
qiyäm qiyam
qom qavm
qubbä qubba
Quddus Quddus, al-
Quddus Quds, al-
qudrät qudrat
quds quds
Quran Qur'an
Qur'an Qur'an
Qur'ani Äzim Qur'an-i ʻAzim
quräysh Quraysh[1]
Quräysh süräsi Quraysh[2]
Qurban bayrimi ʻId al-Azha

Qurban heyiti ʻId al-Azha
qurbanliq qurban
qurwan qurban
Qurwan mäyräm Qurban Bayrami
qutup qutb
rabitä rabita
rabi'ulakhir Rabiʻ al-akhir
rabi'uläwwäl Rabiʻ al-avval
rahib rahib
Rahim Rahim, al-
rahip rahib
ramazan Ramazan
Ramazan bayrimi ʻId al-Fitr
Ramazan heyiti ʻId al-Fitr
ramzan Ramazan
raziallahu änhu razi allahu ʻanhu
Rääd süräsi Raʻd
räb Rabb
rähim rahim
rähim-shäpqat rahm
Rähman Rahman
Rähman Rahman, al-
rähmani rahmani
rähmät rahmat
rähmätliq rahmati
rä'is ra'is[1]
rä'is ra'is[2]
räjäp Rajab
räjim rajim
räjm rajm
räkä'ät rakʻat
räkät rakʻat
rämmal rammal
Räqip Raqib, al-
Räs ahalisi Rass
räsim rasm-rusum
räsul rasul
rät radd
ri'ayä riʻaya
risalä risala
riwayät rivayat
riya riya
riyakar riyakar
riyazät riyazat
riza riza[1]
riziq rizq
rizq rizq
roh ruh[1]
rohani ruhani
rohiy ruhi
Rohulqudus Ruh al-Quddus
roza Ramazan
roza ruza
rukhsat rukhsat
ruku rukuʻ
Rum Rum[1]
sabir sabir
Sabur Sabur, al-
sadir sadr[1]
safar Safar
sahabä sahaba
Salam Salam, al-
salam salam
salamu' äläykum assalamu ʻalaykum
salamu' äläykum salam ʻalaykum
salawat salavat
Salih Salih[2]
sama samaʻ[1]
samawi samavi
sap saf
sapayi safa'il
Saratan Saratan
Sarä Sara
Sarätän Saratan
sawap savab[1]
sawap savab[2]
Sawir Savr
sazayi sazayi
sädiqä sadaqa
Säd süräsi Sad
Säfa Safa
sähär sahar
sähipä sahifa
säjdä sajda[1]
säjdä sujud
säjdägoh sajdagah
sälam salam
sällä salla
Sälsäbil Salsabil
sämawi samavi
Sämud Samud
säna sana[2]
sänäm sanam
säpär Safar
säpär namizi salat al-safar
särap sar-ab
Säritan Saratan
säwäp savab[3]
Säwir Savr
sehir sihr
sehirgär sahir
sehirgärlik sihr
sehirji sahir
shagirt shagird
shahadät shahadat[1]
shahit shahid[1]
shahitliq shahadat[1]
sham salat al-maghrib
sham shamʻ
shamdan shamʻdan
shapa'ät shafaʻat
sharap sharab
Shawwal Shavval
Shä'ban Shaʻban
Shäfi Shafiʻi[1]
shähwät shahvat
shäjirä shajara
shäk shak
shäk shakk
Shäkir Shakur, al-
shäkkäk shakkak
shäk küni shak
shämsiya sana-yi shamsiyya
Shärh süräsi Inshirah
shäriät shariʻat
shärip sharif
shäripa sharifa
shär'iy sharʻan
shär'iy sharʻi
shäykh shaykh
shäytan Shaytan
shäytanat shaytanat
Shehit Shahid, al-
shehit shahid[2]
shehitliq shahadat[2]
sherik sharik
shiä shiʻi
shipa shifa
shipä shifa
shöhrät shuhrat

Shu'äyb Shu'ayb
shübhä shubha
shükür shukr
siddiq siddiq
sihir sihr
sihr sihr
sihrchi sihirbaz
Sirat Sirat[2]
sirat sirat[1]
sopi sufi[1]
sopi sufi[2]
subha subha
subhä subha
subhänalla subhanallah
subhänä ta'ala subhanahu va ta'ala
Sulayman Sulayman
sultan sultan
sumrugh Simurgh
Sunbulä Sunbula
sur sur
sura Än'am An'am
sura Bäqära Baqara
sura Täwbä Tavba[3]
surä Adiyat 'Adiyat
sutkhor sudkhur
sutkhorluq sud
sülih sulh
sünnät sunna
sünnät sunnat[1]
sünnät sunnat[2]
sünni sunni
sünniy sunni
sürä sura
sürä Al Imran Al-i Imran
sürä Äbäsä 'Abasa
sürä Ähqaf Ahqaf
sürä Ähzab Ahzab
sürä Ä'la A'la
sürä Äläq 'Alaq
sürä Änbiya Anbiya[2]
sürä Änfal Anfal
sürä Änkä But 'Ankabut
sürä Ä'raf A'raf[2]
sürä Bayyinä Bayyina
sürä Fatih Fath
sürä Fatihä Fatiha[3]
sürä Fatir Fatir[1]
sürä Fäläq Falaq[2]
sürä Fil Fil
sürä Furqan Furqan[2]
sürä Fussilät Fussilat
sürä Ghafir Ghafir
sürä Ghashiyä Ghashiya
sürä Haqqä Haqqa
sürä Häshr Hashr[2]
sürä Hijr Hijr
sürä Hujurat Hujurat
sürä Infitar Infitar
sürä Inishiqaq Inshiqaq
sürä Inshirah Inshirah
sürä Isra Isra
sürä Jasiyä Jasiya
sürä Jin Jinn[2]
sürä Jümü'ä Jum'a[3]
sürä Kafirun Kafirun
sürä Kähf Kahf
sürä Käwsär Kavsar[2]
sürä Läyl Layl
sürä Loqman Luqman[2]
sürä Ma'arij Ma'arij
sürä Ma'idä Ma'ida
sürä Ma'un Ma'un
sürä Märyäm Maryam[2]
sürä Mäsäd Masad
sürä Mö'minun Mu'minin
sürä Muhämmäd Muhammad[2]
sürä Mulk Mulk[2]
sürä Munafiqun Munafiqun
sürä Mutäffifin Mutaffifin
sürä Muzämmil Muzzammil
sürä Müjadälä Mujadala
sürä Nas Nas
sürä Nazi'at Nazi'at
sürä Näbä Naba
sürä Nähl Nahl
sürä Näjm Najm
sürä Nisa Nisa
sürä Qaf Qaf[1]
sürä Qari'ä Qari'a
sürä Qämär Qamar
sürä Qäsäs Qasas[2]
sürä Qiyamät Qiyamat[2]
sürä Rä'd Ra'd
sürä Sad Sad
sürä Saffat Saffat
sürä Säbä' Saba
sürä Säjdä Sajda[2]
sürä Säp Saff
sürä Shäms Shams
sürä Shu'ära Shu'ara
sürä Shura Shura[2]
sürät surat
sürä Taha Ta ha
sürä Tariq Tariq
sürä Täghabun Taghabun
sürä Tährim Tahrim[2]
sürä Täkasur Takasur
sürä Täkwir Takvir
sürä Tälaq Talaq[2]
sürä Tin Tin
sürä Tur Tur
sürä Waqi'ä Vaqi'a
sürä Yunus Yunus[2]
sürä Yüsüf Yusuf[2]
sürä Zariyat Zariyat
sürä Zälzälä Zilzal
sürä Zuha Zuha
sürä Zukhruf Zukhruf
sürä Zumär Zumar
sütkhor sudkhur
sütkhorluq sud
Ta'ala ta'ala
taäm ta'am
ta'ässup ta'assub
ta'ät ta'at
ta'ät-ibädät ta'at-'ibadat
ta'bir ta'bir
ta'birnama ta'birnama
tabut tabut
talaq talaq[1]
talaqkhät talaq khat
talaq khät talaq khat
talip talib
Tamuq Tamuq
taqwadar taqvadar
tarawi taravih
tarikh tarikh[1]
tawap tavaf[1]
tawap tavaf[2]
täässub ta'assub
täbaräk tabarak
täbiät tabi'at
täbrik tabrik

täharät taharat
tähämmul tahammul
täkbir takbir
tälim ta'lim
tälqin talqin[1]
tälqin talqin[2]
Tängri Tangri
Tänri Tangri
täqdir taqdir
täqwa taqva
tärät taharat
tärätkhana taharatkhana
täriqat tariqat[1]
täriqat tariqat[2]
täsäwwup tasavvuf
Täsnim Tasnim
täswi tasbih
täwäkkül tavakkul[1]
Täwrat Tavrat
täyämmum tayammum
täzir ta'zir
tijarät tijarat
tiläwat tilavat
tugh tugh[1]
tugh tugh[2]
tumar tumar
tümät buhtan
urp 'urf
urpi 'urf
urup 'urf
Usman 'Usman
wa'alaykum ässälam 'alaykim al-salam
wa'iz va'iz
wajip vajib
wakhpä vaqfa
wapa vafa
wapat vafat
waqp vaqf
waris varis
wayiz va'iz
wähi vahi
wäjh vajh
wäkil vakil
wäli vali
wäli'ähd vali ahd
wäräqä varaqa
wärisa varis
wäsiyat vasiyat
wäsiyätnamä vasiyatnama
wäswäsä vasvasa
wätän vatan
wäz va'z
wijdan vijdan
wujut vujud
ya Alla! ya allah
Yahu yahu
yar yar
ya räbbim ya rabbi
Yari ghar Yar-i Ghar
Yasin Ya Sin
yähudi yahud
yähudi yahudi
Yähya Yahya
Yäjäj-Mäjäj Ya'juj va Ma'juj
yä pirim ya pirim
Yä'qub Ya'qub
Yäqüb Ya'qub
yä Ramazan ya ramazan
yitim yatim
Yunus Yunus[1]
Yüsüf Yusuf[1]
zahir zahir
zahit zahid
zakat zakat[1]
zalalät zalalat
zalim zalim
zaratka ziyaratgah
zarzamän zar zaman
zä'ipä za'ifa
zäkat zakat[1]
Zäkäriya Zakariya
Zämzäm Zamzam
Zämzäm quduqi Zamzam
zäpär zafar
zikir zikr
zikirkhana zikrkhana
zikri khup zikr-i khafi
zina zina
zinakar zinakar
zindan zindan
ziya ziya'
ziyarät ziyarat
ziyarätchi ziyaratchi
ziyarätga ziyaratgah
Zulhäjjä Zu'l-hijja
Zulhijjä Zu'l-hijja
Zul-jalälu valikräm Zu'l-jalal va'l-ikram
Zulkifl Zu'l-Kifl
zulm zulm
zulmät zulmat[1]
zulmät zulmat[2]
Zulpiqar Zu'l-fiqar
Zulqarnayn Zu'l-Qarnayn
Zulqä'dä Zu'l-qa'da
Zulqä'idä Zu'l-qa'da
Zulqärnäyn Zu'l-Qarnayn
zulum zulm
zulum zulum
zühä salat al-zuha
zühd zuhd[2]

Uzbek Index

абад abad
Абаса сураси ‘Abasa
абд ‘abd
абдал abdal[1]
абдал abdal[2]
абдал abdal[3]
Абдулла ‘Abdullah[1]
Абдулла ‘Abdullah[2]
абжад abjad
абир ‘abir
абобул қуръон abvab al-Qur’an
аброр abrar
Абу abu
Абу Бакр Abu Bakr
Абу лаҳаб Lahab
Абу Ҳанифа Imam-i A‘zam
Абу Ҳанифа Abu Hanifa
авлиё avliya[1]
авлиё avliya[2]
авлиёзода avliyazada
авлод avlad
аврот ‘avrat
адаб adab
адан ‘adn
Ад-Дорр Zarr, al-
адл ‘adl
адо аҳлияти ahliyyat-i ada
адоват ‘adavat
адолат ‘adl
адолат ‘adalat
аён ayan
ажал ajal
ажам ‘ajam
ажнабий ajnabi
ажр ajr
аза ‘aza
азайимхон ‘azayimkhan
аза тутмоқ ihdad
Азза ва Жалла ‘Azza va Jalla
азиз ‘aziz[1]
азиз ‘aziz[2]
азоб azab
азоби кабир ‘azab al-kabir
Азозил ‘Azazil
азон azan
Азроил ‘Azra’il
Айюб Ayyub
акавачча bachchabaz
акмал akmal
акрам akram
Ал-Аввал Avval, al-
Ал-Авфув ‘Afuv, al-
Ал-Азиз ‘Aziz, al-
Ал-Азим ‘Azim, al-
алайҳис салом ‘alayhi al-salam
Алақ сураси ‘Alaq
Ал-Аҳад Ahad, al-
Ал-Бадий Badi‘, al-
Ал-Барр Barr, al-
Ал-Басир Basir, al-
Ал-Боис Ba‘is, al-
Ал-Бори Bari, al-
Ал-Босит Basit, al-
Ал-Ботин Batin, al-
Ал-Боқий Baqi, al-
ал-Вадуд Vadud, al-
ал-Вакил Vakil, al-
ал-Валий Vali, al-
Ал-Ваҳҳоб Vahhab, al-
Ал-Вожид Vajid, al-
Ал-Ворис Varis, al-
Ал-Воси Vasi‘, al-
Ал-Воҳид Vahid, al-
Ал-Жаббор Jabbar, al-
Ал-Жалил Jalil, al-
Ал-Жомий Jami‘, al-
Алиёса Alyasa‘
Али ибн Абу Толиб ‘Ali
Ал-Исро сураси Isra
алиф лом мим alif lam mim
Ал-Кабир Kabir, al-
Ал-Карим Karim, al-
Ал-Кобуд Qabiz, al-
Аллам ал ғаюб ‘Allam al-ghuyub
Ал-Латиф Latif, al-
аллома ‘allama
Аллоҳ Allah
Аллоҳ ё Аллоҳ Allah ya Allah
Аллоҳи биллаҳи allahi billahi
Аллоҳ мукофоти mukafat
Аллоҳу Акбар Allahu akbar
Аллоҳу аълам Allahu a‘lam bi‘l-savab
Аллоҳу Баширин Allahu Bashirun
Аллоҳу Олимун Allahu ‘Alimun
Аллоҳу! Оллоҳу! Allah hu
Аллоҳу Самиун Allahu Sami‘un
Аллоҳу таолло Allah ta‘ala
Ал-Мажид Majid, al-
Ал-Малик Malik, al-
Ал-Масжид ал-Ақсо Masjid al-Aqsa, al-
Ал масчит ал-Харам Masjid al-Haram, al-
Ал-Метин Matin, al-
алмисоқ misaq
Ал-Моний Mani‘, al-
ал-Муаввазатони Mu‘avvizatan
Ал-Мубдий Mubdi‘, al-
Ал-Музил Muzill, al-
Ал-Мумийт Mumit, al-
Ал-Мунтақийм Muntaqim, al-
Ал-Мусаввир Musavvir, al-
Ал-Мутакаббир Mutakabbir, al-
Ал-Мутаоли Muta‘ali, al-
Ал-Муъид Mu‘id, al-
Ал-Муъиз Mu‘izz, al-
Ал-Муъоххир Mu’akhkhir, al-
Ал-Муқаддим Muqaddim, al-
Ал-Муқит Muqit, al-
Ал-Муқсит Muqsit, al-
Ал-Муқтадир Muqtadir, al-
Ал-Муғний Mughni, al-
Ал-Муҳаймин Muhaymin, al-
Ал-Муҳйи Muhyi, al-
Ал-Муҳсий Muhsi, al-
Ал Мўжиб Mujib, al-
Ал-Мўмин Mu’min, al-
Ал-Одил ‘Adl, al-
Ал-Оли ‘Ali, al-
Ал-Олим ‘Alim, al-
аломат ‘alamat
Ал-Охир Akhir, al-
Ал-Раззоқ Razzaq, al-
Ал-Саттор Sattar, al-
Ал-Фаттоҳ Fattah, al-
ал Фотиҳа! Fatiha, al-
Ал-Хабар Khabir, al-
Ал-Холиқ Khaliq, al-
Ал-Қайюм Qayyum, al-
Ал-Қаҳҳор Qahhar, al-

Ал-Қовий Qavi, al-
Ал-Қодир Qadir, al-
Ал-қориа сураси Qari'a
Ал-Куддус Quddus, al-
Ал-Ғаний Ghani, al-
Ал-Ғафур Ghafur, al-
Ал-Ғаффор Ghaffar, al-
Ал-ҳааққа сураси Haqqa
Ал-Ҳайй Hayy, al-
Ал-Ҳакам Hakam, al-
Ал-Ҳаким Hakim, al-
Ал-Ҳалим Halim, al-
алҳамдулиллоҳ al-hamdullilah
Алҳамдуллилаҳу раббил оламин al-hamdulillahi rabbi'l-'alamin
Ал-Ҳамид Hamid, al-
Ал-Ҳафиз Hafiz, al-[2]
Ал-Ҳақ Haqq, al-
Ал-Ҳодий Hadi, al-
Ал-Ҳосиб Hasib, al-
Ал-Ҳофид Hafiz, al-[1]
амал 'amal
амир amir
амирлик imarat
амирул муслимун amir al-muslimun
амирул мўмин Amir al-mu'minin
амирул умаро amir al-umara
амлок amlak
амният amniyat
амо a'ma
амон ҳирзи hirz
амр amr
амри маъруф amr-i Ma'ruf
анал-ҳақ ana al-haqq
анбар anbar[1]
анбиё anbiya[1]
Анбиё сураси Anbiya[2]
анбор anbar[2]
анвар anvar
андарун andarun
анжуман anjuman
Анкабут сураси 'Ankabut
Ан-нос сураси Nas
Ан-Нофи Nafi', al-
Ан-Нур Nur, al-
ансорлар ansar
ант 'ahd
Анфол сураси Anfal
Анъом сураси An'am
анқо 'Anqa
Арафа shak
арафа 'arafa
арвоҳ arvah
аркон arkan
аросат 'Arasat
Арофат 'Arafat
Арофат куни ruz-i 'arafat
Ар-Рауф Rauf, al-
Ар-Рашид Rashid, al-
Ар-Раҳийм Rahim, al-
Ар-Раҳмон Rahman, al-
Ар-Рофи Rafi', al-
Ар-Роқиб Raqib, al-
арш 'arsh
арши аъло 'arsh-i a'la
арши курси 'arsh-i kursi
Асад Asad
асадулло Asadullah
асар asar
асир asir
асма ул ҳусна asma al-husna
асо 'asa
асорат asarat
аср 'asr[1]
аср намози 'asr[1]
аср намози salat al-'asr
Ас-Сабур Sabur, al-
Ас-Салом Salam, al-
ассалому алайкум assalamu 'alaykum
ассалому алайкум salam 'alaykum
ассалому алайкум ва раҳматуллоҳ taslim[2]
Ас-Самад Samad, al-
Ас-Самий Sami', al-
астағфируллоҳ astaghfirullah
асфаласофилун asfal al-safilin
асфалуссофилин asfal al-safilin
асҳоб ashab
асҳоби Бадр ashab-i Badr
асҳоби жаннат ashab-i jannat
асҳоби кknown ashab-i kiram
асҳоби коф ashab-i kahf
Ат-Таввоб Tavvab, al-
аттаҳият tahiyat, at-
аттор 'attar
Аузи биллаҳи минашайтони рожийм a'uzu billahi min al-shaytani al-rajim
аузи биллоҳи a'uzu billah
Афлотун Aflatun
афсона afsana
афсун afsun
афтода aftada
афюн afyun
ахборот akhbar
ахлоқ akhlaq
ашир ashir
ашр 'ushr
ашрати саат ashrat-i sa'at
ашраф ashraf
ашура 'ashura[2]
ашура 'Ashura[1]
Аш-Шокир Shakur, al-
Аш-Шоҳид Shahid, al-
Аъзам A'zam[2]
аъзам a'zam[1]
аълам a'lam
аълам 'alam[2]
Аъло сураси A'la
аъроф a'raf[1]
Аъроф сураси A'raf[2]
ақида 'aqida
ақиқа 'aqiqa
ақлият 'aqliyat
Ақраб 'Aqrab
ақрабо aqraba
аҳбоб ahbab
аҳд 'ahd
Аҳзоб сураси Ahzab
аҳком ahkam
аҳлал вилоят ahl al-vilayat
аҳли дил ahl-i dil
аҳли зиммат ahl-i zimmat
аҳли Ислом ahl-i Islam
аҳли Китоб ahl-i kitab
аҳли рай ahl-i ra'y
аҳли салб ahl-i salib
аҳли салиб ahl-i salib
аҳли Сунна ahl-i sunna
аҳли тариқат ahl-i tariqat

аҳлияти вужуб ahliyyat-i vujub
аҳли қалам ahl-i qalam
Аҳмад Ahmad
аҳрор ahrar
Аҳқоф сураси Ahqaf
бадал badal
бадали аскарий badal-i askari
бадали нақдий badal-i naqdi
бадали шахсий badal-i shakhsi
баддуо bad-du'a
Бадр Badr
Бадр жанги Badr
Баййина сураси Bayyina
байрам bayram
байрам намози salat al-'idayn
байт bayt
байтул-аҳзон bayt al-ahzan
Байтуллоҳ Baytullah
байтулмол bayt al-mal
Байтул муқаддас Bayt al-muqaddas
Байтул отиқ Bayt al-'atiq, al-
байъат bay'at
Балад сураси Balad
балоғат balaghat
банг bang
бангивор bang
банда banda
бани Ислом bani Islam
Бани Исроил Bani Isra'il[2]
бани Исроил bani Isra'il[1]
баракалла barakullah
баракат barakat
бароат bara'at[1]
Бароат сураси Bara'at[2]
барот barat
Барот кечаси shab-i barat
барқ barq
барҳақ barhaq
басир basir
Батҳо Batha
бахт bakht
бахши bakhshi
бахшиш bakhshish
бачча bachcha
баччабоз bachchabaz
баччабозлик bachchabazi
башарият bashariyat
Башир Bashir
Бақара сураси Baqara
бақо baqa[1]
бақо baqa[2]
бегуноҳ bi gunah
бедиёнат bi diyanat
беиймон bi iman
беимон bi iman
бенамоз bi namaz
бесоқолбозлик bachchabazi
бетаҳорат bi taharat
беҳишт bihisht
биби bibi
Бибимарям Maryam[1]
Биби Ҳожар Hajar
бидъат bid'at
бидъат bid'at-i hasana
бидъати саййи bid'at-i sayyi'a
биллоҳи billahi
Билқийс Bilqis
Бимимайрам Maryam[1]
биродар biradar
бисмиллоҳ bismillah
бисмиллоҳир Раҳмонир Раҳийм bismillah al-Rahman al-Rahim
бисот bisat
бихалфа khalfa[2]
биҳабиллоҳ bihablillah
боб bab
бовар bavar
бож baj
бозгашт baz gasht
бокира bakira
болиғ baligh
бомдод salat al-fajr
бомдод намози bamdad
бомдод намози salat al-fajr
бомдод намози salat al-subh
ботил batil
ботин batin
боқий baqi
бузрук buzurg
Буроқ Buraq
Буруж сураси Buruj
бут but
бутпараст butparast
бутхона butkhana
бўҳтон buhtan
ваалайкум ассалом 'alaykim al-salam
вабол vabal
важ vajh
вażд vajd
ваз va'z
Ва-з-зориёт сураси Zariyat
Ваз-зуҳа сураси Zuha
вазир vazir
вазифа vazifa
вакил vakil
ваколат vakalat
Вал-аср сураси 'Asr[2]
вали vali
валиаҳд vali ahd
валинеъмат vali ni'mat
Вал-лайл сураси Layl
валлоҳи аълам vallahu a'lam bil-savab
валлоҳи аълам билсавоб vallahu a'lam bil-savab
валлоҳи аъламҳ vallahu a'lam
валлоҳу аълам vallahu a'lam
Вал-мурсалот сураси Mursalat
Вал-одиёт сураси 'Adiyat
Вал-фажр сураси Fajr
Ва-н-нажм сураси Najm
Ван-нозиот сураси Nazi'at
вараса varasat
вараса varis
вараъ vara'[1]
вараъ vara'[2]
варақа varaqa
васан vasan
васаний vasani
васваса vasvasa
васият vasiyat
васиятнома vasiyatnama
васиқа vasiqa
васл vasl
Ва-ссаффот сураси Saffat
ватан vatan
Ват-тийн сураси Tin
Ва-т-Тур сураси Tur
вафо vafa
вафот vafat
Ваш-шамс сураси Shams
ваъда va'da

вақф vaqf
вақфа vaqfa
ваҳдади вужуд vahdat-i vujud
ваҳданият vahdaniyat
ваҳи vahi
ваҳий vahi
ваҳобизм Vahhabiya
ваҳобийлик Vahhabiya
ваҳшат vahshat
ваҳшиёна vahshiyana
виждон vijdan
вилдон vildan
вирд vird[1]
вирд vird[2]
вирса virsa
витир намози salat al-vitr
витр vitr
виқор viqar
вожиб vajib
вожибал вужуд vajib al-vujud
воиз va'iz
ворис varis
вос-вос vasvas
восил vasl
Воқеа сураси Vaqi'a
воқиф vaqif[1]
воқиф vaqif[2]
вужуд vujud
вузу vuzu'
вуқуф vuquf
вуқуфи ададии vuquf-i 'adadi
вуқуфи замон vuquf-i zaman
вуқуфи қалбий vuquf-i qalbi
гумбаз gumbaz
гуноҳ gunah
гуноҳкор gunahkar
гўр gur
гўр азоби 'azab-i qabr
гўристон guristan
давир davir
даво da'va[2]
Дажжол Dajjal
Далв Dalv
далил dalil
далили ақлий dalil-i 'aqli
далили нақлий dalil-i naqli
далили шаръий dalil-i shar'i
дарвеш darvish
даргоҳ dargah
дарра darra
дарсхона darskhana
дарус durus
дастор dastar
дастурхон dastarkhan
дастшўй dastshuy
дафн dafn
Даъбба Dabba
даъват da'vat
даъво da'va[1]
Даҳир сураси dahir
даҳр dahr
даҳри дун dahr-i dun
даҳрий dahri
даҳрийлар dahriya
дев div
девон divan
девона divana
диёнат diyanat
диёнаткор diyanatkar
диёнатсиз bi diyanat
дийдор didar
дин din
диндор dindar
диний dini
добба Dabba
домла damulla
домулла damulla
донишманд danishmand
дорилбақо dar al-baqa
дорил ислом dar al-Islam
дорилсалом dar al-salam
дорил сулҳ dar al-sulh
дорилсурур dar al-surur
дорилфано dar al-fana
дорилқазо dar al-qaza
дорилқасос dar al-qasas
дорилғурур dar al-ghurur
дорилҳаводис dar al-havadis
дорилҳарб dar al-harb
дорилҳуффоз dar al-huffaz
доруламон dar al-aman
дубба dubba
Дулдул Duldul
дунё dunya
дунёвий dunyavi
дуо du'a[1]
дуо du'a[2]
дуо du'a[3]
дуогўй du'agu
дуодор du'adar
дуоисалом du'a-yi salam
дуои қунут du'a-yi qunut
дуохон du'akhvan
дуруст durust
духан dukhan[2]
Духон сураси Dukhan[1]
Дўзах Duzakh
дўзахи duzakhi
дўст dust
етим yatim
етти жаннат sab'i samavat
етти само sab'i samavat
ё Аллоҳ! ya allah
ёддошт yad dasht
ёд кард yad kard
ё Пирим ya pirim
ёппирим ya pirim
ёр yar
ё Рабб ! ya rabbi
ё Раббим! ya rabbi
ё Рамазон ya ramazan
ёриоллоҳ yarullah
ёрулло yarullah
Ёсин сураси Ya Sin
Ёқуб Ya'qub
Ёҳу yahu
жабр jabr
Жабройил Jabra'il
Жавзо Javza
жавобнома javabnama
жадид jadid
жадидчилик usul-i jadid
Жадий Jadi
жазб jazb
жазба jazba
жазо jaza
жазо куни ruz-i jaza
Жалла Жалоллоҳ Jalla Jalaluh
жаллод jallad
жалса jalsa
жамоа jama'at[1]
жамоат jama'at[2]
Жамра Jamra
жамъулжамъ jam' al-jam'

жанда janda
Жаннат Jannat
Жаннатул Адн Jannat al-ʻAdn
Жаннатул маъво Jannat al-Ma'va
Жаннатул Фирдавс Jannat al-Firdaus
Жаннатул хулд Jannat al-Khuld
Жаннатун наим Jannat al-Naʻim
жаннат шарораси Tasnim
жаноб janab
жаноби Ҳақ Janab-i haqq
жаноза janaza[1]
жаноза janaza[2]
жаноза намози salat al-janaza
жарима jarima
жасад jasad
жафо jafa
Жаҳаннам Jahannam
жаҳаннам туби Ghayya
жаҳл jahl
жаҳм jahim
жаҳр jahr
Жибрил Jibril
жизия jizya
жилваи раббония jilva-yi rabbaniya
жин jinn[1]
жиноят jinayat
Жин сураси Jinn[2]
Жиржис Jirjis
жиҳод jihad
жиҳоди акбар jihad-i akbar
жиҳоди асгар jihad-i asghar
жоду jadu
жодугар jadugar
жодугар jadugu
жоиз ja'iz
жойнамоз jaynamaz
жоме jamiʻ
жон jan
жон талвасаси talvasa
жон ҳирзи hirz
Жосия сураси Jasiya
жоҳили jahili
жоҳолият jahiliyat
жувут juhud
Жудий Judi
жудо juda
жузъ juz'[1]
жузъ juz'[2]
жузъ juz'[3]
жузъ juz'[4]
жузъя jizya
жума jumʻa[2]
Жумад ал-аввал Jumada al-ula
Жумад ал-охир Jumada al-akhira
жумалик jumalik
жума намози jumʻa[1]
жума намози salat al-jumʻa
жумла jumla
жумъа jumʻa[1]
жумъа salat al-jumʻa
Жумъа сураси Jumʻa[3]
жунун junun[1]
жунун junun[2]
журҳ jurh
жуғрифия jughrafiya
жуҳуд juhud
забиҳа zabiha
забт zabt
Забур Zabur
завия zaviya
завол zaval
заиф zaʻif
заифа zaʻifa
Закариё Zakariya
закот zakat[1]
закотал фитр zakat al-fitr
Залзала сураси Zilzal
залолат zalalat
Замзам Zamzam
замзамий zamzami
занб zanb
зарзамон zar zaman
зарурат zarurat
зарурият zarurat
зафар zafar
заъиф zaʻif
Заққум Zaqqum
заҳодат zahadat
зид zidd
зиё ziya'
зиёрат ziyarat
зиёратгоҳ ziyaratgah
зиёратхона ziyaratkhana
зиёратчи ziyaratchi
зикр zikr
зикри жоҳр zikr-i jahr
зикри хуфи zikr-i khafi
зикрхона zikrkhana
зикрчи zikrchi
зимми zimmi
зиндиқ zindiq
зиндон zindan
зино zina
зинокор zinakar
зифоф zifaf
зовия zaviya
золим zalim
Зоти кибриё Zat-i kibriya
Зоти пок Zat-i pak
зоҳид zahid
зоҳир zahir
Зул-Жалолу вал -Икром Zu'l-jalal va'l-ikram
зулжанаҳайн zu'l-janahayn
Зулиҳсон Zu'l-ihsan
зулм zulm
зулм zulum
зулмат zulmat[1]
зулмат zulmat[2]
зулум zulum
зулфиқор Zu'l-fiqar
Зулқарнайн Zu'l-Qarnayn
Зул Қифл Zu'l-Kifl
Зул-ҳижжа Zu'l-hijja
Зумар сураси Zumar
зуннор zunnar
Зуул-қаъда Zu'l-qaʻda
зуфоф zifaf
Зухруф сураси Zukhruf
зуҳд zuhd[1]
зуҳд zuhd[2]
зуҳо намози salat al-zuha
зуҳр zuhr
зуҳр намози salat al-zuhr
Иблис Iblis
ибодат ʻibadat[1]
ибодат ʻibadat[2]
ибодатгоҳ ʻibadatgah
ибодатхона ʻibadatkhana
ибоҳа ibaha

иброний ʿibrani
Иброҳим Ibrahim[1]
Иброҳим сураси Ibrahim[2]
Ид ал Адҳа ʿId al-Azha
Ид ал Фитр ʿId al-Fitr
идда ʿiddat
иддат ʿiddat
идом iʿdam
Идрис Idris
ижмо ijmaʿ
ижмои уммат ijmaʿ-i ummat
ижоб ijab
ижобат ijabat
ижозат ijazat
ижозатнома ijazatnama
ижтиҳод ijtihad
издивож izdivaj
иззат ʿizzat
изн izn
изор izar
ийд ʿid
иймон iman[1]
иймон iman[2]
иймонсиз bi iman
ийсовият ʿIsaviyat
ийсопараст ʿIsaparast
Илёс Ilyas
иллат ʿillat
илло-билло illa-billah
иллоҳиюн ilahiyun
илм ʿilm[1]
илм ʿilm[2]
илми қол ʿilm-i qal
илми ҳол ʿilm-i hal[1]
илми ҳол ʿilm-i hal[2]
илмул ақоид ʿilm al-ʿaqa'id
илоҳ ilah
илоҳа ilaha
илоҳи ilahi[1]
илоҳи ilahi[3]
илоҳиёт ilahiyat
илоҳий ilahi[2]
илоҳим ilahi[2]
илтижо iltija
илҳад ilhad
илҳом ilham
имом imam[1]
имом imam[2]
имом imam[3]
имом imam[4]
имомал қиблатайн imam al-qiblatayn
имомат imamat[1]
имомат imamat[2]
Имоми Аъзам Imam-i Aʿzam
имон iman[1]
имонсиз bi iman
Имрон ʿImran[1]
Имрон ʿImran[2]
инжизоб injizab
Инжил Injil
инзол inzal
Инна аътайнака ал кавсара inna aʿtaynaka al-kavsara
иноба inabat
инобат inabat
инс-жинс ins-jins
Инсон сураси Insan
инсоф insaf
интихоб intikhab
интиқом intiqam
интиҳо intiha
Инфитор сураси Infitar
Иншиқоҳ сураси Inshiqaq
иншоаллоҳ insha'allah
иншолло insha'allah
иншооллоҳ insha'allah
иона iʿana
ирим irim
ирода irada[1]
ирода irada[2]
ирода irada[3]
иродайи лаязал irada-yi la yazal
иртидод irtidad
иршод irshad
иршоднома irshadnama
исавият ʿIsaviyat
исён ʿisyan
исёнкор ʿisyankar
исёнчилар khavarij
Искандар Iskandar
Ислом Islam
исломият islamiyat
Ислом лашкарлари lashkar-i Islam
исмат ʿismat
исматилла ʿismatullah
исми аъзам ism-i aʿzam
Исмоил Ismaʿil
иснод isnad
Исо ʿIsa
исови ʿIsavi
исовий ʿIsavi
исовият ʿIsaviyat
Исои масиҳ Masih[1]
исопараст ʿIsaparast
Исоқ Ishaq
Исроил Isra'il
исроф israf
Исрофил Israfil
истибдод istibdad
истибро istibra
истидлоли имон istidlali iman
истилоҳат istilahat
истилоҳот istilahat
истинжо istinja
истиншок istinshaq
истислоҳ istislah
истисно istisna
истисқо istisqa
истисқо намози salat al-istisqa
истифор istiʿfar
истихор намози salat al-istikhara
истишод istishhad
истиқбол istiqbal
истиқома istiqamat
истиқомат istiqamat
истиғфор istighfar
истиҳоза istihaza
истиҳора istikhara
истиҳсон istihsan
исқот isqat
Исҳоқ Ishaq
итиқоф iʿtikaf
итлоқ itlaq
итмом itmam
итоат itaʿat
иттиҳод ittihad[1]
иттиҳод ittihad[2]
ифрит ʿifrit
ифта ifta
ифтитоҳ iftitah
ифтор iftar

иффат ʿiffat
ихвон ikhvan
ихлос ikhlas[1]
Ихлос сураси Ikhlas[2]
ихтилоф ikhtilaf
ишорат isharat
ишрок ishrak
ишроқ ishraq
ишроқ намози salat al-ishraq
ишқ ʿishq
иқоб ʿiqab
иқомат iqamat
иқрор iqrar[1]
иқрор iqrar[2]
иқтидо iqtida
иҳдод ihdad
иҳзор ihzar
иҳром ihram
иҳсон ihsan[2]
иҳсор ihsar
иҳсор қурбони ihsar
иҳтижоб ihtijab
иҳтилом ihtilam
йиғи yighi
кабир kabira
Кавсар Kavsar[1]
Кавсар сураси Kavsar[2]
кадар qadar
кажрафтор kajraftar
каламуллоҳ Kalamullah
калима kalima
калимагўй kalimagu
калимаи шаҳодат kalima-yi shahadat
калиматуллоҳ kalimatullah
калиса kalisa
калом kalam
каломи Шариф Kalam-i Sharif
каниз kaniz
канизак kaniz
каниса kanisa
карам karam
Карбало Karbala
каромат karamat
каромат соҳиби sahib-i karamat
кафан kafn
кафил kafalat
кафил kafil
кафолат kafalat
кафорат kaffarat
кашиш kashish
кашишхона kashishkhana
кашкул kashkul
Каъба Kaʿba
Каъбаи мукаррама mukarram
каъбапўш qisvat
каъбатош hajar-i asvad
Каъбатулло Kaʿbatullah
Каъбатуллоҳ Kaʿbatullah
Каҳф сураси Kahf
кироминкотибин kiramin katibin
кисва qisvat
кисса-ул анбиё qisas al-anbiya
китоб kitab
кифоя kifaya
коинот ka'inat
комил akmal
комил инсон insan-i kamil
Корбало Karbala
котиб katib
кофир kafir
кофиристон kafiristan
Кофирун сураси Kafirun
коҳин kahin
кулоҳ kulah
курси kursi
куфр kufr
куфрон kufran
куффор kuffar
лаббай labbay
лаббайка labbayka
лавҳ lavh
лавҳал маҳфуз lavh al-mahfuz, al-
лазо laza
ла илоҳа иллаллаҳ Муҳаммадин расулиллоҳ la ilaha illa allah va muhammadun rasulullah
лайлатилқадр Laylat al-Qadr
лайлатулқадр Laylat al-Qadr
лайн laʿin
лафзан ва маънан lafzan va maʿnan
лафзи куфр lafz-i kufr
лаънат laʿnat
Лаҳаб сураси Lahab
лаҳад lahid[1]
лаҳад lahid[2]
лиллаҳ lillah
лифофа lifafa
ло илоҳа иллоллоҳ Муҳаммадин расулиллоҳ la ilaha illa allah va muhammadun rasulullah
ломакон La makan
лот Lat
Лут Lut
Луқмон Luqman[1]
Луқмони Ҳаким Luqman[1]
Луқмон сураси Luqman[2]
мавжуд mavjud
мавжудот mavjudat
мавзуъ mavzuʿ
мавлавий mavlavi
мавлид Mavlid[1]
мавлид mavlid[2]
мавло Mavla[1]
мавло mavla[2]
мавлоно mavlana
мавлуд Mavlid[1]
мавоза mavʿiza
мавъиза mavʿiza
мавқе mavqiʿ
мавқуф mavquf
мавҳум mavhum
мавҳумот mavhumat
маддоҳ maddah
Мадина Madina
Мадинаи мунаввара Madina-yi munavvara
Мадиналик madini
мадраса madrasa
мадфан madfan
мадҳия madhiya
мажзуб majzub
мажлис majlis
мажнун majnun[1]
мажнун majnun[2]
мажусий majusi
мазлум mazlum
мазмаза mazmaza
мазнуб maznib

мазҳаб mazhab[1]
мазҳаб mazhab[2]
майит mayyit
Макка Makka
маккалик makki
Макка мукаррама mukarram
Маккатулло Makkatullah
Маккатуллоҳ Makkatullah
Макка фатҳи Fath-i Makka
Маккаю мукаррама Makka al-mukarrama
макруҳ makruh
мактаб maktab
малак malak
Малик Malik[1]
малик malik[2]
Маликий Maliki
Маликия Malikiya
малоикот malakut
малойика mala'ika
малъун mal'un[2]
мамлук mamluk
мамот mamat
манасиқ manasik
манзур manzur
маниъ mani'
манкуҳа mankuha
Манот Manat
маноқиб manaqib
маноқибнома manaqibnama
мансаб musab
мансоқ mansak
мантиқ mantiq
мантиқий mantiqi
манфур manfur
манҳу manhi
маоб ma'b
маозаллоҳ ma'az allah
Маориж сураси Ma'arij
маосий ma'asi
маосил maghasil
Марва Marva
мардуд mardud
мариз намози salat al-mariz
маросим marasim
марсия marsiya
марфуъ marfu'
марфуъ сариҳан marfu' sarihan
марфуъ ҳукман marfu' hukman
Марям сураси Maryam[2]
марҳамат marhamat
марҳум marhum
Масад сураси Masad
масала mas'ala
масбуқ masbuq
Масиҳ Masih[1]
масиҳ masih[2]
масиҳи masihi
маст mast
матрука matruka
мафавқал табиат ma favq al-tabi'at
маҳдум makhdum
махзум makhdum
махлуқ makhluq
махлуқот makhluqat
махсум makhdum
мачит masjid
мачити Ақсо Masjid al-Aqsa, al-
машварат mashvarat
машкук mashkuk
машойих mashayikh
машраб mashrab
машру mashru'
машҳад mashhad
машҳадий mashhadi
машҳур mashhur
маъад ma'ad
маъбад ma'bad
маъбуд ma'bud[1]
маъбуд ma'bud[2]
маъжус majus
маъжусият majusiyat
маъзун ma'zun
маъзур ma'zur
маълун Mal'un[1]
маъмур ma'mur
маънавий ma'navi
маънавият ma'naviya
маънан ma'nan
маърака ma'raka
маърифат ma'rifat[1]
маърифат ma'rifat[2]
маъруф ma'ruf
маъсум ma'sum
маъюб ma'yub
мақбара maqbara[1]
мақбара maqbara[2]
мақом maqam
мақоми Иброҳим Maqam-i Ibrahim
мақсура maqsura
мақтул maqtul
мақтуъ maqtu'
мағлуб maghlub
мағриб maghrib
мағриб намози salat al-maghrib
мағфират maghfirat
маҳалла mahalla
маҳафатулла mahafatullah
маҳбус mahbus
Маҳди Mahdi
маҳкам mahkam
маҳкама mahkama
маҳкамаи кубро mahkama-yi kubra
маҳкум mahkum
маҳр mahr[1]
маҳр mahr[2]
маҳрам maharim[1]
маҳрам maharim[2]
маҳрам mahram
маҳрум mahrum
маҳси mahsi
маҳфил mahfil
маҳшар mahshar
маҳшаргоҳ mahshargah
мезана mizana
мезон mizan[1]
Мезон Mizan[3]
мезон mizan[2]
мерос miras
меросхўр miraskhur
меърож mi'raj
меърожия mi'rajiya
меърожнома mi'rajnama
меҳроб mihrab
мизон mizan[1]
Микоил Mika'il
милк milk
милод milad
милодий miladi
Мина Mina
минбар minbar

минора manara
мир mir
мирза mirza
мирзо mirza
мирғазаб mirghazab
мисвок misvak[1]
мисвок misvak[2]
мискин miskin
Миср Misr[2]
миср misr[1]
мисри муаззам misr[1]
миқот Miqat
мовлият mavliyat
моддиюн maddiyun
мозор mazar
мозористон mazaristan
Моида сураси Ma'ida
мол mal
Моликия Malikiya
Моликул-Мулк Malik al-Mulk
молият maliyat
Момо Ҳаво Hava
мотам matam
мотамзада matamzada
мошоллоҳ mashaallah
Моъувн сураси Ma'un
моҳпараст mahparast
муаббир mu'abbir
муаззин mu'azzin
муаккал mu'akkal
муаллим mu'allim
муаллиф mu'allif
муаррих mu'arrikh
муаққад mu'akkad
мубассир mubassir
мубораза mubaraza
муборак mubarak
мубориз mubariz
мубошир mubashir
мубошшир mubashshir
мубоҳ mubah
мубоҳаса mubahasa
мубҳам mubham
муваққат фарз farz-i muvaqqat
муваҳҳид muvahhid
мудаллас mudallas
мударрис mudarris
Муддассир сураси Muddassir
мудофаа mudafa'a
мудрик mudrik
мужассам mujassam
мужда mujda
Мужид Mujid, al-
мужовир mujavir
Мужодала сураси Mujadala
мужоҳада mujahida[1]
мужоҳид mujahid
мужоҳида mujahida[2]
мужтаҳид mujtahid[1]
мужтаҳид mujtahid[2]
Музаммил сураси Muzzammil
музаффар muzaffar
Муздалифа Muzdalifa
мукаллаф mukallaf
мукаммал mukammal
мукаррам mukarram
мукаррир mukarrir
мукофот mukafat
мукошифа mukashifa
мулк amlak
мулк mulk[1]
мулк-амлок mulk-amlak
Мулк сураси Mulk[2]
мулла mulla
муллабачча mullabachcha
мулозим mulazim
мулҳақ mulhaq
мулҳид mulhid
Мумтаҳана сураси Mumtahana
мунаввар munavvar
мунажжим munajjim
муназзал munazzal
мунақаҳат munakahat
мунақиб manaqib
мункар munkar
Мункар-Накир Munkar va Nakir
мункир munkir
муножот munajat[1]
муножот munajat[2]
муножотхона munajatkhana
мунозара munazara
мунофиқ munafiq
Мунофиқун сураси Munafiqun
мунсалик munsalik
муомалат mu'amalat
мурда murda
мурдахона murdakhana
мурдашўй murdashuy
мурдор murdar
мурид murid
мурофаа murafa'a
муроқаба muraqaba
муроҳақа murahaqa
мурсал mursal[1]
мурсал mursal[2]
мурсалин mursalin
муртад murtadd
Муртаза Murtaza
Муртазо Murtaza
муршид murshid
муршиди офоқ murshid-i afaq
мусаб musab
мусалли musalli
мусалло musalla[1]
мусалло musalla[2]
мусбат musbat
мусибат musibat
муслим muslim
муслима muslima
муслимин muslimin
муслимон musulman
муснад musnad
Мусо Musa
мусовий musavi[1]
мусодара musadara
мусолаҳа musalaha
мусофаҳа musafaha
мусофир musafir
мусофир намози salat al-musafir
мустабид mustabidd
мустажоб mustajab
мустакроҳ mustakrah
Мустафо Mustafa
мусташрик mustashrik
мустаҳоб mustahabb
мусулмон musulman
мусурмон musulman
мутааббид muta'abbid
мутаассиб muta'assib
мутавалли mutavalli
мутаваллият mutavalliyat
мутаворрий mutavarri'
мутавотир mutavatir
мутадайин mutadayyin

мутакаллим mutakallim
мутанассир mutanassir
мутасаввиф mutasavvif
Мутаффифун сураси Mutaffifin
муташайх mutashayyikh
мутаҳҳар mutahhar
мутлоқ mutlaq
мутолаа mutala'a
муттасил muttasil
муфассал mufassal
муфассир mufassir
муфсид mufsid[1]
муфсид mufsid[2]
муфсит mufsid[1]
муфти mufti
муфтий mufti
муфтир muftir
мухаддарат mukhaddara
мухлис mukhlis
мухолифатул ҳаводис mukhalifat lil-havadis
мухтасар mukhtasar
мухторият mukhtariyat
мушкулкушод mushkilkushad
мушоҳида mushahida
мушрик mushrik
муъаввизатайн Mu'avvizatayn
муъид mu'id
муътамир mu'tamir
муқаддас muqaddas
муқаллид muqallid
муқарраб muqarrab
муқим muqim
муқовала muqavala
муҳаббат muhabbat
муҳаддис muhaddis
муҳаллил muhallil
Муҳаммад Muhammad[1]
муҳаммадий muhammadi[1]
муҳаммадий muhammadi[2]
Муҳаммад сураси Muhammad[2]
Муҳаррам Muharram[2]
муҳаррамат muharramat
муҳаққиқлар muhaqqiq
муҳиб muhibb
муҳожир muhajir
муҳожират muhajarat
муҳожирун muhajirin
муҳокама muhakama
муҳораба muharaba
муҳосара muhasara
муҳсин muhsin
муҳтади muhtadi
муҳтазир muhtazir
муҳтасиб muhtasib[1]
муҳтасиб muhtasib[2]
мўжиза mu'jiza[1]
мўмин mu'min[1]
мўмина mu'mina
Мўминлар сураси Mu'minin
Мўмин сураси Mu'min[2]
мўсовий musavi[2]
мўъмин mu'min[1]
мўъмина mu'mina
мўътабар mu'tabar
нааш na'sh[1]
нааш na'sh[2]
Набаъ сураси Naba
наби nabi
набивот nabuvat
набиулло nabi'ullah
навкар navkar
Наврўз Navruz
нажас najas
нажасат najasat
нажасати хафиф najasat khafif
нажасати ғализ najasat ghaliz
нажот najat
нажс najis
назар nazar[1]
назар nazar[2]
назар бар қадам nazar bar qadam
назоҳат nazahat
назр nazr[1]
назр nazr[2]
наим Na'im[1]
наим na'im[2]
найран nayran
Намл сураси Naml
намоз salat
намоз namaz
намозгар salat al-'asr
намозгоҳ namazgah
намозгўй namazgu
намозхон namazkhan
Намруд Numrud
насаб nasab
насабнома nasabnama
насиб nasib
насиба nasiba
насил nasl
насиҳат nasihat
насоро nasara
насроний nasrani
насроният nasraniyat
Наср сураси Nasr
настаълиқ nasta'liq
насут nasut
насуҳ nasuh
наузибиллаҳи na'uzu billahi
наузибиллоҳи na'uzu billahi
нафас nafas
нафас солмо nafas
нафақа nafaqa
нафс nafs[1]
нафс nafs[2]
наша afyun
нақиб naqib
нақис naqis
нақлия naqliya
наҳи nahi
Наҳл сураси Nahl
наҳс nahs
наҳу nahu
неъмат ni'mat
нигоҳдошт nigah dasht
ниёз niyaz
низом nizam
никоҳ nikah
Нимруд Numrud
нисаб nisab
нисор nisar
Нисо сураси Nisa
нифос nifas
нихрир nihrir
нишалло nishalla
нишаллофуруш nishallafurush
нишолда nishalla
нишондафуруш nishallafurush
ният niyat
нозил nazil
ноиб na'ib
номашру namashru'

номаҳрам namahram
нопок napak[1]
нопок napak[2]
нораво narava
нот na't
ноти шариф na'-i sharif
нофил nafl
нофила nafila
нофила тавоф tavaf-i nafila
ношаръий nashar'i
ноҳалол nahalal
ноҳақ nahaq
нубуввот nubuvvat
нур nur[1]
нури аршулло nur-i 'arshullah
Нур сураси Nur[2]
нусрат nusrat
нутқ nutq
нушур nushur
Нуҳ Nuh[1]
Нуҳ сураси Nuh[2]
обдаст abdast
обдаста abdasta
обдастхона abdastkhana
обид 'abid
обида abida
обида 'abida
оби Замзам ab-i Zamzam
оби ҳаёт ab-i hayat
овмийн amin[1]
овмин amin[1]
Од 'Ad
Одам Adam
Одам Ато Adam
одат 'adat
одил 'adil
Ойша 'A'isha
олам 'alam[1]
Ол-и Имрон сураси Al-i Imran
олий або al-i aba
олим 'alim
Оллоакбар Allahu akbar
оллоёр allahyar
Оллоҳ ё Оллоҳ Allah ya Allah
омин Amin[2]
омин amin[1]
омонат amanat
омончилик amniyat
ориф 'arif
осий 'asi
осмон asman
оташ atash
оташпараст atashparast
охират akhirat
охират ботқоғи akhirat batqaghi
охирзамон akhir zaman
охун akhund
охунд akhund
ошиқ 'ashiq
оят ayat
ояти карима ayat-i karima
оятул курси ayat al-kursi
оятуллоҳ ayatullah
оятул муташабиҳот ayat al-mutashabihat
оятул муҳкамат ayat al-muhkamat
оқибат 'aqibat
оқибат 'uqba
оҳад ahad
паём payam
пайғамбар payghambar
пайғом paygham
паранжи paranja
парвардигор Parvardigar
пари pari
парихон parikhan
парихонлик parikhani
пешин salat al-zuhr
пешин намози salat al-zuhr
пешқадам pishqadam
пир pir
пири муғон pir-i mughan
пок pak
пора para
порсо parsa
пули Сирот Sirat[2]
пули сирот pul-i sirat
пут put
путпараст putparast
путхона putkhana
раб Rabb
Раббано Rabbana
Рабби Rabbi
Раббил оламин Rabb al-'alamayn
Раббил Фалак Rabb al-Falak
раббим Rabb
раббоний rabbani
рабу ал-аввал Rabi' al-avval
рабу ал-охир Rabi' al-akhir
Равза Ravza
Равзойи мутаҳҳар Ravza-yi mutahhar
раво rava
радд radd
радиаллоҳу анҳу razi allahu 'anhu
ражаб Rajab
ражим rajim
ражм rajm
ражо raja
разиаллоҳу анҳу razi allahu 'anhu
раис ra'is[1]
раис ra'is[2]
ракат rak'at
ракъат rak'at
рамазон Ramazan
Рамазон байрами 'Id al-Fitr
раммол rammal
расм rasm-rusum
расм-русум rasm-rusum
расул rasul
расулона rasulana
Расулуллоҳ Rasulullah
Раъд сураси Ra'd
раъй ra'i
рақс raqs
рағойиб ragha'ib
рағойиб намози salat al-ragha'ib
раҳбон rahban
раҳбонийлик rahbaniyat
раҳийм rahim
раҳим rahim
раҳимли rahim
раҳм rahm
раҳмат rahmat
раҳматли rahmati
раҳмоний rahmani
Раҳмон сураси Rahman
рибо riba
ривоят rivayat

ридо rida[1]
ридо rida[2]
риё riya
риёзат riyazat
риёкор riyakar
рижоал ғайб rijal-i ghayb
Ризвон Rizvan
ризвонуллаҳу алайҳи rizvanullah ʻalayhi[2]
ризо riza[1]
ризо riza[2]
ризқ rizq
ринд rind
риоя riʻaya
рисола risala
рисолат risalat
ришват rishvat
робита rabita
ровий ravi
роҳиб rahib
роҳил rahil
рубобият rububiyat
руку rukuʻ
Рум Rum[1]
Рум сураси Rum[2]
рутба rutba
рухсат rukhsat
рухсатнома rukhsatnama
Руҳ Ruh[2]
руҳ ruh[1]
руҳий ruhi
руҳоний ruhani
руҳоният ruhaniyat
Руҳул-Амин Ruh al-Amin
Руҳуллоҳ Ruhullah
Руҳул Қуддус Ruh al-Quddus
рўза ruza
Рўза байрами ʻId al-Fitr
рўзи жазо ruz-i jaza
Сабаъ сураси Saba
сабр sabr[1]
сабр sabr[2]
сабъаи самовот sabʻi samavat
савмаъа savmaʻa
савоб savab[1]
савоб savab[2]
савоб savab[3]
Савр Savr
садақа sadaqa
садр sadr[1]
садр sadr[2]
садри аъзам sadr[1]
сажда sajda[1]
саждагоҳ sajdagah
саждайи тиловат sajda-yi tilavat
Сажда сураси Sajda[2]
сазойи sazayi
сай saʻi
сайид sayyid
саййийа sayyi'a
сайъи sayyi'a
салават salavat
салавот salavat
салаф salaf
салафи солиҳин salaf-i salihin
салб salb
салиб salb
салиб salib
салибия salibiya
салиблар salibiyun
салла dastar
салла salla
Саллаллоҳу алайҳи васаллам salla allahi ʻalayhu va sallam
саловати нофила salavat-i nafila
салом salam
саломалайкум salam ʻalaykum
салот salat
Салсабил Salsabil
самий samiʻ
само sama
само samaʻ[1]
само samaʻ[2]
самовий samavi
самовий динлар din-i samavi
Самуд Salih[2]
Самуд Samud
сана sana[1]
санаи шамсия sana-yi shamsiyya
санаи қамария sana-yi qamariyya
санайи милодия sana-yi miladiyya
санайи ҳижрия sana-yi hijriyya
санам sanam
сано sana[2]
Сара Sara
Саратон Saratan
сар об sar-ab
сарроф sarraf
сарф sarf
Сафа Safa
сафар Safar
сафар дар ватан safar dar vatan
сафар намози salat al-safar
сафийуллоҳ safi'ullah
сафойил safa'il
сафолият safaliyat
Сафо тоғи Safa
Саф сураси Saff
саховат sakhavat
саъй saʻi
сақар Saqar
сақофат saqafat
сағир saghir
саҳар salat al-subh
саҳар sahar
саҳв sahv
саҳир sahir
саҳифа sahifa
саҳиҳ sahih
саҳоба sahaba
саҳобий sahabi
семурғ Simurgh
семурғ қуши Simurgh
сеҳр sihr
сеҳрбоз sihirbaz
сеҳрий sihri
сибғатиллоҳ sibghatullah
сиддиқ siddiq
Сидратал мунтаҳа Sidrat al-muntaha
сиёрал наби siyar al-nabi
сижжил sijjil
сийрат sirat[1]
сийрати Муҳаммад sirat[1]
силоҳ silah
силсила silsila[1]
силсила silsila[2]
силсиланома silsilanama
сира sirat[1]
Сирот Sirat[2]

Сирот кўприги Sirat[2]
соат sa'at
Сод сураси Sad
сойир sa'ir
Солиҳ Salih[2]
солиҳ salih[1]
соф saf
ссбир sabir
субут subutiya
субутия subutiya
субҳа subha
субҳ намози salat al-subh
субҳон subhan
субҳоналло subhanallah
субҳоналлоҳ subhanallah
субҳоно ва таалло subhanahu va ta'ala
субҳонока subhanaka
суврат surat
судур sudur
судхўр sudkhur
судхўрлик sud
sужуд sujud
суиқасд sui qasd
сукра sukra
сукут sukut
Сулаймон Sulayman
султон sultan
сулук suluk
сулҳ sulh
сунан sunan
Сунбула Sunbula
суннан sunan
суннат sunna
суннат sunnat[1]
суннат sunnat[2]
суннатул муаққада sunnat mu'akkada
суннатул ғайрил муаққада sunnat ghayr-i mu'akkada
сунни sunni
сунний sunni
сур sur
сура sura
сурат surat
сурной surnay
сутра sutra
суфтажо suftajah
суҳуф suhuf
сўфи sufi[1]
сўфи sufi[2]
тааббуд ta'abbud[1]
тааббуд ta'abbud[2]
таавиз ta'avvuz
таассуб ta'assub
табаррук tabarruk
табауттобеин taba'-i tabi'in
табаъа тобиъин taba'-i tabi'in
Таббот Tabbat
табиат tabi'at
табиб tabib
табииюн tabi'iyun
таблиғот tablighat
таборак tabarak
табрик tabrik
таважуҳ tavajjuh
таваккал tavakkul[1]
таваккул tavakkul[2]
таварруқ tavarruq
таваққуф tavaqquf
таваҳҳум tavahhum
тавба tavba[1]
тавба tavba[2]
Тавба сураси Tavba[3]
тавба-тазарру tavba-tazarru
тавба қилувчи ta'ib
тавиз ta'viz[1]
тавиз ta'viz[2]
тавозе tavazi'
таворих tavarikh
тавоф tavaf[1]
тавоф tavaf[2]
тавофи зиёрат tavaf-i ziyarat
тавофи садр tavaf-i sadr
тавофи қудум tavaf-i qudum
Таврот Tavrat
тавсим tavsim
тавсиф tavsif
тавфиқ tavfiq
тавқ tavq
тавқи лаънат tavq
тавҳид tavhid[1]
тавҳид tavhid[2]
тадайин tadayyun[2]
тадаюн tadayyun[1]
тадлис tadlis
тадфин tadfin
тажалли tajalli
тажвид tajvid
тазаҳуд tazahhud
тазвиж tazavij
тазкиратул авлиё tazkirat al-avliya
тазкия tazkiya
тайййба tayyiba[1]
тайййба tayyiba[2]
такбир takbir
такбир takbir al-tahrima
такбири тахрим takbir al-tahrima
Таквир сураси Takvir
такия takiya
такия takya
таклиф taklif
Такосур сураси Takasur
такрир takrir
такфин takfin
такфир takfir
такя takya
талваса talvasa
талоқ talaq[1]
талоқнома talaqnama
Талоқ сураси Talaq[2]
талоқ хати talaq khat
талқин talqin[1]
талқин talqin[2]
талқин talqin[3]
тамаки dukhan[2]
таматтуъ tamattu'
тамжид tamjid
Тамуқ Tamuq
танаввуъ tanavvu'
танавия tanavvu'
танакуҳ tanakuh
танассир tanassur
танасух tanasukh
Тангри Tangri
танзиҳ tanzih[1]
танзиҳ tanzih[2]
тансир tansir
тансур tansir
таоло ta'ala
таом ta'am
таохир ta'akhir

тарака taraka
тарбия tarbiya
тарих tarikh[1]
тарих tarikh[2]
тариқат tariqat[1]
тариқат tariqat[2]
тарки дунё tark-i dunya
тарових salat al-taravih
тарових taravih
тарових намози salat al-taravih
тарових намози taravih
тарсо tarsa
тарғиб targhib
тарғибот targhibat
тасаввуф tasavvuf
тасаддиқ tasadduq
тасаддуқ tasadduq
тасаттур tasattur
тасбеҳ tasbih
тасби tasbih
тасвиб tasvib
тасир tashir
таслим taslim[1]
таслим taslim[2]
Тасним Tasnim
татавву tatavvuʿ
тафрид tafrid
тафсир tafsir
тахрим tahrim[1]
тахримий tahrimi
Тахрим сураси Tahrim[2]
ташаҳуд tashahhud
ташбиҳ tashbih
ташноб tashnab
ташри tashriʿ[1]
ташриқ tashriq
ташриғ tashriʿ[1]
ташриғ tashriʿ[2]
таъабирнома taʿbirnama
таъбир taʿbir
таъвиз taʿviz[1]
таъдил taʿdil
таъдили аркон taʿdil-i arkan
таъзим taʿzim
таъзир taʿzir
таъзия taʿziya
таъкид ta'kid
таълим taʿlim
таълимот taʿlimat
таяммум tayammum
тақаддис taqaddus
тақаддус taqaddus
тақвим taqvim
тақвин takvin
тақво taqva
тақводор taqvadar
тақдир taqdir
тақдир taqdir
тақдис taqdis[1]
тақдис taqdis[2]
тақий taqi
тақия taqiya
тақлид taqlid[1]
тақлид taqlid[2]
тақсир taqsir
Тағобун сураси Taghabun
таҳажжуд tahajjud
таҳажжуд намози salat al-tahajjud
таҳаммул tahammul
таҳлил tahlil
таҳмид tahmid
таҳорат taharat
таҳоратсиз bi taharat
таҳоратхона taharatkhana
таҳриж takhrij
таҳрир tahrir
таҳриф tahrif
таҳя tahiyat
таҳқиқи иймон tahqiqi iman
таҳқиқи имон tahqiqi iman
тиб tibb
тижорат tijarat
тилмиз tilmiz
тиловат tilavat
тилсим tilsim[1]
тилсим tilsim[2]
тилсим tilsim[3]
тоат taʿat
тоат-ибодат taʿat-ʿibadat
тобеъ tabiʿ
тобеъин tabiʿin
тобеъи табиин tabaʿ-i tabiʿin
тобиъин tabiʿin
тобут tabut
тоиб ta'ib
тоифа ta'ifa
тойиб ta'ib
тойиба tayyiba[1]
толе taliʿ
толиб talib
Ториқ сураси Tariq
Тоҳа сураси Ta ha
тоҳир tahir
Туба Tuba
тумор tumar
турба turba
турбат turba
туғ tugh[1]
туғ tugh[2]
тўфон tufan
Увайс ал-Қараний Vays al-Qarani
удум udum
Ужмах Ujmakh
узлат ʿuzlat
узр ʿuzr[1]
узр ʿuzr[2]
уламо ʿulama
Умар ʿUmar
умаро umara
Уммалмўмин Umm al-mu'minin
Уммалмўминин Umm al-mu'minin
уммат ummat
умми ummi
умр ʿumr
умра ʿumra
унс uns
унсур unsur
урф ʿurf
урфи саҳиҳ ʿurf sahih
урфи фосид ʿurf fasid
Усмон ʿUsman
устод ustad
устоз ustaz
усул usul[1]
усул usul[2]
усули жадид usul-i jadid
усули хамса usul-i khamsa
усули қадим usul-i qadim
уқибат ʿuqubat[1]
уқибат ʿuqubat[3]
уқубат ʿuqubat[2]

Уғон Ughan
фазл fazl
файласуф faylasuf
фалак falak[1]
фалак falak[2]
фалақ falaq[1]
Фалақ сураси Falaq[2]
фалсафа falsafa
фан fann
фано fana
фарёд faryad
фарз farz
фарзи айн farz-i ʻayn
фарзиайн farz-i ʻayn
фарзи доим farz-i da'im
фарзи кифоя farz-i kifaya
фарзи муваққат farz-i muvaqqat
фарид farid
фаридал аср farid al-ʻasr
фаришта farishta
фароиз fara'iz[1]
фароиз fara'iz[2]
фарсах farsakh
фаруқ faruq
фасод fasad
фасот fasad
фатво fatva
фатр fatir[2]
Фатҳ сураси Fath
фақир faqir[1]
фақир faqir[2]
фақиҳ faqih
фақоҳат faqahat
фақр faqr
фаҳш fahsh
фидо fida
фидойи fida'i
фидокор fidakyar
фидя fidya
фикрат fikrat
Фил сураси Fil
Фиравн Firaʻun
фирдавс Firdaus
фирқа firqa
фисқ fisq
фитна fitna
фитр fitr[1]
фитр fitr[2]
фитра fitra
фитрат fitrat
фитр закоти zakat al-fitr
фиқҳ fiqh
фожир fajir
фозил fazil
фоиз fa'iz
фол fal
фолбин falbin
фолгўй falgu
фолнома falnama
фоний fani
фосиқ fasiq
Фотима Fatima
Фотир сураси Fatir[1]
фотиҳа fatiha[1]
фотиҳа fatiha[2]
фотиҳагўй fatihagu
фотиҳа сураси Fatiha[3]
фоҳиша fahisha
фузало fuzala
Фурқон Furqan[1]
Фурқон сураси Furqan[2]
Фуссилат Fussilat
футуват futuvat
хабар akhbar
хабар khabar
хабари воҳид khabar-i vahid
хавориж khavarij
хаворижлар khavarij
хавф khavf
хавф намози salat al-khavf
Хадича Khadija
Хайбар Khaybar
хайир khayr[2]
хайр khayr[1]
хайрот khayr[1]
хайр-садақа khayr-sadaqa
халват khalvat
Халилиллоҳ Khalilullah
Халиллуло Khalilullah
Халилуллоҳ Khalilullah
халифа khalifa[1]
халифа khalifa[2]
халифа khilafat[1]
Халифаи Рашидин Khulafa-yi rashidin
халифат khilafat[2]
халифат khilafat[3]
Халлоқ Khallaq
халфа khalfa[1]
халфа khalfa[2]
халқа halqa[2]
хамр khamr
харож kharaj
харажат kharaj
Харам мачити Masjid al-Haram, al-
Харун Harun
хатиб khatib
хатим khatim[2]
хатм khatm[1]
хатм khatm[2]
хат-маҳр khat-mahr
хатми сулук khatm-i suluk
хатми хўжа khatm-i khvajagan
хатми хўжагон khatm-i khvajagan
хатми Қуръон khatm[2]
хатми қутуб khatm-i kutub
хатна khatna
хато khata
хаттот hattat
хеш-ақрабо aqraba
Хизир Khizr
Хизир-Илёс Ilyas
хилват khilvat
хилватгоҳ khalvatgah
хилват дар анжуман khalvat dar anjuman
хилватнишин khalvatgah
хилофа khilafat[1]
Хилофатул Рашидин Khulafa-yi rashidin
хилофи шаърий khilaf-i sharʻ
хилхона khilkhana
хилқат khilqat
хирож kharaj
хирқа khirqa[1]
хирқа khirqa[2]
хирқаи саодат khirqa-yi saʻadat
хирқаи шариф khirqa-yi sharif
хирқапўш khirqa push
хитан khitan
хонақоҳ khanaqa
хотам khatim[1]

хоч khach
хочпараст khachparast
Худо Khuda
Худованд Khudavand
Худовандо khudavanda
худогўй khudaguy
худогўй khudaygu
художўй khudajuy
Худой khuday
худойи khudayi
худойихона khudaykhana
худопараст khudaparast
худотарс khudatars
хул khulʿ
Хулд Khuld
хулия hilya
хулияи саодат hilya-yi saʿadat
хулияи шариф hiliya-yi sharif
хулқ khulq
хумс khums
хунаса khunsa
хурма khurma
хурмо khurma
хурофот khurafat
хусуф намози salat al-khusuf
хутба khutba
хуфтон salat al-ʿisha
хуфтон khuftan
хуфтон намози salat al-ʿisha
хўжа khvaja[1]
хўжа khvaja[2]
хўжазода khvajazada
чалма chalma
чаҳорёр Chahar yar
чилдон childan
чилла chilla[1]
чилла chilla[2]
чиллаёсин chillayasin
чиллахона chillakhana[1]
чиллахона chillakhana[2]
чилтан chiltan
чодира chadra
Шаввал Shavval
шавқ shavq
шажара shajara
шайид shahid[2]
шайтанат shaytanat
шайтон Shaytan
шайтонилаин shaytan al-ʿayn
шайтони лайин shaytan al-ʿayn
шайтони лаъин shaytan al-ʿayn
шайх shaykh
шайхул ислом shaykh al-islam[1]
шайхул ислом shaykh al-islam[2]
шак shakk
шаккок shakkak
шак куни shak
шаклик shaklik
шам shamʿ
шамдон shamʿdan
шамойил shama'il
шамойили шариф shama'il-i sharifa
шариат shariʿat
шарик sharik
шариф sharif
шарифа sharifa
шароб sharab
шарр sharr
Шарх сураси Inshirah
шаръ sharʿ
шаръан sharʿan
шаръий sharʿi
шафоат shafaʿat
Шаъбон Shaʿban
шаҳват shahvat
шаҳид shahid[2]
шаҳидлик shahadat[2]
шаҳодат shahadat[1]
шаҳодат shahadat[2]
шаҳри Рамазон shahr-i ramazan
шиа shiʿi
ширк shirk
шифо shifa
Шиш Shis
шогирд tilmiz
шогирд shagird
Шоймардон Shah-i mardan
шок оқшоми shak
шом намози salat al-maghrib
Шофий Shafiʿi[1]
шофий Shafiʿi[2]
шофийлик Shafiʿiya
шоҳид shahid[1]
шоҳидлик shahadat[1]
Шоҳимардон Shah-i mardan
Шуайб Shuʿayb
Шуаро сураси Shuʿara
шубҳа shubha
шузуз shuzuz
шукр shukr
шуур shuʿur
шўро shura [1]
Шўро сураси Shura[2]
шўҳрат shuhrat
эсма ул ҳусна asma al-husna
эшон ishan
эшонзода ishanzada
эътимод iʿtimad
эътиқод iʿtiqad
эҳром ihram
эҳсон ihsan[1]
эҳтидо ihtida
Юнус Yunus[1]
Юнус сураси Yunus[2]
Юсуф Yusuf[1]
Юсуф сураси Yusuf[2]
Юшо Yushaʿ
Яздон Yazdan
Яратган Yaratqan
ярҳамукалло yarhamukallah
ярҳамукаллоҳ yarhamukallah
Яфас Yafis
Яъжуж-Маъжуж Ya'juj va Ma'juj
Яҳё Yahya
яҳуд yahud
яҳудий yahudi
ўлакса murdar
қабила qabila
қабиҳ qabih
қабоҳат qabahat
қабр qabr
қабр азоби ʿazab-i qabr
қабристон qabristan
қабрлар qubur
қавм qavm
қавом qavam
Қавс Qavs
қадам qadam
қадамгоҳ qadamgah
қадамжой qadamjay
қадар taqdir
қадим Qadim, al-

қадимий qadimi
қадимчилик usul-i qadim
Қадр сураси Qadr[1]
қазо qaza
қазойи муаллақ qaza-yi mu'allaq
қайта тирилиш nushur
қал qal
қалам qalam[1]
қалам qalam[2]
Қалам сураси Qalam[3]
қаландар qalandar
қаландархона qalandarkhana
қалб qalb
қалин sidaq[1]
Қамар сураси Qamar
қамис qamis
қандил кечаси қилинадиган намоз salat al-ragha'ib
қандил намози salat al-ragha'ib
қаноат qana'at
қарз qarz
қасам qasam
қасд qasd
қасис qasis
қасос qasas[1]
қасос qisas
Қасос сураси Qasas[2]
қатл qatl
қатл этилган maqtul
қатъият qat'iyat
қаъда qa'da
қаҳир Qahr, al-
қибла qibla
қиблагоҳ qiblagah
қибланома qiblanama
қиём qiyam
қиёмат qiyamat[1]
қиёмат аломатлари 'alamat
қиёмат ишоратлари ashrat-i sa'at
Қиёмат сураси Qiyamat[2]
қиёмат қойим qiyamat qa'im
қиёс qiyas
қиёси фуқаҳо qiyas-i fuqaha
қимор qimar
қироат qira'at
қироати қурро qurra
қироатхона qira'atkhana
қирон qiran
қирқ ҳадис hadis-i arba'in
қисва qisvat
қисмат qismat
қиссасул анбиё qisas al-anbiya
Қитмир Qitmir
Қобил Qabil
қози qazi
қозизода qazizada
қозихона qazikhana
қоида qa'ida
қомат qamat
қонун qanun
қори qari
қорихона qarikhana
Қоф сураси Qaf[1]
Қоф тоғи Qaf[2]
қубба qubba
Қуббатул Ислом Qubbat al-Islam
қубур qubur
қуддус quddus
Қуддуси шариф Quds, al-
қудрат qudrat
қудс quds
қудси qudsi
қудсият qudsiyat
қулҳу Аллоҳу Аҳад qul hu allah ahad
қунут qunut
қурайш Quraysh[1]
Қурайш сураси Quraysh[2]
қурб qurb
қурбон qurban
Қурбон байрами 'Id al-Azha
Қурбон байрами Qurban Bayrami
қурбонлик qurban
қурро qurra
Қуръон Qur'an
Қуръони Азим Qur'an-i 'Azim
Қуръони Карим Qur'an-i Karim
Қуръони хатим Qur'an khatima
қуръонхона qur'ankhana
қусуф qusuf
қусуф намози salat al-qusuf
қутб qutb
Ғавсал Аъзам Ghavs al-A'zam
ғазаб ghazab
ғазавот ghazavat
ғазо ghaza
ғаййа Ghayya
ғайридин ghayr-i din
ғайридиний ghayr-i din
ғайримашру ghayr-i mashru'
ғайри муаккад ghayr-i mu'akkad
ғайри шаръий ghayr-i shar'i
ғам ghamm[1]
ғам ghamm[2]
Ғамбар Ghambar
ғамхона bayt al-ahzan
ғанимат ghanimat
ғарблик шарқшунос mustashrik
ғариб gharib[1]
ғариб gharib[2]
ғасл ghasl
ғасп ghasb
ғассол ghassal
ғафлат ghaflat[1]
ғафлат ghaflat[2]
ғилмон ghilman
ғози ghazi
ғозий ghazi
ғофил ghafil
Ғофир сураси Ghafir
Ғошия сураси Ghashiya
ғул ghul
ғурбат ghurbat
ғуслхона ghuslkhana
ғусул ghusl
ҳабаш habash
Ҳабашистон Habashistan
Ҳабиб Habib
Ҳабибуллоҳ Habibullah
Ҳабил Habil
ҳавожим havajim
ҳавожис havajis
ҳавола havala
ҳаворилар havari
ҳадд hadd
ҳадди закр hadd-i zakr
ҳадди зино hadd-i zina
ҳадди сиркат hadd-i sirkat
ҳадди шурб hadd-i shurb

ҳадди қазиф hadd-i qazf
Ҳадид сураси Hadid
ҳадис hadis
ҳадиси қудсий hadis-i qudsi
ҳаёё-ҳу hay ya hu
ҳаёти абадия hayat-i abadiya
ҳаёт-мамот mamat
ҳаж hajj[1]
ҳажарул асвод hajar-i asvad
ҳаж бадал hajj badal
ҳаж намози salat al-hajat
Ҳаж сураси Hajj[2]
ҳазрат hazrat
Ҳазрати Али ʻAli
ҳазрати Билол Bilal
ҳазрати Довуд Da'ud
Ҳазрати Муҳаммад Muhammad[1]
ҳазрати Умар ʻUmar
Ҳайдар Haydar
ҳайё-ҳу hay ya hu
ҳайиз hayz
ҳайит ʻid
ҳайит намози salat al-ʻidayn
ҳаким hakim
ҳалим halim
ҳалимхона halimkhana
ҳалиса halim
ҳалисахона halimkhana
ҳалиф halif
ҳалл hall
ҳалол halal
ҳалқа halqa[1]
ҳамал Hamal
ҳамду сано sana[2]
ҳанафий Hanafi
Ҳанафия Hanafiya
ҳанбалий Hanbali
Ҳанбалия Hanbaliya
ҳаниф hanif[1]
ҳаниф hanif[2]
ҳарам haram[2]
ҳарам harim
ҳариф дуо harif duʻa
ҳаром haram[1]
ҳаром muharram[1]
ҳаромзода haramzada
ҳарому занний haram zanni
ҳарому қатъий haram qatʻi
Ҳарут ва Марут Harut va Marut
Ҳасан Hasan[3]
ҳасан hasan[1]
ҳасан hasan[2]
ҳасса ʻasa
ҳафтияк haft-i yak
ҳашир hashr[1]
Ҳашр сураси Hashr[2]
ҳаштияк hasht-i yak
Ҳақ Haqq[2]
ҳақ haqq[1]
ҳақиқат haqiqat
Ҳақ Расул Haqq Rasul
Ҳақ таалло Haqq Taʻala
ҳаққуллоҳ haqqullah
ҳаққул яқин haqq al-yaqin
Ҳибатулоҳ Hibatullah
ҳибоҳ hiba
ҳидоят hidayat
ҳижоб hijab
ҳижра hijra
ҳижрат hijra
ҳижрий hijri
ҳижрия hijriya
Ҳижр сураси Hijr
ҳизб hizb[1]
ҳизб hizb[2]
ҳизбу шайтон hizb al-shaytan
ҳийлаи шаръий hila-yi sharʻi
ҳикмат hikmat
ҳилол hilal
ҳиммат himmat
ҳирз hirz
ҳисс hiss
ҳисси ботиний hiss-i batin
ҳисси зоҳири hiss-i zahiri
ҳовия haviya
ҳовл havl
Ҳожар Hajar
ҳожари асвад hajar-i asvad
ҳожи hajji
ҳол hal
ҳомила hamila
ҳомиладор hamiladar
Ҳомон Haman
Ҳотамул Анбиё Khatam al-anbiyah
Ҳотамул набиин Khatam al-nabiyin
ҳофиз hafiz
ҳу Hu
Ҳуд Hud[1]
Ҳуд сураси Hud[2]
ҳудуд hudud
ҳужра hujra
Ҳужурот сураси Hujurat
ҳукм hukm
ҳукмиллоҳ bihukmillah
ҳукми Самад hukm-i samad
ҳукумат hukumat
ҳулла hulla
ҳулул hulul
Ҳумаза сураси Humaza
ҳур hur
ҳури huri
Ҳусайн Husayn
ҳусн husn
ҳусни адаб husn-i adab
ҳусни ахлоқ husn-i akhlaq
ҳусни тарбия husn-i tarbiya
ҳуснихат husn-i khat
ҳут Hut
ҳуш дар дам khush dar dam

Uzbek Latin Index

abad abad
Abasa surasi ʻAbasa
abd ʻabd
abdal abdal[1]
abdal abdal[2]
abdal abdal[3]
Abdulla ʻAbdullah[1]
Abdulla ʻAbdullah[2]
abjad abjad
abir ʻabir
abobul qur'on abvab al-Qur'an
abror abrar
Abu abu
Abu Bakr Abu Bakr
Abu Hanifa Abu Hanifa
avliyo avliya[1]
avliyo avliya[2]
avliyozoda avliyazada
avlod avlad
avrot ʻavrat
adab adab
adan ʻadn
Ad-Dorr Zarr, al-
adl, adolat ʻadl
ado ahliyati ahliyyat-i ada
adovat ʻadavat
adolat ʻadalat
ayon ayan
ajal ajal
ajam ʻajam
ajnabiy ajnabi
ajr ajr
aza ʻaza
azayimxon ʻazayimkhan
Azza va Jalla ʻAzza va Jalla
aziz ʻaziz[1]
aziz ʻaziz[2]
azob azab
azobi kabir ʻazab al-kabir
Azozil ʻAzazil
azon azan
Azroil ʻAzra'il
Ayyub Ayyub
akmal, komil akmal
akram akram
Al-Avval Avval, al-
Al-Avfuv ʻAfuv, al-
Al-Aziz ʻAziz, al-
Al-Azim ʻAzim, al-
alayhis salom ʻalayhi al-salam
Alaq surasi ʻAlaq
Al-Ahad Ahad, al-
Al-Badiy Badiʻ, al-
Al-Barr Barr, al-
Al-Basir Basir, al-
Al-Bois Baʻis, al-
Al-Bori Bari, al-
Al-Bosit Basit, al-
Al-Botin Batin, al-
Al-Boqiy Baqi, al-
al-Vadud Vadud, al-
al-Vakil Vakil, al-
al-Valiy Vali, al-
Al-Vahhob Vahhab, al-
Al-Vojid Vajid, al-
Al-Voris Varis, al-
Al-Vosi Vasiʻ, al-
Al-Vohid Vahid, al-
Al-Jabbor Jabbar, al-
Al-Jalil Jalil, al-
Al-Jomiy Jamiʻ, al-
Aliyosa Alyasaʻ
Ali ibn Abu Tolib, Hazrati Ali ʻAli
Al-Isro surasi Isra
alif lom mim alif lam mim
Al-Kabir Kabir, al-
Al-Karim Karim, al-
Al-Kobud Qabiz, al-
Allam al g'ayub ʻAllam al-ghuyub
Al-Latif Latif, al-
alloma ʻallama
Alloh Allah
Alloh yo Alloh, Olloh yo Olloh Allah ya Allah
Allohi billahi allahi billahi
Allohu Akbar, Olloakbar Allahu akbar
Allohu a'lam Allahu aʻlam biʻl-savab
Allohu Bashirin Allahu Bashirun
Allohu Olimun Allahu ʻAlimun
Allohu! Ollohu! Allah hu
Allohu Samiun Allahu Samiʻun
Allohu taollo Allah taʻala
Al-Majid Majid, al-
Al-Malik Malik, al-
Al-Masjid al-Aqso, machiti Aqso Masjid al-Aqsa, al-
Al maschit al-Xaram, Xaram machiti Masjid al-Haram, al-
Al-Metin Matin, al-
almisoq misaq
Al-Moniy Maniʻ, al-
al-Muavvazatoni Muʻavvizatan
Al-Mubdiy Mubdiʻ, al-
Al-Muzil Muzill, al-
Al-Mumiyt Mumit, al-
Al-Muntaqiym Muntaqim, al-
Al-Musavvir Musavvir, al-
Al-Mutakabbir Mutakabbir, al-
Al-Mutaoli Mutaʻali, al-
Al-Mu'id Muʻid, al-
Al-Mu'iz Muʻizz, al-
Al-Mu'ohhir Mu'akhkhir, al-
Al-Muqaddim Muqaddim, al-
Al-Muqit Muqit, al-
Al-Muqsit Muqsit, al-
Al-Muqtadir Muqtadir, al-
Al-Mug'niy Mughni, al-
Al-Muhaymin Muhaymin, al-
Al-Muhyi Muhyi, al-
Al-Muhsiy Muhsi, al-
Al Mo'jib Mujib, al-
Al-Mo'min Mu'min, al-
Al-Odil ʻAdl, al-
Al-Oli ʻAli, al-
Al-Olim ʻAlim, al-
alomat, qiyomat alomatlari ʻalamat
Al-Oxir Akhir, al-
Al-Razzoq Razzaq, al-
Al-Sattor Sattar, al-
Al-Fattoh Fattah, al-

al Fotiha! Fatiha, al-
Al-Xabar Khabir, al-
Al-Xoliq Khaliq, al-
Al-Qayyum Qayyum, al-
Al-Qahhor Qahhar, al-
Al-Qoviy Qavi, al-
Al-Qodir Qadir, al-
Al-qoria surasi Qariʿa
Al-Quddus Quddus, al-
Al-G'aniy Ghani, al-
Al-G'afur Ghafur, al-
Al-G'affor Ghaffar, al-
Al-haaqqa surasi Haqqa
Al-Hayy Hayy, al-
Al-Hakam Hakam, al-
Al-Hakim Hakim, al-
Al-Halim Halim, al-
alhamdulilloh al-hamdullilah
Alhamdullilahu rabbil olamin al-hamdulillahi rabbi'l-ʿalamin
Al-Hamid Hamid, al-
Al-Hafiz Hafiz, al-[2]
Al-Haq Haqq, al-
Al-Hodiy Hadi, al-
Al-Hosib Hasib, al-
Al-Hofid Hafiz, al-[1]
amal ʿamal
amir amir
amirlik imarat
amirul muslimun amir al-muslimun
amirul mo'min Amir al-mu'minin
amirul umaro amir al-umara
amlok, mulk amlak
amniyat, omonchilik amniyat
amo aʿma
amr amr
amri ma'ruf amr-i Maʿruf
anal-haq ana al-haqq
anbar anbar[1]
anbiyo anbiya[1]
Anbiyo surasi Anbiya[2]
anbor anbar[2]
anvar anvar
andarun andarun
anjuman anjuman
Ankabut surasi ʿAnkabut
An-nos surasi Nas
An-Nofi Nafiʿ, al-
An-Nur Nur, al-
ansorlar ansar
Anfol surasi Anfal
An'om surasi Anʿam
anqo ʿAnqa
arafa ʿarafa
arvoh arvah
arkon arkan
arosat ʿArasat
Arofat ʿArafat
Arofat kuni ruz-i ʿarafat
Ar-Rauf Rauf, al-
Ar-Rashid Rashid, al-
Ar-Rahiym Rahim, al-
Ar-Rahmon Rahman, al-
Ar-Rofi Rafiʿ, al-
Ar-Roqib Raqib, al-
arsh ʿarsh
arshi a'lo ʿarsh-i aʿla
arshi kursi ʿarsh-i kursi
Asad Asad
asadullo Asadullah
asar asar
asir asir
asma ul husna, esma ul husna asma al-husna
asorat asarat
asr, asr namozi ʿasr[1]
asr namozi, namozgar salat al-ʿasr
As-Sabur Sabur, al-
As-Salom Salam, al-
assalomu alaykum assalamu ʿalaykum
assalomu alaykum, salomalaykum salam ʿalaykum
As-Samad Samad, al-
As-Samiy Samiʿ, al-
astag'furulloh astaghfirullah
asfalasofilun, asfalussofilin asfal al-safilin
ashob ashab
ashobi Badr ashab-i Badr
ashobi jannat ashab-i jannat
ashobi kirom ashab-i kiram
ashobi kof ashab-i kahf
At-Tavvob Tavvab, al-
attahiyat tahiyat, at-
attor ʿattar
Auzi billahi minashaytoni rojiym aʿuzu billahi min al-shaytani al-rajim
auzi billohi aʿuzu billah
Aflotun Aflatun
afsona afsana
afsun afsun
aftoda aftada
afyun, nasha afyun
axborot, xabar akhbar
axloq akhlaq
ashir ashir
ashr ʿushr
ashrati saat, qiyomat ishoratlari ashrat-i saʿat
ashraf ashraf
ashura ʿAshura[1]
ashura ʿashura[2]
Ash-Shokir Shakur, al-
Ash-Shohid Shahid, al-
a'zam aʿzam[1]
A'zam Aʿzam[2]
a'lam aʿlam
a'lam ʿalam[2]
A'lo surasi Aʿla
a'rof aʿraf[1]
A'rof surasi Aʿraf[2]
aqida ʿaqida
aqiqa ʿaqiqa
aqliyat ʿaqliyat
Aqrab ʿAqrab
aqrabo, xesh-aqrabo aqraba
ahbob ahbab
ahd, ant ʿahd
Ahzob surasi Ahzab
ahkom ahkam
ahlal viloyat ahl al-vilayat
ahli dil ahl-i dil
ahli zimmat ahl-i zimmat
ahli Islom ahl-i Islam
ahli Kitob ahl-i kitab
ahli ray ahl-i ra'y

ahli salb, ahli salib ahl-i salib
ahli Sunna ahl-i sunna
ahli tariqat ahl-i tariqat
ahliyati vujub ahliyyat-i vujub
ahli qalam ahl-i qalam
Ahmad Ahmad
ahror ahrar
Ahqof surasi Ahqaf
badal badal
badali askariy badal-i askari
badali naqdiy badal-i naqdi
badali shaxsiy badal-i shakhsi
badduo bad-duʿa
Badr, Badr jangi Badr
Bayyina surasi Bayyina
bayram bayram
bayram namozi, hayit namozi salat al-ʿidayn
bayt bayt
Baytulloh Baytullah
baytulmol bayt al-mal
Baytul muqaddas Bayt al-muqaddas
Baytul otiq Bayt al-ʿatiq, al-
bay'at bayʿat
Balad surasi Balad
balog'at balaghat
bang, bangivor bang
banda banda
bani Islom bani Islam
bani Isroil bani Isra'il[1]
Bani Isroil Bani Isra'il[2]
barakalla barakullah
barakat barakat
baroat bara'at[1]
Baroat surasi Bara'at[2]
barot barat
Barot kechasi shab-i barat
barq barq
barhaq barhaq
basir basir
Batho Batha
baxt bakht
baxshi bakhshi
baxshish bakhshish
bachcha bachcha
bachchaboz, akavachcha bachchabaz
bachchabozlik, besoqolbozlik bachchabazi
bashariyat bashariyat
Bashir Bashir
Baqara surasi Baqara
baqo baqa[1]
baqo baqa[2]
begunoh bi gunah
bediyonat, diyonatsiz bi diyanat
beimon, beiymon, imonsiz, iymonsiz bi iman
benamoz bi namaz
betahorat, tahoratsiz bi taharat
behisht bihisht
bibi bibi
Bibimaryam, Bimimayram Maryam[1]
bid'at bidʿat
bid'at bidʿat-i hasana
bid'ati sayyi bidʿat-i sayyi'a
billohi billahi
Bilqiys Bilqis
birodar biradar
bismilloh bismillah
bismillohir Rahmonir Rahiym bismillah al-Rahman al-Rahim
bisot bisat
bihabilloh bihablillah
bob bab
bovar bavar
boj baj
bozgasht baz gasht
bokira bakira
bolig' baligh
bomdod namozi bamdad
bomdod namozi, bomdod salat al-fajr
bomdod namozi, sahar, subh namozi salat al-subh
botil batil
botin batin
boqiy baqi
buzruk buzurg
Buroq Buraq
Buruj surasi Buruj
but but
butparast butparast
butxona butkhana
bo'hton buhtan
vaalaykum assalom ʿalaykim al-salam
vabol vabal
vaj vajh
vajd vajd
vaz vaʿz
Va-z-zoriyot surasi Zariyat
Vaz-zuha surasi Zuha
vazir vazir
vazifa vazifa
vakil vakil
vakolat vakalat
Val-asr surasi ʿAsr[2]
vali vali
valiahd vali ahd
valine'mat vali niʿmat
Val-layl surasi Layl
vallohi a'lamh, vallohu a'lam vallahu aʿlam
vallohi a'lam, vallohi a'lam bilsavob vallahu aʿlam bil-savab
Val-mursalot surasi Mursalat
Val-odiyot surasi ʿAdiyat
Val-fajr surasi Fajr
Va-n-najm surasi Najm
Van-noziot surasi Naziʿat
varasa varasat
varasa, voris varis
vara' varaʿ[1]
vara' varaʿ[2]
varaqa varaqa
vasan vasan
vasaniy vasani
vasvasa vasvasa
vasiyat vasiyat
vasiyatnoma vasiyatnama
vasiqa vasiqa
Va-ssaffot surasi Saffat
vatan vatan

Vat-tiyn surasi Tin
Va-t-Tur surasi Tur
vafo vafa
vafot vafat
Vash-shams surasi Shams
va'da va‘da
vaqf vaqf
vaqfa vaqfa
vahdadi vujud vahdat-i vujud
vahdaniyat vahdaniyat
vahiy, vahi vahi
vahobiylik, vahobizm Vahhabiya
vahshat vahshat
vahshiyona vahshiyana
vijdon vijdan
vildon vildan
vird vird[1]
vird vird[2]
virsa virsa
vitir namozi salat al-vitr
vitr vitr
viqor viqar
vojib vajib
vojibal vujud vajib al-vujud
voiz va‘iz
vos-vos vasvas
vosil, vasl vasl
Voqea surasi Vaqi‘a
voqif vaqif[1]
voqif vaqif[2]
vujud vujud
vuzu vuzu’
vuquf vuquf
vuqufi adadi vuquf-i ‘adadi
vuqufi zamon vuquf-i zaman
vuqufi qalbiy vuquf-i qalbi
gumbaz gumbaz
gunoh gunah
gunohkor gunahkar
go'r gur
go'riston guristan
davir davir
davo da‘va[2]
Dajjol Dajjal
Dalv Dalv
dalil dalil
dalili aqliy dalil-i ‘aqli
dalili naqliy dalil-i naqli
dalili shar'iy dalil-i shar‘i
darvesh darvish
dargoh dargah
darra darra
darsxona darskhana
darus durus
dastor, salla dastar
dasturxon dastarkhan
dastsho'y dastshuy
dafn dafn
Da'bba, dobba Dabba
da'vat da‘vat
da'vo da‘va[1]
Dahir surasi dahir
dahr dahr
dahri dun dahr-i dun
dahriy dahri
dahriylar dahriya
dev div
devon divan
devona divana
diyonat diyanat
diyonatkor diyanatkar
diydor didar
din din
dindor dindar
diniy dini
domulla, domla damulla
donishmand danishmand
dorilbaqo dar al-baqa
doril islom dar al-Islam
dorilsalom dar al-salam
doril sulh dar al-sulh
dorilsurur dar al-surur
dorilfano dar al-fana
dorilqazo dar al-qaza
dorilqasos dar al-qasas
dorilg'urur dar al-ghurur
dorilhavodis dar al-havadis
dorilharb dar al-harb
dorilhuffoz dar al-huffaz
dorulamon dar al-aman
dubba dubba
Duldul Duldul
dunyo dunya
dunyoviy dunyavi
duo du‘a[1]
duo du‘a[2]
duo du‘a[3]
duogo'y du‘agu
duodor du‘adar
duoisalom du‘a-yi salam
duoi qunut du‘a-yi qunut
duoxon du‘akhvan
durust durust
duxan, tamaki dukhan[2]
Duxon surasi Dukhan[1]
Do'zax Duzakh
do'zaxi duzakhi
do'st dust
yetim yatim
yo Alloh! ya allah
yoddosht yad dasht
yod kard yad kard
yoppirim, yo Pirim ya pirim
yor yar
yo Rabb !, yo Rabbim! ya rabbi
yo Ramazon ya ramazan
yoriolloh, yorullo yarullah
Yosin surasi Ya Sin
Yoqub Ya‘qub
Yohu yahu
jabr jabr
Jabroyil Jabra’il
Javzo Javza
javobnoma javabnama
jadid jadid
Jadiy Jadi
jazb jazb
jazba jazba
jazo jaza
Jalla Jalolloh Jalla Jalaluh
jallod jallad
jalsa jalsa
jamoa jama‘at[1]
jamoat jama‘at[2]
Jamra Jamra
jam'uljam' jam‘ al-jam‘
janda janda
Jannat Jannat
Jannatul Adn Jannat al-‘Adn
Jannatul ma'vo Jannat

al-Ma'va
Jannatul Firdavs Jannat al-Firdaus
Jannatul xuld Jannat al-Khuld
Jannatun naim Jannat al-Na'im
janob janab
janobi Haq Janab-i haqq
janoza janaza[1]
janoza janaza[2]
janoza namozi salat al-janaza
jarima jarima
jasad jasad
jafo jafa
Jahannam Jahannam
jahl jahl
jahm jahim
jahr jahr
Jibril Jibril
jiziya, juz'ya jizya
jilvai rabboniya jilva-yi rabbaniya
jin jinn[1]
jinoyat jinayat
Jin surasi Jinn[2]
Jirjis Jirjis
jihod jihad
jihodi akbar jihad-i akbar
jihodi asgar jihad-i asghar
jodu jadu
jodugar jadugar
jodugar jadugu
joiz ja'iz
joynamoz jaynamaz
jome jami'
jon jan
Josiya surasi Jasiya
johili jahili
joholiyat jahiliyat
Judiy Judi
judo juda
juz' juz'[1]
juz' juz'[2]
juz' juz'[3]
juz' juz'[4]
juma jum'a[2]
Jumad al-avval Jumada al-ula
Jumad al-oxir Jumada al-akhira
jumalik jumalik
juma namozi, jum'a jum'a[1]
juma namozi, jum'a salat al-jum'a
jumla jumla
Jum'a surasi Jum'a[3]
junun junun[1]
junun junun[2]
jurh jurh
jug'rifiya jughrafiya
juhud, juvut juhud
zabiha zabiha
zabt zabt
Zabur Zabur
zavol zaval
zaifa za'ifa
zaif, za'if za'if
Zakariyo Zakariya
zakot zakat[1]
zakotal fitr, fitr zakoti zakat al-fitr
Zalzala surasi Zilzal
zalolat zalalat
Zamzam Zamzam
zamzamiy zamzami
zanb zanb
zarzamon zar zaman
zarurat, zaruriyat zarurat
zafar zafar
Zaqqum Zaqqum
zahodat zahadat
zid zidd
ziyo ziya'
ziyorat ziyarat
ziyoratgoh ziyaratgah
ziyoratxona ziyaratkhana
ziyoratchi ziyaratchi
zikr zikr
zikri johr zikr-i jahr
zikri xufi zikr-i khafi
zikrxona zikrkhana
zikrchi zikrchi
zimmi zimmi
zindiq zindiq
zindon zindan
zino zina
zinokor zinakar
zoviya, zaviya zaviya
zolim zalim
Zoti kibriyo Zat-i kibriya
Zoti pok Zat-i pak
zohid zahid
zohir zahir
Zul-Jalolu val -Ikrom Zu'l-jalal va'l-ikram
zuljanahayn zu'l-janahayn
Zulihson Zu'l-ihsan
zulm zulm
zulmat zulmat[1]
zulmat zulmat[2]
zulm, zulum zulum
zulfiqor Zu'l-fiqar
Zulqarnayn Zu'l-Qarnayn
Zul Qifl Zu'l-Kifl
Zul-hijja Zu'l-hijja
Zumar surasi Zumar
zunnor zunnar
Zuul-qa'da Zu'l-qa'da
zufof, zifof zifaf
Zuxruf surasi Zukhruf
zuhd zuhd[1]
zuhd zuhd[2]
zuho namozi salat al-zuha
zuhr zuhr
Iblis Iblis
ibodat 'ibadat[1]
ibodat, 'ibadat[2]
ibodatgoh 'ibadatgah
ibodatxona 'ibadatkhana
iboha ibaha
ibroniy 'ibrani
Ibrohim Ibrahim[1]
Ibrohim surasi Ibrahim[2]
Id al Adha, Qurbon bayrami 'Id al-Azha
Id al Fitr, Ramazon bayrami, Ro'za bayrami 'Id al-Fitr
idda, iddat 'iddat
idom i'dam
Idris Idris
ijmo ijma'

ijmoi ummat ijmaʿ-i ummat
ijob ijab
ijobat ijabat
ijozat ijazat
ijozatnoma ijazatnama
ijtihod ijtihad
izdivoj izdivaj
izzat ʿizzat
izn izn
izor izar
iymon iman[2]
Ilyos, Xizir-Ilyos Ilyas
illat ʿillat
illo-billo illa-billah
illohiyun ilahiyun
ilm ʿilm[1]
ilm ʿilm[2]
ilmi qol ʿilm-i qal
ilmi hol ʿilm-i hal[1]
ilmi hol ʿilm-i hal[2]
ilmul aqoid ʿilm al-ʿaqa'id
iloh ilah
iloha ilaha
ilohi ilahi[1]
ilohi ilahi[3]
ilohiyot ilahiyat
ilohiy, ilohim ilahi[2]
iltijo iltija
ilhad ilhad
ilhom ilham
imom imam[1]
imom imam[2]
imom imam[3]
imom imam[4]
imomal qiblatayn imam al-qiblatayn
imomat imamat[1]
imomat imamat[2]
Imomi A'zam, Abu Hanifa Imam-i Aʿzam
imon, iymon iman[1]
Imron ʿImran[1]
Imron ʿImran[2]
injizob injizab
Injil Injil
inzol inzal
Inna a'taynaka al kavsara inna aʿtaynaka al-kavsara
inoba, inobat inabat
ins-jins ins-jins
Inson surasi Insan
insof insaf
intixob intikhab
intiqom intiqam
intiho intiha
Infitor surasi Infitar
Inshiqoh surasi Inshiqaq
inshoalloh, inshoolloh, inshollo insha'allah
iona iʿana
irim irim
iroda irada[1]
iroda irada[2]
iroda irada[3]
irodayi layazal irada-yi la yazal
irtidod irtidad
irshod irshad
irshodnoma irshadnama
isyon ʿisyan
isyonkor ʿisyankar
Iskandar Iskandar
Islom Islam
islomiyat islamiyat
Islom lashkarlari lashkar-i Islam
ismat ʿismat
ismatilla ʿismatullah
ismi a'zam ism-i aʿzam
Ismoil Ismaʿil
isnod isnad
Iso ʿIsa
isovi, isoviy ʿIsavi
isoviyat, iysoviyat, isaviyat ʿIsaviyat
isoparast, iysoparast ʿIsaparast
Isoq, Ishoq Ishaq
Isroil Isra'il
isrof israf
Isrofil Israfil
istibdod istibdad
istibro istibra
istidloli imon istidlali iman
istilohot, istilohat istilahat
istinjo istinja
istinshok istinshaq
istisloh istislah
istisno istisna
istisqo istisqa
istisqo namozi salat al-istisqa
istifor istiʿfar
istixor namozi salat al-istikhara
istishod istishhad
istiqbol istiqbal
istiqoma, istiqomat istiqamat
istig'for istighfar
istihoza istihaza
istihora istikhara
istihson istihsan
isqot isqat
itiqof iʿtikaf
itloq itlaq
itmom itmam
itoat itaʿat
ittihod ittihad[1]
ittihod ittihad[2]
ifrit ʿifrit
ifta ifta
iftitoh iftitah
iftor iftar
iffat ʿiffat
ixvon ikhvan
ixlos ikhlas[1]
Ixlos surasi Ikhlas[2]
ixtilof ikhtilaf
ishorat isharat
ishrok ishrak
ishroq ishraq
ishroq namozi salat al-ishraq
ishq ʿishq
iqob ʿiqab
iqomat iqamat
iqror iqrar[1]
iqror iqrar[2]
iqtido iqtida
ihdod, aza tutmoq ihdad
ihzor ihzar
ihson ihsan[2]
ihsor, ihsor qurboni ihsar

ihtijob ihtijab
ihtilom ihtilam
yig'i yighi
kabir kabira
Kavsar Kavsar[1]
Kavsar surasi Kavsar[2]
kadar qadar
kajraftor kajraftar
kalamulloh Kalamullah
kalima kalima
kalimago'y kalimagu
kalimai shahodat kalima-yi shahadat
kalimatulloh kalimatullah
kalisa kalisa
kalom kalam
kalomi Sharif Kalam-i Sharif
kaniz, kanizak kaniz
kanisa kanisa
karam karam
karomat karamat
karomat sohibi sahib-i karamat
kafan kafn
kafil kafil
kafil, kafolat kafalat
kaforat kaffarat
kashish kashish
kashishxona kashishkhana
kashkul kashkul
Ka'ba Ka'ba
ka'bapo'sh, qisva, kisva qisvat
Ka'batulloh, Ka'batullo Ka'batullah
Kahf surasi Kahf
kiromin kotibin kiramin katibin
kitob kitab
kifoya kifaya
koinot ka'inat
komil inson insan-i kamil
Korbalo, Karbalo Karbala
kotib katib
kofir kafir
kofiriston kafiristan
Kofirun surasi Kafirun
kohin kahin
kuloh kulah
kursi kursi
kufr kufr
kufron kufran
kuffor kuffar
labbay labbay
labbayka labbayka
lavh lavh
lavhal mahfuz lavh al-mahfuz, al-
lazo laza
la iloha illallah Muhammadin rasulilloh, lo iloha illolloh Muhammadin rasulilloh la ilaha illa allah va muhammadun rasulullah
laylatulqadr, laylatilqadr Laylat al-Qadr
layn la'in
lafzan va ma'nan lafzan va ma'nan
lafzi kufr lafz-i kufr
la'nat la'nat
Lahab surasi, Abu lahab Lahab
lahad lahid[1]
lahad lahid[2]
lillah lillah
lifofa lifafa
lomakon La makan
lot Lat
Lut Lut
Luqmon, Luqmoni Hakim Luqman[1]
Luqmon surasi Luqman[2]
mavjud mavjud
mavjudot mavjudat
mavzu' mavzu'
mavlaviy mavlavi
mavlid mavlid[2]
mavlid, mavlud Mavlid[1]
mavlo Mavla[1]
mavlo mavla[2]
mavlono mavlana
mavoza, mav'iza mav'iza
mavqe mavqi'
mavquf mavquf
mavhum mavhum
mavhumot mavhumat
maddoh maddah
Madina Madina
Madinai munavvara Madina-yi munavvara
Madinalik madini
madrasa madrasa
madfan madfan
madhiya madhiya
majzub majzub
majlis majlis
majnun majnun[1]
majnun majnun[2]
ma€usiy majusi
mazlum mazlum
mazmaza mazmaza
maznub maznib
mazhab mazhab[1]
mazhab mazhab[2]
mayit mayyit
Makka Makka
makkalik makki
Makkatullo, Makkatulloh Makkatullah
Makka fathi Fath-i Makka
Makkayu mukarrama Makka al-mukarrama
makruh makruh
maktab maktab
malak malak
Malik Malik[1]
malik malik[2]
Malikiy Maliki
Malikiya, Molikiya Malikiya
maloikot malakut
maloyika mala'ika
mal'un mal'un[2]
mamluk mamluk
mamot, hayot-mamot mamat
manasiq manasik
manzur manzur
mani' mani'
mankuha mankuha
Manot Manat
manoqibnoma manaqibnama

mansoq mansak
mantiq mantiq
mantiqiy mantiqi
manfur manfur
manhu manhi
maob ma'b
maozalloh ma'az allah
Maorij surasi Ma'arij
maosiy ma'asi
maosil maghasil
Marva Marva
mardud mardud
mariz namozi salat al-mariz
marosim marasim
marsiya marsiya
marfu' marfu'
marfu' sarihan marfu' sarihan
marfu' hukman marfu' hukman
Maryam surasi Maryam[2]
marhamat marhamat
marhum marhum
Masad surasi Masad
masala mas'ala
masbuq masbuq
masih masih[2]
masihi masihi
Masih, Isoi masih Masih[1]
mast mast
matruka matruka
mafavqal tabiat ma favq al-tabi'at
maxdum, maxsum, maxzum makhdum
maxluq makhluq
maxluqot makhluqat
machit masjid
mashvarat mashvarat
mashkuk mashkuk
mashoyix mashayikh
mashrab mashrab
mashru mashru'
mashhad mashhad
mashhadiy mashhadi
mashhur mashhur
ma'ad ma'ad
ma'bad ma'bad
ma'bud ma'bud[1]
ma'bud ma'bud[2]
ma'jus majus
ma'€usiyat majusiyat
ma'zun ma'zun
ma'zur ma'zur
ma'lun Mal'un[1]
ma'mur ma'mur
ma'naviy ma'navi
ma'naviyat ma'naviya
ma'nan ma'nan
ma'raka ma'raka
ma'rifat ma'rifat[1]
ma'rifat ma'rifat[2]
ma'ruf ma'ruf
ma'sum ma'sum
ma'yub ma'yub
maqbara maqbara[1]
maqbara maqbara[2]
maqom maqam
maqomi Ibrohim Maqam-i Ibrahim
maqsura maqsura
maqtul, qatl etilgan maqtul
maqtu' maqtu'
mag'lub maghlub
mag'rib maghrib
mag'firat maghfirat
mahalla mahalla
mahafatulla mahafatullah
mahbus mahbus
Mahdi Mahdi
mahkam mahkam
mahkama mahkama
mahkamai kubro mahkama-yi kubra
mahkum mahkum
mahr mahr[1]
mahr mahr[2]
mahram maharim[1]
mahram maharim[2]
mahram mahram
mahrum mahrum
mahsi mahsi
mahfil mahfil
mahshar mahshar
mahshargoh mahshargah
mezana mizana
mezon mizan[2]
Mezon Mizan[3]
meros miras
merosxo'r miraskhur
me'roj mi'raj
me'rojiya mi'rajiya
me'rojnoma mi'rajnama
mehrob mihrab
mizon, mezon mizan[1]
Mikoil Mika'il
milk milk
milod milad
milodiy miladi
Mina Mina
minbar minbar
minora manara
mir mir
mirza, mirzo mirza
mirg'azab mirghazab
misvok misvak[1]
misvok misvak[2]
miskin miskin
Misr Misr[2]
misr, misri muazzam misr[1]
miqot Miqat
movliyat mavliyat
moddiyun maddiyun
mozor mazar
mozoriston mazaristan
Moida surasi Ma'ida
mol mal
Molikul-Mulk Malik al-Mulk
moliyat maliyat
Momo Havo Hava
motam matam
motamzada matamzada
mosholloh mashaallah
Mo'uvn surasi Ma'un
mohparast mahparast
muabbir mu'abbir
muazzin mu'azzin
muakkal mu'akkal
muallim mu'allim
muallif mu'allif
muarrix mu'arrikh
muaqqad mu'akkad
mubassir mubassir

muboraza mubaraza
muborak mubarak
muboriz mubariz
muboshir mubashir
muboshshir mubashshir
muboh mubah
mubohasa mubahasa
mubham mubham
muvahhid muvahhid
mudallas mudallas
mudarris mudarris
Muddassir surasi Muddassir
mudofaa mudafaʻa
mudrik mudrik
mujassam mujassam
mujda mujda
Mujid Mujid, al-
mujovir mujavir
Mujodala surasi Mujadala
mujohada mujahida[1]
mujohid mujahid
mujohida mujahida[2]
mujtahid mujtahid[1]
mujtahid mujtahid[2]
Muzammil surasi Muzzammil
muzaffar muzaffar
Muzdalifa Muzdalifa
mukallaf mukallaf
mukammal mukammal
mukarram, Ka'bai mukarrama, Makka mukarrama mukarram
mukarrir mukarrir
mukofot, Alloh mukofoti mukafat
mukoshifa mukashifa
mulk mulk[1]
mulk-amlok mulk-amlak
Mulk surasi Mulk[2]
mulla mulla
mullabachcha mullabachcha
mulozim mulazim
mulhaq mulhaq
mulhid mulhid
Mumtahana surasi Mumtahana
munavvar munavvar
munajjim munajjim
munazzal munazzal
munaqahat munakahat
munaqib, manoqib manaqib
munkar munkar
Munkar-Nakir Munkar va Nakir
munkir munkir
munojot munajat[1]
munojot munajat[2]
munojotxona munajatkhana
munozara munazara
munofiq munafiq
Munofiqun surasi Munafiqun
munsalik munsalik
muomalat muʻamalat
murda murda
murdaxona murdakhana
murdasho'y murdashuy
murdor, o'laksa murdar
murid murid
murofaa murafaʻa
muroqaba muraqaba
murohaqa murahaqa
mursal mursal[1]
mursal mursal[2]
mursalin mursalin
murtad murtadd
Murtaza, Murtazo Murtaza
murshid murshid
murshidi ofoq murshid-i afaq
musab, mansab musab
musalli musalli
musallo musalla[1]
musallo musalla[2]
musbat musbat
musibat musibat
muslim muslim
muslima muslima
muslimin muslimin
musnad musnad
Muso Musa
musoviy musavi[1]
musodara musadara
musolaha musalaha
musofaha musafaha
musofir musafir
musofir namozi salat al-musafir
mustabid mustabidd
mustajob mustajab
mustakroh mustakrah
Mustafo Mustafa
mustashrik, g'arblik sharqshunos mustashrik
mustahob mustahabb
musulmon, muslimon, musurmon musulman
mutaabbid mutaʻabbid
mutaassib mutaʻassib
mutavalli mutavalli
mutavalliyat mutavalliyat
mutavorriy mutavarriʻ
mutavotir mutavatir
mutadayin mutadayyin
mutakallim mutakallim
mutanassir mutanassir
mutasavvif mutasavvif
Mutaffifun surasi Mutaffifin
mutashayx mutashayyikh
mutahhar mutahhar
mutloq mutlaq
mutolaa mutalaʻa
muttasil muttasil
mufassal mufassal
mufassir mufassir
mufsid mufsid[2]
mufsid, mufsit mufsid[1]
muftiy, mufti mufti
muftir muftir
muxaddarat mukhaddara
muxlis mukhlis
muxolifatul havodis mukhalifat lil-havadis
muxtasar mukhtasar
muxtoriyat mukhtariyat
mushkulkushod mushkilkushad
mushohida mushahida
mushrik mushrik
mu'avvizatayn Muʻavvizatayn
mu'id muʻid
mu'tamir muʻtamir

muqaddas muqaddas
muqallid muqallid
muqarrab muqarrab
muqim muqim
muqovala muqavala
muhabbat muhabbat
muhaddis muhaddis
muhallil muhallil
muhammadiy muhammadi[1]
muhammadiy muhammadi[2]
Muhammad surasi Muhammad[2]
Muhammad, Hazrati Muhammad Muhammad[1]
Muharram Muharram[2]
muharramat muharramat
muhaqkiqlar muhaqqiq
muhib muhibb
muhojir muhajir
muhojirat muhajarat
muhojirun muhajirin
muhokama muhakama
muhoraba muharaba
muhosara muhasara
muhsin muhsin
muhtadi muhtadi
muhtazir muhtazir
muhtasib muhtasib[1]
muhtasib muhtasib[2]
mo'jiza mu‘jiza[1]
mo'mina, mo''mina mu’mina
Mo'minlar surasi Mu’minin
mo'min, mo''min mu’min[1]
Mo'min surasi Mu’min[2]
mo'soviy musavi[2]
mo''tabar mu‘tabar
naash na‘sh[1]
naash na‘sh[2]
Naba' surasi Naba
nabi nabi
nabivot nabuvat
nabiullo nabi’ullah
navkar navkar
Navro'z Navruz
najas najas
najasat najasat
najasati xafif najasat khafif
najasati g'aliz najasat ghaliz
najot najat
najs najis
nazar nazar[1]
nazar nazar[2]
nazar bar qadam nazar bar qadam
nazohat nazahat
nazr nazr[1]
nazr nazr[2]
naim Na‘im[1]
naim na‘im[2]
nayran nayran
Naml surasi Naml
namoz namaz
namozgoh namazgah
namozgo'y namazgu
namozxon namazkhan
nasab nasab
nasabnoma nasabnama
nasib nasib
nasiba nasiba
nasil nasl
nasihat nasihat
nasoro nasara
nasroniy nasrani
nasroniyat nasraniyat
Nasr surasi Nasr
nasta'liq nasta‘liq
nasut nasut
nasuh nasuh
nauzibillohi, nauzibillahi na‘uzu billahi
nafas, nafas solmo nafas
nafaqa nafaqa
nafs nafs[1]
nafs nafs[2]
naqib naqib
naqis naqis
naqliya naqliya
nahi nahi
Nahl surasi Nahl
nahs nahs
nahu nahu
ne'mat ni‘mat
nigohdosht nigah dasht
niyoz niyaz
nizom nizam
nikoh nikah
Nimrud, Namrud Numrud
nisab nisab
nisor nisar
Niso surasi Nisa
nifos nifas
nixrir nihrir
nishallo, nisholda nishalla
nishallofurush, nishondafurush nishallafurush
niyat niyat
nozil nazil
noib na’ib
nomashru namashru‘
nomahram namahram
nopok napak[1]
nopok napak[2]
noravo narava
not na‘t
noti sharif na‘t-i sharif
nofil nafl
nofila nafila
nofila tavof tavaf-i nafila
noshar'iy nashar‘i
nohalol nahalal
nohaq nahaq
nubuvvot nubuvvat
nur nur[1]
nuri arshullo nur-i ‘arshullah
Nur surasi Nur[2]
nusrat nusrat
nutq nutq
nushur, qayta tirilish nushur
Nuh Nuh[1]
Nuh surasi Nuh[2]
obdast abdast
obdasta abdasta
obdastxona abdastkhana
obid ‘abid
obida ‘abida
obida abida
obi Zamzam ab-i Zamzam
obi hayot ab-i hayat
Od ‘Ad

Odam, Odam Ato Adam
odat ʻadat
odil ʻadil
Oysha ʻAʼisha
olam ʻalam[1]
Ol-i Imron surasi Al-i Imran
oliy abo al-i aba
olim ʻalim
olloyor allahyar
omin Amin[2]
omin, ovmin, ovmiyn amin[1]
omonat amanat
orif ʻarif
osiy ʻasi
osmon asman
otash atash
otashparast atashparast
oxirat akhirat
oxirat botqog'i akhirat batqaghi
oxirzamon akhir zaman
oxun, oxund akhund
oshiq ʻashiq
oyat ayat
oyati karima ayat-i karima
oyatul kursi ayat al-kursi
oyatulloh ayatullah
oyatul mutashabihot ayat al-mutashabihat
oyatul muhkamat ayat al-muhkamat
oqibat ʻaqibat
oqibat ʻuqba
ohad ahad
payom payam
payg'ambar payghambar
payg'om paygham
paranji paranja
parvardigor Parvardigar
pari pari
parixon parikhan
parixonlik parikhani
peshin namozi, zuhr namozi, peshin salat al-zuhr
peshqadam pishqadam
pir pir
piri mug'on pir-i mughan
pok pak
pora para
porso parsa
puli sirot pul-i sirat
put put
putparast putparast
putxona putkhana
Rabbano Rabbana
Rabbi Rabbi
Rabbil olamin Rabb al-ʻalamayn
Rabbil Falak Rabb al-Falak
rabboniy rabbani
rab, rabbim Rabb
rabu al-avval Rabiʻ al-avval
rabu al-oxir Rabiʻ al-akhir
Ravza Ravza
Ravzoyi mutahhar Ravza-yi mutahhar
ravo rava
radd radd
rajab Rajab
rajim rajim
rajm rajm
rajo raja
raziallohu anhu, radiallohu anhu razi allahu ʻanhu
rais raʼis[1]
rais raʼis[2]
rakat, rak'at rakʻat
ramazon Ramazan
rammol rammal
rasm-rusum, rasm rasm-rusum
rasul rasul
rasulona rasulana
Rasululloh Rasulullah
Ra'd surasi Raʻd
ra'y raʼi
raqs raqs
rag'oyib raghaʼib
rag'oyib namozi, qandil namozi, qandil kechasi qilinadigan namoz salat al-raghaʼib
rahbon rahban
rahboniylik rahbaniyat
rahim, rahiym, rahimli rahim
rahm rahm
rahmat rahmat
rahmatli rahmati
rahmoniy rahmani
Rahmon surasi Rahman
ribo riba
rivoyat rivayat
rido rida[1]
rido rida[2]
riyo riya
riyozat riyazat
riyokor riyakar
rijoal g'ayb rijal-i ghayb
Rizvon Rizvan
rizvonullahu alayhi rizvanullah ʻalayhi[2]
rizo riza[1]
rizo riza[2]
rizq rizq
rind rind
rioya riʻaya
risola risala
risolat risalat
rishvat rishvat
robita rabita
roviy ravi
rohib rahib
rohil rahil
rubobiyat rububiyat
ruku rukuʻ
Rum Rum[1]
Rum surasi Rum[2]
rutba rutba
ruxsat rukhsat
ruxsatnoma rukhsatnama
ruh ruh[1]
Ruh Ruh[2]
ruhiy ruhi
ruhoniy ruhani
ruhoniyat ruhaniyat
Ruhul-Amin Ruh al-Amin
Ruhulloh Ruhullah
Ruhul Quddus Ruh al-Quddus
ro'za ruza

ro'zi jazo, jazo kuni ruz-i jaza
Saba' surasi Saba
sabr sabr[1]
sabr sabr[2]
sab'ai samovot, etti samo, etti jannat sab'i samavat
savma'a savma'a
savob savab[1]
savob savab[2]
savob savab[3]
Savr Savr
sadaqa sadaqa
sadr sadr[2]
sadr, sadri a'zam sadr[1]
sajda sajda[1]
sajdagoh sajdagah
sajdayi tilovat sajda-yi tilavat
Sajda surasi Sajda[2]
sazoyi sazayi
sayid sayyid
sayyiya, say'i sayyi'a
say, sa'y sa'i
salavot, salavat salavat
salaf salaf
salafi solihin salaf-i salihin
salib salib
salibiya salibiya
saliblar salibiyun
salib, salb salb
salla salla
Sallallohu alayhi vasallam salla allahi 'alayhu va sallam
salovati nofila salavat-i nafila
salom salam
salot, namoz salat
Salsabil Salsabil
samiy sami'
samo sama
samo sama'[1]
samo sama'[2]
samoviy samavi
samoviy dinlar din-i samavi
Samud Samud
sana sana[1]
sanai shamsiya sana-yi shamsiyya
sanai qamariya sana-yi qamariyya
sanayi milodiya sana-yi miladiyya
sanayi hijriya sana-yi hijriyya
sanam sanam
sano, hamdu sano sana[2]
Sara Sara
Saraton Saratan
sar ob sar-ab
sarrof sarraf
sarf sarf
safar Safar
safar dar vatan safar dar vatan
safar namozi salat al-safar
Safa, Safo tog'i Safa
safiyulloh safi'ullah
safoyil safa'il
safoliyat safaliyat
Saf surasi Saff
saxovat sakhavat
saqar Saqar
saqofat saqafat
sag'ir saghir
sahar sahar
sahv sahv
sahir sahir
sahifa sahifa
sahih sahih
sahoba sahaba
sahobiy sahabi
semurg', semurg' qushi Simurgh
sehr sihr
sehrboz sihirbaz
sehriy sihri
sibg'atilloh sibghatullah
siddiq siddiq
Sidratal muntaha Sidrat al-muntaha
siyoral nabi siyar al-nabi
sijjil sijjil
siyrat, sira, siyrati Muhammad sirat[1]
siloh silah
silsila silsila[1]
silsila silsila[2]
silsilanoma silsilanama
Sirot, puli Sirot, Sirot ko'prigi Sirat[2]
soat sa'at
Sod surasi Sad
soyir sa'ir
solih salih[1]
Solih, Samud Salih[2]
sof saf
ssbir sabir
subut, subutiya subutiya
subha subha
subhon subhan
subhonalloh, subhonallo subhanallah
subhono va taallo subhanahu va ta'ala
subhonoka subhanaka
sudur sudur
sudxo'r sudkhur
sudxo'rlik sud
sujud sujud
suiqasd sui qasd
sukra sukra
sukut sukut
Sulaymon Sulayman
sulton sultan
suluk suluk
sulh sulh
sunan, sunnan sunan
Sunbula Sunbula
sunnat sunna
sunnat sunnat[1]
sunnat sunnat[2]
sunnatul muaqqada sunnat mu'akkada
sunnatul g'ayril muaqqada sunnat ghayr-i mu'akkada
sunniy, sunni sunni
sur sur
sura sura
surat, suvrat surat
surnoy surnay
sutra sutra
suftajo suftajah
suhuf suhuf
so'fi sufi[1]

so'fi sufi[2]
taabbud ta‘abbud[1]
taabbud ta‘abbud[2]
taaviz ta‘avvuz
taassub ta‘assub
tabarruk tabarruk
Tabbot Tabbat
tabiat tabi‘at
tabib tabib
tabiiyun tabi‘iyun
tablig'ot tablighat
taborak tabarak
tabrik tabrik
tavajuh tavajjuh
tavakkal tavakkul[1]
tavakkul tavakkul[2]
tavarruq tavarruq
tavaqquf tavaqquf
tavahhum tavahhum
tavba tavba[1]
tavba tavba[2]
Tavba surasi Tavba[3]
tavba-tazarru tavba-tazarru
taviz ta‘viz[2]
taviz, ta'viz ta‘viz[1]
tavoze tavazi‘
tavorix tavarikh
tavof tavaf[1]
tavof tavaf[2]
tavofi ziyorat tavaf-i ziyarat
tavofi sadr tavaf-i sadr
tavofi qudum tavaf-i qudum
Tavrot Tavrat
tavsim tavsim
tavsif tavsif
tavfiq tavfiq
tavq, tavqi la'nat tavq
tavhid tavhid[1]
tavhid tavhid[2]
tadayin tadayyun[2]
tadayun tadayyun[1]
tadlis tadlis
tadfin tadfin
tajalli tajalli
tajvid tajvid
tazahud tazahhud
tazvij tazavij
tazkiratul avliyo tazkirat al-avliya
tazkiya tazkiya
tayyiba tayyiba[2]
tayyiba, toyiba tayyiba[1]
takbir takbir
takbir, takbiri taxrim takbir al-tahrima
Takvir surasi Takvir
takiya takiya
takiya, takya takya
taklif taklif
Takosur surasi Takasur
takrir takrir
takfin takfin
takfir takfir
talvasa, jon talvasasi talvasa
taloq talaq[1]
taloqnoma talaqnama
Taloq surasi Talaq[2]
taloq xati talaq khat
talqin talqin[1]
talqin talqin[2]
talqin talqin[3]
tamattu' tamattu‘
tamjid tamjid
Tamuq Tamuq
tanaviya, tanavvu' tanavvu‘
tanakuh tanakuh
tanassir tanassur
tanasux tanasukh
Tangri Tangri
tanzih tanzih[1]
tanzih tanzih[2]
tansur, tansir tansir
taolo ta‘ala
taom ta‘am
taoxir ta’akhir
taraka taraka
tarbiya tarbiya
tarix tarikh[1]
tarix tarikh[2]
tariqat tariqat[1]
tariqat tariqat[2]
tarki dunyo tark-i dunya
tarovix namozi, tarovix salat al-taravih
tarovix namozi, tarovix taravih
tarso tarsa
targ'ib targhib
targ'ibot targhibat
tasavvuf tasavvuf
tasadduq, tasaddiq tasadduq
tasattur tasattur
tasbeh, tasbi tasbih
tasvib tasvib
tasir tashir
taslim taslim[1]
taslim, assalomu alaykum va rahmatulloh taslim[2]
Tasnim, jannat sharorasi Tasnim
tatavvu tatavvu‘
tafrid tafrid
tafsir tafsir
taxrim tahrim[1]
taxrimiy tahrimi
Taxrim surasi Tahrim[2]
tashahud tashahhud
tashbih tashbih
tashnob tashnab
tashriq tashriq
tashrig' tashri‘[2]
tashrig', tashri tashri‘[1]
ta'abirnoma ta‘birnama
ta'bir ta‘bir
ta'dil ta‘dil
ta'dili arkon ta‘dil-i arkan
ta'zim ta‘zim
ta'zir ta‘zir
ta'ziya ta‘ziya
ta'kid ta’kid
ta'lim ta‘lim
ta'limot ta‘limat
tayammum tayammum
taqaddis, taqaddus taqaddus
taqvim taqvim
taqvin takvin
taqvo taqva
taqvodor taqvadar
taqdir taqdir
taqdir, qadar taqdir
taqdis taqdis[1]
taqdis taqdis[2]

taqiy taqi
taqiya taqiya
taqlid taqlid[1]
taqlid taqlid[2]
taqsir taqsir
Tag'obun surasi Taghabun
tahajjud tahajjud
tahajjud namozi salat al-tahajjud
tahammul tahammul
tahlil tahlil
tahmid tahmid
tahorat taharat
tahoratxona taharatkhana
tahrij takhrij
tahrir tahrir
tahrif tahrif
tahya tahiyat
tahqiqi imon, tahqiqi iymon tahqiqi iman
tib tibb
tijorat tijarat
tilmiz, shogird tilmiz
tilovat tilavat
tilsim tilsim[1]
tilsim tilsim[2]
tilsim tilsim[3]
toat ta'at
toat-ibodat ta'at-'ibadat
tobe' tabi'
tobe'in, tobi'in tabi'in
tobe'i tabiin, taba'a tobi'in, tabauttobein taba'-i tabi'in
tobut tabut
toifa ta'ifa
toyib, toib, tavba qiluvchi ta'ib
tole tali'
tolib talib
Toriq surasi Tariq
Toha surasi Ta ha
tohir tahir
Tuba Tuba
tumor tumar
turbat, turba turba
tug' tugh[1]
tug' tugh[2]
to'fon tufan
Uvays al-Qaraniy Vays al-Qarani
udum udum
Ujmax Ujmakh
uzlat 'uzlat
uzr 'uzr[1]
uzr 'uzr[2]
ulamo 'ulama
umaro umara
Umar, hazrati Umar 'Umar
Ummalmo'min, Ummalmo'minin Umm al-mu'minin
ummat ummat
ummi ummi
umr 'umr
umra 'umra
uns uns
unsur unsur
urf 'urf
urfi sahih 'urf sahih
urfi fosid 'urf fasid
Usmon 'Usman
ustod ustad
ustoz ustaz
usul usul[1]
usul usul[2]
usuli jadid, jadidchilik usul-i jadid
usuli xamsa usul-i khamsa
usuli qadim, qadimchilik usul-i qadim
uqibat 'uqubat[1]
uqibat 'uqubat[3]
uqubat 'uqubat[2]
Ug'on Ughan
fazl fazl
faylasuf faylasuf
falak falak[1]
falak falak[2]
falaq falaq[1]
Falaq surasi Falaq[2]
falsafa falsafa
fan fann
fano fana
faryod faryad
farz farz
farziayn, farzi ayn farz-i 'ayn
farzi doim farz-i da'im
farzi kifoya farz-i kifaya
farzi muvaqqat, muvaqqat farz farz-i muvaqqat
farid farid
faridal asr farid al-'asr
farishta farishta
faroiz fara'iz[1]
faroiz fara'iz[2]
farsax farsakh
faruq faruq
fasod, fasot fasad
fatvo fatva
fatr fatir[2]
Fath surasi Fath
faqir faqir[1]
faqir faqir[2]
faqih faqih
faqohat faqahat
faqr faqr
fahsh fahsh
fido fida
fidoyi fida'i
fidokor fidakyar
fidya fidya
fikrat fikrat
Fil surasi Fil
Firavn Fira'un
firdavs Firdaus
firqa firqa
fisq fisq
fitna fitna
fitr fitr[1]
fitr fitr[2]
fitra fitra
fitrat fitrat
fiqh fiqh
fojir fajir
fozil fazil
foiz fa'iz
fol fal
folbin falbin
folgo'y falgu
folnoma falnama
foniy fani
fosiq fasiq
Fotima Fatima
Fotir surasi Fatir[1]

fotiha fatiha[1]
fotiha fatiha[2]
fotihago'y fatihagu
fotiha surasi Fatiha[3]
fohisha fahisha
fuzalo fuzala
Furqon Furqan[1]
Furqon surasi Furqan[2]
Fussilat Fussilat
futuvat futuvat
xabar khabar
xabari vohid khabar-i vahid
xavorij, xavorijlar, isyonchilar khavarij
xavf khavf
xavf namozi salat al-khavf
Xadicha Khadija
Xaybar Khaybar
xayir khayr[2]
xayr-sadaqa khayr-sadaqa
xayr, xayrot khayr[1]
xalvat khalvat
Xalililloh, Xalillulo, Xalilulloh Khalilullah
xalifa khalifa[1]
xalifa khalifa[2]
xalifat khilafat[2]
xalifat khilafat[3]
xalifa, xilofa khilafat[1]
Xalloq Khallaq
xalfa khalfa[1]
xalfa, bixalfa khalfa[2]
xalqa halqa[2]
xamr khamr
xaraj, xarajat, xiroj kharaj
Xarun Harun
xatib khatib
xatim khatim[2]
xatm khatm[1]
xat-mahr khat-mahr
xatmi suluk khatm-i suluk
xatmi xo'jagon, xatmi xo'ja khatm-i khvajagan
xatmi qutub khatm-i kutub
xatm, xatmi Qur'on khatm[2]
xatna khatna
xato khata
xattot hattat
Xizir Khizr
xilvat khilvat
xilvatgoh, xilvatnishin khalvatgah
xilvat dar anjuman khalvat dar anjuman
Xilofatul Rashidin, Xalifai Rashidin Khulafa-yi rashidin
xilofi sha'riy khilaf-i sharʿ
xilxona khilkhana
xilqat khilqat
xirqa khirqa[1]
xirqa khirqa[2]
xirqai saodat khirqa-yi saʿadat
xirqai sharif khirqa-yi sharif
xirqapo'sh khirqa push
xitan khitan
xonaqoh khanaqa
xotam khatim[1]
xoch khach
xochparast khachparast
Xudo Khuda
Xudovand Khudavand
Xudovando khudavanda
xudogo'y khudaguy
xudogo'y khudaygu
xudojo'y khudajuy
Xudoy khuday
xudoyi khudayi
xudoyixona khudaykhana
xudoparast khudaparast
xudotars khudatars
xul khulʿ
Xuld Khuld
xuliya hilya
xuliyai saodat hilya-yi saʿadat
xuliyai sharif hiliya-yi sharif
xulq khulq
xums khums
xunasa khunsa
xurmo, xurma khurma
xurofot khurafat
xusuf namozi salat al-khusuf
xutba khutba
xufton khuftan
xufton namozi, xufton salat al-ʿisha
xo'ja khvaja[1]
xo'ja khvaja[2]
xo'jazoda khvajazada
chalma chalma
chahoryor Chahar yar
childon childan
chilla chilla[1]
chilla chilla[2]
chillayosin chillayasin
chillaxona chillakhana[1]
chillaxona chillakhana[2]
chiltan chiltan
chodira chadra
Shavval Shavval
shavq shavq
shajara shajara
shaytanat shaytanat
shayton Shaytan
shaytonilain, shaytoni la'in, shaytoni layin shaytan al-ʿayn
shayx shaykh
shayxul islom shaykh al-islam[1]
shayxul islom shaykh al-islam[2]
shak shakk
shakkok shakkak
shak kuni, Arafa, shok oqshomi shak
shaklik shaklik
sham shamʿ
shamdon shamʿdan
shamoyil shama'il
shamoyili sharif shama'il-i sharifa
shariat shariʿat
sharik sharik
sharif sharif
sharifa sharifa
sharob sharab
sharr sharr
Sharx surasi Inshirah
shar' sharʿ

shar'an shar'an
shar'iy shar'i
shafoat shafa'at
Sha'bon Sha'ban
shahvat shahvat
shahid, shayid shahid[2]
shahodat, shahidlik shahadat[2]
shahodat, shohidlik shahadat[1]
shahri Ramazon shahr-i ramazan
shia shi'i
shirk shirk
shifo shifa
Shish Shis
shogird shagird
shom namozi, mag'rib namozi salat al-maghrib
Shofiy Shafi'i[1]
shofiy Shafi'i[2]
shofiylik Shafi'iya
shohid shahid[1]
Shohimardon, Shoymardon Shah-i mardan
Shuayb Shu'ayb
Shuaro surasi Shu'ara
shubha shubha
shuzuz shuzuz
shukr shukr
shuur shu'ur
sho'ro shura [1]
Sho'ro surasi Shura[2]
sho'hrat shuhrat
eshon ishan
eshonzoda ishanzada
e'timod i'timad
e'tiqod i'tiqad
ehrom, ihrom ihram
ehson ihsan[1]
ehtido ihtida
Yunus Yunus[1]
Yunus surasi Yunus[2]
Yusuf Yusuf[1]
Yusuf surasi Yusuf[2]
Yusho Yusha'
Yazdon Yazdan
Yaratgan Yaratqan
yarhamukallo, yarhamukalloh yarhamukallah
Yafas Yafis
Ya'juj-Ma'juj Ya'juj va Ma'juj
Yahyo Yahya
yahud yahud
yahudiy yahudi
qabila qabila
qabih qabih
qabohat qabahat
qabr qabr
qabr azobi, go'r azobi 'azab-i qabr
qabriston qabristan
qavm qavm
qavom qavam
Qavs Qavs
qadam qadam
qadamgoh qadamgah
qadamjoy qadamjay
qadim Qadim, al-
qadimiy qadimi
Qadr surasi Qadr[1]
qazo qaza
qazoyi muallaq qaza-yi mu'allaq
qal qal
qalam qalam[1]
qalam qalam[2]
Qalam surasi Qalam[3]
qalandar qalandar
qalandarxona qalandarkhana
qalb qalb
qalin sidaq[1]
Qamar surasi Qamar
qamis qamis
qanoat qana'at
qarz qarz
qasam qasam
qasd qasd
qasis qasis
qasos qasas[1]
qasos qisas
Qasos surasi Qasas[2]
qatl qatl
qat'iyat qat'iyat
qa'da qa'da
qahir Qahr, al-
qibla qibla
qiblagoh qiblagah
qiblanoma qiblanama
qiyom qiyam
qiyomat qiyamat[1]
Qiyomat surasi Qiyamat[2]
qiyomat qoyim qiyamat qa'im
qiyos qiyas
qiyosi fuqaho qiyas-i fuqaha
qimor qimar
qiroat qira'at
qiroatxona qira'atkhana
qiron qiran
qirq hadis hadis-i arba'in
qismat qismat
qissasul anbiyo, kissa-ul anbiyo qisas al-anbiya
Qitmir Qitmir
Qobil Qabil
qozi qazi
qozizoda qazizada
qozixona qazikhana
qoida qa'ida
qomat qamat
qonun qanun
qori qari
qorixona qarikhana
Qof surasi Qaf[1]
Qof tog'i Qaf[2]
qubba qubba
Qubbatul Islom Qubbat al-Islam
qubur, qabrlar qubur
quddus quddus
Quddusi sharif Quds, al-
qudrat qudrat
quds quds
qudsi qudsi
qudsiyat qudsiyat
qulhu Allohu Ahad qul hu allah ahad
qunut qunut
quraysh Quraysh[1]
Quraysh surasi Quraysh[2]
qurb qurb
Qurbon bayrami Qurban Bayrami

qurbon, qurbonlik qurban
qurro, qiroati qurro qurra
Qur'on Qur'an
Qur'oni Azim Qur'an-i ʿAzim
Qur'oni Karim Qur'an-i Karim
Qur'oni xatim Qur'an khatima
qur'onxona qur'ankhana
qusuf qusuf
qusuf namozi salat al-qusuf
qutb qutb
G'avsal A'zam Ghavs al-Aʿzam
g'azab ghazab
g'azavot ghazavat
g'azo ghaza
g'ayya, jahannam tubi Ghayya
g'ayridin, g'ayridiniy ghayr-i din
g'ayrimashru ghayr-i mashruʿ
g'ayri muaqqad ghayr-i mu'akkad
g'ayri shar'iy ghayr-i sharʿi
g'am ghamm[1]
g'am ghamm[2]
G'ambar Ghambar
g'amxona, baytul-ahzon bayt al-ahzan
g'animat ghanimat
g'arib gharib[1]
g'arib gharib[2]
g'asl ghasl
g'asp ghasb
g'assol ghassal
g'aflat ghaflat[1]
g'aflat ghaflat[2]
g'ilmon ghilman
g'ozi, g'oziy ghazi
g'ofil ghafil
G'ofir surasi Ghafir
G'oshiya surasi Ghashiya
g'ul ghul
g'urbat ghurbat
g'uslxona ghuslkhana
g'usul ghusl
habash habash
Habashiston Habashistan
Habib Habib
Habibulloh Habibullah
Habil Habil
havojim havajim
havojis havajis
havola havala
havorilar havari
hadd hadd
haddi zakr hadd-i zakr
haddi zino hadd-i zina
haddi sirkat hadd-i sirkat
haddi shurb hadd-i shurb
haddi qazif hadd-i qazf
Hadid surasi Hadid
hadis hadis
hadisi qudsiy hadis-i qudsi
hayoyo-hu, hayyo-hu hay ya hu
hayoti abadiya hayat-i abadiya
haj hajj[1]
haj badal hajj badal
haj namozi salat al-hajat
Haj surasi Hajj[2]
hazrat hazrat
hazrati Bilol Bilal
hazrati Dovud Da'ud
Haydar Haydar
hayiz hayz
hayit, iyd ʿid
hakim hakim
halimxona, halisaxona halimkhana
halim, halisa halim
halif halif
hall hall
halol halal
halqa halqa[1]
hamal Hamal
hanafiy Hanafi
Hanafiya Hanafiya
hanbaliy Hanbali
Hanbaliya Hanbaliya
hanif hanif[1]
hanif hanif[2]
haram haram[2]
haram harim
harif duo harif duʿa
harom haram[1]
harom muharram[1]
haromzoda haramzada
haromu zanniy haram zanni
haromu qat'iy haram qatʿi
Harut va Marut Harut va Marut
hasan hasan[1]
hasan hasan[2]
Hasan Hasan[3]
hassa, aso ʿasa
haftiyak haft-i yak
hashir hashr[1]
Hashr surasi Hashr[2]
hashtiyak hasht-i yak
haq haqq[1]
Haq Haqq[2]
haqiqat haqiqat
Haq Rasul Haqq Rasul
Haq taallo Haqq Taʿala
haqqulloh haqqullah
haqqul yaqin haqq al-yaqin
Hibatuloh Hibatullah
hiboh hiba
hidoyat hidayat
hijob hijab
hijra, hijrat hijra
hijriy hijri
hijriya hijriya
Hijr surasi Hijr
hizb hizb[1]
hizb hizb[2]
hizbu shayton hizb al-shaytan
hiylai shar'iy hila-yi sharʿi
hikmat hikmat
hilol hilal
himmat himmat
hirz, amon hirzi, jon hirzi hirz
hiss hiss
hissi botiniy hiss-i batin
hissi zohiri hiss-i zahiri
hoviya haviya
hovl havl
Hojar, Bibi Hojar Hajar
hojari asvad, hajarul

asvod, ka'batosh hajar-i asvad
hoji hajji
hol hal
homila hamila
homilador hamiladar
Homon Haman
Hotamul Anbiyo Khatam al-anbiyah
Hotamul nabiin Khatam al-nabiyin
hofiz hafiz
hu Hu
Hud Hud[1]
Hud surasi Hud[2]
hudud hudud
hujra hujra
Hujurot surasi Hujurat
hukm hukm
hukmilloh bihukmillah
hukmi Samad hukm-i samad
hukumat hukumat
hulla hulla
hulul hulul
Humaza surasi Humaza
hur hur
huri huri
Husayn Husayn
husn husn
husni adab husn-i adab
husni axloq husn-i akhlaq
husni tarbiya husn-i tarbiya
husnixat husn-i khat
hut Hut
hush dar dam khush dar dam

Subject Index

Divine Names

Adl, al-
ʿAfuv, al-
Ahad, al-
Akhir, al-
ʿAli, al-
ʿAlim, al-
Allah
Allah taʿala
Allahu ʿAlimun
ʿAllam al-ghuyub
Avval, al-
ʿAzim, al-
ʿAziz, al-
Badiʿ, al-
Baʿis, al-
Baqi, al-
Bari, al-
Barr, al-
Basir, al-
Basit, al-
Batin, al-
Fattah, al-
Ghaffar, al-
Ghafur, al-
Ghani, al-
Hadi, al-
Hafiz, al-[1]
Hafiz, al-[2]
Hakam, al-
Hakim, al-
Halim, al-
Hamid, al-
Haqq, al-
Haqq Taʿala
Hasib, al-
Hayy, al-
Hu
ilah
Jabbar, al-
Jalil, al-
Jamiʿ, al-
Janab-i haqq
Kabir, al-
Kardigar
Karim, al-
Khabir, al-
Khaliq, al-
Khallaq
Khuda
Khudavand
khuday
La makan
Latif, al-
Majid, al-
Malik, al-
Malik al-Mulk
Maniʿ, al-
Matin, al-
Mavla[1]
Mu'akhkhir, al-
Mubdiʿ, al-
Mughni, al-
Muhaymin, al-
Muhsi, al-
Muhyi, al-
Muʿid, al-
Muʿizz, al-
Mujib, al-
Mujid, al-
Mu'min, al-
Mumit, al-
Muntaqim, al-
Muqaddim, al-
Muqit, al-
Muqsit, al-
Muqtadir, al-
Musavvir, al-
Mutaʿali, al-
Mutakabbir, al-
Muzill, al-
Nafiʿ, al-
Nur, al-
Parvardigar
Qabiz, al-
Qadim, al-
Qadir, al-
Qahhar, al-
Qahr, al-
Qavi, al-
Qayyum, al-
Quddus, al-
Rabb
Rabb al-Falak
Rabbana
Rafiʿ, al-
Rahim, al-
Rahman, al-
Raqib, al-
Rashid, al-
Rauf, al-
Razzaq, al-
Sabur, al-
Salam, al-
Samad, al-
Samiʿ, al-
Satir, al-
Sattar, al-
Sattar al-ʿuyub
Shahid, al-
Shakur, al-
taʿala
Tangri
Tavvab, al-
Ughan
Vadud, al-
Vahhab, al-
Vahid, al-
Vajid, al-
Vakil, al-
Vali, al-
Varis, al-
Vasiʿ, al-
Yaratqan
Yazdan
Zarr, al-
Zat-i kibriya
Zat-i pak
Zu'l-ihsan
Zu'l-jalal va'l-ikram

Hadith

ahad
ahliyyat-i ada
akhbar
asar
ʿaziz[2]
gharib[2]
hadis
hadis-i arbaʿin
hadis-i qudsi

hasan[2]
ʿillat
isnad
jurh
juz'[4]
khabar
khabar-i vahid
lafzan va maʿnan
maqtuʿ
mardud
marfuʿ
marfuʿ hukman
marfuʿ sarihan
mashhur
mavquf
mavzuʿ
mursal[2]
musbat
musnad
mutavatir
muttasil
ravi
rivayat
sahih
sunan
taʿdil
tadlis
takhrij
zaʿif

Hajj

ʿabir
ab-i Zamzam
anbar[1]
ʿArafat
badal
Batha
hajj badal
hajji
hajjikhana
ihram
ihsar
Jamra
labbayka
manasik
Maqam-i Ibrahim
Marva
Mina
Miqat
murahaqa
Muzdalifa
qiran
ruz-i ʿarafat
Safa
saʿi
tamattuʿ
tavaf[1]
tavaf-i nafila
tavaf-i qudum
tavaf-i sadr
tavaf-i ziyarat
tavsim
vaqfa
vuquf
Zamzam
zamzami

Historical

abiz
ʿAd
amir al-muslimun
amir al-umara
ansar
ashab
ashab-i Badr
ashab-i kahf
ashab-i kiram
Badr
bani Isra'il[1]
bayt al-mal
Chahar yar
dar al-sulh
Firaʿun
hijra
imam[2]
imam[4]
Isagujikhvan
jadid
jahiliyat
Karbala
khalifa[1]
Khaybar
khilafat[1]
khilafat[2]
khilafat[3]
Khulafa-yi rashidin
lashkar-i Islam
Lat
Manat
manshur
muhajirin
muhasara
muhtasib[2]
mustashrik
prighuvur
qadimi
Quraysh[1]
Rum[1]
sahaba
Samud
tabaʿ-i tabiʿin
tabiʿin
ukaz
Umm al-kitab
ustabika
usul-i jadid
usul-i qadim
Vahhabiya

Law

ʿadat
ahl-i ra'y
ahrar
aʿlam
amanat
amlak
aqraba
asarat
asir
ʿavrat
balaghat
baligh
bara'at[1]
buhtan
dalil
dalil-i ʿaqli
dalil-i naqli
dalil-i sharʿi
darra
diyat
dukhan[2]

faqahat
faqih
faqir[1]
fara'iz[1]
farz
farz-i 'ayn
fatva
fiqh
ghanimat
gharib[1]
ghasb
ghayr-i mashru'
ghayr-i misr
ghayr-i mu'akkad
ghayr-i shar'i
ghul
hadd
hadd-i qazf
hadd-i shurb
hadd-i sirkat
hadd-i zakr
hadd-i zina
halal
halif
hamiladar
Hanafi
Hanafiya
Hanbali
Hanbaliya
haram[1]
haram qat'i
haramzada
haram zanni
hasht-i yak
havala
hiba
hila-yi shar'i
hudud
hukm
hurr
'ibadat[2]
i'dam
'iddat
ifta
ihzar
ijab
ijma'
ijma'-i ummat
ikhtilaf
imam[3]
insaf
intiqam
'iqab
iqrar[2]
israf
istihsan
istislah
i'tiqadat
itlaq
jallad
jarima
jaza
jinayat
juda
junun[1]
kafalat
kafil
kaniz
khamr
khat-mahr
khilaf-i shar'
khul'
khunsa
khvaja[2]
maghlub
maharim[1]
maharim[2]
mahbus
mahkama
mahkum
mahr[2]
mahram
majnun[2]
makruh
makruh tahrima
makruh tanzih
mal
Maliki
Malikiya
mamluk
ma'mur
ma'nan
manhi
maqtul
ma'ruf
mashkuk
mashru'
matruka
ma'yub
mazhab[1]
milk
miras
miskin
misr[1]
mu'akkad
mu'amalat
mubah
mubahasa
mudallas
mufsid[2]
mufti
muhakama
muhallil
muharram[1]
muharramat
mujtahid[2]
mukatib
mukhaddara
mukhasamat
mukhtasar
mulk[1]
mulk-amlak
munakahat
muqim
murafa'a
murdar
musadara
mustahabb
mustakrah
mu'tamir
nafaqa
nahalal
namahram
namashru'
narava
nashar'i
nazar[1]
nizam
qanun
qasas[1]
qatl
qatl 'amd
qatl sabab
qatl shubha 'amd

qazi
qazikhana
qimar
qisas
qiyas
qiyas-i fuqaha
radd
ra'i
rajm
rasm-rusum
rava
rishvat
rutba
saghir
sarraf
sazayi
Shafi'i[2]
Shafi'iya
shar'
sharab
shar'an
shar'i
shari'at
shubha
shuzuz
sidaq[1]
sidaq[2]
suftajah
sui qasd
sunna
sunnat[1]
sunnat ghayr-i mu'akkada
sunnat mu'akkada
tahrim[1]
tahrimi
taklif
takrir
talaq[1]
talaq khat
talaqnama
taraka
tashri'[1]
tashri'[2]
tatliq
tavq
tazavij
ta'zir
'ulama
umm-i valad
'uqubat[2]
'uqubat[3]
'urf
'urf fasid
'urf sahih
usul[2]
'uzr[2]
vajib
vaqif[2]
varasat
varis
vasiqa
vasiyat
vasiyatnama
virsa
yatim
zina
zinakar

Personal Names

'Abdullah[1]
'Abdullah[2]
Abu Bakr
Abu Hanifa
Adam
Aflatun
Ahmad
'Ali
Alyasa'
Asadullah
Ayyub
'Azazil
'Azra'il
Bashir
Bilal
Buraq
Dajjal
Da'ud
Duldul
Fatima
Ghambar
Habibullah
Habil
Hajar
Haman
Haqq Rasul
Harun
Harut va Marut
Hasan[3]
Hava
Haydar
Hibatullah
Hud[1]
Husayn
Iblis
Ibrahim[1]
Idris
Ilyas
Imam-i A'zam
'Imran[1]
'Imran[2]
Ishaq
Iskandar
Isma'il
Israfil
Isra'il
Jabra'il
Jibril
Jirjis
Khadija
Khalilullah
Khizr
Luqman[1]
Lut
Mahdi
Malik[1]
Mal'un[1]
Maryam[1]
Masih[1]
Mika'il
Muhammad[1]
Musa
Qabil
Rabb al-'alamayn
Rasulullah
Rizvan
Ruh[2]
Ruh al-Amin
Ruh al-Quddus
Ruhullah
Salih[2]
Sara
Shah-i mardan
Shaytan

Shis
Shu'ayb
Sulayman
'Umar
'Usman
Vays al-Qarani
Yafis
Yahya
Ya'juj va Ma'juj
Ya'qub
Yasu'
Yunus[1]
Yusha'
Yusuf[1]
Zakariya
Zu'l-Kifl
Zu'l-Qarnayn

Qur'an

'Abasa
abvab al-Qur'an
'Adiyat
Ahzab
A'la
'Alaq
alif lam mim
Al-i Imran
An'am
Anbiya[2]
Anfal
'Ankabut
A'raf[2]
'Asr[2]
ayat
ayat al-kursi
ayat al-muhkamat
ayat al-mutashabihat
ayat-i karima
bab
Balad
Bani Isra'il[2]
Baqara
Bara'at[2]
barat
Bayyina
Buruj
dahir
dar al-huffaz
Dukhan[1]
Fajr
Falaq[2]
Fath
Fatiha[3]
Fatir[1]
Fil
Furqan[1]
Furqan[2]
Fussilat
Ghafir
Ghashiya
Hadid
Hajj[2]
Haqqa
Hashr[2]
Hijr
hizb[2]
Hud[2]
Hujurat
Humaza
huri
Ibrahim[2]
Ikhlas[2]
Infitar
inna a'taynaka al-kavsara
Insan
Inshiqaq
Inshirah
Isra
Jasiya
Jinn[2]
Jum'a[3]
juz'[1]
juz'[2]
juz'[3]
Kafirun
Kahf
Kalamullah
Kavsar[2]
khatm[1]
khulq
Lahab
lavh
Layl
Luqman[2]
Ma'arij
madini
mahkam
Ma'ida
makki
Maryam[2]
Masad
Ma'un
Mu'avvizatan
Mu'avvizatayn
mubham
Muddassir
mufassir
Muhammad[2]
Mujadala
Mu'jiza[2]
Mulk[2]
Mu'min[2]
Mu'minin
Mumtahana
Munafiqun
muqallid
Mursalat
mushaf
Mutaffifin
Muzzammil
Naba
Nahl
Najm
Naml
Nas
Nasr
Nazi'at
nazil
Nisa
Nuh[2]
Nur[2]
nushur
para
Qadr[1]
Qaf[1]
Qalam[3]
Qamar
qari
Qari'a
qarikhana
Qasas[2]
qira'at
qira'atkhana

Qiyamat[2]
qul hu allah ahad
Qur'an
Qur'an-i 'Azim
Qur'an-i Karim
Qur'an-i Majid
qur'ankhana
Qur'an khatima
Quraysh[2]
qurra
Ra'd
Rahman
Rum[2]
Saba
Sad
Saff
Saffat
safi'ullah
Sajda[2]
Shams
Shu'ara
Shura[2]
sijjil
sura
tabarak
Tabbat
Taghabun
Ta ha
Tahrim[2]
ta'ib
tajvid
Takasur
Takvir
Talaq[2]
tamjid
Tariq
Tavba[3]
tilavat
Tin
Tur
Vaqi'a
Ya Sin
Yunus[2]
Yusuf[2]
Zariyat
Zilzal
Zuha
Zukhruf
Zumar

Ritual

akhirat batqaghi
akmal
Allah hu
amin[1]
'aqiqa
'arafa
'Ashura[1]
'ashura[2]
'asr[1]
azan
azar
'azayimkhan
bamdad
bayram
bayt al-ahzan
childan
chilla[2]
chillakhana[2]
chillayasin
dafn
dastarkhan
dastshuy
da'vat
davir
du'akhvan
du'a-yi qunut
durud
durust
farz-i da'im
farz-i kifaya
farz-i muvaqqat
Fath-i Makka
Fatiha, al-
fida
fidya
fitr[1]
fitr[2]
ghasl
ghassal
ghusl
halim
halimkhana
havl
hulla
'id
'Id al-Azha
'Id al-Fitr
iftar
iftitah
iqamat
iqtida
ishraq
isqat
istibra
istihaza
istinja
istinshaq
istiqbal
istisqa
i'tikaf
itmam
izar
ja'iz
jalsa
janaza[1]
janaza[2]
jaynamaz
jum'a[1]
junub
kafn
kalima
kalima-yi shahadat
khata
khatib
khatna
khirqa[2]
khitan
khuftan
khurma
khutba
kifaya
la havla
lahid[2]
la ilaha illa allah va muhammadun rasulullah
Laylat al-Qadr
lifafa
ma'b
maghrib
mahsi
mani'
ma'raka

masbuq
mashhadi
masih[2]
matam
matamzada
Mavlid[1]
mazmaza
ma'zur
minbar
mi'raj
misvak[1]
misvak[2]
mudrik
mufsid[1]
muftir
muhtazir
munajat[1]
munajat[2]
munajatkhana
muqavala
murdakhana
murdashuy
musafaha
musafir
mushkilkushad
nafila
nahs
najasat
najasat ghaliz
najasat khafif
namaz
naqis
na'sh[1]
na'sh[2]
Navruz
nifas
nikah
nisar
nishalla
nishallafurush
niyat
nutq
qa'da
qamat
qamis
qavam
qaza
qibla
qiblagah
qiblanama
qiyam
qunut
qurban
Qurban Bayrami
qusuf
ragha'ib
rak'at
rida[1]
ruku'
ruza
sahar
sahv
sajda[1]
sajda-yi tilavat
salat
salat al-'asr
salat al-fajr
salat al-hajat
salat al-'idayn
salat al-'isha
salat al-ishraq
salat al-istikhara
salat al-istisqa
salat al-janaza
salat al-jum'a
salat al-khavf
salat al-khusuf
salat al-maghrib
salat al-mariz
salat al-musafir
salat al-qusuf
salat al-ragha'ib
salat al-safar
salat al-subh
salat al-tahajjud
salat al-taravih
salat al-tasbih
salat al-vitr
salat al-zuha
salat al-zuhr
salavat-i nafila
shab-i barat
shahr-i ramazan
shak
shaklik
sham'
shama'il-i sharifa
sham'dan
subhanaka
sujud
sukut
sunnat[2]
sutra
ta'abbud[2]
ta'akhir
ta'at-'ibadat
ta'avvuz
tadfin
ta'dil-i arkan
tahajjud
taharat
taharatkhana
tahiyat
tahiyat, at-
tahlil
tahmid
takbir
takbir al-tahrima
takfin
talqin[2]
tanakuh
tankih
taqlid[2]
taravih
tasadduq
tasbih
tashahhud
tashnab
tashriq
taslim[2]
tasvib
tatavvu'
tavarruq
tayammum
ta'ziya
'umra
'uzr[1]
vird[1]
vitr
ya ramazan
yighi
zabiha
zakat[2]
zakat al-fitr

zifaf
ziyaratchi

Sufism

abdal[3]
ahbab
ahl-i dil
ahl-i tariqat
akhi
a'ma
'ashiq
asitana
atash
baz gasht
chilla[1]
chillakhana[1]
dargah
darvish
didar
divana
faqr
futuvat
ghaflat[2]
ghamm[2]
Ghavs al-A'zam
ghurbat
hal
haqq al-yaqin
havajim
havajis
hay ya hu
himmat
hiss
hiss-i batin
hiss-i zahiri
hulul
ijazat
ijazatnama
'ilm-i hal[2]
'ilm-i qal
inabat
injizab
insan-i kamil
irada[3]
irshad
irshadnama
ishan
ishanzada
isharat
'ishq
ittihad[2]
izn
jahr
jam' al-jam'
janda
jazb
jazba
jilva-yi rabbaniya
junun[2]
karamat
kashkul
khalifa[2]
khalvat
khalvat dar anjuman
khalvatgah
khanaqa
khatm-i khvajagan
khatm-i suluk
khavf
khilvat
khirqa[1]
khirqa push
khush dar dam
kulah
majnun[1]
majzub
manaqibnama
maqam
ma'rifat[2]
mashayikh
mashrab
mast
muhabbat
muhaqqiq
muhibb
mujahida[2]
mukashifa
mulhaq
munazara
muraqaba
murid
murshid
murshid-i afaq
mushahida
mutasavvif
mutashayyikh
nazar bar qadam
nigah dasht
pir
pir-i mughan
qalandar
qalandarkhana
qurb
qutb
rabita
raja
raqs
rida[2]
rijal-i ghayb
riza[2]
rukhsat
rukhsatnama
sabr[2]
sadr[2]
safa'il
safar dar vatan
sahib-i karamat
sama'[1]
shavq
shaykh
silsila[1]
sufi[1]
sukra
suluk
tafrid
tajalli
takiya
talqin[3]
tariqat[1]
tariqat[2]
tasavvuf
tavakkul[2]
tavba[2]
uns
'uzlat
vahdat-i vujud
vajd
vali
vara'[2]
vasl
vird[2]
vuquf-i 'adadi
vuquf-i qalbi

vuquf-i zaman
yad dasht
yad kard
yar
zikr
zikrchi
zikr-i jahr
zikr-i khafi
zuhd[2]
zu'l-janahayn

Taxation

ashir
badal-i askari
badal-i naqdi
badal-i shakhsi
baj
fitra
haqqullah
jizya
kharaj
khums
maliyat
mubashir
nisab
tazkiya
ʿushr
zakat[1]

Theology

baqa[2]
basir
batil
hashr[1]
hayan
ʿilm[2]
irada[2]
istidlali iman
istilahat
ittihad[1]
jahl
Jannat
kajraftar
kalam
karam
kavnayn
maddiyun
maʿnaviya
mavjud
mavjudat
mufassal
mujassam
mukhalifat lil-havadis
mukhtariyat
mutakallim
mutlaq
muvahhid
nasuh
qatʿiyat
qidam
qiyam binafsihi
rububiyat
salibiya
samiʿ
shirk
subutiya
tabiʿiyun
tahqiqi iman
takvin
tanasukh
tanavvuʿ
tanzih[1]
taqlid[1]
tashbih
tavhid[1]
usul-i khamsa
vahdaniyat
vajib al-vujud

The Dictionary

A

abad ابد ARABIC *n.* eternity

BAS: әбәд
KAR: абат
TAJ: абад
TAT: әбәд
UYG: abad
UZB: абад

'Abasa عبس ARABIC *Qur'an n.* the 80th sura of the Qur'an

KAR: Әбәсә сүўреси
KAZ: Ғабәсә сүресі
TAJ: сураи Абас
UYG: Abäsa süräsi, sürä Äbäsä
UZB: Абаса сураси

'abd عبد ARABIC *n.* creature, slave (of God)

BAS: ғәбит
KAR: абд, әбд
KAZ: абд, ғабд
TAJ: абд
TAT: габед
TUR: абд
UYG: äbd
UZB: абд

abdal[1] ابدال ARABIC *n.* religious man, holy man

KAR: абдал
TAJ: абдал
TAT: әбдал
UYG: abdal
UZB: абдал

abdal[2] ابدال ARABIC *n.* one who performs circumcisions

KAR: әбдәл
TAJ: абдал
TAT: сөннәтче бабай
UYG: abdal
UZB: абдал

abdal[3] ابدال ARABIC *Sufism n.* unseen spirits of saints ☞ ***rijal al-ghayb***

KAR: әбдәл
TAJ: абдалон
TAT: абдаллар
UZB: абдал

abdast آبدست PERSIAN *n.* ablutions ☞ ***taharat***

KAR: абдәст
TAJ: обдаст
TAT: абдәст, әбъдәст
UYG: abdäst, äbdäst
UZB: обдаст

abdasta آبدسته PERSIAN *n.* pitcher (for performing ablutions) ☞ ***abdast***

KAR: абдәсте
TAJ: обдаста, офтоба
UYG: abdasta
UZB: обдаста

abdastkhana آدستخانه PERSIAN *n.* place for performing ablutions ☞ ***taharatkhana***

KAR: абдәстехана
TAT: абдәстханә, әбъдәстханә
UYG: abdästkhanä
UZB: обдастхона

'Abdullah[1] عبدالله ARABIC *pn.* Slave of God (epithet of the prophets Abraham and Jesus)

KAR: Әбдулле, Абдулла, Абдылла
TAJ: Абдулло
TAT: Габдулла
TUR: Абдылла
UYG: Abdalla
UZB: Абдулла

'Abdullah[2] عبدالله ARABIC *pn.* name of the prophet Muhammad's father

KAR: Әбдулле
TAJ: Абдулло
TAT: Габдулла
TUR: Абдылла
UYG: Abdalla
UZB: Абдулла

ab-i hayat آب حیات PERSIAN *np.* the Water of Life, water believed to provide eternal life

BAS: абелхаят
KAR: абыҳәят
TAJ: оби ҳаёт
TAT: абелхәят
UYG: abihayat, abu hayat
UZB: оби ҳаёт

ab-i Zamzam آب زمزم PERSIAN *Hajj np.* water from the well of Zamzam ☞ ***Zamzam***

BAS: Зәмзәм һыуы
KAR: Абызәмзәм, Зәмзәм суўы, Зәмзәм абы, Әбизәмзәм
KYR: замзам суусу, абузамзам суусу

TAJ: оби Замзам
TAT: Зәмзәм суы
UYG: Abizamzam
UZB: оби Замзам

ʻabid عابد ARABIC *n.* devotee, worshiper
BAS: ғабид
KAR: абыт
KYR: абид
TAJ: обид
TAT: габид ① *devotee, worshiper* ② *Sufi*
UYG: abid
UZB: обид

ʻabida عابده ARABIC *n.* religious woman, pious woman
KAR: абытә
TAJ: обида
UYG: abidä
UZB: обида

abida آبيده ARABIC *n.* tombstone
KAR: абыдә
TAJ: обида
UYG: abidä
UZB: обида

ʻabir عبير ARABIC *Hajj n.* perfume, musk (typically given to pilgrims during the hajj)
KAR: абыр
TAJ: абир
UYG: abir, ipar
UZB: абир

abiz آبيض TURKIC *Historical n.* one possessing a religious education, learned in religion ☞ ***hafiz***
BAS: абыз
KAZ: абыз ① *one possessing a religious education, learned in religion* ② *soothsayer, fortune-teller*
KYR: апыз ① *learned person* ② *poet* ③ *singer*
TAT: абыз

abjad ابجد ARABIC *n.* ordering of Arabic letters in which each letter is accorded a numeric value; system used to form chronograms
BAS: әбжәт
KAR: абжат
KAZ: абжəд, əбжет
KYR: абжат
TAJ: абҷад
UYG: abjad
UZB: абжад

abrar ابرار ARABIC *adj.* pious, godly
BAS: әбрәр
KAR: әбрар
TAJ: аброр
TAT: әбрар
UYG: abrar
UZB: аброр

abu ابو ARABIC *n.* father
BAS: Әбү
KAR: Абу, Әбу
KAZ: Әбу
KYR: Абу
TAJ: Абу
TAT: Әбу
TUR: Абу
UYG: Abu
UZB: Абу

Abu Bakr ابو بكر ARABIC *pn.* the prophet Muhammad's father-in-law and the first of the four righteous caliphs
BAS: Әбүбәкер Ситдик
KAR: Әбу Бакр, Әбуўбәкир
KAZ: Әбу Бакр, Әбу Бакір
KYR: Абубакир, Абубакр
TAJ: Абу Бакр
TAT: Әбу Бәкер
TUR: Абу Бекир
UYG: Abu Bekr
UZB: Абу Бакр

Abu Hanifa ابو حنيفه ARABIC *n.* legal scholar and theologian, after whom the Hanafi school of jurisprudence (699-767)
KAR: Әбу Қанифе
TAJ: Абу Ҳанифа
TAT: Әбү Хәнифә
UYG: Abu Hanipa
UZB: Абу Ҳанифа

abvab al-Qur'an ابواب القرآن ARABIC *Qur'an np.* suras, parts of the Qur'an
TAJ: абобил қуръон
UZB: абобул қуръон

ʻAd عاد ARABIC *Historical pn.* a tribe, mentioned in the Qur'an, to which the prophets Hud and Salih were sent
KAR: Әд
KAZ: Ғад
TAJ: Ад

TAT: Гад
TUR: Ад
UYG: Äd, Ad
UZB: Од

adab ادب ARABIC *n.* good behavior, ethical behavior, politeness, manners
BAS: әҙәп
KAR: әдеп
KYR: адеп
TAJ: адаб
TAT: әдәб
TUR: эдеп
UYG: adäb
UZB: адаб

'adalat عدالت PERSIAN *n.* fairness, justice
BAS: ғәҙәләт
KAR: әдалат
KAZ: әділет
KYR: адилат
TAJ: адолат
TAT: гадаләт
UYG: adalät
UZB: адолат

Adam آدم ARABIC *pn.* the prophet Adam
BAS: Әҙәм
KAR: Адам әлеусәләм
KAZ: Адамата, Адам Ата
KYR: Адам
TAJ: Одам
TAT: Адәм, Адәм ата, Әдәм
TUR: Адам, Адамата, Адам ата
UYG: Adämata
UZB: Одам, Одам Ато

'adat عادات ARABIC *Law n.* custom, esp. customary law practiced in Muslim societies
BAS: ғәҙәт
KAR: әдет
KAZ: әдет, ғадет
KYR: адат
TAJ: одат
TAT: гадәт
TUR: адат
UYG: adät ① *custom, tradition (in contrast to Islamic law)* ② *superstition*
UZB: одат

'adavat عداوة ARABIC *n.* enmity
KAR: адаўат
TAJ: адоват
TAT: гадавәт
UYG: adävät
UZB: адоват

'adil عادل ARABIC *adj.* just, fair
BAS: ғәҙел
KAR: әдыл, әдил
KAZ: әділ, ғаділ ① *just, fair* ② *righteous*
KYR: адил, адел
TAJ: одил
TAT: гадил
UYG: adil
UZB: одил

'Adiyat عاديات ARABIC *Qur'an n.* the 100th sura of the Qur'an
KAR: Әдыят суўреси
KAZ: Ғадят сүресі
TAJ: сураи Одиёт
UYG: surä Adiyat
UZB: Вал-одиёт сураси

'adl عدل ARABIC *n.* justice, correctness
BAS: ғәҙел
KAR: әдл
KAZ: ғадл
TAJ: адл
TAT: гадел
UYG: ädl
UZB: адл, адолат

'Adl, al- العادل ARABIC *n.* name of God: the Just
KAR: Әдил
TAJ: Одил
TUR: ал-Адл
UYG: Adil
UZB: Ал-Одил

'adn عدن ARABIC *n.* Heaven, Paradise, Eden
☞ ***jannat, jannat al-firdaus***
KAR: адан
KAZ: ғадн, ғадын
TAJ: адан
TAT: гаден
UZB: адан

Aflatun افلاطون ARABIC *pn.* Plato (the ancient Greek philosopher)
KAR: Әплатун
TAJ: Афлотун
TAT: Әфләтун
UZB: Афлотун

afsana افسانه PERSIAN *n.* legend, fairy tale
- **KAR:** эпсана
- **TAJ:** афсона
- **TAT:** әфсанә
- **UYG:** äpsana, äpsanä
- **UZB:** афсона

afsun افسون PERSIAN *n.* sorcery, divination
- **KAR:** эпсын
- **TAJ:** афсун
- **TAT:** әфсун
- **UYG:** äpsun
- **UZB:** афсун

aftada افتاده PERSIAN *n.* poor, modest, weakened
- **KAR:** пахыр
- **TAJ:** афтода
- **UYG:** aptädä
- **UZB:** афтода

'Afuv, al- العفو ARABIC *n.* name of God: the Pardoner
- **BAS:** Ғәфү
- **KAR:** Әпиў
- **TAJ:** Авфу
- **TAT:** Гафу
- **TUR:** ал-Афу
- **UZB:** Ал-Авфув

afyun افيون PERSIAN *n.* narcotics
- **KAR:** неше
- **TAJ:** афьюн
- **UZB:** афюн, наша

ahad آحد ARABIC *Hadith adj.* not directly transmitted (as a category of hadith)
- **UZB:** оҳад

Ahad, al- الاحد ARABIC *n.* name of God: the One
- **KAR:** Әҳед
- **TAJ:** Аҳад
- **TUR:** ал-Ахад, Еке-тәк
- **UYG:** Ahäd
- **UZB:** Ал-Аҳад

ahbab احباب ARABIC *Sufism n.* Sufis (lit. "friends") ☞ ***muhibb***
- **KAR:** әхбаб
- **TAJ:** аҳбоб
- **TAT:** әхбаб
- **UYG:** ähbäb
- **UZB:** аҳбоб

'ahd عهد ARABIC *n.* promise, oath
- **KAR:** ўәде
- **KAZ:** ахд, ант
- **KYR:** ант
- **TAJ:** аҳд
- **TAT:** гаһед, ант
- **TUR:** ант
- **UYG:** ähd
- **UZB:** аҳд, ант

ahkam احكام ARABIC *n.* rulings, judgments, verdicts (on the basis of Islamic law)
- **BAS:** әхкәм
- **KAZ:** ахкам
- **TAJ:** аҳком
- **TAT:** әхкям
- **UYG:** ähkäm
- **UZB:** аҳком

ahl al-vilayat اهل الولايت ARABIC *np.* holy persons (descendants of sahabas, tabi'un, etc.)
- **TAJ:** аҳлал вилоят
- **TAT:** әһлел-виляят
- **UZB:** аҳлал вилоят

ahl-i dil اهل دل PERSIAN *Sufism np.* Sufis, dervishes (lit. people of the heart)
- **TAJ:** аҳли дил
- **UZB:** аҳли дил

ahl-i Islam اهل اسلام PERSIAN *n.* Muslims, followers of Islam
- **BAS:** әһле Ислам
- **KAR:** әҳли Ислам
- **TAJ:** аҷли Ислом
- **TAT:** әһле Ислам
- **UYG:** ähli Islam
- **UZB:** аҳли Ислом

ahl-i kitab اهل كتاب PERSIAN *n.* People of the Book; adherents of the teaching of the Torah, Gospels and of the Qur'an; Muslims, Christians, and Jews (collectively)
- **KAR:** әҳли китап
- **KAZ:** аһл әл-кітаб, жазу адамдары, әһли кітап
- **TAJ:** аҳли Китоб
- **TAT:** әһле Китап
- **TUR:** ахл ал-китап
- **UYG:** ähli kitap
- **UZB:** аҳли Китоб

ahl-i qalam اهل قلم PERSIAN *np.* bureaucrats
- **BAS:** әһле ҡәләм
- **KAR:** әҳли қәлем
- **TAJ:** аҳли қалам

UYG: ähli qäläm
UZB: аҳли қалам

ahl-i ra'y اهل رأی ARABIC *Law np.* scholars who solve primarily theological and juridical disputes using reason
KAR: әҳли рәй
TAJ: аҳли рай
UYG: ähli räy
UZB: аҳли рай

ahl-i salib اهل صليب PERSIAN *n.* People of the Cross, Christians; Crusaders
KAR: әҳли селиб
TAJ: аҳли салиб
TAT: әһле салиб
UYG: ähli salib *Crusaders*
UZB: аҳли салб, аҳли салиб

ahl-i sunna اهل سنّه PERSIAN *np.* people of the Sunna, Sunnis
KAR: әҳли сунна
KAZ: ахл ал-сунна, сунниттер
TAJ: аҳли Сунна
TAT: әһлес-сөннә, әһле сөннәт
UZB: аҳли Сунна

ahl-i tariqat اهل طريقت PERSIAN *Sufism np.* Sufis (lit. people of the tariqa)
KAR: әҳли тәриқет
KAZ: әһли тариқат
TAJ: аҳли тариқат
UYG: ähli täriqat
UZB: аҳли тариқат

ahl-i zimmat اهل زمّة PERSIAN *np.* Christians or Jews inhabiting a Muslim country
TAJ: аҳли зиммат
UZB: аҳли зиммат

ahliyyat-i ada اهليّت ادا PERSIAN *Hadith np.* permission to teach hadith
TAJ: аҳлияти адо
UZB: адо аҳлияти

ahliyyat-i vujub اهليّت وجوب PERSIAN *n.* human rights conferred by God
TAJ: аҳлияти вуҷуб
UZB: аҳлияти вужуб

Ahmad احمد ARABIC *pn.* the most praised, epithet of the prophet Muhammad
BAS: Әхмәд
KAR: Ақмет
KAZ: Ахмәд
TAJ: Аҳмад
TAT: Әхмәд
UYG: Äkhmät
UZB: Аҳмад

Ahqaf احقاف ARABIC *n.* the 46th sura of the Qur'an
KAR: Әхқәф суўреси
KAZ: Ахқаф сүресі
TAJ: сураи Аҳқоф
UYG: Ahqäp süräsi, sürä Ähqaf
UZB: Аҳқоф сураси

ahrar احرار ARABIC *Law n.* free man (singular)
KAR: ақрар
TAJ: аҳрор
TAT: әхрар
UYG: ahrär
UZB: аҳрор

Ahzab احزاب ARABIC *Qur'an n.* the 33rd sura of the Qur'an
KAR: Әҳзап суўреси
KAZ: Ахзап сүресі
TAJ: сураи Аҳзоб
UYG: Ahzäb süräsi, sürä Ähzab
UZB: Аҳзоб сураси

ʻA'isha عائشه ARABIC *pn.* the wife of the prophet Muhammad and the daughter of the Caliph Abu Bakr
BAS: Ғәйшә
KAR: Айша
KAZ: Айша
TAJ: Оиша
TAT: Гайшә
TUR: Айша
UZB: Ойша

ajal اجل ARABIC *n.* the appointed time, the moment of death
BAS: әжәл
KAR: әжел
KAZ: ажал
KYR: ажал
TAJ: аҷал
TAT: әҗәл
TUR: аҗал
UYG: äjal, äjäl
UZB: ажал

ʻajam عجم ARABIC *n.* Iranian, non-Arab
KAR: әжем

KAZ: ғажем
TAJ: ачам
TAT: гаҗәм
UYG: äjäm *Persian*
UZB: ажам

ajnabi اجنابی ARABIC *n.* strange, foreign (for people)
KAR: әжнебы
TAJ: ачнабӣ
UYG: äjnabi, äjnibi
UZB: ажнабий

ajr اجر ARABIC *n.* reward, recompense
KAR: әжр
TAJ: ачр
TAT: әҗер
UYG: ajr
UZB: ажр

akbar ☞ ***allahu akbar***

akhbar اخبار ARABIC *Hadith n.* traditions of the prophet Muhammad, synonymous with hadith ☞ ***hadith***
KAR: ақпар, хабар
KAZ: ақпар, ахбар
KYR: кабарлар
TAJ: ахбор
TAT: әхбар
TUR: ахбар, хабарлар
UZB: ахборот, хабар

akhi اخی ARABIC *Sufism n.* brother in a Sufi order, fellow Sufi
TAT: әхи, ахи

Akhir, al- الآخر ARABIC *n.* name of God: the Last
KAR: Ақыр
TAJ: Охир
TUR: ал-Ахир
UZB: Ал-Охир

akhir zaman آخر زمان ARABIC *n.* apocalypse, the End of the World, the end of life on earth (as foretold in the Qur'an)
BAS: ахыры заман, заман ахыры, ахыр заман
KAR: ақырзаман
KAZ: заман ақыр, ақырзаман
KYR: акыр заман
TAJ: охирзамон
TAT: ахыр заман
TUR: ахырзаман, ахырзамана
UYG: akhir zaman
UZB: охирзамон

akhirat آخرت PERSIAN *n.* the afterlife
BAS: әхирәт
KAR: ақырат
KAZ: ақырет, ахирет, ақирет, ақырет күні, ахар ① *the afterlife* ② *burial shroud*
KYR: акырет, акрет
TAJ: охират
TAT: ахирәт ① *the afterlife* ② *loyal friend*
TUR: ахырет
UYG: akhirät
UZB: охират

akhirat batqaghi آخرت باطقاغی TURKIC *Ritual np.* part of the burial shroud covering the body from the neck to the feet
TAT: ахирәт күлмәге
UZB: охират ботқоғи

akhiravi آخراوی ARABIC *adj.* pertaining to the afterlife
TAT: әхыйрави

akhlaq اخلاق ARABIC *n.* morals, ethics ☞ ***husn-i akhlaq***
BAS: әхләк
KAR: әхлақ
KAZ: әхлақ, ахлақ
KYR: ахлак
TAJ: ахлоқ
TAT: әхлакъ
TUR: ахлак
UYG: äkhlaq
UZB: ахлоқ

akhun آخون ☞ ***akhund***

akhund آخوند PERSIAN *n.* learned figure, usually a senior authority in Islamic law (the sense of this term, however, varies widely in the Islamic world as a whole, as well as within various regions of Inner Asia)
BAS: ахун ① *authority in Islamic law* ② *an official title in the imperial Russian period signifying the head of official Islamic scholars in a given district.*
KAR: ақун, ахун ① *senior religious scholar* ② *title held by Uyghurs*
KAZ: ахун, ақын ① *authority in Islamic law* ② *an official title in the imperial Russian period signifying the head of official Islamic scholars in a given district* ③ *poet*
KYR: акун, ахун, акын ① *person possessing religious authority* ② *poet poet-scribe* ③ *person who has*

received training in the Kashgar madrasas ④ *Uyghur*

TAJ: охун, охунд ① *person possessing high religious authority* ② *teacher,* ③ *wise man, master*

TAT: ахун, ахунд ① *authority in Islamic law* ② *an official title in the imperial Russian period signifying the head of official Islamic scholars in a given district.*

TUR: ахун

UYG: akhun

UZB: охун, охунд ① *person possessing high religious authority* ② *intelligent man* ③ *Uyghur*

akmal اکمل ARABIC *Ritual adj.* complete, sufficient, full (a status of acts of devotion)

TAJ: комил

TAT: әкмал

UYG: äkmäl

UZB: акмал, комил

akram اکرم *adj.* generous, most noble

KAR: әкрем

TAJ: акром

TAT: әкрәм

UYG: äkräm

UZB: акрам

A'la اعلى ARABIC *Qur'an pn.* the 87th sura of the Qur'an

KAR: Әьла суўреси

KAZ: Ағла сүресі

TAJ: сураи Аъло

TAT: Әгъла сүрәсе

UYG: A'la süräsi, sürä Ä'la

UZB: Аъло сураси

a'lam اعلم ARABIC *Law n.* expert in Islamic law

KAR: әълэм

TAJ: аълам

TAT: әгъләм

UYG: a'läm

UZB: аълам

'alam [1] عالم ARABIC *n.* the World, the Universe

BAS: ғаләм

KAR: әлем

KAZ: әлем, ғалам

KYR: аалам

TAJ: олам

TAT: галәм

TUR: әлем

UYG: aläm

UZB: олам

'alam [2] علم flag, banner (esp. carried in processions during Muharram)

KAZ: әлем *standard placed at a shrine of a Muslim saint*

TAJ: аълам

TAT: әләм

UYG: äläm

UZB: аълам

'alamat علامات ARABIC *n.* warning signs of Judgment Day

TAJ: аломат

TAT: галямәт

UZB: аломат, қиёмат аломатлари

'Alaq علق ARABIC *Qur'an n.* the 96th sura of the Qur'an

KAR: Алақ суўреси

KAZ: Ғалақ сүресі

TAJ: сураи Алақ

TUR: сураи Алак, сураи Ыкра

UYG: sürä Äläq

UZB: Алақ сураси

'alaviyat علويات ARABIC *n.* realm of the heavens, the heavens and their contents

TAT: галәвият

'alayhi al-salam عليه السلام ARABIC *intj.* peace be upon him (pious phrase uttered after saying the name of a prophet)

BAS: ғәләйһәссәләм, ғәлиәссәләм

KAZ: ғалаhиссалам, ғаләйhиссәләм

KYR: алик, алейсалам, алей салам

TAJ: алайҳисалом

TAT: галәйһиссәлам

TUR: алейхис салам, алейхэссалам

UYG: äläyhissalam

UZB: алайҳис салом

'alaykim al-salam و عليكم السلام ARABIC *intj.* and peace be upon you (said in response to the greeting "peace be upon you")

BAS: вәғәләйкүм, вәғәләйкүм әссәләм

KAR: алейким-у-салам

KAZ: уағалайкүмуссәләм, әлейкүмуссәлем

KYR: валекиме салам, алейкүм-ассалам, алейки-салам, алейкиме салам

TAJ: ва алайкум ассалом

UYG: wa'alaykum ässälam

UZB: ваалайкум ассалом

al-hamdulillahi rabbi'l-'alamin الحمد لله رب العالمين ARABIC Praise be to Allah, the Lord of the Worlds
- **KAR:** Әлҳәмдиллилау реббил аламин
- **TAJ:** Алҳамдуллилоҳу раббил оламин
- **TAT:** әлхәмдүллилаh раббелгаләмийн
- **TUR:** элхамдү лилләхи реббил әлеминә
- **UZB:** Алҳамдуллилаҳу раббил оламин

al-hamdullilah الحمدلله ARABIC *intj.* praise God
- **BAS:** әлхәмделилла
- **KAR:** әлҳәмдиллила, әлҳәмдулла
- **KYR:** алкамду лиила, алхамдуллила алхамду лилла
- **TAJ:** алҳамдулилло
- **TAT:** әлхәмде лилля, хәмеде лилләh, әлхәмдүллилаh
- **TUR:** алхамдиллила
- **UZB:** алҳамдулиллоҳ

'Ali علی ARABIC *pn.* the fourth of the four righteous caliphs
- **BAS:** Ғали
- **KAR:** Әли, Әлий
- **KAZ:** Әлі, Әзірет Әлі
- **KYR:** Аалы, Азирет Аалы
- **TAJ:** Али ибн Толиб, Ҳазрат Али
- **TAT:** Гали
- **TUR:** Алы
- **UZB:** Али ибн Абу Толиб, Ҳазрати Али

al-i aba آل ابا ARABIC *np.* descendants of the prophet Muhammad
- **TAJ:** олӣабо
- **UZB:** олий або

'Ali, al- العلی ARABIC *n.* name of God: the Lofty
- **KAR:** Әлий
- **KAZ:** Ғали
- **TAJ:** Олӣ
- **TUR:** ал-Алы
- **UZB:** Ал-Оли

Al-i Imran آل عمران ARABIC *Qur'an n.* the 3rd sura of the Qur'an
- **KAR:** Әли Имран суўреси
- **KAZ:** Әли Ғымран сүресі
- **TAJ:** сураи Оли Имрон
- **TAT:** Гыймран сүрәсе
- **UYG:** Imrän, sürä Al Imran
- **UZB:** Ол-и Имрон сураси

alif lam mim ا ل م ARABIC *Qur'an n.* initial part of the 2nd Sura
- **BAS:** әлиф
- **KAR:** әлип
- **TAJ:** алиф лом мим
- **UYG:** alip, elip
- **UZB:** алиф лом мим

'alim عالم ARABIC *n.* scholar, esp. legal scholar ☞ ***'ulama***
- **BAS:** ғалим
- **KAR:** әлим, алым
- **KAZ:** ғалым
- **KYR:** аалым, аалим, алым
- **TAJ:** олим
- **TAT:** галим
- **TUR:** алым
- **UYG:** alim
- **UZB:** олим

'Alim, al- العليم ARABIC *pn.* name of God: the Knower
- **KAR:** Әлим
- **KAZ:** Ғалим
- **TAJ:** Олим
- **TAT:** Галим
- **TUR:** ал-Алим
- **UZB:** Ал-Олим

Allah الله ARABIC *n.* God, Allah
- **BAS:** Алла
- **KAR:** Алла
- **KAZ:** Алла
- **KYR:** Алда, Алла, Алло, Олдо
- **TAJ:** Оллоҳ
- **TAT:** Алла, Аллаh
- **TUR:** Алла, Пелек
- **UYG:** Alla
- **UZB:** Аллоҳ

Allah hu الله هو ARABIC *Ritual intj.* God exists! (a formulation used especially in performing dhikr)
- **KAR:** Аллау!
- **KYR:** олдо үй
- **TAJ:** Аллоҳу!
- **UZB:** Аллоҳу! Оллоҳу!

Allah ta'ala الله تعالی ARABIC *np.* God, God the Exalted
- **BAS:** Алла тәғәлә
- **KAR:** Алла тағала, аллатала, Алла тәала, Алла тала
- **KAZ:** Алла тағала
- **KYR:** Алда Таала
- **TAJ:** Аллоҳу таволло

TAT: Аллаһ тәгалә, Аллатәгалә
TUR: Алла тагала, Аллатагала
UYG: allahi ta'ala
UZB: Аллоҳу таолло

Allah ya Allah الله يا الله ARABIC *intj.* God oh God! (an invocation affirming God's oneness)
BAS: Я алла
KAR: Алла-Алла!
KYR: алда-жалда
TAJ: Аллоҳ ё Аллоҳ
UZB: Аллоҳ ё Аллоҳ, Оллоҳ ё Оллоҳ

allahi billahi الله با لله ARABIC *intj.* God is a witness! (expression of pious astonishment)
KAR: Алла билла
KYR: олдо-бүлдө
TAJ: Аллаҳи биллаҳ
UZB: Аллоҳи биллаҳи

Allahu akbar الله اكبر ARABIC *np.* God is great ☞ ***takbir***
BAS: аллаһы әкбәр
KAR: Аллакбар, аллаакбар
KAZ: аллаһу-акбар, Алла-акпар, аллаһу-әкбәр,
KYR: алдоо акпар, алло акпар, алооки акбар, акбар, акпар
TAJ: Оллоҳу Акбар, Аллоҳу Акбар
TAT: аллаһу әкбәр
TUR: аллаху акбер, аллаху экбер
UYG: allahuäkbär, allahu äkbär
UZB: Аллоҳу Акбар, Оллоакбар

Allahu aʿlam biʾl-savab الله أعلم بالصواب ARABIC *np.* only God knows the right of it
TUR: Аллахы аглам бес соваб
UZB: Аллоҳу аълам

Allahu ʿAlimun الله عالم ARABIC *np.* God the knower ☞ ***zikr-i khafi***
KAR: Алла Алим
TAJ: Аллоҳу Олимун
UZB: Аллоҳу Олимун

Allahu Bashirun الله بشير ARABIC *np.* God the Seer
KAR: Алла Бәшир
TAJ: Аллоҳу Баширун
UZB: Аллоҳу Баширин

Allahu Samiʿun الله سميع ARABIC *np.* God the Hearer
KAR: Алла Сәми
TAJ: Аллоҳу Самиун
UZB: Аллоҳу Самиун

allahyar الله يار PERSIAN *n.* friend of God; your worship (form of address to a an authoritative religious figure)
KAR: аллыяр, аллияр, аллаяр
KAZ: алдияр
KYR: алдаяр, аллаяр, элдияр
TAJ: аллаёр
UZB: оллоёр

ʿAllam al-ghuyub علّام الغيوب ARABIC *pn.* Who knows the shortcomings of people (epithet of God)
TAJ: Аллам ал ғаюб
TAT: Галлямелгоюб
UZB: Аллам ал ғаюб

ʿallama علّامه ARABIC *n.* eminent scholar, erudite scholar
KAR: әлламе
KAZ: ғаллама
TAJ: аллома
TAT: галлямә
UYG: allämä
UZB: аллома

Alyasaʿ اليسع ARABIC *pn.* the prophet Alyasa'
KAR: Әляса
KAZ: Әлясаға
TAJ: Алийоса
TUR: Элиеса
UYG: Ilyäsä'
UZB: Алиёса

aʿma اعما ARABIC *Sufism n.* blind, i.e. one who is learned but is unaware of the truth
TAJ: амо
UZB: амо

ʿamal عمل ARABIC *n.* action (in fulfilling faith)
BAS: ғәмәл
KAR: әмел
KAZ: ғамал
KYR: амал
TAJ: амал
TAT: гамәл
UYG: amäl, ämäl
UZB: амал

ʿamama عمامه ARABIC *n.* turban ☞ ***chalma***
KAR: сәлле
KAZ: имама
TAJ: аммома
TAT: гамамә

amanat امانات ARABIC *Law n.* securities, a branch of civil jurisprudence involving safekeeping, pledges, etc. ☞ ***mu'amalat***

KAR: аманат
KYR: аманат
TAT: әманәт
TUR: аманат
UZB: омонат

'amd ☞ ***qatl 'amd, qatl shubha 'amd***

amin[1] آمين ARABIC *Ritual intj.* amen, let it be so

BAS: амин
KAR: әмин, әмийин, әўмийин
KYR: амин, омийин, оомийн, оомийин
TAJ: омин
TAT: амин, әмин, амийн
TUR: әмин
UYG: amin
UZB: омин, овмин, овмийн

Amin[2] امين ARABIC *pn.* the Reliable, the Trustworthy, the Honest (epithet of the prophet Muhammad)

KAR: әмин
TAJ: омин
TAT: амин, әмин
TUR: әмин
UYG: amin
UZB: омин

amir امير ARABIC *n.* emir, commander; prince

BAS: әмир
KAR: әмир
KAZ: әмір, мір
KYR: амир, амыр
TAJ: амир
TAT: әмир
TUR: эмир, амр
UYG: ämir
UZB: амир

Amir al-mu'minin امير المؤمنين ARABIC *np.* Commander of the Faithful, Caliph

KAR: әмирул мүмин
TAJ: амирул мумин
TAT: Әмирел-мөәминин
TUR: эмир эл-мөмин
UYG: ämirul möminin, ämirulmu'minin
UZB: амирул мўмин

amir al-muslimun امير المسلمون ARABIC *Historical np.* Commander of the Muslims (e.g., the Prophet Muhammad, the Caliphs, etc.)

TAJ: амир ал муслимун
UZB: амирул муслимун

amir al-umara امير الامرا ARABIC *Historical np.* Commander of the commanders (epithet of the Prophet Muhammad)

KAR: әмирул-үмера
TAJ: амир ал умаро
UZB: амирул умаро

amlak املاك ARABIC *Law n.* property (plural form) ☞ ***mulk***

KAR: әмлак
TAJ: амлок
TAT: әмляк
UYG: amläk
UZB: амлок, мулк

amniyat امنيت ARABIC *n.* peace, security

KAR: әмниет
TAJ: амн, амният
TAT: әминият
UYG: ämniyät
UZB: амният, омончилик

amr امر ARABIC *n.* order, command (of a ruler)

KAR: әмр
TAJ: амр
UYG: ämr
UZB: амр

amr-i Ma'ruf امر معروف PERSIAN *np.* commanding the good (Islamic moral imperative)

KAR: әмри меруп
TAJ: амри маъруф
UYG: ämri märüp
UZB: амри маъруф

ana al-haqq انا الحقّ ARABIC *intj.* I'm right! (phrase attributed to the Sufi Mansur Hallaj)

KAR: әнел-ҳақ
TAJ: анал-хақ
UYG: änäl haq
UZB: анал-ҳақ

An'am انعام ARABIC *Qur'an n.* the 6th sura of the Qur'an

KAR: Әнъәм суўреси
KAZ: Әнғам сүресі
TAJ: сураи Анъом
TAT: Әл-Әнгам сүрәсе, Әнгәм сүрәсе
UYG: An'äm süräsi, sura Än'am
UZB: Анъом сураси

anbar [1] عنبر ARABIC *Hajj n.* ambergris (given to pilgrims during the hajj)

BAS: ғәмбәр
KAR: әнбер
TAJ: анбар
TAT: ганбәр
UYG: änbär
UZB: анбар

anbar [2] عنبر ARABIC *n.* Jewish scholars, rabbis

TAJ: анбор
UZB: анбор

anbiya [1] انبياء ARABIC *n.* prophets (plural of nabi) ☞ ***nabi***

BAS: әнбия *prophet*
KAR: әнбия
KAZ: әнбие
KYR: анбия *prophet (singular)*
TAJ: анбиё
TAT: әнбия
UYG: änbiya ① *prophet* ② *fortune-teller*
UZB: анбиё

Anbiya [2] انبياء ARABIC *Qur'an n.* the 21st sura of the Qur'an

KAR: Әнбия суўреси
KAZ: Әнбия сүресі
TAJ: сураи Анбиё
TAT: Әнбия сурәсе
UYG: sürä Änbiya
UZB: Анбиё сураси

andarun اندرون PERSIAN *n.* inner part; section of a house restricted to women

TAJ: андарун
TAT: әндәрун
UZB: андарун

Anfal انفال ARABIC *Qur'an n.* the 8th sura of the Qur'an

KAR: Әнпал суўреси
KAZ: Әнфал сүресі
TAJ: сураи Анфол
UYG: Anpol süräsi, sürä Änfal
UZB: Анфол сураси

anjuman انجمن PERSIAN *n.* meeting (of scholars); society

KAR: әнжумен
TAJ: анчуман
TAT: әнҗемән
UYG: änjumän
UZB: анжуман

'Ankabut عنكبوت ARABIC *Qur'an pn.* the 29th sura of the Qur'an

KAR: Әнкәбут суўреси
KAZ: Ғанкәбұт сүресі
TAJ: сураи Анкабут
UYG: Änkabut süräsi, sürä Änkä But
UZB: Анкабут сураси

'Anqa عنقا ARABIC *pn.* name of a mythical bird

KAR: әнқә
TAJ: анқо
TAT: ганка
UZB: анқо

ansar انصار ARABIC *Historical n.* helpers; the inhabitants of the city of Medina who invited the prophet Muhammad and his followers to their city

KAR: әнсар
KAZ: әл-ансар, ансар
TAJ: ансор
TAT: әнсар
TUR: ансар ① *helpers of the prophet Muhammad* ② *Christian*
UYG: ansär
UZB: ансорлар

anvar انوار ARABIC *n.* divine light

BAS: әнүәр
KAR: әнўәр
KYR: анвар
TAJ: анвор
TAT: әнвәр
UYG: änwär
UZB: анвар

'aqibat عاقبت ARABIC *n.* Judgment Day, the End of the World

KAR: ақибат
KAZ: ғақибат
TAJ: оқибат
TAT: гакыйбәт
UYG: äqibat
UZB: оқибат

'aqida عقيده ARABIC *n.* article of faith, dogma, creed

BAS: ғәкидә
KAR: ақидә
KAZ: акида
TAJ: ақида
TAT: гакыйдә
TUR: акыда

UYG: äqidä
UZB: ақида

'aqiqa عقيقه ARABIC *Ritual n.* sacrifice performed on the seventh day after the birth of a child
TAJ: ақиқа
TAT: гакыйка корбаны
UYG: äqiqä
UZB: ақиқа

'aqliyat عقليات ARABIC *n.* philosophical conceptions (as a topic in the madrasa curriculum)
KAZ: ғақлия
TAJ: ақлият
TAT: гаклыять
UZB: ақлият

'Aqrab عقرب ARABIC *pn.* 9th month of the Hidjri Solar year; Scorpio
BAS: Ғәкрәп
KAR: әқреб, ақрап
KAZ: Ғақраб
TAJ: Ақраб
TAT: Гакрәб
UYG: Äqrap
UZB: Ақраб

aqraba اقربا ARABIC *Law n.* relatives
TAJ: ақрабо
TAT: экъриба
UZB: ақрабо, хеш-ақрабо

a'raf [1] اعراف ARABIC *n.* purgatory
BAS: әғраф
KAR: әъраф
KAZ: ағраф
TAJ: аъраф
TAT: эгъраф
UZB: аъроф

A'raf [2] اعراف ARABIC *Qur'an n.* the 7th sura of the Qur'an
KAR: Әъраф суўреси
KAZ: Ағраф сүресі
TAJ: сураи Аъроф
TAT: Әгъраф сүрәсе, Әл-эгъраф сүрәсе
TUR: сураи Аграф
UYG: A'räp, sürä Ä'raf
UZB: Аъроф сураси

'arafa عرفة ARABIC *Ritual n.* last day of the month of Ramadan; the 9th day of Zu'lhijja, when the the pilgrims assemble at mount 'Arafat near Mecca ☞ ***shak***
BAS: ғәрәфә, ғәрәфә көн, әрәпә
KAR: әрапә
KAZ: арафа күні, арапа күні
KYR: арапа
TAJ: арафа
TAT: гарәфә
TUR: арафа
UYG: äripä, äräpä, ärpat, harpa
UZB: арафа

'Arafat عرفات ARABIC *Hajj pn.* the name of a hill near Mecca which pilgrims climb as part of the hajj
BAS: Ғәрәфәт
KAR: Әрапат
KAZ: Арафат, Ғарапат
TAJ: Арофат
TAT: Гарәфәт
TUR: Арафат
UYG: Arapat
UZB: Арофат

'Arasat عرصات ARABIC *n.* a plain near Mecca where those who will be resurrected on Judgment Day are to be assembled ☞ ***hashir***
BAS: ғәрәсәт
KAR: әресат
KAZ: Ғарасат, Ғарасат мейданы
KYR: Арасат, Аразат
TAJ: арасот
TAT: гарәсат, Гарәсат мәйданы
UZB: аросат

'arif عارف ARABIC *n.* wise, informed, learned; a Sufi who knows God's qualities
KAR: әрип
TAJ: ориф
TAT: гариф
UZB: ориф

arkan اركان ARABIC *n.* supports, pillars (epithet of major figures in early Islamic history); pillars of faith, essential tenets of Islam ☞ ***rukn***
KAR: әркан
TAJ: аркон
TAT: әркян
UYG: ärkän
UZB: аркон

'arsh عرش ARABIC *n.* the location of God's throne in the Ninth Heaven
BAS: ғәреш
KAR: әрш

KAZ: ғарыш
KYR: арш
TAJ: арш
TAT: гареш, гәрш
TUR: арш, арыш
UYG: ärsh
UZB: арш

'arsh-i a'la عرش اعلا PERSIAN *n.* the summit of Heaven ☞ ***'arsh***
KAR: әршала
KYR: арши агла
TAJ: аршӣ аъло
TAT: гарше әгъля
UYG: ärsh-äla, ärshi a'la
UZB: арши аъло

'arsh-i kursi عرش کرسی PERSIAN *n.* God's throne in the Ninth Heaven ☞ ***'arsh***
BAS: ғәрше көрси
KYR: арыш-корш
TAJ: аршӣ курси
TAT: гарше көрси
UZB: арши курси

arvah ارواح ARABIC *n.* ghost, spirit; ancestral spirits ☞ ***ruh***
BAS: әруах
KAR: арўақ, әрўақ
KAZ: аруақ
KYR: арбак, обурак, абырак ① *ancestral spirits* ② *holy, sacred*
TAJ: арвоҳ
TAT: әрвәх
TUR: ал-арвах
UYG: ärwah, ärway
UZB: арвоҳ

'asa عصا ARABIC *n.* staff, rod (especially carried by the prophets Moses and Noah, and also by itinerant Sufis)
BAS: ғаса
KAR: ҳаса, аса
KAZ: аса, аса-муса
KYR: аса, аса-муса
TAJ: асо
TAT: гаса
TUR: хаса
UZB: ҳасса, асо

Asad اسد ARABIC *pn.* Leo; the sixth month of the Hidjri Solar year
BAS: Әсәд
KAR: асед, әсет
KAZ: Асад
TAJ: Асад
TAT: Әсәд
UYG: äsäd
UZB: Асад

Asadullah اسدالله ARABIC *pn.* the Lion of God (epithet of the Caliph 'Ali)
BAS: Асадулла
KAR: аседулла
TAJ: асадулоҳ
TAT: Әсәдулла
TUR: Эседулла
UYG: Asadulla
UZB: асадулло

asar اثر ARABIC *Hadith n.* hadith
TAT: әсәр
UZB: асар

asarat اسارت ARABIC *Law n.* captivity, imprisonment
KAR: асерет
TAJ: асорат
TAT: әсарәт
UYG: asärät
UZB: асорат

asfal al-safilin اسفل السافلین ARABIC *n.* the lowest of the low; Hell
TAJ: асфалуссофилин
TAT: әсфалессафилин
UZB: асфаласофилун, асфалуссофилин

ashab اصحاب ARABIC *Historical n.* companions of the prophet Muhammad ☞ ***sahaba***
BAS: әсхаб
KAR: әсҳаб
KAZ: асхаб, асхап
KYR: асаб
TAJ: асҳоб
TAT: әсхаб
TUR: асхаб, асхап
UYG: äshap
UZB: асҳоб

ashab al-rass ☞ ***Rass***

ashab-i Badr اصحاب بدر PERSIAN *Historical n.* companions who fought with the prophet Muhammad at the Battle of Badr
TAJ: азҳоби Бадр
UZB: асҳоби Бадр

ashab-i jannat اصحاب جنّت PERSIAN *n.* the blessed, inhabitants of Paradise
KAR: әсҳабул жәннат
KAZ: асхабу-л-жаннә
KYR: асабул жаннат
TAJ: асҳоби ҷаннат
UZB: асҳоби жаннат

ashab-i kahf اصحاب کهف PERSIAN *Historical pn.* followers of the prophet Muhammad said to have lived in a cave with their dogs; Christians who fled to a cave when they were persecuted because of their faith
KAZ: асхаб әл-кахф
TAJ: асҳобил кахф
TAT: әсхабе кәһәф
TUR: асхаб ал-кахф
UYG: äshabi kähäf
UZB: асҳоби коф

ashab-i kiram اصحاب کرام PERSIAN *Historical n.* the great companions (of the prophet Muhammad)
TAJ: асҳоби киром
UZB: асҳоби киром

'ashiq عاشق ARABIC *Sufism n.* Sufi, Sufi adept, one who loves God
TAJ: ошиқ
TAT: гашыйк, гашикъ
UZB: ошиқ

ashir عاشر ARABIC *Taxation n.* collector of Islamic taxes
TAT: гашир
UYG: ashir
UZB: ашир

ashraf اشرف ARABIC *n.* exalted, i.e. descendants of the prophet Muhammad ☞ ***sharif***
KAR: әшреп
TAJ: ашраф
UYG: äshräp
UZB: ашраф

ashrat-i sa'at اشرط ساعت PERSIAN *np.* signs of the arrival of Judgment Day
TAJ: ишорати қиёмат
UZB: ашрати саат, қиёмат ишоратлари

'Ashura [1] عاشورا ARABIC *Ritual n.* festival held on the 10th of Muharram commemorating the martyrdom of Husayn, the son of the Caliph Ali; the festival is primarily celebrated by Shi'ites ☞ ***muharram***
KAR: әшура
KAZ: ашура
KYR: ашура
TAJ: ашура
TAT: гашура, гашурә
TUR: ашура, мәхеррем
UYG: ghashura, äshurä, Äshurä bayrimi
UZB: ашура

ashura [2] عاشورا ARABIC *Ritual n.* a voluntary fast day, observed on the tenth of the Muharram
TAJ: ашура
UYG: äshurä
UZB: ашура

'asi عاصی ARABIC *adj.* sinner
BAS: ғаси
KAZ: ғаси
TAT: гасый
UYG: asi
UZB: осий

asir اسیر ARABIC *Law n.* captive, war prisoner
BAS: әсир
KAR: әсир
TAJ: асир
TAT: әсир
TUR: есир
UYG: äsir ① *captive* ② *slave*
UZB: асир

asitana آستانه PERSIAN *Sufism n.* the location of the residence or tomb of a Sufi order's chief shaykh; lit. threshold, beginning
BAS: астәнә
TAT: аситанә, астәнә

asma al-husna اسما الحسنه ARABIC *np.* the ninety-nine names of Allah (collectively)
KAZ: әл-асма әл-хусна
TAJ: эсма ул ҳусна
UZB: асма ул ҳусна, эсма ул ҳусна

asman اسمان PERSIAN *n.* the heavens; the sky, the firmament
BAS: асман, әсман
KAR: аспан, асман
KAZ: аспан
KYR: асман
TAJ: осмон
TAT: әсман
TUR: асман
UYG: asman

UZB: осмон

'asr[1] عصر ARABIC *Ritual n.* obligatory afternoon prayer ☞ ***salat al-'asr***

BAS: ғасыр

KAR: аср

TAJ: аср

TAT: гасыр

UYG: äsr

UZB: аср, аср намози

'Asr[2] عصر ARABIC *Qur'an n.* the 103rd sura of the Qur'an

KAR: Аср суўреси

KAZ: Ғасыр сүресі

TAJ: сураи Аср

TAT: гасыр сүрәсе

UYG: Äsr süräsi

UZB: Вал-аср сураси

assalamu 'alaykum السلام عليكم ARABIC *intj.* peace be upon you (greeting)

BAS: әссәләмәғәләйкүм

KAR: сәлем

KAZ: ассалаумағалайкум

KYR: ассалам алейкүм, ассалам алйким, ассалам алейкоом, атсалоому алейкүм, салам алейкүм, ассалоому алейкум, салоом алеки, салоом алейкүм

TAJ: салом, ассалому алайкум

TAT: әссәламе галәйкем

TUR: салавмалейким

UYG: salamu' äläykum

UZB: ассалому алайкум

astaghfirullah استغفرالله ARABIC *intj.* God forgive me

BAS: әстәғәфирулла

KAR: астапыралла, әстапыралла

KYR: астапурулда, астакпурулда, астакпырылда, астахбурулла

TAJ: астағфируллоҳ

TAT: әстәгъфируллаh

UYG: ästaghpurulla

UZB: астағфуруллоҳ

astana ☞ ***asitana***

atash آتش PERSIAN *Sufism n.* flame, esp. the flame of divine love

TAJ: оташ

TAT: атәш

UZB: оташ

atashparast آتشپرست PERSIAN *n.* Zoroastrian; fire worshipper ☞ ***majus***

KAR: әтешпәрест

TAJ: оташпараст

TAT: атәшпәрәст

TUR: аташ берес

UYG: atäshpäräs, atäshpäräst

UZB: оташпараст

'attar عطّار ARABIC *n.* seller (of Islamic articles)

KAR: аттар

TAJ: аттор

UYG: attär

UZB: аттор

a'uzu billah اعوذ بالله ARABIC *intj.* God help [me] (appeal for divine aid); name of a prayer spoken before undertaking any action

BAS: әлғаязы билләhи

KAR: әғузибилләә

KAZ: ағузы, ағузү білла

KYR: агузу, агузу биллаахи

TAJ: аузи биллоҳи

TAT: әгузе биллаhи

UYG: auzibilla

UZB: аузи биллоҳи

a'uzu billahi min al-shaytani al-rajim اعوذ بالله من الشيطان الرجيم ARABIC *intj.* God protect me from Satan, the accursed

KAR: Әузибилле мынешетан режым

TAJ: Аузи биллоҳи минашайтони раҷим

TAT: Әгүзү билләhи минәш-шәйтанир-рәҗим

TUR: әузу биллэхи минеш шейтаныр ражым

UYG: Auzibillahu minäshaytani räjiym

UZB: Аузи биллаҳи минашайтони рожийм

avlad اولاد ARABIC *n.* descendant; dynasty

BAS: әүләд

KAR: әўлад

KAZ: әулет

KYR: авлад, овлад, оолат

TAJ: авлод

TAT: әүляд

TUR: өвлат, өвләт ① *saint, holy person* ② *the six Turkmen holy tribes believed to be descended from one of the four righteous Caliphs*

UYG: äwläd

UZB: авлод *generation descendant*

avliya[1] اوليا ARABIC *n.* Muslim saint (singular); saintly person ☞ ***vali***

BAS: әүлиә, изге

KAR: әўлийе ① *Muslim saint* ② *Muslim saint's tomb, shrine, cemetery* ③ *prophet, one who can predict he future*

KAZ: әулие ① *Muslim saint (singular) saintly person* ② *prophet, one who can predict the future*

KYR: олуя, ыйык ① *Muslim saint (singular) saintly person* ② *prophet, one who can predict the future*

TAJ: авлиё

TAT: әүлия, изге, яхшы ① *Muslim saint (singular) saintly person* ② *prophet, one who can predict the future*

TUR: өвлүйә ① *Muslim saint* ② *Muslim saint's tomb, shrine, cemetery*

UYG: äwliya

UZB: авлиё

avliya[2] اوليا ARABIC *adj.* holy; sacred (restricted to people)

KAR: әўлийе

TAJ: авлиё

UYG: äwliya, äwliyaliq

UZB: авлиё

avliyazada اوليا زاده ARABIC *n.* son or male descendant of a Muslim saint

KAR: әўлийезадә

KYR: олуя заада

TAJ: авлиёзода

UZB: авлиёзода

'avrat عورت ARABIC *Law n.* parts of the body that, by religious law, have to be covered

BAS: ғәүрәт

KAR: әврат

TAJ: аврат

TAT: гаурәт ① *parts of the body that, by religious law, have to be covered* ② *woman, girl*

TUR: оврат

UYG: awrät

UZB: аврот

Avval, al- الاوّل ARABIC *n.* name of God: the First

KAR: Әўел

TAJ: Аввал

TUR: ал-Аввал

UYG: Awwal

UZB: Ал-Аввал

ayan ایان PERSIAN *adj.* aware (e.g. Muhammad's state upon receiving prophecy)

KAR: аян

TAJ: аён

UYG: äyän

UZB: аён

ayat آیت ARABIC *Qur'an n.* Qur'anic verse

BAS: аят

KAR: аят

KAZ: аят

KYR: аят

TAJ: оя

TAT: аять

TUR: аят

UYG: ayät

UZB: оят

ayat al-kursi آیت الکرسی *Qur'an n.* the 256th verse of the second sura, called the "Throne of the Qur'an"

KAZ: аятүл-күрси

TAJ: оятул курси

TAT: аятелкөрси

UZB: оятул курси

ayat al-muhkamat آیت المحکمت PERSIAN *Qur'an np.* concrete verses (as a category of Qur'anic verse)

TAJ: оятул мухкамат

UZB: оятул муҳкамат

ayat al-mutashabihat آیت المتشبهت ARABIC *Qur'an np.* non-concrete verses, verses requiring metaphoric interpretations (as a category of Qur'anic verse)

TAJ: оятул муташабиҳот

UZB: оятул муташабиҳот

ayat-i karima آیت کریمه ARABIC *Qur'an np.* noble verse, i.e. incontrovertible, without doubt (as a category of Qur'anic verse)

UZB: ояти карима

ayatullah ایت الله ARABIC *n.* highest rank of legal scholar (almost exclusively restricted to Shi'ites)

KAR: аяталла

KAZ: аятолла

TAJ: оятулло

TAT: аятулла

TUR: аятолла

UZB: оятуллоҳ

'ayn ☞ ***farz-i 'ayn***

Ayyub ایّوب ARABIC *pn.* the prophet Job

KAR: Айып

KAZ: Айып, Әйуп

TAJ: Аюб

TAT: Әйүп

TUR: Эйюп

UYG: Ayüp

UZB: Айюб

'aza عزا ARABIC *n.* mourning, lamenting (the dead)

KAR: аза

KAZ: аза ① *mourning, lamenting (the dead)* ② *the custom of providing material help to the family of he deceased and of conducting the funeral procession and repasts*

KYR: аза ① *mourning, lamenting (the dead)* ② *that which is brought to a funerary repast by the relatives of the deceased (e.g. livestock)*

TAJ: азо

TUR: аза

UYG: aza, haza

UZB: аза

azab عذاب ARABIC *n.* torture, torment

BAS: ғазап

KAR: азап

KAZ: азап, ғазап

KYR: азап

TAJ: азоб

TAT: газап

TUR: азап

UYG: äzäp, azap

UZB: азоб

'azab al-kabir عذاب الكبير ARABIC *np.* the torment of the grave (inflicted on sinners by interrogating angels) ☞ ***'azab al-qabr***

KAR: азап

TAJ: азоби кабир

TUR: азап ал-кебир

UZB: азоби кабир

'azab-i qabr عذاب قبر ARABIC *np.* the torment of the grave (inflicted on sinners by interrogating angels)

KAR: азапул қәбир

KAZ: азаб ал-қабр

KYR: көр азабы

TAJ: азоби қабр

TAT: кабер газабы

TUR: азап ал-кабр

UZB: қабр азоби, гўр азоби

a'zam [1] اعظم ARABIC *adj.* great, magnificent

BAS: әғзәм

KAR: ағзам

KYR: агзам

TAJ: аъзам

TAT: әгъзам

UYG: äzäm

UZB: аъзам

A'zam [2] اعظم ARABIC *adj.* great, magnificent (as an epithet of God)

BAS: Әғзәм

KAR: Әзем

KYR: Агзам

TAJ: Аъзам

TAT: Әгъзам

UYG: Äzäm

UZB: Аъзам

azan اذان ARABIC *Ritual n.* call to prayer; early morning

BAS: аҙан

KAR: азан

KAZ: азан

KYR: азан

TAJ: азон

TAT: азан

TUR: азан

UYG: äzan, äzän

UZB: азон

azar آزار PERSIAN *Ritual n.* portion of the burial shroud covering the body from the top of the head to the bottom of the feet

TAT: азар

'azayimkhan عزائم خوان PERSIAN *Ritual n.* one who invokes spirits to perform religious ceremonies, esp. healing ceremonies, a type of shaman

TAJ: азоимхон

UZB: азайимхон

'Azazil عزازيل ARABIC *pn.* Satan, the Devil ☞ ***Shaytan***

BAS: Ғазазил

KAR: Әзазил

KAZ: Әзәзіл, Ғазазыл, Ғазезіл

KYR: Азезил, Азазил

TAJ: Азозил

TAT: Газазил

TUR: Азазыл

UZB: Азозил

'Azim, al- العظيم ARABIC *n.* name of God: the Mighty

BAS: Ғәзим

KAR: Әзим

KAZ: Ғазим

KYR: Азым

TAJ: Азим

TAT: Газыйм

TUR: ал-Азым
UYG: Al-Azim
UZB: Ал-Азим

'aziz [1] عزيز ARABIC *adj.* dear, beloved ☞ ***avliya***
BAS: ғәзиз ① *dear, beloved* ② *Muslim saint*
KAR: әзийз, әзиз
KAZ: ғазиз, әзиз
KYR: азиз ① *dear, beloved* ② *Muslim saint*
TAJ: азиз
TAT: газиз ① *dear, beloved* ② *Muslim saint*
TUR: эзиз
UYG: äziz
UZB: азиз ① *dear, beloved* ② *holy*

'aziz [2] عزيز ARABIC *Hadith adj.* tradition related by only two sources
TAT: газиз
UZB: азиз

'Aziz, al- العزيز ARABIC *n.* name of God: the Mighty
KAR: Әзийз
KAZ: Ғазиз, әл-Әзиз
TAJ: Азиз
TUR: ал-Эзиз
UYG: Äziz
UZB: Ал-Азиз

'Azra'il عزرائل ARABIC *pn.* the Angel of Death
BAS: Ғазраил
KAR: Әзиреил
KAZ: Әзірейіл
KYR: Азирейил, Асрейил
TAJ: Азроил
TAT: Газраил, Гыйзраил
TUR: Эзрайыл, Җаналгыч
UYG: Äzra'il
UZB: Азроил

'Azza va Jalla عزوجل ARABIC *np.* Greatness and Splendor (an epithet of God)
TAJ: Аззау Ҷалла
TAT: Газзә вә Җәллә
UZB: Азза ва Жалла

B

bab باب ARABIC *Qur'an n.* sura, Qur'anic verse ☞ ***sura***
BAS: баб
KAR: бап
KAZ: баб
TAJ: боб, фасл
TAT: баб
UYG: bab
UZB: боб

bachcha بچّه PERSIAN *n.* boy, dancing boy; object of pedophilia
KAR: баччә
TAJ: бачча
TAT: бәччә
UZB: бачча

bachchabaz بچّه باز PERSIAN *n.* pedophile
KAR: баччебәз
TAJ: баччабоз
UZB: баччабоз, акавачча

bachchabazi بچّه بازى PERSIAN *n.* pedophilia
KAR: баччебәзлиқ
TAJ: баччабозӣ
TAT: бәччәбазлык
UZB: баччабозлик, бесоқолбозлик

badal بدل ARABIC *Hajj n.* substitute (e.g. for a conditional obligation); holy personage
BAS: бәдәл
KAR: бәдел
KYR: бадал
TAJ: бадал
TAT: бәдәл
UYG: bädäl
UZB: бадал

badal-i askari بدل عسكرى PERSIAN *Taxation np.* tax for non-Muslims exempting them from military service
TAJ: бадали асакарӣ
UZB: бадали аскарий

badal-i naqdi بدل نقدى PERSIAN *Taxation n.* tax for Muslims exempting them from military service
TAJ: бадали накдӣ
UZB: бадали накдий

badal-i shakhsi بدل شخصى PERSIAN *Taxation n.* tax for Muslims exempting them from military service
TAJ: бадали шахсӣ
UZB: бадали шахсий

bad-du'a بددعا PERSIAN *n.* malediction, curse
BAS: бәддоға
KAR: бәддиўа
TAJ: баддуо
TAT: бәддога

UYG: bäddua
UZB: баддуо

Badiʿ, al- البديع *n.* name of God: the Incomparable
KAR: Бәдый
TAJ: Бадӣ
TUR: ал-Бады
UYG: Badi
UZB: Ал-Бадий

Badr بدر ARABIC *Historical n.* the first full military confrontation between the Muslims and the Meccans
KAR: Бәдр
TAJ: Бадр
UYG: Badr
UZB: Бадр, Бадр жанги

Baʿis, al- الباعث ARABIC *pn.* name of God: the Resurrector
KAR: Байыс
TAJ: Боис
TUR: ал-Баис
UYG: Bais
UZB: Ал-Боис

baj باج ARABIC *Taxation n.* tax; duty
KAR: бáж
TAJ: боҷ
TAT: баҗ
UYG: baj
UZB: бож

bakhshi بخشى TURKIC *n.* shaman, healer; bard, performer and improviser of oral epics
KAR: бақсы
KAZ: бақсы
KYR: бакшы
TAJ: бахшӣ ① *shaman, healer* ② *secretary, scribe* ③ *Buddhist monk*
TUR: багшы
UYG: bakhshi ① *shaman* ② *secretary, scribe*
UZB: бахши ① *performer and improvisor of oral epics* ② *healer* ③ *tribal name* ④ *secretary, scribe*

bakhshish بخشيش PERSIAN *n.* alms, gift, charity
TAJ: бахшиш
TAT: бәхшиш
UZB: бахшиш

bakht بخت *n.* fate, fortune
BAS: бәхет
KAR: бахыт, бақыт
KAZ: бақыт
KYR: бак, бакт, бакты, бакыт
TAJ: бахт
TAT: бәхт ① *fate, fortune* ② *luck, good fortune*
TUR: багт
UYG: baqt, bäkhit
UZB: бахт

bakira باكره ARABIC *n.* innocence, absence of guilt; virgin
KAR: бакира
TAJ: бокира
UYG: bakira
UZB: бокира

Balad بلد ARABIC *Qur'an n.* the 90th sura of the Qur'an
KAR: Бәләд сүўреси
KAZ: Бәлад сүресі
TAJ: сураи Балад
UYG: Balad süräsi
UZB: Балад сураси

balaghat بلاغت ARABIC *Law n.* legal age, adult
KAR: бәлагат
TAJ: балоғат
TUR: балагат
UYG: balagat
UZB: балоғат

baligh بالغ ARABIC *Law adj.* adult, of age
BAS: балиғ, бәлиғ
TAT: балиг
TUR: балыг
UYG: baligh
UZB: болиғ

bamdad بامداد PERSIAN *Ritual n.* morning prayer
☞ ***salat al-subh, salat al-fajr***
KAR: бамдат намазы
TAJ: намози бомдод
UYG: bamdat, bamdat namizi, namaz bamdat
UZB: бомдод намози

banda بنده PERSIAN *n.* creature, servant (of God)
BAS: бәндә
KAR: бәнде, бенде
KAZ: бенде, пенде, бәнде
KYR: бенде, пенде
TAJ: банда
TAT: бәндә
TUR: бенде ① *creature, servant (of God)* ② *slave*
UYG: bändä
UZB: банда

bang بنگ PERSIAN *n.* narcotics
KAR: банги
TAJ: банг
UYG: bäng *hashish*
UZB: банг, бангивор

bani hashimi بنی هاشمی ARABIC *np.* descendants of the prophet Muhammad
TUR: бени хашымы

bani Islam بنی اسلام ARABIC *np.* the people of Islam, Muslims
KAR: бани Ислам
TAJ: бани Ислом
TAT: бәни Ислам
UZB: бани Ислом

bani Isra'il [1] بنی اسرائیل ARABIC *Historical np.* Jews, the Children of Israel
BAS: бәни исраил
KAR: бани Исраил
KAZ: бәни Исраил, бану Исраил
KYR: Бани Ысрайыл, Бани Ысырайыл
TAJ: бани Исроил
TAT: Бәни-Исраил
TUR: Бени исраил
UYG: bani Isra'il
UZB: бани Исроил

Bani Isra'il [2] بنی اسرائیل ARABIC *Qur'an n.* alternate name of the 17th sura of the Qur'an ☞ ***Isra***
KAZ: Бәни Ісраил сүресі
TAJ: Бани Исроил
TAT: Бәни-Исраил сүрәсе
TUR: сураи Бени исраил
UZB: Бани Исроил

baqa [1] بقا ARABIC *n.* eternity
KAR: бәқә, мәнгилик
KAZ: бақа
TAJ: бақо
TAT: бәка
UYG: bäqä
UZB: бақо

baqa [2] بقا ARABIC *Theology n.* eternity (a distinguishing quality of God)
TAJ: бақо
TAT: бәка
UZB: бақо

Baqara بقره ARABIC *Qur'an pn.* the second sura of the Qur'an
KAR: Бәқәре сүўреси
KAZ: Бақара сүресі
TAJ: сураи Бақара
TAT: Бәкара сүрәсе
UYG: sura Bäqära
UZB: Бақара сураси

baqi باقی ARABIC *adj.* eternal
BAS: баҡый
KAR: бақый
KAZ: бақи
KYR: бакы
TAJ: боқӣ
TAT: бакый
TUR: бакы
UYG: baqi
UZB: боқий

Baqi, al- الباقی ARABIC *pn.* name of God: the Enduring
KAR: Бақый
TAJ: Боқӣ
TUR: ал-Баки
UYG: Baqi
UZB: Ал-Боқий

bara'at [1] برائت ARABIC *Law n.* innocence, absence of guilt
TAJ: бароат
TAT: бәраәт
UYG: bara'ät
UZB: бароат

Bara'at [2] برائت ARABIC *Qur'an n.* alternate name of the 9th sura of the Qur'an ☞ ***Tavba***
KAZ: Бәра-ат сүресі
TAJ: сураи Бароат
UZB: Бароат сураси

barakat برکت ARABIC *n.* blessing, divine grace; abundance; prosperity
BAS: бәрәкәт
KAR: бәрекет, берекет
KAZ: берекет
KYR: баракат, береке, берекет, жайбаракат
TAJ: баракат
TAT: бәрәкәт ① *blessing, abundance* ② *interjection expressing surprise*
TUR: берекет, барака
UYG: bäräkät
UZB: баракат

barakullah بارك الله ARABIC *intj.* the blessing of God!, well done! congratulations!

BAS: бәрәкалла
KAR: бәрекелла, аллабәрекелла
KAZ: бәрекелде
KYR: баракелде, баракелди
TAJ: баракалло
TAT: барәкәаллаһ
TUR: берекелла
UYG: bäräkällä
UZB: баракалла

barat برات ARABIC *Qur'an n.* absolution (document)
KAR: бәрат
TAJ: барот
UYG: bärät
UZB: барот

barhaq برحق PERSIAN *n.* absolute truth
KAR: бәрҳақ
TAJ: барақ
UYG: barhaq
UZB: барҳақ

Bari, al- البارى ARABIC *n.* The Creator (an epithet of God)
KAZ: әл-Бари
TAJ: Борӣ
TAT: Бари
TUR: ал-Бари
UZB: Ал-Бори

barq برق ARABIC *n.* divine light ☞ ***nur***
TAJ: барқи саодат
TAT: бәрык
UZB: барқ

Barr, al- البرّ ARABIC *n.* name of God: the Benefactor
KAR: Бәрр
TAJ: Барр
TUR: ал-Барр
UYG: Barr
UZB: Ал-Барр

bashariyat بشريت PERSIAN *n.* mankind; the world
KAR: бәшериет
TAJ: башарият
TAT: бәшәрият
UYG: bäshäriyät
UZB: башарият

Bashir بشير ARABIC *pn.* Herald of Joy (epithet of the prophet Muhammad)
KAZ: Бәшир
TAT: Бәшир
UZB: Башир

basir بصير ARABIC *Theology n.* all-seeing (an established quality of God)
TAT: бәсар, бәсыйр
UZB: басир

Basir, al- البصير ARABIC *n.* name of God: the Seer
KAR: Бәсыр
KAZ: Басар
TAJ: Басир
TAT: Басыйр
TUR: ал-Басир
UYG: Basir
UZB: Ал-Басир

Basit, al- الباسط ARABIC *pn.* name of God: the Expander
KAR: Бәсит
TAJ: Босит
TUR: ал-Басид
UYG: Bäsit
UZB: Ал-Босит

Batha بطحه ARABIC *Hajj pn.* name of a flat location in Mecca
KAR: Бәтхә
TAJ: Батҳо
UYG: Bathä
UZB: Батҳо

batil باطل ARABIC *Theology n.* this world, the false world
BAS: батыл
KAR: батыл
KAZ: батыл
KYR: батыл
TAJ: ботил
TAT: батыйль
TUR: батыл
UYG: batil
UZB: ботил

batin باطن ARABIC *adj.* esoteric, internal (as a category of sciences)
KAR: бәтин
KYR: батын
TAJ: ботин
TAT: бәтын, батыйн
UYG: batin
UZB: ботин

Batin, al- الباطن ARABIC *pn.* name of God: Who Penetrates into the Internal

KAR: Бэтин
TAJ: Ботин
TUR: ал-Батин
UYG: Batin
UZB: Ал-Ботин

bavar باور PERSIAN *n.* faith, belief
TAJ: бовар
TAT: бавэр
UYG: bawär
UZB: бовар

bay'at بيعت ARABIC *n.* handshake, pledge (typically signifying a formal pledge of submission of a pupil to his Sufi master)
BAS: бэйғэт
KAR: бэят
KAZ: байа
TAJ: баят
TAT: бэйгать, бигать
UYG: bayät
UZB: байъат

bayram بيرام TURKIC *Ritual n.* religious festival ☞ *'id*
BAS: байрэм
KAR: байрам, мереке, ҳайт
KAZ: майрам, байрам
KYR: майрам, байрам
TAJ: байрам
TAT: бэйрам
TUR: байрам *religious festival the month of Shavval*
UYG: bayram, mäyräm
UZB: байрам

bayt بيت ARABIC *n.* house (esp. of the Prophet)
KAR: байт
KAZ: бейіт *tomb, grave*
KYR: бейт, бейит ① *tomb, grave (with a structure placed on top)* ② *prayer performed for the deceased forty days after death*
TAJ: байт
TAT: бэйт
UYG: bayt
UZB: байт

bayt al-ahzan بيت الاحزان ARABIC *Ritual np.* house which is in a state of mourning
KAR: байтулэҳзан
TAJ: байтулаҳзон
UYG: baytul ähzän
UZB: ғамхона, байтул-аҳзон

Bayt al-'atiq, al- البيت العطيق ARABIC *pn.* epithet of the Ka'ba (lit. "the ancient house")
KAR: Байтул этиқ
TAJ: Байтул атиқ
TAT: элбэйтүл гатикъ
UZB: Байтул отиқ

bayt al-mal بيت المال ARABIC *Historical n.* treasury; bank
KAR: байтулмал
TAJ: байтулмол
TAT: бэйтелмал
TUR: бейтил мал
UYG: baytulmal
UZB: байтулмол

Bayt al-muqaddas بيت المقدس ARABIC *pn.* Jerusalem
KAR: байтулкэрамат
TAJ: Байтулмуқаддас
TAT: Бэйтелмөкаддэс, Бэйтүлмөкаддэс, Бэйтел Кодес
TUR: Бейтулмукаддес
UYG: Baytul muqaddas, Bäytulmuqäddäs
UZB: Байтул муқаддас

Baytullah بيت الله ARABIC *pn.* Gods house; epithet of the Mosque in Mecca
BAS: бэйтулла
KAR: байтулла
TAJ: Байтуллоҳ
TAT: Бэйтулла ① *Gods house epithet of the Mosque in Mecca* ② *mosque*
UYG: Baytulla *mosque*
UZB: Байтуллоҳ

Bayyina بيّنه ARABIC *Qur'an n.* the 98th sura of the Qur'an
KAR: Бэййина суўреси
KAZ: Бэййіна сүресі
TAJ: сураи Байинна
UYG: Bayyina süräsi, sürä Bayyinä
UZB: Баййина сураси

baz gasht باز گشت PERSIAN *Sufism np.* restraining one's thoughts during dhikr (one of the eight principles of the Naqshbandi Sufi order)
TAJ: бозгашт
TAT: бяз гэшт
UZB: бозгашт

bi diyanat بی دیانت PERSIAN *adj.* impious
KAR: бидиянет
TAJ: бедиёнат
TAT: бидиянэт

UYG: bidyänät
UZB: бедиёнат, диёнатсиз

bi gunah بی گناه PERSIAN *adj.* sinless, innocent
KAR: бигуна, бийгүна
KAZ: бейкүнә, бикүнә, бигүнә
KYR: бейкүнөө, бейгүнөө
TAJ: бегунох̣
TAT: бигөнаh
TUR: бигүнә
UYG: biguna
UZB: бегунох̣

bi iman بی ایمان PERSIAN *n.* unbeliever; atheist
KAR: бийиман
TAJ: беимон
UZB: беимон, бейимон, имонсиз, иймонсиз

bi namaz بی نماز PERSIAN *np.* a person who does not perform the namaz; infidel, unbeliever
KAR: бинамаз
KYR: бейнамаз
TAJ: бенамоз
UYG: binamaz
UZB: бенамоз

bi taharat بی طهارت PERSIAN *n.* one who behaves like a non-Muslim
KAR: бийдәрет
TAJ: бетах̣орат
UZB: бетах̣орат, тах̣оратсиз

bibi بی بی، بیبی ARABIC *n.* woman, especially learned and authoritative woman ☞ ***Maryam***
KAR: бийби
TAJ: биби
TAT: биби
UZB: биби

Bibi Maryam ☞ ***Maryam***

bid'at بدعت ARABIC *n.* illicit innovation, heresy; the opposite of sunna
BAS: бидғәт
KAR: бидәт
TAJ: бидъа, бидъат
TAT: бидгать ① *illicit innovation, heresy* ② *atheism*
UYG: bid'ät
UZB: бидъат

bid'at-i hasana بدعت حسنه ARABIC *np.* useful innovation
KAR: бидәт
TAJ: бидъа, бидъат
TAT: бидгать хәсәнә
UYG: bid'at
UZB: бидъат

bid'at-i sayyi'a بدعت سیئه ARABIC *np.* pernicious innovation
TAT: бидгать сәййиъәh
UYG: bid'ati säyyi
UZB: бидъати саййи

bihablillah بحبل الله ARABIC *intj.* with God's help (lit. by [clinging to] the branch of God)
TAJ: бих̣абиллах̣
TAT: бихәблиллаh
UZB: бих̣абиллох̣

bihisht بهشت PERSIAN *n.* Heaven, Paradise ☞ ***jannat***
KAR: бейиш, бихишт
KYR: бейиш
TAJ: бих̣ишт
TAT: биhишт
TUR: бехишт
UYG: biyish
UZB: бех̣ишт

bihukmillah بحکم الله ARABIC *intj.* by the decree of God
TAT: бихөкмиллаh
UZB: х̣укмиллох̣

Bilal بلال ARABIC *pn.* the first mu'azzin
BAS: Билал
KAR: Билал
TAJ: Билол
UYG: Bilal
UZB: х̣азрати Билол

billahi با لله ARABIC *intj.* by God!, I swear to God!
BAS: билләhи, билләhи-вәлләhи
KAR: биллаў
TAJ: биллах̣и
TAT: биллаhи
UYG: billahi
UZB: биллох̣и

Bilqis بلقيس ARABIC *pn.* Bilqis, Queen of Saba' (a Qur'anic figure who appears in the story of the prophet Solomon)
KAZ: Былқыс, Билқис
TAJ: Билқийс
TAT: Билкыйс
TUR: Былкыс
UYG: Bilqis
UZB: Билқийс

biradar برادر PERSIAN *n.* brother, fellow Muslim ☞ ***ikhvan***
- **KAR:** пирадер
- **KAZ:** пірәдар *brother Sufi, disciple to a Sufi master*
- **TAJ:** бародар
- **UYG:** birädär
- **UZB:** биродар

bisat بساط ARABIC *n.* trousseau (of a bride)
- **BAS:** бисә
- **KAR:** бисат
- **TAJ:** бисот
- **UYG:** bisat
- **UZB:** бисот

bismillah بسم الله ARABIC *intj.* in the name of God (to be spoken by Muslims before any action; typically spoken before speeches or written at the beginning of a document)
- **BAS:** бисмилла
- **KAR:** бисмилла
- **KAZ:** бісмилла, бісміллә, пісміллә
- **KYR:** бысмылда, бистымылда, бисмилла
- **TAJ:** бисмилло
- **TAT:** бисмиллаh
- **TUR:** бисмилла, бисимилла, биссимилла
- **UYG:** bismilla
- **UZB:** бисмиллоҳ

bismillah al-Rahman al-Rahim بسم الله الرحمن الرحيم ARABIC *np.* In the Name of God, the Compassionate, the Merciful
- **KAR:** бисмиллахир рахманыр рәйим, бисмилла ирахма ниррахим
- **KAZ:** бісміллаhір-Рахманір-Рахим, Бисмиллаhир рахманир рахим
- **KYR:** бысмыллаи-ррахманы ррахым
- **TAJ:** бисмуллоҳу Раҳмону Раҳим
- **TAT:** Бисмилләhир-рахмәнир-рахим
- **TUR:** Бисмиллахыр рахманыр рахым
- **UYG:** bismillahir Rähmanir Rähim
- **UZB:** бисмиллоҳир Раҳмонир Раҳийм

buhtan بهتان ARABIC *Law n.* slander, false accusation
- **KAR:** дәўмет
- **TAJ:** буҳтон
- **TAT:** бөhтан
- **UYG:** tümät
- **UZB:** бўҳтон

Buraq براق ARABIC *pn.* the animal which the prophet Muhammad mounted for his ascension to Heaven
- **BAS:** Бораҡ
- **KAR:** Бурақ
- **KAZ:** Бурақ, Пырақ, әл-Бурақ
- **KYR:** Бурак, Бурак Ат
- **TAJ:** Буроқ
- **TAT:** Борак, Бурак ① *the animal which the prophet Muhammad mounted for his ascension to Heaven* ② *the Wailing Wall (in Jerusalem)*
- **TUR:** Бырак
- **UYG:** buräq
- **UZB:** Буроқ

Buruj بروج ARABIC *Qur'an pn.* the 85th sura of the Qur'an
- **KAR:** Буруж суўреси
- **KAZ:** Бұруж сүресі
- **TAJ:** сураи Буруҷ
- **UYG:** Burj süräsi
- **UZB:** Буруж сураси

but بت PERSIAN *n.* idol ☞ ***put***
- **BAS:** бот, бут, буты
- **KAR:** бут *the Buddha*
- **KAZ:** бұт
- **KYR:** бут ① *idol* ② *the Buddha*
- **TAJ:** бут
- **TAT:** бот
- **TUR:** бут
- **UYG:** but ① *idol* ② *icon*
- **UZB:** бут

butkhana بتخانه PERSIAN *n.* temple (of idolaters) ☞ ***putkhana***
- **KAR:** бутқана, бутхана
- **KYR:** бутkана
- **TAJ:** бутхона
- **TAT:** ботханә
- **TUR:** бутхана ① *temple (of idolaters)* ② *church*
- **UYG:** butkhana
- **UZB:** бутхона

butparast بتپرست PERSIAN *n.* idolater, idol-worshipper ☞ ***putparast***
- **KAR:** бутпәрест
- **KYR:** бутпарас
- **TAJ:** бутпараст
- **TAT:** ботпәрәст
- **TUR:** бутпараз
- **UYG:** butpäräs
- **UZB:** бутпараст

buzurg بزرگ PERSIAN *adj.* holy; great, powerful

KAR: бузурук
TAJ: бузург
UYG: büzrük
UZB: бузрук

C

chadra چادره PERSIAN *n.* chador, a type of cloak worn by some Muslim women covering the entire head and body)
KAR: шадыр
KAZ: шадыра, чадра *veil*
KYR: чадыра
TAJ: чодра
TAT: чадра
TUR: чадра
UYG: chadir
UZB: чодира

Chahar yar چهار یار PERSIAN *Historical pn.* the first four Caliphs (Abu Bakr, 'Umar, 'Uthman, and 'Ali)
KAR: шәряр
KYR: чарыяр, төрт чарыяр, чалыяр, чаряр
TAJ: чорёр, чаҳорёр
TAT: чәһар яр, чәһәр яр, чәр яр,
TUR: чарыяр, дөртчарыяр
UYG: charyar
UZB: чаҳорёр

chalma چالما TURKIC *n.* turban
KAR: шәлме
KAZ: шалма
KYR: чалма
TAJ: чалма
TAT: чалма
TUR: чалма
UYG: chalma
UZB: чалма

childan چلدان PERSIAN *Ritual n.* ceremonial dipper used to wash newborns
KAR: шылдан
TAJ: чилдон
UYG: childän
UZB: чилдон

chilla [1] چله PERSIAN *Sufism n.* forty-day period of religious seclusion and prayer (for Sufis)
KAR: шилде, шилле
TAJ: чилла
UYG: chillä
UZB: чилла

chilla [2] چله PERSIAN *Ritual n.* forty-day period following the birth of a child, or following someone's death
KAR: шилде, шилле
KAZ: шілде
KYR: чилде
TAJ: чилла
TUR: чиле
UYG: chillä
UZB: чилла

chillakhana [1] چله خانه PERSIAN *Sufism n.* place where forty-day religious seclusions are held (traditionally attended by Sufis)
KAR: шилдехана
TAJ: чиллахона
UZB: чиллахона

chillakhana [2] چله خانه PERSIAN *Ritual n.* place where a baby is washed forty days after its birth
KAR: шилде
KAZ: шілдехана
TAJ: чиллахона
TAT: чилләханә
UYG: chilläkhana
UZB: чиллахона

chillayasin چله یاسین PERSIAN *Ritual n.* ceremony for healing the sick involving repeated ablutions and prayers
KAR: шилясын
TAJ: чиллаёсин
UYG: chilyasin
UZB: чиллаёсин

chiltan چلتن PERSIAN *n.* forty invisible spirits believed to live among people
☞ ***rijal al-ghayb, abdal***
KAR: шылтан
KAZ: қырық шілтен
KYR: чилтен, кырк чилтен
TAJ: чилтан
TAT: кырыклар
UYG: chiltan
UZB: чилтан

D

Dabba دابّه ARABIC *pn.* name of an animal mentioned in the Qur'an that will appear just before Judgment Day
TAJ: Даъбба, добба
TAT: даббә
UZB: Даъбба, добба

dafn دفن ARABIC *Ritual n.* burial, funeral
BAS: дәфен
KAR: дәпн
TAJ: дафн
TAT: дәфен
UYG: dapn
UZB: дафн

dahir ARABIC *Qur'an n.* alternate name of the 76th sura of the Qur'an ☞ ***Insan***
KAZ: Даһыр сүресі
TAJ: сураи Даҳр
UZB: Даҳир сураси

dahr دهر ARABIC *n.* world, time, period
TAJ: даҳр
TAT: дәһер
UZB: даҳр

dahri دهری ARABIC *adj.* atheist; materialistic
BAS: дәһри
KAR: кудайсыз
TAJ: даҳрӣ, бедин
TAT: дәһри
UYG: dähri
UZB: даҳрий *atheist*

dahr-i dun دهر دون PERSIAN *np.* this world, the faulty world
TAJ: даҳри дун
UZB: даҳри дун

dahriya دهریه ARABIC *n.* unbelievers, atheists; materialists
KAR: кудайсызлар
TAJ: даҳриҳо
UYG: dährilik
UZB: даҳрийлар

Dajjal دجّال ARABIC *pn.* the Deceiver (who is said will appear before Judgment Day and will try to lead believers astray)
BAS: Дәжжәл
KAR: Тәжжал
KAZ: Тажал
KYR: Дажаал, Тажаал
TAJ: Даҷҷол
TAT: Дәҗҗал
TUR: Дечҗал, Хартечҗал
UYG: Däjjäl
UZB: Дажжол

dalil دلیل ARABIC *Law n.* proof, evidence
BAS: дәлил
KAR: дәлил
TAJ: далил
TAT: дәлил
UYG: delil, dälil
UZB: далил

dalil-i ʿaqli دلیل عقلی PERSIAN *Law n.* speculative proof (i.e. not by tradition)
KAR: дәлилы ақылынан
TAJ: далили ақлӣ
TAT: дәлил гакъли, дәлиле гакыли
UZB: далили ақлий

dalil-i naqli دلیل نقلی PERSIAN *Law np.* proof received from tradition (e.g. from the Qur'an, prophets etc.)
KAR: дәлилы нәқылынан
TAJ: далили нақлӣ
TAT: дәлил нәкъли, дәлиле нәкъли
UZB: далили нақлий

dalil-i sharʿi دلیل شرعی ARABIC *Law np.* authoritative proof (based on authoritative testimony)
KAR: дәлилы шәрият
TAJ: далили шаръӣ
TAT: дәлил шәргый
UZB: далили шаръий

Dalv دلو ARABIC *pn.* Aquarius, 12th month of the Hidjri Solar year
BAS: Дәлү
KAR: далп, дәлуў
KAZ: дәлү
TAJ: Далв
TAT: Дәлү
UYG: delu
UZB: Далв

damulla داملّا PERSIAN *n.* erudite teacher, learned scholar (often used as an honorific)
BAS: дамолла
KAR: дамулла
KAZ: дамолла

KYR: дамбылда, дамылда ① *legal expert* ② *erudite teacher* ③ *imam* ④ *respected person possessing religious knowledge*
TAJ: домулло
TAT: дамелля
UYG: damolla
UZB: домулла, домла

danishmand دانشمند PERSIAN *n.* scholar; erudite scholar
BAS: данишмэн
KAR: данишпан
KAZ: данышпан
KYR: данышман
TAJ: донишманд
TAT: данишмэнд
UYG: dänishpand
UZB: донишманд

dar al-aman دار الآمان ARABIC *np.* abode of peace
KAR: дәрүламан
TAJ: доруламон
UZB: доруламон

dar al-baqa دارالبقا ARABIC *np.* the afterlife, the abode of eternity ☞ ***akhirat***
KAR: дәрүлбәқа
TAJ: дорулбақо
TAT: дарелбэка
UYG: därulbäqä, darulbaqa
UZB: дорилбақо

dar al-fana دارالفنا ARABIC *np.* This world, the abode of the living
KAR: дәрүлфәна
TAJ: дорулфано
TAT: дарелфэна
UYG: därulpanä, darulpäna
UZB: дорилфано

dar al-ghurur دارالغرور ARABIC *np.* this world, the abode of delusion
KAR: дәрүларшыллық
TAJ: дорулғурур
UYG: därulghürür
UZB: дорилғурур

dar al-harb دار الحرب ARABIC *np.* territories not ruled by Islamic sovereigns, lit. "the abode of war"
BAS: дарелхэреб
KAR: дәрүлхәрб
KAZ: дар ал-харб, дәрілхараб
TAJ: дорулҳарб
TAT: дарелхэреб
TUR: дар ал-харб
UYG: därilharp
UZB: дорилҳарб

dar al-havadis دار الحوادث ARABIC *np.* this world, the world of the living
KAR: дәрүлхәўадис
TAJ: дорулҳаводис
UYG: däril häwädis
UZB: дорилҳаводис

dar al-huffaz دار الحفّاظ ARABIC *Qur'an np.* mind (in which the Qur'an has been memorized)
KAR: дәрүлхуппаз
TAJ: дорулуффоз
UYG: däril huppäz
UZB: дорилҳуффоз

dar al-Islam دار الاسلام ARABIC *np.* the dominions of Islam, territory ruled by Muslims
KAR: дәрүлислам
KAZ: дар ал-ислам
TAJ: дорулислом
TUR: дар ал-ыслам
UYG: däril islam
UZB: дорил ислом

dar al-qasas دار القصاص ARABIC *np.* the Next World (where revenge is taken)
KAR: дәрүлқәсас
TAJ: дорулқарор
UYG: därulqäsäs
UZB: дорилқасос

dar al-qaza دار القضا ARABIC *np.* court of law
KAR: дәрүлқәза
TAJ: дорулқазо
UYG: därulqäzä
UZB: дорилқазо

dar al-salam دارالسلام ARABIC *np.* Paradise
KAR: дәрүлсәлем
TAJ: дорулсалом
UYG: därussalam
UZB: дорилсалом

dar al-sulh دار الصلح ARABIC *Historical np.* non-Muslim territories subordinate to Muslims on the basis of treaties
KAR: дәрүлсулух
KAZ: дар ас-сулх
TAJ: дорул сулҳ
TUR: дар ал-сулх

UYG: däril sulh
UZB: дорил сулҳ

dar al-surur دار السرور ARABIC *np.* Paradise
KAR: дәрүлсурур
TAJ: дорилсурур
UYG: däris surur
UZB: дорилсурур

darayn دارين ARABIC *n.* the Two Realms (the realm of the living and the realm of the dead)
TAT: дарәйн

dargah درگاه PERSIAN *Sufism n.* Sufi lodge; residence of a Sufi master; holy place of God ☞ ***khanaqah***
BAS: дәргәһ
KAR: дәрга, дәргаҳ
KYR: даргөй
TAJ: даргоҳ
TAT: дәргяһ ① *Sufi lodge* ② *threshold, threshold of Paradise*
TUR: дергәх
UYG: dargäh
UZB: даргоҳ

darra درّه PERSIAN *Law n.* lash (as a punishment)
KAR: дәрре
TAJ: дарра
UYG: därrä
UZB: дарра

darskhana درسخانه PERSIAN *n.* classroom (in a madrasa)
BAS: дәресхана
KAR: дәрысхана, сабақхана, класс
KAZ: дәрісхана
KYR: дарыскана
TAJ: дарсхона
TAT: дәресханә
UYG: därskhana
UZB: дарсхона

darvish درويش PERSIAN *Sufism n.* dervish, itinerant Sufi, member of a Sufi order, ascetic
BAS: дәрүиш
KAR: дервиш, дәрўиш
KAZ: дәруіш
KYR: дербиш, дервиш, дарвыш, дарвиш
TAJ: дарвеш
TAT: дәрвиш
TUR: дервүш
UYG: därwish
UZB: дарвеш

dastar دستار PERSIAN *n.* turban
KAR: сәлле
TAJ: дастор, салла
UYG: dästar *cloth for a turban*
UZB: дастор, салла

dastarkhan دسترخان PERSIAN *Ritual n.* tablecloth considered obligatory for serving food during all Islamic festivals and holidays
BAS: дәстәрхан
KAR: дастурқан, дәстурхан
KAZ: дастарқан
KYR: дасторкон, тасторкон
TAJ: дастурхон
TAT: дәстәрхан
TUR: дессерхан
UYG: dastikhan, dästar
UZB: дастурхон

dastshuy دست شوئی PERSIAN *Ritual n.* vessel, tub (for ablutions)
TAJ: дастшӯяк
UYG: das, aptuwa
UZB: дастшўй

Da'ud داود ARABIC *pn.* the prophet David
BAS: Дауыт
KAR: Дәўуд
KAZ: Дауіт, Дауыт
KYR: Дөөтү, Даут *the prophet David and the patron saint of blacksmiths*
TAJ: Довуд
TAT: Давыт, Дауд
TUR: Давут *the prophet David and the patron saint of blacksmiths*
UYG: Dawut, Dawud
UZB: ҳазрати Довуд

da'va [1] دعوا، دعوى ARABIC *n.* summoning; demand; conflict, controversy
BAS: дәғүә
KAR: даў
KAZ: дағуа, дау
KYR: доо
TAT: дәгъва, дау
TUR: дава
UYG: däwä
UZB: даъво

da'va [2] دعوا، دعوى ARABIC *n.* accusation or arraignment in civil and criminal law
BAS: дәғүә

KAR: даў
TAJ: даъво
UYG: däwä
UZB: даво

da'vat دعوت ARABIC *Ritual n.* Islamic missionary work; Islamic activism
KAR: дәўәт, шақырыў
TAJ: даъват
TAT: дәгъвәт
UYG: däwät
UZB: даъват

davir دور ARABIC *Ritual n.* exculpatory sacrifice
KAR: дәўир ① *exculpatory sacrifice* ② *offerings given to a mulla for performing an exculpatory sacrifice*
KAZ: дәуір
TAJ: давр
TAT: дәвер
UZB: давир

didar دیدار PERSIAN *Sufism n.* meeting with God; looking upon God's beauty
TAJ: дидор
TAT: дидар
UZB: дийдор

din دین ARABIC *n.* religion, religious system (especially Islam)
BAS: дин
KAR: дин
KAZ: дін
KYR: дин
TAJ: дин
TAT: дин, ден
TUR: дин
UYG: din
UZB: дин

dindar دیندار PERSIAN *n.* pious person, religious person, righteous person; religious official
BAS: диндар
KAR: диншил
KAZ: діндар
KYR: диндар
TAJ: диндор
TAT: диндар
TUR: диндар
UYG: dindar
UZB: диндор

dini دینی ARABIC *adj.* religious
BAS: дини
KAR: дини
KAZ: діни
KYR: диний
TAJ: динӣ
TAT: дини
TUR: дини
UYG: dini
UZB: диний

din-i samavi دین سماوی PERSIAN *np.* Judaism, Christianity and Islam (collectively)
KAR: сәмәўи дин
TAJ: дини самовӣ
UZB: самовий динлар

div دیو PERSIAN *n.* div (a type of jinn)
KAR: дәў
KYR: дөө
TAJ: дев
TUR: дөв
UYG: dew
UZB: дев

divan دیوان PERSIAN *n.* council, cabinet
BAS: диуан
KAR: дәўән
TAJ: девон
TAT: диван
UYG: diwan
UZB: девон

divana دیوانه *Sufism n.* holy fool, madman
BAS: диуана
KAR: диййўана, дәўәна
KAZ: диуана *devout person*
KYR: дубана, дийвана, дувана, думана
TAJ: девона
TAT: дивана
TUR: дивана
UYG: diwanä
UZB: девона

diyanat دیانت ARABIC *n.* piety, religiosity
BAS: диянәт
KAR: дийәнәт
TAJ: диёнат
TAT: диянәт
TUR: диянат
UYG: diyänät
UZB: диёнат

diyanatkar دیانتکار PERSIAN *n.* pious person, religious person

KAR: дийәнәткар
TAJ: диёнаткор
TAT: диянәткяр
UYG: diyänätchi
UZB: диёнаткор

diyat دية ARABIC *Law n.* monetary compensation for the shedding of blood
TAT: диять
TUR: диет

du'a [1] دعا ARABIC *n.* prayer, blessing
BAS: доға
KAR: дуўа, дуға
KAZ: дұға
KYR: дуба, дуга, дува ① *prayer, blessing* ② *hello (southern dialect)*
TAJ: дуо
TAT: дога
TUR: дога
UYG: du'a
UZB: дуо

du'a [2] دعا ARABIC *n.* spell
KAR: дуўа, дуға *sorcery*
KAZ: дуа
KYR: дуба, дуга, дува
TAJ: дуо
TAT: дога
TUR: дога
UYG: du'a
UZB: дуо

du'a [3] دعا ARABIC *n.* prayer amulet (an amulet containing a written prayer)
KAR: дуўа, дуға
KAZ: дуа
KYR: дуба, дуга, дува *verses written in an amulet*
TAJ: дуо
TUR: дога
UYG: du'a
UZB: дуо

du'adar دعادار PERSIAN *n.* one who has a wish or request (from God)
KAR: дуўадар
KYR: дугадар
TAJ: дуодор
UYG: du'adär
UZB: дуодор

du'agu دعاگو PERSIAN *n.* one who casts spell, sorcerer
KAR: дуўагөй, дуўаши
KAZ: дұғагөй, дұғакөй, дұғагой
KYR: дубагөй, дубакөй, дувакөй
TAJ: дуогӯй
TUR: догагөй
UYG: du'agoy
UZB: дуогӯй

du'akhvan دعاخوان PERSIAN *Ritual n.* one who performs prayers (e.g. for the sick)
KAR: дуўахан, дуўаши
TAJ: дуохон
UYG: du'akhan
UZB: дуохон

du'a-yi qunut دعای قنوت PERSIAN *Ritual np.* prayer performed after the obligatory night prayer
TUR: догаи кунут
UZB: дуои кунут

du'a-yi salam دعاءسلام PERSIAN *np.* greeting, well-wishing, blessing
BAS: доғаи сәләм
KAR: дуўаисәлам
KYR: дубай салам, дугай салам, салам-дуба, дубайы салам
TAJ: дуоисалом
UYG: du'ayisalam
UZB: дуоисалом

dubba دبّه PERSIAN *n.* small round skullcap ☞ ***taqiya***
KAR: дуббә
KYR: топу
TAJ: дубба
UYG: dubbä, doppa
UZB: дубба

Duha ☞ ***Zuha***

Dukhan [1] دخان ARABIC *Qur'an pn.* the 44th sura of the Qur'an
KAR: Духан суўреси
KAZ: Дұхан сүресі
TAJ: сураи Духон
TAT: Духан сүрәсе, Сүрәтүл-дөхан
UYG: Dukhän süräsi
UZB: Духон сураси

dukhan [2] دخان ARABIC *Law n.* tobacco (as an illicit substance)
KAR: тәмәки, шылым, ирик
KAZ: темекі
TAJ: духан, тамоки
TAT: дөхан, тәмәке

TUR: теммэки
UYG: dukhän
UZB: духан, тамаки

Duldul دلدل ARABIC *pn.* name of the horse of the Caliph Ali
BAS: Дөлдөл
KAR: Дүлдүл
KAZ: Дүлдүл
KYR: Дулдул
TAJ: Дулдул
TAT: Дөлдөл
TUR: Дүлдүл
UYG: Duldul
UZB: Дулдул

dunya دنيا ARABIC *n.* This world, the world of the living
BAS: донъя
KAR: дүнья
KAZ: дүние, дүния
KYR: дүйнө, дүнүйө
TAJ: дуньё
TAT: дөнья
TUR: дүнйә, дүнъе
UYG: dunya
UZB: дунё

dunyavi دنياوي ARABIC *adj.* secular, pertaining to this world
BAS: донъяуи
KAR: дүньяўи
KAZ: дүнияуи
TAJ: дуньёвӣ
TAT: дөньяви ① *secular* ② *profane*
TUR: дүнйәви, дүнъеви
UYG: dunyawiy
UZB: дунёвий

durud درود PERSIAN *Ritual n.* thanks, thanksgiving (e.g. a type of prayer)
TUR: дуруд

durus دروس ARABIC *n.* lessons, classes
UZB: дарус ① *lessons, classes* ② *student (among Hizb ut-Tahrir)*

durust درست PERSIAN *Ritual adj.* valid, correct, proper, appropriate (e.g. a prayer)
BAS: дөрөç
KAR: дурыс
KAZ: дұрыс
KYR: дурус
TAJ: дуруст
TAT: дөрес, дөрест
TUR: дүрс, дүрст
UYG: durus
UZB: дуруст

dust دوست PERSIAN *n.* friend, companion; God (in Sufi contexts); epithet of the Prophet Muhammad
BAS: дуç
KAR: дос, жан дос
KAZ: дос
KYR: дос
TAJ: дӯст
TAT: дус, дуст
TUR: дост
UYG: dost
UZB: дўст

Duzakh دوزخ PERSIAN *n.* Hell
BAS: Дозах
KAR: Дозақ
KAZ: Дозақ, Тозақ
KYR: Тозок
TAJ: Дӯзах
TAT: Дузэх
TUR: Довзах
UYG: Dozaq
UZB: Дўзах

duzakhi دوزخی ARABIC *n.* sinner, one who is bound for Hell
KAR: дозақи
KAZ: тозақы
KYR: тозоку
TAJ: дӯзахӣ
TUR: довзахы
UYG: dozaqi
UZB: дўзахи

F

fahisha فاحشه ARABIC *n.* immoral woman, prostitute
BAS: фэхишэ
KAR: пэхишэ, жэлеп
TAJ: фоҳиша
TAT: фахишэ
UYG: pahisha
UZB: фоҳиша

fahsh فحش ARABIC *n.* continuous obscene behavior, lewdness

BAS: фәхеш
KAR: пәхыш
TAJ: фаҳш
TAT: фәхеш
UYG: pahsh
UZB: фаҳш

fa’iz فائض ARABIC *n.* interest (e.g. on a loan)
KAR: пәис
TAJ: фоиз
TAT: фаиз
UYG: päiz
UZB: фоиз

fajir فاجر ARABIC *n.* lewd person, immoral person
TAJ: фоҷир
TAT: фаҗир
UYG: päjir
UZB: фожир

Fajr فجر ARABIC *Qur'an pn.* the 89th sura of the Qur'an
KAR: Фәжр суўреси
KAZ: Фәжір сүресі
TAJ: сураи Фаҷр
TAT: фәҗер сүрәсе
UYG: Fajr süräsi
UZB: Вал-фажр сураси

fal فال ARABIC *n.* fortune telling, divination; fortune, fate
BAS: фал
KAR: пал, бал
KAZ: бал
KYR: бал, пал
TAJ: фол
TAT: фал
TUR: пал
UYG: pal
UZB: фол

falak [1] فلك ARABIC *n.* sky, firmament
BAS: фәләк
KAR: пәләк
TAJ: фалак
TAT: фәләк
TUR: пелек ① *sky, firmament* ② *God*
UYG: paläk
UZB: фалак

falak [2] فلك ARABIC *n.* fate, fortune
BAS: фәләк
KAR: пәләк
TAJ: фалак
TAT: фәләк
TUR: пелек
UYG: paläk, päläk
UZB: фалак

falaq [1] فلق ARABIC *n.* special board used in madrasas to punish students, on which the guilty student's legs are placed and struck by the teacher
KAR: пәлақ
TAJ: фалақ
UYG: palaq
UZB: фалақ

Falaq [2] فلق ARABIC *Qur'an pn.* the 113th sura of the Qur'an ☞ ***Mu’avvizitan, Mu’avvizitayn***
KAR: Пәлақ суўреси
KAZ: Фалақ сүресі
TAJ: сураи Фалақ
TAT: Фәлакъ сүрәсе
UYG: Palaq süräsi, sürä Fäläq
UZB: Фалақ сураси

falbin فالبين PERSIAN *n.* fortune teller
KAR: палбын
TAJ: фолбин
UZB: фолбин

falgu فالگو PERSIAN *n.* fortune teller
KAR: палшы
KAZ: балгөй
KYR: балчы
TAJ: фолгӯ
TAT: фалчы
TUR: палчы
UZB: фолгўй

falnama فالنامه PERSIAN *n.* oracular book used for divination
BAS: фалнама
KAR: палнама
KAZ: балдама
TAJ: фолнома
UYG: palnamä
UZB: фолнома

falsafa فلسفه ARABIC *n.* philosophy (as an Islamic science)
BAS: фәлсәфә
KAR: философия
KAZ: фәлсәпа
TAJ: фалсафа
TAT: фәлсәфә

TUR: пелсепе
UYG: pälsäpä
UZB: фалсафа

fana فنا ARABIC *n.* passing away, non-existence
BAS: фәна
KAR: пәнә
TAJ: фано
TAT: фәна
UYG: pänä
UZB: фано

fani فانى ARABIC *adj.* temporal, of this world
KAR: пәний
KAZ: фани
TAJ: фонӣ
TAT: фани
UYG: päni
UZB: фоний

fann فنّ ARABIC *n.* discipline, field of study, science
BAS: фән
KAR: пән
KAZ: пән
TAJ: фан
TAT: фән
UYG: pän
UZB: фан

faqahat فقاهت ARABIC *Law n.* the comprehension of Islamic law
TAJ: фақоҳат
TAT: фәкаһәт
UZB: фақоҳат

faqih فقيه ARABIC *Law n.* expert in Islamic law
KAR: пәқих
KAZ: факих
TAJ: фақиҳ
TAT: фәкыйһ
TUR: факих
UYG: päqih
UZB: фақиҳ

faqir [1] فقير ARABIC *Law n.* poor person, needy person, signifying both a legal status allowing exemption from zakat and other forms of Islamic taxation, as well as a category of needy person who is allowed to receive charity
BAS: фаҡир
KAR: пәқыр
KAZ: пақыр
KYR: бакыр
TAJ: фақир
TAT: фәкыйр
TUR: пахыр, пакыр, факыр
UYG: paqir
UZB: фақир

faqir [2] فقير ARABIC *n.* one who is in need, either physically or spiritually; self-identifying epithet of an author of a given text
BAS: фаҡир
KAR: пақыр, пәқыр
KYR: бакыр
TAJ: фақр
TAT: фәкыйр
UYG: paqir
UZB: фақир

faqr فقر ARABIC *Sufism n.* renouncement of worldly life (as a precondition of embarking on the Sufi path)
BAS: фәҡр
KAR: пәкыр
TAJ: фақр
TAT: фәкыр
UYG: paqir
UZB: фақр

fara'iz [1] فرائض ARABIC *Law n.* rules for the distribution of inheritances
BAS: фараиз
KAR: парыз
TAJ: фароиз
TAT: фәраиз
UYG: pärz
UZB: фароиз

fara'iz [2] فرائض ARABIC *n.* religious obligations (plural form) ☞ ***farz***
KAR: парыз
KYR: барайыз
TAJ: фароиз
TAT: фәраиз
UYG: pärz
UZB: фароиз

farid فريد ARABIC *adj.* peerless, without equal, unique
KAR: пәрид
TAJ: фарид
TAT: фәрид
UYG: parid
UZB: фарид

farid al-'asr فريدالعصر ARABIC *np.* the most outstanding of the age (epithet given to eminent scholars)
- TAJ: фаридал аср
- TAT: фәриделгасыр
- UYG: paridal asr
- UZB: фаридал аср

farishta فرشته PERSIAN *n.* angel
- BAS: фәрештә
- KAR: перуште, пәрийшта
- KAZ: періште
- KYR: периште, бериште
- TAJ: фаришта
- TAT: фәрештә
- TUR: перишде
- UYG: pärishtä, perishtä
- UZB: фаришта

farsakh فرسخ PERSIAN unit of measurement equal to 6.24 kilometers
- TAJ: фарсанг, фарсах
- TAT: фәрсәх
- UYG: pärsäkh
- UZB: фарсах

faruq فاروق ARABIC *n.* one who can distinguish well between good and evil (epithet of the Caliph 'Umar)
- KAR: пәрух
- TAJ: форуқ
- TAT: фарук
- UYG: pärüq
- UZB: фаруқ

faryad فرياد PERSIAN *n.* cry for help, supplication
- BAS: фәрьяд
- KAR: пәряд, парияд, пәрияд, фарьяд
- TAJ: фарёд
- TAT: фәрьяд, фөрьяд
- TUR: феряд
- UYG: paryäd
- UZB: фарёд

farz فرض ARABIC *Law n.* obligatory religious activity, religious obligation
- BAS: фарыз
- KAR: парыз
- KAZ: парыз, параз
- KYR: парыз, парз, барыз, барз, фарыз
- TAJ: фарз
- TAT: фарыз
- TUR: парз, фарз
- UYG: pärz ① *obligatory religious activity, religious obligation* ② *circumcision ritual*
- UZB: фарз

farz-i 'ayn فرض عين PERSIAN *Law np.* group of religious obligations applicable to all
- KAR: парзайн
- TAJ: фарзайн
- TAT: фарыз гаен, фарыз гайн
- UYG: pärzi ayn
- UZB: фарзиайн, фарзи айн

farz-i da'im فرض دائم PERSIAN *Ritual np.* permanent obligation, a category of religious obligation required at all times, i.e. the obligation of faith
- TAT: фарыз даим
- UZB: фарзи доим

farz-i kifaya فرض كفايه PERSIAN *Ritual np.* religious obligation incumbent on one person (at a minimum) at one point in time, and not on all Muslims
- KAR: парзы кипая
- TAJ: фарзи кифоят
- TAT: фарыз кифая
- TUR: парз кефая
- UYG: pärzi kipäyä
- UZB: фарзи кифоя

farz-i muvaqqat فرض موقّت PERSIAN *Ritual np.* provisional obligation, temporal obligation (a category of religious obligation), i.e. performing the hajj
- KAR: мувәққат
- TAJ: фарзи муваққат
- TAT: фарыз мувәккать
- UZB: фарзи муваққат, муваққат фарз

fasad فساد ARABIC *n.* licentiousness, immorality; rebellion, sedition
- BAS: фәсад
- KAR: пасәд
- KAZ: фасат
- TAJ: фасод
- TAT: фәсад
- TUR: фасд
- UYG: päsat
- UZB: фасод, фасот

fasiq فاسق ARABIC *n.* immoral person, licentious person
- BAS: фасиҡ
- KAR: пасық
- KAZ: пасық, фасық *ignorant person unclean*

forbidden

TAJ: фосиқ

TAT: фасик, фасыйк, фасикъ ① *immoral, licentious person* ② *atheist, unbeliever* ③ *fornicator*

UYG: päsiq

UZB: фосиқ

Fath فتح ARABIC *Qur'an pn.* the 48th sura of the Qur'an

KAR: Патых суўреси

KAZ: Фатах сүресі

TAJ: сураи Фатҳ

UYG: Pätkh süräsi, sürä Fatih

UZB: Фатҳ сураси

Fath-i Makka فتح مكّه PERSIAN *Ritual np.* the Conquest of Mecca (festival observed on the 21st of Ramadan commemorating the Prophet Muhammad's victory in 632 over the Meccan forces, resulting in the conquest of that city

KAR: Мәкке пәтхи

TAJ: Фатҳи Макка

TAT: Фәтхе Мәккә, Фәтех Мәккә

UYG: Mäkkä pathi

UZB: Макка фатҳи

fatiha [1] فاتحه ARABIC *n.* prayer (the act)

BAS: фатиха, бата

KAR: пәтия

KAZ: бата

KYR: бата

TAJ: фотиҳа

TAT: фатиха

UYG: patihä, pätä *short prayer*

UZB: фотиҳа

fatiha [2] فاتحه ARABIC *n.* blessing, benediction

BAS: фатиха, бата

KAR: пәтия

KAZ: бата, патиха, фатиха

KYR: бата

TAJ: фотиҳа

TAT: фатиха ① *blessing, benediction* ② *prayer for the dead*

TUR: пата, патыха ① *blessing (usually from a Sufi master or master craftsman)* ② *memorial feast*

UYG: patihä

UZB: фотиҳа

Fatiha [3] فاتحه ARABIC *Qur'an pn.* the first sura of the Qur'an

KAR: Пәтия суўреси

KAZ: Фатиха сүресі, Бата, Патиха

KYR: Бата

TAJ: сураи Фотиҳа

TAT: фатиха, Фатиха сүрәсе, Әлхәм сүрәсе

TUR: Фатыха сүреси

UYG: Patihä, sürä Fatihä

UZB: фотиҳа сураси

Fatiha, al- الفاتحه ARABIC *Ritual intj.* invitation to perform the Fatiha prayer

TAJ: ал Фотиҳа!

UZB: ал Фотиҳа!

fatihagu فاتحه گو PERSIAN *n.* one who gives blessings

KAR: пәтиягөй

KYR: батакөй

TAJ: фотиҳагӯ

UZB: фотиҳагўй

Fatima فاطمه ARABIC *pn.* daughter of the prophet Muhammad and wife of the Caliph 'Ali

BAS: Фатима

KAR: Патыйма

KAZ: Фатима, Батима

KYR: Фатима

TAJ: Фотима

TAT: Фатыймә

TUR: Патма

UYG: Patima

UZB: Фотима

Fatir [1] فاطر ARABIC *Qur'an n.* the 35th sura of the Qur'an

KAR: Пәтыр суўреси

KAZ: Фатыр сүресі

TAJ: сураи Фотир

TAT: Фатир сүрәсе

UYG: sürä Fatir

UZB: Фотир сураси

fatir [2] فاطر ARABIC *n.* one who violates the fast

TAJ: фатр

TAT: фатыйр

TUR: патер

UZB: фатр

Fattah, al- الفتّاح ARABIC *n.* name of God: the Opener

KAR: Паттах

TAJ: Фаттоҳ

TUR: ал-Фаттах

UYG: Pättäh

UZB: Ал-Фаттоҳ

fatva فتوى ARABIC *Law n.* formal legal opinion
- BAS: фәтүә
- KAR: пәтӯә, патӯә, пәтӯа
- KAZ: пәтуа, бәтуа, фатуа
- KYR: батуба, батыба
- TAJ: фатво
- TAT: фәтва
- TUR: питива, фетва
- UYG: pätiwa, pätwa
- UZB: фатво

faylasuf فيلسوف ARABIC *n.* philosopher
- BAS: фәйләсуф
- KAR: философ
- TAJ: файласуф
- TAT: фәйләсуф
- UYG: päylasup
- UZB: файласуф

fazil فاضل ARABIC *adj.* eminent, erudite (epithet of especially learned scholars)
- BAS: фазыл
- KAR: пазыл
- TAJ: фозил
- TAT: фазыйл
- TUR: пазыл
- UYG: pazil
- UZB: фозил

fazl فضل ARABIC *n.* erudition, eminence
- KAR: пазыл
- KAZ: пазыл
- TAJ: фазл
- TAT: фазыл
- TUR: пазыл
- UYG: pazil
- UZB: фазл

fida فدا ARABIC *Ritual n.* victim, that which is sacrificed
- BAS: фиҙа
- KAR: пида, пидә, фида
- KAZ: пида
- KYR: пида
- TAJ: фидо
- TAT: фида
- TUR: пейда
- UYG: pida
- UZB: фидо

fida'i فدائى ARABIC *n.* one who sacrifices himself
- BAS: фидаи
- KAR: пидәи
- KAZ: фидаи
- TAJ: фидой
- TAT: фидаи
- UYG: pidayi
- UZB: фидойи

fidakyar فداكار PERSIAN *n.* one who sacrifices himself ☞ ***fida'i***
- KAR: пидакер
- TAJ: фидокор
- TAT: фидакяр
- UYG: pidakar
- UZB: фидокор

fidya فديه ARABIC *Ritual n.* offerings made to redeem the sins of a deceased person
- BAS: фидия
- KAR: пыдия
- KAZ: пiдия, фiдие
- KYR: пидия, бидия
- TAJ: фидья
- TAT: фидия
- TUR: фидъе
- UYG: pidya
- UZB: фидя

fikrat فكرت ARABIC *n.* science, scholarship (among Hizb ut-Tahrir)
- UZB: фикрат

Fil فيل ARABIC *Qur'an n.* the 105th sura of the Qur'an
- KAR: Пыл сүўреси
- KAZ: Фiл сүресi
- TAJ: сураи Фил
- UYG: Pil süräsi, sürä Fil
- UZB: Фил сураси

fiqh فقه ARABIC *Law n.* Islamic law, Islamic jurisprudence
- BAS: фикһе
- KAR: пикх
- KAZ: фикх
- TAJ: фиқеҳ
- TAT: фикъһе, фикыһ
- TUR: фикх
- UZB: фиқҳ

Fira'un فرعون ARABIC *Historical pn.* Pharaoh; tyrant, oppressor
- BAS: Фирғаүен
- KAR: Пирғаўын
- KAZ: Перғауын, Пырғғауын, Фәрғауын

KYR: Фараон
TAJ: Фиръавн
TAT: Фиргавен
TUR: Фираун, Пыргаун
UYG: Pir'äwn
UZB: Фиравн

Firdaus فردوس PERSIAN *pn.* Heaven, Paradise ☞ ***Jannat al-Firdaus***
BAS: фирҙәүес
KAR: пирдаўс
KAZ: фырдаус
TAJ: фирдавс
TAT: фирдәвес
UYG: pirdäws
UZB: фирдавс

firqa فرقه ARABIC *n.* sect, group, party
BAS: фирҡа
KAR: пирқә
KAZ: фирка
TAJ: фирқа
TAT: фирка
UYG: pirqa
UZB: фирқа

fisq فسق ARABIC *n.* obscene behavior, lewdness; rebellion
TAJ: фасх
TAT: фисык
UYG: pisq
UZB: фисқ

fitna فتنه ARABIC *n.* sedition, mutiny, rebellion; civil war
KAR: питнә
KAZ: пітіне, фітне
KYR: фитне
TAJ: фитна
TAT: фитнә, фетнә
TUR: питне
UYG: pitnä
UZB: фитна

fitr [1] فطر ARABIC *Ritual n.* breaking the fast (especially after Ramazan) ☞ ***'Id al-Fitr***
BAS: фытыр
KAR: питир
KAZ: пітір
KYR: битир, питир
TAJ: фитр
TAT: фитыр
TUR: питре, фитре
UYG: pitir
UZB: фитр

fitr [2] فطر ARABIC *Ritual n.* offerings given in honor of breaking the fast, considered a form of zakat ☞ ***zakat al-fitr***
BAS: фытыр саҙаҡаһы
KAR: питир ① *offerings given in honor of breaking the fast* ② *sacrifice performed after the harvest*
KAZ: пітір
KYR: битир, питир
TAJ: фитр
TAT: фитыр, фитыр садакасы
TUR: питре
UYG: pitir
UZB: фитр

fitra فطره ARABIC *Taxation n.* voluntary offerings made at the end of Ramadan, considered a form of zakat ☞ ***zakat al-fitr***
TAJ: фитра
TAT: фитра садакасы
TUR: фитре
UZB: фитра

fitrat فطرة ARABIC *n.* character, esp. Islamic character
KAZ: фытрат
TAJ: фитрат
TAT: фитрәт
UZB: фитрат

Furqan [1] فرقان ARABIC *Qur'an pn.* the Qur'an
KAR: Пурқән
KAZ: Фуркан, Фұрқан
TAJ: Фурқон
TAT: Фөркан, Фуркан, Форкан
UYG: Purqän
UZB: Фурқон

Furqan [2] فرقان ARABIC *Qur'an pn.* the 25th sura of the Qur'an
KAR: Пурқән суўреси
KAZ: Фұрқан сүресі
TAJ: сураи Фурқон
TUR: сураи Фуркан
UYG: Purqän süräsi, sürä Furqan
UZB: Фурқон сураси

Fussilat فصّلت ARABIC *Qur'an pn.* the 41st sura of the Qur'an
KAR: Пуссиләт суўреси
KAZ: Фұссилат сүресі

TAJ: сураи Фуссилат
TAT: Фуссыйлэт сүрэсе
UYG: sürä Fussilät
UZB: Фуссилат

futuvat فتوت ARABIC *Sufism n.* good morals; generosity; chivalry, bonds of brotherhood (between Sufis or craftsmen)
UYG: putuwat
UZB: футуват

fuzala فضلا ARABIC *n.* learned men of Islam, clergy
KAR: пузалә
TAJ: фузало
TAT: фозала
UZB: фузало

G

Ghaffar, al- الغفّار ARABIC *pn.* name of God: the Forgiver
BAS: Ғәффар
KAR: Ғаппар
KAZ: Ғаффар
TAJ: Ғаффор
TUR: ал-Гаффар
UYG: Ghappar
UZB: Ал-Ғаффор

ghafil ARABIC *adj.* ignorant
BAS: ғафил
KAR: ғәпил, ғапыл
KAZ: ғафіл
TAJ: ғофил
TAT: гафил
UYG: ghapil
UZB: ғофил

Ghafir غافر ARABIC *Qur'an pn.* the 40th sura of the Qur'an ☞ ***Mu'min***
BAS: Ғафир
KAR: Ғәпыр сүўреси
KAZ: Ғафыр сүресі
TAJ: сураи Мӯмин (Ғофир)
UYG: Ghäpir süräsi, sürä Ghafir
UZB: Ғофир сураси

ghaflat [1] غفلت ARABIC *n.* negligence, inattention
BAS: ғәфләт
KAR: ғаплэт, ғаплат
KAZ: ғафлет
TAJ: ғафлат
TAT: гафләт
UYG: Ghäplät
UZB: ғафлат

ghaflat [2] غفلت ARABIC *Sufism n.* heedlessness, carelessness; living at a great spiritual distance from God
KAZ: ғафлет
TAJ: ғафлат
TAT: гафләт
UZB: ғафлат

Ghafur, al- الغفور ARABIC *n.* name of God: the Forgiving
KAR: Ғәпыр
KAZ: Ғафұр
TAJ: Ғафур
TUR: ал-Гафур
UYG: Ghapur
UZB: Ал-Ғафур
ghaliz ☞ ***najasat ghaliz***

Ghambar غامبر PERSIAN *pn.* the groom of the Caliph Ali's horse Duldul
BAS: Ғәмбәр
KAR: Ғамбәр
KYR: Камбар, Камбар Ата ① *the groom of the Calip Ali's horse Duldul* ② *the patron saint of horses* ③ *a name given to a horse possessing the best qualities within a herd*
TAJ: Ғамбар
TUR: Баба Гаммар
UYG: Ghambar
UZB: Ғамбар

ghamm [1] غمّ ARABIC *n.* grief, anxiety
BAS: ғәм
KAR: ғам
TAJ: ғам
TAT: гамь
UYG: ghäm
UZB: ғам

ghamm [2] غمّ ARABIC *Sufism n.* grieving, sensing (of a Sufi regarding God or regarding the temporal world)
TAJ: ғам
TAT: гамь
UZB: ғам

Ghani, al- الغنى ARABIC *pn.* name of God: the Self-Sufficient
BAS: Ғәни

KAR: Ғәний
KAZ: Ғани
TAJ: Ғанӣ
TUR: ал-Ганы
UYG: Ghaniy
UZB: Ал-Ғаний

ghanimat غنيمت ARABIC *Law n.* spoil, booty (as regulated in Islamic law)
BAS: ғәнимәт
KAR: ғәнийбет
KAZ: ганима, ғанимат
KYR: канимет
TAJ: ганимат
TAT: ганимәт
TUR: ганымат
UYG: ghanimät
UZB: ғанимат

gharib[1] غريب ARABIC *Law n.* poor person; stranger; solitary person (who receives alms); itinerant Sufi
BAS: ғәрип
KAR: ғәрип, малсыз
TAJ: ғариб
UYG: gharip
UZB: ғариб

gharib[2] غريب ARABIC *Hadith adj.* tradition related by only one source
TAT: гариб
UZB: ғариб

ghasb غصب ARABIC *Law n.* capture or seizure of another's property
TAJ: ғасб
TAT: гасб
UZB: ғасп

Ghashiya غاشيه ARABIC *Qur'an pn.* the 88th sura of the Qur'an
KAR: Ғәшия сүўреси
KAZ: Ғашия сүресі
TAJ: сураи Ғошия
UYG: sürä Ghashiyä
UZB: Ғошия сураси

ghasl غسل ARABIC *Ritual n.* washing the corpse before burial and performing prayers
TAJ: ғасл
UZB: ғасл

ghassal غسّال ARABIC *Ritual n.* person who washes the corpse before burial and performs prayers
TAJ: ғассол
UYG: ghässäl
UZB: ғассол

Ghavs al-A'zam غوث الاعظم ARABIC *Sufism pn.* mediator; a title given to a Muslim saint, usually below the rank of Qutb; esp. 'Abd al-Qadir al-Gilani (lit. the greatest help)
KAZ: Ғаусыл Ағзам
KYR: Коосул аазам, капсылазам
TAJ: Ғавс ал Аъзам
TAT: Гаус
UYG: Ghavsal A'zam
UZB: Ғавсал Аъзам

ghayb ☞ ***rijal al-ghayb***

ghayr-i din غير دين PERSIAN *adj.* unislamic, irreligious
KAR: ғәйрыдин, кудайсыз
KYR: кайрыдин, кара дин, диникайыр
TAJ: ғайридин, ғайр динӣ
UYG: ghäyridin, ghäyridiniy
UZB: ғайридин, ғайридиний

ghayr-i mashru' غير مشروع PERSIAN *Law adj.* counter to Islamic law
KAR: ғайры мәшру
TAJ: ғайр машруҳ
UYG: ghayrimashrü
UZB: ғайримашру

ghayr-i misr غير مصر PERSIAN *Law np.* lacking the legal status of a city, i.e. small towns or villages
TUR: гайры мусур

ghayr-i mu'akkad قير مؤكّد PERSIAN *Law adj.* unconfirmed, uncorroborated (as a classification of sunnat) ☞ ***mu'akkad***
KAZ: ғайрі мү'аккад
TAJ: ғайри муъаққат
UYG: ghäyri muäqqäd
UZB: ғайри муаққад

ghayr-i shar'i غير شرع ARABIC *Law adj.* counter to Islamic law
KAR: ғәйры шарий
TAJ: ғайр шарӣ
UYG: ghayrishar'iy
UZB: ғайри шаръий

Ghayya غيّا ARABIC *pn.* the name of a well in the deepest part of Hell; the pit of Hell
TAJ: ғаййа
UZB: ғаййа, жаҳаннам туби

ghaza غزا ARABIC *n.* raid, attack, conquest; holy war, war for the faith (fought against infidels) ☞ ***ghazavat***

KAR: ғаза
TAJ: ғазо, ғазв, ғазва
TAT: газа
UZB: ғазо

ghazab غضب ARABIC *n.* divine anger

KAR: ғазап
TAJ: ғазаб
UYG: ghazab, ghäzäp
UZB: ғазаб

ghazavat غزوات *n.* holy war, war for the faith (against infidels) ☞ ***jihad***

KAR: ғазабат
KAZ: ғазауат, ғазабат
KYR: казат, газават, нээти казат
TAJ: ғазва
TAT: газават, газәват
TUR: газават
UYG: ghazavät
UZB: ғазавот

ghazi غازی ARABIC *n.* warrior for the faith, holy warrior

BAS: ғази
KAR: ғазий
KAZ: гази
KYR: казы, казатчы
TAJ: ғозӣ
TAT: газый
TUR: гази, газы
UYG: ghäzi, ghazi
UZB: ғози, ғозий

ghilman غلمان ARABIC *n.* servants in Paradise; servants

BAS: ғилман
KAR: ғилмән
KAZ: ғилман
TAJ: ғилмон
TAT: гыйльман
UYG: ghilman
UZB: ғилмон

ghul غل ARABIC *Law n.* fetters, chains

TAJ: ғулл
TAT: гол
UYG: ghul
UZB: ғул

ghurbat غربت PERSIAN *Sufism n.* separation from one's homeland; exile in the transitory world

TAJ: ғурбат
TAT: горбәт
UZB: ғурбат

ghusl غسل ARABIC *Ritual n.* major ablution, involving washing the whole body

BAS: ғөсөл
KAR: ғусыл
KAZ: ғұсыл
KYR: кусул, кусулдаарат
TAJ: ғусл
TAT: госел
TUR: гусул
UYG: ghusl, chong tärät
UZB: ғусул

ghuslkhana غسلخانه PERSIAN *n.* building or location for performing the major ablution

BAS: ғөсөлхана
KAR: ғусылхана
TAT: госелханә
UYG: ghuslkhana
UZB: ғуслхона

gumbaz گنبذ PERSIAN *n.* cupola, dome (of a mosque or mausoleum)

BAS: көмбәҙ, гөмбәҙ
KAR: гүмбез ① *cupola* ② *mausoleum*
KAZ: күмбез
KYR: күмбөз
TAJ: гумбаз
TAT: гөмбәз
TUR: гүммез
UYG: gümbäz
UZB: гумбаз

gunah گناه PERSIAN *n.* sin, transgression

BAS: гөнаһ
KAR: гүна
KAZ: күнә, кінә
KYR: күнө, күнөө
TAJ: гуноҳ
TAT: гөнаһ
TUR: гүнә
UYG: guna, gunah
UZB: гуноҳ

gunahkar گناهکار PERSIAN *n.* sinner ☞ ***gunah***

BAS: гөнаһҡар
KAR: гүнакар, гүнәкәр

KAZ: күнəкар
KYR: күнөөкөр
TAJ: гунохкор
TAT: гөнаһкяр
TUR: гүнәкәр, гүнәли
UYG: gunakar
UZB: гуноҳкор

gur گور PERSIAN *n.* tomb, grave
BAS: гүр
KAR: гөр
KAZ: көр
KYR: көр, гөр
TAJ: гӯр
TAT: гүр
TUR: гөр
UYG: gör, gor
UZB: гўр

guristan گورستان PERSIAN *n.* cemetery, graveyard
BAS: гүрстан
KAR: гөрыстəн, гөристан
KYR: көрүстөн
TAJ: гӯристон
TAT: гүрстан, гүрестан
UYG: görüstan, goristan
UZB: гўристон

gurkhana گورخانه PERSIAN *n.* mausoleum, tomb
KAZ: гөрхана
KYR: көркана

H

habash حبش ARABIC *n.* Ethiopian, Abyssinian
BAS: хəбəш
KAR: ҳəбаш
TAJ: ҳабаш
TAT: хəбəш
UYG: häbäsh
UZB: ҳабаш

Habashistan حبشستان PERSIAN *pn.* Ethiopia, Abyssinia
KAR: Ҳəбашистəн
TAJ: Ҳабашистон
TAT: Хəбəшстан, Хəбəш
UYG: Häbäshistan, Hawashstan
UZB: Ҳабашистон

Habib حبيب ARABIC *pn.* Beloved (epithet of the Prophet Muhammad)
KAR: ҳəбиб
TAJ: Ҳабиб
TAT: Хəбиб
UYG: Häbib
UZB: Ҳабиб

Habibullah حبيب الله ARABIC *pn.* epithet of the prophet Muhammad (God's beloved)
BAS: Хəбибулла, Хабибулла
KAR: Ҳəбиййбулла
TAJ: Ҳабиби Оллоҳ
TUR: Хабыбылла
UYG: Habibullah
UZB: Ҳабибуллоҳ

Habil هابيل ARABIC *pn.* Abel, the son of the prophet Adam
KAR: Ҳабыл
KAZ: Хабыл
TAJ: Ҳабил
TAT: Һабыл
TUR: Абыл
UYG: Habil
UZB: Ҳабил

hadd حدّ ARABIC *Law n.* limit, boundary; punishment (for violations against Islamic law)
KAR: ҳадд
KAZ: хадд
TAJ: ҳад, андоза, дарача
TAT: хəдд
TUR: хадд
UYG: hädd
UZB: ҳадд

hadd-i qazf حدّ قذف PERSIAN *Law np.* category of punishment for slander; category of punishment given to a person who unjustly accuses an honest woman of being a prostitute
TAJ: ҳадди қазф
UZB: ҳадди қазиф

hadd-i shurb حدّ شرب PERSIAN *Law np.* category of punishment for wine-drinking
TAJ: ҳадди шароб
UZB: ҳадди шурб

hadd-i sirkat حدّ سرکة PERSIAN *Law np.* category of punishment for theft, commonly involving the amputation of a hand
TAJ: ҳадди сиркат
UZB: ҳадди сиркат

hadd-i zakr PERSIAN *Law np.* name of a punishment given to a person who has consumed intoxicants of a sort other than wine
TAJ: ҳадди закр
UZB: ҳадди закр

hadd-i zina حدّ زنا PERSIAN *Law np.* category of punishments for having committing fornication
TAJ: ҳадди зино
UZB: ҳадди зино

Hadi, al- الهادى ARABIC *pn.* name of God: the Guide
BAS: һади
KAR: Ҳәдий
TAJ: Ҳодӣ
TAT: һади
TUR: ал-Хади
UYG: Hädiy
UZB: Ал-Ҳодий

Hadid حديد ARABIC *Qur'an pn.* the 57th sura of the Qur'an
KAR: Ҳадид суўреси
KAZ: Хадид сүресі
TAJ: сураи Ҳадид
TAT: Хәдид сүрәсе
UYG: Hädid süräsi
UZB: Ҳадид сураси

hadis حديث ARABIC *Hadith n.* hadith, traditions and sayings attributed to the Prophet Muhammad
BAS: хәдис
KAR: ҳәдийс
KAZ: хадис
KYR: адыс
TAJ: ҳадис
TAT: хәдис, хадисе шәриф
TUR: хадыс
UYG: hädis
UZB: ҳадис

hadis-i arbaʿin حديث اربعين PERSIAN *Hadith np.* collection of forty hadiths (as a literary genre)
TAT: хәдиси әрбагыйн, кырык хәдис
UZB: қирқ ҳадис

hadis-i qudsi حديث قدسى PERSIAN *Hadith np.* sacred tradition, a tradition spoken by the Prophet Muhammad and attributable to God
UZB: ҳадиси қудсий

hafiz حافظ ARABIC *n.* one who has memorized the entire Qur'an
BAS: абыз
KAR: ҳәпиз
KAZ: абыз
KYR: апыз, капыз, хафыз ① *learned person* ② *poet* ③ *singer*
TAJ: ҳофиз
TAT: хафиз, коръәнхафиз
TUR: хапыз *reciter of poetry, one who knows poetry by heart*
UYG: hapiz ① *one who has memorized the entire Qur'an* ② *singer, hafiz* ③ *performer at Sufi zikr rituals*
UZB: ҳофиз ① *one who has memorized the entire Qur'an* ② *singer*

Hafiz, al- [1] الحافظ ARABIC *pn.* name of God: the protector
KAR: Ҳәпит
TAJ: Ҳофид
TAT: Хафиз
TUR: ал-Хафид
UZB: Ал-Ҳофид

Hafiz, al- [2] الحفيظ ARABIC *pn.* name of God: the Guardian
KAR: Ҳәпиз
TAJ: Ҳафиз
TUR: ал-Хафиз
UYG: Hapiz
UZB: Ал-Ҳафиз

haft-i yak هفتيك PERSIAN *n.* one-seventh of the Qur'an (as a separate book)
BAS: әфтиәк, һәфтиәк
KAR: ҳәптияк, әптийәк, әптүйек
KAZ: әптиек
KYR: аптиек, аптээк
TAJ: ҳафтияк
TAT: һәфтеяк
UYG: haptiyak
UZB: ҳафтияк

Hajar هاجر ARABIC *pn.* Hagar, the wife of Abraham
BAS: һажер
KAR: Ҳажар
KAZ: Хаджар
TAT: һаҗәр
TUR: Хажар
UYG: Häjar, Hajär
UZB: Ҳожар, Биби Ҳожар

hajar-i asvad حجر اسود PERSIAN *pn.* the sacred black stone in the southeastern corner of the Ka'ba in Mecca

BAS: кәғбә ташы, ҡара таш
KAZ: қара тас
KYR: кара таш
TAJ: ҳочари асвад, ҳачарул асвад
TAT: хәҗәре әсвәд, кара таш, караташ
TUR: гара даш
UYG: häjari-äsväd
UZB: ҳожари асвад, ҳажарул асвод, каъбатош

hajj[1] حج ARABIC *n.* the pilgrimage to Mecca (a conditional obligation) or the pilgrimage to Mecca, Arafat and Mina; the fifth of the five pillars of Islam
BAS: хаж
KAR: ҳаж
KAZ: қажы, хажы, қажылық, әл-хажж, хаж
KYR: ажы
TAJ: ҳаҷҷ
TAT: хаҗ
TUR: хач, хаҗ
UYG: haj, häj
UZB: ҳаж

Hajj[2] حج ARABIC *Qur'an pn.* the 22nd sura of the Qur'an
KAR: Ҳаж суўреси
KAZ: Хаж сүресі
TAJ: сураи Ҳаҷ
TAT: Хаҗ
TUR: сураи Хаҗ
UYG: Häj süräsi
UZB: Ҳаж сураси

hajj badal حج بدل ARABIC *Hajj np.* substituting the hajj by another pious deed, which is considered the equivalent of the hajj (usually by providing support to a substitute to go on the hajj)
BAS: бәдәл хаж
KAR: ҳаж бәдәл
KYR: ажы бедел
TAJ: бадали ҳаҷ
UYG: haj badal
UZB: ҳаж бадал

hajji حاجّی ARABIC *Hajj n.* one who has performed the pilgrimage to Mecca
BAS: хажи, хажый
KAR: ҳажы
KAZ: қажы, хажы
KYR: ажы
TAJ: ҳоҷи
TAT: хаҗи
TUR: хаҗы
UYG: haji
UZB: ҳожи

hajjikhana حاجّی خانه PERSIAN *Hajj n.* guesthouse for those going on the hajj
KAR: хажыхана

Hakam, al- الحکم ARABIC *pn.* name of God: the Judge
TAJ: Ҳакам
TUR: ал-Хакам
UYG: Hakam
UZB: Ал-Ҳакам

hakim حکیم ARABIC *n.* philosopher, wise man
KAR: ҳәким
KAZ: хакім, кәким
TAJ: ҳаким ① *doctor, physician* ② *philosopher, wise man*
TAT: хәким
TUR: хеким ① *doctor, physician* ② *philosopher, wise man*
UYG: hakim
UZB: ҳаким ① *doctor, physician* ② *philosopher, wise man*

Hakim, al- الحکیم ARABIC *pn.* name of God: the Wise
BAS: Хәким
KAR: Ҳәким
TAJ: Ҳаким
TUR: ал-Хаким
UYG: Hakim
UZB: Ал-Ҳаким

hal حال ARABIC *Sufism n.* state, mystical state
BAS: хәл
KAR: ҳал
KAZ: хал
KYR: ал
TAJ: ҳол
TAT: хәл
TUR: хал
UYG: hal
UZB: ҳол

halal حلال ARABIC *Law n.* licit, canonically lawful, permitted
BAS: хәләл ① *licit, canonically lawful, permitted* ② *married*
KAR: ҳадал, ҳадал
KAZ: адал, халал ① *licit, canonically lawful, permitted* ② *honorable, honest*
KYR: адал ① *licit, canonically lawful, permitted* ②

washing, cleaning (of the dead) ③ *honorable, honest*

TAJ: ҳалол

TAT: хәләл, хәлял

TUR: халал

UYG: halal

UZB: ҳалол ① *licit, canonically lawful, permitted* ② *honorable, honest*

halif حليف ARABIC *Law n.* one who enjoys the protection of a tribe but does not belong to it by blood

KAR: халиф

TAJ: ҳалиф

UZB: ҳалиф

halim حليم ARABIC *Ritual n.* name of a dish made from of wheat porridge and meat and especially prepared during Novruz

KAZ: халим

TAJ: ҳалиса, ҳалим

UYG: hälim

UZB: ҳалим, ҳалиса

Halim, al- الحليم ARABIC *pn.* name of God: the Gentle

KAR: Ҳәлим

TAJ: Ҳалим

TUR: ал-Халим

UYG: Hälim

UZB: Ал-Ҳалим

halimkhana حليمخانه PERSIAN *Ritual n.* place where halim is prepared during Novruz

KAZ: халимхана

TAJ: ҳалисахона, ҳолимхона

UYG: hälimkhana

UZB: ҳалимхона, ҳалисахона

hall حلّ ARABIC *n.* absolution of sins

KAR: ҳалл

KYR: ал

TAJ: ҳалл

TAT: хәлл, хәл

UYG: hall

UZB: ҳалл

halqa [1] حلقه ARABIC *n.* circle of madrasa students

TAJ: ҳалқа

TAT: хилка, халка

UYG: halqa

UZB: ҳалқа

halqa [2] حلقه ARABIC *n.* circle of students (among Hizb ut-Tahrir)

UZB: ҳалқа

Hamal حمل ARABIC *pn.* Aries, second month of the Hidjri Solar year

BAS: Хәмәл

KAR: ҳәмәл, ҳәмал

KAZ: Хамал

TAJ: ҳамал

TAT: Хәмәл

UYG: Hämäl

UZB: ҳамал

Haman هامان ARABIC *pn.* name of the Pharaoh's minister who is mentioned in the Qur'an

KAZ: Һаман

TAJ: Ҳомон

UYG: Haman

UZB: Ҳомон

Hamid, al- الحميد ARABIC *pn.* name of God: the Praiseworthy

BAS: Хәмид

KAR: Хәмийт

TAJ: Ҳамид

TUR: ал-Хамыт

UYG: Hamid

UZB: Ал-Ҳамид

hamila حامله ARABIC *n.* fetus; pregnant

KAR: ҳамилә

TAJ: ҳомила

TAT: хамилә

UYG: hamilä

UZB: ҳомила

hamiladar حامله دار PERSIAN *Law n.* pregnant (as a legal condition)

KAR: жукли, қабат

TAJ: ҳомиладор

UYG: hämiläliq, hamilidar

UZB: ҳомиладор

Hanafi حنفى ARABIC *Law n.* follower of the Hanafi school of jurisprudence

KAR: қанапий

KAZ: ханафит

TAJ: ҳанафӣ

TAT: хәнәфи

TUR: ханафи

UYG: hanapi

UZB: ҳанафий

Hanafiya حنفيه ARABIC *Law pn.* one of the four major schools of Sunni jurisprudence, founded by Abu

Hanifa (699-767 AD); historically the Muslims of Central Asia and the Volga-Ural region have mainly belonged to this school ☞ ***mazhab***

KAR: Қанапия, Қанафия
KAZ: Ханафиттік мазхаб
TAJ: Ҳанафия
TAT: Хәнәфи
TUR: Ханафи
UYG: Hanapiya
UZB: Ҳанафия

Hanbali حنبلی ARABIC *Law n.* a follower of he Hanbali school of jurisprudence ☞ ***Hanbaliya***

KAR: ҳанбалий
KAZ: ханбалшы, ханбалит, ханбалдық
TAJ: ҳанбалӣ
TAT: хәнбәли ① *a follower of he Hanbali school of jurisprudence* ② *one who strictly follows religious precepts*
TUR: ханбали
UYG: hanbaliy
UZB: ҳанбалий

Hanbaliya حنبلیه ARABIC *Law n.* one of the four major schools of Sunni jurisprudence, founded by Ahmad ibn Hanbal (780-855 AD) ☞ ***mazhab***

KAR: Ҳанбалия
TAJ: Ҳанбалия
TAT: Хәнбәли
TUR: Ханбали
UYG: Hanbaliya
UZB: Ҳанбалия

hanif[1] حنیف ARABIC *n.* monotheist; follower of the religion of Abraham (in the time before the prophet Muhammad)

BAS: хәниф
KAR: қанип
TAJ: ҳаниф
TAT: хәниф
UYG: hanip
UZB: ҳаниф

hanif[2] حنیف ARABIC *adj.* sincere, devout, orthodox (in Islam)

BAS: хәниф
KAR: қанип
KAZ: ханіф
TAJ: ҳаниф
TAT: хәниф
UZB: ҳаниф

haqiqat حقیقة ARABIC *n.* divine truth

BAS: хәкикәт
KAR: ҳақыйқат
KAZ: ақиқат
KYR: акыйкат
TAJ: ҳақиқат
TAT: хәкыйкать, хакыйкать
TUR: хакыкат
UYG: häqiqät
UZB: ҳақиқат

haqq[1] حقّ ARABIC *adj.* true, real, genuine

BAS: хаҡ
KAR: ҳақ
KAZ: ақ, хақ, қақ, ақы
KYR: ак ① *true, real, genuine* ② *licit, permitted by Islamic law, halal*
TAJ: ҳақ
TAT: хак, хәкъ
TUR: хак
UYG: häqq, häq
UZB: ҳақ

Haqq[2] حقّ ARABIC *pn.* God ☞ ***Haqq, al-***

BAS: хаҡ
KAR: Ҳақ
KAZ: Хақ
KYR: Ак, Хак
TAJ: Ҳақ
TAT: Хак
TUR: Хак, Хакк
UYG: Häqq
UZB: Ҳақ

Haqq, al- الحقّ ARABIC *pn.* name of God: the Truth

KAR: Ҳақ
KAZ: Хақ
TAJ: Ҳақ
TUR: ал-Хак
UYG: Häq
UZB: Ал-Ҳақ

haqq al-yaqin حقّ الیقین ARABIC *Sufism np.* conviction of God and the truth, reality of certitude (as a degree of spiritual knowledge)

TAJ: ҳаққул яқин
UZB: ҳаққул яқин

Haqq Rasul حقّ رسول ARABIC *pn.* the prophet Muhammad

KAR: Рәсул
KYR: Ак Расул

TAJ: Ҳақ Расул
UYG: Häq Rasul
UZB: Ҳақ Расул

Haqq Ta'ala حق تعالى ARABIC *pn.* the Exalted, God
BAS: Хаҡ тәғәлә
KAR: Ҳақ тала
KYR: Ак Таала
TAJ: Ҳақ таолло
TAT: Хак тәгала
TUR: Хактагала
UYG: Häq ta'ala
UZB: Ҳақ таалло

Haqqa حاقّه ARABIC *Qur'an pn.* the 69th sura of the Qur'an
KAR: Ҳәққа сүўреси
KAZ: Хаққа сүресі
TAJ: сураи Ҳоққа
UYG: Haqqa süräsi, sürä Haqqä
UZB: Ал-ҳааққа сураси

haqqullah حق الله ARABIC *Taxation n.* a type of agricultural tax
KAR: ҳаққулла
TAJ: ҳаққуллоҳ
UZB: ҳаққуллоҳ

haram[1] حرام ARABIC *Law adj.* illicit, forbidden, contravening Islamic law
BAS: хәрәм
KAR: ҳарам, ҳәрем
KAZ: арам, харам
KYR: арам, карам ① *illicit, forbidden, contravening Islamic law* ② *illegitimate (e.g. a child)*
TAJ: ҳаром
TAT: хәрам
TUR: харам
UYG: haram
UZB: ҳаром ① *illicit, forbidden, contravening Islamic law* ② *illegitimate (e.g. a child)*

haram[2] حرم ARABIC *n.* sacred territory, especially in the cities of Mecca and Medina
KAR: ҳәрем
TAJ: ҳарам
TAT: хәрәм
TUR: харам
UYG: haram
UZB: ҳарам

haram qat'i حرم قطعى ARABIC *Law np.* categorical prohibition
TAJ: ҳарому қатъӣ
TAT: хәрәм катгый
UZB: ҳарому қатъий

haram zanni حرم ظنّى ARABIC *Law np.* conjectural prohibition
TAJ: ҳарому занний
TAT: хәрәм занни
UZB: ҳарому занний

Haramayn حرمين ARABIC *pn.* the sacred cities of Mecca and Medina
KAZ: екі Харам
TAT: Хәрәмәен
UYG: ikki häräm

haramzada حرامزاده PERSIAN *Law n.* illegitimate child, bastard
KAR: ҳарамзада, ҳәреми
KAZ: арамза, арамзада
KYR: арамза, аранзаа, арамзаада
TAJ: ҳаромзода
TAT: хәрамзадә
TUR: харамзада
UYG: haramzadä
UZB: ҳаромзода

harif du'a حريف دعا ARABIC *np.* sorcery, magic (performed in partnership of two people)
KAR: ҳәрипдуўа
KYR: арып дуба
TAJ: ҳариф дуо
UYG: harip du'a
UZB: ҳариф дуо

harim حريم ARABIC *n.* harem, women's portion of a house which is forbidden to male visitors
BAS: хәрәм һарайы
KAR: ҳәрем
TAJ: ҳарам
TAT: хәрим
TUR: харем
UYG: häräm, mährämkhana
UZB: ҳарам

Harun هارون ARABIC *pn.* the prophet Aaron, the brother of Moses
BAS: һарун
KAR: Ҳарун
KAZ: Харун, Һарұн
KYR: Карун, Карынбай, Карымбай
TAJ: Ҳарун
TAT: һарун

TUR: Карун, Харун
UYG: Harun, Qarun
UZB: Харун

Harut va Marut هاروت و ماروت ARABIC *pn.* the names of two angels who were sent to earth to be tempted
KAZ: Харут-Марут
TAJ: Ҳарут ва Марут
TAT: һарут вә Марут
UYG: Harut-Marut, Harut wä Marut
UZB: Ҳарут ва Марут

hasan[1] حسن ARABIC *adj.* good, desirable, beautiful (in a moral context)
BAS: хәсән
KAR: асан
KAZ: хасан
TAJ: ҳасан
TAT: хәсән
UYG: hasan
UZB: ҳасан

hasan[2] حسن ARABIC *Hadith adj.* mediocre, a hadith whose narrator's moral qualities are established, but whose transmission is nonetheless questionable
TAT: хәсән
UZB: ҳасан

Hasan[3] حسن ARABIC *pn.* son of the Caliph Ali and of Fatima, daughter of the prophet Muhammad
BAS: Хәсән
KAR: Асан, Әсен
KAZ: Хасан
KYR: Асан
TAJ: Ҳасан
TAT: Хәсән
TUR: Хасан
UYG: Hasan
UZB: Ҳасан

hasana ☞ ***bid'at-i hasana***

hashr[1] حشر ARABIC *Theology n.* the gathering of the resurrected dead on Judgment Day ☞ ***'arasat***
BAS: хәшер
KAR: ҳашр
KAZ: хашыр
TAJ: ҳашр
TAT: хәшер
UYG: hashir
UZB: ҳашир

Hashr[2] حشر ARABIC *Qur'an pn.* the 59th sura of the Qur'an
KAR: Ҳашр суўреси
KAZ: Хашыр сүресі
TAJ: сураи Ҳашр
TAT: Хәшер сүрәсе
UYG: Hashr süräsi, sürä Häshr
UZB: Ҳашр сураси

hasht-i yak هشت یاک PERSIAN *Law n.* one-eighth of an inheritance designated for the widow of the deceased, according to Islamic law
KAR: ҳәштыяк
TAJ: ҳаштьяк
UYG: hashtiyak
UZB: ҳаштияк

Hasib, al- الحسيب ARABIC *pn.* name of God: the Reckoner
TAJ: Ҳосиб
TUR: ал-Хасиб
UYG: Häsib
UZB: Ал-Ҳосиб

hattat خطّاط ARABIC *n.* calligrapher
KAR: ҳәттат
TAJ: ҳаттот
TAT: хәттат
UYG: khättat
UZB: хаттот

Hava هوا ARABIC *pn.* Eve, the First Woman
BAS: һауа
KAR: Ҳәўа
KAZ: Хауа, Хауаана
KYR: Обо эне, Умай эне
TAJ: момои Бараҳна
TAT: Хәува, Хава
TUR: Хов, Хов Эне
UYG: Hawa
UZB: Момо Ҳаво

havajim هواجم ARABIC *Sufism n.* assaults, shocks, that which enters the heart without desire or intention
TAJ: ҳавочим
UZB: ҳавожим

havajis هواجس ARABIC *Sufism n.* thoughts, worldly thoughts of the heart
TAJ: ҳавочис
UZB: ҳавожис

havala هوالة ARABIC *Law n.* the removal or transfer of debt
KAR: ҳәвале
TAJ: ҳавола

UYG: hawalä
UZB: ҳавола

havari حواری ARABIC *n.* apostles (of the prophet Jesus)
KAZ: хауари
TAJ: ҳавориён
TAT: хәвари
UYG: häwari, häwariyun
UZB: ҳаворилар

haviya هاوية ARABIC *n.* deepest division of the Hell, the bottomless pit for hypocrites
KAR: ҳаўия
TAJ: ҳавия
TAT: һавия
UZB: ҳовия

havl هول ARABIC *Ritual n.* prayer performed in the evening on the day of a funeral
TAJ: ҳави
TAT: һәул, һәвел
UYG: häwl
UZB: ҳовл

hay ya hu حی یا هو ARABIC *Sufism np.* formula performed during dhikr
TAJ: ҳаёҳу
UZB: ҳаёё-ҳу, ҳайё-ҳу

hayan حياً ARABIC *Theology adv.* living, alive (an established quality of God)
TAT: хәйан

hayat-i abadiya حیات ابدیه PERSIAN *np.* eternal life
TAJ: ҳаёти абадия
TAT: хәят әбәдия
UZB: ҳаёти абадия

Haydar حیدر PERSIAN *n.* the Lion (epithet of the Caliph Ali) ☞ ***'Ali***
BAS: Айдар
KAR: Айдар
KAZ: Айдар
KYR: Айдар
TAJ: Ҳайдар
TAT: Хәйдәр, Айдар
TUR: Хайдар
UYG: Haydar
UZB: Ҳайдар

Hayy, al- الحیّ ARABIC *pn.* name of God: the Living
KAZ: әл-Хайи
TAJ: Ҳай
TAT: Хәййү, Хәй
TUR: ал-Хайй
UYG: Hayy
UZB: Ал-Ҳайй

hayz حیض ARABIC *n.* menstruation, period (as a condition of ritual impurity)
BAS: хәйез
KAR: ҳәйыз, етеги келиў
KAZ: хайыз
KYR: кайыз
TAJ: ҳайз
TAT: хәез, хәйз
TUR: хайыз
UYG: haiz
UZB: ҳайиз

hazrat حضرت PERSIAN *n.* honorific applied especially to authoritative religious figures
BAS: хәҙрәт
KAR: ҳазирет, азрет
KAZ: әзірет, қазірет, хазірет
KYR: азирет, хазрет
TAJ: ҳазрат
TAT: хәзрәт
TUR: хезрет
UYG: häzrät
UZB: ҳазрат

hiba هبه ARABIC *Law n.* debt or gift, a transfer of property made immediately and without any exchange
TAJ: ҳибаҳ
TAT: һибә
UYG: hibäh
UZB: ҳибоҳ

Hibatullah هبة الله ARABIC *pn.* epithet of the prophet Seth ☞ ***Shis***
TAJ: Ҳибатулло
TAT: һибәтулла
UYG: Hibatulla
UZB: Ҳибатулоҳ

hidayat هدايت ARABIC *n.* God's guidance, the Divine Path
BAS: һидайәт
KAZ: һидайәт
TAJ: ҳидоят
TAT: һидаят, һидая
UYG: hidäyät
UZB: ҳидоят

hijab حجاب ARABIC *n.* covering, headscarf worn by Muslim women

BAS: хижаб
KAR: хиджаб, бет перде, тор
KAZ: хиджаб
TAJ: ҳиҷоб
TAT: хиҗаб ① *covering, headscarf* ② *amulet*
TUR: хыҗап
UYG: hijab
UZB: ҳижоб

Hijr حجر ARABIC *Qur'an pn.* the 15th sura of the Qur'an

KAR: Ҳижр суўреси
KAZ: Хыжыр сүресі
TAJ: сураи Ҳиҷр
UYG: sürä Hijr
UZB: Ҳижр сураси

hijra هجره ARABIC *Historical n.* Muhammad's flight from Mecca to Medina in 622 (from which date the Muslim calendar begins)

BAS: һижрə, һижрəт
KAR: хиджре
KYR: ижарат, ижират
TAJ: ҳиҷра, ҳиҷрат
TAT: һиҗрəт
UYG: hijrä, hijrät ① *Muhammad's flight from Mecca to Medina in 622* ② *festival held on the ninth of Rabi' al-avval commemorating Muhammad's flight from Mecca to Medina*
UZB: ҳижра, ҳижрат

hijri هجری ARABIC *adj.* pertaining to the hijri calendar (the Islamic calendar calculated from the time of the prophet Muhammad's flight from Mecca to Medina)

BAS: һижри
KAR: хиджрия
TAJ: ҳиҷрӣ
TAT: һиҗри
TUR: хиҗри
UYG: hijriyä
UZB: ҳижрий

hijriya هجريه ARABIC *n.* hijri calendar (the Islamic calendar calculated from the time of the prophet Muhammad's flight from Mecca to Medina)

KAR: хижре
KAZ: хижра, хиджра
TAJ: ҳиҷрия
TAT: һиҗрия
TUR: хиҗрия
UYG: hijriyä
UZB: ҳижрия

hikmat حکمت ARABIC *n.* wisdom, knowledge; philosophy; God's wisdom

BAS: хикмəт
KAR: ҳикмет
KAZ: хикмат, хикмет, хікмет
KYR: икмет
TAJ: ҳикмат
TAT: хикмəт
TUR: хикмет
UYG: hikmät
UZB: ҳикмат

hilal هلال ARABIC *n.* the new moon, crescent moon

KAR: ҳилал
TAJ: ҳилол
TAT: һилял
UYG: hiläl
UZB: ҳилол

hila-yi shar'i حيلهء شرعی PERSIAN *Law np.* legal stratagem for fraud that does not violate the letter of the shari'a

TAJ: ҳилаи шарӣ
UYG: hiyläi shä'ri
UZB: ҳийлаи шаръий

hiliya-yi sharif حليهء شريف PERSIAN *np.* poetic work describing the personal qualities and virtues of the prophet Muhammad ☞ ***hilya***

TAT: хилйəи шəриф
UZB: хулияи шариф

hilya حليه ARABIC *n.* poetic work describing the personal qualities and virtues of the prophet Muhammad

TAT: хилйə
UZB: хулия

hilya-yi sa'adat حليهء سعادت PERSIAN *np.* poetic work describing the personal qualities and virtues of the prophet Muhammad

TAT: хилйəи сəгадəт
UZB: хулияи саодат

himmat همّة ARABIC *Sufism n.* resolution, strength, power (esp. of a shaykh)

KAR: химмəт, қайырқом
TAJ: ҳиммат
TAT: һиммəт

UYG: himmät
UZB: ҳиммат

hirz حرز ARABIC *n.* amulet
TAJ: ҳирз, ҳирзи амон, ҳирзи ҷон
TAT: хирз
UZB: ҳирз, амон ҳирзи, жон ҳирзи

hiss حسّ ARABIC *Sufism n.* understanding, sense
KAR: ҳис, сәзим
TAJ: ҳис
UYG: his
UZB: ҳисс

hiss-i batin حسّ باطن PERSIAN *Sufism np.* inner feeling, inner sense
TAJ: ҳисси ботинӣ
TAT: хиссе батыйн
UZB: ҳисси ботиний

hiss-i zahiri حسّ ظاهری PERSIAN *Sufism np.* physical feeling, physical sensation
TAJ: ҳисси зоҳирӣ
TAT: хиссе заһири
UZB: ҳисси зоҳири

hizb [1] حزب ARABIC *n.* group, party ☞ ***ahzab***
KAR: хизб
TAJ: ҳизб
TAT: хизеб
UYG: hizp
UZB: ҳизб

hizb [2] حزب ARABIC *Qur'an n.* one-sixtieth portion of the Qur'an
KAR: хизб
TAJ: ҳизб
TAT: хизеб
UYG: hizp
UZB: ҳизб

hizb al-shaytan حزب الشيطان ARABIC *np.* allies of Satan, followers Satan
KAR: ҳизбу шайтан
TAJ: ҳизбу шайтон
UZB: ҳизбу шайтон

Hu هو PERSIAN *pn.* He, God
KAZ: Хуya
KYR: үү
TAJ: ҳу
TAT: һуyə, һу
UZB: ху

hubb حبّ ARABIC *n.* love toward God and man (as a moral quality)
TAT: хөб

Hud [1] هود ARABIC *pn.* the prophet Hud
KAR: Худ
KAZ: Құт, Худ, Һуд
TAJ: Ҳуд
TAT: Һуд
TUR: Хут
UYG: Hud
UZB: Ҳуд

Hud [2] هود ARABIC *Qur'an pn.* the 11th sura of the Qur'an
KAR: Худ
KAZ: Һұд сүресі
TAJ: сураи Ҳуд
UYG: Hud
UZB: Ҳуд сураси

hudud حدود ARABIC *Law n.* legal punishments for certain grave crimes against the rights of God (e.g. wine-drinking, murder, fornication etc.) ☞ ***hadd***
KAR: худуд
TAJ: ҳудуд
TAT: хөдүд
UYG: hudud
UZB: ҳудуд

hujra حجره ARABIC *n.* cell, small room (inhabited by students in madrasas or Sufis)
BAS: хөжрә
KAR: ҳужрә
KAZ: құжыра
KYR: үжүрө
TAJ: ҳуҷра
TAT: хөҗрә
TUR: хүҗре
UYG: hujra
UZB: ҳужра

Hujurat حجرات ARABIC *Qur'an pn.* the 49th sura of the Qur'an
KAR: Хужурәт сүўреси
KAZ: Хұжрат сүресі
TAJ: сураи Ҳуҷурот
UYG: Hujurät süräsi, sürä Hujurat
UZB: Ҳужурот сураси

hukm حكم ARABIC *Law n.* verdict, decision
BAS: хөкөм ① *verdict, decision* ② *court*
KAR: ҳүким
KAZ: өкім, хүкім

KYR: өкум
TAJ: ҳукм
TAT: хөкем
TUR: хөкүм
UYG: hüküm
UZB: ҳукм

hukm-i samad حکم صمد PERSIAN *np.* eternal verdict, verdict of God
KAR: ҳүкми Сәмат
TAJ: ҳукми Самад
TAT: хөкеме самәд
UYG: hökmu Samat
UZB: ҳукми Самад

hukumat حکومت ARABIC *n.* power, authority, rule, government, administration
BAS: хөкөмәт
KAR: ҳүкимет
KAZ: өкімет, үкімет
KYR: өкмөт, өкүмөт
TAJ: ҳукумат
TAT: хөкүмәт
TUR: хөкүмет
UYG: hökümät
UZB: ҳукумат

hulla حلّه ARABIC *Ritual n.* burial shroud, cloth used for a burial shroud
TAJ: ҳулла
TAT: хөлләә
UZB: ҳулла

hulul حلول ARABIC *Sufism n.* descending; incarnation; the indwelling light in the soul of man
TAJ: ҳулул
UZB: ҳулул

Humaza همزه ARABIC *Qur'an pn.* the 104th sura of the Qur'an
KAR: Хумаза сүўреси
KAZ: һұмәзә сүресі
TAJ: сураи Ҳумиза
UYG: Humäzä süräsi
UZB: Ҳумаза сураси

hur خور PERSIAN *n.* houri, virgin servant-girl in Paradise
BAS: хур, хур ҡыҙы
KAR: ҳор, ҳүр
KAZ: хор
KYR: нур, нургунча, ур
TAJ: ҳур
TAT: хур
TUR: хүйр
UYG: hör
UZB: ҳур

huri خوری PERSIAN *Qur'an n.* houri, virgin servant-girl in Paradise
KYR: нур, нургунча, ур
TAJ: ҳури
TAT: хури
UYG: hör qizi, hör-päri
UZB: ҳури

hurr حرّ *Law*. ☞ ***ahrar***

Husayn حسین ARABIC *pn.* Husayn ibn 'Ali (626-680), grandson of the prophet Muhammad
BAS: Хөсәйен
KAR: Усен
KAZ: Хұсайын
TAJ: Ҳусайн
TUR: Хүсейин
UYG: Hösain
UZB: Ҳусайн

husn حسن ARABIC *n.* beauty; good quality (as a moral characteristic)
KAR: ҳусн
TAJ: ҳусн
TAT: хөсен
UYG: hösün
UZB: ҳусн

husn-i adab حسن ادب PERSIAN *np.* ethics, good morals (as a subject of education) ☞ ***adab***
KAR: ҳусни әдап
TAJ: ҳусни адаб
TAT: хөсне әдәб
UYG: hösünu adäb
UZB: ҳусни адаб

husn-i akhlaq حسن اخلاق PERSIAN *np.* morality, ethics
KAR: ҳусни әхлақ
TAJ: ҳусни ахлоқ
TAT: хөсне әхлак
UYG: hösünu ahläq
UZB: ҳусни ахлоқ

husn-i khat حسن خط PERSIAN *np.* calligraphy, penmanship (as a subject of education)
KAR: ҳусни хат
TAJ: ҳусни хат
TAT: хөсне хат
UYG: hösünu khät

UZB: ҳуснихат

husn-i tarbiya حسن تربیه PERSIAN *np.* ethics, morality (as a subject of education)

KAR: хусни тәрбие
TAJ: ҳусни тарбия
TAT: хөсне тәрбия
UZB: ҳусни тарбия

Hut حوت ARABIC *pn.* Pisces, the name of the first month in the Persian solar calendar

BAS: Хут
KAR: хут
KAZ: Хұт
KYR: Үт
TAJ: хут
TAT: Хут
UYG: Hut
UZB: хут

I

i'ana اعانة ARABIC *n.* alms, offering (lit. help)

BAS: иғәнә, иғанә, иғәнәт
TAJ: ионат
TAT: иганә, иганәт
UYG: i'anä
UZB: иона

'ibadat [1] عبادت ARABIC *n.* worship; acts of worship incumbent upon all Muslims

BAS: ғибәҙәт
KAR: ибадат, табыныў
KAZ: ғибадат
KYR: ибадат, ыйбадат
TAJ: ибодат
TAT: гыйбадәт
TUR: ыбадат
UYG: ibadät
UZB: ибодат

'ibadat [2] عبادات ARABIC *Law n.* devotions (one of the five divisions of Islamic law)

TAT: гыйбадат
UZB: ибодат,

'ibadatgah عبادتگاه PERSIAN *n.* place for performing devotions

KAR: ибадатгаҳ
TAJ: ибодатгоҳ
UYG: ibadätgah
UZB: ибодатгоҳ

'ibadatkhana عبادتخانه PERSIAN *n.* place of worship; house of worship (Muslim or non-Muslim)

BAS: ғибәҙәтхана, ғибәҙәт йорто
KAR: ибадатхана
KAZ: ғибадатхана
KYR: ибадаткана, ыйбадаткана
TAJ: ибодатхона
TAT: гыйбадәтханә
TUR: ыбадатхана
UYG: ibadätkhana
UZB: ибодатхона

ibaha اباحه ARABIC *n.* permission; full freedom of action; licentiousness

TAJ: ибоҳа
TAT: ибахә
UYG: ibähä
UZB: ибоҳа

Iblis ابلیس ARABIC *pn.* Satan, the Devil ☞ ***Shaytan***

BAS: Иблис
KAR: Ыблыс
KAZ: Ібіліс, Ыбылыс
KYR: Ибилис
TAJ: Иблис
TAT: Иблис
TUR: Иблис
UYG: Iblis
UZB: Иблис

Ibrahim [1] ابراهیم ARABIC *pn.* the prophet Abraham

BAS: Ибраһим
KAR: Ыбрайым, Ибирайым
KAZ: Ибраһим, Ібраһим, Ыбырайым
KYR: Ыбрайым
TAJ: Иброҳим
TAT: Ибраһим, Ибраһим Хәлил
TUR: Ыбрайым
UYG: Ibrahim
UZB: Иброҳим

Ibrahim [2] ابراهیم ARABIC *Qur'an pn.* the 14th sura of the Qur'an

KAR: Ыбрайым суўреси
KAZ: Ібраһим сүресі
TAJ: сураи Иброҳим
TAT: Ибраһим сүрәсе
UYG: Ibrahim süräsi
UZB: Иброҳим сураси

'ibrani عبرانی ARABIC *adj.* Jewish, Hebrew
- KAR: ыбрани
- TAJ: иброни̅
- TAT: гыйбрани
- UYG: ibräniy
- UZB: иброний

'id عید ARABIC *Ritual n.* religious feast
☞ ***'Id al-Fitr, 'Id al-Azha,***
- BAS: ғәйет
- KAR: ҳайт, айт
- KAZ: айт
- KYR: айт
- TAJ: ид
- TAT: гайд, гает ① *religious feast* ② *'Id al-Fitr (the feast held at the conclusion of Ramadan fasting)*
- TUR: ид, айыд
- UYG: heyit, heyt
- UZB: ҳайит, ийд

'Id al-Azha عید الاضحی ARABIC *Ritual pn.* Qurban Bayram, the Feast of the Sacrifice
☞ ***qurban bayrami***
- BAS: Ҡорбан байрамы, Ҡорбан, Ҡорбан ғәйете
- KAR: қурбан ҳайт, қурбан айты, қурбан
- KAZ: Ид әл-Адха, Құрбан айт
- KYR: Курман айт
- TAJ: Идал Адха, Иди Қурбон
- TAT: Корбан бәйрәме, Гайде әзхия, Корбан гаете, Гайдел әдха, Гайдел-корбан
- TUR: Ид ал-адха, Гурбан байрамы
- UYG: Qurban bayrimi, Qurban heyiti
- UZB: Ид ал Адҳа, Қурбон байрами

'Id al-Fitr عید الفطر ARABIC *Ritual pn.* feast held at the conclusion of Ramadan fasting
- BAS: Ураҙа, Фытыр бәйрамы, Ураҙа ғәйете
- KAR: Рамазан байрамы, Ораза ҳайт
- KAZ: Ораза айты
- TAJ: Идал Фитр, иди Рамазон, Рӯза
- TAT: Ураза бәйрәме, Гайде фитыр, Гает, Фитыр гаете, Рамазан гаете, Гайдел-фитыр
- TUR: Ид ал-фитр, Ораза байрамы
- UYG: Ramazan bayrimi, Ramazan heyiti
- UZB: Ид ал Фитр, Рамазон байрами, Рўза байрами

i'dam اعدام ARABIC *Law n.* death penalty, execution
- BAS: иғдам
- KAR: идәм
- TAJ: иъдом
- TAT: игъдам
- UZB: идом

'iddat عدّة ARABIC *Law n.* three-month period following a woman's divorce or a four-month plus ten-day period following the death of a woman's husband during which she is not permitted to remarry
- KAR: иддә
- KAZ: ғиддат
- TAJ: идда, иддат
- TAT: гыйддәт, гыйддәт чоры
- UYG: idda, iddät *the 100-day period after divorce during which it is determined whether or not the divorced woman is pregnant*
- UZB: идда, иддат

Idris ادریس ARABIC *pn.* the prophet Idris
- BAS: Иҙрис, Идрис
- KAR: Ыдрыс
- KAZ: Ыдырыс, Идрис, Ыдріс
- KYR: Идирис
- TAJ: Идрис
- TAT: Идрис
- TUR: Идрис
- UYG: Idris
- UZB: Идрис

'iffat عفّت ARABIC *n.* virginity, chastity
- TAJ: иффат
- TAT: гыйффәт
- UYG: ippät
- UZB: иффат

'ifrit عفریت ARABIC *n.* malicious demon, malicious jinn
- BAS: ғифрит
- KAR: иприт
- KAZ: ифрит
- KYR: ифрит
- TAJ: ифрит
- TAT: гыйфрит
- TUR: ыфрит
- UYG: iprit
- UZB: ифрит

ifta افتا ARABIC *Law n.* issuing a fatwa ☞ ***fatva***
- TAJ: ифта
- TAT: ифта
- UYG: ipta
- UZB: ифта

iftar افطار ARABIC *Ritual n.* breaking the fast (after

sundown during Ramadan); feast held to commemorate breaking the fast

BAS: ифтар
KAR: иптар
KAZ: ауыз ашар
KYR: ыптар
TAJ: ифтор
TAT: ифтар, ифтар мәҗлесе, авыз ачу
TUR: ифтар, агзачар
UYG: iptar
UZB: ифтор

iftitah افتتاح ARABIC *Ritual n.* formally beginning worship by chanting "Allahu Akbar"

KAZ: іфтитах, іфтітах
TAJ: ифтитоҳ
TAT: ифтитах
TUR: ифтитах төвири
UYG: iptitäh
UZB: ифтитоҳ

ihdad احداد ARABIC *n.* the period of mourning observed by a widow for her husband, namely, four months and ten days

TAJ: иҳдод
UZB: иҳдод, аза тутмоқ

ihram احرام ARABIC *Hajj n.* usually white seamless garment worn by pilgrims in Mecca

KAR: ихрам
KAZ: ихрам, ыхрам
TAJ: эҳром
TAT: ихрам
TUR: ыхрам, ихрам
UYG: ehram
UZB: эҳром, иҳром

ihsan [1] احسان ARABIC *n.* conferring favors, performing an action in a perfect manner, esp. giving alms

BAS: ихсан
KAR: иҳсан
TAJ: эҳсон
TAT: ихсан
UYG: ehsan
UZB: эҳсон

ihsan [2] احسان ARABIC *n.* marriage that is in keeping with Muslim standards

KAR: иҳсан
TAJ: иҳсан
UYG: ihsän
UZB: иҳсон

ihsar احصار ARABIC *Hajj n.* reason for a pilgrim's delay in performing the hajj or 'umra (e.g. sickness, accident), which necessitates sending an animal ahead to be sacrificed in Mecca

TAJ: иҳсор
UZB: иҳсор, иҳсор қурбони

ihtida اهتدا ARABIC *n.* being correctly guided

KAZ: іһтида
TAJ: эҳтидоъ
TAT: иһтида
UZB: эҳтидо

ihtijab احتجاب ARABIC *n.* covering with a hijab

KAR: ихтижаб
TAJ: иҳтиҷоб
TAT: ихтиҗаб
UZB: иҳтижоб

ihtilam احتلام ARABIC *n.* seminal emission (after which ghusul is absolutely necessary)

TAJ: иҳтилам
TUR: ыхтылам
UYG: ehtilam
UZB: иҳтилом

ihzar احضار ARABIC *Law n.* summons to appear before an Islamic judge

TAJ: иҳзор
UZB: иҳзор

ijab ايجاب ARABIC *Law n.* initial offer (of marriage or other contract)

BAS: ижап, ижап-ҡабул
KAR: ийжап
TAJ: иҷоб
UYG: ijab
UZB: ижоб

ijabat اجابت ARABIC *n.* favorable answer (to a prayer)

KAR: ийжабат
TAJ: иҷобат
TAT: иҗабәт
UYG: ijabät
UZB: ижобат

ijazat اجازة ARABIC *Sufism n.* permission (esp. for transferring Sufi knowledge)

BAS: ижазәт
KAR: ийжазат, рухсат етиў
KYR: ижаза
TAJ: иҷозат

TAT: иҗазә, иҗазәт ① *permission* ② *license, diploma*
TUR: эжҗаза
UYG: ijazat
UZB: ижозат

ijazatnama اجازة نامه PERSIAN *Sufism n.* license, diploma (given by a Sufi master to his disciple)
KAR: ийжазатнаме
TAJ: иҷозатнома
TAT: иҗазәтнамә
UYG: ijazätnama
UZB: ижозатнома

ijma' اجماع ARABIC *Law n.* consensus, general agreement of legal experts (considered a principle of Islamic law)
KAZ: ұжым
TAJ: иҷмо
TAT: иҗмаг
TUR: иҗма
UYG: ijmä
UZB: ижмо

ijma'-i ummat اجماع امّة PERSIAN *Law np.* general consensus of legal experts
TAT: әҗмәгу өммәт
UZB: ижмои уммат

ijtihad اجتهاد ARABIC *n.* interpretation, independent reasoning (in jurisprudence and theology) on the source texts of Islam; effort ☞ ***qiyas***
BAS: иҗтиһад
KAR: ежтыҳәт
KAZ: ежтиһат, іжтиһат, ыждағат
TAJ: иҷтиҳод
TAT: иҗтиһад
TUR: иҗтихат
UYG: ijtihäd, ijtihät
UZB: ижтиҳод

ikhlas [1] اخلاص ARABIC *n.* devotion, sincerity (in belief)
BAS: ихлас
KAR: ихлас
KAZ: ықылас
TAJ: ихлос
TAT: ихляс
TUR: ыхлас
UYG: ikhlas
UZB: ихлос

Ikhlas [2] اخلاص ARABIC *Qur'an pn.* the 112th sura of the Qur'an
KAR: Ыхлас сүўреси
KAZ: Ыхлас сүресі
TAJ: сураи Ихлос
TAT: Ихлас сүрәсе, Әл-Ихлас сүрәсе, Колһуаллаһ сүрәсе
UYG: Ikhlas süräsi
UZB: Ихлос сураси

ikhtilaf اختلاف ARABIC *Law v.* difference of opinion; difference of views
BAS: ихтилаф
TAJ: ихтилоф
TAT: ихтиляф
UYG: ikhtilaf
UZB: ихтилоф

ikhvan اخوان ARABIC *n.* brothers, brethren; brotherhood ☞ ***ahbab***
BAS: ихуан
KAZ: ихван
TAJ: ихван
TAT: ихван
TUR: ихван
UYG: ikhvan
UZB: ихвон

ilah اله ARABIC *n.* God
BAS: илаһ
KAR: илаҳ
KAZ: әл-Илах
TAJ: илоҳ
TAT: илаһ
TUR: ылах
UYG: ilah
UZB: илоҳ

ilaha الهه ARABIC *n.* goddess (in pre-Islamic beliefs)
BAS: илаһә
KAR: илаҳа
TAJ: илоҳа
TAT: илаһә, алиһә
UYG: ilaha
UZB: илоҳа

ilahi [1] الهى ARABIC *adj.* divine, pertaining to God
BAS: илаһи
KAR: илаҳий
KAZ: илаһи
KYR: алдо уй, лайым, ылайым
TAJ: илоҳи
TAT: илаһи

TUR: ылахы
UYG: ilahi
UZB: илоҳи

ilahi[2] الهى ARABIC *intj.* My God!, Oh God!
BAS: илаһым
KAR: илаҳий
KAZ: илаһи
KYR: ылаайым, ылайым
TAJ: илоҳӣ
TAT: илаһи
UYG: ilahiy
UZB: илоҳий, илоҳим

ilahi[3] الهى ARABIC *adj.* godly, pious
BAS: илаһи
KAR: илаҳи
KAZ: илаһи
TAJ: илоҳӣ
TAT: илаһи
UYG: ilahiy
UZB: илоҳи

ilahiyat الهيات ARABIC *n.* theology
KAR: илаҳият
TAJ: илоҳиёт
TAT: илаһият
UYG: ilahiyät
UZB: илоҳиёт

ilahiyun الهيون ARABIC *n.* theologians, theological philosophers
KAR: илаҳиун
TAJ: иллоҳиун
TAT: илаһиун
UZB: иллоҳиюн

ilhad الحاد ARABIC *n.* heresy, atheism
KAZ: ілхад
TAJ: илҳад
UYG: ilhäd
UZB: илҳад

ilham الهام ARABIC *n.* inspiration
BAS: илһам
KAR: илҳәм, илҳам
KAZ: ілхам
KYR: илхам
TAJ: илҳом
TAT: илһам
TUR: ылхам
UYG: ilham
UZB: илҳом

illa-billah الاّ بالله ARABIC *intj.* I swear to God
KAR: илла-биллә
TAJ: биллаҳ
UZB: илло-билло

ʿillat علّة ARABIC *Hadith n.* weakness, defect (of a hadith tradition)
TAT: гыйлләт
UZB: иллат

ʿilm[1] علم ARABIC *n.* Islamic science, field of study; knowledge
BAS: ғилем
KAR: илим
KAZ: ғылым, ілім
KYR: илим
TAJ: илм
TAT: гыйлем
TUR: ылым
UYG: ilm
UZB: илм

ʿilm[2] علم ARABIC *Theology n.* all-knowing (an established quality of God)
KAZ: ғылым
TAT: гыйлем
UZB: илм

ʿilm al-ʿaqa'id علم العقائد ARABIC *np.* dogmatic theology (as an Islamic science)
UZB: илмул ақоид

ʿilm-i hal[1] علم حال PERSIAN *np.* religious primer, catechism (esp. for children)
KAR: илимҳал
KAZ: ғылымхал
TAJ: илми ҳол
UYG: ilimihal
UZB: илми ҳол

ʿilm-i hal[2] علم حال PERSIAN *Sufism np.* Sufi ethics
KAR: илимҳал
TAT: гыйлме хал
UYG: ilimhal
UZB: илми ҳол

ʿilm-i qal علم قال PERSIAN *Sufism np.* Islamic sciences as based on the interpretation of the literal meaning of Islamic tradition
KAR: илимқал
UYG: ilimqal
UZB: илми қол

iltija التجا ARABIC *n.* prayer, plea for protection

(before God)
- KAR: илтийжа
- TAJ: илтиҷо
- TAT: илтиҗа
- UYG: iltija
- UZB: илтижо

Ilyas الياس ARABIC *pn.* the prophet Ilyas (often associated with the prophet Elijah in the Old Testament and with the Islamic prophet Khizr) ☞ ***Khizr***
- BAS: Ильяс
- KAR: Илияс
- KAZ: Ілияс, Іляс
- KYR: Илияс, Кызыр-Илияс *the prophet Khizr-Ilyas, who is also the patron saint of abundance and plenty*
- TAJ: Илёс
- TAT: Ильяс
- TUR: Ылияс
- UYG: Ilyas
- UZB: Илёс, Хизир-Илёс

imam [1] امام ARABIC *n.* person who leads the prayer in a congregation; official who administers a mosque and leads the prayers in the mosque
- BAS: имам
- KAR: иймам
- KAZ: имам
- KYR: ыймам, имам
- TAJ: имом
- TAT: имам
- TUR: ымам
- UYG: imam
- UZB: имом

imam [2] امام ARABIC *Historical n.* (among Sunnis) Caliph, religious and political leader of all Muslims
- BAS: имам
- KAR: иймам
- KAZ: имам
- KYR: ыймам, имам
- TAJ: имом
- TAT: имам
- TUR: ымам
- UYG: imam
- UZB: имом

imam [3] امام ARABIC *Law n.* title borne by the founders of the four Sunni schools of jurisprudence (Shafi'i, Malik, Ibn Hanbal, Abu Hanifa);
- KAR: иймам
- KAZ: имам
- KYR: ыймам, имам
- TAJ: имом
- TAT: имам
- TUR: ымам
- UYG: imam
- UZB: имом

imam [4] امام ARABIC *Historical n.* (among Shi'ites) title borne by Ali and his descendants
- KAR: иймам
- KAZ: имам
- KYR: ыймам, имам
- TAJ: имом
- TAT: имам
- TUR: ымам
- UYG: imam
- UZB: имом

imam al-qiblatayn امام القبلتين ARABIC *np.* title for the most erudite of scholars
- TAJ: имомал қиблатайн
- TAT: имамү кыйблатәйн
- UZB: имомал қиблатайн

imamat [1] امامت ARABIC *n.* the office or position of imam ☞ ***imam***
- BAS: имамат
- KAR: иймамат
- KAZ: имамат
- TAJ: имомат
- TAT: имамәт
- UYG: imamat
- UZB: имомат

imamat [2] امامت ARABIC *n.* imamate, a state headed by an imam ☞ ***imam***
- BAS: имамат
- KAR: иймамат
- KAZ: имамат
- TAJ: имомат
- TAT: имамәт
- UYG: imamat
- UZB: имомат

Imam-i A'zam امام‌اعظام PERSIAN *pn.* Abu Hanifa (699-767 AD), founder of the Hanafi school of jurisprudence ☞ ***Hanafi***
- KAR: Әбу Қанифа
- KAZ: Имам Ағзам

KYR: Имам Агзам *also the patron saint of merchants*
TAJ: Абу Ҳанифа
UYG: imam A'zam
UZB: Имоми Аъзам, Абу Ҳанифа

iman [1] ايمان ARABIC *n.* faith, belief (in Islam)
BAS: иман
KAR: ийман
KAZ: иман
KYR: ыйман, ыман
TAJ: имон
TAT: иман
TUR: иман
UYG: iman
UZB: имон, иймон

iman [2] ايمان ARABIC *n.* faith, religion (synonymous with Islam)
BAS: иман
KAR: ийман
KAZ: иман
TAJ: имон
TAT: иман
TUR: иман
UYG: iman
UZB: иймон

imarat امارت ARABIC *n.* emirate, a territory ruled by an emir
BAS: әмират
KAR: әмирәт
TAJ: амират
TAT: әмарәт
TUR: эмирлик
UZB: амирлик

'Imran [1] عمران ARABIC *pn.* the father of the prophet Moses ☞ ***Al-i 'Imran***
BAS: Ғимран
KAR: Имран
TAJ: Имрон
UYG: Imran
UZB: Имрон

'Imran [2] عمران ARABIC *pn.* the father of the Virgin Mary ☞ ***Al-i 'Imran***
BAS: Ғимран
KAR: Имран
KAZ: Имран
TAJ: Имрон
UYG: Imran
UZB: Имрон

inabat انابة ARABIC *Sufism n.* appointment as an authorized deputy (esp. of a Sufi shaykh)
TAJ: иноба
TAT: инабәт
UZB: иноба, инобат

Infitar انفطار ARABIC *Qur'an n.* the 82nd sura of the Qur'an
KAR: Ынпитар суўреси
KAZ: Ынфитар сүресі
TAJ: сураи Инфитор
UYG: Inpitar süräsi, sürä Infitar
UZB: Инфитор сураси

Injil اينجيل ARABIC *pn.* the New Testament, the Gospels
BAS: Инжил
KAR: Инжил
KAZ: інжил, інжіл
KYR: Инжил
TAJ: Инҷил
TAT: Инҗил
TUR: Инҗил
UYG: Injil
UZB: Инжил

injizab انجذاب ARABIC *Sufism n.* being attracted (by God); a form a assistance that helps the adept along the Sufi path
TAJ: инҷизоб
UZB: инжизоб

inna a'taynaka al-kavsara انّا اعطينك الكوثر ARABIC *Qur'an np.* the first verse of the 108th sura (al-kavsar)
KYR: инна а тайна
TAJ: Инна аттайнака алкавсара
UZB: Инна аътайнака ал кавсара

insaf انصاف ARABIC *Law n.* justice, equity, fairness
BAS: инсаф
KAR: инсап
KAZ: нысап, ынсап
KYR: ынсап
TAJ: инсоф
TAT: инсаф
TUR: ынсап *conscience, scruples*
UYG: insap
UZB: инсоф

Insan انسان ARABIC *Qur'an pn.* the 76th sura of the Qur'an

KAR: Инсан суўреси
KAZ: Інсан сүресі
TAJ: сураи Инсон
UYG: Insan süräsi
UZB: Инсон сураси

insan-i kamil انسان كامل PERSIAN *Sufism np.* the perfect man, the Prophet Muhammad; a Sufi who has reached spiritual perfection
TAJ: инсони комил
TAT: инсан-уль камил
UZB: комил инсон

insha'allah انشاء الله ARABIC *intj.* if God wills it, God willing
BAS: иншалла
KAR: иншалла
KAZ: иншалла
KYR: иншаалла, иншахалла, нишалла
TAJ: иншооллоҳ
TAT: инша алла
TUR: эншалла
UYG: insha'alla, inshalla
UZB: иншоаллоҳ, иншооллоҳ, иншолло

Inshiqaq انشقاق ARABIC *Qur'an pn.* the 84th sura of the Qur'an
KAR: Иншиқақ суўреси
KAZ: Іншиқақ сүресі
TAJ: сураи Иншиқоқ
TAT: Иншикак
UYG: Inshiqäq süräsi, sürä Inishiqaq
UZB: Иншиқоҳ сураси

Inshirah انشراح ARABIC *Qur'an pn.* the 94th sura of the Qur'an
KAR: Шарх суўреси
KAZ: Шарх сүресі
TAJ: сураи Иншироҳ
TAT: инширах сүрәсе
UYG: Shärh süräsi, sürä Inshirah
UZB: Шарх сураси

ins-jins انس جنس ARABIC *n.* jinns and humans (as a category of beings)
KAR: инис-жинис
TAJ: инс-чинс
UYG: ins-jins, insi-jins
UZB: инс-жинс

intiha انتها ARABIC *n.* end, expiration (philosophical term)
BAS: интиһа
TAJ: интиҳо
UYG: intihä
UZB: интиҳо

intikhab انتخاب ARABIC *n.* election (e.g. of an imam)
TAJ: интихоб
TAT: интихаб
UZB: интихоб

intiqam انتقام ARABIC *Law n.* revenge, vengeance
BAS: интиҡам
KAR: интиқам, өш
TAJ: интиқом
TAT: интикам
UYG: intiqam
UZB: интиқом

inzal انزال ARABIC *n.* that which is sent from Heaven, e.g. rain, revelation
KAZ: інзәл
TAJ: инзал
TAT: инзал
UYG: inzal
UZB: инзол

'iqab عقاب ARABIC *Law n.* punishment (as a category in fiqh)
KAZ: үкім
TAJ: иқаб
TAT: гыйкаб
UZB: иқоб

iqamat اقامت ARABIC *Ritual n.* introductory prayer said before performing an obligatory daily prayer
BAS: иҡамат
KAZ: иқамет
TAJ: иқомат
TAT: икамәт
UYG: iqämät
UZB: иқомат

iqrar[1] اقرار ARABIC *n.* confession, admission (of a sin)
BAS: иҡрар
KAR: иқрар
KYR: икрар
TAJ: иқрор
TAT: икърар
UYG: iqrar
UZB: иқрор

iqrar[2] اقرار ARABIC *Law n.* acknowledgment, confession (legal term for the avowal of the right of another upon one's self in sales, contracts and

divorce)
KAR: иқрар
TAJ: иқрор
UYG: iqrar
UZB: иқрор

iqtida اقتدا ARABIC *Ritual n.* imitation (of an imam during prayers)
TAJ: иқтидо
TAT: икътидаэ
UZB: иқтидо

irada [1] اراده ARABIC *n.* fate, destiny, will (of God)
KAZ: ираде
TAJ: ирода
TAT: ирадә
UYG: iradä
UZB: ирода

irada [2] اراده ARABIC *Theology n.* willing, providing (an established quality of God)
TAT: ирадә
UZB: ирода

irada [3] اراده ARABIC *Sufism n.* flame of love in the heart of an adept, who desires unity with God
KAR: ираде, жигер
TAJ: ирода
TAT: ирадә
UYG: irädä
UZB: ирода

irada-yi la yazal ارادهٔ لایزال ARABIC *np.* God's eternal will, God's command
TAJ: иродаи лайазал
TAT: ирадәи ля язаль
UZB: иродайи лаязал

irim اریم TURKIC *n.* ceremony; superstitious ritual, superstition
BAS: ырым
KAR: ирим
KAZ: ырым
TAJ: ирим
TUR: ырым
UYG: irim
UZB: ирим

irshad ارشاد ARABIC *Sufism n.* instruction, guidance (of an adept by a master)
BAS: иршад
KAR: иршат
TAJ: иршод
TAT: иршад
UYG: irshat
UZB: иршод

irshadnama ارشادنامه PERSIAN *Sufism n.* license, diploma (to teach Sufism)
KAR: иршатнама
TAJ: иршоднома
TAT: иршаднамә
UYG: irshatnama
UZB: иршоднома

irtidad ارتداد ARABIC *n.* apostasy (from Islam)
☞ ***murtadd***
TAJ: иртидод
TAT: иртидад
UZB: иртидод

'Isa عیسی ARABIC *pn.* the prophet Jesus
BAS: Ғайса, Ғәйсә
KAR: Ийса
KAZ: Иса, Ғайса, Ғиса
KYR: Иса
TAJ: Исо
TAT: Гайсә, Гыйсә
TUR: Иса
UYG: Isa
UZB: Исо

Isagujikhvan ایساغوجی خوان PERSIAN *Historical n.* student who has reached the middle level of the madrasa curriculum in which the work Eisagoge was studied (i.e. the Isagoge of Porphyry (234 - c. 305 AD), widely translated and adapted by Muslim authors)
TAT: исагуҗихан

'Isaparast عیسی پرست PERSIAN *n.* Christian
KAR: ийсапәрест
KYR: испарас
TAJ: исопараст
UYG: Isapäräs
UZB: исопараст, ийсопараст

'Isavi عیسوی ARABIC *adj.* Christian
KAR: ийсави
TAJ: исовӣ
TAT: гыйсави
TUR: исайы
UYG: isawi, isiwi
UZB: исови, исовий

'Isaviyat عیسویت ARABIC *n.* Christianity
KAR: ийсавият
TAJ: исовият

TAT: гыйсавиять
UYG: isawiyat
UZB: исовият, ийсовият, исавият

ishan ايشان PERSIAN *Sufism n.* Sufi master, Sufi shaykh
BAS: ишан
KAR: ийшан
KAZ: ишан
KYR: эшен
TAJ: эшон
TAT: ишан
TUR: ишан
UYG: ishän, ishan
UZB: эшон

ishanzada ايشان زاده PERSIAN *Sufism n.* son of an ishan; descendant of an ishan
TAJ: эшонзода
UZB: эшонзода

Ishaq اسحاق ARABIC *pn.* the prophet Isaac
BAS: Исхаҡ
KAR: Ийсақ, Ысқақ
KAZ: Ысқақ, Исхақ, Ысхақ
TAJ: Исоқ
TAT: Исхак
TUR: Исхак
UYG: Isaq, Ishaq
UZB: Исоқ, Исҳоқ

isharat اشارة ARABIC *Sufism n.* symbol, sign; advice, instruction; sign of the Zodiac
KAZ: ишара
TAJ: ишорат
TAT: ишарәт
UZB: ишорат

'ishq عشق *Sufism n.* love, divine love; the highest stage of love
BAS: ғишыҡ
KAR: ишиқ
KYR: ышкы
TAJ: ишқ
TAT: гыйшык
TUR: ышк
UYG: ishq
UZB: ишқ

ishrak اشراك ARABIC *n.* paganism, idolatry
KAZ: ішрак
TAJ: ишрак
TAT: ишрәк
UYG: ishräk
UZB: ишрок

ishraq اشراق ARABIC *Ritual n.* optional prayer performed following the morning prayer and after sun has risen
BAS: ишраҡ *optional prayer performed following the morning prayer and after sun has risen, especially performed by Sufis*
TAJ: ишроқ
TAT: ишракъ
UYG: ishräq
UZB: ишроқ

Iskandar اسكندر ARABIC *pn.* the prophet Alexander the Great ☞ ***Zu'l-Qarnayn***
BAS: Искәндәр
KAR: Искендер
KAZ: Іскендір
KYR: Искендер
TAJ: Искандар
TAT: Искәндәр
TUR: Исгендер
UYG: Iskändär
UZB: Искандар

Islam اسلام ARABIC *n.* Islam
BAS: Ислам
KAR: Ислам
KAZ: Ислам
KYR: Ислам, Ыслам
TAJ: Ислом
TAT: Ислам
TUR: Ыслам
UYG: Islam
UZB: Ислом

islamiyat اسلاميت ARABIC *n.* the Islamic world; the Islamic religion
BAS: исламиат
KAR: исламият
TAJ: исломият
TAT: ислямиять
UYG: islamiyät
UZB: исломият

Isma'il اسماعيل ARABIC *pn.* the prophet Ishmael, son of the patriarch Abraham
BAS: Исмағил
KAR: Исмайыл, Ысмайыл
KAZ: Ысмайыл, Исмаил, Ісмағил, Ысмағил
TAJ: Исмоил

TAT: Исмәгыйл
TUR: Ысмайыл
UYG: Isma'il
UZB: Исмоил

ʻismat عصمة ARABIC *n.* being a good Muslim, avoiding illicit things (a quality attributed to prophets)
TAJ: исмат
TAT: гыйсмәт
UZB: исмат

ʻismatullah عصمة الله ARABIC *adj.* honorable, sinless; servant of God
TAJ: исматилло
UZB: исматилла

ism-i aʻzam اسم اعظام PERSIAN *np.* the name of God (i.e. "Allah," "Hu"), esp. recited in dhikr
KYR: исми агзам
TAJ: исми аъзам
UZB: исми аъзам

isnad اسناد ARABIC *Hadith n.* the chain of transmission of hadiths (from the prophet Muhammad to the compiler of a hadith collection and beyond)
BAS: иснад
KAR: иснад
KAZ: иснад
TAJ: иснод
TAT: иснад
TUR: иснат
UYG: isnäd
UZB: иснод

isqat اسقاط ARABIC *Ritual n.* ritual by which the sins of the deceased are assumed by person who have accepted money from the relatives of the deceased
BAS: иҫкат
TAJ: исқот
TAT: искат
UYG: isqät
UZB: исқот

Isra اسرا ARABIC *Qur'an n.* the 17th sura of the Qur'an (i.e. the prophet Muhammad's midnight journey to the seven heavens)
KAR: Исрә суўреси
KAZ: Ісра сүресі
TAJ: сураи Исуро
TAT: Исраэ, Исраи, Сүрәтүл-исраэ
UYG: Isrä süräsi, sürä Isra
UZB: Ал-Исро сураси

israf اسراف ARABIC *Law n.* wasting, extravagance in religious duties, i.e. doing more than is required by the law
BAS: исраф
KAR: исрәп
KAZ: ысырап
TAJ: исроф
TAT: исраф
UYG: israp
UZB: исроф

Israfil اسرافيل ARABIC *pn.* the Archangel Israfil
BAS: Исрафил
KAR: Исрапил
KAZ: Ісрафил, Исрафил
KYR: Ысырапыл, Исрафил
TAJ: Исрофил
TAT: Исрафил
TUR: Эсрафыл
UYG: Israpil
UZB: Исрофил

Isra'il اسرائيل *pn.* surname of the prophet Jacob ☞ ***Ya'qub, Bani Isra'il***
KAZ: Исраил
TAJ: Исроил
UYG: Isra'il
UZB: Исроил

istibdad استبداد ARABIC *n.* absolutism, autocracy
BAS: истибдад
KAR: истибдәд
TAJ: истибдод
TAT: истибдад
UYG: istibdäd, istibat
UZB: истибдод ① *oppression, despotism* ② *absolutism, autocracy*

istibra استبرا ARABIC *Ritual n.* minor ablution performed after urination
BAS: истибра
KAZ: істібра
TAT: истибра
UZB: истибро

istidlali iman استدلالی ایمان ARABIC *Theology np.* demonstrated faith, faith acquired by means of proof ☞ ***tahqiqi iman***
TAT: истидлали иман, истидляли иман
UZB: истидлоли имон

istiʻfar استعفار ARABIC *n.* request for forgiveness, request for absolution

BAS: истиғфар
KYR: ыстыкпар
TAJ: истифор
TAT: истигъфар
UYG: istipär
UZB: истифор

istighfar استغفار PERSIAN *n.* request for forgiveness (from God)
BAS: истиғфар
KAZ: істіғфар
TAJ: истиғфор
TAT: истигъфар
UYG: istighpär
UZB: истиғфор

istihaza استحاضه ARABIC *Ritual n.* the issue of menstrual blood, during which time women are ritually unclean
TAJ: истиҳоза
TAT: истихазә
TUR: истыхаза
UZB: истиҳоза

istihsan استحسان ARABIC *Law n.* equity (as a legal principle guiding analogical reasoning in Islamic law)
KAZ: истихсан
TAJ: истихсон
TAT: истихсан
UZB: истиҳсон

istikhara استخاره ARABIC *n.* divination on the basis of dreams; divination by means of opening the Qur'an or another Islamic text and selecting a random passage
BAS: истихара *prayer to make what was dreamt come true*
TAJ: истиҳора
TAT: истихарә, истихара
UZB: истиҳора

istilahat اصطلاحات ARABIC *Theology n.* terminology
BAS: истилах
KAR: истиләҳат
TAJ: истилоҳот
UZB: истилоҳот, истилоҳат

istinja استنجا ARABIC *Ritual n.* major ablutions performed after relieving oneself
KAR: истинжа
KAZ: істінжа, истинжа
TAJ: истинҷо
TAT: истинҗа
UYG: istinja
UZB: истинжо

istinshaq استنشاق ARABIC *Ritual n.* inhaling of water through the nose (as a part of the ablution)
TAJ: истиншоқ
UZB: истиншок

istiqamat استقامة ARABIC *n.* rectitude of life, purity of life, being constant in religion according to the rules of the Qur'an
BAS: истиҡамат
TAJ: истиқома
TAT: истикамәт
UYG: istiqamät
UZB: истиқома, истиқомат

istiqbal استقبال ARABIC *Ritual n.* turning the face towards Mecca for prayer
BAS: истиҡбал
KAR: истиқбал
TAJ: истиқбол
TAT: истикъбаль
UYG: istiqbal
UZB: истиқбол

istishhad استشهاد ARABIC *n.* martyrdom, dying as a martyr
TAJ: истисшод
TAT: истишхад
UZB: истишод

istislah استسلاح ARABIC *Law n.* public interest, public welfare (as a legal principle guiding analogical reasoning in Islamic law)
KAZ: истислах
TAJ: истисло
UZB: истислоҳ

istisna استثنا ARABIC *n.* accepting, conditioning one's plan on God's will
KAR: истисна
TAJ: истисно
UYG: istisna
UZB: истисно

istisqa استسقا ARABIC *Ritual n.* rain prayer
BAS: истисҡа
KAZ: истисқа
TAJ: истисқо
TAT: истиска
UZB: истисқо

'isyan عصيان ARABIC *n.* rebellion (esp. against God)
KAR: исён, қозғалан
TAJ: исён
TAT: гыйсъян
UZB: исён

'isyankar عصيانكار PERSIAN *n.* rebel
KAR: исёнкәр
TAJ: исёнгар
UZB: исёнкор

ita'at اطاعت ARABIC *n.* obeying, submitting
BAS: итәғәт, итәғә
KAR: итәат
TAJ: итоат
TAT: итагать
UYG: ita'ät
UZB: итоат

i'tikaf اعتكاف ARABIC *Ritual n.* extended period of voluntary prayer and contemplation conducted in a mosque during the month of Ramadan
KAZ: ығтикәф
TAJ: итиқоф
TAT: игътикяф
UYG: etikap
UZB: итиқоф

i'tikafkhana اعتكافخانه PERSIAN *n.* place for performing i'tikaf
UYG: etikapkhana

i'timad اعتماد ARABIC *n.* belief, reliance (upon faith)
TAJ: эътимод
TAT: игътимад
UYG: etimät
UZB: эътимод

i'tiqad اعتقاد ARABIC *n.* belief, faith (that a thing is so); the tenets of faith, theology
BAS: иғтикад
KAR: итиқат
KAZ: итикад, иғтиқад, иғтиқат
TAJ: эътиқод
TAT: игътикад
TUR: ыгтыкат
UYG: etiqat, etiqad
UZB: эътиқод

i'tiqadat اعتقادات ARABIC *Law n.* one of the five branches of Islamic law governing the articles of the Islamic faith
TAT: игътикадат

itlaq اطلاق ARABIC *Law n.* divorce (from a woman)
BAS: итлаҡ
TAJ: итлоқ
TAT: итлак
UZB: итлоқ

itmam اتمام ARABIC *Ritual n.* completion (of a prayer)
KAR: итмам
TAJ: итмом
TAT: итмам
UZB: итмом

ittihad [1] اتّحاد ARABIC *Theology n.* becoming one, union (as a metaphoric philosophical term)
BAS: иттиһад
KAR: иттиҳад
KAZ: иттихад
TAJ: иттиҳод
TAT: иттихад
UZB: иттиҳод

ittihad [2] اتّحاد ARABIC *Sufism n.* becoming one with God, unification with God; monism (as a Sufi school, esp. of Ibn 'Arabi)
BAS: иттиһад
KAR: иттиҳад
KAZ: иттихад
KYR: итихад
TAJ: иттиҳод
TAT: иттихад
UZB: иттиҳод

izar ازار ARABIC *Ritual n.* portion of the burial shroud that covers the body from the waist to the feet
KAZ: изар
TAJ: изор, эзор
TAT: изар
UZB: изор

izdivaj ازدواج ARABIC *n.* matrimony, marriage
TAJ: издивоч
TAT: издиваҗ
UZB: издивож

izn اذن ARABIC *Sufism n.* permission; license to transmit Sufi knowledge ☞ ***irshadnama, ijazat***
BAS: иҙен
KAR: изн
KAZ: ізін
TAJ: изн
TAT: изен
UZB: изн

ʻizzat عزّة ARABIC *n.* honor, might, high rank
BAS: ғиззәт
KAR: иззет
KAZ: ғыззет
TAJ: иззат
TAT: гыйззәт
UYG: izzät *respect, honor*
UZB: иззат

J

Jabbar, al- الجبّار ARABIC *pn.* the Powerful, the Awesome (name of God)
BAS: Жәббар
KAR: Жаппар
KAZ: әл-Жаббар
KYR: Жапар
TAJ: Ҷаббор
TAT: Җәббар
TUR: ал-Җепбар
UYG: Jäppär
UZB: Ал-Жаббор

jabr جبر ARABIC *n.* oppression
BAS: йәбер
KAR: жебир
TAJ: ҷабр
TAT: җәбер *oppression offense*
UZB: жабр

Jabra'il جبرائيل ARABIC *pn.* the Archangel Gabriel
BAS: Ябраил, Жабраил
KAR: Жабрайыл
KAZ: Жебірейіл, Жебрәйіл, Жабрил
KYR: Жебирейил, Жибирейил, Жебреил ① *the Archangel Gabriel* ② *the Angel of Death*
TAJ: Ҷаброил
TAT: Җәбраил
TUR: Җебрайыл
UYG: Jibri'il, Jäbra'il
UZB: Жаброийл

Jadi جدى ARABIC *pn.* Capricorn, 11th month of the Hidjri Solar year
BAS: Жәди
KAR: жәдий, жедди
KAZ: Жәди
TAJ: ҷадӣ
TAT: Җәди
UYG: Jedi
UZB: Жадий

jadid جديد ARABIC *Historical n.* adherent of the usul-i jadid; Islamic modernist ☞ ***usul-i jadid***
BAS: йәдит
KAR: жәдит
KAZ: жәдит, жәдитші
KYR: жадит
TAJ: ҷадид
TAT: җәдид
TUR: җезит
UYG: jädit
UZB: жадид

jadu جادو PERSIAN *n.* sorcerer
KAR: жәди
KAZ: жады
KYR: жады, жаду
TAJ: ҷоду
TAT: җаду
TUR: җады
UYG: jadu
UZB: жоду

jadugar جادوگر PERSIAN *n.* sorcerer, magician
KAR: жәдигар, дуўахан
KYR: жадыгер
TAJ: ҷодугар
UYG: jadugär
UZB: жодугар

jadugu جادو گو PERSIAN *n.* sorcerer, wizard
KAR: жадигөй, жадүгар, жәдигөй
KYR: жадыгөй, жадугөй, жадыкөй
TAJ: ҷодугар
TUR: җадыгөй
UYG: jadugär, jaduchi
UZB: жодугар

jafa جفا ARABIC *n.* torment, repression, harshness
KAR: жапа
TAJ: ҷафо
TAT: җәфа
UZB: жафо

Jahannam جهنّم ARABIC *pn.* Hell, Hellfire; damnation
BAS: Йәһәннәм
KAR: Жәҳәннем
KAZ: Жаһаннам
KYR: Жааннам, Жаханнам
TAJ: Ҷаҳаннам
TAT: Җәһәннәм
TUR: Җәхеннем

UYG: Jähännäm
UZB: Жаҳаннам

jahili جاهلی ARABIC *adj.* pre-Islamic, pertaining to unbelief and idolatry
BAS: яһил, жаһил
KAR: жәхыл
KAZ: жаһіл, жаһил
KYR: жаал, жаалы, жайыл ① *pre-Islamic* ② *ignorant*
TAJ: ҷоҳили
TAT: җаһили
UYG: jahalät
UZB: жоҳили

jahiliyat جاهلیت ARABIC *Historical n.* the time of darkness, the pre-Islamic period
BAS: жаһилиә
KAR: жахылият
KAZ: жаһилийа, жаһилия
TAJ: ҷоҳилият
TAT: җаһилиять
UYG: jahalätlik
UZB: жоҳолият

jahim جحیم ARABIC *n.* Hellfire
TAJ: ҷаҳм
TAT: җәхим
UYG: jahm
UZB: жаҳм

jahl جهل ARABIC *Theology n.* ignorance of religious truths
BAS: йәһел
KAR: жахыл, ашыў
KAZ: жаһыл
TAJ: ҷаҳл
UYG: jähl
UZB: жаҳл

jahr جهر ARABIC *Sufism n.* loud dhikr, prayer performed aloud (among specific Sufi orders)
TAJ: ҷаҳр
TAT: җәһр
UZB: жаҳр

ja'iz جائز ARABIC *Ritual adj.* appropriate, correct
TAT: җаиз
TUR: җайыз
UZB: жоиз

Jalil, al- الجلیل ARABIC *pn.* name of God: the Majestic
BAS: Йәлил
KAR: Жалил
TAJ: Ҷалил
TAT: Җәлил
TUR: ал-Җелил
UZB: Ал-Жалил

Jalla Jalaluh جلّ جلاله ARABIC *intj.* May His Glory be Exalted
TAT: Җәллә Җәләлуһ
UZB: Жалла Жалоллоҳ

jallad جلّاد ARABIC *Law n.* executioner
BAS: йәлләт, жәлләд
KAR: жаллат, жәллат
TAJ: ҷаллод
TAT: җәлляд
UYG: jällat
UZB: жаллод

jalsa جلسه ARABIC *Ritual n.* sitting (in prayer)
KAR: жалса
TAJ: ҷалса
TAT: җәлсә
UZB: жалса

jam' al-jam' جمع الجمع ARABIC *Sufism np.* the plural of a plural, highest position of the perfect man (i.e. someone who has collected the wisdom of all wisdom in his person)
TAJ: ҷамулҷамъ
UZB: жамъулжамъ

jama'at [1] جماعت ARABIC *n.* community, group of people, public; the Muslim community
BAS: йәмәғәт, жәмәғәт
KAR: жәмәат, жамаат
KAZ: жамағат
KYR: жамаат, жамагат
TAJ: ҷамоа
TAT: җәмагать, җәмәгать
TUR: җемагат
UYG: jama'ä
UZB: жамоа

jama'at [2] جماعت ARABIC *n.* family, household
BAS: йәмәғәт, жәмәғәт ① *family, household* ② *wife*
KAR: жәмийет
KAZ: жамағат *wife*
KYR: жамаат *wife*
TAJ: ҷамоат
TAT: җәмагать, җәмәгать ① *family, household* ② *wife*
UYG: jama'ät
UZB: жамоат

jami' جامع ARABIC *n.* Friday mosque (containing a minbar and where the khutba is performed)
- BAS: ямиғ
- KAR: жәмы, мешит
- TAJ: ҷомеъ
- TAT: җамигъ
- TUR: җами, җума метҗиди
- UZB: жоме

Jami', al- الجامع ARABIC *pn.* name of God: the Gatherer
- KAR: Жәмий
- TAJ: Ҷамӣ
- TUR: ал-Җамы
- UZB: Ал-Жомий

Jamra جمره ARABIC *Hajj pn.* a location near Mecca, at the Three Pillars of Mina, where pilgrims cast seven stones; the pillars mark the locations where Satan is said to have appeared successively to Adam, Abraham, and Ishmael
- KAR: Жамра
- KAZ: Жамра
- TAJ: Ҷамра
- UZB: Жамра

jan جان PERSIAN *n.* soul; spirit
- BAS: йән
- KAR: жан
- KAZ: жан
- KYR: жан
- TAJ: ҷон
- TAT: җан
- TUR: җан
- UYG: jan
- UZB: жон

janab جناب ARABIC *n.* your highness (form of address)
- KAR: жанап, жаныў
- TAJ: ҷаноб
- TAT: җәнаб
- TUR: җенаб
- UZB: жаноб

Janab-i haqq جناب حق PERSIAN *pn.* God
- KAR: жанапи Ҳақ
- TAJ: ҷаноби Ҳаққ
- TAT: Җәнабе хак, Җәнаби хак
- TUR: Җенаб-и хакк
- UZB: жанобии Ҳақ

janaza[1] جنازه ARABIC *Ritual n.* deceased, prepared for burial
- BAS: йыназа
- KAR: жаназа, жиназа, жыназа
- KAZ: жаназа
- KYR: жаназа
- TAJ: ҷаноза
- TAT: җәназа
- TUR: җыназа
- UYG: jinaza
- UZB: жаноза

janaza[2] جنازه ARABIC *Ritual n.* funeral, funeral rites; funeral prayer
- BAS: жиназа, йыназа
- KAR: жаназа, аза, матам
- KAZ: жаназа, жаназа намазы
- KYR: ассалоошу жаназа
- TAJ: ҷаноза
- TAT: җәназа, җеназа, җеназа намазы
- TUR: җыназа, җыназа намазы
- UYG: jinaza ① *funeral, funeral rites funeral prayer* ② *funerary bier*
- UZB: жаноза

janda جنده PERSIAN *Sufism n.* patched robe worn by itinerant Sufis
- KAR: жәнде
- UYG: jändä
- UZB: жанда

Jannat جنّت ARABIC *Theology pn.* Heaven, Paradise ☞ *'Adn*
- BAS: Йәннәт, Жәннәт
- KAR: Жәннет
- KAZ: Жәннәт, Жаннат
- KYR: Жаннат
- TAJ: Ҷаннат
- TAT: Җәннәт, Оҗмах
- TUR: Җеннет
- UYG: Jännät
- UZB: Жаннат

Jannat al-'Adn جنّت العدن ARABIC *pn.* the gardens of Eden, paradise ☞ *'Adn*
- KAZ: ғадын жаннаты
- TAJ: Ҷаннату Адн
- UZB: Жаннатул Адн

Jannat al-Firdaus جنّت الفردوس ARABIC *np.* the Garden of Paradise ☞ *'Adn*
- BAS: Фирҙәүес
- KAR: Жәннетул Пирдаўс

KAZ: Фірдауыс жаннаты
TAJ: Ҷаннатул Фирдавс
TAT: Фирдавес
UZB: Жаннатул Фирдавс

Jannat al-Khuld جنّت الخلد ARABIC *pn.* the Garden of Eternity ☞ ***'Adn***
TAJ: Ҷаннатул хулд
UZB: Жаннатул хулд

Jannat al-Ma'va جنّت المأوى ARABIC *pn.* the Garden of Refuge, Paradise
KAZ: Мәуа жаннаты
TAJ: Ҷаннатул маъво
UZB: Жаннатул маъво

Jannat al-Na'im جنّت النعيم ARABIC *pn.* the Garden of Delight, Paradise
KAZ: Нағым жаннаты
TAJ: Ҷаннатун наъим
UZB: Жаннатун наим

jarima جريمه ARABIC *Law n.* fine, contravention
KAR: ыштарап
TAJ: ҷарима
TAT: җәримә ① *fine* ② *crime, sin*
TUR: җериме
UYG: jarimanä
UZB: жарима

jasad ARABIC *n.* corpse
KAR: жасат, өлик
TAJ: ҷасад
UYG: jäsät
UZB: жасад

Jasiya جاثيه ARABIC *Qur'an pn.* the 45th sura of the Qur'an
KAR: Жәсия суўреси
KAZ: Жасия сүресі
TAJ: сураи Ҷосия
UYG: sürä Jasiyä
UZB: Жосия сураси

javabnama جوابنامه PERSIAN *n.* paper inscribed with Quranic verses and wrapped in the shroud before burial (thought to enable the deceased to answer questions in the next world)
BAS: яуаплама
KAR: жаўәпнама
UZB: жавобнома

Javza جوزا ARABIC *pn.* Gemini, the fourth month of the Hidjri Solar year
BAS: Жәүзә
KAR: жәўзә, жаўза, заўза
KAZ: Зауза
TAJ: ҷавзо
TAT: Җәүза
UYG: Jawza, Joza
UZB: Жавзо

jaynamaz جانماز PERSIAN *Ritual n.* prayer rug
BAS: намаҙлыҡ
KAR: жайнамаз
KAZ: жайнамаз, намаздық
KYR: жайнамаз
TAJ: ҷойинамоз
TAT: намазлык
TUR: намазлык
UYG: jaynamaz
UZB: жойнамоз

jaza جزا ARABIC *Law n.* punishment
BAS: яза
KAR: жаза
KAZ: жаза
TAJ: ҷазо
TAT: җәза, җәзаә
UZB: жазо

jazb جذب *Sufism n.* a state of ecstasy reached during worship
TAJ: ҷазб
TAT: җәзеб
UZB: жазб

jazba جذبه ARABIC *Sufism n.* attraction, the state of yearning after the divine being
TAJ: ҷазбаъ
UZB: жазба

Jibril جبريل ARABIC *pn.* the Archangel Gabriel ☞ ***Jabra'il***
KAZ: Жибрил
TAT: Җибрил
UZB: Жибрил

Jibt جبت ARABIC *pn.* name of an idol of the Qurayish mentioned in the Qur'an
KAZ: Жыбт

jihad جهاد ARABIC *n.* effort, internal effort; holy war, war for the faith
BAS: йыһат, жиһат
KAR: жыхад
KAZ: жихад, жиһат
TAJ: ҷиҳод

TAT: җиһад
TUR: җыхад, җихад
UZB: жиҳод

jihad-i akbar جهاد اكبر PERSIAN *np.* the greater effort, i.e. the struggle for self mastery over inner appetites
TAJ: ҷиҳоди акбар
UZB: жиҳоди акбар

jihad-i asghar جهاد اصغر PERSIAN *np.* the lesser effort, i.e. war against infidels
TAJ: ҷиҳоди асгар
UZB: жиҳоди асгар

jilva-yi rabbaniya جلوهء ربانيّة PERSIAN *Sufism np.* forgetting one's self at the time when the Sufi is united with God (lit. "unveiling of the Lord")
TAJ: ҷилваи раббонӣ
UZB: жилваи раббония

jinayat جنايت ARABIC *Law n.* crime
BAS: енәйәт
KAR: жинаят
TAJ: ҷиноят
TAT: җинаять
TUR: җенаят
UYG: jinayät
UZB: жиноят

jinaza ☞ ***janaza***

jinn [1] جنّ ARABIC *n.* jinn, spirit, demon
BAS: ен
KAR: жин, жын
KAZ: жын
KYR: жин *jinn, spirit, demon (also a tutelary spirits to a shaman)*
TAJ: ҷин
TAT: җен, җин
TUR: җын, айҗын
UYG: jin
UZB: жин

Jinn [2] جنّ ARABIC *Qur'an n.* the 72nd sura of the Qur'an
KAR: Жин суўреси
KAZ: Жын сүресі
TAJ: сураи Ҷин
TAT: Җен сүрәсе
UYG: sürä Jin
UZB: Жин сураси

Jirjis جرجس ARABIC *pn.* Saint George (a prophet in Islamic tradition)
TAJ: Ҷирҷис
TUR: Җирҗис
UZB: Жиржис

jizya جزيه ARABIC *Taxation n.* poll tax traditionally paid by non-Muslims living under Muslim rule
KAZ: жизья
TAJ: ҷизя, ҷузъя
TAT: җизия, җәзия
TUR: җизья
UZB: жизия, жузъя

juda جدا ARABIC *Law n.* loss, deprivation, mourning (as a regulated behavior)
KAR: жуда
TAJ: ҷудо
TAT: җөда
UZB: жудо

Judi جودى ARABIC *pn.* name of a mountain on which, according to one Qur'anic tradition, Noah's Ark came to rest
KAZ: Жуди тауы
TAJ: Ҷудӣ
UYG: Jüdi teghi
UZB: Жудий

jughrafiya جغرافيا ARABIC *n.* geography (as an Islamic science)
KAR: жуғрәпия, география
TUR: җуграфия
UYG: jughrapiya
UZB: жуғрифия

juhud جهود PERSIAN *n.* Jew ☞ ***yahud***
KAR: жөҳит
TAJ: ҷуҳуд
TAT: җөһүд
UYG: johut
UZB: жуҳуд, жувут

jum'a [1] جمعه ARABIC *Ritual n.* collective prayer, Friday prayer
BAS: йома, йома намаҙы
KAR: жума
KAZ: жұма, жұма
KYR: жума намаз
TAJ: ҷумъа
TAT: җомга
TUR: җума, җума, җумга намазы
UYG: jumä, jümä
UZB: жума намози, жумъа

jum'a [2] جمعه ARABIC *n.* Friday, the day on which communal prayers are held

BAS: йома
KAR: жума
KAZ: жұма ① *Friday, the day on which communal prayers are held* ② *week*
KYR: жума
TAJ: чумъа
TAT: җомга
TUR: анна, җума
UYG: jumä
UZB: жума

Jum'a [3] جمعه ARABIC *Qur'an pn.* the 62nd sura of the Qur'an
KAR: Жума суўреси
KAZ: Жұма сүресі
TAJ: Сураи чумъа
UYG: sürä Jümü'ä
UZB: Жумъа сураси

Jumada al-akhira جمادی الآخره ARABIC *n.* the sixth month of the Islamic lunar calendar
BAS: Йомадилахыр, Жөмадиәлахыр
KAR: Жумадул-ахир, Жумәдиүссәни
TAJ: Ҷумадалохир
TAT: Җөмадиәлахир
TUR: Җумадилахыр
UYG: Jumadil-akhir
UZB: Жумад ал-охир

Jumada al-ula جمادی الاولا ARABIC *n.* the fifth month of the Islamic lunar calendar
BAS: Йомадиләүүәл, Жөмадиәләүүәл
KAR: Жумадул-әўўал, Жумадиүләўәл
TAJ: Ҷумадалаввал
TAT: Җөмадиәләүвәл
TUR: Җумадиловвал
UYG: Jumadil-äwwäl
UZB: Жумад ал-аввал

jumalik جمعه لك TURKIC *n.* Friday alms which student bring to their teachers in madrasas and maktabs
KAR: жумалиқ
UZB: жумалик

jumla جمله ARABIC *n.* gathering of people for prayer
BAS: йөмлә
KAR: жумлә
TAJ: чумла
UZB: жумла

junub جنب ARABIC *Ritual n.* state of major ritual impurity; person in a state of major ritual impurity
TUR: җүнүп, җүнүб

junun [1] جنون ARABIC *Law adj.* insane (as a legal category of persons)
TAJ: чунун
TAT: җөнүн
TUR: җунун
UZB: жунун

junun [2] جنون ARABIC *Sufism n.* possession (by the love of God)
TAJ: чунун
TAT: җөнүн
UZB: жунун

jurh جرح ARABIC *Hadith n.* rejection and replacement of a hadith tradition by a scholar
UZB: журҳ

juz' [1] جزء ARABIC *Qur'an n.* one thirtieth part of the Qur'an
TAJ: чуз
TAT: җөзэ
UZB: жузъ

juz' [2] جزء ARABIC *Qur'an n.* manuscript Qur'an consisting of twenty pages
TAJ: чуз
TAT: җөзэ
UZB: жузъ

juz' [3] جزء ARABIC *Qur'an n.* incomplete printed edition consisting of one or several sections of the Qur'an
TAJ: чуз
UZB: жузъ

juz' [4] جزء ARABIC *Hadith n.* hadith volume
TAJ: чуз
TAT: җөзэ
UZB: жузъ

K

Ka'ba كعبه ARABIC *n.* Kaaba, the sanctuary at Mecca
BAS: Ҡәғбә
KAR: Кәба, Каба
KAZ: Кағба
KYR: Кааба, Кеаба, Кава
TAJ: Каъба
TAT: Кәгъбә
TUR: Кәбе, Кәъбе
UYG: Käbä
UZB: Каъба

Ka'batullah كعبة الله ARABIC *pn.* Ka'ba, the sanctuary at Mecca ☞ ***Ka'ba***
- BAS: Ҡәғбәтулла
- KAR: Кәбатулла
- TAJ: Каъбатулло
- TAT: Кәгъбәтулла
- UZB: Каъбатуллоҳ, Каъбатулло

Kabir, al- الكبير ARABIC *n.* name of God: the Great
- BAS: Кәбир
- KAR: Кәбыр
- TAJ: Кабир
- TAT: Кәбир
- TUR: ал-Кабир
- UZB: Ал-Кабир

kabira كبيره ARABIC *n.* heinous sin, deadly sin
- KAR: кәбыр
- KAZ: кабира
- TAJ: кабира
- TAT: кәбирә
- UZB: кабир

kafalat كفالت ARABIC *Law n.* pledge given to a creditor to secure a loan
- BAS: кәфаләт
- KAR: кәпил
- TAJ: кафилӣ
- TAT: кәфаләт
- UZB: кафил, кафолат

kaffarat كفّارت ARABIC *n.* atonement, expiation (for a sin); compensation (legal)
- BAS: кәфарәт
- KAR: кәппарат
- KAZ: кәппарат, кәффәрат
- KYR: кеперет
- TAJ: кафорат
- TAT: кәффарәт
- TUR: кефарат
- UYG: kuparät
- UZB: кафорат

kafil كفيل ARABIC *Law n.* guarantor
- BAS: кәфил
- KAR: кәпил, кепил
- KAZ: кефил
- TAJ: кафил
- TAT: кәфил
- UZB: кафил

kafir كافر ARABIC *n.* infidel, unbeliever
- BAS: кафыр
- KAR: кәпир
- KAZ: кәпір, кәфір
- KYR: капыр, каапыр
- TAJ: кофир
- TAT: кяфир ① *unbeliever, infidel* ② *atheist*
- TUR: капыр, кяфир, кәфир
- UYG: kapir, kupur
- UZB: кофир

kafiristan كافرستان PERSIAN *n.* the land of the infidels
- KAR: кәпиристан
- TAJ: кофиристон
- TAT: кяфирстан
- UYG: kupuristan
- UZB: кофиристон

Kafirun كافرون ARABIC *Qur'an pn.* the 109th sura of the Qur'an
- KAR: Кәпирун суўреси
- KAZ: Кәфирұн сүресі
- TAJ: сураи Кофурун
- TAT: Кәфирун сүрәсе
- UYG: sürä Kafirun
- UZB: Кофирун сураси

kafn كفن ARABIC *Ritual n.* shroud (in which the deceased is wrapped for an Islamic burial)
- BAS: кәфен
- KAR: кепин, кәпин, кебин
- KAZ: кебін
- KYR: кепин
- TAJ: кафан
- TAT: кәфен
- TUR: кепен, кефен
- UYG: kapan, kipin
- UZB: кафан

Kahf كهف ARABIC *Qur'an pn.* the 18th sura of the Qur'an
- KAR: Қахп суўреси
- KAZ: Кеһф сүресі
- TAJ: сураи Каҳф
- TAT: Кәһәф сүрәсе, Кәһф сүрәсе
- UYG: sürä Kähf
- UZB: Каҳф сураси

kahin كاهن ARABIC *n.* priest (of a non-Muslim faith); seer, soothsayer ☞ ***falbin***
- KAR: кәхин
- KAZ: кахин
- TAJ: коҳин
- TAT: кяһин *seer, soothsayer*

TUR: кахин
UYG: kahin
UZB: коҳин ① *religious person* ② *fortune teller*

ka'inat كائنات ARABIC *n.* the universe, all things existing
KAR: әлем
TAJ: коинот
TAT: кяинат
UZB: коинот

kajraftar کج رفتار PERSIAN *Theology adj.* deceiving, having two aspects (e.g. the world)
TAJ: каҷрафтор
UZB: кажрафтор

kalam كلام ARABIC *Theology n.* dogma (as a field of study), scholastic theology
BAS: кәлам
KAR: кәлам
KAZ: кәләм, калам, қалам
KYR: келем
TAJ: калом
TAT: кәлям
TUR: келам
UZB: калом

Kalam-i Sharif كلام شريف PERSIAN *np.* the Qur'an ☞ ***Qur'an***
KAR: кәлами Шарип
KYR: келем шарып, келеме шарып
TAJ: каломи Шариф
TAT: Кәляме шәриф, Каләме Шәриф
UZB: каломи Шариф

Kalamullah كلام الله ARABIC *Qur'an n.* the Qur'an ☞ ***Qur'an***
KAR: кәламулла
KYR: Келе молдо
TAJ: каламулло
TAT: Кәлямулла
TUR: келамулла, келамылла
UZB: каламуллоҳ

kalima كليمه ARABIC *Ritual n.* the profession of faith (there is no God but Allah and Muhammad is his prophet)
BAS: кәлимә
KAR: кәлимә, кәлийма
KYR: келме
TAJ: калима
TAT: кәлимә
UZB: калима

kalimagu كلمه گو PERSIAN *n.* pious person, one who professes his faith ☞ ***kalimullah***
KAR: кәлимагөй
KYR: келмекөй
UZB: калимагўй

kalimatullah كليمة الله ARABIC *n.* the Word of God; epithet of the prophet Moses
TAJ: калиматулло
UZB: калиматуллоҳ

kalima-yi shahadat كليمهٔ شهادت PERSIAN *Ritual n.* the profession of faith
KAR: кәлимаи шахәдат
KYR: келме шаадат
TAJ: калимаи шаҳодат
TAT: кәлимәи шәһәдәт
TUR: келеме шахадат
UZB: калимаи шаҳодат

kalimullah كليم الله ARABIC *n.* pious person, one who professes his faith ☞ ***kalimagu***
TAJ: калимулло

kalisa كليسه ARABIC *n.* church (Christian)
BAS: кәлисә *cathedral (Christian)*
KAR: ширкеў
TAJ: калисо, калисиё, калисьё
TAT: кәлисә, чиркәү
TUR: килисе
UYG: kilisä
UZB: калиса

kanisa كنيسه ARABIC *n.* church
TAJ: каниса
TAT: кәнисә
UZB: каниса

kaniz كنز ARABIC *Law n.* female slave
KAR: кәниз, кәнизек
TAJ: каниз
UZB: каниз, канизак

karam كرم ARABIC *Theology n.* Gods love, Divine love
BAS: кәрәм
KAR: кәрам
TAJ: карам
TAT: кәрәм
UZB: карам

karamat كرامت ARABIC *Sufism n.* miracle (typically performed by a Sufi or a Muslim saint)
BAS: кәрәмәт
KAR: кәрамат, қарамат

KAZ: керемет
KYR: керемет
TAJ: каромот
TAT: кәрамәт
TUR: керамат
UYG: karamät
UZB: кароmat

Karbala كربلا ARABIC *Historical pn.* the location in Iraq where the imam Husayn was slain in October 680
KAR: Кәрбалә
KAZ: Кербала
KYR: Кербала
TAJ: Карбало
UZB: Корбало, Карбало

Kardigar كردگار PERSIAN *pn.* God, the Creator
TAT: Кәрдигяр

Karim, al- الكريم ARABIC *pn.* name of God: the Generous
BAS: Кәрим
KAR: Кәрим
TAJ: Карим
TAT: Кәрим
TUR: ал-Керим
UZB: Ал-Карим

kashish كشيش ARABIC *n.* Christian priest; monk
TAJ: кашиш
TAT: кәшиш
UZB: кашиш

kashishkhana كشيشخانه PERSIAN *n.* Christian monastery
TAJ: кашишхона
TAT: кәшишханә
UZB: кашишхона

kashkul كشكول PERSIAN *Sufism n.* kashkul, small badge worn by dervishes for eliciting donations
TAJ: кашкӯл
UZB: кашкул

katib كاتب ARABIC *n.* clerk, scribe
KAR: қәтип
TAJ: котиб
TAT: кятиб
UZB: котиб

kavnayn كونين ARABIC *Theology n.* the two worlds, the material and spiritual worlds
TAT: кәунәен

Kavsar [1] كوثر ARABIC *pn.* name of a spring or well in Paradise
BAS: Кәусәр, Хәүзе Кәусәр
KAR: Кәўсар, абы Кәўсар
KAZ: Кәусар, Кеусер, Каусар
KYR: абзи Көвсар, абыз Көөсар, Көөсөр
TAJ: Кавсар
TAT: Кәусәр
UYG: Käwsar
UZB: Кавсар

Kavsar [2] كوثر ARABIC *Qur'an pn.* the 108th sura of the Qur'an
KAR: Каўсар сүўреси
KAZ: Кәусәр сүресі
TAJ: сураи Кавсар
TAT: Кәусәр сурәсе
UYG: sürä Käwsär
UZB: Кавсар сураси

khabar خبر ARABIC *Hadith n.* hadith, tradition
☞ ***hadis, akhbar***
KAR: хабар
KAZ: хабар
TAJ: хабар
TAT: хәбәр
UZB: хабар

khabar-i vahid خبر واحد PERSIAN *Hadith np.* hadith having a single source
TAJ: хабари воҳид
UZB: хабари воҳид

Khabir, al- الخبير ARABIC *pn.* name of God: the Aware
KAR: Хәбар
KAZ: Хабир
TAJ: Хабар
TAT: Хәбир
TUR: ал-Хабир
UZB: Ал-Хабар

khach خاچ PERSIAN *n.* cross (esp. of Christians)
BAS: хач
KAR: хәч
TAJ: хоч
TAT: хач
TUR: хач
UZB: хоч

khachparast خاچپرست PERSIAN *n.* Christian
KAR: хәчпәрэст
TAJ: хочпараст
TUR: хачпараст, хачпараз

UZB: хочпараст

Khadija ARABIC *n.* Muhammad's first wife

KAR: Хедийша, Қатыйша

KAZ: Қадиша

TAJ: Хадича

TUR: Хатыҗа

UZB: Хадича

khafif ☞ ***najasat khafif***

khalaqa خلقه ARABIC *n.* the end of a turban that hangs over the shoulder

KAR: ҳалақа

khalfa [1] خلفه ARABIC *n.* junior instructor in a madrasa

BAS: хәлфә

KAR: халфе, халфа ① *junior instructor in a madrasa* ② *senior shagird in a madrasa*

KAZ: халфе

KYR: калпа ① *teacher, instructor* ② *disciple to an ishan* ③ *madrasa student in charge of instructing a group of junior students*

TAJ: халфа

TAT: хәлфә

UYG: khälpä, khälpät *assistant reader of the Qur'an in a madrasa*

UZB: халфа

khalfa [2] خلفه ARABIC *n.* female performer of religious songs

KAR: халиф

TAJ: бихалфа

UYG: khälpä

UZB: халфа, бихалфа

khalifa [1] خليفه ARABIC *Historical n.* caliph

BAS: хәлифә

KAR: халийфа, хәлип

KAZ: халифа

KYR: калыпа, халиф

TAJ: халифа

TAT: хәлифә

TUR: халиф

UYG: khälpä

UZB: халифа

khalifa [2] خليفه ARABIC *Sufism n.* a shaykh's deputy

BAS: хәлифә

KAR: хәлип

KAZ: халифа

KYR: калыпа, халиф

TAJ: халифа

TAT: хәлифә

TUR: халиф

UYG: khälpä

UZB: халифа

Khalilullah خليل الله ARABIC *pn.* epithet of the prophet Abraham (lit. God's friend)

KAR: Хәлилулла

KAZ: Халил Алла

KYR: Халил Аллах

TAJ: Халилулло

TUR: Халылылла

UYG: Khelilulla

UZB: Халилиллоҳ, Халиллуло, Халилуллоҳ

Khaliq, al- الخالق ARABIC *pn.* name of God: the Creator

KAR: Ҳалық, Ҳәлиқ, Қалық

KAZ: Халық, әл-Халиқ

KYR: Калык

TAJ: Ҳолиқ

TAT: Халикъ

TUR: ал-Халык

UZB: Ал-Холиқ

Khallaq خلّاق ARABIC *n.* God, the Creator

KAR: Хәлләқ

TAJ: Ҳаллоқ

TAT: Хәллякъ

UZB: Халлоқ

khalvat خلوت ARABIC *Sufism n.* retirement for devotion (among Sufis)

BAS: хилүәт

KAR: хилўәт

KAZ: халуа

TAJ: халват

TAT: хәлвәт

UYG: khilwät

UZB: халват

khalvat dar anjuman خلوت در انجمن PERSIAN *Sufism np.* solitude in the crowd (one of the eight principles of the Naqshbandi Sufi order)

TAT: хәлвәт дәр энҗән

UZB: хилват дар анжуман

khalvatgah خلوتگاه PERSIAN *Sufism n.* place of seclusion (esp. for Sufis)

KAR: хилўәтга

TAJ: хилватгоҳ, хилватхона, хилватнишин, хилватсарой

TAT: хәлвәтгяһ

UYG: khilätgoh

UZB: хилватгоҳ, хилватнишин

khamr خمر ARABIC *Law n.* wine, alcohol (as a category of prohibition)

BAS: хәмер

KAR: қамр

TAJ: хамир

TAT: хәмер

UYG: khimir

UZB: хамр

khanaqa خانقا PERSIAN *Sufism n.* Sufi lodge

BAS: ханаҡа

KAR: ханақа

KAZ: ханака

TAJ: хонақоҳ, хонақаҳ ① *Sufi lodge* ② *interior chamber of a mosque or madrasa*

TAT: ханәка

TUR: ханака

UYG: khaniqa ① *Sufi lodge* ② *mosque*

UZB: хонақоҳ ① *Sufi lodge* ② *interior chamber of a mosque or madrasa*

kharaj خراج ARABIC *Taxation n.* land tax, agricultural tax

BAS: хираж

KAR: қарж

TAJ: харач, хироч, хароч

UZB: хараж, харажат, хирож

khata خطا ARABIC *Ritual n.* unconditional mistake (in performing worship) ☞ ***qaza***

BAS: хата

KAR: қәте

KAZ: қате

KYR: ката

TAJ: хато

TAT: хата

TUR: хата

UYG: khata

UZB: хато

Khatam al-anbiyah خاتم الانبيا ARABIC *pn.* the Last (lit. seal) of all the Prophets (i.e. Muhammad)

TAJ: Ҳотамул Анбиё

UZB: Ҳотамул Анбиё

Khatam al-nabiyin خاتم النبين ARABIC *pn.* the Last Prophet (epithet of the Prophet Muhammad)

TAJ: Ҳотамул набиун

TAT: Хатәменнәбини

UZB: Ҳотамул набиин

khatib خطيب ARABIC *Ritual n.* one who performs the khutba in a mosque, preacher ☞ ***khutba***

BAS: хатип ① *one who performs the khutba in a mosque* ② *one who gives sermons*

KAR: хатиб, қатип

KAZ: хатиб

TAJ: хатиб, хутбахон

TAT: хатиб ① *one who performs the khutba in a mosque* ② *one who gives sermons*

TUR: хатып

UYG: khätib

UZB: хатиб

khatim [1] خاتم ARABIC *n.* seal (i.e. of a document)

BAS: хәтем

KAR: қәтам

TAJ: хотам

TAT: хатим

UZB: хотам

khatim [2] خاتم ARABIC *n.* one who reads the Qur'an through to completion

BAS: хатим

KAR: қатым

TAJ: хатим

TAT: хатим

TUR: хатым

UYG: khätmä

UZB: хатим

khatm [1] ختم ARABIC *Qur'an n.* reading the Qur'an to completion

KAR: қатым

KAZ: хатым

KYR: катым

TAJ: хатм

UYG: khätmä

UZB: хатм

khatm [2] ختم ARABIC *n.* prayer meeting (where the Qur'an is recited)

KAR: қатым

TAJ: хатми Қуръон

UYG: khätma, khätmä Quran

UZB: хатм, хатми Қуръон

khat-mahr خط مهر ARABIC *Law n.* official document determining ownership of property between spouses

TAJ: хати маҳр

UZB: хат-маҳр

khatm-i khvajagan ختم خواجه گان PERSIAN *Sufism np.* litany of the Naqshbandi Sufis
- TAT: хэтем хуҗа
- UZB: хатми хўжагон, хатми хўжа

khatm-i kutub ختم كتب ARABIC *n.* graduation (from school), completion of studies
- TAJ: хатми қутб
- TAT: хэтме кѳтиб
- UZB: хатми қутуб

khatm-i suluk ختم سلوك PERSIAN *Sufism np.* completion of the Sufi path
- TAJ: хатми сулук
- TAT: хэтме сѳлүк
- UYG: khätmä sülük
- UZB: хатми сулук

khatna ختنه ARABIC *Ritual n.* circumcision ☞ ***sunnat***
- TAJ: хатна
- UYG: khätnä
- UZB: хатна

khavarij خوارج ARABIC *n.* heretics; separatists
- KYR: кабарыж
- TAJ: хаворич, хоричӣ
- TAT: хэвариҗ
- TUR: харыҗы
- UYG: khawarich, khawarish *apostate, renegade*
- UZB: хавориж, хаворижлар, исёнчилар

khavf خوف ARABIC *Sufism n.* division, doubt, i.e. from belief to unbelief (as a stage on the Sufi path); fear (of God)
- TAJ: хавф, тарс
- UZB: хавф

Khaybar خيبر ARABIC *Historical pn.* the name of an oasis north of Medina, inhabited by Jews, and the site of one of the prophet Muhammad's earliest expeditions in 628 CE
- KAZ: Хайбар
- KYR: Кайбар
- TAJ: Хайбар
- UYG: Khäybär
- UZB: Хайбар

khayr [1] خير ARABIC *n.* charity, alms
- BAS: хэйер
- KAR: қайир, хайыр
- KAZ: қайыр
- KYR: кайыр
- TAJ: хайр, хаират
- TAT: хэер
- TUR: хайыр
- UYG: khäyr
- UZB: хайр, хайрот

khayr [2] خير ARABIC *n.* goodness, benefit; sympathy
- BAS: хэйер
- KAZ: қайыр
- KYR: кайыр
- TAJ: хайир
- TAT: хэер
- TUR: хайыр
- UYG: khäyr
- UZB: хайир

khayr-sadaqa خير صدقه ARABIC *np.* alms
- BAS: хэер-саҙаҡа
- KAR: қайир-садақа, қайыр-садақа
- KAZ: қайыр-садақа
- KYR: садага-кайыр
- TAJ: хайр-садақа
- TAT: хэер-садака
- UYG: khäyr-sädiqä
- UZB: хайр-садақа

khilafat [1] خلافت ARABIC *Historical n.* the title of Caliph
- KAR: халифа
- KAZ: халифат
- TAJ: хилофа, халифа
- TAT: хилафэт
- TUR: халыфат
- UYG: khälipä
- UZB: халифа, хилофа

khilafat [2] خلافت ARABIC *Historical n.* territory ruled by a caliph
- KAR: халифатлық
- KAZ: халифат, хилофат
- TAJ: халифат
- TAT: хилафэт
- TUR: халыфат
- UYG: khälipä
- UZB: халифат

khilafat [3] خلافت ARABIC *Historical n.* the era of a caliph's rule
- KAR: халифатлық
- KAZ: халифат
- TAJ: халифат
- TAT: хилафэт
- UYG: khälipä

UZB: халифат

khilaf-i shar' خلاف شرع ARABIC *Law adj.* contravening Islamic law

TAJ: хилофи шаръӣ

TAT: хилафе шәрыг

TUR: хылаф

UZB: хилофи шаърий

khilkhana خلخانه PERSIAN *n.* portion of a cemetery belonging to a specific family

UZB: хилхона

khilqat خلقت ARABIC *n.* Creation, the Creation of the Universe

BAS: хилҡәт

TAJ: хилқат

TAT: хилкать, хилкате галәм

UZB: хилқат ① *Creation, the Creation of the Universe* ② *the afterlife*

khilvat خلوت ARABIC *Sufism n.* seclusion ☞ ***khalvat***

BAS: хилүәт

TAJ: хилват

TAT: хәлвәт

UZB: хилват

khirqa [1] خرقه ARABIC *Sufism n.* type of robe worn by dervishes

KAZ: хирқа

TAJ: хирқа

TAT: хирка

TUR: хырка

UZB: хирқа

khirqa [2] خرقه ARABIC *Ritual n.* portion of the woman's burial shroud (covering the area from the bust to the midriff)

KAZ: хырқа

TAJ: хирқа

TUR: хырка

UZB: хирқа

khirqa push خرقه پوش PERSIAN *Sufism n.* dervish, one who wears a khirqa

TAJ: хирқапӯш

TAT: хирка пуш, хиркапуш

UZB: хирқапўш

khirqa-yi sa'adat خرقهء سعادت PERSIAN *np.* type of robe worn by Muhammad

TAJ: хирқаи саодат

UZB: хирқаи саодат

khirqa-yi sharif خرقهء شریف PERSIAN *np.* type of robe presented by the prophet Muhammad

TAJ: хирқаи шариф

UZB: хирқаи шариф

khitan ختان *Ritual n.* circumcision ritual

TAJ: хитон

TAT: хитан

UZB: хитан

Khizr خضر ARABIC *pn.* the prophet Khizr ☞ ***Ilyas***

BAS: Хызыр

KAR: Қызыр, Қыдыр

KAZ: Қызыр, Қыдыр, Хыдыр, Қадыр

KYR: Кызыр, Кыдыр *the prophet Khizr, who is also the patron saint of abundance and plenty*

TAJ: хӯҷаи Хизр

TAT: Хизыр, Хозыр, Хөзер

TUR: Хыдыр *the prophet Khizr, who is also the patron saint of abundance and plenty*

UZB: Хизир

Khuda خدا PERSIAN *n.* God

BAS: Хоҙа

KAR: Кудай

KYR: Кудаа

TAJ: Худо

TAT: Хода

UYG: Khuda

UZB: Худо

khudaguy خداگو PERSIAN *adj.* religious man

KAR: кудайгөй

TAJ: худогӯй

UYG: khudagöy

UZB: худогўй

khudajuy خداجوی PERSIAN *n.* religious man

KAR: кудайжөй

TAJ: худоҷӯй

UYG: khudajöy

UZB: художўй

khudaparast خداپرست PERSIAN *adj.* religious man

KAR: кудайпәрест

TAJ: худопараст

UYG: khudapäräs

UZB: худопараст

khudatars خداترس PERSIAN *n.* God-fearing

TAJ: худонотарс

UYG: khudatärs

UZB: худотарс

Khudavand خداوند PERSIAN *pn.* God

KAR: Кудайўан

TAJ: Худованд
UYG: Khudawänd
UZB: Худованд

khudavanda خداونده PERSIAN *intj.* Oh God!
BAS: Хоҙаүәндә *God*
KAR: Кудайўандә
TAJ: Худовандо
UYG: Khudawändä
UZB: Худовандо

khuday خدای PERSIAN *n.* God
BAS: Хоҙай
KAR: Кудай
KAZ: Құдай, Құдайы
KYR: Кудай
TAJ: Худой
TAT: Ходай
TUR: Худай
UYG: Khuday
UZB: Худой

khudaygu خدای گو PERSIAN *n.* God-fearing person, pious person
KAR: кудайгөй
KYR: кудайкөй
TAJ: худогӯй
UYG: khudagöy
UZB: худогӯй

khudayi خدائی PERSIAN *adj.* godly, pious
KAR: кудайи
KAZ: құдайы
KYR: кудайы
TAJ: худойи
TAT: ходаи
UYG: khudayi
UZB: худойи

khudaykhana خدایخانه PERSIAN *n.* place for giving alms to poor people
KAR: кудайихана
TAJ: худойихона
UZB: худойихона

khuftan ARABIC *Ritual n.* time for late evening prayers ☞ ***salat al-'isha***
KAR: куптан
TAJ: хуфтон
UYG: khuptän, namaz khuptan
UZB: хуфтон

khul' خلع ARABIC *Law n.* money or property given or returned to a wife to effect a divorce
TAJ: хул
UZB: хул

Khulafa-yi rashidin خلفای راشدین PERSIAN *Historical np.* the four Caliphs (Abu Bakr, Umar, 'Usman and 'Ali)
TAJ: Хилофатул Рашиддин
TAT: Хөләфаи рашидин
UZB: Хилофатул Рашидин, Халифаи Рашидин

Khuld خلد ARABIC *pn.* Heaven, Paradise
TAJ: Хулд
TAT: Холд
UZB: Хулд

khulq ARABIC *Qur'an n.* good qualities of person
TAJ: хулқ
UZB: хулқ

khums خمس ARABIC *Taxation n.* one fifth (as a tax rate in Islamic law)
KAZ: хумс
TAJ: хумс
TAT: хомес
UYG: khums
UZB: хумс

khunsa خنثی ARABIC *Law n.* hermaphrodite
TAJ: хунасо, хунсо
TAT: хонса, хонәса
UZB: хунаса

khurafat خرافات ARABIC *n.* superstition
BAS: хөрәфәт
KAR: курапәт, хурапет
TAJ: хурофот
TAT: хорафат
UYG: khurapat
UZB: хурофот

khurma خرما ARABIC *Ritual n.* date (the fruit), typically eaten to break the daily fast during Ramadan
BAS: хөрмә
KAR: курмә, курма, хурма
TAJ: хурмо
TAT: хөрмә
TUR: хурма
UYG: khorma
UZB: хурмо, хурма

khush dar dam خوش در دم PERSIAN *Sufism np.* awareness in breathing; awareness of God while breathing (one of the eight principles of the

Naqshbandi Sufi order)

TAT: хуш дәр дәм

UZB: хуш дар дам

khutba خطبه ARABIC *Ritual n.* Friday or holiday sermon performed, usually by a khatib, in a mosque

BAS: хөтбә ① *Friday sermon performed, usually by an imam, in a Friday mosque* ② *prayer performed during a wedding*

KAR: қутбә, хутбә

KAZ: құтба, хұтба, хұтпа

KYR: кутпа, кутпа дубасы ① *Friday sermon performed, usually by an imam, in a Friday mosque* ② *sermon performed at a wedding*

TAJ: хутба, хутбат

TAT: хотбә, хөтбә

TUR: хутба

UYG: khutbä

UZB: хутба

khvaja [1] خواجه PERSIAN *n.* descendant of the Prophet Muhammad or of one of the four caliphs ☞ ***sayyid***

KAR: хожа, қожа

KAZ: қожа, хожа ① *descendant of the Prophet Muhammad or of one of the four caliphs* ② *One of the several holy tribes among the Kazakhs claiming descent from the prophet Muhammad, the Caliph Ali, and numerous Central Asian saints*

KYR: кожо

TAJ: хӯҷа

TUR: хоҗа ① *descendant of the Prophet Muhammad or of one of the four caliphs* ② *One of the six Turkmen holy tribes claiming descent from the prophet Muhammad of from the Caliph Ali*

UYG: khoja, khojä, ghoja

UZB: хўжа

khvaja [2] خواجه PERSIAN *Law n.* owner, possessor

BAS: хужа

KAR: хожа

KAZ: қожа

KYR: кожо

TAJ: хӯҷа

TAT: хуҗа

TUR: хоҗа

UYG: khoja, ghoja

UZB: хўжа

khvajazada خواجه زاده PERSIAN *n.* descendant of a khoja

KAR: хожазада

UZB: хўжазода

kifaya كفايه ARABIC *Ritual n.* sufficiency; sufficient, satisfactory; non-binding (e.g. a religious obligation) ☞ ***farz-i kifaya***

BAS: кифая

KAZ: кіпая, кіфая

TAJ: кифоя

TAT: кифая

TUR: кифая

UYG: kipayä

UZB: кифоя

kiramin katibin كرام كاتبين PERSIAN *n.* angels who record the sins and good deeds of people

TAJ: киромин котибун

TAT: кирамен кятибин

UZB: киромин котибин

kitab كتاب ARABIC *n.* book, especially the four holy books (the Torah, Psalms, Gospels and the Qur'an) ☞ ***ahl-i kitab***

BAS: китап

KAR: китап

KAZ: кітап

KYR: китеп

TAJ: китоб

TAT: китап

TUR: китап

UYG: kitap

UZB: китоб

kuffar كفّار ARABIC *n.* unbelievers (plural form of kafir) ☞ ***kafir***

BAS: көффар

KAR: куппар

TAJ: куффор

TAT: көффар

UYG: kupar, kupurluq

UZB: куффор

kufr كفر ARABIC *n.* unbelief, unbelief in a single God, infidelity ☞ ***kafir***

BAS: көфөр ① *unbelief, blasphemy* ② *atheism, heresy* ③ *adj. sinful*

KAR: купур

KAZ: күпір, күпірлик, күфір

KYR: күпүр

TAJ: куфр

TAT: көфер, көферлек ① *unbelief* ② *atheism*

UYG: kupur

UZB: куфр

kufran كفران ARABIC *n.* unbelief (in God); ingratitude
KAR: купран
TAJ: куфрон
TAT: кафран
UYG: kupran
UZB: куфрон

kulah کلاه، کله PERSIAN *Sufism n.* conical hat worn by dervishes
KAR: кулах
TAJ: кулоҳ, кула
UZB: кулоҳ

kursi كرسى ARABIC *n.* throne (esp. of God); chair
BAS: көрси
KAR: курсы
KYR: көрсү
TAJ: курсӣ
UZB: курси

L

la havla لا حول ARABIC *Ritual np.* powerless, without strength (the first word of the prayer Everything is God's Will)
BAS: лә хәүлә, ләхәүлә
TAT: ля хәүлә

la ilaha illa allah va muhammadun rasulullah لا اله الا الله و محمد رصول لله *Ritual intj.* There is no God but Allah and Muhammad is his messenger (the Muslim profession of faith ☞ ***kalima, shahadat***
BAS: лә илаhи илла алла
KYR: ла илахи иллалла Мухаммед Расул Алла, лаилахаилалла, иллалда, илдалда
TAJ: ло илоҳо иллоллоҳ Муҳаммадин расулиллоҳ
TAT: лә иләhә иллал-лаh Мөхәммәдин Рәсүллүла
TUR: лә иләха иллелах Мухаммедүр ресулуллах
UZB: ла илоҳа иллаллаҳ Муҳаммадин расулиллоҳ, ло илоҳа иллоллоҳ Муҳаммадин расулиллоҳ

La makan لا مكان ARABIC *pn.* The Omnipresent (an epithet of God)
TAJ: ломакон
TAT: ля мәкян
UZB: ломакон

labbay لبّى ARABIC *intj.* yes, God! ☞ ***labbayka***
KAR: ләббәй, ләббай
KYR: лаббай, ляббай, ылаббай
TAJ: лаббай
UZB: лаббай

labbayka لبّيك ARABIC *Hajj intj.* invocation made while performing the hajj (lit. here I am)
BAS: ләбәйкә
KAR: ләббайка
KYR: лаббайка, лапайка, ылаббайка
TAJ: лабайка, лаббайк
TUR: ляббейка
UYG: läbbaykä
UZB: лаббайка

lafzan va ma'nan لفظاً و معناً ARABIC *Hadith adv.* literally and in meaning (e.g. a hadith where the prophet's literal words and his sense in undisputed)
TAT: ләфзан вә мәгънан
UZB: лафзан ва маънан

lafz-i kufr لفظ کفر PERSIAN *np.* blasphemy, blasphemous statement
TAJ: лафзи куфур
TAT: ләфзы көфер
UZB: лафзи куфр

Lahab لهب ARABIC *Qur'an pn.* alternate name of the 111th sura of the Qur'an ☞ ***Masad***
KAZ: Ләһеп сүресі
TAJ: сураи Лаҳаб
UZB: Лаҳаб сураси, Абу лаҳаб

lahid [1] لحد ARABIC *n.* tomb, grave
BAS: ләхет
KAR: ләхад
KYR: лахат
TAJ: лаҳад
TAT: ләхед
TUR: лахат
UYG: lähät
UZB: лаҳад

lahid [2] لحد ARABIC *Ritual n.* niche dug in a grave for placing the body
BAS: ләхет
KAR: ләхад
KAZ: лақат
TAJ: лаҳад
TAT: ләхед, ләхет
UYG: lähät
UZB: лаҳад

la'in لعن ARABIC *n.* curse, malediction ☞ ***la'nat***
BAS: ләгин
KAR: лайн, қарғыс

TAJ: лаин
TAT: лэгын
UYG: lä'in
UZB: лайн

la'nat لعنت ARABIC *n.* curse, malediction
BAS: лэғнэт
KAR: нэлет
KAZ: лағынат, лағынет, лағнат, нэлет
KYR: лаанат, ылаанат, наалат
TAJ: лаънат
TAT: лэгнэт
TUR: лагнат
UYG: lä'nat, länät
UZB: лаънат

lashkar-i Islam لشکر اسلام PERSIAN *Historical np.* warriors of Islam
KAR: Ислам лэшкерлэри
TAJ: Лашкари Ислом
UZB: Ислом лашкарлари

Lat لات ARABIC *Historical pn.* the name of an idol venerated by the pre-Islamic Meccans
KAR: Латманат ① *the name of an idol of the ancient Arabs* ② *the Buddhist God*
KYR: лат, лаат, ыланат
TAJ: лот
UZB: лот

Latif, al- اللطيف ARABIC *pn.* name of God: the Subtle
BAS: Латиф
KAR: Латип
TAJ: Латиф
TAT: Лэтыйф
TUR: ал-Латиф
UZB: Ал-Латиф

lavh لوح ARABIC *Qur'an n.* desk (esp. for reading the Qur'an)
BAS: лэүх
KYR: лавих
TAJ: лавҳ
TAT: лэүх
UZB: лавҳ

lavh al-mahfuz, al- اللوح المحفوظ ARABIC *np.* the Book of Fate (which is preserved in Heaven and in which the fates of all people are inscribed)
BAS: лэүх эл-мэхфүз
KYR: лоух махфуз
TAJ: лавхал маҳфуз
TAT: лэүхелмэхфуз, лэүхел-мэхфуз
UZB: лавҳал маҳфуз

Layl ليل ARABIC *Qur'an pn.* the 92nd sura of the Qur'an
KAR: Лайил суўреси
KAZ: Лэйіл сүресі
TAJ: сураи Лайл
TAT: Лэел сүрэсе
UYG: sürä Läyl
UZB: Вал-лайл сураси

Laylat al-Qadr ليلة القدر ARABIC *Ritual np.* the Night of Atonement, held on the 27th day of Ramazan
BAS: Ҡэҙыр төн
KAR: лэлатулкедр, лэйлэтулқэдир, қэдир түн, қэдир ақшамы
KAZ: қадыр кеші
KYR: кадыр түн
TAJ: лайлатул қадр
TAT: лэйлэт эл-кадр, кадер кичэсе
TUR: лейлят ал-кадр, гадыр гижеси
UYG: qadir, qadir kechisi
UZB: лайлатулқадр, лайлатилқадр

laza لظى ARABIC *n.* hellfire
TAJ: лазо
UZB: лазо

lifafa لفافه ARABIC *Ritual n.* portion of the burial shroud that covers the body from head to foot and is closed at the ends
KAZ: лифафа
TAJ: лифафа
TAT: лифафэ
TUR: лифафа
UZB: лифофа

lillah لله ARABIC *intj.* for God's sake
TAJ: лиллоҳ
TAT: лиллаһ
UZB: лиллаҳ

Luqman [1] لقمان ARABIC *pn.* Luqman, Qur'anic figure, renowned for proverbial wisdom
BAS: Лоҡман
KAR: Луқман
KAZ: Лұқман, Лұқпан
TAJ: Луқмон
TUR: Лукман, лукма Хеким
UYG: Lokhmen, Loqman, Loqman Häkim
UZB: Луқмон, Луқмони Ҳаким

Luqman [2] لقمان ARABIC *Qur'an pn.* the 31st sura of the Qur'an

KAR: Луқман суўреси
KAZ: Лұқман сүресі
TAJ: сураи Луқмон
UYG: sürä Loqman
UZB: Луқмон сураси

Lut لوط ARABIC *pn.* the prophet Lot
KAR: Лут
KAZ: Лұт
TAJ: Лут
TAT: Лут
TUR: Лут
UYG: Lut
UZB: Лут

M

ma favq al-tabi'at مافوق الطبيعت ARABIC *adj.* supernatural
TAJ: мафавқал табиат
TAT: ма фәвыкыттабигать
UZB: мафавқал табиат

ma'ad معاد *n.* the Afterlife
TAJ: мааъд
TAT: мәгад
UZB: маъад

Ma'arij معارج ARABIC *Qur'an n.* the 70th sura of the Qur'an
KAR: Маәриж суўреси
KAZ: Мағарыж сүресі
TAJ: сураи Маъориҷ
UYG: sürä Ma'arij
UZB: Маориж сураси

ma'asi معاصى ARABIC *n.* sinful deeds, sins
BAS: мәғаси
TAJ: маосӣ
TAT: мәгасый
UZB: маосий

ma'az allah معاذ الله ARABIC *intj.* God protect us, God help us (lit. the refuge is with God)
BAS: мәғаз алла
TAJ: маозоллоҳ
TAT: мәгаз алла
UZB: маозаллоҳ

ma'b مآب ARABIC *Ritual n.* place where prayers are performed (e.g. a mosque or other location); refuge
TAJ: маоб
TAT: мәаб
UZB: маоб

ma'bad معبد ARABIC *n.* place of worship, house of worship (Muslim or non-Muslim)
☞ ***'ibadatkhana***
BAS: мәғбәд
TAJ: маъбад
TAT: мәгъбәд
UZB: маъбад

ma'bud [1] معبود ARABIC *n.* that which is worshiped
BAS: мәғбүд
TAJ: маъбуд
TAT: мәгъбүд
UZB: маъбуд

ma'bud [2] معبود ARABIC *n.* idol, god (non-Muslim)
BAS: мағбүд
TAJ: маъбуд
TAT: мәгъбүд
UYG: mä'bud
UZB: маъбуд

maddah مدّاح ARABIC *n.* professional narrator of the lives of Islamic saints
BAS: мәҙхиәсе
KAR: маддах
TAJ: маддоҳ
TAT: мәддах *panegyrist*
UYG: maddah, madda
UZB: маддоҳ

maddiyun مادّيون ARABIC *Theology n.* materialists
KAR: маддылиқ
TAJ: моддӣ
TAT: маддиюн
UYG: maddiliq
UZB: моддиюн

madfan مدفن ARABIC *n.* cemetery, burial ground
TAJ: мадфан
TAT: мәдфән
UZB: мадфан

madhiya مدحيه ARABIC *n.* praise poem (esp. addressed to the prophet Muhammad)
BAS: мәҙхиә
TAJ: мадҳия
TAT: мәдхия
UYG: mädhiya
UZB: мадҳия

Madina مدينه ARABIC *pn.* Medina (the city)

BAS: Мәҙинә
KAR: Мәдийна, Мәдина
KAZ: Медине, Медіне
KYR: Медина
TAJ: Мадина
TAT: Мәдинә ① *the city of Medina* ② *city*
TUR: Медине
UYG: Madina
UZB: Мадина

Madina-yi munavvara مدينهٔ منوّره PERSIAN *np.* Medina the Illuminated ☞ ***munavvar***
TAJ: Мадинаи мунаввир
TAT: Мәдинаи мунәүвәрә
UZB: Мадинаи мунаввара

madini مدنى ARABIC *Qur'an adj.* Medinan, i.e., those suras revealed to the prophet Muhammad after the flight from Mecca
KAZ: мединелік
TAT: Мәдини, Мәдинәнеке
UZB: Мадиналик

madrasa مدرسه ARABIC *n.* school for advanced religious studies
BAS: мәҙрәсә
KAR: медресе
KAZ: медресе
KYR: медресе, медиресе
TAJ: мадраса
TAT: мәдрәсә
TUR: медресе
UYG: mädris, mädrisä
UZB: мадраса

maghasil مغاسل ARABIC *n.* place for washing the dead
TAJ: маосил
TAT: мәгасил
UZB: маосил

maghfirat مغفرت ARABIC *n.* forgiveness of sins
KAR: мәқпират
KAZ: мағфире
TAJ: мағфират
TAT: мәгъфирәт
UYG: mäghpirät
UZB: мағфират

maghlub مغلوب ARABIC *Law n.* defeated, conquered
BAS: мәғлүб
KAR: мәғлуп
TAJ: мағлуб
TAT: мәгълүб
UYG: mäghlub
UZB: мағлуб

maghrib مغرب ARABIC *Ritual n.* the obligatory prayer, that is performed right after the sun sets over the horizon. ☞ ***salat al-maghrib***
BAS: мәғрип
KAR: мағрип
TAJ: магриб
TAT: мәгриб
UYG: mäghrib
UZB: мағриб

mahafatullah محافت الله ARABIC *n.* the fear of God
TAJ: маҳафатулла
TAT: мәхафатуллаh
UZB: маҳафатулла

mahalla محله ARABIC *n.* neighborhood; congregation (of a mosque)
BAS: мәхәллә
KAR: мәҳәлле
KYR: маала
TAJ: маҳалла
TAT: мәхәллә
TUR: мәхелле
UYG: mähällä
UZB: маҳалла

maharim [1] محارم ARABIC *Law n.* that which is forbidden, that which is haram ☞ ***haram***
KAR: маҳрәм
TAJ: маҳрам
TAT: мәхарим
UYG: mähräm
UZB: маҳрам

maharim [2] محارم ARABIC *Law n.* close relatives to whom marriage to one another is forbidden
KAR: маҳрәм
TAJ: маҳрам
TAT: мәхарим
UYG: mähräm
UZB: маҳрам

mahbus محبوس ARABIC *Law n.* prisoner, convict
BAS: мәхбус
KAR: мәҳбус
TAJ: маҳбус
TAT: мәхбус
UYG: mähbus
UZB: маҳбус

Mahdi مهدی ARABIC *pn.* restorer of religion and justice before the end of the world
- BAS: Мәһди, Мәһҙи
- KAR: Мәҳди
- KAZ: Мәһди, Мәди
- KYR: Маади
- TAJ: Маҳди
- TAT: Мәһди
- UZB: Маҳди

mahfil محفل ARABIC *n.* meeting, congregation, assembly
- TAJ: маҳфил
- TAT: мәхфил
- UYG: mähpil
- UZB: маҳфил

mahkam محکم ARABIC *Qur'an adj.* incontrovertible (as a category of Quranic verse)
- KAR: мәҳкәм
- TAJ: маҳкам
- UYG: mähkäm
- UZB: маҳкам

mahkama محکمه ARABIC *Law n.* court, tribunal
- BAS: мәхкәмә
- KAR: мәҳкәма
- TAJ: маҳкама
- TAT: мәхкәмә
- UYG: mähkimä
- UZB: маҳкама

mahkama-yi kubra محکمهء کبره PERSIAN *np.* Judgment Day
- UZB: маҳкамаи кубро

mahkum محکوم ARABIC *Law adj.* judged; sentenced, convicted
- BAS: мәхкүм
- KAR: мәҳкум
- TAJ: маҳкум
- TAT: мәхкүм
- UYG: mähkum
- UZB: маҳкум

mahparast ماه پرست PERSIAN *n.* moon-worshipper; pagan
- KAR: мәҳпәрәст
- TAJ: мохпарастй
- TAT: мәһпәрәст
- UZB: моҳпараст

mahr [1] مهر ARABIC *n.* kindness, compassion
- KAR: мәхр
- KAZ: мейір, мейірім
- KYR: мээр, мейир
- TAJ: маҳр
- UYG: mähr, mehir
- UZB: маҳр

mahr [2] مهر ARABIC *Law n.* a share of property guaranteed to a woman after marriage; dowry, setting a dowry
- BAS: мәһәр
- KAR: маҳр
- KAZ: махр, мәһір
- TAJ: маҳр
- TAT: мәһәр
- TUR: мәхр, махр
- UYG: mähr
- UZB: маҳр

mahram محرم ARABIC *Law adj.* forbidden by Islamic law
- KAR: мәҳрем, мәрем
- TAJ: маҳрам
- TAT: мәхрәм
- TUR: мәхрем
- UYG: mähräm
- UZB: маҳрам *rule determining which family members a husband and a wife are permitted to openly*

mahrum محروم ARABIC *adj.* devoid; deprived
- BAS: мәхрүм
- KAR: маҳрум
- TAJ: маҳрум
- UYG: mährum
- UZB: маҳрум

mahshar محشر ARABIC *n.* Judgment Day ☞ ***qiyamat***
- BAS: мәхшәр
- KAR: мәқшер, маҳшер, маҳшер күни
- KAZ: махшар
- KYR: макшар, махшар, таңгы макшар, таңды макшар, махшар майдан. машыр, машар
- TAJ: маҳшар
- TAT: мәхшәр
- TUR: магшар
- UYG: mähshär
- UZB: маҳшар

mahshargah محشر گاه PERSIAN *n.* the location where Muslims will gather on Judgment Day
- KAR: маҳшер

TAJ: махшаргох, хашргох
UYG: mähshärgah
UZB: махшаргох

mahsi محسى ARABIC *Ritual n.* type of tall heelless boots worn by Muslim men inside mosques
KAR: мəгси
TAJ: масси
UZB: махси

Ma'ida مائده ARABIC *Qur'an pn.* the 5th sura of the Qur'an
KAR: Мəида сүўреси
KAZ: Мəида сүресі
TAJ: сураи Моида
TAT: Маидə сүрəсе, Əл-Маидə сүрəсе
UYG: sürä Ma'idä
UZB: Моида сураси

Majid, al- المجيد ARABIC *adj.* name of God: the Glorious
BAS: Мəжит
TAJ: Мачид
TAT: Мəҗид
TUR: ал-Межит
UYG: Mäjit
UZB: Ал-Мажид

majlis مجلس ARABIC *n.* gathering of Muslim scholars or Sufis
BAS: мəжлес
KAR: мажилис, мəжилис
KAZ: мəжіліс
KYR: мажилис
TAJ: мачлис
TAT: мəҗлес, мəҗлис
TUR: меҗлис
UYG: mäjlis
UZB: мажлис

majnun[1] مجنون ARABIC *Sufism n.* attracted (to God), possessed, insane; holy fool
BAS: мəжнүн
TAJ: мачнун
TAT: мəҗнүн
UZB: мажнун

majnun[2] مجنون ARABIC *Law n.* insane person (as a legal category)
KAR: мəжнүн
TAJ: мачнун
TAT: мəҗнүн
TUR: меҗнун
UZB: мажнун

majus مجوس ARABIC *n.* pagan (i.e. neither a Muslim, Christian, or Jew); Zoroastrian
BAS: мəжүс
KAR: мəджүс
KAZ: мəжүс
KYR: мажус
TAJ: мачус
TAT: мəҗүс
UYG: mäjus
UZB: маъжус

majusi مجوسى ARABIC *adj.* pagan (neither Muslim, Christian, or Jewish); Zoroastrian
BAS: мəжүси
KAR: мəджус
KAZ: мəжуси
KYR: мажусу
TAJ: мачусй
TAT: мəҗүси
UYG: mäjusi, mäjusiy
UZB: мажусий

majusiyat مجوسيت ARABIC *n.* paganism; Zoroastrianism
BAS: мəжүсилек
KAR: мəджусия
TAJ: мачусият
TAT: мəҗүсиять
UYG: mäjusiyät
UZB: маъжусият

majzub مجذوب ARABIC *Sufism adj.* ecstatic (as a stage on the Sufi path)
TAJ: мачзуб
TAT: мəҗзүб
UZB: мажзуб

makhdum مخدوم ARABIC *n.* master, high-ranking religious figure
BAS: мəхзүм *the son of a religious figure*
KAR: мақсым ① *Sufi* ② *son of an ishan*
TAJ: махдум
TAT: мəхдүм ① *master, high-ranking religious figure* ② *son of a religious figure*
UYG: mähdum
UZB: махдум, махсум, махзум

makhluq مخلوق ARABIC *n.* being, creature
BAS: мəхлуҡ, алла мəхлуғы
KAR: мақлуқ
KAZ: махлұқ

TAJ: махлуқ
TAT: мəхлук
UYG: mähluq
UZB: махлуқ

makhluqat مخلوقات ARABIC *n.* creatures, humans and animals
KAR: мақлуқат
KYR: маклукат
TAJ: махлукот
TAT: мəхлукат
UZB: махлуқот

Makka مکّه ARABIC *pn.* Mecca (the city)
BAS: Мəккə
KAR: Мəкке
KAZ: Мекке
KYR: Меке
TAJ: Макка
TAT: Мəккə
TUR: Мекге
UYG: Mäkkä, Bäkkä
UZB: Макка

Makka al-mukarrama مکّه المکرّمه ARABIC *pn.* Mecca the Venerated
TAT: Мəккə ал-мөкəррəмə
UYG: Mäkkä mukärrämä
UZB: Маккаю мукаррама

Makkatullah مکّة الله ARABIC *pn.* Mecca (the city)
KAR: Мəккетуллла
KYR: Маккатулла
TAJ: Маккатулло
UYG: Mäkkätulla
UZB: Маккатулло, Маккатуллоҳ

makki مکّی ARABIC *Qur'an adj.* Meccan, i.e., those suras revealed to the prophet Muhammad before the flight from Mecca
KAZ: меккелік
TAJ: маккӣ
TAT: Мəкки, Мəккəнеке
UZB: маккалик

makruh مکروه ARABIC *Law adj.* loathsome, not prohibited by Islamic law, but discouraged
BAS: мəкруһ
KAR: мəкруў, мəкируў
KAZ: мəкрук, мəкрҮк, мəкрҮһ
KYR: макирөө, мекирин, макрөө, макҮрөө, макҮр, мекирик
TAJ: макруҳ
TAT: мəкруһ
TUR: мекру
UYG: mäkru, mäkruh
UZB: макруҳ

makruh tahrima مکروه تحریمی ARABIC *Law np.* loathsome and approaching the unlawful
TUR: мекру тахрымы

makruh tanzih مکروه تنزیه ARABIC *Law np.* loathsome, but approaching the lawful
TUR: мекру тəнзих

maktab مکتب ARABIC *n.* Islamic primary school
BAS: мəктəп
KAR: мəктеп
KAZ: мектеп
KYR: мектеп
TAJ: мактаб
TAT: мəктəп
TUR: мектеп
UYG: maktap
UZB: мактаб

mal مال ARABIC *Law n.* possessions, property (as a legal category)
BAS: мал
KAR: мал
TAJ: мол
TAT: мал
TUR: мал
UYG: mal
UZB: мол

mala'ika ملائکه ARABIC *n.* angels
BAS: мəлаик
KAR: пəриште
TAJ: малоика, малоик
TAT: мəляикə
UYG: mala'ika
UZB: малойика

malak ملك ARABIC *n.* angel
BAS: мəлəк
KAR: малақ
TAJ: малак
TAT: мəлəк
TUR: мелек
UYG: malak
UZB: малак

malakut ملکوت ARABIC *n.* heavenly kingdom; the world of the angels
BAS: мəлəкҮт

KAZ: малакут
TAJ: малоикот
TAT: мәләкут
UYG: malakiyat
UZB: малоикот

malakutiyat ملكوتية ARABIC *n.* piety, purity
TAT: мәләкутиять

Malik[1] مالك ARABIC *pn.* name of an angel who is the keeper of Hell
BAS: Малик
KAR: Мәлийк
KAZ: Мәлік
KYR: Малик
TAJ: Малик
TAT: Малик
UYG: Mälik
UZB: Малик

malik[2] ملك ARABIC *n.* king, lord, sovereign
BAS: малик
KAR: малийк
TAJ: малик
TAT: малик
TUR: мәлик
UYG: mälik
UZB: малик

Malik, al- الملك ARABIC *pn.* name of God: the King
BAS: Малик
KAR: Малийк
KAZ: әл-Мәлік
TAJ: Малик
TAT: Малик
TUR: ал-Мәлик
UYG: Mälik
UZB: Ал-Малик

Malik al-Mulk مالك الملك ARABIC *pn.* name of God: the Ruler of the Kingdom
TAJ: Моликулмулк
TUR: Мәлик ал-Мүлк
UYG: Mälikul-Mulk
UZB: Моликул-Мулк

Maliki مالكي ARABIC *Law n.* adherent of the Maliki school of jurisprudence
KAR: Мәлики
KAZ: Мәлікші
TAJ: Моликӣ
TAT: Малики
UZB: Маликий

Malikiya مالكيه ARABIC *Law pn.* one of the four major schools of Sunni jurisprudence, founded by Malik b. Anas (d. 795 AD)
KAR: мәликия
KAZ: маликтік мазхаб
TAJ: Моликия
UZB: Маликия, Моликия

maliyat ماليت ARABIC *Taxation n.* tax
KAR: мәлғият
TAJ: молият
UYG: mäliyät
UZB: молият

Mal'un[1] ملعون ARABIC *pn.* the Accursed One (a name of Satan)
BAS: мәлғүн ① *the Accursed One (a name of Satan)* ② *cursed*
KAR: мәлун
KAZ: мәлғұн, малғұн
KYR: малгун ① *the Accursed One (a name of Satan)* ② *evil spirit*
TAJ: маълун
TAT: мәлгун, мәлгунь
TUR: мелгун
UYG: Mäl'un
UZB: маълун

mal'un[2] ملعون ARABIC *adj.* cursed, damned
BAS: мәлғүн
KAR: мәлун, мәлғүн
KAZ: малғұн
TAJ: малъун
TAT: мәлгун
UYG: mäl'un
UZB: малъун

mamat ممات ARABIC *n.* death
KAR: мәмат
TAJ: мамот
TAT: мәмат
UZB: мамот, ҳаёт-мамот

mamluk مملوك ARABIC *Law n.* slave, (lit. that which is owned)
BAS: мәмлүк
TAJ: мамлук, ғулом
TAT: мәмлүк
UYG: mämluk
UZB: мамлук

ma'mur مأمور ARABIC *Law n.* that which is ordered, that which is good; licit (as a category of actions)

KAR: мәмур
TAJ: маъмур
TAT: мәэмүр
UZB: маъмур

ma'nan معناً ARABIC *Law adv.* in sense, in idea (e.g. a hadith where the prophet's literal words are unclear, but his sense is undisputed)
☞ ***lafzan va ma'nan***
TAT: мәгънан
UZB: маънан

manaqib مناقب ARABIC *n.* qualities, miracles (esp. of Sufis or other learned figures)
TAJ: мунақиб
TAT: мәнакыйб
UZB: мунақиб, маноқиб

manaqibnama مناقبنامه PERSIAN *Sufism n.* literary work describing the qualities and miracles of a Muslim saint, hagiography
TAT: мәнакыйбнамә
UZB: маноқибнома

manara مناره ARABIC *n.* minaret (of a mosque)
BAS: манара
KAR: минара
KAZ: мұнара
KYR: мунар, мунара, бурана
TAJ: минора
TAT: манара
TUR: минара
UYG: munärä, minara, munar
UZB: минора

manasik مناسك ARABIC *Hajj n.* rites, custom (for those performing the hajj)
TAT: мәнасик
UZB: манасиқ

Manat منات ARABIC *Historical pn.* the name of an idol of the ancient Arabs
KAR: Латманат ① *the name of an idol of the ancient Arabs* ② *the Buddhist God*
KYR: Манат, Лат-Манат, Ыланат
TAJ: Манот
TAT: Мәнат
UYG: Manat
UZB: Манот

ma'navi معنوى ARABIC *adj.* speculative; pertaining to meaning; abstract
TAJ: маънавӣ
TAT: мәгънәви
UZB: маънавий

ma'naviya معنويه ARABIC *Theology n.* values that can be inferred, i.e., a category of qualities attributed to God
TAT: мәгънәвия
UZB: маънавият

manfur منفور ARABIC *n.* disgusting, repulsive (i.e. morally)
BAS: мәнфүр
KAR: мәнпур
TAJ: манфур
TAT: мәнфур
UYG: mänpur
UZB: манфур

manhi منهى ARABIC *Law adj.* forbidden, illicit (as a category of actions)
TAJ: манҳи
TAT: мәнһи
TUR: менхи
UZB: манҳу

mani' منيع ARABIC *Ritual adj.* insurmountable obstacle, impediment (e.g. a status which forbids participation in specific ritual activity)
TUR: меньıг
UZB: маниъ

Mani', al- المانع ARABIC *n.* name of God: the Preventer
KAR: Мәний
TAJ: Монӣ
TAT: Манигъ
TUR: ал-Мани
UYG: Mäniy
UZB: Ал-Моний

mankuha منكوحه ARABIC *n.* wife, (legally) married woman
TAJ: манкуҳа
TAT: мәнкүхә
UYG: mänkuha
UZB: манкуҳа

mansak منسك ARABIC *n.* place for prayer and performing sacrifice
KAR: масәк
TAJ: мансак
UZB: мансоқ

manshur منشور ARABIC *Historical n.* license (during the imperial Russian period, allowing an imam or mu'azzin to serve in a specific mosque) (restricted to the Volga-Ural region and Kazakhstan) ☞ ***ukaz***

BAS: мәншүр

TAT: мәншүр

mantiq منطق ARABIC *n.* logic (as a field of Islamic science)

BAS: мантик

KAR: мәнтиқ

KAZ: мантық

TAJ: мантиқ

TAT: мантыйк

UYG: mäntiq

UZB: мантиқ

mantiqi منطقی ARABIC *n.* logician, dialectician

BAS: мантиксы

KAR: мәнтиқий

TAJ: мантиқӣ

TAT: мәнтыйкый

UYG: mäntiqiy

UZB: мантиқий

manzur منذور ARABIC *n.* promised, vowed (to God) ☞ ***nazr***

BAS: мәнзур

KAR: манзур

TAJ: манзур

TAT: мәнзур

UZB: манзур

maqam مقام ARABIC *Sufism n.* stage in a Sufi's spiritual path ☞ ***silk, salik***

BAS: маҡам

KAR: мәқәм, мақам

KAZ: мақам

KYR: мукам

TAJ: мақом

TAT: мәкам

UYG: muqam

UZB: мақом

Maqam-i Ibrahim مقام ابراهیم PERSIAN *Hajj pn.* the Tomb of Abraham (at Mecca)

KAR: Ыбрайым мәқәмы

TAJ: мақоми Иброҳим

TAT: мәкаме Ибраһим

UZB: мақоми Иброҳим

maqbara[1] مقبره ARABIC *n.* tomb, grave; mausoleum

BAS: мәкбәрә

KAR: мазар

TAJ: мақбара

TAT: мәкъбәрә

UYG: mäqbärä

UZB: мақбара

maqbara[2] مقبره ARABIC *n.* cemetery, graveyard

KAR: мазар

TAJ: мақбара

TAT: мәкъбәрә

UYG: mäqbärä

UZB: мақбара

maqsura مقصوره ARABIC *n.* private enclosure in a mosque for a sovereign; enclosure around a grave

KAZ: мақсура

TAJ: мақсура

TAT: мәкъсурә *a woman prohibited from leaving the house*

UZB: мақсура

maqtuʿ مقطوع ARABIC *Hadith adj.* intersected (a category of hadith which is traced to a companion of a companion of the Prophet Muhammad)

TAT: мәкътуг

UZB: мақтуъ

maqtul مقتول ARABIC *Law adj.* killed, murdered

TAJ: мақтул

TAT: мәкътул

UZB: мақтул, қатл этилган

maʿraka معرکه ARABIC *Ritual n.* memorial service, memorial repast; battlefield

KAR: мәрака

TAJ: маърака

TAT: мәгърәкә *battlefield*

UZB: маърака

marasim مراسم ARABIC *n.* ceremonies, rituals

BAS: мәрасим

KAR: мәрасим

TAJ: маросим

TAT: мәрасим

UYG: murasim

UZB: маросим

mardud مردود ARABIC *Hadith adj.* rejected, refused (i.e. an untrustworthy hadith)

TAJ: мардуд

TAT: мәрдуд

UZB: мардуд

marfuʿ مرفوع ARABIC *Hadith adj.* exalted (a category of hadith which is attributed to the prophet, regardless of whether the isnad is complete or not)

TAT: мәрфугъ

UZB: марфуъ

marfu‘ hukman مرفوع حكماً ARABIC *Hadith np.* legally considered to derive directly from the prophet Muhammad (as a category of hadith) ☞ ***marfu’***
UZB: марфуъ ҳукман

marfu‘ sarihan مرفوع صريحاً ARABIC *Hadith np.* explicitly clear (as a category of hadith that derives directly from the prophet Muhammad) ☞ ***marfu’***
UZB: марфуъ сариҳан

marhamat مرحمت ARABIC *n.* kindness, benevolence
BAS: мәрхәмәт
KAR: мәрҳәмат
KAZ: мәрхамет
KYR: маркабат, маркамат
TAJ: марҳамат
TAT: мәрхәмәт
TUR: мерхемет
UYG: märhämät
UZB: марҳамат

marhum مرحوم ARABIC *adj.* deceased, late
BAS: мәрхүм
KAR: марҳум
KAZ: марқұм
KYR: маркум, маркун
TAJ: марҳум
TAT: мәрхүм
UYG: märhum
UZB: марҳум

ma‘rifat [1] معرفت ARABIC *n.* religious knowledge, spiritual knowledge, education
BAS: мәғрифәт
KAR: мәрипат, марапат
KAZ: мағрифат
KYR: магрифат, марифат, магрыбыт
TAJ: маърифат
TAT: мәгърифәт
TUR: марифет
UYG: märipät
UZB: маърифат

ma‘rifat [2] معرفت ARABIC *Sufism n.* spiritual knowledge (a stage on the Sufi path)
TAJ: маърифат
TAT: мәгърифәт
UZB: маърифат

marsiya مرثيه ARABIC *n.* elegy (originally, and primarily, performed to commemorate the martyrdom of Husayn)
BAS: мәрҫиә
KAR: мәрсия
TAJ: марсия, марсият
TAT: мәрсия
UYG: märsiya
UZB: марсия

ma‘ruf معروف ARABIC *Law n.* knowledgeable (in an Islamic science)
BAS: мәғруф
KAZ: мағруф
TAJ: маъруф
UYG: ma’rup
UZB: маъруф

Marva مروه ARABIC *Hajj pn.* a mound near the Ka'bah that is referred to in the Quran as one of the symbols of Allah
KAR: Мәрва
KAZ: Марв, ал-Маруа
TAJ: Марва
TAT: Мәрвә, Мәрвә тауы
UYG: Marwa, Märwä
UZB: Марва

Maryam [1] مريم ARABIC *pn.* Mary, the mother of the prophet Jesus
BAS: Мәрйәм Ана
KAR: Бийбимерям, Мәрьям
KAZ: Мәриям
KYR: Бүбү Мариям
TAJ: бибӣ Марям
TAT: Мәрьям
TUR: Меръем
UYG: Märyäm
UZB: Бибимарям, Бимимайрам

Maryam [2] مريم ARABIC *Qur'an pn.* the 19th sura of the Qur'an
KAR: Мәриям суўреси
KAZ: Мерям сүресі
TAJ: сураи Марям
TAT: Мәрьям сүрәсе, Мәрйәм
TUR: сураи Меръем
UYG: sürä Märyäm
UZB: Марям сураси

Masad مسد ARABIC *Qur'an n.* the 111th sura of the Qur'an
KAR: Масад суўреси
KAZ: Мәсәд сүресі
TAJ: сураи Масад

UYG: Masad süräsi, sürä Mäsäd
UZB: Масад сураси

mas'ala مسئله ARABIC *n.* issue discussed by religious scholars
BAS: мәсьәлә
KAR: мәсәла
TAJ: масали
TAT: мәсьәлә
TUR: меселе
UYG: mäsilä
UZB: масала

masbuq مسبوق ARABIC *Ritual n.* person who was late to public prayer but who finished first raka't privately with the imam (i.e. who arrived after the first rak'at)
TAJ: масбук
TAT: мәсбук
UZB: масбуқ

mashaallah ما شا الله ARABIC *intj.* Wonderful! (lit. What wonders God has willed)
BAS: машалла
KYR: машаалла
TAJ: мошолло
TAT: машалла, мәшә алла
UYG: masha'alla
UZB: мошоллоҳ

mashayikh مشايخ ARABIC *Sufism n.* ishans, Sufi masters, shaykhs (collectively) ☞ ***ishan, shaykh***
KAR: масайиқ *shrine, Muslim saint's tomb*
KAZ: машайық, машайих
KYR: машайык, машаяк ① *chief figure among Sufis* ② *title for a high ranking religious figure*
TAJ: машойих
TAT: мәшаих
UYG: mashayikh
UZB: машойих

mashhad مشهد ARABIC *n.* tomb of a martyr; place of martyrdom; a city in Iran where the tomb of Imam Riza is located
KAR: мәшқад
KAZ: машхад
KYR: машат
TAJ: машхад
TAT: мәшхәд
UYG: mashhad *theologian jurist teacher*
UZB: машҳад

mashhadi مشهدی ARABIC *Ritual n.* title of a person who has performed the pilgrimage to the tomb of Imam Riza in the Iranian city of Mashhad
TAJ: машхадӣ
TUR: мешхеди
UZB: машҳадий

mashhur مشهور ARABIC *Hadith adj.* tradition narrated by at least three sources (as a category of hadith)
KAR: мәшқур
TAT: мәшһүр
UZB: машҳур

mashkuk مشكوك ARABIC *Law adj.* doubtful (i.e. the classification of an action or status as not forbidden or unclean, but nevertheless doubtful)
TAT: мәшкүк
TUR: мешкук
UZB: машкук

mashrab مشرب ARABIC *Sufism n.* dervish, Sufi; school of learning (lit. source)
TAJ: машраб
TAT: мәшрәб
UZB: машраб

mashru' مشروع ARABIC *Law adj.* licit, legal, allowed by the shari'a
KAR: мәшру
TAJ: машрух
TAT: мәшруг
UYG: mashru
UZB: машру

mashvarat مشورت ARABIC *n.* meeting, consultation, deliberation
TAJ: машоварат
UYG: mashparat
UZB: машварат

Masih [1] مسيح ARABIC *pn.* Messiah, epithet of the prophet Jesus ☞ ***'Isa***
KAR: Мәсих
KAZ: Мәсих
TAJ: Масих
TAT: Мәсих
UZB: Масиҳ, Исои масиҳ

masih [2] مسيح ARABIC *Ritual n.* wiping with the hands (during ablutions)
BAS: мәсих
KAR: мәсих
KAZ: мәсих
TAJ: масих

TAT: мэсих
TUR: месих
UZB: масиҳ

masihi مسيحى ARABIC *n.* Christian
KAR: мэсихи
TAJ: масиҳи
TAT: мэсихи
UZB: масиҳи

masjid مسجد ARABIC *n.* mosque
BAS: мэсет
KAR: мешит
KAZ: мешит
KYR: мечит
TAJ: масчид
TAT: мэчет, мэсжид, мэсжед
TUR: метжит, месжид
UYG: machit, michit
UZB: мачит

Masjid al-Aqsa, al- المسجد الاقسا ARABIC *pn.* the Mosque in Jerusalem located on the Temple Mount
KAR: мешит Акса
TAJ: масчиди Акco
TAT: Мэсжидел Әкъса
UYG: Mäsjidi Äqsa
UZB: Ал-Масжид ал-Акco, мачити Акco

Masjid al-Haram, al- المسجد الحرام ARABIC *pn.* the Mosque in Mecca (including the Ka'ba)
KAR: мешит Харам
TAJ: Масчиди Харам
TAT: Мэсжиде хэрам, Мэсжиделхэрэм
UYG: Mäsjidi häram
UZB: Ал масчит ал-Харам, Харам мачити

mast مست PERSIAN *Sufism adj.* drunk, intoxicated (by divine love)
KAR: мэс
TAJ: маст
TAT: мэст
TUR: мест
UZB: маст

ma'sum معصوم ARABIC *adj.* innocent, sinless
BAS: мэғсүм
TAJ: маъсум
TAT: мэгъсум
UYG: ma'sum, mä'sum
UZB: маъсум

matam ماتم ARABIC *Ritual n.* mourning, grief; the mourning ceremony
BAS: матэм
KAR: матам
TAJ: мотам
TAT: матэм
TUR: матам
UYG: matäm, mätäm
UZB: мотам

matamzada ماتمزاده PERSIAN *Ritual n.* one who is in mourning
KAR: матамзада
TAJ: мотамзада
TAT: матэмзадэ
UYG: matämlik
UZB: мотамзада

Matin, al- المتين ARABIC *pn.* name of God: the Firm
KAR: Метин
TAJ: Метин
TAT: Мэтин
TUR: ал-Матин
UYG: Metin
UZB: Ал-Метин

matruka متروكه ARABIC *Law n.* woman who has been given a divorce (by her husband)
BAS: мэтрүкэ *estate, property left by a deceased person*
TAJ: матрука
TAT: мэтрүкэ
UZB: матрука

Ma'un ماعون ARABIC *Qur'an pn.* the 107th sura of the Qur'an
KAR: Мәуўн сүўреси
KAZ: Мағұн сүресі
TAJ: сураи Моъун
UYG: Mä'uwn süräsi, sürä Ma'un
UZB: Моъувн сураси

mavhum موهوم ARABIC *adj.* abstract, imaginary, fantastic
KAR: мәўхум
TAJ: мавҳум
TAT: мэүһүм
UYG: mäwhüm
UZB: мавҳум

mavhumat موهومات ARABIC *n.* superstition, prejudice
TAJ: мавҳумот
TAT: мэүһүмат
UZB: мавҳумот

mav'iza موعظه ARABIC *n.* sermon, preaching
TAJ: мавъиза

TAT: мәүгазә
UZB: мавоза, мавъиза

mavjud موجود ARABIC *Theology adj.* existent
BAS: мәүжүд
KAR: мәўжуд
KAZ: мәужүд
TAJ: мавҷуд
TAT: мәүҗүд
UYG: mäwjud, mäwjut
UZB: мавжуд

mavjudat موجودات ARABIC *Theology n.* existence (as a whole), all things created (collectively)
BAS: мәүжүдәт
KAR: мәўжудат
TAJ: мавҷудот
TAT: мәүҗүдат
UYG: mäwjudiyät, mäwjudat
UZB: мавжудот

Mavla [1] مولا ARABIC *n.* name of God: the Master
BAS: мәүлә
KAR: мәўла
TAJ: мавло
TAT: мәүла
UYG: mäwlä
UZB: мавло

mavla [2] مولى ARABIC *n.* master; client
BAS: мәүлә
KAR: мәўла
TAJ: мавло
TAT: мәүла
UYG: mäwlä
UZB: мавло *master servant a person of slave origin who does not have tribal protection*

mavlana مولانا ARABIC *n.* honorific title of a learned Muslim (literally "our master")
KAR: мәўлана
TAJ: мавлоно
TAT: мәүләна
UYG: mävlänä
UZB: мавлоно

mavlavi مولوى ARABIC *n.* learned Muslim
KAR: мәўлаўи
TAJ: мавлавӣ
TAT: мәүләви
UZB: мавлавий

Mavlid [1] مولد ARABIC *Ritual n.* the time, location or commemoration of the birth of a holy person, esp. Muhammad (12th of Rabi' al-avval)
BAS: мәүлит бәйрамы ① *festival commemorating the birthday of the prophet Muhammad* ② *prayer performed at this festival*
KAR: мәўлит
KAZ: мәуліт
KYR: моолут
TAJ: мавлид, мавлуд
TAT: мәүлид, мәүлүд, гайдел мәүлид
TUR: мавлид, маулид, мөвлит
UYG: mäwlut, mäwlud
UZB: мавлид, мавлуд

mavlid [2] مولد ARABIC *n.* poem celebrating the birth of the Prophet Muhammad
KAR: мәўлит
TAJ: мавлид
TAT: мәүлид
UZB: мавлид

mavliyat ماوليت ARABIC *n.* ceremonies (birthdays of prophets, holy days, etc.)
UZB: мовлият

mavqiʿ موقع ARABIC *n.* place, goal (of a believer's religious development)
BAS: мәүкиғ
TAJ: мавқеъ
TAT: мәүкыйг
UZB: мавқе

mavquf موقوف ARABIC *Hadith adj.* interrupted (a category of hadith that can only be traced as far back as one of the companions of the Prophet Muhammad)
TAT: мәүкуф
UZB: мавқуф

mavzuʿ موضوع ARABIC *Hadith adj.* absolutely false, invented (as a category of hadith)
TAJ: мавзу
TAT: мәүзугъ
UZB: мавзуъ

maʿyub معيوب ARABIC *Law n.* guilty, culpable
BAS: мәғъюб
TAJ: маъюб
TAT: мәгъюб
UZB: маъюб

mayyit ميّت ARABIC *n.* deceased, body, corpse
BAS: мәйет
KAR: мәйит
KAZ: мәйіт

KYR: мейит
TAJ: майит
TAT: мэет
TUR: мейит
UYG: meyit
UZB: майит

mazalim مظالم ARABIC *n.* cruelties, oppressions, injustices
KAR: мәзлум
KAZ: мазалим

mazar مزار ARABIC *n.* tomb, grave; Muslim saint's tomb; cemetery, graveyard
BAS: маҙар
KAR: мазар
KAZ: мазар
KYR: мазар
TAJ: мазор
TAT: мәзар
TUR: мазар
UYG: mazar
UZB: мозор

mazaristan مزارستان PERSIAN *n.* cemetery, graveyard
KAR: мазарстан
TAJ: мазористон
TAT: мәзарстан
TUR: мазарыстан, мазарыстанлык
UYG: mazaristan
UZB: мозористон

mazarkarda مزاركرده PERSIAN *n.* shrine, sacred tomb
KYR: мазаркерде
TAJ: мазоркарда

mazhab [1] مذهب ARABIC *Law n.* school of Islamic jurisprudence; doctrine, teaching
☞ ***hanafi, maliki, hanbali, shafi'i***
BAS: мәҙһап
KAR: мәзҳәп
KAZ: мазһаб
KYR: мазап, мусап
TAJ: мазҳаб
TAT: мәзһәб
TUR: мезхеп, мессеп
UYG: mäzhäp
UZB: мазҳаб

mazhab [2] مذهب ARABIC *n.* sect; religion
BAS: мәҙһап
KAR: мәзхеп
KYR: мазап, мусап
TAJ: мазҳаб
TAT: мәзһәб
TUR: мезхеп, мессеп
UYG: mäzhäp
UZB: мазҳаб

mazlum مظلوم ARABIC *adj.* oppressed, tyrannized
KAR: мәзлум
KAZ: мазлұм
TAJ: мазлум
TAT: мәзлум
UYG: mäzlum
UZB: мазлум

mazmaza مضمضه ARABIC *Ritual n.* washing of the mouth (as part of the ghusl)
TAT: мәзмәзә
UZB: мазмаза

maznib مذنب ARABIC *n.* sinner
TAJ: мазнуб
TAT: мөзниб
UZB: мазнуб

ma'zun مأذون ARABIC *n.* person authorized by a qazi to perform marriages and administer divorces
TAJ: маъзун
TAT: мәэзүн
UZB: маъзун

ma'zur معذور ARABIC *Ritual n.* one who is exempt from specific ritual obligations
TAT: мәгъзүр
TUR: магзур
UZB: маъзур

mihrab محراب ARABIC *n.* conical niche in a mosque placed in the direction of Mecca
BAS: михрап, михраб ① *conical niche in a mosque placed in the direction of Mecca* ② *shrine*
KAR: михрап
KAZ: мұхраб, михраб
KYR: михрап
TAJ: меҳроб
TAT: михраб ① *conical niche in a mosque placed in the direction of Mecca* ② *shrine*
TUR: мэхрап, мэхраб
UYG: mehrap, mihrab
UZB: меҳроб

Mika'il ميكائل، ميكال ARABIC *pn.* the Archangel Michael
KAR: Микәйыл
KAZ: Микәйіл, Микаил, Микал, Михаил

KYR: Мекейил, Омейил
TAJ: Микаил
TAT: Микаил
TUR: Микайыл, Мыкайыл
UYG: Mikäil, Mika'il
UZB: Микоил

milad میلاد ARABIC *n.* the birth of the prophet Jesus; Christian era, Common era, A.D.
BAS: милад, бәндәл милад
KAR: милэд
KAZ: милад
TAJ: милод
TAT: миляд
TUR: милад
UYG: milad
UZB: милод

miladi میلادی ARABIC *adj.* pertaining to the Christian era, Common era, A.D.
BAS: милади
KAR: милэди
TAJ: милодй
TAT: миляди
TUR: милады
UYG: miladi
UZB: милодий

milk ملك ARABIC *Law n.* private property (as a category in Islamic law) ☞ ***mulk***
BAS: милек
KAR: мулк
KAZ: милк
KYR: мүлк
TAJ: мулк
TAT: милек
UYG: mülük
UZB: мулк

Mina منى ARABIC *Hajj pn.* a sacred valley in the hills east of Mecca in which part of the ceremony of the pilgrimage takes place
KAR: Мына
KAZ: Мина
TAJ: Мина
TAT: Мина
TUR: Мина
UYG: Mina
UZB: Мина

minbar منبر ARABIC *Ritual n.* pulpit from which a khatib performs his sermon
BAS: мөнбәр
KAR: минбер
KAZ: мінбе, мінбар
KYR: минбар
TAJ: минбар
TAT: минбәр
TUR: меммер, мүнбер
UYG: munbar, minbar, munbär
UZB: минбар

Miqat میقات ARABIC *Hajj pn.* name of a location on the way to Mecca where pilgrims don the ihram and declare their intention to perform the hajj
TAT: микат
UZB: миқот

mir میر PERSIAN *n.* commander, leader ☞ ***amir***
BAS: мир
KAR: мыр
TAJ: мир
TAT: мир
UYG: mir
UZB: мир

mi'raj معراج ARABIC *Ritual pn.* ascent to Heaven, especially the Prophet Muhammad's miraculous journey to heaven (the 27th of Rajab) ☞ ***Isra***
BAS: миғраж, миғраж көнө
KAR: мираж
KAZ: мираж, меғраж
TAJ: меъроҷ
TAT: мигъраҗ
TUR: мираж, миграж
UYG: miräj, miraj
UZB: меърож ① *the prophet Muhammad's ascent to heaven* ② *place of ascension ladder especially ladder by which souls and angels ascend to heaven*

mi'rajiya معراجيّه ARABIC *n.* type of poem recounting the Prophet Muhammad's miraculous ascent to Heaven
KAR: миражия
TAJ: меъроҷия
TAT: мигъраҗия
UZB: меърожия

mi'rajnama معراجنامه PERSIAN *n.* type of poem recounting the Prophet Muhammad's miraculous ascent to Heaven
KAR: миражнэма
TAJ: меъроҷнома

TAT: мигъраждамә
UZB: меърожнома

miras میراث ARABIC *Law n.* inheritance, patrimony (as determined by Islamic inheritance law); cultural and religious patrimony of a people
BAS: мираç
KAR: мийрас
KAZ: мийрас
KYR: мурас, мирас
TAJ: мерос
TAT: мирас
TUR: мирас
UYG: miras
UZB: мерос

miraskhur میراث خور PERSIAN *n.* inheritor, heir ☞ ***varis***
KAR: мийрасхор
KAZ: мийрасхор
TAJ: меросхӯр
TAT: мирас хор
UYG: miraskhor
UZB: меросхўр

mirghazab میر غضب PERSIAN *n.* executioner, hangman
TAJ: мириғазаб
UYG: mirghazap
UZB: мирғазаб

mirza میرزا PERSIAN *n.* scribe; clerk
BAS: мырҙа, мирза
KAR: мирза
TAJ: мирзо
TAT: мирза
UYG: mirzä, mirza
UZB: мирза, мирзо

misaq میثاق ARABIC *n.* pact made between God and mankind shortly after Creation; the time of Creation
BAS: әлмисаҡ
KAR: әлмысак, әлимсақ
KAZ: әлмисақ
KYR: алмустак
TAJ: алмисоқ
TAT: мисак
UZB: алмисоқ

miskin مسکین ARABIC *Law n.* destitute person; homeless person; a category of people defined as possessing only a single day's sustenance and possessing the ability to receive alms; self-reference made by the author of a literary work
KAR: мискин
KYR: мискин
TAJ: мискин
TAT: мискин, мескен
TUR: мисгин
UYG: miskin
UZB: мискин

misr [1] مصر ARABIC *Law n.* city (in a legal sense, a city possessing requisite size for specific rituals to be legally conducted) ☞ ***ghayr-i misr***
KAR: миср
TAJ: миср
TAT: мисыр
TUR: мусур, мусыр
UYG: misir
UZB: миср, мисри муаззам

Misr [2] مصر ARABIC *pn.* Egypt
KAR: Миср
KAZ: Мысыр
KYR: Мисир ① *Egypt* ② *blessed location*
TAJ: Миср
TAT: Мисыр
TUR: Мүсүр
UYG: Misir
UZB: Миср

misvak [1] مسواك ARABIC *Ritual n.* cleaning the teeth, which constitutes the first part of the vuzu' ablution ritual
BAS: мисүәк
KAR: мисўәк, мәсиўек
KAZ: місуак
KYR: мисибек, мисбек
TAJ: мисвок
TAT: мисвәк
TUR: месвах
UYG: miswak
UZB: мисвок

misvak [2] مسواك ARABIC *Ritual n.* toothpick; toothbrush (esp. used for ablutions)
BAS: мисүәк
KAR: мисўәк, мәсиўек
KAZ: місуак
KYR: мисибек, мисбек
TAJ: мисвок
TAT: мисвәк
TUR: месвах

UYG: miswak
UZB: мисвок

mizan [1] ميزان ARABIC *n.* scales used to weigh sins on Judgment Day
KAR: мизән
TAJ: мизон
TAT: мизан
UZB: мизон, мезон

mizan [2] ميزان ARABIC *n.* Judgment Day
BAS: мизан көнө, миҙам көнө
KAR: мийзан
TAJ: мизан
UZB: мезон

Mizan [3] مزان ARABIC *pn.* Libra, 8th month of the Hidjri Solar year
BAS: Мизан
KAR: мийзан
KAZ: Мизан
TAJ: Мизон
TAT: Мизан
UYG: Mizan
UZB: Мезон

mizana مئذنة، ميذنة ARABIC *n.* minaret
KAR: мийзана
TAJ: мизана
UYG: mizänä
UZB: мезана

mu'abbir معبّر ARABIC *n.* interpreter of dreams
BAS: мөғаббир
TAT: мөгаббир
UZB: муаббир

Mu'akhkhir, al- المؤخّر ARABIC *pn.* name of God: the Deferrer
TAJ: Муоъхҳир
TAT: Мөәххәр
TUR: ал-Мувахxир
UYG: Muähhir
UZB: Ал-Муъоҳҳир

mu'akkad مؤكّد ARABIC *Law adj.* confirmed, corroborated (as a classification of sunnat)
KAZ: мү'әккад
TAJ: муаққад
TAT: мөәккәд, мөъәккәт
TUR: муәккет
UZB: муаққад
mu'akkada ☞ ***sunnat mu'akkada***

mu'akkal مؤكّل ARABIC *n.* angel ☞ ***farishta***
KYR: мубакил, мукил
UYG: mu'äkkäl
UZB: муаккал

mu'allif مؤلّف ARABIC *n.* author (of a composition)
BAS: мөәллиф
TAJ: муаллиф
TAT: мөәллиф
UYG: mu'allip
UZB: муаллиф

mu'allim معلّم ARABIC *n.* teacher, instructor
BAS: мөғәллим
KAR: муғаллим
KAZ: мұғалім
KYR: мугалим
TAJ: муаллим
TAT: мөгаллим
TUR: мугаллим
UYG: mu'ällim
UZB: муаллим

mu'amalat معاملات ARABIC *Law n.* civil jurisprudence, one of the five formal divisions of Islamic law governing interpersonal relations
TAJ: муомалат
TAT: мөгамәлә
UYG: mu'amilä
UZB: муомалат

mu'arrikh مؤرّخ ARABIC *n.* historian
BAS: мөүәррих, тарихсы
KAR: тарийхшы
KAZ: тарихшы
KYR: тарыхчы
TAJ: муаррих
TAT: мөәррих, тарихчы
UZB: муаррих

Mu'avvizatan معوّذتان ARABIC *Qur'an pn.* collective title for the last two suras of the Qur'an, suras 113 and 114
UZB: ал-Муаввазатони

Mu'avvizatayn معوّذتين ARABIC *Qur'an pn.* collective title for the last two suras of the Qur'an, suras 113 and 114
TAT: Мәгүзәтәйн
UZB: муъаввизатайн

mu'azzin مؤذّن ARABIC *n.* one who calls the faithful to prayer ☞ ***azan***

BAS: мэзин
KAR: мүэзин, мэзин
KAZ: муэзин, муаззин, азаншы
KYR: мазин, азанкеш
TAJ: муаззин
TAT: мөэззин, азанчы
TUR: муэззин, мүъүззен, азанчы
UYG: mäzin
UZB: муаззин

mubah مباح ARABIC *Law n.* permissible, neither prescribed nor forbidden by Islamic law
BAS: мөбах
KAR: мубәх
KAZ: мубах
TAJ: мубоҳ
TAT: мөбах
TUR: мубах
UZB: мубоҳ

mubahasa مباحثه ARABIC *Law n.* debate, discussion (e.g. of a fatva)
KAR: мубәхиса
TAJ: мубоҳиса
TAT: мөбахәсә
UYG: mubahisä
UZB: мубоҳаса

mubarak مبارك ARABIC *adj.* blessed, congratulated
BAS: мөбәрәк
KAR: мүбәрек
KAZ: мүбарак
KYR: мубарек, маарек, муварек, мубайрек
TAJ: муборак
TAT: мөбарәк
UYG: mubaräk
UZB: муборак

mubaraza مبارزه ARABIC *n.* fighting, combat (esp. for he faith)
KAR: мубәриза
TAJ: мубориза
TAT: мөбарәзә
UYG: mubarizä
UZB: мубораза

mubariz مبارز ARABIC *n.* fighter, warrior (esp. for the faith)
BAS: мөбариҙ
KAR: муғбәриз
TAJ: мубориз
TAT: мөбариз
UYG: mubäriz
UZB: мубориз

mubashir مباشر ARABIC *Taxation n.* tax collector, inspector
KAR: муғбәшыр
TAJ: мубошир
TAT: мөбашир *bureaucrat, supervisor*
UYG: mubashir
UZB: мубошир

mubashshir مبشّر ARABIC *n.* missionary, one who spreads the faith
KAR: муғбәшыр
TAJ: мубошшир
TAT: мөбәшшир
UZB: мубошшир

mubassir مبصّر superintendent (of a mosque or madrasa), assistant (to a senior religious figure), usher (of a mosque)
BAS: мөбассир
TAJ: мубассир
TAT: мөбассыйр
UZB: мубассир

Mubdi', al- المبدع ARABIC *pn.* name of God: the Innovator, the Originator
TAJ: Мубдӣ
TAT: Мөбдигъ
TUR: ал-Мубтди
UYG: Mubdiy
UZB: Ал-Мубдий

mubham مبهم ARABIC *Qur'an n.* indefinite; obscure (i.e. as a category of Qur'anic verses)
BAS: мөбһәм
KAR: мубхәм
TAJ: мубҳам
TAT: мөбһәм
UYG: mubhäm
UZB: мубҳам

mudafa'a مدافعه ARABIC *n.* defense, resistance
KAR: қорғай
TAJ: мудофиа
TAT: мөдафәгә
UYG: mudapiä
UZB: мудофаа

mudallas مدلّس ARABIC *Law n.* person who knowingly sells defective goods
TAJ: мудаллас
UZB: мудаллас

mudarris مدرّس ARABIC *n.* teacher, instructor (in a madrasa)
BAS: мөдәррис
KAR: мүдәрис, мудәррис
KAZ: мударис
KYR: мударис
TAJ: мударрис
TAT: мөдәррис
UYG: mudärris
UZB: мударрис

Muddassir مدثّر ARABIC *Qur'an pn.* the 74th sura of the Qur'an
KAR: Мүддассир сүўреси
KAZ: Мүддәссір сүресі
TAJ: сураи Мудассир
UYG: Muddässir süräsi
UZB: Муддассир сураси

mudrik مدرك ARABIC *Ritual n.* person who was late to public prayer but who finished first raka't privately with the imam (i.e. who came during the first rak'at)
KAR: мудрик
TAJ: мудрик
UZB: мудрик

mufassal مفصّل ARABIC *Theology adj.* complete, full, in detail (as a category of faith)
KAR: муфәссәл, толық
KAZ: мүфассал
TAJ: муфассал
TAT: мөфассал
UYG: mupässäl
UZB: муфассал

mufassir مفسّر ARABIC *Qur'an n.* commentator (esp. on the Qur'an), author of a tafsir
BAS: мөфәссир
TAJ: муфассир
TAT: мөфәссир
UZB: муфассир

mufsid [1] مفسد ARABIC *Ritual n.* person who spoils an act of devotion (e.g. a fast, namaz, etc.)
KAZ: мүпсіт, муфсит
TAJ: муфсид, муфсит
TAT: мөфсид
TUR: муфсит, муфсид
UZB: муфсид, муфсит

mufsid [2] مفسد ARABIC *Law n.* person who commits a mortal sin
TAT: мөфсид
UZB: муфсид

mufti مفتی ARABIC *Law n.* senior legal figure authorized to issue fatwas; administrative head of Muslim religious figures ☞ ***fatva***
BAS: мөфтөй, мөфти
KAR: мүпти
KAZ: муфти, мүфти
KYR: мупту
TAJ: муфтӣ
TAT: мөфти
TUR: мүфти
UYG: mupti, mufti
UZB: муфтий, муфти

muftir مفتر ARABIC *Ritual n.* one who breaks the fast
KAR: мүптыр
TAJ: муфтир
TAT: мофтыйр
UZB: муфтир

Mughni, al- المغنی ARABIC *n.* name of God: the Enricher
TAJ: Муғнӣ
TAT: Могни
TUR: ал-Мугни
UYG: Mughniy
UZB: Ал-Муғний

muhabbat محبّت ARABIC *Sufism n.* love for God (as a stage of the Sufi path)
BAS: мөхәббәт
KAR: мухаббат
TAJ: мухаббат
TAT: мәхәббәт
TUR: мухаббет
UYG: muhäbbät
UZB: муҳаббат

muhaddis محدّث ARABIC *n.* traditionist, expert in hadith study
KAR: муҳәдийс
KAZ: мүхаддис
TAJ: мухаддис
UYG: muhäddis
UZB: муҳаддис

muhajarat مهاجرت ARABIC *n.* the state of being a refugee or emigrant ☞ ***muhajir***
KAR: муҳәжирәт
TAJ: муҳоҷират

TAT: мөһаҗәрәт
UYG: muhajirät
UZB: муҳожират

muhajir مهاجر ARABIC *n.* refugee, emigrant (usually referring to Muslims fleeing religious persecution)
BAS: мөһажир
KAR: муҳәжир
KYR: можур
TAJ: муҳоҷир
TAT: мөһаҗир
TUR: мухаҗир
UYG: muhajir
UZB: муҳожир

muhajirin مهاجرين ARABIC *Historical n.* Meccans who followed the prophet Muhammad in his flight to Medina; plural form of muhajir ☞ ***muhajir***
KAR: муҳәжир
KAZ: мұхаджир
TAJ: муҳоҷирун
TAT: мөһаҗирин, әлмөһаҗир
TUR: мухаҗир
UYG: muhajirun
UZB: муҳожирун

muhakama محاكمه ARABIC *Law n.* hearing a case in court
BAS: мөхакәмә
KAR: муҳәкәмә
KAZ: мұхакама
TAJ: муҳокама
TAT: мөхакәмә
UYG: muhakimä
UZB: муҳокама

muhallil محلّل ARABIC *Law n.* one who makes lawful
TAJ: муҳаллил
TAT: мөхәллил
UZB: муҳаллил

Muhammad[1] محمّد ARABIC *pn.* the prophet Muhammad
BAS: Мөхәммәт
KAR: Муқамбет, Мақамбет, Мәмбет
KAZ: Мұхаммед
KYR: Мухаммед, Мукамбет
TAJ: Муҳаммад, ҳазрати Муҳаммад
TAT: Мөхәммәт
TUR: Мухаммат
UYG: Muhämmät, Mähmät
UZB: Муҳаммад, Ҳазрати Муҳаммад

Muhammad[2] محمّد ARABIC *Qur'an pn.* the 47th sura of the Qur'an
KAR: Муқамбет сүўреси
KAZ: Мұхаммед сүресі
TAJ: сураи Муҳаммад
TAT: Мөхәммәт сүрәсе
UYG: sürä Muhämmäd
UZB: Муҳаммад сураси

muhammadi[1] محمّدى ARABIC *n.* Muslim, follower of the Islamic faith
TAJ: муҳаммадӣ
TAT: мөхәммәди
UYG: muhämmäti
UZB: муҳаммадий

muhammadi[2] محمّدى ARABIC *adj.* Muslim, Islamic
TAJ: муҳаммадӣ
TAT: мөхәммәди
UYG: muhämmäti
UZB: муҳаммадий

muhaqqiq محقّق ARABIC *Sufism n.* Sufi who has witnessed God, high ranking Sufi or scholar
TAT: мөхәкъкыйк
UZB: муҳаққиқлар

muharaba محاربه ARABIC *n.* war, battle, conflict
TAJ: муҳориба
TAT: мөхарәбә
UYG: muhariba
UZB: муҳораба

muharram[1] محرّم ARABIC *Law adj.* illicit, forbidden
KAR: ҳарам
KYR: макрам
TAJ: ҳаром
TAT: мөхәррәм
UYG: haram
UZB: ҳаром

Muharram[2] محرّم ARABIC *pn.* the first month of the Islamic lunar calendar
BAS: мөхәррәм
KAR: Мухаррәм, Мухәррәм
KAZ: Мұхаррам, Мұһаррам
TAJ: Муҳаррам
TAT: Мөхәррәм
TUR: Мухаррам, Мәхеррем, Ашыр
UYG: Muhärräm, Äshur
UZB: Муҳаррам

muharramat محرّمات ARABIC *Law n.* women with

whom it is not lawful to contract marriage
TAJ: мухаррамат
UZB: муҳаррамат

muhasara محاصره ARABIC *Historical n.* siege (e.g. of Mecca), blockade
TAJ: муҳосира
TAT: мөхасарә
UYG: muhasira
UZB: муҳосара

Muhaymin, al- المهيمن ARABIC *pn.* name of God: the Vigilant
KAZ: әл-Мухаймин
TAJ: Мухаймин
TUR: ал-Мухаймин
UYG: Muhaymin
UZB: Ал-Муҳаймин

muhibb محبّ ARABIC *Sufism n.* Sufi amateur, one who is only loosely affiliated with a Sufi order of shaykh
TAJ: муҳиб
UZB: муҳиб

Muhsi, al- المحصى ARABIC *n.* name of God: the Counter
TAJ: Мухсӣ
TUR: ал-Мухси
UYG: Muhsiy
UZB: Ал-Муҳсий

muhsin محسن ARABIC *n.* benefactor; legally eligible for marriage (e.g. being free, Muslim etc.)
BAS: мөхсин
TAJ: муҳсин
TAT: мөхсин
UZB: муҳсин

muhtadi مهتدى ARABIC *n.* one who has accepted Islam
TAJ: муҳтадӣ
TAT: мөһтәди
UZB: муҳтади

muhtasib [1] محتسب ARABIC *n.* enforcer of Islamic moral norms and requirements
BAS: мөхтәсиб
KAR: мухтәсиб
KAZ: мұхтасиб
TAJ: муҳтасиб
TAT: мөхтәсиб ① *enforcer of Islam moral norms and requirements* ② *religious scholar*
UZB: муҳтасиб

muhtasib [2] محتسب ARABIC *Historical n.* superintendent of weights and measures in markets
KAR: мухтәсиб
KAZ: мұхтасиб
TAJ: мухтасиб
TAT: мөхтәсиб
UZB: муҳтасиб

muhtazir محتضر ARABIC *Ritual n.* person who is on the verge of death
TAT: мохтазир, мөхтәзыйр
TUR: мухтазар
UZB: муҳтазир

Muhyi, al- المحيى ARABIC *n.* name of God: the Life-Giver
TAJ: Мухӣ
TUR: ал-Мухйи
UYG: Muhiy
UZB: Ал-Муҳйи

mu'id معيد ARABIC *n.* drillmaster (of pupils in a school), tutor
TAJ: муъиз
UZB: муъид

Mu'id, al- المعيد ARABIC *n.* name of God: the Restorer
TAJ: Муъид
TUR: ал-Мувид
UYG: Muid
UZB: Ал-Муъид

Mu'izz, al- المعزّ ARABIC *pn.* name of God: Who gives honor and strength
TAJ: Муъиз
TUR: ал-Муизз
UYG: Muiz
UZB: Ал-Муъиз

Mujadala مجادله ARABIC *Qur'an n.* the 58th sura of the Qur'an
KAR: Мужәдала суўреси
KAZ: Мұжадәлә сүресі
TAJ: сураи Муҷодала
UYG: Mujädälä süräsi, sürä Müjadälä
UZB: Мужодала сураси

mujahid مجاهد ARABIC *n.* fighter for the faith
BAS: мөжәһид
KAR: мужәҳид
TAJ: муҷоҳид
TAT: мөҗаһид
TUR: муҗахид
UZB: мужоҳид

mujahida[1] مجاهده ARABIC *n.* effort (esp. in jihad)
UZB: мужоҳада

mujahida[2] مجاهده ARABIC *Sufism n.* effort (in one's fight against one's own appetites)
UZB: мужоҳида

mujassam مجسّم ARABIC *Theology adj.* corporal, being bodily
BAS: мөжәссәм
TAJ: муҷассам
TAT: мөҗәссәм
UYG: mujässäm
UZB: мужассам

mujavir مجاور ARABIC *n.* custodian of a tomb or shrine; visitor to a shrine (esp. at Medina)
TAJ: муҷавир
TAT: мөҗавир
TUR: мүҗевир, мүҗевүр ① *custodian of a tomb or shrine* ② *name of one of the six Turkmen holy tribes*
UZB: мужовир

mujda مجده ARABIC *n.* joyful message (from God)
KAR: мүждә
TAJ: муҷда
UZB: мужда

Mujib, al- المجيب ARABIC *pn.* name of God: the Responder
KAR: Мужип
TAJ: Муҷиб
TAT: Мөҗиб
TUR: ал-Муҗиб
UYG: Mujib
UZB: Ал Мўжиб

Mujid, al- الموجد ARABIC *n.* name of God: the Creator
TAT: Муҗид
UZB: Мужид

mu'jiza[1] معجزة ARABIC *n.* prophetic miracle
BAS: мөғжизә
KAZ: мұджиза, мұғжиза
TAJ: мӯъҷиза
TAT: могҗиза
TUR: мугжуза
UYG: möjizä
UZB: мўжиза

Mu'jiza[2] معجزة ARABIC *Qur'an pn.* the Qur'an
TAT: Могҗиза

mujtahid[1] مجتهد ARABIC *n.* one who practices ijtihad (i.e. draws legal conclusions on the basis of the Qur'an and sunna); one who strives to acquire knowledge
BAS: мөжтаһид
KAZ: мұджтахит, мұжжағид, мұжтаһід
KYR: мужтахит, мужтаид
TAJ: муҷтаҳид
TAT: мөҗтәһид, мөҗтәһит
TUR: мужтахид
UZB: мужтаҳид

mujtahid[2] مجتهد ARABIC *Law n.* senior mufti
☞ ***mufti***
TAJ: муҷдаҳид
UZB: мужтаҳид

mukafat مكافاة ARABIC *n.* reward (from God)
KAR: Алла мукәпати
TAJ: мукофоти Худой
TAT: мөкяфәт
UYG: mukapat
UZB: мукофот, Аллоҳ мукофоти

mukallaf مكلّف ARABIC *n.* one who has accepted a burden, one who has accepted the obligations of Islam, i.e., an adult
KAR: мукәлләп
TAJ: мукаллаф
TAT: мөкәлләф
UZB: мукаллаф

mukammal مكمّل *adj.* complete, perfect, excellent
BAS: мөкәммәл
KAR: мукәммәл
TAJ: мукаммал
TAT: мөкәммәл
UYG: mukämäl
UZB: мукаммал

mukarram مكرّم ARABIC *adj.* respected, honored (commonly used to refer to the Ka'ba and to Mecca)
☞ ***Makka al-mukarrama***
BAS: мөкәрәм
KAR: мукәррем
TAJ: мукаррам, Каъбаи мукаррам
TAT: мөкәррәм, Мәккәи Мөкәррәмә
UYG: mukärräm, Mäkkä mükärrämä
UZB: мукаррам, Каъбаи мукаррама, Макка мукаррама

mukarrir مكرّر ARABIC *n.* instructor at a madrasa
TAJ: мукаррир
TAT: мөкәррир

UYG: mukärrir
UZB: мукаррир

mukashifa مكاشفه ARABIC *Sufism n.* beginning to understand the divine secrets (a stage on the Sufi path)
TAT: мөкяшәфә
UZB: мукошифа

mukatib مكاتب ARABIC *Law n.* one who has made an agreement to free his slave upon receipt of a specific amount from the slave
TUR: мукәтеб, мукатеб

mukhaddara مخدّرة ARABIC *Law n.* girl kept in seclusion; veiled woman
TAJ: мухаддарат
UZB: мухаддарат

mukhalifat lil-havadis مخالفة للحوادیث ARABIC *Theology np.* independent of events (a distinguishing quality of God)
TAT: мөхалифәтүн лилхәвадис
UZB: мухолифатул ҳаводис

mukhasamat مخاصمات ARABIC *Law n.* altercations (a category of civil jurisprudence addressing disputes) ☞ ***mu'amalat***
TAJ: мухосамат

mukhlis مخلص ARABIC *n.* believer, pious person
TAJ: мухлис
UYG: mukhlis
UZB: мухлис

mukhtariyat مختاریت ARABIC *Theology n.* free will, freedom of choice
BAS: мохтариәт
TAJ: мухторият
TAT: мохтарияць
UYG: mukhtariyät
UZB: мухторият

mukhtasar مختصر ARABIC *Law adj.* shortened, abbreviated (e.g. a treatise); the name of several authoritative works on Islamic law
BAS: мохтасар
KYR: муктасар
TAJ: мухтасар
UYG: mukhtasär
UZB: мухтасар

mulazim ملازم ARABIC *n.* official, servant (of the state)
KAR: мулазим
TAJ: мулозим
TAT: мөлязим
UYG: mulazim
UZB: мулозим

mulhaq ملحق *Sufism* person attached to a shaykh; absorbed, united (the condition of human soul when it is absorbed into the essence of God)
TAJ: мулҳақ
TAT: мөлхак
UZB: мулҳақ

mulhid ملحد ARABIC *n.* heretic; apostate; atheist
TAJ: мулҳид
TAT: мөлхид
UZB: мулҳид

mulk [1] ملك ARABIC *Law n.* private property (as a category in Islamic law) ☞ ***milk***
KAR: мулк, мулик
KAZ: мүлік
KYR: мүлк, мүлүк
TAJ: мулк
TAT: мөлек
TUR: мулк
UYG: mülük
UZB: мулк

Mulk [2] ملك ARABIC *Qur'an pn.* the 67th sura of the Qur'an ☞ ***tabarak***
KAR: Мүлк суўреси
KAZ: Мүлік сүресі
TAJ: сураи Мулк
TAT: Мөлек сүрәсе
UYG: Mulik süräsi, sürä Mulk
UZB: Мулк сураси

mulk-amlak ملك املاك ARABIC *Law np.* property (as a whole)
KAR: мулки амләк
TAJ: мулки амлок
TAT: мөлкәт
UYG: mulik-ämläk
UZB: мулк-амлок

mulla ملا ARABIC *n.* person possessing religious authority; commonly a synonym for imam ☞ ***imam***
BAS: мулла
KAR: молла
KAZ: молда
KYR: молдо, молла, молло ① *person possessing religious authority* ② *imam* ③ *instructor in an old-method madrasa* ④ *hist. official scribe of a*

local leader

TAJ: мулла

TAT: мулла, молла, мөлля

TUR: молла

UYG: molla

UZB: мулла

mullabachcha ملّابچّه PERSIAN *n.* student of a mulla; son of a mulla

TAJ: муллобачча

UZB: муллабачча

mu'min [1] مؤمن ARABIC *n.* faithful (person), believer ☞ ***Amir al-mu'minin,***

BAS: мөьмин

KAR: мумин

KAZ: мумин, муъмін, мү'мін

KYR: момун

TAJ: мӯъмин

TAT: мөэмин, мөъмин

TUR: мөмин, мүмин, мүъмүн

UYG: mömin

UZB: мўмин, мўъмин

Mu'min [2] مؤمن ARABIC *Qur'an n.* alternate name of the 40th sura of the Qur'an ☞ ***Ghafir,***

KAZ: Мүмін сүресі

TAJ: сураи Мӯмин

UZB: Мўмин сураси

Mu'min, al- المؤمن ARABIC *n.* name of God: the One with Faith

KAR: Мумин

KAZ: әл-Мумин

TAJ: Мумин

TUR: ал-Мумин

UYG: Mömin

UZB: Ал-Мўмин

mu'mina مؤمنه ARABIC *n.* female Muslim

TAJ: мӯъмина

UZB: мўмина, мўъмина

Mu'minin مؤمنين ARABIC *Qur'an n.* the 23rd sura of the Qur'an

KAR: Муминун суўреси

KAZ: Мұминұн сүресі

TAJ: сураи Мӯъминун

TAT: Мөэминнәр сүрәсе

UYG: Möminin süräsi, sürä Mö'minun

UZB: Мўминлар сураси

Mumit, al- المميت ARABIC *pn.* name of God: the Slayer

TAJ: Мумит

TUR: ал-Мумит

UYG: Mumiyt

UZB: Ал-Мумийт

Mumtahana ممتحنه ARABIC *Qur'an pn.* the 60th sura of the Qur'an

KAR: Мумтахана суўреси

KAZ: Мүмтахина сүресі

TAJ: сураи Мумтаҳана

UYG: Mumtahana süräsi

UZB: Мумтаҳана сураси

munafiq منافق ARABIC *n.* hypocrite

BAS: мөнафиҡ

KAR: мунапиқ

KAZ: мұнафиқ, мұнапық

KYR: мунапык

TAJ: мунофиқ

TAT: монафикъ

TUR: мунафык

UYG: munapiq

UZB: мунофиқ

Munafiqun منافقون ARABIC *Qur'an n.* the 63rd sura of the Qur'an

KAR: Мунапиқиун суўреси

KAZ: Мұнафиқұн сүресі

TAJ: сураи Мунофиқун

UYG: Munapiqun süräsi, sürä Munafiqun

UZB: Мунофиқун сураси

munajat [1] مناجات ARABIC *Ritual n.* fervent prayer, supplication (to God)

BAS: мөнәжәт

KAR: минәжат

KAZ: мінажат

KYR: мунажат, мунажаат

TAJ: муноҷат

TAT: мөнаҗат

TUR: мунаҗат

UYG: munajat

UZB: муножот

munajat [2] مناجات ARABIC *Ritual n.* piece or song used as a prayer in religious music

BAS: мөнәжәт

KAR: минәжат

TAJ: муноҷат

TAT: мөнаҗат

UYG: munajat

UZB: муножот

munajatkhana مناجاتخانه PERSIAN *Ritual n.* location where munajat prayers are performed ☞ ***munajat***
KAR: минәжатхана
KAZ: мінажатхана
UYG: munajathana
UZB: муножотхона

munajjim منجّم ARABIC *n.* astrologer
BAS: мөнәжжим ① *astrologer* ② *astronomer*
KAR: мунәжжым
TAJ: муначчим
TAT: мөнәҗҗим ① *astrologer* ② *astronomer*
UYG: munäjjim
UZB: мунажжим

munakahat مناكحات ARABIC *Law n.* nuptials, a category of civil jurisprudence addressing issues of marriage ☞ ***mu'amalat***
TAT: мөнакәхә
UZB: мунақаҳат

munavvar منوّر ARABIC *adj.* illuminated by divine light (used especially as an epithet for the city of Medina) ☞ ***Madina-yi munavvara***
BAS: мөнәүүәр
KAR: мунәўар, мунәўўер
TAJ: мунаввар
TAT: мөнәүвәр
UYG: münäwwär
UZB: мунаввар

munazara مناظرة ARABIC *Sufism n.* presenting the soul to God in the performance of dhikr
KAR: муназәра
TAJ: мунозара
UZB: мунозара

munazzal منزّل ARABIC *n.* sent down from heaven
TAJ: муназзал
TAT: мөнәззәл
UZB: муназзал

munkar منكر ARABIC *adj.* sinful, illicit
BAS: мөнкәр
KAR: мункәр
TAJ: мункар
TAT: мөнкәр
UYG: munkir
UZB: мункар

Munkar va Nakir منكر و نكير ARABIC *pn.* names of two angels who question the dead about the conduct of their lives
BAS: Мөнкир вә Нәнкир
KAR: Мункәр-Нәкир
KAZ: Мұңкір мен Нәңкір
KYR: Мункур-Нанкир, Үнкур-Нанкир, Мункур-Накир
TAJ: Мункар-Накир
TAT: Мөнкир һәм Нәкир, Мөнкир-Нәкир
TUR: Мұңкур ве Некир
UYG: Munkir- Näkir
UZB: Мункар-Накир

munkir ARABIC *n.* atheist
BAS: мөнкир
KAR: мункир
TAJ: мункиршавӣ
UYG: munkir
UZB: мункир

munsalik منسلك ARABIC *adj.* belonging to a sect or religion
TAT: мөнсәлик
UZB: мунсалик

Muntaqim, al- المنتقم ARABIC *pn.* name of God: the Avenger
TAJ: Мунтақим
TAT: Мөнтәкыйм
TUR: ал-Мунтаким
UYG: Muntaqiym
UZB: Ал-Мунтақийм

muqaddas مقدّس ARABIC *adj.* sacred, holy
BAS: мөҡәддәс
KAR: муқәддәс
KYR: мукаддас
TAJ: муқаддас
TAT: мөкаддәс ① *sacred, holy* ② *pious, religious*
TUR: мукаддес
UYG: muqäddäs
UZB: муқаддас

Muqaddim, al- المقدّم ARABIC *pn.* name of God: the Expediter
TAJ: Муқаддим
TUR: ал-Мукаддим
UYG: Muqaddim
UZB: Ал-Муқаддим

muqallid مقلّد ARABIC *Qur'an n.* person who recites the Qur'an by imitating the style of another
KAR: муқаллит
TAJ: муқаллид
UZB: муқаллид

muqarrab مقرّب ARABIC *adj.* near, close (esp. to God)
KYR: мукарап, мукараб, мукиреб, төрт мукиреб *the four archangels*
TAJ: муқарраб
TAT: мөкаррəб
UZB: муқарраб

muqavala مقاوله ARABIC *Ritual pn.* method of public Qur'an recitation
TAJ: муқавала
UZB: муқовала

muqim مقيم ARABIC *Law n.* being resident, one who is at home and not traveling (as a status governing specific ritual obligations)
TAT: мокыйм
TUR: мукым
UZB: муқим

Muqit, al- المقيت ARABIC *pn.* name of God: the Nourisher
TAJ: Муқит
TUR: ал-Мукит
UYG: Muqit
UZB: Ал-Муқит

Muqsit, al- المقسط ARABIC *pn.* name of God: the Equitable
TAJ: Муқсит
TUR: ал-Муксит
UYG: Muqsit
UZB: Ал-Муқсит

Muqtadir, al- المقتدر ARABIC *pn.* name of God: the Powerful
TAJ: Муқтадир
TAT: Моктадир
TUR: ал-Муктадир
UYG: Muqtadir
UZB: Ал-Муқтадир

murafa'a مرافعه ARABIC *Law n.* trial; lawsuit
TAJ: мурофаъ
TAT: морафəга
UYG: müräpä
UZB: мурофаа

murahaqa مراهقة ARABIC *Hajj n.* arriving in Mecca when the ceremonies of the hajj are nearly finished
TAJ: мурохақа
UZB: мурохақа

muraqaba مراقبه ARABIC *Sufism n.* watching and controlling one's senses; contemplation and asceticism
TAJ: муроқиба
TAT: моракабə, муракабə
UYG: muraqabä
UZB: муроқаба

murda مرده PERSIAN *n.* deceased, corpse
KAR: мурда, өлик
KAZ: мүрде
KYR: мүрдө
TAJ: мурда
UYG: murda
UZB: мурда

murdakhana مرده خانه PERSIAN *Ritual n.* place where a corpse is kept and washed before burial
TAJ: мурдахона
UZB: мурдахона

murdar مردار PERSIAN *Law n.* carrion, an animal that has died of natural causes (an‰ hence haram); a bad person
BAS: үлəkhə
KAR: өликсе
KAZ: өлексе, мəйте
KYR: мурдар, мырдар
TAJ: мурдор
TAT: мөрдар, үлəксə
TUR: лəш
UYG: murdär
UZB: мурдор, ўлакса

murdashuy مرده شوی PERSIAN *Ritual n.* person who washes the corpse before burial and performs prayers ☞ ***ghassal***
TAJ: мурдашўй
UZB: мурдашўй

murid مريد ARABIC *Sufism n.* follower of a Sufi master
BAS: мөрит
KAR: мүрид
KAZ: мүрид
KYR: мурид, мурут
TAJ: мурид
TAT: мөрид
TUR: мүрит
UYG: murit
UZB: мурид

mursal [1] مرسل ARABIC *n.* envoy, prophet
KAR: мурсал
TAJ: мурсал
TAT: мөрсəл

UZB: мурсал

mursal [2] مرسل ARABIC *Hadith adj.* attributed to the prophet Muhammad by one of his companions (as a category of hadith)

TAT: мөрсәл
UZB: мурсал

Mursalat مرسلات ARABIC *Qur'an n.* the 77th sura of the Qur'an

KAR: Ўал-мурсалэт суўреси
KAZ: Мүрсәлат сүресі
TAJ: сураи Мурсалот
TAT: Мөрсәлат сүрәсе
UZB: Вал-мурсалот сураси

mursalin مرسلين ARABIC *n.* messengers; prophets

BAS: мөрсәлин
KAR: мурсалин
TAJ: мурсалин
UZB: мурсалин

murshid مرشد ARABIC *Sufism n.* instructor, teacher
☞ ***pir***

BAS: мөршит, мөршид
KAR: муршит
KAZ: міршіт
TAJ: муршид
TAT: мөршид
TUR: мүршит
UYG: murshit
UZB: муршид

murshid-i afaq مرشد آفاق PERSIAN *Sufism np.* Sufi master who is renowned throughout the world (lit. murshid of all the horizons)

UZB: муршиди офоқ

murtadd مرتدّ ARABIC *n.* apostate (i.e. from Islam)

BAS: мөртәт
KAR: муртад
KYR: мүртөс
TAJ: муртад
TAT: мөртәд
TUR: мүртөз, муртад
UYG: murtäd
UZB: муртад

Murtaza مرتضى ARABIC *pn.* epithet of the Caliph 'Ali

BAS: Мортаза
KAR: Мыртаза
TAJ: Муртазо
TUR: Муртаза
UYG: Murtaza
UZB: Муртаза, Муртазо

Musa موسى ARABIC *pn.* the prophet Moses

BAS: Муса
KAR: Муса
KAZ: Мұса
KYR: Муса
TAJ: Мусо
TAT: Муса
TUR: Муса
UYG: Musa
UZB: Мусо

musab مثاب ARABIC *adj.* rewarded by God for good deeds

TAJ: мусаб
TAT: мөсаб
UZB: мусаб, мансаб

musadara مصادره ARABIC *Law n.* confiscation (i.e. as a punishment), fine

KAR: мусадәра
TAJ: мусодира
TAT: мөсадәрә
UYG: musadirä, musadira
UZB: мусодара

musafaha مصافحه ARABIC *Ritual n.* using both hands to take the hands (of a person) while greeting

TAJ: мусофаҳа
TAT: мосафәхә
UZB: мусофаҳа

musafir مسافر ARABIC *Ritual n.* pilgrim; traveler (as a legal status for involving specific ritual obligations and exemptions)

BAS: мосафир
KAR: мүсәпир *poor person*
KAZ: мүсәпір ① *pilgrim,* ② *poor person*
KYR: мусапыр
TAJ: мусофир
TAT: мөсафир
UYG: musapir
UZB: мусофир ① *pilgrim,* ② *poor person*

musalaha مصالحه ARABIC *n.* pacifying, bringing about peace, making peace

BAS: мосаләхә
TAJ: мусолиҳа
TAT: мосаләхә
UYG: musälähä
UZB: мусолаҳа

musalla[1] مصلّى ARABIC *n.* place for performing prayers
- KAZ: мұсалла
- TAJ: мусалла
- TAT: мосалла
- UZB: мусалло

musalla[2] مصلّى ARABIC *n.* prayer-rug
- TAJ: мусалла
- TAT: мосалла
- UZB: мусалло

musalli مصلّى ARABIC *n.* one who prays
- TAJ: мусалли
- TAT: мосалли
- UZB: мусалли

musavi[1] موسوى ARABIC *adj.* Jewish; Jewish person
- KAR: мусаўи
- TAJ: мусовӣ
- TAT: мусави
- TUR: мусайы
- UYG: musawi
- UZB: мусовий

musavi[2] موسوى ARABIC *n.* descendant of the seventh Shi'ite imam Musa al-Kazim
- TAJ: мӯсовӣ
- UZB: мўсовий

Musavvir, al- المصوّر ARABIC *pn.* name of God: the Fashioner
- BAS: Мосауыир
- KAR: Мусәўўыр
- KAZ: әл-Мұсаввир
- TAJ: Мусаввир
- TAT: Мосаувир
- TUR: ал-Мусаввир
- UYG: Musawwir
- UZB: Ал-Мусаввир

musbat مثبت ARABIC *Hadith adj.* confirmed, established (as a category of hadith)
- KAR: мусбэт
- TAJ: мусбат
- TAT: мөсбэт
- UZB: мусбат

mushaf مصحف ARABIC *Qur'an n.* the Qur'an
- BAS: мосхэф
- TAT: Мосхэф, Мосхэф Шэриф

mushahida مشاهده ARABIC *Sufism n.* a stage on the Sufi path; lit. comprehending God's oneness or beauty
- TAJ: мушоҳида
- UZB: мушоҳида

mushkilkushad مشکلکشاد PERSIAN *Ritual n.* ceremony (i.e. for solving a specific problem)
- TAJ: мушкилкушо
- UZB: мушкулкушод

mushrik مشرك ARABIC *n.* polytheist, pagan, infidel, one who ascribes partners to God
- BAS: мөшрик
- KAR: мушрик
- KAZ: мүшрік
- TAJ: мушрик
- TAT: мөшрик
- UYG: mushrik
- UZB: мушрик

musibat مصيبت ARABIC *n.* misfortune, disaster (e.g. which Muslims are obligated to help relieve)
- BAS: мосибэт
- KAR: мусибэт
- TAJ: мусибат
- TAT: мосыйбэт
- UYG: musibät *funeral, mourning*
- UZB: мусибат

muslim مسلم ARABIC *n.* Muslim, follower of the Islamic faith
- BAS: мөслим
- KAR: мусырман, мусылман
- KAZ: мұслим, мұслім
- KYR: муслим
- TAJ: мусулмон
- TAT: мөслим
- UYG: muslim
- UZB: муслим

muslima مسلمه ARABIC *n.* female Muslim
- BAS: мөслимэ
- KAR: муслыма
- TAJ: муслима
- TAT: мөслимэ
- UZB: муслима

muslimin مسلمين ARABIC *n.* Muslims
- KAR: муслымун
- TAJ: муслимин
- TAT: мөслимин
- UZB: муслимин

musnad مسند ARABIC *Hadith adj.* supported, uninterruptedly traced to a companion of the

prophet Muhammad (as a category of hadith)
TAT: мөснәд
UZB: муснад

mustabidd مستبدّ ARABIC *n.* tyrant, oppressor
BAS: мөстәбид
KAR: мустәбит
TAJ: мустабид
TAT: мөстәбид
UYG: mustäbit
UZB: мустабид

Mustafa مصطفى ARABIC *n.* the Chosen (an epithet of the Prophet Muhammad)
BAS: Мостафа
KAR: Мустафа
KAZ: Мұстапа, Мұстафа
KYR: Мустапа
TAJ: Мустафо
TAT: Мостафа
TUR: Мустафа
UYG: Mustapa
UZB: Мустафо

mustahabb مستحبّ ARABIC *Law adj.* recommended but not enjoined by Islamic law
KAZ: мұстахап
KYR: мустахаб
TAJ: мустаҳобб
TAT: мөстахәб
TUR: мустахаб, мустахап
UZB: мустаҳоб

mustajab مستجاب ARABIC *n.* one whose prayers are answered
KAR: мустәжәб
TAJ: мустаҷоб
TAT: мөстәҗаб
UYG: mustajäb
UZB: мустажоб

mustakrah مستكره ARABIC *Law adj.* abominable, loathsome
TAT: мөстәкрәһ
UZB: мустакроҳ

mustashrik مستشريق ARABIC *Historical n.* Western Orientalist
TAJ: мусташрик
UZB: мусташрик, ғарблик шарқшунос

musulman مسلمان ARABIC *n.* Muslim, follower of the Islamic faith
BAS: мосолман
KAR: мусылман, мусырман
KAZ: мұсылман
KYR: бусурман, бусулман, мусулман, мусурман
TAJ: мусулмон
TAT: мөселман
TUR: мўсулман
UYG: musulman
UZB: мусулмон, муслимон, мусурмон

muta'abbid متعبّد ARABIC *adj.* pious, religious, God-fearing
TAJ: мутаъббид
TAT: мөтәгаббид
UZB: мутааббид

Muta'ali, al- المتعالى ARABIC *pn.* name of God: the Exalted
KAR: Мутәли
TAJ: Мутаолӣ
TAT: Мөтәгали
TUR: ал-Мутавали
UYG: Mutaäli
UZB: Ал-Мутаоли

muta'assib متعصّب ARABIC *n.* fanatic, radical (used in a negative sense)
BAS: мөтәғәссиб
KAR: мутәссип
TAJ: мутаассиб
TAT: мөтәгассыйб
UYG: mutä'assip, mutä'ässip *conservative*
UZB: мутаассиб

mu'tabar معتبر ARABIC *adj.* authoritative, trustworthy (e.g. scholars)
KAR: ылайық
KYR: мутабар, мөтабар
TAJ: мўътабар
UYG: mu'tabär
UZB: мўътабар

mutadayyin متديّن ARABIC *adj.* pious, religious
TAJ: мутадаййин
TAT: мөтәдәйин
UZB: мутадайин

Mutaffifin مطفّفن ARABIC *Qur'an pn.* the 83rd sura of the Qur'an
KAR: Мутаффипин сүўреси
KAZ: Мұтаффифун сүресі
TAJ: сураи Мутаффифин
UYG: Mutäppipun süräsi, sürä Mutäffifin
UZB: Мутаффифун сураси

mutahhar مطهّر ARABIC *adj.* sacred, holy; purified ☞ ***ravza-yi mutahhar***
- **KAR:** мутаххәр
- **TAJ:** мутаҳҳар
- **TAT:** мотаhhәр
- **UZB:** мутаҳҳар

Mutakabbir, al- المتكبّر ARABIC *pn.* name of God: the Imperious
- **KAR:** Мутәкәппир
- **KAZ:** әл-Мутакаббир
- **TAJ:** Мутакаббир
- **TAT:** Мөтәкәббир
- **TUR:** ал-Мутакаббир
- **UYG:** Mutäkäbbir
- **UZB:** Ал-Мутакаббир

mutakallim متكلّم ARABIC *Theology n.* scholar of Islamic dogma, scholar of kalam ☞ ***kalam***
- **KAR:** мутәкәллим
- **KAZ:** мутакаллим, мұтакаллим
- **TAJ:** мутакаллим
- **TAT:** мөтәкәллим
- **TUR:** мутакаллим, келамчы
- **UZB:** мутакаллим

mutala'a مطالعة ARABIC *v.* study, studying
- **TAJ:** мутолиа
- **UYG:** mutälää
- **UZB:** мутолаа

mu'tamir معتمر ARABIC *Law n.* a performer of the Umrah
- **TAJ:** муътамир
- **UZB:** муътамир

mutanassir متنصّر ARABIC *n.* one who has converted to Christianity
- **TAT:** мөтәнассыйр
- **UZB:** мутанассир

mutasavvif متصوّف ARABIC *Sufism n.* Sufi
- **KAR:** мутасаўўип
- **TAJ:** мутасаввиф
- **TAT:** мөтасаувыф
- **UZB:** мутасаввиф

mutashayyikh متشيّخ ARABIC *Sufism n.* pseudo-shaykh, one who pretends to be a Sufi shaykh
- **KAR:** муташайих
- **TAJ:** муташайх
- **TAT:** мөтәшәйех
- **UZB:** муташайх

mutavalli متولّى ARABIC *n.* administrator of an Islamic institution or foundation (vaqf, shrine, mosque, etc.)
- **BAS:** мөтәүәлли
- **KAR:** мутавәли
- **TAJ:** мутаваллӣ
- **TAT:** мөтәвәлли
- **UYG:** mutiwälli
- **UZB:** мутавалли *guardian of a mosque*

mutavalliyat متولّيت ARABIC *n.* administrative board of a mosque or other Islamic institution
- **KAR:** мутәўллият
- **TAJ:** муталлият
- **TAT:** мөтәвәллият
- **UYG:** mutiwälliyät
- **UZB:** мутаваллият

mutavarri' متورّع ARABIC *adj.* pious, godly
- **TAT:** мөтәвәрриг
- **UZB:** мутаворрий

mutavatir متواتر ARABIC *Hadith adj.* transmitted from multiple authorities and considered reliable (as a category of hadith)
- **TAT:** мөтәватир
- **UZB:** мутавотир

mutlaq مطلق ARABIC *Theology adj.* absolute, unconditional (e.g. as a quality of God)
- **BAS:** мотлаҡ
- **KAR:** мутләқ
- **TAJ:** мутлақ
- **TAT:** мотлак
- **TUR:** мутлак
- **UYG:** mutläq
- **UZB:** мутлоқ

muttasil متّصل ARABIC *Hadith adj.* connected, having an unbroken chain of transmission (as a category of hadith)
- **KAR:** муттәсил
- **TAT:** мөтассил
- **TUR:** муттасыл
- **UZB:** муттасил

muvahhid موحّد ARABIC *Theology n.* monotheist
- **BAS:** мөүәххит
- **TAJ:** муваҳҳид
- **TAT:** мовәххид
- **UZB:** муваҳҳид

muvaqqat ☞ ***farz-i muvaqqat***

muzaffar مظفّر ARABIC *adj.* winner, victor; epithet of the prophet Muhammad
- KAR: музаппар
- TAJ: музаффар
- TAT: мозаффар
- UYG: muzäppär
- UZB: музаффар

Muzdalifa مزدلفه ARABIC *Hajj pn.* location in Mecca between 'Arafat and the valley of Mina where pilgrims returning from 'Arafat spend the night between 9th and 10th Zu'l-hijja
- KAR: Муздəлип
- KAZ: Муздəлипа, Муздалиф
- TAJ: кӯҳи Муздалиф
- TAT: Мөздəлифə
- TUR: Муздалиф дагы
- UZB: Муздалифа

Muzill, al- المذلّ ARABIC *pn.* name of God: the Abaser
- KAR: Музил
- TAJ: Музил
- TUR: ал-Музилл
- UYG: Muzil
- UZB: Ал-Музил

Muzzammil مزمّل ARABIC *Qur'an n.* the 73rd sura of the Qur'an
- KAR: Музəммил суўреси
- KAZ: Мұззəммiл сүресi
- TAJ: сураи Музаммил
- TAT: Мүзəммил сүрəсе
- UYG: Muzammil süräsi, sürä Muzämmil
- UZB: Музаммил сураси

N

Naba نبا ARABIC *Qur'an pn.* the 78th sura of the Qur'an
- KAR: Нəбə суўреси
- KAZ: Нəбə сүресi
- TAJ: сураи Набо
- UYG: Nabää süräsi, sürä Näbä
- UZB: Набаъ сураси

nabi نبی ARABIC *n.* prophet ☞ ***payghambar***
- BAS: нəби
- KAR: нəби, нəбий
- KAZ: нəби
- KYR: набий
- TAJ: набӣ
- TAT: нəби
- TUR: неби
- UYG: näbi
- UZB: наби

nabi'ullah نبی الله ARABIC *n.* prophet of God
- KAR: нəбиалла
- TAJ: набиулло
- TAT: нəбиулла
- UYG: näbiulla
- UZB: набиулло

nabuvat نبوت ARABIC *n.* prophetic mission, prophethood
- BAS: нəбүəт
- KAR: набиўəт
- TAJ: набивот
- TAT: нəбүвəт
- UZB: набивот

nafaqa نفقه ARABIC *Law n.* alimony, money or goods intended for the support of orphans or divorced women
- BAS: нəфəкə
- KAR: нəпақа
- KAZ: нəфақа
- KYR: напака
- TAJ: нафақа
- TAT: нəфəка
- UYG: napaqa
- UZB: нафақа

nafas نفس ARABIC *n.* breath, breathing
☞ ***sahib-i nafas***
- KAR: нəпес
- TAJ: нафас
- TAT: нəфəс
- TUR: непес
- UZB: нафас, нафас солмо

Nafi', al- النافع ARABIC *n.* name of God: the Benefactor
- KAR: Нəпий
- TAJ: Нофӣ
- TAT: Нафигъ
- TUR: ан-Нафи
- UYG: Näpi
- UZB: Ан-Нофи

nafila نافله ARABIC *Ritual n.* optional actions, supplementary action (esp. prayer, alms, etc.)
- KAR: нəпилə намаз
- TAJ: намози нофила
- TAT: нафилə

TUR: нефил
UYG: näpilä
UZB: нофила

nafl نفل ARABIC *adj.* optional, supplementary (in worship)
BAS: нәфел
KAR: нәпилә
KAZ: нәпіл
KYR: напил
TAJ: нофил
TAT: нәфел
UYG: näpil
UZB: нофил

nafs[1] نفس ARABIC *n.* passion; desire
BAS: нәфес
KAR: напс
TAJ: нафс
TAT: нәфес
UYG: näps
UZB: нафс

nafs[2] نفس ARABIC *n.* soul
BAS: нәфес
KAR: напс
KAZ: нәпсі, нәфс
TAJ: нафс
TAT: нәфес
UYG: näps
UZB: нафс

nahalal نا حلال PERSIAN *Law adj.* forbidden, illicit
KAR: нәхалал
TAJ: ноҳалол
TAT: нахәлял
UZB: ноҳалол

nahaq نا حق PERSIAN *adj.* illegal, unjust
BAS: нахаҡ
KAR: наҳақ, нәхақ
TAJ: ноҳақ
TAT: нахак
UYG: nahäq
UZB: ноҳақ

nahi نهی ARABIC *n.* forbidding (an act or deed)
BAS: нәһи
TAT: нәһи
UZB: наҳи

Nahl نحل ARABIC *Qur'an pn.* the 16th sura of the Qur'an
KAR: Нахл суўреси
KAZ: Нахыл сүресі
TAJ: сураи Наҳул
TAT: Нәхел сүрәсе
TUR: сураи Нахыл
UYG: Nahl süräsi, sürä Nähl
UZB: Наҳл сураси

nahs نحس ARABIC *Ritual n.* one who has not performed ghusl
BAS: нәхес *ill-omened, unlucky*
KAR: нәхс
TAJ: наҳс
UZB: наҳс

nahu نحو ARABIC *n.* syntax (as an Islamic science)
BAS: нәхеү
TAJ: наҳу
TAT: нәхү
UZB: наҳу

na'ib نائب ARABIC *n.* deputy
BAS: наиб
KAR: найып, нәиб, найб
TAJ: ноиб
TAT: наиб
TUR: найып
UYG: näib
UZB: ноиб

Na'im[1] نعيم ARABIC *n.* a name for Paradise
KAR: нәим
TAJ: наим
TAT: нәгыйм
UYG: näim
UZB: наим

na'im[2] نعيم ARABIC *n.* God's bounty to his creatures
KAR: нәим
TAJ: наим
TAT: нәгыйм
UYG: näim
UZB: наим

najas نجس ARABIC *n.* rubbish, trash, filth
KAR: нәжас
TAJ: начас
UYG: najas
UZB: нажас

najasat نجاست ARABIC *Ritual n.* impurity, uncleanliness, filth
KAR: нәжасәт, нәжас
TAT: нәҗасәт
UZB: нажасат

najasat ghaliz نجاسط غليظ ARABIC *Ritual np.* foul impurity (the greater degree of an impure substance)

TAT: нәҗасәт газиз

UZB: нажасати ғализ

najasat khafif نجاست خفيف ARABIC *Ritual np.* lesser impurity (the lesser degree of an impure substance)

TAT: нәҗасәт хәфиф

UZB: нажасати хафиф

najat نجات ARABIC *n.* salvation

BAS: нәжәт

KAR: нәжат

TAJ: наҷот

TAT: нәҗат

UYG: najat

UZB: нажот

najis نجس ARABIC *adj.* filthy, unclean, impure

BAS: нәжес

KAR: нажәс

KAZ: нажес, нажіс, нажес

TAJ: наҷис

TAT: нәҗес

TUR: нежис

UYG: nijis

UZB: нажс

Najm نجم ARABIC *Qur'an pn.* the 53rd sura of the Qur'an

KAR: Ўан-нажм суўреси

KAZ: Нежім сүресі

TAJ: сураи Наҷм

TAT: Нәҗем сүрәсе

TUR: сураи Вен нежим

UYG: sürä Näjm

UZB: Ва-н-нажм сураси

namahram نا محرم PERSIAN *Law adj.* not banned, not illicit (not in violation of laws concerning marriage to distant relatives)

KAR: намәҳрәм

TAJ: номаҳрам

TAT: намәхрәм

TUR: нәмәхрем

UYG: namährämp

UZB: номаҳрам *a rule determining which family members of a husband and a wife are allowed to be openly seen*

namashru' نامشروع PERSIAN *Law adj.* violating Islamic law

KAR: нәмашру

TAJ: номашру

TAT: намәшруг

UZB: номашру

namaz نماز PERSIAN *Ritual n.* one of the daily prayers required by Islamic tradition

☞ ***salat; salat al-fajr, salat al-subh, salat al-zuhr, s-alat al-'asr, salat al-maghrib, salat al-'isha', salavat -i nafila***

BAS: намаҙ

KAR: намаз ① *one of the daily prayers required by Islamic tradition* ② *reading of the Qur'an at a burial*

KAZ: намаз

KYR: намаз

TAJ: намоз

TAT: намаз

TUR: намаз

UYG: namaz

UZB: намоз

namazgah نمازگاه PERSIAN *n.* open air place of public worship

KAR: намазгөҳ

TAJ: намозгоҳ

TUR: намазгәх

UYG: namazgah

UZB: намозгоҳ

namazgu نماز گو PERSIAN *n.* one who performs the daily prayer, pious person

KAR: намазгөй

KYR: намазгөй

TAJ: намозгӯ

UYG: namazgo

UZB: намозгўй

namazkhan نمازخوان PERSIAN *n.* one who performs the daily prayers, reader of prayers

KAR: намазхан

TAJ: намозхон

UYG: namazkhan

UZB: намозхон

Naml نمل ARABIC *Qur'an pn.* the 27th sura of the Qur'an

KAR: Намл суўреси

KAZ: Нәміл сүресі

TAJ: сураи Намл

TAT: Нәмел сүрәсе

TUR: сураи Немл

UYG: Naml süräsi
UZB: Намл сураси

napak [1] نا پاك PERSIAN *adj.* unclean, impure
KAR: нәпак
TAJ: нопок
TAT: напакь
UYG: napak
UZB: нопок

napak [2] نا پاك PERSIAN *n.* menstruating woman
KAR: нәпак
TAJ: нопок
TAT: напакь
UYG: napak
UZB: нопок

naqib نقيب ARABIC *n.* elder, chief, head
KAR: нәқип
KAZ: нақып
TAJ: нақиб
TAT: нәкыйб
UZB: нақиб

naqis ناقص ARABIC *Ritual adj.* insufficient, short, defective (as a status of acts of devotion)
BAS: наҡыҫ
TAJ: нақс
TAT: накыйс
UZB: нақис

naqliya نقليه ARABIC *n.* that which pertains to Islamic tradition
KAR: нақлия
KAZ: нақлия
TAJ: нақлия
TAT: нәкълият
UZB: нақлия

narava ناروا PERSIAN *Law adj.* unlawful (according to Islamic law)
TAT: нарәва
UZB: нораво

Nas ناس ARABIC *Qur'an pn.* the 114th sura of the Qur'an ☞ ***Mu'avvizitan, Mu'avvizitayn***
KAR: Аннәс суўреси
KAZ: Нас сүресі
TAJ: сураи Нос
TAT: Нас сүрәсе, ән-Нас сүрәсе
UYG: Annäs süräsi, sürä Nas
UZB: Ан-нос сураси

nasab نسب ARABIC *n.* lineage, genealogy
BAS: нәсәп
KAR: нәсап
TAJ: насаб
TAT: нәсәб
UYG: nasap
UZB: насаб

nasabnama نسبنامه PERSIAN *n.* genealogy, genealogical treatise
KAR: нәсапнамә
KAZ: насабнама
TAJ: насабнома
UZB: насабнома

nasara نصارا ARABIC *n.* Christians
KAR: насәрә
KAZ: насара
TAJ: насоро
TAT: нәсара
UYG: näsara
UZB: насоро

na'sh [1] نعش ARABIC *Ritual n.* coffin containing a body
KAR: нәәш
TAJ: нааш
TAT: нәгыш
UZB: нааш

na'sh [2] نعش ARABIC *Ritual n.* body placed in a coffin
KAR: нәәш
TAJ: нааш
TAT: нәгыш
UZB: нааш

nashar'i ناشرعى PERSIAN *Law adj.* illicit, unlawful, contravening Islamic law
KAR: нәшари
TAJ: ношаръӣ
UYG: nashar'iy
UZB: ношаръий

nasib نصيب ARABIC *n.* fate, that which is ordained by fate
BAS: насип
KAR: несип, нәсип
KYR: насип, насып
TAJ: насиб
TAT: нәсыйб
TUR: несип
UYG: näsip
UZB: насиб

nasiba نصيبه ARABIC *n.* fate
- **KAR:** несийбе
- **TAJ:** насиба
- **UYG:** näsibä
- **UZB:** насиба

nasihat نصيحت ARABIC *n.* admonition, precepts, advice, good counsel
- **BAS:** нэсихэт
- **KAR:** нэсийҳат, нэсихат, нэсият
- **KAZ:** насихат
- **KYR:** насыят, насият, насаат
- **TAJ:** насиҳат
- **TAT:** насыйхэт
- **TUR:** несихат
- **UYG:** näsihät
- **UZB:** насиҳат

nasl نسل ARABIC *n.* descendants
- **BAS:** нэçел
- **KAR:** нэсил
- **KAZ:** нэсіл
- **KYR:** насил
- **TAJ:** насил
- **TAT:** нэсел
- **TUR:** несил
- **UZB:** насил

Nasr نصر ARABIC *Qur'an pn.* the 110th sura of the Qur'an
- **KAR:** Наср суўреси
- **KAZ:** Насыр сүресі
- **TAJ:** сураи Наср
- **TAT:** Нэсыр сүрэсе
- **UYG:** Nasr süräsi
- **UZB:** Наср сураси

nasrani نصرانى ARABIC *adj.* Christian
- **KAR:** насрани
- **KAZ:** насрани
- **TAJ:** насронӣ
- **TAT:** нэсрани
- **UYG:** näsara
- **UZB:** насроний

nasraniyat نصرانيت ARABIC *n.* Christianity
- **KAR:** насраният
- **TAJ:** насроният
- **TAT:** нэсраниять
- **UYG:** näsara
- **UZB:** насроният

nasta'liq نستعليق ARABIC *n.* a style of calligraphic handwriting of the Arabic script
- **KYR:** насталик
- **TAJ:** настаълиқ
- **UZB:** настаълиқ

nasuh نصوح ARABIC *Theology n.* sincere repentance
- **TAJ:** насух
- **UZB:** насуҳ

nasut ناسوت ARABIC *n.* human nature
- **KAZ:** насут
- **TAJ:** насу
- **TAT:** насут
- **UZB:** насут

na't نعت ARABIC *n.* genre of poetic work in which the Prophet Muhammad is praised
- **TAT:** нэгыть
- **UZB:** нот

na't-i sharif نعت شريف PERSIAN *np.* genre of poetic work in which the Prophet Muhammad is praised
- **TAT:** нэгъти шэриф
- **UZB:** ноти шариф

na'uzu billahi نعوذ بلله ARABIC *intj.* God help us
- **TAT:** нэгузе биллаһи
- **UZB:** наузибиллоҳи, наузибиллаҳи

navkar نوكر PERSIAN *n.* servant (e.g. of a sovereign); soldier
- **BAS:** нөгэр, нэүкэр, нөгөр, нүкэр
- **KAR:** нөкер, нэвкер
- **KAZ:** нөкер
- **KYR:** нөкөр
- **TAJ:** навкар
- **TUR:** нөкер
- **UYG:** nawkar
- **UZB:** навкар

Navruz نوروز PERSIAN *Ritual pn.* solar New Year's festival observed on March 21st which is widely celebrated among Muslims in Central Asia and the Volga-Ural region
- **BAS:** Нэүруз
- **KAR:** Наўруз
- **KAZ:** Наурыз
- **KYR:** Нооруз, Оруздама
- **TAJ:** Наврӯз
- **TAT:** Нэүруз, Нэүрүз
- **TUR:** Новруз
- **UYG:** Näwbahar

UZB: Наврўз

nayran نیران ARABIC *n.* hellfire
TAJ: найрон
TAT: нәйран
UZB: найран

nazahat نزاهت ARABIC *n.* purity (i.e. moral)
TAJ: назоҳат
TAT: нәзаһәт
UZB: назоҳат

nazar [1] نظر ARABIC *Law n.* view, opinion (esp. in Islamic law)
BAS: назар
KAR: нәзар
KAZ: назар
KYR: назар
TAJ: назар
TAT: нәзар
UZB: назар

nazar [2] نظر ARABIC *n.* theory (as opposed to practice; in Islamic philosophy)
BAS: назар
KAR: нәзар
KAZ: назар
TAJ: назар
TAT: нәзар
UZB: назар

nazar bar qadam نظر بر قدم PERSIAN *Sufism np.* watching over one's steps (one of the eight principles of the Naqshbandi Sufi order)
TAT: назар бер кадәм
UZB: назар бар қадам

Nazi'at نزعت ARABIC *Qur'an pn.* the 79th sura of the Qur'an
KAR: Ўан-нәзиәт сўуреси
KAZ: Насиғат сүресі
TAJ: сураи Нозиъот
UYG: sürä Nazi'at
UZB: Ван-нозиот сураси

nazil نازل ARABIC *Qur'an adj.* sent down from God (i.e. Qur'anic verses)
KAR: нәзил
TAJ: нозил
TAT: назил
TUR: назыл
UZB: нозил

nazr [1] نذر ARABIC *n.* vow, promise (esp. to God)
BAS: нәҙер
KAR: нәзир
KAZ: нәзір
TAJ: назр
TAT: нәзер
UYG: näzr ① *vow, promise (esp. to God)* ② *memorial repast*
UZB: назр

nazr [2] نذر ARABIC *n.* alms, charity
KAR: нәзр
KAZ: нәзр
KYR: назир, назр, назыр
TAJ: назр
TAT: нәзер
TUR: незир
UYG: näzir, näzr
UZB: назр

nifas نفاس ARABIC *Ritual n.* bleeding following giving birth (as a condition of ritual impurity)
KAZ: нифас
KYR: нифас
TAJ: нифос
TAT: нифас
TUR: нефас
UZB: нифос

nigah dasht نگاه داشت PERSIAN *Sufism np.* watching over one's thoughts, protecting one's thoughts (one of the eight principles of the Naqshbandi Sufi order)
TAT: нигяһ дәшт
UZB: нигоҳдошт

nihrir نحریر ARABIC *adj.* extremely learned, erudite (epithet for a scholar)
TAJ: нихрир
TAT: нихрир
UZB: нихрир

nikah نکاح ARABIC *Ritual n.* wedding, marriage
BAS: никах
KAR: неке
KAZ: неке
KYR: нике
TAJ: никоҳ
TAT: никях, никах
TUR: ника
UYG: nika, nikah
UZB: никоҳ

ni'mat نعمت ARABIC *n.* abundance, favor, blessings
BAS: ниғмәт

KAR: нигмет
KAZ: негмат, нигмэт, ныгмат
TAJ: неъмат
TAT: нигъмэт
UZB: неъмат

Nisa نسا ARABIC *Qur'an pn.* the 4th sura of the Qur'an
KAR: Нисə суўреси
KAZ: Ниса сүресі
TAJ: сураи Нисо
TAT: Ниса сүрəсе, Нисаэ сүрəсе
UYG: Nisä süräsi, sürä Nisa
UZB: Нисо сураси

nisab نصاب ARABIC *Taxation n.* minimum property qualification (for paying zakat) ☞ ***zakat***
KAR: нисап
KAZ: нысап
TAJ: нисаб
TAT: нисаб
UZB: нисаб

nisar نثار ARABIC *Ritual n.* money scattered about at a wedding
TAJ: нисор
TAT: нисар
UYG: nisär
UZB: нисор

nishalla نشتاله PERSIAN *Ritual n.* confection prepared from eggs and sugar and eaten during Ramadan
TAJ: нишалло
UZB: нишалло, нишолда

nishallafurush نشتاله فروش PERSIAN *Ritual n.* seller of nishalla ☞ ***nishalla***
TAJ: нишаллофурӯш
UZB: нишаллофуруш, нишондафуруш

niyat نیت ARABIC *Ritual n.* intention (i.e. as a required initial state before performing a religious devotion)
BAS: ниэт
KAR: нийет, ниет
KAZ: ниет
KYR: ниэт, ниет
TAJ: ният
TAT: ният
TUR: ниет
UYG: niyat, niyät
UZB: ният

niyaz نیاز ARABIC *n.* prayer, request
BAS: нияз
KAR: нияз
KYR: нияз, ныяз ① *prayer, request* ② *alms*
TAJ: ниёз
TAT: нияз
TUR: ныяз
UZB: ниёз

nizam نظام ARABIC *Law n.* law, rule, precept
BAS: низам
KAR: низам, ныэам
KAZ: низам
TAJ: низом
TAT: низам
UYG: nizam
UZB: низом

nubuvvat نبوّت ARABIC *n.* prophethood, being a prophet ☞ ***nabuvat***
TAJ: нубувват
TAT: нөбүвэт, нөбөввэт
UZB: нубуввот

Nuh [1] نوح ARABIC *pn.* the prophet Noah
BAS: Нух, Ноҡ
KAR: Нух
KAZ: Нұх, Нуh
KYR: Нух
TAJ: Нуҳ
TAT: Нух
TUR: Нух
UYG: Nuh
UZB: Нуҳ

Nuh [2] نوح ARABIC *Qur'an n.* the 71st sura of the Qur'an
KAR: Нух суўреси
KAZ: Нұх сүресі
TAJ: сураи Нуҳ
TAT: Нух сүрəсе
UYG: Nuh süräsi
UZB: Нуҳ сураси

Numrud نمرود ARABIC *pn.* Nimrod, a Qur'anic figure said to have been a persecutor of the prophet Abraham
KAR: Нимрут, Нəмруд
TAJ: Нумруд, Намруд
TAT: Нэмруд
TUR: Немрут
UYG: Namrut
UZB: Нимруд, Намруд

nur [1] نور ARABIC *n.* light, ray; divine light
BAS: нур

KAR: нур
KAZ: нұр
KYR: нур
TAJ: нур
TAT: нур
TUR: нур
UYG: nur
UZB: нур

Nur ² نور ARABIC *Qur'an pn.* the 24th sura of the Qur'an
KAR: Нур суўреси
KAZ: Нұр сүресі
TAJ: сураи Нур
TAT: Нур сүрәсе
UYG: Nur süräsi
UZB: Нур сураси

Nur, al- النور ARABIC *n.* name of God: Divine Light
BAS: Нур
KAR: Нур
TAJ: Нур
TAT: Нур
TUR: ан-Нур
UYG: Nur
UZB: Ан-Нур

nur-i 'arshullah نور عرش الله PERSIAN *np.* divine light emanating from God's throne
KAR: нури аршиалла
TAJ: нури аршулло
TAT: нуре гаршеллаһ
UZB: нури аршулло

nushur نشور ARABIC *Qur'an n.* God's resurrecting the dead
TAJ: нушур
UZB: нушур, қайта тирилиш

nusrat نصرت ARABIC *n.* help, aid; success, victory
BAS: носрат
KAR: нусрет
KAZ: нұсрат
TAJ: нусрат
TAT: носрәт
UZB: нусрат

nutq نطق ARABIC *Ritual n.* sermon, khutba; speech ☞ ***khutba***
BAS: нотоҡ
KAR: сөз, нутиқ
TAJ: нутқ
TAT: нотык
UZB: нутқ

P

pak پاك PERSIAN *adj.* pure, clean
BAS: пак
KAR: пәк
KAZ: пак
KYR: пак
TAJ: пок
TAT: пакь
UYG: pak
UZB: пок

para پاره PERSIAN *Qur'an n.* section, portion (of a sacred text)
BAS: пара
KAR: пәра, пара
KAZ: пара
TAT: парә
UYG: parä
UZB: пора

paranja پرنجه PERSIAN *n.* long robe covering the entire body worn by Muslim women
BAS: пәрәнжә
KAR: пәренже, паранжи
KAZ: пәренже
KYR: паранжы, баранжы
TAJ: фаранҷи, чодар
TAT: пәрәнҗә
TUR: перенҗи, бүренҗек, пүренҗек
UYG: päränjä
UZB: паранжи

pari پری PERSIAN *n.* fairy, spirit, sprite (belonging to the category of jinns) ☞ ***jinn***
BAS: бәрей, пәрей
KAR: пери, фери
KAZ: пері ① *fairy, spirit, sprite* ② *angel*
KYR: пери, бери
TAJ: парӣ
TAT: пәри
TUR: пери
UYG: päri, piri
UZB: пари *angel*

parikhan پری خوان PERSIAN *n.* shaman, one who invokes spirits to perform religious ceremonies, esp. healing ceremonies
KAR: перихан

TAJ: парихон
UYG: pirikhon
UZB: парихон

parikhani پری خوانی PERSIAN *n.* ceremony of invoking spirits
TAJ: парихони
UYG: pirikhonluq
UZB: парихонлик

parsa پارسا PERSIAN *adj.* pious, godly
TAJ: порсо
TAT: парса
UZB: порсо

Parvardigar پروردگار PERSIAN *n.* the Creator, God
KAR: перўардигар
KAZ: пәруардигәр
KYR: пербердигер, бербердигер, барбардигер
TAJ: парвардигор
TAT: пәрвәрдикяр
UYG: pärwärdigar
UZB: парвардигор

payam پیام PERSIAN *n.* revelation from God ☞ ***paygham***
TAJ: паём
TAT: пәям
UZB: паём

paygham پیغم PERSIAN *n.* revelation from God
KAR: пайғәм
TAJ: пайғом
TAT: пәйгам
UZB: пайғом

payghambar پیغمبر PERSIAN *n.* prophet
BAS: пәйғәмбәр, бәйғәмбәр
KAR: пайғамбар
KAZ: пайғамбар
KYR: пайгамбар, байгамбар
TAJ: пайғамбар
TAT: пәйгамбәр, пигамбәр
TUR: пыгамбер
UYG: päyghämbär, höküma
UZB: пайғамбар

pir پیر PERSIAN *Sufism n.* master, spiritual master (of Sufi adepts, craft apprentices etc.); patron saint (of livestock, trades, etc.); title given to a Sufi master or Muslim saint
BAS: пир
KAR: пир
KAZ: пiр
KYR: пир, бир
TAJ: пир
TAT: пир
TUR: пир
UYG: pir
UZB: пир

pir-i mughan پیر موغان PERSIAN *Sufism np.* shaykh, Sufi master (lit. wine dealer)
KAR: пирмуған
TAJ: пири муғон
UZB: пири муғон

pishqadam پیشقدم PERSIAN *n.* a respected person who had completed an advanced course of study in a madrasa
BAS: пишҡәдәм
KAR: пешқәдәм
TAJ: пешқадам
TAT: пишкадәм
UZB: пешқадам

prighuvur پریغوور ,پریغور RUSSIAN *Historical n.* nomination (during the imperial Russian period in which the congregation of a mosque officially selected its nominee) (restricted to the Volga-Ural region and Kazakhstan)
BAS: приговор
TAT: приговор

pul-i sirat پل صراط PERSIAN *np.* name of the bridge that passes over Hell, ☞ ***Sirat***
KAR: пулсират
TAJ: пули сирот
TUR: Сырат көпрүси
UYG: pilsirat
UZB: пули сирот

purtaqsir پرتقصیر PERSIAN *adj.* loaded down with sins; insufficient, lacking (often used by authors to refer to themselves)
TAT: пәртакъсыйр

put پت PERSIAN *n.* idol, image ☞ ***but***
BAS: бот
KAR: бут ① *idol* ② *Buddha (the person)*
KAZ: пұт
KYR: пут, бут
TAJ: пут
TAT: пот ① *idol* ② *icon, image* ③ *cross*
UZB: пут

putkhana پتخانه PERSIAN *n.* temple, shrine (of idol worshipers)

KAR: бутқана
KYR: буткана
TAJ: путхона
TAT: потханә
UZB: путхона

putparast پتپرست PERSIAN *n.* idol worshiper
☞ ***butparast***
KAR: бутпәрәст
KYR: бутпарас
TAJ: путпараст
TAT: потпәрәст
UZB: путпараст

Q

qabahat قباحت ARABIC *n.* fault, sin, offense; shame, disgrace
BAS: ҡәбәхәт
KAR: қәбахәат
TAJ: қабоҳат
TAT: кабахәт, кабәхәт
UZB: қабоҳат

qabih قبیح ARABIC *adj.* repugnant, ugly (in a moral context)
BAS: ҡәбих
KAR: қабих
KAZ: кабих
TAJ: қабиҳ
TAT: кабих
UZB: қабиҳ

Qabil قابیل ARABIC *pn.* Cain, the son of the prophet Adam
KAR: Қабыл
KAZ: Қабыл
TAJ: Қобил
TAT: Кабил
TUR: Кабыл
UYG: Qabil
UZB: Қобил

qabila قبیله ARABIC *n.* tribe, clan
BAS: ҡәбилә
KAR: қәбийле
TAJ: қабила
TAT: кабилә
UYG: qabilä, qäbilä
UZB: қабила

Qabiz, al- القابض ARABIC *pn.* name of God: the Contractor
KAR: Кәбуд
TAJ: Кобуд
TAT: Кабиз
TUR: ал-Кабид
UYG: Käbud
UZB: Ал-Кобуд

qabr قبر ARABIC *n.* tomb, grave
BAS: ҡабер
KAR: қәбир
KAZ: қабір, қабыр
KYR: кабыр
TAJ: қабр
TAT: кабер
TUR: габыр
UYG: qäwrä, qäbr
UZB: қабр

qabristan قبرستان PERSIAN *n.* graveyard, cemetery
KAR: қәбристан, қәбирстан
TAJ: қабристон
TAT: каберстан
TUR: габрыстан, габрыстанлык
UYG: qawristan, göristan
UZB: қабристон

qa'da قعده ARABIC *Ritual n.* sitting position assumed by males during prayer
TAJ: қаъда
TAT: кагъдә, кагадә
UZB: қаъда *funeral services held at a relative's home instead of at the deceased's home*

qadam قدم ARABIC *n.* pace, step
BAS: ҡәдәм
KAR: қәдем
TAJ: қадам
TAT: кадәм
UYG: qädäm
UZB: қадам

qadamgah قدمگاه PERSIAN *n.* holy place, shrine
KAR: қәдемгөх
TAJ: қадамгоҳ
UYG: qädämgah
UZB: қадамгоҳ

qadamjay قدمجای PERSIAN *n.* holy place, shrine
KAR: қәдемжөй
TAJ: қадамҷой
UYG: qädämjay

UZB: қадамжой

qadar قدر ARABIC *n.* fate
BAS: ҡәҙәр
KAR: кәдер
TAJ: қадар
TAT: кадәр
UZB: қадар

Qadim, al- القديم ARABIC *pn.* name of God: the One without Beginning
KAR: қадым
TAJ: қадим
TAT: Кадим
UZB: қадим

qadimi قديمى *Historical adj.* traditionalist, qadimist, pertaining to traditionalist opposition to jadidism
☞ ***usul-i qadim***
BAS: ҡәҙими, ҡәҙимсе
KAR: қадыми
KAZ: қадыми, қадими
KYR: кадими
TAJ: қадимӣ
TAT: кадими
UZB: қадимий

Qadir, al- القدير ARABIC *n.* name of God: the Great, the All Powerful
BAS: Ҡадир
KAR: Қәдир
KYR: Кадыр, Кадыр алла, Кадыр Ак
TAJ: Қодир
TAT: Кадир, әл-Кадыйр
TUR: ал-Кадир
UYG: Qadir
UZB: Ал-Қодир

Qadr [1] قدر ARABIC *Qur'an pn.* the 97th sura of the Qur'an
BAS: ҡәҙер
KAR: Қадр суўреси
KAZ: Қадыр сүресі
KYR: кадыр, кадыр алла, кадыр ак
TAJ: сураи Қадр
TAT: Кадер сүрәсе, Сүрәтүл-кадри
UYG: Qädir süräsi
UZB: Қадр сураси

qadr [2] قدر ☞ ***laylat al-qadr***

Qaf [1] قاف ARABIC *Qur'an pn.* the 50th sura of the Qur'an
KAR: Қәф суўреси
KAZ: Қаф сүресі
TAJ: сураи Қоф
TAT: Каф сүрәсе
UYG: Qäp süräsi, sürä Qaf
UZB: Қоф сураси

Qaf [2] قاف ARABIC *pn.* mythical mountain range surrounding the world, and generally equated with the Caucasus range
BAS: Ҡаф тауы
KAR: Қәф тәғи
KYR: Кап тоо, Көйкап тоо
TAJ: кӯҳи Қоф
UZB: Қоф тоғи

Qahhar, al- القهّار ARABIC *pn.* name of God: the Dominant
BAS: Ҡәһһар
KAR: Қаххәр, Қәҳәр
TAJ: Қаҳҳор
TUR: ал-Каххар
UYG: Qähhär
UZB: Ал-Қаҳҳор

Qahr, al- القاهر ARABIC *pn.* name of God: the Compeller
KAR: қаҳыр
TAJ: қаҳр
UZB: қаҳир

qaʻida قاعده ARABIC *n.* rule, principle, precept, foundation
BAS: ҡағиҙа
KAR: қағыйда, қаыдә
KAZ: қағида
KYR: каада
TAJ: қоида
TAT: кагыйдә
UYG: qa'idä
UZB: қоида

qal قال ARABIC *n.* that which is acquired by learning (as opposed to that which is known intuitively)
☞ ***hal***
KAZ: қал
TAJ: қал
UZB: қал

qalam [1] قلم ARABIC *n.* fate, predestination
BAS: ҡәләм
KAR: қәләм
KAZ: қалам
KYR: калам

TAJ: қалам
UYG: qalam
UZB: қалам

qalam[2] قلم ARABIC *n.* pen (thought to be the first thing created by God)

KAR: қәлем, қәләм
KAZ: қалам
KYR: калем
TAJ: қалам
TAT: каләм
TUR: галам
UZB: қалам

Qalam[3] قلم ARABIC *Qur'an pn.* the 68th sura of the Qur'an

KAR: Қәлем сүўреси
KAZ: Қалам сүресі
KYR: Калем, Калам
TAJ: сураи Қалам
TAT: Каләм сүрәсе
UYG: Qalam süräsi
UZB: Қалам сураси

qalandar قلندر PERSIAN *Sufism n.* itinerant Sufi, dervish; wanderer; free dervish (not restricted by a master); beggar dervish

KAR: қәлендер
KYR: календер
TAJ: қаландар
TAT: каләндәр
TUR: галандар
UYG: qäländär
UZB: қаландар

qalandarkhana قلندرخانه PERSIAN *Sufism n.* Sufi lodge, house for itinerant Sufis

KAR: қәлендерханә, қәлендерхана
KYR: календеркана
TAJ: қаландархона
UYG: qäländärkhana
UZB: қаландархона

qalb قلب ARABIC *n.* heart; spirituality; in Sufi contexts, the location of God on earth; the location of divine love

BAS: ҡәлб
KAR: қалп
TAJ: қалб
TAT: кальб
UYG: qälb
UZB: қалб

Qamar قمر ARABIC *Qur'an pn.* the 54th sura of the Qur'an

KAR: Қамәр сүўреси
KAZ: Қамар сүресі
TAJ: сураи Қамар
TAT: Камәр сүрәсе
UYG: Qamar süräsi, sürä Qämär
UZB: Қамар сураси

qamat قامت ARABIC *Ritual n.* mu'azzin's call signaling the beginning of a namaz; preliminary prayer performed standing up

BAS: ҡамәт
KAR: қәмәт
KYR: коомат
TAJ: қомат
TAT: камәт
UZB: қомат

qamis قميص ARABIC *Ritual n.* shirt; part of the burial clothes

KAZ: қамис
TAJ: қамис
TAT: камис
UZB: қамис

qana'at قناعت ARABIC *n.* satisfaction; conviction, belief

BAS: ҡәнәғәт
TAJ: қаноат
TAT: канагать
UYG: qänäät
UZB: қаноат

qanun قانون ARABIC *Law n.* laws (of the state), secular law (as opposed to Islamic law)

BAS: ҡанун
KAR: қәнун, нызам, закон
TAJ: қонун
TAT: канун
TUR: канун
UYG: qanun
UZB: қонун

qari قارئ ARABIC *Qur'an n.* Qur'an reciter, one who has memorized the Qur'an

BAS: ҡарый
KAR: қары, қарый
KAZ: қари
KYR: кары, карыя
TAJ: қорӣ
TAT: кари, кариэ

TUR: кары
UYG: qari
UZB: қори

Qariʻa قارعه ARABIC *Qur'an pn.* the 101st sura of the Qur'an
KAR: Ал-қәрия суўреси
KAZ: Қариға сүресі
TAJ: сураи Қориъа
TAT: Каригаһ сүрәсе
UYG: Qäriya süräsi, sürä Qari'ä
UZB: Ал-қориа сураси

qarikhana قاری خانه PERSIAN *Qur'an n.* school for Qur'an recitation
KAR: қарыханә
TAJ: қорихона
UYG: qarikhana
UZB: қорихона

qarz قرض ARABIC *n.* debt (i.e. of life given by God); loan
BAS: ҡарыз
KAR: қарыз
TAJ: қарз
TAT: карз
UYG: qärz
UZB: қарз

qasam قسم ARABIC *n.* oath, pledge
KAR: қасәм
TAJ: қасам
TAT: касәм
UYG: qäsäm
UZB: қасам

qasas [1] قصاص ARABIC *Law n.* revenge, vengeance (as a legal right defined in Islamic law, but in a restricted capacity compared with pre-Islamic law)
KAR: қасәс
TAJ: қасос
UYG: qisas
UZB: қасос

Qasas [2] قصص ARABIC *Qur'an pn.* the 28th sura of the Qur'an
KAR: Қасәс суўреси
KAZ: Қасас сүресі
TAJ: сураи Қисас
UYG: sürä Qäsäs
UZB: Қасос сураси

qasd قصد ARABIC *n.* intention, goal; evil intention, revenge
KAR: қасыт
TAJ: қасд
TAT: касд
UYG: qäst
UZB: қасд

qasis قسيس ARABIC *n.* Christian saint
TAJ: қасис
TAT: касис
UZB: қасис

qatʻi ☞ ***haram qat'i***

qatʻiyat قتعيت ARABIC *Theology n.* explicitness, being unshakable (as a condition of belief)
TAJ: қатъият
UZB: қатъият

qatl قتل ARABIC *Law n.* homicide, murder; putting to death
BAS: ҡәтел
KAR: қатл
TAJ: қатл
TAT: кател
TUR: катыл
UZB: қатл

qatl ʻamd قتل عمد ARABIC *Law np.* willful murder
TUR: катыл амыд

qatl sabab قتل سبب ARABIC *Law np.* murder by an intermediate cause, for which the person charged is not directly responsible
TUR: катыл себәб

qatl shubha ʻamd قتل شبه عمد ARABIC *Law np.* manslaughter, murder carried out with a stick or rod
TUR: катыл шубхе амыд

qavam قوام ARABIC *Ritual n.* the motion of raising oneself between the ruku' and the sajda
TAJ: қавом
UZB: қавом

Qavi, al- القوى ARABIC *n.* name of God: the Strong
BAS: Ҡәүи
KAR: Қавий
TAJ: Қовӣ
TAT: Кави
TUR: ал-Кавп
UZB: Ал-Қовий

qavm قوم ARABIC *n.* tribe; group; congregation that attends the same mosque; nation
BAS: ҡәүем ① *clan, descent group* ② *nation, people*

KAR: қәуим, қауым, мешитқәуим ① *community* ② *tribe*
KYR: коом
TAJ: қавм
TAT: каум
UYG: qom
UZB: қавм

Qavs قوس ARABIC *pn.* Sagittarius, the 10th month of the Hidjri Solar year
BAS: Ҡәүес
KAR: қауыс
KAZ: Қаус
TAJ: қавс
TAT: Кавәс
UYG: Qaws, Kewus
UZB: Қавс

Qayyum, al- القيّوم ARABIC *n.* name of God: the Self-Subsistent
KAR: Қаййим
KAZ: Қаййұм, әл-Қаййум
TAJ: Қаюм
TUR: ал-Каййум
UZB: Ал-Қайюм

qaza قضا ARABIC *Ritual n.* the subsequent performance of an act of worship which had been previously omitted from the proper time
BAS: ҡаза
KAR: қаза, ғаза ① *the subsequent performance of an act of worship which had been previously omitted at the proper time* ② *death*
KAZ: қаза ① *the subsequent performance of an act of worship which had been previously omitted at the proper time* ② *death*
KYR: каза ① *the subsequent performance of an act of worship which had been previously omitted at the proper time* ② *fate* ③ *death*
TAJ: қазо ① *the subsequent performance of an act of worship which had been previously omitted at the proper time* ② *fate* ③ *death*
TAT: каза ① *the subsequent performance of an act of worship which had been previously omitted from the proper time* ② *divine punishment*
TUR: каза
UZB: қазо ① *the subsequent performance of an act of worship which had been previously omitted at the proper time* ② *fate* ③ *death*

qaza-yi mu'allaq قضای معلّق ARABIC *np.* inevitability of death
TAJ: қазову муаллақ
UZB: қазойи муаллақ

qazi قاضی ARABIC *Law n.* judge (of Islamic law)
BAS: ҡазый
KAR: қазы
KAZ: қазы, қади
KYR: казы, казый
TAJ: қозӣ
TAT: казый, кади
TUR: казы
UYG: qazi
UZB: қози

qazikhana قاضی خانه PERSIAN *Law n.* Islamic court
KAR: қазыхана
TAJ: қозихона
UYG: qazikhana
UZB: қозихона

qazizada قاضی زاده PERSIAN *n.* judge's son
KAR: қазызәдә
TAJ: қозизода
UYG: qazizada
UZB: қозизода

qibla قبله ARABIC *Ritual n.* the direction of Mecca (toward which Muslims are obligated to pray) (this term can also denote a cardinal point, equivalent to the south or southwest)
BAS: ҡибла, ҡыбла
KAR: қиплә
KAZ: құбыла
KYR: кыбыла, кыбла
TAJ: қибла
TAT: кыйбла
TUR: кыбла
UYG: qiblä, qiwla
UZB: қибла

qiblagah قبله گاه ARABIC *Ritual n.* the direction of the Qibla
KAR: қипләгә
TAJ: қиблагоҳ
UYG: qibligah
UZB: қиблагоҳ ① *the direction of the Qibla* ② *respected man*

qiblanama قبله نامه ARABIC *Ritual n.* compass (used mainly for determining the direction of Mecca)
BAS: ҡибланма
KAR: қипләнамә
KAZ: құбыланама

TAJ: қибланамо
TAT: кыйбланамә
TUR: кыбланама
UYG: qiblänama
UZB: қибланома

qidam قدم ARABIC *Theology n.* timelessness, eternal existence in the past (a distinguishing quality of God)
KAZ: қыдем
TAT: кыйдәм

qimar قمار ARABIC *Law n.* gambling
BAS: ҡомар
KAR: қимәр
TAJ: қимор
UYG: qimär
UZB: қимор

qira'at قرائت ARABIC *Qur'an n.* Qur'an recitation
BAS: ҡираәт
KAR: қирәет, қыраат
KAZ: қираға, қира'әт, қирағат
KYR: кыраат
TAJ: қироат
TAT: кыйраәт, кыйраьәт
TUR: кырагат, кыраат ① *Qur'an recitation* ② *performing a brief Qur'anic verse three times during a namaz*
UYG: qira'at
UZB: қироат

qira'atkhana قرائتخانه PERSIAN *Qur'an n.* room for reading the Quran
BAS: ҡираәтхана
TAJ: қироатхона
TAT: кыйраәтханә
UYG: qira'atkhana
UZB: қироатхона

qiran قران ARABIC *Hajj n.* the act of performing the 'umra pilgrimage and the hajj simultaneously; a lucky alignment of planets
KAR: қиран
KAZ: қыран
TAJ: қирон
UZB: қирон

qisas قصاص ARABIC *Law n.* retaliation, reprisal
☞ *qasas*
BAS: ҡисас
KAR: қасәс
KAZ: қысас
TAJ: қасос
TAT: кыйсас
TUR: кысас
UYG: qisas
UZB: қасос

qisas al-anbiya قصص الانبيا ARABIC *np.* history of the prophets (as a literary genre)
TAT: кыйссасел-әнбия
UYG: qissasul-änbiya
UZB: қиссасул анбиё, кисса-ул анбиё

qismat قسمت ARABIC *n.* destiny; fate
BAS: ҡисмәт
KAR: қисмәт
TAJ: қисмат
TAT: кыйсмәт
UYG: qismät
UZB: қисмат

qisvat قسوة ARABIC *n.* the cloth covering placed over the Ka'ba
KAR: қысўа
KAZ: қисуа
TAJ: каъбапӯш
TAT: кисвә, кыйсва, кисвәт әл-Кәъбә
UZB: каъбапўш, қисва, кисва

Qitmir قطمير ARABIC *pn.* name of the dog which accompanied the Seven Sleepers
KAR: Қитмир
TAJ: Қитмир
UZB: Қитмир

qiyam قيام ARABIC *Ritual n.* standing position in prayer
BAS: ҡыям
KAZ: қыям
TAJ: қиём
TAT: кыям
TUR: кыям
UYG: qiyäm, qiyam
UZB: қиём

qiyam binafsihi قيام بنفسه ARABIC *Theology np.* inherent in himself (a distinguishing quality of God)
KAZ: қыям бі-нәфсіһі
TAT: кыйам бинәфсиниһи

qiyamat[1] قيامت ARABIC *n.* Judgment Day, the End of the World
BAS: ҡиәмәт, ҡиәмәт көнө, мәхшәр көнө ① *Judgment Day* ② *the afterlife*

KAR: қыямат, қиямәт
KAZ: қиямет, қиямет күні
KYR: кыямат ① *Judgement Day* ② *this world*
TAJ: қиёмат
TAT: кыямәт, кыямәт көне
TUR: кыямат, кыямат гүни
UYG: qiyamät
UZB: қиёмат

Qiyamat 2 قيامت ARABIC *Qur'an pn.* the 75th sura of the Qur'an
KAR: Қиямәт суўреси
KAZ: Қиямет сүресі
TAJ: сураи Қиёмат
TAT: Кыямәт сүрәсе
UYG: sürä Qiyamät
UZB: Қиёмат сураси

qiyamat qa'im قيامت قائم ARABIC *np.* Judgment Day ☞ ***akhir zaman***
BAS: ҡиәмәт ҡайымы
KAR: қиямәт қәйим
KYR: кыямат кайым ① *Judgement Day* ② *this world*
TAJ: қиёмат қойим
UZB: қиёмат қойим

qiyas قياس ARABIC *Law n.* comparison, analogy in Islamic law (concerning issues not directly addressed in the Qur'an or the Sunna); one of the four "roots" of Islamic law, synonymous with ijtihad ☞ ***ijtihad***
BAS: ҡыяс
KAR: қияс, қыяс
KAZ: қийас, қыяс
TAJ: қиёс
TAT: кыяс
TUR: кияс
UYG: qiyas
UZB: қиёс

qiyas-i fuqaha قياس فقها PERSIAN *Law np.* analogy of legal experts
TAT: кыйасе фөкаһа
UZB: қиёси фуқаҳо

qubba قبّه ARABIC *n.* dome, cupola
BAS: ҡоббә
KAR: қубба
KYR: купа
TAJ: қубба
TAT: коббә
UYG: qubbä
UZB: қубба

Qubbat al-Islam قبّة الاسلام ARABIC *np.* the Dome of Islam (epithet for the city of Basra)
KAR: Қуббатул Ислам
TAJ: Қуббатул Ислом
TAT: Куббәтүл ислами
UZB: Қуббатул Ислом

qubur قبور ARABIC *n.* graves (plural) ☞ ***qabr***
TAJ: қубур
TAT: кобур
UZB: қубур, қабрлар

quddus قدّوس ARABIC *adj.* holy, sacred
BAS: ҡөддөс
KAR: қуддус
TAJ: қуддус
TAT: коддус
UZB: қуддус

Quddus, al- القدّوس ARABIC *adj.* name of God: the Holy
BAS: Ҡөддөс
KAR: Қуддус
KAZ: әл-Құддыс
TAJ: Қуддус
TAT: Коддус
TUR: ал-Куддус
UYG: Quddus
UZB: Ал-Қуддус

qudrat قدرت ARABIC *n.* power, strength; divinity
BAS: ҡөҙрәт
KAR: қудрәт, қудирет
KAZ: құдірет
KYR: кудурет, кудрет
TAJ: қудрат
TAT: кодрәт
TUR: гудрат
UYG: qudrät
UZB: қудрат

quds قدس ARABIC *n.* sanctity, holiness, purity
BAS: ҡодес
KAR: қудс
TAJ: қудс
TAT: кодес
UYG: quds
UZB: қудс

Quds, al- القدس ARABIC *pn.* Jerusalem
KAR: Қуддуси Шарип

KAZ: Иерусалим
TAJ: Қуддус
TAT: эл-Кодес, Кудс
TUR: Куддус, Кудс
UYG: Quddus
UZB: Қуддуси шариф

qudsi قدسى ARABIC *adj.* pure, unsullied, sacred
BAS: ҡөдси
KAR: қудс
TAJ: қудсӣ
TAT: кодси
UZB: қудси

qudsiyat قدسيت ARABIC *n.* sanctity, holiness
BAS: ҡөдсиэт
TAJ: қудсият
TAT: кодсиять
UZB: қудсият

qul hu allah ahad قل هو الله احد ARABIC *Qur'an np.* the first verse of the 112th sura ☞ ***Ikhlas***
BAS: ҡөлһыуалла
KAR: қулхиаллаахад
KYR: кулкулдабат
TAJ: қулҳи Аллоҳу Аҳад
TAT: колһуаллаһ
UZB: қулҳу Аллоҳу Аҳад

qunut قنوت ARABIC *Ritual n.* worshiping God humbly and obediently ☞ ***du'a-yi qunut***
KAZ: құнұт
KYR: кунут
TAJ: қунут
TAT: конут, кунут
TUR: кунут
UZB: қунут

Qur'an قرآن ARABIC *Qur'an pn.* the Qur'an, the holy book of Islam transmitted by God to the Prophet Muhammad
BAS: Ҡөрьән
KAR: Қуран
KAZ: Құран
KYR: Куран ① *the Qur'an, the holy book of Islam transmitted by God to the Prophet Muhammad* ② *reading a portion of the Qur'an for the dead (performed by a person who was not at the burial and is visiting the family of the deceased for the first time)*
TAJ: Қуръон
TAT: Коръан
TUR: Гурхан, Куръан, Куран
UYG: Qur'an, Quran
UZB: Қуръон

Qur'an khatima قرآن خاتمه ARABIC *Qur'an np.* reading the Qur'an from beginning to end for the benefit of one's ancestors
KAR: Қурани қатим
KYR: Куран катма
TAJ: Қуръони хотима
UZB: Қуръони хатим

Qur'an-i 'Azim قرآن عظيم ARABIC *Qur'an np.* the Glorious Qur'an
KAR: Қурани Азийм
TAJ: Қуръони Азим
TAT: Корьэн-Газыйм, Корьэн-Газим
UYG: Qur'ani Äzim
UZB: Қуръони Азим

Qur'an-i Karim قرآن كريم ARABIC *Qur'an np.* the Holy Qur'an
KAR: Қуран Кәрим
KAZ: Құр'аны Кәрим, Құран-Кәрім
TAJ: Қуръони Карим
TAT: Коръане Кәрим, Көрьэни-Кәрим, Коръэн-Кәрим
UZB: Қуръони Карим

Qur'an-i Majid قرآن مجيد PERSIAN *Qur'an np.* the Glorious Qur'an
TAJ: Қуръони Маҷид
TAT: Коръэн-Мәҗид

qur'ankhana قرآنخانه PERSIAN *Qur'an n.* a pupil who is already able to read the Qur'an
KAR: Қуранханә
KYR: куранкана
TAJ: қуръон хона
UZB: қуръонхона

Quraysh[1] قريش ARABIC *Historical pn.* the tribe of the prophet Muhammad
KAR: қурәйиш
KAZ: құрайыш
TAJ: қурайш
TAT: көрәйш
TUR: курайыш, курейиш
UYG: quräysh
UZB: қурайш

Quraysh[2] قريش ARABIC *Qur'an pn.* the 106th sura of the Qur'an
KAR: Қурәйиш суўреси

KAZ: Құрайш сүресі
TAJ: сураи Қурайш
TAT: Көрәйш сүрәсе
UYG: Quräysh süräsi
UZB: Қурайш сураси

qurb قرب ARABIC *Sufism n.* the adept's feeling that God is close to him
TAT: корб
UZB: қурб

qurban قربان *Ritual n.* sacrifice; victim
BAS: ҡорбан ① *sacrifice, victim* ② *'Id al-Adha*
KAR: қурбан, қурбанлиқ
KAZ: құрбан, құрман
KYR: курман, курбан
TAJ: қурбонӣ
TAT: корбан
TUR: гурбан ① *sacrifice victim* ② *the month of Zu'lhijja*
UYG: qurwan, qurbanliq
UZB: қурбон, қурбонлик

Qurban Bayrami قربان بيرامی TURKIC *Ritual np.* 'Id al-Azha ☞ ***'Id al-Azha***
BAS: Ҡорбан байрамы, Ҡорбан
KAR: Қурбан айти
KAZ: Қорбан мейрамы, Қорбан айты
KYR: Курман айт
TAJ: ийди Қурбон
TAT: Корбан бәйрәме
TUR: Гурбан байрамы
UYG: Qurwan mäyräm
UZB: Қурбон байрами

qurra قرا ARABIC *Qur'an n.* person who in addition to being able to recite the Qur'an in seven different styles and explaining the Qur'an in ten different ways, possesses additional Qur'an reciting abilities
TAJ: қироати қурро
TAT: корра *Qur'an recitation*
UZB: қурро, қироати қурро

qusuf قصوف ARABIC *Ritual n.* eclipse (of the moon or sun)
TAJ: кусуф
TAT: косуф ① *eclipse* ② *prayer to stop rain*
UZB: қусуф

qutb قطب ARABIC *Sufism n.* lit. pole (of the earth); a title given to a Sufi thought to be the highest ranking saint on earth
BAS: ҡотоп
KAZ: құтб
TAJ: кутб, кутуб
TAT: котып
TUR: кутб
UYG: qutup
UZB: қутб

R

Rabb ربّ ARABIC *pn.* name of God: the Master
BAS: раббы, рабби
KAR: рабб
KAZ: рабб
TAJ: рабб
TAT: Раббе
TUR: Реб
UYG: räb
UZB: раб, раббим

Rabb al-'alamayn ربّ العلمين ARABIC *np.* name of God: Lord of the Two Worlds
BAS: Раббы әл-ғаләмин
KAR: Раббил әламин
TAJ: Раббил оламин
UZB: Раббил оламин

Rabb al-Falak ربّ الفلك ARABIC *np.* name of God: Lord of Heaven
BAS: Раббы әл-фәләк
TAJ: Раббил Фалак
UZB: Раббил Фалак

Rabbana ربّنا ARABIC *intj.* our God ☞ ***rabb***
KAR: Раббанә
TAJ: Раббано
TAT: Раббәна
UZB: Раббано

rabbani ربّانی ARABIC *adj.* pious, godly
TAJ: раббонӣ
TAT: рәббәни
UZB: раббоний

Rabbi ربّی ARABIC *intj.* my God ☞ ***rabb***
BAS: рабби, я рабби
KAR: Рабби
KAZ: Раббы
KYR: рабби
TAJ: Рабби
TAT: Рабби
UZB: Рабби

Rabi' al-akhir ربيع الآخر ARABIC *pn.* fourth month of the Islamic lunar calendar
- BAS: рабиғылахыр, рабиғылəссани
- KAR: рəбийҮссəни, рабиӱул ақыр
- KAZ: Ребиғул-ақыр
- TAJ: рабеулохир
- TAT: рабигылахыр
- TUR: ребигилсани
- UYG: rabi'ulakhir
- UZB: рабу ал-охир

Rabi' al-avval ربيع الاوّل ARABIC *pn.* third month of the Islamic lunar calendar
- BAS: рабиғылəҮҮəл
- KAR: Рəбийүлəӱəл, Рабиӱул аввəл
- KAZ: Ребиғул-əууəл
- TAJ: рабеулаввал
- TAT: рабигылəҮвəл
- TUR: ребигиловвал
- UYG: rabi'uläwwäl
- UZB: рабу ал-аввал

rabita رابطه ARABIC *Sufism n.* bond, tie; Sufi technical term signifying the connection of the adept with the spiritual master
- KAR: рəбита
- KAZ: рабита
- TAJ: робита
- TAT: рабита
- UYG: rabitä
- UZB: робита

Ra'd رعد ARABIC *Qur'an pn.* the 13th sura of he Qur'an
- KAR: Раъд суӱреси
- KAZ: Рағыд сүресі
- TAJ: сураи Раъд
- TAT: Рəгыд сүрəсе, Əррагд сүрəсе
- TUR: сураи Рагт
- UYG: Rääd süräsi, sürä Rä'd
- UZB: Раъд сураси

radd ردّ ARABIC *Law n.* refutation, rejection
- BAS: рəд, радд
- UYG: rät
- UZB: радд

Rafi', al- الرافع ARABIC *pn.* name of God: the Exalter
- KAR: Рəпи
- TAJ: Рофӣ
- TUR: ар-Рафи
- UZB: Ар-Рофи

ragha'ib رغائب ARABIC *Ritual n.* festival observed on the first Friday of the month Rajab
- KAR: рағəйип
- KAZ: реғайып
- TAJ: рагойиб
- TAT: Рəгаиб, Рəгаиб кичəсе
- UZB: рағойиб

rahban رهبان ARABIC *n.* ascetic; monk
- TAJ: раҳбон
- TAT: рəһбан
- UZB: раҳбон

rahbaniyat رهبانيت ARABIC *n.* asceticism; monasticism
- TAJ: раҳбония
- TAT: рəһбаниять
- UZB: раҳбонийлик

rahib راهب ARABIC *n.* monk (i.e. non-Muslim)
- KAR: рəхип
- TAJ: роҳиб
- TAT: раһиб
- UYG: rahib, rahip
- UZB: роҳиб

rahil رحل ARABIC *n.* bookstand in mosques and Islamic schools
- TAJ: рахил
- UZB: роҳил

rahim رحيم ARABIC *adj.* merciful, compassionate
- BAS: рəхим
- KAR: рəйим, рəҳим
- KAZ: рақым, рахым, рахим
- TAJ: раҳим
- TAT: рахим
- TUR: рехим
- UYG: rähim
- UZB: раҳим, раҳийм, раҳимли

Rahim, al- الرحيم ARABIC *pn.* name of God: the Merciful
- BAS: Рəхим
- KAR: Рəйим
- KAZ: ар-Рахим
- TAJ: Раҳим
- TUR: ал-Рахым
- UYG: Rahim
- UZB: Ар-Раҳийм

rahm رحم ARABIC *n.* mercy, compassion
- KAZ: рақым, рахым

KYR: райым, ракым, ырайым
TAJ: раҳм
TAT: рәхем
TUR: рахым
UYG: rähim-shäpqat
UZB: раҳм

Rahman رحمن ARABIC *Qur'an pn.* the 55th sura of the Qur'an
KAR: Рахман суўреси
KAZ: Рахман сүресі
TAJ: сураи Рахмон
TAT: Рәхман сүрәсе
UYG: Rähman
UZB: Раҳмон сураси

Rahman, al- الرحمن ARABIC *pn.* name of God: the Compassionate
BAS: Рахман
KAR: Рахман
KAZ: ар-Рахман
TAJ: Раҳмон
TAT: ар-Рәхман
TUR: ар-Рахман
UYG: Rähman
UZB: Ар-Раҳмон

rahmani رحمنی ARABIC *adj.* pious, godly; divine
TAJ: раҳмонӣ
TAT: рәхмани
UYG: rähmani
UZB: раҳмоний

rahmat رحمت ARABIC *n.* mercy, compassion
BAS: рәхмәт
KAR: рәҳмәт, рахмет
KAZ: рақмет, рахмат, рахмет
KYR: ыракмат, ракмат, рахмат
TAJ: раҳмат
TAT: рәхмәт
TUR: рахмет
UYG: rähmät
UZB: раҳмат

rahmati رحمتی ARABIC *n.* deceased
KAR: рахметли
TAJ: раҳматӣ
UYG: rähmätliq
UZB: раҳматли

ra'i رأی ARABIC *Law n.* idea, opinion (in Islamic law)
BAS: рай
KAZ: рай
TAJ: раъй
TAT: раи
UZB: раъй

ra'is[1] رئیس ARABIC *n.* figure who presides over religious ceremonies (esp. in Central Asia proper)
BAS: рәис
KAR: рәйис, райыс
KAZ: райыс
KYR: райис, раис
TAJ: раис
TAT: рәис
UYG: rä'is
UZB: раис

ra'is[2] رئیس ARABIC *n.* officially appointed administrator of religious ceremonies and procedures (esp. in Central Asia proper)
KAR: райыс
KAZ: райыс
TAJ: раис
UYG: rä'is
UZB: раис

raja رجا ARABIC *Sufism n.* hope, requesting (a stage on the Sufi path)
BAS: рәжа
UZB: ражо

Rajab رجب ARABIC *pn.* the seventh month of the Islamic lunar calendar
BAS: рәжәп
KAR: рәжәп, рәжап
KAZ: ережеп
TAJ: раҷаб
TAT: рәҗәб
TUR: реҗеп
UYG: räjäp
UZB: ражаб

rajim رجیم ARABIC *pn.* Beaten with Stones (an epithet of the Devil)
KAR: рәжым
TAJ: раҷим
TAT: рәҗим
UYG: räjim
UZB: ражим

rajm رجم ARABIC *Law n.* stoning to death (as a punishment given to women who are unfaithful to their husbands)
BAS: рәжем
KAR: рәжм

KAZ: раджм, таспен ату
TAJ: рачм
TAT: рәҗем
TUR: ражм
UYG: räjm
UZB: ражм

rak'at ركعت ARABIC *Ritual n.* kneeling in prayer
☞ ***namaz***
BAS: рәкәғәт
KAR: рәкет
KAZ: рікғат, ракат
KYR: ирекет, рекет
TAJ: ракъат
TAT: рәкәгать
TUR: рекагат
UYG: räkät, räkä'ät
UZB: ракат, ракъат

Ramazan رمضان ARABIC *pn.* the ninth month of the Islamic lunar calendar; the month of fasting for Muslims
BAS: рамаҙан, рамаҙан шәриф
KAR: Рамазан
KAZ: рамазан, ораза айы
KYR: жарамазан, рамазан, орозо айы, ырамазан
TAJ: рамазон
TAT: рамазан
TUR: ремезан
UYG: ramazan, ramzan, roza
UZB: рамазон

ramazaniya رمضانيّه ARABIC *n.* eulogies written on the occasion of Ramadan
TAT: рамазания

rammal رمّال ARABIC *n.* fortune-teller
TAJ: раммол
UYG: rämmal
UZB: раммол

Raqib, al- الرقيب ARABIC *pn.* name of God: the Guardian
BAS: Рәкип
KAR: Рәқип
TAJ: Роқиб
TAT: Рәкыйб
TUR: ар-Ракып
UYG: Räqip
UZB: Ар-Роқиб

raqs رقص ARABIC *Sufism n.* dance, dancing
KAR: ойын, бий
KAZ: рақыс
TAJ: рақс
TAT: рәкыс
UZB: рақс

Rashid, al- الرشيد ARABIC *pn.* name of God: the Rightly Guided
BAS: Рәшит
KAR: Рәшит
TAJ: Рашид
TAT: Рәшид
TUR: ар-Рашид
UZB: Ар-Рашид

rasm-rusum رسم رسوم ARABIC *Law n.* folk customs, customary law
KAR: рәсим, үрп-әдет
TAJ: расм-русум
UYG: räsim
UZB: расм-русум, расм

Rass رسّ ARABIC *pn.* name of a group or tribe mentioned in the Qur'an
TAJ: асҳоби расс
UYG: Räs ahalisi, äshaburräs

rasul رسول ARABIC *n.* emissary, messenger; the prophet Muhammad
BAS: рәсүл, хәҙрәте рәсүл
KAR: рәсул, рәсӯл
KAZ: рәсул
KYR: расул, ырасул
TAJ: расул
TAT: рәсүл
TUR: ресул
UYG: räsul
UZB: расул

rasulana رسولانه PERSIAN *adj.* prophet-like
TAJ: расулона
UZB: расулона

Rasulullah رسول الله ARABIC *pn.* Messenger of God (epithet of the prophet Muhammad)
BAS: Рәсүле алла
KAR: Рәсулалла, Расулалла, Рәсӯлалла
KYR: Расулулла
TAJ: Расулуллоҳ
TAT: Расүлуллаһ, Рәсүлулла
TUR: Ресулуллах
UZB: Расулуллоҳ

Rauf, al- الروف ARABIC *n.* name of God: the Pardoner
KAR: Рәуп

TAJ: Рауф
TAT: Рәүф
TUR: ар-Равуф
UZB: Ар-Рауф

rava روا PERSIAN *Law adj.* lawful, permitted (in Islamic law) ☞ ***mashru'***
BAS: рәуа
TAJ: раво
TAT: рәва
UZB: раво

ravi راوی ARABIC *Hadith n.* narrator, teller, esp. a transmitter of hadith
BAS: рауи
TAJ: ровӣ
TAT: рави
TUR: равы
UZB: ровий

Ravza روضه ARABIC *pn.* Paradise, heaven
BAS: Рауза
KAR: Рәвза
TAJ: Равза
TAT: Рәуза, Рәүзә
UZB: Равза

Ravza-yi mutahhar روضهء متهّر PERSIAN *pn.* the tomb of the prophet Muhammad in Medina, lit. "the immaculate garden"
TAT: Рәүзаи мотаhhәр
UZB: Равзойи мутаҳҳар

razi allahu ʿanhu رضی الله عنه ARABIC *intj.* may Allah be pleased with him (eulogy for companions of the Prophet)
TAJ: разиаллоҳу анҳу
TAT: разы Аллаhу ганhе
UYG: raziallahu änhu
UZB: разиаллоҳу анҳу, радиаллоҳу анҳу

Razzaq, al- الرزّاق ARABIC *pn.* name of God: the Provider
BAS: Рәзәҡ
KAR: Разақ
TAJ: Раззоқ
TAT: Рәззак
TUR: ар-Раззак
UZB: Ал-Раззоқ

riʿaya رعایه ARABIC *n.* observance; esteem, respect
BAS: риғәйә, риғәйәт
TAJ: риоя
TAT: ригая, ригаять
UYG: ri'ayä
UZB: риоя

riba ربا ARABIC *n.* usury ☞ ***sud***
KAZ: риба
TAJ: рибо
TAT: риба
TUR: риба
UZB: рибо

rida [1] ردا ARABIC *Ritual n.* portion of the burial shroud that covers the body from the feet to the shoulders
KAZ: рида
TAJ: ридо
UZB: ридо

rida [2] ردا ARABIC *Sufism n.* a long garment worn by dervishes
TAJ: ридо
TAT: рида
UZB: ридо

rijal-i ghayb رجال غیب PERSIAN *Sufism n.* lit. "the men of the unseen," a group of saints who can see far-away events and appear wherever they choose ☞ ***chiltan***
BAS: ғәйеп ирәндәр
KAR: ғайып ерен *"the unseen man," tutelary spirits of people and animals*
KAZ: ғайыперен
KYR: кайып эрен, кайберен, кайып эр ① *lit. "the men of the unseen," a group of saints who can see far-away events and appear wherever they choose* ② *the powers of the "men of the unseen"*
TAJ: риҷоал ғайб
TAT: рижале гайб, рижалел-гаиб, гайб ирәннәр
UZB: рижоал ғайб

rind رند PERSIAN *n.* irreligious person; one who refuses to submit to Islamic law
TAJ: ринд
UZB: ринд

risala رساله ARABIC *n.* treatise, prose text
BAS: рисәлә
KAR: рисале
KAZ: рисале
KYR: ирсаалы, рисала
TAJ: рисола
TAT: рисалә
TUR: рисала
UYG: risalä

UZB: рисола ① *treatise* ② *rule, regulation*

risalat رسالت ARABIC *n.* prophetic mission

BAS: рисаләт
KAZ: рисалат
TAJ: рисолат
TAT: рисаләт
UZB: рисолат

rishvat رشوت ARABIC *Law n.* bribery

BAS: ришүәт
TAJ: ришват
TAT: ришвәт
UZB: ришват

rivayat روایت ARABIC *Hadith n.* narration, account, transmission of a hadith

BAS: риүәйәт
KAR: рәўият, ривәят
KAZ: рауаят
KYR: рабаят, риваят
TAJ: ривоят
TAT: риваять
TUR: роваят
UYG: riwayät
UZB: ривоят

riya ریا ARABIC *adj.* hypocrisy

BAS: рыя
TAJ: риё
TAT: рия
UYG: riya
UZB: риё

riyakar ریاکار PERSIAN *n.* hypocrite ☞ ***munafiq***

TAJ: риёкор
TAT: риякяр
UYG: riyakar
UZB: риёкор

riyazat ریاضت ARABIC *adj.* austerity, fastidiousness (i.e. with food); Sufi exercises (of technique)

BAS: риязәт
KAR: риязат
TAJ: риёзат
TAT: риязәт
UYG: riyazät
UZB: риёзат

riza[1] رضا ARABIC *n.* satisfaction, resignation (esp. with the decrees of God)

BAS: риза
KAR: риза
KAZ: риза, ырза
TAJ: ризо
TAT: риза
UYG: riza
UZB: ризо

riza[2] رضا ARABIC *Sufism n.* purification of the heart (a stage on the Sufi path)

TAT: риза
UZB: ризо

rizq رزق ARABIC *n.* daily sustenance (provided by God)

BAS: ризыҡ
KAR: ризиқ
KAZ: рызық, рыздық
TAJ: ризқ
TAT: ризык
UYG: rizq, riziq
UZB: ризқ

Rizvan رضوان ARABIC *pn.* name of the flower garden's watchman in Paradise

BAS: Ризуан
KAR: Ризвән
TAJ: Ризвон
TAT: Ризван
TUR: Ридван
UZB: Ризвон

rizvanullah ʻalayhi[2] رضوان الله علیه ARABIC *intj.* may God be satisfied

TAJ: ризвонулоҳу алайҳи
TAT: ридвану аллаһу галәйһи
UZB: ризвонуллаҳу алайҳи

rububiyat ربوبیت ARABIC *Theology n.* God's being the Master

TAJ: рубобият
TAT: рөбүбиять
UZB: рубобият

ruh[1] روح ARABIC *n.* spirit, soul

BAS: рух
KAR: рух, руўх
KAZ: рух, рҰх ① *spirit, soul* ② *the Qur'an*
KYR: урук, орой, рух, үрөй
TAJ: руҳ
TAT: рух
TUR: рух
UYG: roh
UZB: руҳ

Ruh[2] روح ARABIC *pn.* epithet of the Archangel Gabriel

TAT: Рух

UZB: Руҳ

Ruh al-Amin روح الامين ARABIC *pn.* epithet of the Archangel Gabriel ☞ ***Jabra'il***

KAZ: Рұх

TAJ: Руҳул Амин

TAT: Рухыл-Әмин

UZB: Руҳул-Амин

Ruh al-Quddus روح القدّوس ARABIC *pn.* epithet of the Archangel Gabriel

UYG: Rohulqudus

UZB: Руҳул Куддус

ruhani روحانى ARABIC *n.* religious figure; clergyman; spiritual

BAS: рухани

KAR: руханий, рухани

KAZ: рухани

KYR: руханий

TAJ: руҳонӣ

TAT: рухани ① *religious figure clergyman* ② *spiritual, inner* ③ *spirit, demon*

TUR: руханы

UYG: rohani

UZB: руҳоний

ruhaniyat روحانيت ARABIC *n.* spirituality

KAR: руханият

TAJ: руҳоният

TAT: руханиять

UZB: руҳоният

ruhi روحى ARABIC *adj.* spiritual, pertaining to the soul

BAS: рухи

KAR: руҳый, руўхый, руўхий

KYR: рухий ① *soul* ② *spiritual, pertaining to the soul*

TAJ: руҳий

TAT: рухи

TUR: рухы

UYG: rohiy

UZB: руҳий

Ruhullah روح الله ARABIC *pn.* Spirit of God (epithet of the prophet Jesus)

KYR: Рух Аллах

TAJ: Руҳуллоҳ

TAT: Рухулла

UZB: Руҳуллоҳ

rukhsat رخصت ARABIC *Sufism n.* permission, authorization (to transmit Sufi teachings)

BAS: рөхсәт

KAR: рухсат, рухсәт, руўхсат, урықсат

KAZ: рұқсат

KYR: уруксат, руксат, улуксат

TAJ: рухсат

TAT: рөхсәт

TUR: ругсат

UYG: rukhsat

UZB: рухсат

rukhsatnama رخصتنامه PERSIAN *Sufism n.* certificate of graduation, license (conferred by a Sufi master to his adept)

BAS: рөхсәтнамә

KAR: рухсәтнәма

TAJ: рухсатнома

TAT: рөхсәтнамә

TUR: ругсатнаме

UZB: рухсатнома

ruku' ركوع ARABIC *Ritual n.* bowing in prayer so that the hands touch the knees

BAS: рөкүғ

KAZ: рукүғ, рукұғ

KYR: руку, уруку

TAJ: руку

TAT: рөкүгъ, рукугы

TUR: руку, рекуг

UYG: ruku

UZB: руку

Rum [1] روم ARABIC *Historical pn.* Rome; Greece, Byzantium; Turkey, the Ottoman Empire

KAR: Рум

KAZ: Рұм

TAJ: Рум

TAT: Рум

TUR: Рум

UYG: Rum

UZB: Рум

Rum [2] روم ARABIC *Qur'an pn.* the 30th sura of the Qur'an

KAR: Рум суўреси

KAZ: Рұм сүресі

TAJ: сураи Рум

TAT: Рум сүрәсе

UZB: Рум сураси

rutba رتبه ARABIC *Law n.* rank, position

BAS: рәтбә

KAR: рутбә

TAJ: рутба

TAT: рөтбә

UZB: рутба

ruza روزه PERSIAN *Ritual n.* the fast during Ramadan; fasting; the month of Ramadan

BAS: ураҙа

KAR: ораза, руўза

KAZ: ораза

KYR: орозо

TAJ: рӯза

TAT: рузә, ураза

TUR: ораза

UYG: roza

UZB: рўза

ruz-i 'arafat روز عرفات PERSIAN *Hajj np.* the 9th of Zu'lhijja, the day when the pilgrims pass the Hill of 'Arafa ☞ ***'arafat***

KAR: Арапат күн

TAJ: рӯзи Арафат

TAT: гарәфә көне

UYG: äripä

UZB: Арофат куни

ruz-i jaza روز جزا PERSIAN *np.* Judgment Day

TAJ: рӯзи ҷазо

UZB: рўзи жазо, жазо куни

S

sa'at ساعة ARABIC *n.* hour (a term frequently used in the Qur'an for Judgment Day)

KAR: саат, сағат

TAJ: соат

UZB: соат

Saba سبا ARABIC *Qur'an pn.* the 34th sura of the Qur'an

KAR: Сабә суўреси

KAZ: Сәбә сүресі

TAJ: сураи Сабо

UYG: sürä Säbä'

UZB: Сабаъ сураси

sabab ☞ ***qatl sabab***

sabi' صابئ *n.* one who worships the stars

KAR: сәбр

KAZ: саби

TAT: сабиэ, сабидар

sab'i samavat سبع سموات ARABIC *np.* the Seven Heavens

TAT: сәбгы сәмәват

UZB: сабъаи самовот, етти само, етти жаннат

sabir صابر ARABIC *adj.* patient

BAS: сабыр

KAR: сәбр

KAZ: сабыр

TAJ: собир

TAT: сабир

TUR: сабыр

UYG: sabir

UZB: ссбир

sabr [1] صبر ARABIC *n.* patience (as an Islamic virtue)

KAR: сәбр

TAJ: сабр

TAT: сабыр

UZB: сабр

sabr [2] صبر ARABIC *Sufism n.* patience, endurance (a stage on the Sufi path)

KAR: сәбр

KYR: сабыр

TAT: сабыр

UZB: сабр

Sabur, al- الصبور ARABIC *pn.* name of God: the Patient

KAR: Сәбр

TAJ: Сабр

TUR: ас-Сабур

UYG: Sabur

UZB: Ас-Сабур

Sad ص ARABIC *Qur'an pn.* the 38th sura of the Qur'an

KAR: Сәд суўреси

KAZ: Сад сүресі

TAJ: сураи Сод

TAT: Сад

TUR: сураи Сат

UYG: Säd süräsi, sürä Sad

UZB: Сод сураси

sadaqa صدقه ARABIC *n.* offerings, alms, charity

BAS: саҙаҡа

KAR: садақа, сәдәқе, садаға ① *offerings, alms, charity* ② *sacrifice* ③ *funeral repast*

KAZ: садақа

KYR: садака, садага, сакаба

TAJ: садақа

TAT: садака, сәдака

TUR: садака

UYG: sädiqä

UZB: садақа

sadr [1] صدر ARABIC *n.* chief of a religious group; chief administrator of a vaqf

TAJ: садр
TAT: садыр
UYG: sadir
UZB: садр, садри аъзам

sadr [2] صدر ARABIC *Sufism n.* highest stage attained by a Sufi; ecstasy reached while performing dhikr

TAJ: садр
UZB: садр

saf صاف ARABIC *adj.* clean, pure

BAS: саф
KAR: сап
KAZ: саф
KYR: сап
TAJ: соф
TAT: саф
UYG: sap
UZB: соф

Safa صفا، الصفا ARABIC *Hajj pn.* a location near Mecca visited by pilgrims

KAR: Сапа
KAZ: Сапа, Сафа, ас-Сафа
TAJ: Сафа
TAT: Саффа, Саффа тауы, Сафа тауы
TUR: Сафа дагы
UYG: Säfa
UZB: Сафа, Сафо тоғи

safa'il سفائل ARABIC *Sufism n.* flute-like instrument traditionally played by itinerant dervishes

TAJ: сафойл
UYG: sapayi
UZB: сафойил

safaliyat سفليات ARABIC *n.* the realm of the earth, the earth and its contents

TAT: сәфәлият
UZB: сафолият

Safar صفر ARABIC *pn.* the second month of the Islamic lunar calendar

BAS: сәфәр
KAR: сапар, сәпәр
KAZ: сапар
KYR: сапар
TAJ: сафар
TAT: сәфәр
TUR: сапар
UYG: säpär, safar
UZB: сафар

safar dar vatan سفر در وطن PERSIAN *Sufism np.* internal journey (one of the eight principles of the Naqshbandi Sufi order)

TAT: сәфәр дәр ватан
UZB: сафар дар ватан

Saff صف ARABIC *Qur'an pn.* the 61st sura of the Qur'an

KAR: Сәп сүўреси, Саф сүўреси
KAZ: Саф сүресі
TAJ: сураи Саф
TAT: Саф сүрәсе
UYG: sürä Säp
UZB: Саф сураси

Saffat صفّت ARABIC *Qur'an pn.* the 37th sura of the Qur'an

KAR: Ўа-саппәт сүўреси
KAZ: Саффат сүресі
TAJ: сураи Соффот
TAT: Саффат сүрәсе
UYG: sürä Saffat
UZB: Ва-ссаффот сураси

safi'ullah صفى الله ARABIC *Qur'an pn.* God's good slave, Adam

TAJ: сафийилло
UZB: сафийуллоҳ

saghir صغير ARABIC *Law n.* orphan

KAR: сағир, жетим
TAJ: сағир
UZB: сағир

sahaba صحابه ARABIC *Historical n.* companion of the prophet Muhammad

BAS: сәхәбә
KAR: сахәба, саҳаба
KAZ: сахаба
KYR: сааба, сакаба
TAJ: саҳоба
TAT: сәхабә, сахабә
TUR: сахаба
UYG: sahabä
UZB: саҳоба

sahabi صحابى ARABIC *n.* companion of the Prophet Muhammad ☞ ***sahaba***

UZB: саҳобий

sahar سحر ARABIC *Ritual n.* the meal which is taken before the dawn of day during the Ramazan

BAS: сәхәр
TAJ: саҳар, таъоми саҳарӣ
TAT: сәхәр
UYG: sähär
UZB: саҳар

sahib-i karamat صاحب‌کرامت PERSIAN *Sufism np.* Sufi, Sufi master; one who performs miracles
TAJ: соҳиби кароmат
TAT: сахибе кәрамәт
UZB: каромат соҳиби

sahifa صحيفه ARABIC *n.* prophetic revelation, esp. received by the prophets Adam, Seth, Idris, and Abraham ☞ ***suhuf***
BAS: сәхифә
KAZ: сахипа
TAJ: саҳифа
TAT: сахифә, сәхифә
UYG: sähipä
UZB: саҳифа

sahih صحيح ARABIC *Hadith adj.* sound, correct, genuine (as a classification of hadith) ☞ ***'urf sahih***
BAS: сахих
KAZ: сахих
TAJ: саҳих
TAT: сәхих, сахих
UZB: саҳиҳ

sahir ساحر ARABIC *n.* sorcerer
BAS: сахир
KAZ: сиқыршы
TAJ: сахир
TAT: сахир
UYG: sehirji, sehirgär
UZB: саҳир

sahv سهو ARABIC *Ritual n.* negligence (in performing a prayer or other devotion)
KAZ: сәһу
TAJ: саҳв
TAT: сәһив, сәһү
TUR: сәхив, сәхув
UZB: саҳв

sa'i سعى ARABIC *Hajj n.* performing the circumambulation of the Ka'ba
BAS: сәғи
TAJ: саъӣ
TAT: сәгый
UZB: сай, саъй

sa'ir سعير ARABIC *n.* hellfire; Hell
TAJ: сойир
TAT: сәгыйр
UZB: сойир

sajda [1] سجده ARABIC *Ritual n.* prostration (in prayer)
BAS: сәждә
KAR: сәжде
KAZ: сәжда, сажде, сәжде
KYR: сажда, сежде, сейде, сажыда
TAJ: саҷда
TAT: сәждә
TUR: сежде
UYG: säjdä
UZB: сажда

Sajda [2] سجده ARABIC *Qur'an pn.* the 32nd sura of the Qur'an
KAR: Сәжде сүўреси
KAZ: Сәжде сүресі
TAJ: сураи Саҷда
TAT: Сәждә
TUR: сураи Сежде
UYG: sürä Säjdä
UZB: Сажда сураси

sajdagah سجده گاه PERSIAN *n.* place for praying
KAR: сәждегах
TAJ: саҷдагоҳ
UYG: säjdägoh
UZB: саждагоҳ

sajda-yi tilavat سجدهٔ تلاوت PERSIAN *Ritual np.* prayer, namaz
KAZ: тилауәт сәждесі
TAT: сәждәи тилавәт
TUR: сеждәи тилеват, сеждети тилеват
UZB: саждайи тиловат

sakhavat سخاوت ARABIC *n.* generosity, munificence, liberality (as an Islamic moral quality)
KAR: сахәват
KYR: сакабат
TAJ: саховат
TAT: сәхавәт
TUR: сахават
UZB: саховат

salaf سلف ARABIC *n.* ancestors, predecessors
KAR: салап
TAJ: салаф
TAT: сәләф

UZB: салаф

salaf-i salihin سلف صالحين PERSIAN *np.* sacred ancestors, the pious forefathers

TAJ: салафи солиҳин
TAT: сәләфе салихин
UZB: салафи солиҳин

salam سلام ARABIC *intj.* peace, hello; greeting ☞ ***al-salam 'alaykim,***

BAS: сәләм
KAR: сәлем, салам
KAZ: сәлем
KYR: салам
TAJ: салом
TAT: сәлам
UYG: salam, sälam
UZB: салом

Salam, al- السلام ARABIC *intj.* name of God: the Peace

BAS: Сәләм
KAR: Сәлем
KAZ: әс-Салам
TAJ: Салом
TAT: Сәлям
TUR: ал-Салам
UYG: Salam
UZB: Ас-Салом

salam 'alaykum سلام عليكم ARABIC peace be upon you; greeting

KAR: сәлем алейкум, ассалаўма әлейкум, салаўмәлейкум
TAJ: ассалому алайкум
UYG: salamu' äläykum
UZB: ассалому алайкум, саломалайкум

salat صلات ARABIC *Ritual n.* prayer, ritual prayer ☞ ***namaz***

BAS: һалат
KAR: намаз
KAZ: салат, ассалату
TAJ: салот, намоз
TAT: салат, саләт
TUR: салят
UYG: namaz
UZB: салот, намоз

salat al-'asr صلات العصر ARABIC *Ritual np.* the obligatory afternoon prayer

BAS: икенде намаҙы
KAR: намаздигер, намаздыгер
KAZ: екінті намазы, екінді намазы
KYR: дигер, намаздигер, намазгер
TAJ: намози дигар
TAT: икенде намазы
TUR: икинди намазы, намаз дийгер
UYG: digär, namaz digär
UZB: аср намози, намозгар

salat al-fajr صلات الفجر ARABIC *Ritual np.* the obligatory morning prayer ☞ ***salat al-subh***

BAS: иртәнге намаҙы
KAR: пәмдет намаз
KAZ: таң намазы, памдат намазы
KYR: багымдат, багымдат намаз
TAJ: намози субҳ, намози бомдод
TAT: иртәнге намаз, сабах намазы, сәхәр намазы
TUR: даң намазы, эртир намазы
UYG: bamdat, bamdat namizi, namaz bamdat
UZB: бомдод намози, бомдод

salat al-hajat صلات الحاجت ARABIC *Ritual np.* four or twelve rak'ats performed during the hajj

KAR: ҳаж намаз
TAJ: намози ҳаҷ
TAT: хаҗәт намазы
UZB: ҳаж намози

salat al-'idayn صلات العيدين ARABIC *Ritual np.* holiday prayers

BAS: гәйет намаҙы
KAR: ҳайт намаз
TAJ: намози ийд
UZB: байрам намози, ҳайит намози

salat al-'isha صلات العشا ARABIC *Ritual np.* the obligatory evening prayer

BAS: ястү намаҙы, йәсиғ намаҙы
KAR: хуптән намаз, қуптан
KAZ: жашыйық намазы, ясту намазы
KYR: куптан намазы
TAJ: намози хуфтон
TAT: ястү намазы, йәстү намазы, йәсигъ намазы
TUR: яссы намазы, намаз хуфтан
UYG: khuptän, namaz khuptän
UZB: хуфтон намози, хуфтон

salat al-ishraq صلات الاشراق ARABIC *Ritual np.* voluntary prayer, performed when the sun has well risen

BAS: ишраҡ
TAJ: намози ишроқ
TAT: ишракъ намазы
UZB: ишроқ намози

salat al-istikhara صلاة الاستخارة ARABIC *Ritual np.* prayers for success or guidance

BAS: истихара
TAJ: намози истиҳора
TAT: истихара намазы
UZB: истихор намози

salat al-istisqa صلاة الاستسقا ARABIC *Ritual np.* two rak'at of prayers performed in time of drought to bring rain

TAJ: намози истисқо
TAT: истиска намазы
UZB: истисқо намози

salat al-janaza صلاة الجنازه ARABIC *Ritual np.* prayers performed at a funeral

BAS: йыназа намаҙы
KAR: жыназа намаз
TAJ: намози ҷаноза
UZB: жаноза намози

salat al-jum'a صلاة الجمعه ARABIC *Ritual np.* the Friday prayer, consisting of two rak'ats after the daily noontime prayer

BAS: йома намаҙы
KAR: жума намаз
TAJ: намози ҷумаъ
UZB: жума намози, жумъа

salat al-khavf صلاة الخوف ARABIC *Ritual np.* prayers performed in time of danger, especially performed by troops in time of war

TAJ: намози хауф
TAT: хәүф намазы
UZB: хавф намози

salat al-khusuf صلاة الخسوف ARABIC *Ritual np.* two rak'ats performed at the time of an eclipse of the moon

TAJ: намози хусуф
TAT: хосуф намазы
UZB: хусуф намози

salat al-maghrib صلاة المغرب ARABIC *Ritual np.* the obligatory sunset prayer

BAS: аҡшам намаҙы, киске намаҙ
KAR: намазшам
KAZ: ақшам намазы
KYR: шам намаз, намазшам
TAJ: намози шом, намози мағриб
TAT: ахшам намазы
TUR: агшам намазы, намаз шам
UYG: sham, namaz sham
UZB: шом намози, мағриб намози

salat al-mariz صلاة المريض ARABIC *Ritual np.* prayers performed in times of illness

KAR: мариз намаз
TAJ: намози мариз
UZB: мариз намози

salat al-musafir صلاة المسافر ARABIC *Ritual n.* prayers performed by a traveler, consisting of two rak'at instead of the usual number during the meridian, afternoon and night prayers

KAR: мусәпир намаз
TAJ: намози мусофир
TAT: сәфәр намазы
UZB: мусофир намози

salat al-qusuf صلاة القصوف ARABIC *Ritual np.* two rak'ats prayers at the time of an eclipse of the sun

TAJ: намози кусуф
TAT: косуф намазы
UZB: қусуф намози

salat al-ragha'ib صلاة الرغايب ARABIC *Ritual np.* prayer candle night, the first Friday in the month of Rajab

TAJ: намози рағойиб
TAT: рәгаиб намазы
UZB: рағойиб намози, қандил намози, қандил кечаси қилинадиган намоз

salat al-safar صلاة السفر ARABIC *Ritual np.* travel prayer, an abbreviated prayer for travelers

BAS: сәфәр намаҙы
KAR: сапар намазы
KAZ: сапар намазы, жолаушының намазы
KYR: сапар намазы
TAJ: намози сафар
TAT: сәфәр намазы
UYG: säpär namizi
UZB: сафар намози

salat al-subh صلاة الصبح ARABIC *Ritual np.* the obligatory morning prayer ☞ ***salat al-fajr***

BAS: иртәнге намаҙ
KAR: пәмдет намаз
KAZ: таң намазы, памдат намазы
KYR: багымдат
TAJ: намози бомдод, намози субҳ
TAT: иртәнге намаз, сабах намазы
TUR: даң намазы, эртир намазы
UZB: бомдод намози, саҳар, субҳ намози

salat al-tahajjud صلات التهجّد ARABIC *Ritual np.* voluntary prayer, performed after midnight

TAJ: намози таҳаччуд
TAT: тәһәҗҗуд намазы
UZB: таҳажжуд намози

salat al-taravih صلات التراويح ARABIC *Ritual np.* twenty rak'at recited every evening during Ramadan, immediately after the fifth daily prayer ☞ ***taravih***

KAR: тәрәўих намаз
TAJ: намози тарових
TAT: тәравих намазы
UZB: тарових намози, тарових

salat al-tasbih صلات التسبيح ARABIC *Ritual np.* litanies spoken while counting on prayer beads

TAT: тәсбих намазы, саләт әт-тәсбих
TUR: тесбих

salat al-vitr صلات الوتر ARABIC *Ritual np.* a supplemental prayer performed after the obligatory night prayer

KAR: ўитр намаз
TAJ: намози витр
TUR: вүтир намазы, витир намазы
UZB: витир намози

salat al-zuha صلات الضحا ARABIC *Ritual np.* optional prayer performed in the forenoon

KAZ: зұха
TAJ: намози част
TAT: зоха намазы, доха намазы
UYG: zühä
UZB: зуҳо намози

salat al-zuhr صلات الظهر ARABIC *Ritual np.* the obligatory noon prayer

BAS: өйлә намаҙы
KAR: түс намз
KAZ: бесін намазы
KYR: бешим
TAJ: намози пешин, намози зуҳр
TAT: өйлә намазы
TUR: өйле намазы, пейшин намазы
UYG: peshin namaz, namaz peshin
UZB: пешин намози, зуҳр намози, пешин

salavat صلوات ARABIC *n.* prayers, praise (plural form of salat) ☞ ***salat***

BAS: салауат
KAR: салаўат
KAZ: салауат
KYR: салават, салабат ① *prayer* ② *mutual forgiveness of grievances*
TAJ: салавот
TAT: салават ① *prayers (in general)* ② *obligatory prayers*
TUR: салават
UYG: salawat
UZB: салавот, салават

salavat-i nafila صلوات نافله PERSIAN *Ritual np.* optional prayers (in addition to the five obligatory daily prayers)

BAS: нафел намаҙы
KAZ: нәпіл намазы
KYR: напил намаз
TAJ: саловати нофила
TAT: салаваты нафилә, нәфилә намазы
UZB: саловати нофила

salb صلب ARABIC *n.* crucifixion

KAR: салип
TAJ: салиб
TAT: салеб
UZB: салиб, салб

salib صليب ARABIC *n.* cross

TAJ: салиб
TAT: салиб
UZB: салиб

salibiya سلبيه ARABIC *Theology n.* distinguishing qualities, i.e., a category of qualities attributed to God

TAT: сәлибия
UZB: салибия

salibiyun صليبيون ARABIC *n.* Christians; Crusaders

TAJ: салибиун
TAT: салибиюн
UYG: ählisälip
UZB: салиблар

salih [1] صالح ARABIC *adj.* righteous, devout

BAS: салиҡ
KAR: сәлих
KAZ: салих
TAJ: солеҳ
TAT: салих
TUR: салых
UZB: солиҳ

Salih [2] صالح ARABIC *pn.* the prophet Salih

BAS: Салих
KAR: Сәлих

KAZ: Салих
TAJ: Солеҳ
TAT: Салих
TUR: Салых
UYG: Salih
UZB: Солиҳ, Самуд

salla سله ARABIC *n.* turban
BAS: сәллә
KAR: сәлле
KAZ: сәлде
KYR: селде
TAJ: салла
TAT: сәллә
UYG: sällä
UZB: салла

salla allahi 'alayhu va sallam صلّى الله عليه و سلّم ARABIC *intj.* May the blessings and the peace of Allah be upon him (Muhammad)
BAS: салла аллаһө ғалиһө вә сәлләм
KYR: Салейли галейхи вассалам
TAJ: Саллаллоҳу алайҳи васаллам
TAT: Салләллаһү галәйһи вәсәлләм
UZB: Саллаллоҳу алайҳи васаллам

Salsabil سلسبيل ARABIC *pn.* the name of a fountain in Paradise
BAS: Сәлсәбил
KAZ: Сәлсәбил
TAJ: Салсабил
TAT: Сәлсәбил
UYG: Sälsäbil
UZB: Салсабил

sama سما ARABIC *n.* heaven
BAS: сәма
KAR: аспан
TAJ: само
TAT: сәма
UZB: само

sama' [1] سماع ARABIC *Sufism n.* hearing of music (as a devotional practice leading to an emotional state of mind)
KAR: сема
KAZ: семағ, сама
TAJ: само
UYG: sama
UZB: само

sama' [2] سماع ARABIC *n.* process or certification of listening to a teacher's instruction
KAZ: сама
TAJ: само
UZB: само

Samad, al- الصمد ARABIC *pn.* name of God: the Eternal
BAS: Самат
KAR: Сәмат
TAJ: Самад
TAT: Самәд
TUR: ас-Самад
UZB: Ас-Самад

samavi سماوى ARABIC *adj.* heavenly ☞ ***din-i samavi***
BAS: сәмауи
KAR: аспаний
TAJ: самовӣ
TAT: сәмави
TUR: семави
UYG: sämawi, samawi
UZB: самовий

sami' سميع ARABIC *Theology n.* all-hearing (an established quality of God)
KAZ: сәмиғ
TAT: сәмигъ
UZB: самий

Sami', al- السميع ARABIC *pn.* name of God: the Hearer
KAR: Сәми
KAZ: Семіғ
TAJ: Самӣ
TAT: Сәмигъ
TUR: ас-Сами
UZB: Ас-Самий

Samud ثمود ARABIC *Historical pn.* a tribe, mentioned in the Qur'an, to which the prophet Salih was sent ☞ ***Salih***
KAR: Самут
KAZ: Сәмуд, Сәмут
TAJ: Самуд
TAT: Сәмуд, Сәмүт
TUR: Семут
UYG: Sämud
UZB: Самуд ① *a tribe, mentioned in the Qur'an, to which the prophet Salih was sent* ② *name of the prophet Salih*

sana [1] سنه ARABIC *n.* year
BAS: сәнә
KYR: сана
TAJ: сана
TAT: сәнә

TUR: сене
UZB: сана

sana [2] ثنا ARABIC *n.* praise for God or for a prophet
TAJ: сано
TAT: сәна
UYG: säna
UZB: сано, ҳамду сано

sanam صنم ARABIC *n.* idol, image
BAS: санам
KAR: сәнам
TAJ: санам
TAT: санәм
UYG: sänäm
UZB: санам

sana-yi hijriyya سنهء هجريّه PERSIAN *np.* hijri calendar (the Islamic calendar calculated from the time of the prophet Muhammad's flight from Mecca to Medina). ☞ ***hijra***
KAR: хижри жыл
TAJ: санаи ҳиҷрия
TAT: сәнәи һиҗрия
UZB: санайи ҳижрия

sana-yi miladiyya سنهء ميلاديّه PERSIAN *np.* the Christian calendar (calculated from the birth of Christ) ☞ ***miladiya***
KAR: милат жыл
TAJ: санаи милодия
TAT: сәнәи миладия
UZB: санайи милодия

sana-yi qamariyya سنهء قمريّه PERSIAN *np.* lunar year, lunar calendar
KAR: қамар жыл, қамария жыл
TAJ: санаи қамария
TAT: сәнәи камәрия
TUR: камары йыл
UZB: санаи қамария

sana-yi shamsiyya سنهء شمسيّه PERSIAN *np.* solar year, solar calendar
KAR: шамс жыл
TAJ: санаи шамсия
TAT: сәнәи шәмсия
UYG: shämsiya
UZB: санаи шамсия

saqafat ثقافت ARABIC *n.* culture, Islamic culture
UZB: сақофат ① *culture, Islamic culture* ② *teacher, master (among Hizb ut-Tahrir)*

Saqar سقر ARABIC *pn.* Hell, the Underworld
BAS: сәкар
TAJ: сақар
TAT: Сәкарь
UZB: сақар

Sara ساره ARABIC *pn.* Sarah, the wife of the prophet Abraham
KAR: Сара
TAJ: Сара
TAT: Сара
TUR: Сара
UYG: Sarä
UZB: Сара

sar-ab سر آب، سراب PERSIAN *np.* mirage, Fata Morgana
TAJ: сар об
TAT: сәраб
UYG: särap
UZB: сар об

Saratan سرطان ARABIC *pn.* Cancer, the 5th month of the Hidjri Solar year
BAS: Саратан
KAR: Саратән, Саратан
KAZ: Саратан
TAJ: Саратон
TAT: Саратан
UYG: Saratan, Sarätän, Säritan
UZB: Саратон

sarf صرف ARABIC *n.* morphology (as an Islamic science)
BAS: сарыф
TAJ: сарф
TAT: сарф, сарыф, гыйлмус сарф
UZB: сарф

sarraf صرّاف ARABIC *Law n.* money-changer, banker (e.g. one who conducts licit financial dealing, as opposed to a money-lender)
TAJ: саррофф
TAT: сарраф
UZB: саррофф

Satir, al- الساتر ARABIC *pn.* name of God: the Concealer
TAT: Сатир

Sattar, al- الستّار ARABIC *n.* name of God: the Concealer
KAR: Саттәр

TAJ: Саттор
TAT: Сəттар
TUR: Саттар,
UZB: Ал-Саттор

Sattar al-'uyub ستّار العيوب ARABIC *np.* name of God: the Veiler of Imperfections
TUR: Саттарул уюб

savab[1] ثواب compensation, reward
KAR: саўэп
TAJ: савоб
TAT: сəваб
UYG: sawap
UZB: савоб

savab[2] صواب ARABIC *n.* good deed, pious deed
BAS: һауап, сауап
KAR: саўэп, саўап
KAZ: сауап
KYR: ссоп, собоп
TAJ: савоб
TAT: сəваб
TUR: согап
UYG: sawap
UZB: савоб

savab[3] صواب ARABIC *n.* that which is correct, correct opinion
KAR: саўэп
KAZ: сауап
KYR: сооп, собоп
TAJ: савоб
TAT: саваб
UYG: säwäp *cause, reason, pretext*
UZB: савоб

savma'a صومعه ARABIC *n.* hermitage, cell; monastery (Christian)
TAJ: савмаъ
TAT: соумəга
UZB: савмаъа

Savr ثور ARABIC *pn.* Taurus, the third month of the Hidjri Solar year
BAS: Сəуер
KAR: Саўр, Сəўир
KAZ: Сəуiр
TAJ: Савр
TAT: Сəвер
UYG: Säwir, Sawir
UZB: Савр

sayyi'a سيئه ARABIC *n.* wicked act, pernicious act
☞ ***bid'at-i sayyi'a***
TAJ: саййийа
TAT: сəййиъəһ
UZB: саййийа, сайъи

sayyid سيّد ARABIC *n.* descendant of the prophet Muhammad ☞ ***khvaja, sharif***
BAS: сəйет
KAR: сайит, сейит
KAZ: сайид, сейiт
KYR: сейит
TAJ: сайид
TAT: сəед, сəйид
TUR: сейит ① *descendant of the prophet Muhammad* ② *one of the six Turkmen holy tribes*
UZB: сайид

sazayi سزايى ARABIC *Law n.* a type of public punishment for violation of the shari'a
KAR: сазəйи
UYG: sazayi
UZB: сазойи *a type of public punishment for violation of the shari'a involving having the legs bound and being publicly ridden on a horse*

Sha'ban شعبان ARABIC *n.* the eighth month of the Islamic lunar calendar
BAS: Шағбан
KAR: Шəбəн, Шəбан
KAZ: Шағбан
TAJ: Шаъбон
TAT: Шəгбан
TUR: Шагбан, Мерет
UYG: Shä'ban, Barat
UZB: Шаъбон

shab-i barat شب برات PERSIAN *Ritual np.* festival held on the fifteenth day of Sha'ban, at which time it is believed God records all of the good and bad deeds that mankind is to perform in the coming year
BAS: Бəрат, Бəрат кисəһе
KAR: Бəрəт
KAZ: Берат кешi
TAJ: Шаъби барот
TAT: Бəраəт кичəсе, Бəрат
TUR: Лəйлят ал-бараа
UYG: Bara'ät
UZB: Барот кечаси

shafa'at شفاعت ARABIC *n.* intercession, help; mediation

BAS: шәфәғәт
KAR: шапаат
KAZ: шафағат
TAJ: шафоат
TAT: шәфагәт
UYG: shapa'ät
UZB: шафоат

Shafi'i [1] شفعی ARABIC *n.* Imam Shafi'i, founder of Shafi'i school of jurisprudence
KAR: шәпи
TAJ: Шофӣ
TAT: Шафиг
UYG: Shäfi
UZB: Шофий

Shafi'i [2] شفعی ARABIC *Law n.* follower of the Shafi'i legal school
KAR: шәпи
KAZ: шафиит
TAJ: шофӣ
TAT: Шафигый
TUR: шафи
UZB: шофий

Shafi'iya شافعیه ARABIC *Law n.* one of the four major schools of Islamic jurisprudence, founded by Imam Shafi'i ☞ ***mazhab***
KAR: шәпилық
KAZ: шафии, шафиғалық мазхаб
TAJ: шофия
TAT: шафигый
TUR: шафи, шафыгы мезхеби
UZB: шофийлик

shagird شاگرد PERSIAN *n.* student in a madrasa
BAS: шәкерт
KAR: шәкирт
KAZ: шәкірт
KYR: шакирт, шекит, шекирт
TAJ: шогирд
TAT: шәкерт
TUR: шәгирт
UYG: shagirt
UZB: шогирд

shahadat [1] شهادت ARABIC *n.* witnessing, testimonial; Islamic profession of faith
BAS: шәһаҙәт
KAR: шаҳәдет
KYR: шаадат
TAJ: шаҳодат
TAT: шәһадәт, шаһәдәт
TUR: шахадат
UYG: shahadät, shahitliq
UZB: шаҳодат, шоҳидлик

shahadat [2] شهادت ARABIC *n.* martyrdom
KAR: шаҳәдет
TAJ: шаҳодат
TAT: шәһадәт, шаһәдәт
TUR: шахадат
UYG: shehitliq
UZB: шаҳодат, шаҳидлик

Shah-i mardan شاه مردان PERSIAN *pn.* King of the People (epithet of the Caliph 'Ali)
KAR: Шаймәрдән, Шаҳмардан
KAZ: Шаймерден
KYR: Шаймерден
TAJ: Шоҳмардон
TUR: Шаймердан
UZB: Шоҳимардон, Шоймардон

shahid [1] شاهد ARABIC *n.* witness
BAS: шаһит
KAR: шәхит, гүўа
KAZ: шахид
TAJ: шоҳид
TAT: шаһит
UYG: shahit
UZB: шоҳид

shahid [2] شهيد ARABIC *n.* martyr (for the faith)
BAS: шәһит
KAR: шейит, шахид
KAZ: шейт, шахид, шеһит
KYR: шейит
TAJ: шаҳид
TAT: шәһит
TUR: шехит
UYG: shehit
UZB: шаҳид, шайид

Shahid, al- الشاهد ARABIC *np.* name of God: the Witness
BAS: Шаһит
KAR: шәхит
TAJ: Шоҳид
TAT: Шаһит
TUR: аш-Шахид
UYG: Shehit
UZB: Аш-Шоҳид

shahr-i ramazan شهر رمضان PERSIAN *Ritual np.* the period of Ramadan, the month of Ramadan
- **KAR:** ярамазан *religious songs sung during Ramadan*
- **KAZ:** жарапазан, жарамазан *religious songs sung during Ramadan*
- **KYR:** жарамазан
- **TAJ:** шаҳри Рамазон
- **UZB:** шаҳри Рамазон

shahvat شهوت ARABIC *n.* lust, desire
- **BAS:** шәhүәт
- **TAT:** шәhвәт
- **TUR:** шәхвет
- **UYG:** shähwät
- **UZB:** шаҳват

shajara شجره ARABIC *n.* family tree, genealogy
- **BAS:** шәжәрә
- **KAR:** шәжире, шежәрә
- **KAZ:** шежіре
- **KYR:** санжыра, шежире, чажыра, чежире
- **TAJ:** шаҷара
- **TAT:** шәҗәрә
- **TUR:** шеҗере
- **UYG:** shäjirä
- **UZB:** шажара

shak شك PERSIAN *Ritual n.* eve of Ramadan
- **KAR:** шәк
- **KYR:** шак
- **TAJ:** рӯзи шак
- **UYG:** shäk, shäk küni
- **UZB:** шак куни, Арафа, шок оқшоми

shakk شكّ ARABIC *n.* doubt (i.e. in faith)
- **KAR:** шәк
- **TAJ:** шак
- **TAT:** шәк, шик
- **TUR:** шек
- **UYG:** shäk
- **UZB:** шак

shakkak شكّاك PERSIAN *n.* doubter, skeptic
- **KAR:** шәккәк
- **TAJ:** шаккок
- **UYG:** shäkkäk
- **UZB:** шаккок

shaklik TURKIC *Ritual n.* women's mourning ceremony on the eve of Ramazan
- **KAR:** шәклиқ
- **UZB:** шаклик

Shakur, al- الشكور ARABIC *pn.* name of God: the Grateful
- **BAS:** Шәкүр
- **KAR:** Шәкир
- **KAZ:** Шәкүр
- **TAJ:** Шокир
- **TAT:** Шәкүр
- **TUR:** аш-Шакур
- **UYG:** Shäkir
- **UZB:** Аш-Шокир

sham' شمع ARABIC *Ritual n.* candle
- **BAS:** шәм
- **KAR:** шәм, шам
- **TAJ:** шамъ, шамъчароғ
- **TAT:** шәмгъ
- **UYG:** sham
- **UZB:** шам

shama'il شمائل ARABIC *n.* moral character, traits; features
- **TAJ:** шамоил
- **TAT:** шәмаил ① *moral character, traits* ② *religious texts or illustrations placed on the edges of a document or wall*
- **UZB:** шамойил

shama'il-i sharifa شمائل شريفه PERSIAN *Ritual np.* moral qualities of the prophets
- **TAJ:** шамоили шариф
- **UZB:** шамойили шариф

sham'dan شمعدان PERSIAN *Ritual n.* candle holder (esp. used in women's religious ceremonies)
- **KAR:** шамадан
- **TAJ:** шамъдон
- **TAT:** шәмгыдан
- **UYG:** shamdan
- **UZB:** шамдон

Shams شمس ARABIC *Qur'an pn.* the 91st sura of the Qur'an
- **KAR:** Ўаш-шамс суўреси
- **KAZ:** Шәміс сүресі
- **TAJ:** сураи Шамс
- **TAT:** шәмес сүрәсе
- **UYG:** sürä Shäms
- **UZB:** Ваш-шамс сураси

shar' شرع ARABIC *Law n.* Islamic law, canonical law
- **BAS:** шәрғе
- **KAR:** шәр
- **TAJ:** шаръ

TAT: шәргъ
UZB: шаръ

sharab شراب ARABIC *Law n.* wine, alcoholic beverage
BAS: шарап
KAR: шарап, шарәп
TAJ: шароб
TAT: шәраб
UYG: sharap
UZB: шароб

shar'an شرعاً ARABIC *Law adv.* according to Islamic law
KAR: шәрән
TAJ: шаръан
TAT: шәрган
UYG: shär'iy
UZB: шаръан

shar'i شرعی ARABIC *Law adv.* legal, in accordance with Islamic law ☞ ***dalil shar'i***
BAS: шәрғи
KAR: шәрий
TAJ: шаръӣ
TUR: шергы
UYG: shär'iy
UZB: шаръий

shari'at شریعت ARABIC *Law n.* Islamic law, canonical law
BAS: шәриғәт
KAR: шәрият
KAZ: шариғат, шариға
KYR: шарыят, шараат
TAJ: шариат
TAT: шәригать
TUR: шеригат
UYG: shäriät
UZB: шариат

sharif شریف noble; title borne by descendants of the Prophet Muhammad
BAS: шариф ① *noble* ② *holy, sacred*
KAR: шәрип
KAZ: шариф
KYR: шарип, шарып
TAJ: шариф
TAT: шәриф
TUR: шерип
UYG: shärip
UZB: шариф

sharifa شریفه ARABIC *n.* distinguished woman, educated woman
KAR: шәрипа
TAJ: шарифа
UYG: shäripa
UZB: шарифа

sharik شریك ARABIC *n.* partner, holder of a joint position (e.g. with an imam, reciter of prayers etc.)
KAR: шерик
KAZ: шерік
KYR: шерик
TAJ: шарик
TAT: шәрик
TUR: шәрик
UYG: sherik
UZB: шарик

sharr شرّ ARABIC *n.* evil, wickedness
BAS: шәрр
KAZ: шарр
TAJ: шарр
TAT: шәр, шәрр
UZB: шарр

shavq شوق ARABIC *Sufism n.* longing (for God), passion, ecstasy (one of the stages of Sufi knowledge)
BAS: шәүеҡ
TAT: шәүк
UZB: шавқ

Shavval شوّال ARABIC *n.* the tenth month of the Islamic lunar calendar
BAS: Шәүүәл
KAR: Шәўәл, Шаўўал
KAZ: Шәуәл
TAJ: Шаввол
TAT: Шәүәл
TUR: Шаввал, Байрам
UYG: Shawwal
UZB: Шаввал

shaykh شیخ ARABIC *Sufism n.* Sufi master, ishan
BAS: шәйех
KAR: шейих, шәйих
KAZ: шайқы, шейх
KYR: шайык
TAJ: шайх
TAT: шәех
TUR: шых, шейх ① *Sufi master* ② *one of the six Turkmen holy tribes* ③ *title accorded to notable*

Sufis and Muslim saints
UYG: shäykh ① *Sufi master, ishan* ② *theologian, judge*
UZB: шайх ① *head of an Islamic religious order* ② *collector of alms at cemeteries and holy places*

shaykh al-islam[1] شيخ الاسلام ARABIC *n.* among Sunnis title of dignitary responsible for matters of canonical law (since the collapse of the Soviet Union, some figures have begun adopting this title)
KAR: шейихул-ислам, шәйихул ислам
KAZ: шейхы әл-ислам
KYR: шайых-ул-ислам, шайхул ислам
TAJ: шайхул ислом
TAT: шәйхелислам
UZB: шайхул ислом

shaykh al-islam[2] شيخ الاسلام ARABIC *n.* mufti (among Shi'ites)
KAR: шәйихул ислам
TAJ: шайхул ислом
TAT: шәйхелислам
UZB: шайхул ислом

Shaytan شيطان ARABIC *pn.* Satan, the Devil
BAS: шайтан
KAR: шайтан
KAZ: сайтан, шайтан
KYR: шайтан
TAJ: шайтон
TAT: шәйтан
TUR: шейтан
UYG: shäytan
UZB: шайтон

shaytan al-ʿayn شيطان العين ARABIC *n.* the evil eye
BAS: ләғин
TAJ: шайтонлайин
UZB: шайтонилаин, шайтони лаъин, шайтони лайин

shaytanat شيطنت ARABIC *n.* group of devils in one location, demonic activity
KAR: шайтанат
TAJ: шайтанат
TAT: шәйтанәт
UYG: shäytanat
UZB: шайтанат

shifa شفاء ARABIC *n.* healing, treating (esp. by means of Qur'an recitation)
BAS: шифа
KAR: шипа
KAZ: шипа
TAJ: шифо
TAT: шифа
UYG: shipä, shipa
UZB: шифо

shiʿi شيعى ARABIC *n.* Shi'ite, Shi'a
KAR: шиит
KAZ: шиит, шиашы, шейіт
KYR: шейит
TAJ: шиа, шеа
TAT: шигый
TUR: шайы, шехит
UYG: shiä
UZB: шиа

shirk شرك ARABIC *Theology n.* polytheism (lit. attributing partners to God)
KAR: ширик
KAZ: ширк, шерк
TAJ: ширк
TAT: ширек
TUR: ширк, мүшриклик
UZB: ширк

Shis شيث ARABIC *pn.* the prophet Seth
KAZ: Шис
TAT: Шис
TUR: Шейс
UZB: Шиш

Shuʿara شعرا ARABIC *Qur'an pn.* the 26th sura of Qur'an
KAR: Шуғара сүўреси
KAZ: Шұғара сүресі
TAJ: сураи Шуъаро
TAT: Шөгарә сүрәсе
UYG: sürä Shu'ära
UZB: Шуаро сураси

Shuʿayb شعيب ARABIC *pn.* the prophet Shu'ayb
KAR: Шуайип
KAZ: Шуайб, Шуғайб, Шұғайып
TAJ: Шуайб
TAT: Шогаип
TUR: Шугайп
UYG: Shu'äyb
UZB: Шуайб

shubha شبه ARABIC *Law n.* doubt (as a legal concept)
☞ ***qatl shubha ʿamd***
BAS: шөбһа
KAR: шубҳә

TAJ: шубҳа
TAT: шөбһә
TUR: шүбхе
UYG: shübhä
UZB: шубҳа

shuhrat شهرت ARABIC *n.* glory, fame
BAS: шөхрәт
TAJ: шӯҳрат
TAT: шөһрәт
UYG: shöhrät
UZB: шуҳрат

shukr شکر ARABIC *n.* thanks, gratitude
BAS: шөкөр
KAR: шүкир, шукур
KAZ: шүкір
TAJ: шукр
TAT: шөкер
UYG: shükür
UZB: шукр

shura [1] شورا ARABIC *n.* consultation, council; soviet
BAS: шура
KAR: шурә
TAJ: шӯро
TAT: шура
UZB: шўро

Shura [2] شورا ARABIC *Qur'an n.* the 42nd sura of the Qur'an
KAR: Шурә сүўреси
KAZ: Шұра сүресі
TAJ: сураи Шӯро
TAT: Шура сүрәсе
UYG: sürä Shura
UZB: Шўро сураси

shu'ur شعور ARABIC *n.* awareness, understanding, comprehension (e.g. of the meaning of the Qur'an)
TAJ: шуур
TAT: шөгур
UZB: шуур

shuzuz شذوذ ARABIC *Law n.* irregularity, peculiarity
UZB: шузуз

sibghat صبغة ARABIC *n.* teaching, sect
TAT: сыйбгать

sibghatullah صبغة الله ARABIC *n.* God's religion, the true faith
TAJ: сибгатилло
UZB: сибғатиллоҳ

sidaq [1] صداق ARABIC *Law n.* bride price, money given by a groom or his family to the bride's family
KAR: қалын, қалынлиқ
KAZ: қалың мал
TAT: сыйдак
TUR: галың
UZB: қалин

sidaq [2] صداق ARABIC *Law n.* dowry, money given by a bride to her husband
TAT: сыйдак

siddiq سدّيق ARABIC *adj.* truthful, who tells the truth (esp. an epithet of the Caliph Abu Bakr)
BAS: ситдик
TAJ: сиддиқ
TAT: сыйддикъ
UYG: siddiq
UZB: сиддиқ

Sidrat al-muntaha سدرة المنتهى ARABIC *pn.* the tree from which the prophet Muhammad saw God
TAJ: Сидратал мунтаҳа
TAT: Сидрәтелмөнтәһа
UZB: Сидратал мунтаҳа

sihirbaz سحرباز PERSIAN *n.* sorcerer
BAS: сыхырсы
KYR: сыйкырчы ① *sorcerer* ② *hypnotist*
TAJ: сеҳрбоз
TAT: сихырбаз, сихерче
UYG: sihrchi
UZB: сеҳрбоз

sihr سحر ARABIC *n.* sorcery, witchcraft, black magic
BAS: сихыр
KAR: сыйқыр
KAZ: сиқыр, сыхр, сықыршылық
KYR: сыйкыр, сээр, зыйкыр ① *sorcery, witchcraft* ② *hypnosis*
TAJ: сеҳр
TAT: сихыр, сихер
UYG: sehir, sihr, sihir, sehirgärlik
UZB: сеҳр

sihri سحرى ARABIC *adj.* magical, bewitching
BAS: сихри
KAR: сыйқырлы
TAJ: сеҳрий
TAT: сихри
UZB: сеҳрий

sijjil سجّيل ARABIC *Qur'an pn.* stones baked by the

flames of Hell, on which the names are written of those who will be tormented by them
BAS: сижжил
TAJ: сиччил
TAT: сиҗҗил
UZB: сижжил

silah سلاح ARABIC *n.* weapon
KAR: силәх
TAJ: силоҳ
TAT: силах
UZB: силоҳ

silsila[1] سلسله ARABIC *Sufism n.* Sufi chain of initiation
BAS: силсилә
KAR: силсилә
KAZ: силсила
TAJ: силсила
TAT: силсилә
UZB: силсила

silsila[2] سلسله ARABIC *n.* genealogy, chain of descent
BAS: силсилә
KAZ: силсила
TAJ: силсила
TAT: силсилә
UZB: силсила

silsilanama سلسله نامه PERSIAN *n.* family tree, genealogical treatise
TAJ: силсиланома
TAT: силсилә намә
UZB: силсиланома

Simurgh سیمرغ PERSIAN *pn.* in Persian mythology a wise bird that dwells on mount Qaf ☞ ***Qaf***
TAJ: симурғ
UYG: sumrugh
UZB: семурғ, семурғ қуши

sirat[1] سیرة ARABIC *n.* biography (especially of the prophet Muhammad)
BAS: сират
KAZ: сира
TAJ: сирот
TAT: сирәт, сирә, сирәтен-нәби
TUR: сира
UYG: sirat
UZB: сийрат, сира, сийрати Муҳаммад

Sirat[2] صراط ARABIC *pn.* name of the bridge that passes over Hell, over which he righteous will pass into Heaven and from which the damned will fall into Hell
BAS: Сират күпере
KAR: Сират
KAZ: Сират
KYR: Сырат көпүрөө
TAJ: Сирот, пули Сирот
TAT: Сыйрат, Сыйрат күпере, Сират күпере
TUR: Сырат, Сырат көпрүси
UYG: Sirat
UZB: Сирот, пули Сирот, Сирот кўприги

siyar al-nabi سیرالنبی ARABIC *np.* literary genre recounting the campaigns of the prophet Muhammad, biography of the prophet Muhammad
TAJ: сиёр ал набӣ
TAT: сияреннәби, сийәр эн-нәби
UZB: сиёрал наби

subha سبحه ARABIC *n.* prayer beads ☞ ***tasbih***
TAJ: субҳа, тасбеҳ
UYG: subhä, subha
UZB: субҳа

subhan سبحان ARABIC *n.* praise (to God)
BAS: собхан
KAR: субхән
KAZ: сұбхан, сүбхан
TAJ: субҳон
TAT: сөбхан
UZB: субҳон

subhanahu va ta'ala سبحانه و تعالی ARABIC *intj.* God be praised and exalted
KAR: субхәнәтала
TAJ: субҳоно атаалло
UYG: subhänä ta'ala
UZB: субҳоно ва таалло

subhanaka سبحانك ARABIC *Ritual n.* the name of a prayer beformed at the beginning of the namaz following the takbir
KAR: субхәнәка
KAZ: субханәкә
TAJ: субҳонака
TAT: сөбханәкә
UZB: субҳонока

subhanallah سبحان الله ARABIC *intj.* formula praising God and expressing surprise or fright
BAS: собхан алла
KAR: субхәналла
KYR: субханалла
TAJ: субҳоноллоҳ

TAT: сөбхан алла
TUR: субхан Алла
UYG: subhänalla
UZB: субҳоналлоҳ, субҳоналло

subutiya ثبوتيه ARABIC *Theology n.* qualities that can be illustrated and explained with clear proofs, established qualities, i.e., a category of qualities attributed to God
TAT: субутия
UZB: субут, субутия

sud سود PERSIAN *n.* usury, money lending ☞ ***riba***
KAR: судхүр
KYR: сүт
TAJ: судхӯри
TUR: сүйтхорлык
UYG: sutkhorluq, sütkhorluq
UZB: судхўрлик

sudkhur سودخوار PERSIAN *n.* moneylender
KAR: судхүр, сүтхор
KYR: сүткер, сүткөр, сүткор
TAJ: судхӯр
TUR: сүйтхор
UYG: sutkhor, sütkhor
UZB: судхўр

sudur صدور ARABIC *n.* issuing, emanating (as a philosophical term)
KAZ: судур
TAJ: судур
TAT: содур
UZB: судур

sufi [1] صوفى ARABIC *Sufism n.* Muslim mystic, Sufi, member of a Sufi order
BAS: суфый
KAR: супы, сопы, суўпы
KAZ: сопы
KYR: сопу ① *Muslim mystic, Sufi member if a Sufi order* ② *muezzin*
TAJ: сӯфӣ
TAT: суфи
TUR: сопы ① *Muslim mystic, Sufi, member of a Sufi order* ② *adept, initiate, apprentice to a mulla*
UYG: sopi
UZB: сўфи

sufi [2] صوفى ARABIC *n.* pious person, godly person
BAS: суфый
KAR: сопы
KAZ: сопы
KYR: сопу
TAJ: сӯфӣ
TAT: суфи
TUR: сопы
UYG: sopi ① *pious person, godly person* ② *mu'azzin*
UZB: сўфи

suftajah سفتجه ARABIC *Law n.* the delivery of property by way of loan, and not by way of trust, that is forbidden in the Sunni jurisprudence
TAJ: суфтаҷо
UZB: суфтажо

suhuf صحف ARABIC *n.* prophetic revelation, esp. received by the prophets Adam, Seth, Idris, and Abraham ☞ ***sahifa***
KAZ: сүхұф
TAJ: суҳуф, суҳаф
TAT: сохоф
UZB: сухуф

sui qasd سؤ قصد PERSIAN *Law n.* suicide (as a religious prohibition)
TAJ: суиқасд
UZB: суиқасд

sujud سجود ARABIC *Ritual n.* prostrations, prostrating oneself in prayer (pl. form of sajda) ☞ ***sajda***
KAR: сажда
KAZ: сүжұд
TAJ: саҷда
TAT: сәҗуд
TUR: сүҗүт
UYG: säjdä
UZB: сужуд

sukra سکره PERSIAN *Sufism n.* intoxication, drunkenness
UZB: сукра

sukut سکوت ARABIC *Ritual n.* silence (as part of the prayer ritual)
KAR: сукут
TAJ: сукут
TAT: сөкүт
UZB: сукут

Sulayman سليمان ARABIC *pn.* the prophet Solomon
BAS: Сөләймән, Сөләйман
KAR: Сүләйман
KAZ: Сүлейман, Сүлеймен патша
KYR: Сулайман
TAJ: Сулаймон
TAT: Сөләйман

TUR: Сулейман *the prophet Solomon and patron saint of carpetmakers*
UYG: Sulayman
UZB: Сулаймон

sulh صلح ARABIC *n.* reconciliation; truce
BAS: солох
KAR: сулих
TAJ: сулҳ
TAT: солых
UYG: sülih
UZB: сулҳ

sultan سلطان ARABIC *n.* ruler, sovereign
BAS: солтан
KAR: султэн
KAZ: сұлтан ① *ruler, sovereign* ② *son of a Chingisid khan*
KYR: султан, солтон
TAJ: султон
TAT: солтан
TUR: солтан
UYG: sultan
UZB: султон

suluk سلوك ARABIC *Sufism n.* the Sufi path to God, esp. its spiritual techniques and ethical norms ☞ ***khatm-i suluk***
BAS: сөлүк
TAJ: сулук
TAT: сөлүк
UZB: сулук ① *the path bringing the murid closer to God* ② *Sufi*

sunan سنن ARABIC *Hadith n.* category of hadiths attributed to the traditions of the prophet Muhammad
UZB: сунан, суннан

Sunbula ARABIC *pn.* Virgo, the 7th month of the Hidjri Solar year
BAS: Сөмбәлә, Сөнбәлә
KAR: сунбулә, сүнбиле
KAZ: Сүмбіле
TAJ: Сунбула
TAT: Сөнбелә
UYG: Sunbulä
UZB: Сунбула

sunna سنّه ARABIC *Law n.* practices and rules derived from the prophet Muhammad's own actions and words ☞ ***sunnat***
BAS: сөннәт
KAR: сунна, сүннет
KAZ: сүннәт, сунна
KYR: сөннөт, сүннөт, суннет, сүрнөт
TAJ: суннат
TAT: сөннәт, сөннә
TUR: сүнне, сүннет
UYG: sünnät
UZB: суннат

sunnat [1] ARABIC *Law n.* custom, tradition ☞ ***sunna***
BAS: сөннәт
KAR: сүннет
KAZ: сүннәт, сунна
KYR: сөннөт
TAJ: суннат
TAT: сөннәт
TUR: сүннет
UYG: sünnät
UZB: суннат

sunnat [2] ARABIC *Ritual n.* circumcision ☞ ***khatna***
BAS: сөннәт
KAR: сүннет
KAZ: сүндет
KYR: сүннөт, суннет, сүрнөт
TAJ: суннат
TAT: сөннәт
TUR: сүннет
UYG: sünnät
UZB: суннат

sunnat ghayr-i mu'akkada سنّت غيرى مؤكّده PERSIAN *Law np.* that which the Prophet did not do consistently do (as a category of sunna)
TAT: сөннәт гайре мөвәкдә
UZB: суннатул ғайрил муаққада

sunnat mu'akkada سنّه مؤكّده ARABIC *Law np.* that which he Prophet emphatically enjoined his followers (as a category of sunna)
TAT: сөннәт мөвәкдә
UZB: суннатул муаққада

sunni سنّى ARABIC *n.* the Sunni branch of Islam; a follower of the Sunni branch of Islam ☞ ***sunna***
BAS: сөнни
KAR: суннит, суннизм
KAZ: суннит
TAJ: суннӣ
TAT: сөнни
TUR: сунни, сүңңи
UYG: sünni, sünniy

UZB: сунний, сунни

sur صور ARABIC *n.* trumpet (which the Archangel Israfil will play to announce the arrival of Judgment Day)

KAZ: сұр
TAJ: сур
TAT: сур
UYG: sur
UZB: сур

sura سوره ARABIC *Qur'an n.* sura, chapter of the Qur'an

BAS: сүрә
KAR: сүўре, сүре
KAZ: сүре, сүре
KYR: сүрө, сөрөө
TAJ: сура
TAT: сүрә
TUR: сүре, суура, сүрәт
UYG: sürä
UZB: сура

surat صورت ARABIC *n.* image, depiction

BAS: һүрәт, сүрәт
KAZ: сурет
KYR: сүрөт
TAJ: сурат
TAT: сурәт
TUR: сурат
UYG: sürät
UZB: сурат, сиврат

surnay سورنای PERSIAN *n.* trumpet (which the Archangel Israfil will play to announce the arrival of Judgment Day) ☞ ***sur***

KYR: сурайыл
TAJ: сурной
TUR: сурнай
UZB: сурной

sutra ستره ARABIC *Ritual n.* veil, chador

TAT: сөтрә
UZB: сутра

T

Ta ha تا ها ARABIC *Qur'an pn.* the 20th sura of the Qur'an

KAR: Таха сүўреси
KAZ: Taha сүресі
TAJ: сураи Тоҳо
TAT: Таһә сүрәсе
UYG: sürä Taha
UZB: Тоҳа сураси

ta'abbud [1] تعبّد ARABIC *n.* piety, godliness

TAT: тәгаббед
UZB: тааббуд

ta'abbud [2] تعبّد ARABIC *Ritual n.* prayer directed exclusively toward God (rather than toward specific prophets or saints)

KAR: тәәббут
TAJ: тааббуд
UZB: тааббуд

ta'akhir تأخر ARABIC *Ritual n.* delay (e.g. in performing a prayer)

TAT: тәәхир
TUR: тәьәхир, тәъәхыр
UZB: таохир

ta'ala تعالى ARABIC *n.* the Most High (a praise formula to refer to God)

BAS: тәғәлә
KAR: тәала, тала
KAZ: тағала
KYR: Таала
TAJ: таоло
TAT: тәгалә
TUR: тагалла
UYG: Ta'ala
UZB: таоло

ta'am طعام ARABIC *n.* food (as a category of religious distinction)

BAS: тәғәм
KAR: тамақ
TAJ: таом
TAT: тәгам
UYG: taäm
UZB: таом

ta'assub تعصّب ARABIC *n.* extremism, fanaticism

BAS: тәғәссөб
TAJ: таассуб
TAT: тәгассыб
UYG: täässub, ta'ässup
UZB: таассуб

ta'at طاعت ARABIC *n.* obedience, submission (to God); worship, veneration, prayer

BAS: тағат
KAR: тәат
KAZ: тағат

KYR: таат
TAJ: тоат
TAT: тагать
TUR: тагат
UYG: ta'ät
UZB: тоат

ta'at-'ibadat طاعت عبادت ARABIC *Ritual n.* obedience and worship; continuous prayer
KAR: тәат-ибадат
KAZ: тағат-ғибадат
TAJ: тоат-ибодат
UYG: ta'ät-ibädät
UZB: тоат-ибодат

ta'avvuz تعوّذ ARABIC *Ritual n.* saying the phrase a'uzu billahi (God help me) ☞ ***a'uzu billah***
TAJ: таавиз
TAT: тәгаввез
UZB: таавиз

taba'-i tabi'in تبع تابعين PERSIAN *Historical np.* followers of the followers of the sahabas ☞ ***tabi'in***
BAS: тәбғи табиғин
TAJ: тобеъи табиин, табауттобеъин
TAT: тәбгы табигыйн
UZB: тобеъи табиин, табаъа тобиъин, табауттобеин

tabarak تبارك ARABIC *Qur'an n.* alternate name of the 67th sura of the Qur'an ☞ ***Mulk***
BAS: тәбәрәк сүрәhе
KAR: табәрак
TAJ: таборак
TAT: тәбарәк
UYG: täbaräk
UZB: таборак

tabarruk تبرّك ARABIC *n.* blessing
BAS: тәбәррек
KAR: теберик, тәберик *blessing, blessing from a saint*
KAZ: тәберік, тәбәрік
KYR: табарик *sacred, holy*
TAJ: табаррук *sacred*
TAT: тәбәррек
UZB: табаррук *sacred*

Tabbat تبّت ARABIC *Qur'an pn.* alternate name of the 111th sura of the Qur'an ☞ ***Masad***
KAR: Тәббәт
KAZ: Тәббет
UZB: Таббот

tabi' تابع ARABIC *n.* follower, student, disciple
BAS: табиғ
KAR: тәбе
TAJ: тобеъ
TAT: табигъ
UZB: тобеъ

tabi'at طبيعت ARABIC *n.* nature, the natural realm
BAS: тәбиғәт
KAR: тәбият,тәбийғат
KAZ: табиғат
KYR: табият, табийет, табыйгат
TAJ: табиат
TAT: табигыят
TUR: тебигат
UYG: täbiät
UZB: табиат

tabib طبيب ARABIC *n.* healer, doctor (esp. one who uses Islamic scripture in medicine)
BAS: табип, табиб
KAR: тәўип
KAZ: тәуіп
KYR: табип, табып, табыпчы
TAJ: табиб
TAT: табиб
TUR: тебиб
UZB: табиб

tabi'in تابعين ARABIC *Historical n.* followers, those who were closely associated with sahabas ☞ ***sahaba***
BAS: тәбиғин
KAR: табынун
TAJ: тобъеин
TAT: табигыйн
UZB: тобеъин, тобиъин

tabi'iyun طبيعيون ARABIC *Theology n.* materialists
KAR: табыун
TAJ: табиию н
UZB: табиию н

ta'bir تعبير ARABIC *n.* dream interpretation, prognostication
BAS: тәғбир
TAJ: таъбир
TAT: тәгъбир
UYG: ta'bir
UZB: таъбир

ta'birnama تعبيرنامه PERSIAN *n.* manual of dream

interpretation
BAS: тәғбирнамә
TAJ: таъбирнома
TAT: тәгъбирнамә
UYG: ta'birnama
UZB: таъабирнома

tablighat تبليغات ARABIC *n.* propagation of Islam, spreading of Islam, missionary work
KAR: тәблиғат
KYR: ташбыйкат
TAJ: таблиғот
TAT: тәблигат
UZB: таблиғот

tabrik تبريك ARABIC *n.* blessing, benediction
KAR: тәберик
TAT: тәбрик
UYG: täbrik
UZB: табрик

tabut تابوت ARABIC *n.* coffin, casket; bier
BAS: табут
KAR: табыт
KAZ: табыт
KYR: табыт
TAJ: тобут
TAT: табут
TUR: табыт
UYG: tabut
UZB: тобут

tadayyun [1] تديّن ARABIC *n.* religiosity, piety
TAJ: тадаюн
TAT: тәдәйен
UZB: тадаюн

tadayyun [2] تديّن ARABIC *n.* acceptance (of a religion)
TAJ: тадайин
TAT: тәдәйен
UZB: тадайин

tadfin تدفين ARABIC *Ritual n.* burial, funeral
TAJ: тадфин
TAT: тәдфин
UZB: тадфин

ta'dil تعديل ARABIC *Hadith n.* acceptance and confirmation of a hadith tradition by a scholar
TAT: тәгъдил
UZB: таъдил

ta'dil-i arkan تعديل اركان PERSIAN *Ritual np.* to perform a namaz perfectly without any mistakes
TAJ: таъдили аркон
UZB: таъдили аркон

tadlis تدليس ARABIC *Hadith n.* knowingly creating a false hadith
TAJ: тадлис
UZB: тадлис

tafrid تفريد ARABIC *Sufism n.* renunciation, asceticism (esp. among Sufis)
BAS: тәфрит
TAJ: тафрид
TAT: тәфрид
UZB: тафрид

tafsir تفسير ARABIC *n.* commentary (esp. on the Qur'an)
BAS: тәфсир
KAR: тәпсир, тапсир
KAZ: тәпсир, тәфсир тәпсір
KYR: тапсир
TAJ: тафсир
TAT: тәфсир
TUR: тефсир
UZB: тафсир

Taghabun تغابن ARABIC *Qur'an pn.* the 64th sura of the Qur'an
KAR: Тағәбун суўреси
KAZ: Тағабұн сүресі
TAJ: сураи Тағобун
UYG: sürä Täghabun
UZB: Тағобун сураси

tahajjud تهجّد ARABIC *Ritual n.* the night prayer, which is generally not considered obligatory and not counted among the five daily prayers
☞ ***salat al-tahajjud***
BAS: тәһәжжед
KAZ: тахажжұд
TAJ: таҳаччуд
TAT: тәһәҗҗид, тәһәҗҗүд, тәһәҗҗуд
TUR: техеҗҗуд намазы
UZB: таҳажжуд

tahammul تحمّل ARABIC *n.* tolerance, forbearance
TAJ: тахаммул
TAT: тәхәммел
UYG: tähämmul
UZB: таҳаммул

taharat طهارت ARABIC *Ritual n.* ablution, ritual of canonical purification; purity
BAS: тәһәрәт

KAR: тәҳарет, дәрет
KAZ: дәрет, дәрет алу
KYR: даарат
TAJ: таҳорат
TAT: таһарәт
TUR: тахара, тәрет, тәхәрет
UYG: tärät, täharät
UZB: таҳорат

taharatkhana طهارتخانه PERSIAN *Ritual n.* place for ablutions, washroom for ablutions
KAR: тәҳарәтхана, дәретхана
KAZ: дәретхана
KYR: дааратканa
TAJ: таҳоратхона
UYG: tärätkhana
UZB: таҳоратхона

tahir طاهر ARABIC *adj.* pure, immaculate; innocent, without sin
KAR: тәхир
TAJ: тоҳир
TAT: таһир
UZB: тоҳир

tahiyat تحيات ARABIC *Ritual n.* salutary prayer (performed while kneeling)
KAR: тәхия
TAJ: таҳия
TAT: тәһийәтүл-мәчет *prayer performed upon entering a mosque*
UZB: таҳя

tahiyat, at- التحيات ARABIC *Ritual n.* prayers performed while kneeling, greeting prayers
KAR: әттәхият
KAZ: әт-тәхият, тақият
TAJ: аттаҳият
TAT: әттәхият, әттәхийәт, әт-тәхият, тәхийәт
TUR: эттехиат
UZB: аттаҳият

tahlil تهليل ARABIC *Ritual n.* saying the phrase "there is no god but God"
☞ ***la ilaha illa allaha va muhammadun rasulullah***
BAS: тәһлил
KAR: тәхлил
TAJ: таҳлил
TAT: тәһлил ① *saying the phrase "there is no god but God"* ② *reciting the Qur'an over the deceased at a funeral*
UZB: таҳлил

tahmid تحميد ARABIC *Ritual n.* uttering the phrase "praise be to God" (al-hamdullilah)
☞ ***alhamdullilah***
TAJ: таҳмуд
TAT: тәхмид
UZB: таҳмид

tahqiqi iman تحقيقى ايمان ARABIC *Theology np.* certain faith, faith accepted on the basis of experience (e.g. faith held by a prophet) ☞ ***istidlali iman***
TAT: тәхкыйкый иман
UZB: таҳқиқи имон, таҳқиқи иймон

tahrif تحريف ARABIC *n.* corruption, distortion (e.g. of a sacred text)
KAR: тәхрип
TAJ: таҳриф
TAT: тәхриф
UZB: таҳриф

tahrim [1] تحريم ARABIC *Law n.* prohibition, ban
KAR: такрим
KAZ: тақрим, тахрим
TAJ: тахрим
TAT: тәхрим
UZB: тахрим

Tahrim [2] تحريم ARABIC *Qur'an n.* the 66th sura of the Qur'an
KAR: Такрим суўреси
KAZ: Тахрим сүресі
TAJ: сураи Таҳрим
TAT: Тәхрим сүрәсе
UYG: sürä Tährim
UZB: Тахрим сураси

tahrimi تحريمى ARABIC *Law adj.* prohibited, banned
KAR: такримий
TAJ: тахримӣ
TAT: тәхрими
UZB: тахримий

tahrir تحرير ARABIC *n.* liberating, liberation, freeing
BAS: тәхрир
KAR: тәхрир
TAJ: тахрир
TAT: тәхрир
UZB: таҳрир

ta'ib تائب ARABIC *Qur'an n.* one who repents
KAR: тәйиб
TAJ: тоиб
UZB: тойиб, тоиб, тавба қилувчи

ta'ifa طائفه ARABIC *n.* group of people; religious community

BAS: тэифə
KAR: тийпе
KAZ: тайпа, тайфа *clan*
KYR: тайпа
TAJ: тоифа
TAT: таифə
TUR: тайпа *tribe*
UZB: тоифа

tajalli تجلّى ARABIC *Sufism n.* manifestation of God to man

KAR: тəжалли
TAJ: таҷалли
TAT: тəҗəлли, тəҗəлла
UZB: тажалли

tajvid تجويد ARABIC *Qur'an n.* rules for the proper pronunciation in Qur'an recitation

BAS: тəжүит
KAZ: таджвид
TAJ: таҷвид
TAT: тəҗвид
UZB: тажвид

Takasur تكاثر ARABIC *Qur'an n.* the 102nd sura of Qur'an

KAR: Тəкəсур сүўреси
KAZ: Тəкəсүр сүресі
TAJ: сураи Такосур
UYG: sürä Täkasur
UZB: Такосур сураси

takbir تكبير ARABIC *Ritual n.* the affirmation "God is great" (allahu akbar) ☞ ***tashriq***

BAS: тəкбир
KAR: такбир
KAZ: такбир, тəкпір
KYR: депкир, текпир
TAJ: такбир
TAT: тəкбир
TUR: такбир, текбир, төвир, дога-төвир
UYG: täkbir
UZB: такбир

takbir al-tahrima تكبير التحريه ARABIC *Ritual n.* standing during prayer with the thumbs touching the lobules of the ears and the open hands on each side of the face

KAR: такбир
TAJ: такбир
TAT: тəкбир, тəкбир əйтү
TUR: текбир тахрыма
UZB: такбир, такбири тахрим

takfin تكفين ARABIC *Ritual n.* wrapping up a corpse in a shroud

KAR: такпин
TAJ: такфин
TAT: тəкфин
UZB: такфин

takfir تكفير ARABIC *n.* accusation of heresy or unbelief

TAJ: такфир
TAT: тəкфир
UZB: такфир

takhrij تخريج ARABIC *Hadith n.* determining the original narrator of a hadith

KAR: тəхриж
TAJ: тахриҷ
TAT: тəхриҗ
UZB: таҳриж

ta'kid تأكيد ARABIC *n.* confirmation

KAR: тəкит
TAJ: таъкид
TUR: такид
UZB: таъкид

takiya تكيه ARABIC *Sufism n.* Sufi lodge ☞ ***khanaqah***

KAR: тəкия
KAZ: тəкия
TAJ: такъя
TAT: тəкия
TUR: текке
UZB: такия

taklif تكليف ARABIC *Law n.* proposal, offer, proposition

BAS: тəклиф
KAR: тəклип
KAZ: тəклиф
TAJ: таклиф
TAT: тəклиф
UZB: таклиф

takrir تكرير ARABIC *Law n.* that part of the sunna that the prophet Muhammad saw, heard, and did not reject

UZB: такрир

takvin تكوين ARABIC *Theology n.* making to be,

creating (an established quality of God)
- **TAT:** тәквин
- **UZB:** тақвин

Takvir تكوير ARABIC *Qur'an pn.* the 81st sura of the Qur'an
- **KAR:** Такўир суўреси
- **KAZ:** Текуир сүресі
- **TAJ:** сураи Таквир
- **UYG:** sürä Täkwir
- **UZB:** Таквир сураси

takya تكيه ARABIC *n.* place of repose (in Central Asia, these places are often simply marked by a few stones and a flag, but are held to be sacred)
- **KAR:** тәкия
- **TAJ:** такия, такя
- **UZB:** такия, такя

talaq[1] طلاق ARABIC *Law n.* divorce (from a wife)
- **BAS:** талаҡ
- **KAR:** талақ, таләқ
- **KAZ:** талақ
- **KYR:** талак
- **TAJ:** талоқ
- **TAT:** талак
- **TUR:** талак
- **UYG:** talaq
- **UZB:** талоқ

Talaq[2] طلاق ARABIC *Qur'an n.* the 65th sura of the Qur'an
- **KAR:** Таләқ суўреси
- **KAZ:** Талақ сүресі
- **TAJ:** сураи Талоқ
- **TAT:** Талак сүрәсе
- **UYG:** sürä Tälaq
- **UZB:** Талоқ сураси

talaq khat طلاق خط PERSIAN *Law np.* divorce decree (from a husband)
- **BAS:** талаҡ хаты, талаҡ ҡағыҙы
- **KAR:** таләқхат
- **KAZ:** талақ хат
- **KYR:** талак кат
- **TAJ:** талоқхат
- **UYG:** talaq khät, talaqkhät
- **UZB:** талоқ хати

talaqnama طلاقنامه PERSIAN *Law n.* divorce decree (from a husband)
- **KAR:** таләқнәме
- **TAJ:** талоқхат
- **UZB:** талоқнома

tali' طالع ARABIC *n.* fate
- **BAS:** талиғ
- **KAR:** тәле
- **TAJ:** толеъ
- **TAT:** талигъ *happy fate, good fortune*
- **UZB:** толе

talib طالب ARABIC *n.* student, madrasa student
- **BAS:** талип
- **KAR:** тәлип
- **KAZ:** талиб
- **TAJ:** толиб
- **TAT:** талиб
- **TUR:** талып
- **UYG:** talip
- **UZB:** толиб

ta'lim تعليم ARABIC *n.* teaching, instruction
- **BAS:** тәғлим
- **KAR:** тәлим
- **KAZ:** тәлім, тағлим
- **KYR:** таалым, таалим
- **TAJ:** таълим
- **TAT:** тәгълим
- **UYG:** tälim
- **UZB:** таълим

ta'limat تعليمات ARABIC *n.* teachings, instructions
☞ ***ta'lim***
- **BAS:** тәғлимәт
- **KAR:** тәлимат
- **TAJ:** таълимот
- **TAT:** тәгълимат
- **UZB:** таълимот

talqin[1] تلقين ARABIC *n.* explanation, interpretation
- **BAS:** тәлҡин
- **KAR:** тәлқин
- **TAJ:** талқин
- **TAT:** тәлкыйн
- **UYG:** tälqin
- **UZB:** талқин *preaching, religious speech*

talqin[2] تلقين ARABIC *Ritual n.* the reading of a prayer after the burial of a deceased person
- **BAS:** тәлҡин
- **KAR:** тәлқин
- **TAJ:** талқин
- **TAT:** тәлкыйн
- **UYG:** tälqin
- **UZB:** талқин

talqin [3] تلقين ARABIC *Sufism n.* teaching the litanies or the articles of faith to a novice (especially a novice to a Sufi order)
BAS: тәлкин
KAR: тәлқин
TAJ: талқин
TAT: тәлкыйн
UZB: талқин

talvasa تلواسه PERSIAN *n.* inner turmoil (as a state before death)
KAR: тәлӯәса
TAJ: талвоса
UZB: талваса, жон талвасаси

tamattuʻ تمتّع ARABIC *Hajj n.* the act of completing the 'umrah pilgrimage, and then performing the hajj as a separate ceremony
KAZ: тәмәттүғ
TAJ: таматтуъ
TAT: тәмәттег
UZB: таматтуъ

tamjid تمجيد ARABIC *Qur'an n.* the expression, "La haula wa la quwwata illa bi-llahi l-'aliyi l-'azim" (There is no power and strength but in God, the Lofty One, the Great)
TAJ: тамчид
TAT: тәмҗид *praise*
UZB: тамжид

Tamuq تاموق، تاموغ TURKIC *n.* Hell
BAS: Тамук
KAZ: Тамұқ
TAT: Тәмуг, Тәмугъ
UYG: Tamuq
UZB: Тамуқ

tanakuh تناكح ARABIC *Ritual n.* wedding, marrying
TAT: тәнакех
UZB: танакуҳ

tanassur تنصّر ARABIC *n.* baptism; conversion to Christianity
KAR: тәнассыр
KAZ: шоқыну
TAJ: танассир
TAT: тәнәссыр, чукыныру
TUR: чокундырмаклык
UZB: танассир

tanasukh تناسخ ARABIC *Theology n.* reincarnation, metempsychosis, the passing of a soul after death into a body of the same species
KAZ: танасух
TAJ: танассух
TAT: тәнасых
TUR: танасух
UZB: танасух

tanavvuʻ تنوّع ARABIC *Theology n.* dualism; light and darkness
TAJ: танаввӯъ
TAT: тәнәүвыг
UZB: танавия, танаввуъ

Tangri تنكرى TURKIC *n.* God
BAS: Тәңре
KAR: Тәнир, Тәнри
KAZ: Тәңір
KYR: Теңир
TAJ: Тангрӣ
TAT: Тәңре
TUR: Таңры
UYG: Tänri, Tängri
UZB: Тангри

tankih تنكيح ARABIC *Ritual n.* marrying, wedding
TAT: тәнких

tansir تنصير ARABIC *n.* baptism; converting to Christianity
TAT: тәнсыйр
UZB: тансур, тансир

tanzih [1] تنزيه ARABIC *Theology n.* declaring and believing God to be free from human qualities (i.e. rejecting anthropomorphism)
KAZ: танзих
TAJ: танзиҳ
TAT: тәнзиә
UZB: танзиҳ

tanzih [2] تنزيه ARABIC *n.* absolutory (as category of sunna)
TAJ: танзиҳ
TAT: тәнзиһ
UZB: танзиҳ

taqaddus تقدّس ARABIC *n.* holiness, sanctity
TAJ: тақаддис
TAT: тәкаддес
UZB: тақаддис, тақаддус

taqdir تقدير ARABIC *n.* fate, predestination
BAS: тәкдир
KAR: тәғдир

KAZ: тағдыр
KYR: тагдыр, такдыр
TAJ: тақдир
TAT: тәкъдир
TUR: такдыр
UYG: täqdir
UZB: тақдир

taqdir تقدير ARABIC *n.* decrees of God, fate
BAS: тәкдир
KAR: тәғдир
TAJ: тақдир
UZB: тақдир, қадар

taqdis [1] تقديس ARABIC *n.* canonization (of a Christian saint)
TAJ: тақдис
TAT: тәкъдис
UZB: тақдис

taqdis [2] تقديس ARABIC *n.* sacralizing, making sacred
TAJ: тақдис
TAT: тәкъдис
UZB: тақдис

taqi تقى ARABIC *adj.* pious, God-fearing; righteous
TAJ: тақий
TAT: тәкый
UZB: тақий

taqiya طقيه ARABIC *n.* small round skullcap
KAR: тақыя, тәқия
KAZ: тақия
KYR: такыя
TAJ: тақия
TAT: такыя
TUR: тахя
UZB: тақия

taqiyyat تقيّت ARABIC *n.* concealing one's religious convictions out of fear of persecution (esp. among Shi'ites)

taqlid [1] تقليد ARABIC *Theology n.* imitation; imitation of and implicit obedience toward previous or contemporary authorities in matters of dogma, ritual, and law (without one's own inquiry into source texts)
BAS: тәклид
KAR: тәқлит
KAZ: тақлид, тәқлид
TAJ: тақлид
TAT: тәкълид
UZB: тақлид

taqlid [2] تقليد ARABIC *Ritual n.* placing a wreath around the neck of an animal intended for sacrifice at Mecca
TAJ: тақлид
UZB: тақлид

taqsir تقصير ARABIC *n.* your grace, your honor (form of address to an authoritative religious figure)
BAS: тәксир
KAR: тақсыр
KAZ: тақсыр
KYR: таксыр
TAJ: тақсир
TAT: тәкъсыйр
TUR: тагсыр
UZB: тақсир

taqva تقوى ARABIC *n.* piety, godliness
BAS: тәкүә
KAR: тақўа, тәқўа, тақыўа
KAZ: тақуа ① *piety, godliness* ② *pious person*
KYR: такыба, такыбаа, таква ① *piety, godliness* ② *pious person*
TAJ: тақво
TAT: тәкъва
TUR: таква
UYG: täqwa
UZB: тақво *belief*

taqvadar تقوى دار PERSIAN *n.* pious person
KAR: тәқўәдәр
TAJ: тақводор
UYG: taqwadar
UZB: тақводор

taqvim تقويم ARABIC *n.* calendar; astronomical chart
KAZ: тақуім
TAJ: тақвим
TAT: тәкъвим
UZB: тақвим

taraka تركه ARABIC *Law n.* estate of a deceased person; division of an inheritance
TAJ: тарака
TUR: тереке
UZB: тарака

taravih تراويح ARABIC *Ritual n.* additional night prayer performed during Ramadan
☞ ***salat al-taravih***
BAS: тәрәүех, тәрүәх
KAR: тарәвих намаз
KAZ: тарауық, таравих

KYR: тараба, тарабих
TAJ: намози таровеҳ
TAT: тəравих
TUR: тарава намазы
UYG: tarawi
UZB: тарових намози, тарових

tarbiya تربيه ARABIC *n.* training, education
☞ ***husn-i tarbiya***
BAS: тəрбиə
KAR: тəрбия
KAZ: тəрбие
KYR: тарбия
TAJ: тарбия
TAT: тəрбия
TUR: тербие
UZB: тарбия

targhib ترغيب ARABIC *n.* exhorting, conducting Islamic missionary activity
TAJ: тарғиб
TAT: тəргыйб
UZB: тарғиб

targhibat ترغيبات ARABIC *n.* exhortations, Islamic missionary activity
KAR: тəрғибəт
TAJ: тарғибот
UZB: тарғибот

tarikh [1] تاريخ ARABIC *n.* history (as an Islamic field of study)
BAS: тарих
KAR: тарийх
KAZ: тарих
KYR: тарых, тарих
TAJ: таърих
TAT: тарих
TUR: тарых
UYG: tarikh
UZB: тарих *era chronology history*

tarikh [2] تاريخ ARABIC *n.* date (in a calendar)
KAR: тарийх
TAJ: тарих
TAT: тарих
UZB: тарих

Tariq طارق ARABIC *Qur'an n.* the 86th sura of the Qur'an
KAR: Тəриқ суўреси
KAZ: Тарық сүресі
TAJ: сураи Ториқ
TAT: Тарик сүрəсе
UYG: sürä Tariq
UZB: Ториқ сураси

tariqat [1] طريقت ARABIC *Sufism n.* Sufi order, religious order
BAS: тарик
KAR: тəриқəт, тəрийқа
KAZ: тариқа, тариқат
KYR: тарийка, тарыхат
TAJ: тариқат, тариқ
TAT: тарикать
TUR: тарыкат
UYG: täriqat
UZB: тариқат

tariqat [2] طريقت ARABIC *Sufism n.* the Sufi Path
BAS: тарик
KAR: тəриқə
KAZ: тариқа, тариқат
KYR: тарийка, тарыхат
TAJ: тариқат, тариқ
TAT: тарикать
TUR: тарыкат
UYG: täriqat
UZB: тариқат

tark-i dunya ترك دنيا PERSIAN *np.* asceticism, (lit, leaving the world)
KAR: тəркдунья
KAZ: тəркдуния
KYR: тарки дүйнө
TAJ: тарки дунё
TUR: теркидүнйəлик
UZB: тарки дунё

tarsa ترسا ARABIC *n.* Christian
KYR: тарса
TAJ: тарсо ① *Christian* ② *atheist*
TAT: тəрса
UZB: тарсо ① *Christian* ② *atheist*

tasadduq تصدّق ARABIC *Ritual n.* offering, sacrifice
KAR: тасаттық
KAZ: тасаттық ① *offering, sacrifice* ② *rain prayer*
TAJ: тасаддиқ
TAT: тəссадык
UZB: тасаддуқ, тасаддиқ

tasattur تستّر *n.* the process of covering up the parts of the body that Islamic law requires to be covered; veiling
TAT: тəсəттер

TUR: тесеттур
UZB: тасаттур

tasavvuf تصوّف ARABIC *Sufism n.* Sufism, Islamic mysticism
BAS: тэсауыф, суфыйлык
KAR: тасаўўуп
KAZ: тасаввуф
TAJ: тасаввуф
TAT: тэсаувыф, суфичылык ① *Sufism* ② *piety, godliness*
TUR: сопучылык
UYG: täsäwwup
UZB: тасаввуф

tasbih تسبيح ARABIC *Ritual n.* prayer beads ☞ ***salat al-tasbih***
BAS: тэсбих
KAR: тэсби
KAZ: тэсбих, тасбық
KYR: теспе, таспи
TAJ: тасбеҳ
TAT: тэсбих, дисбе ① *prayer beads* ② *saying "subhanullah"*
TUR: тесби
UYG: täswi
UZB: тасбеҳ, тасби

tashahhud تشهّد ARABIC *Ritual n.* profession of faith affirming the unity of God and the prophethood of Muhammad ☞ ***tahiyat, al-***
KAZ: тәшәhhуд
TAJ: ташахудд
TAT: тәшәhhөд
TUR: тешеххуд
UZB: ташаҳуд ① *profession of faith affirming the unity of God and the prophethood of Muhammad* ② *raising the first finger of the right hand in prayer*

tashayyu' تشيع ARABIC *n.* Shi'ism
TAT: тэшэйегъ

tashbih تشبيه ARABIC *Theology n.* allegory, analogy, comparison (esp. the anthropomorphic interpretation of God)
BAS: тэшбиһ
KAR: тэшбих
KAZ: ташбих
TAJ: ташбеҳ
TAT: тэшбиһ
UZB: ташбиҳ

tashir تسحير ARABIC *n.* sorcery, practicing sorcery
KAR: тэсир
KAZ: тесхир
TAJ: тасир
TAT: тэсхир
UZB: тасир

tashnab تشناب PERSIAN *Ritual n.* place were ablutions are performed ☞ ***taharatkhana***
TAJ: ташноб
UZB: ташноб

tashri' [1] تشريع ARABIC *Law n.* legislating, laying forth the law
TAJ: ташриғ
TAT: тэшригъ
UZB: ташриғ, ташри

tashri' [2] تشريع ARABIC *Law n.* conducting matters on the basis of Islamic law
TAJ: ташриғ
TAT: тэшригъ
UZB: ташриғ

tashriq تشريق ARABIC *Ritual n.* saying the phrase "Allahu akbar" following the service of worship during 'Id al-Azha; recognizing the unity of God
KAZ: тәшрық
TAJ: ташриқ
TAT: тэшрик, тэшрикъ, такбир тэшрыйк
UZB: ташриқ

taslim [1] تسليم ARABIC *n.* submission, obedience
BAS: тэслим
KAR: тэслим
KAZ: тэслім
KYR: таслим
TAJ: таслим
TAT: тэслим
UZB: таслим

taslim [2] تسليم *Ritual.* the benediction at the close of the usual form of prayer, "The peace and mercy of Allah be with you"
KAR: тэслим
TAJ: таслим
TAT: эттэслиму *the prayer performed at the conclusion of the azan*
UZB: таслим, ассалому алайкум ва раҳматуллоҳ

Tasnim تسنيم ARABIC *pn.* the name of a fountain in Paradise
KAZ: Тэсним

TAJ: Тасним
UYG: Täsnim
UZB: Тасним, жаннат шарораси

tasvib تثويب ARABIC *Ritual n.* voluntary prayer; reward
TAJ: тасвиб
UZB: тасвиб

tatavvu' تطوّع ARABIC *Ritual n.* act of voluntary devotion
TAJ: татавву
UZB: татавву

tatliq تطليق ARABIC *Law n.* divorce (of a wife by a husband)
TAT: татликъ

tavaf[1] طواف ARABIC *Hajj n.* circumambulation (performed seven times counter-clockwise around the Ka'ba)
BAS: тәуаф
KAR: таўап
KAZ: тауап, тәуап, тауап ету, тәуеп ету
KYR: тооп, тобоп
TAJ: тавоф
TAT: тәваф, тәуваф
TUR: таваф, тавах
UYG: tawap
UZB: тавоф

tavaf[2] طواف ARABIC *n.* circumambulation (performed seven times counter-clockwise around a Muslim shrine)
BAS: тәуаф
KAR: таўап, тәўап ① *circumambulation* ② *visiting holy places or sacred people*
KAZ: тауап, тәуап, тауап ету, тәуеп ету, тауаф
KYR: тооп, тобоп
TAJ: тавоф
TAT: тәваф
TUR: таваф
UYG: tawap
UZB: тавоф ① *circumambulation* ② *visiting holy places or sacred people*

tavaf-i nafila طواف نافله PERSIAN *Hajj np.* optional circumambulation of the Ka'ba, in addition to the three required circumambulations
TAJ: тавофи нофила
UZB: нофила тавоф

tavaf-i qudum طواف قدوم PERSIAN *Hajj np.* one of the required circumambulations of the Ka'ba performed by those who have come to Mecca from elsewhere
TAJ: тавофи кудум
UZB: тавофи кудум

tavaf-i sadr طواف صدر PERSIAN *Hajj np.* one of the required circumambulations of the Ka'ba performed after throwing stones at the Devil in Mina
TAJ: тавофи садр
UZB: тавофи садр

tavaf-i ziyarat طواف زيارت PERSIAN *Hajj np.* one of the required circumambulations of the Ka'ba performed by one who has returned from Arafat
TAJ: тавофи зиёрат
UZB: тавофи зиёрат

tavahhum توهّم ARABIC *n.* panic, fear (as a state attained before divine judgment); deception by false ideas
TAJ: таваххум
TAT: тәвәһһем
UZB: таваххум

tavajjuh توجّه ARABIC *n.* prayer; pleading
BAS: тәуәжжеһ
KAR: тәўәжжух
TAJ: таваҷҷӯх
TAT: тәвәжжеһ
UZB: таважуҳ

tavakkul[1] توكّل ARABIC *n.* hope, trust, confidence (in God)
BAS: тәүәккәл
KAR: тәўекел, тәўәккәл
KAZ: тәуеккел, таваккул, тәуәккүл
KYR: тобокел
TAJ: таваккал
TAT: тәвәккел
UYG: täwäkkül
UZB: таваккал

tavakkul[2] توكّل ARABIC *Sufism n.* trust in God, conviction that everything comes from God (a stage on the Sufi path)
UZB: таваккул

tavaqquf توقّف ARABIC *n.* patience, restraint
TAJ: тавақкуф
TAT: тәвәкъкыф
TUR: товаккуф
UZB: тавақкуф

tavarikh تواريخ ARABIC *n.* chronicles, histories (plural form of tarikh) ☞ ***tarikh***
BAS: тәуарих
KAR: тауәрих
TAJ: таворих
TAT: тәварих
UZB: таворих

tavarruq تورّق ARABIC *Ritual n.* kneeling position assumed by females during prayer
TAJ: таваррук
TAT: тәвәррүк
UZB: таваррук

tavazi' تواضع ARABIC *n.* reverence, modesty, humility
KAR: тауәзы
TAJ: табозӯъ
TAT: тәвазыг, тәвазыйг
UZB: тавозе

tavba [1] توبه ARABIC *n.* repentance; vow not to repeat an offense
BAS: тәүбә
KAR: тәубе, тәубә, тоба
KAZ: тәубе
KYR: тобо
TAJ: тавба
TAT: тәүбә
TUR: тоба
UZB: тавба

tavba [2] توبه ARABIC *Sufism n.* repentance, return to God (a stage on the Sufi path)
KAR: тәубе
KAZ: тәубә
UZB: тавба

Tavba [3] توبه ARABIC *Qur'an n.* the 9th sura of the Qur'an
KAR: Тәубе сүуреси
KAZ: Тәубе сүресі
TAJ: сураи Тавба
TAT: Тәүбә сүрәсе
UYG: sura Täwbä
UZB: Тавба сураси

tavba-tazarru توبه تضرّع ARABIC *np.* repentance and humiliation in order to obtain forgiveness
KAR: тәубе ету
TAJ: тавба-тазаррӯ
TAT: тәүбә-тәзәррыг
UZB: тавба-тазарру

tavfiq توفيق ARABIC *n.* accommodation to the will of God; good fortune
BAS: тәүфик
KAR: таупиқ
TAJ: тавфиқ
TAT: тәүфыйк
UZB: тавфиқ

tavhid [1] توحيد ARABIC *Theology n.* monotheism; the expression of monotheism
KAR: таухид
KAZ: таухид
TAJ: тавҳид
TAT: тәухид
TUR: еке-тәк
UZB: тавҳид

tavhid [2] توحيد ARABIC *n.* poetic work praising the qualities of the prophet Muhammad
TAT: тәухид
UZB: тавҳид

ta'viz [1] تعويذ ARABIC *n.* incantation, spell
TAJ: таъвиз
TAT: тәгъвиз
UZB: тавиз, таъвиз

ta'viz [2] تعويذ ARABIC *n.* amulet
TAJ: таъвиз
TAT: тәгъвиз
UZB: тавиз

tavq طوق ARABIC *Law n.* type of yoke placed around the neck of prisoners
KAR: тауқ
TAJ: тавқ, тавқи бандагӣ
TAT: таук
UZB: тавқ, тавқи лаънат

Tavrat تورات ARABIC *pn.* the Torah
BAS: Таурат, Тәүрат
KAR: Таурәт
KAZ: Таурат
KYR: Тоорат, ат-Таура
TAJ: Таврот
TAT: Тәурат, Тәурат
TUR: Төврат
UYG: Täwrat
UZB: Таврот

tavsif توصيف ARABIC *n.* description of qualities (e.g. of God)
BAS: тәүсиф

TAJ: тавсиф
TAT: тәусыйф
UZB: тавсиф

tavsim توسيم ARABIC *Hajj n.* the arrival of pilgrims in Mecca at the appointed time
TAJ: тавсим
TAT: тәвсим
UZB: тавсим

Tavvab, al- التواّب ARABIC *pn.* name of God: the Acceptor of Repentance
TAJ: Таввоб
TAT: Тәүваб
TUR: ат-Таввап
UZB: Ат-Таввоб

tayammum تيمم ARABIC *Ritual n.* performing ablutions with sand, earth, rags, cotton, etc. (in the absence of water)
BAS: тәйәммөм
KAZ: тәяммүм, тәям соғу
TAJ: таяммум
TAT: тәяммәм, тәйәммүм
TUR: тейим
UYG: täyämmum
UZB: таяммум

tayyiba[1] طيّبة ARABIC *n.* the profession of faith ☞ ***shahada***
TAJ: таййиба
UZB: таййиба, тойиба

tayyiba[2] طيّبة ARABIC *pn.* the fragrant (epithet for the city of Madina)
TAJ: таййиба
UZB: таййиба

tazahhud تزهّد ARABIC *n.* asceticism; piety, godliness
TAJ: тазахуд
TAT: тәзәhhед
UZB: тазаҳуд

tazavij تزوج ARABIC *Law n.* joining, marriage contract
BAS: тәзәүүеж
TAJ: тазвиҷ
TAT: тәзәүвеҗ
UZB: тазвиж

ta'zim تعظيم ARABIC *n.* reverence, respect
BAS: тәғзим
KAR: тағзым
KAZ: тағзым
KYR: таазим
TAJ: таъзим
UZB: таъзим

ta'zir تعزير ARABIC *Law n.* punishment (of a crime)
BAS: тәғзир
TAJ: таъзир
TAT: тәгъзир
UYG: täzir *one of the four types of punishment established in the shari'a*
UZB: таъзир

ta'ziya تعزيه ARABIC *Ritual n.* condolences, consolations, wake; mourning
BAS: тәғзиә
KYR: тазия, тажия
TAJ: таъзия
TAT: тәгъзия
UZB: таъзия

tazkirat al-avliya تذكرة الاوليه ARABIC *n.* biographical treatise on a Muslim saint, hagiography
KAZ: тазкират әл-әулие
TAT: тәзкирәтел-әүлия
UZB: тазкиратул авлиё

tazkiya تزكيه ARABIC *Taxation n.* paying of the zakat tax ☞ ***zakat***
TAJ: тазкия
TAT: тәзкия
UZB: тазкия

tibb طبّ ARABIC *n.* medicine (as a science)
TAJ: тибб
TAT: тыйбб
UZB: тиб

tijarat تجارت ARABIC *n.* trade, commerce (as an activity expressly enjoined by the prophet Muhammad)
BAS: тижарәт
TAJ: тиҷорат
TAT: тиҗарәт
UYG: tijarät
UZB: тижорат

tilavat تلاوت ARABIC *Qur'an n.* recitation, chanting (of the Qur'an)
TAJ: тиловат
TAT: тилавәт
TUR: тылавет, тилеват
UYG: tiläwat
UZB: тиловат

tilmiz تيلمذ ARABIC *n.* student, disciple
TAJ: тилмиз, тирмизак

TAT: тилмиз
UZB: тилмиз, шогирд

tilsim [1] طلسم ARABIC *n.* riddle, enigma
KAR: тилсим
KAZ: тылсым
KYR: тилсим
UZB: тилсим

tilsim [2] طلسم ARABIC *n.* witchcraft
KAR: тилсим ① *witchcraft* ② *amulet*
KAZ: тылсым
KYR: тилсим ① *witchcraft* ② *amulet*
UZB: тилсим

tilsim [3] طلسم ARABIC *n.* magic words, magic phrase
KAR: тилсим
KAZ: тылсым
KYR: тилсим
UZB: тилсим

Tin تين ARABIC *Qur'an n.* 95th sura of the Qur'an
KAR: Ўат-тийин суўреси
KAZ: Тин сүресі
TAJ: сураи Тин
UYG: sürä Tin
UZB: Ват-тийн сураси

Tuba طوبى ARABIC *pn.* the name of a tree in Paradise
TAJ: Туба
TAT: Туба
UZB: Туба

tufan طوفان ARABIC *n.* typhoon; the Deluge
BAS: туфан
TAJ: тӯфон
TAT: туфан
TUR: тупан
UZB: тўфон

tugh [1] طوغ، توغ TURKIC *n.* banner (traditionally carried in processions during Muharram)
UYG: tugh
UZB: туғ

tugh [2] طوغ، توغ TURKIC *n.* banner, standard (on which prayer flags are tied; often placed at shrines or used in healing rituals)
UYG: tugh
UZB: туғ

tumar طومار ARABIC *n.* triangle-shaped cloth amulet (usually prepared by a mulla and containing texts of prayers or Qur'anic verses) ☞ ***du'a***
BAS: бетеү
KAZ: тұмар, бойтұмар
KYR: тумар
TAJ: тумор
TUR: тумар
UYG: tumar
UZB: тумор

Tur طور ARABIC *Qur'an n.* the 52nd sura of the Qur'an
KAR: Ўат-Тур суўреси
KAZ: Тұр сүресі
TAJ: сураи Тур
UYG: sürä Tur
UZB: Ва-т-Тур сураси

turba تربه ARABIC *n.* tomb, grave, mausoleum
BAS: төрбә, торба, кәшәнә
KAZ: кесене
TAJ: турбат
TAT: төрбә
UZB: турбат, турба

U

udum ARABIC *n.* tradition
TAJ: удум
UZB: удум

Ughan اوغان TURKIC *pn.* God
BAS: Уған
UZB: Уғон

Ujmakh اوجماخ ARABIC *n.* Heaven, Paradise
BAS: Өзмах, ожмах
KAZ: Ұжмақ, Ұшпақ, Ұжмақ, Жұмақ
KYR: Учмак, Ужмак
TAJ: Очмах
TAT: Оҗмах
UZB: Ужмах

ukaz اوكاز، اوقاز RUSSIAN *Historical n.* license (during the imperial Russian period allowing an imam or mu'azzin to serve in a specific mosque) (restricted to the Volga-Ural region and Kazakhstan) ☞ ***manshur***
BAS: указ
TAT: указ

ukhravi اخروی ARABIC *adj.* pertaining to the Other World
BAS: охрауи
TAT: охрави

'ulama علما ARABIC *Law n.* scholars, especially legal

scholars (collective plural form of 'alim) ☞ *'alim*
BAS: ғөләмә
KAR: улама
KAZ: ғұлама
KYR: улама
TAJ: уламо
TAT: голяма
TUR: улама
UYG: ölima
UZB: уламо

'Umar عمر ARABIC *pn.* the second of the four righteous caliphs
BAS: Ғумер
KAR: Омар
KAZ: Омар
KYR: Омор
TAJ: Умар
TUR: Омар
UZB: Умар, ҳазрати Умар

umara امرا ARABIC *n.* commanders (plural form of amir) ☞ ***amir***
TAJ: умаро
TAT: өмәра
UZB: умаро

Umm al-kitab امّ الكتاب ARABIC *Historical np.* the Qur'an
TAT: Өммелкитаб

Umm al-mu'minin امّ المؤمنين ARABIC *n.* title given to each of the prophet Muhammad's wives (lit. mother of the faithful)
TAJ: Уммалмӯмин
TAT: Өммелмүъминин
UZB: Уммалмўмин, Уммалмўминин

ummat امّت ARABIC *n.* the followers of a given prophet; followers of the prophet Muhammad, the community of Muslims as a whole
☞ ***ijma'-i ummat***
BAS: өммәт
KAR: умбәт, әләўмет
KAZ: үмбет, әлеумет, умма, үммет
KYR: үмөт, үммөт
TAJ: уммат
TAT: өммәт
TUR: умма, ыммат
UZB: уммат

ummi امّى ARABIC *n.* a person, often a prophet, who is unable to read or write, but who possesses great knowledge
TAJ: умми
UZB: умми

umm-i valad امّ ولد PERSIAN *Law np.* slave mother to her owner's child
TUR: үмивелед

'umr عمر ARABIC *n.* life, existence
BAS: ғүмер
KAR: омр
KAZ: өмір, ғұмыр
KYR: өмүр
TAJ: умр
TAT: гомер
TUR: өмүр
UYG: ömür
UZB: умр

'umra عمره ARABIC *Ritual n.* optional pilgrimage to Mecca, performed at any time of the year
KAR: умрә
KAZ: умра, ғұмра
TAJ: умра
TAT: гөмрә, өмрә
TUR: умра
UZB: умра

uns انس ARABIC *Sufism n.* intimacy (a stage on the Sufi path)
UZB: унс

unsur عنصر ARABIC *n.* enemy, unbeliever
KAR: унсур
TAJ: унсур
UZB: унсур

'uqba عقبى ARABIC *n.* the afterlife
BAS: ғоҡба
KAR: әкибәт
TAJ: оқибат
TAT: гокба
UZB: оқибат

'uqubat [1] عقوبت ARABIC *n.* torture, punishment (in this life and in the afterlife)
KAR: өкибәт
TAJ: уқибат
TAT: гокубәт
UZB: уқибат

'uqubat [2] عقوبت ARABIC *Law n.* punishment inflicted at the discretion of the magistrate
KAR: өкибәт, азап, жәбирлеў

TAJ: укубат
UZB: укубат

'uqubat [3] عقوبات ARABIC *Law n.* punishments, one of the five branches of Islamic law governing punishments
TAT: гокубә
UZB: укибат

'urf عرف ARABIC *Law n.* custom (in contrast to Islamic law) ☞ ***'adat, rasm-rusum***
BAS: ғөрөф
KAR: урип, үрп
KAZ: ғұрып
KYR: үрп, урп
TAJ: урф
TAT: гореф
TUR: урп
UYG: urpi, örp, urp, urup ① *custom (in contrast to Islamic law)* ② *superstition*
UZB: урф

'urf fasid عرف فاسد ARABIC *Law np.* vicious custom (i.e. a custom that contravenes Islamic law)
TAT: гореф фәсид
UZB: урфи фосид

'urf sahih عرف صحیح ARABIC *Law np.* correct custom (i.e. a custom that does not contravene Islamic law)
TAT: гореф сахих
UZB: урфи саҳиҳ

'ushr عشر ARABIC *Taxation n.* tax paid by Muslims consisting of one tenth of agricultural produce or income
BAS: ғөшөр, кәтмән
KAR: ушр
KAZ: ушр, үшір
KYR: үшүр, ошур
TAJ: ушр
TAT: гошер
TUR: хүшүр, үшүр
UYG: öshrä
UZB: ашр

'Usman عثمان ARABIC *pn.* the third of the four righteous caliphs
BAS: Ғосман
KAR: Осман, Оспан
KAZ: Осман, Оспан
KYR: Осмон
TAJ: Усмон
TAT: Госман
TUR: Осман
UYG: Usman
UZB: Усмон

ustabika اوسته بیکه TURKIC *Historical n.* the wife of an imam (specific to the Volga-Ural region and Kazakhstan)
BAS: оҫтабикә
TAT: остабикә

ustad استاد ARABIC *n.* master, teacher ☞ ***ustaz***
BAS: остаҙ
KAR: устәз
KAZ: ұстаз
KYR: устат
TAJ: устод
TAT: остад, өстад
TUR: уссат
UZB: устод

ustaz استاذ ARABIC *n.* master, teacher ☞ ***ustad***
BAS: остаҙ
KAR: устәз, устаз
KAZ: ұстаз
KYR: устаз
TAJ: устоз
TAT: остаз, өстаз
TUR: уссат
UZB: устоз

usul [1] اصول ARABIC *n.* method, means
BAS: ысул
KAR: усыл
KAZ: усул
KYR: усул
TAJ: усул
TAT: осул
TUR: усул
UZB: усул

usul [2] اصول ARABIC *Law n.* roots, foundations (of Islamic law)
BAS: ысул
KAR: усыл
TAJ: усул
UZB: усул

usul-i jadid اصول جدید PERSIAN *Historical np.* jadidism (a brand of Islamic modernism current among a very small segment of the Muslim population in imperial Russia and in the early Soviet period)
BAS: ысулы йәдит, йәдитселек

KAR: усылжадит
KAZ: жәдитшілдік
KYR: усул жадит
TAJ: усули чадид
TAT: осуле җәдид, җәдидчелек
TUR: җәзитчилик
UYG: jäditlik
UZB: усули жадид, жадидчилик

usul-i khamsa اصول خمسه PERSIAN *Theology np.* the five precepts of the Islamic religion collectively (namaz, hajj, fasting, zakat, and the profession of faith), the five pillars of faith
TAJ: усули хамса
UZB: усули хамса

usul-i qadim اصول قديم PERSIAN *Historical np.* qadimism, (a term encompassing traditionalist opposition to jadidism) ☞ ***usul-i jadid***
BAS: ҡәҙимселек
KAR: қадимшилик
KAZ: қадімшілдік
KYR: усул кадим
TAJ: усули қадим
TAT: осуле кадим, кадимчелек
UZB: усули қадим, қадимчилик

'uzlat عزلت ARABIC *Sufism n.* retirement, religious life of retirement from the world
KAR: узләт
TAJ: узлат
TAT: гозләт
UZB: узлат

'uzr [1] عذر ARABIC *Ritual n.* reason, cause, pretext (e.g. that which exempts one from performing a religious obligation) ☞ ***ma'zur***
BAS: ғөҙөр
KAR: озр
KAZ: ғұзыр
TAJ: узр
TAT: гозер
TUR: узур
UZB: узр

'uzr [2] عذر ARABIC *Law n.* excuse, (legal term for claim or an objection)
KAR: өтиниў
TAJ: узр
UZB: узр

V

vabal وبال ARABIC *n.* harm, evil, sin (that will be punished in the next world
KYR: убал
TAJ: вабол
TAT: вәбал
UZB: вабол

va'da وعده ARABIC *n.* promise
BAS: вәғәҙә
KAR: ўәде, ўадә
KAZ: уәде
TAJ: ваъда
TAT: вәгъдә
UZB: ваъда

Vadud, al- الودود ARABIC *n.* name of God: the Loving
TAJ: Вудуд
TUR: ал-Вадуд
UZB: ал-Вадуд

vafa وفاء ARABIC *n.* pledge, promise
BAS: вафа
KAR: ўапа, ўапә
KAZ: опа
KYR: бапа, опаа *goodness, benefit*
TAJ: вафо
TAT: вафа
UYG: wapa *faithfulness, trustworthiness*
UZB: вафо *faithfulness*

vafat وفات ARABIC *n.* death
BAS: вафат
KAR: ўапәт
TAJ: вафот
TAT: вафат
TUR: вепат
UYG: wapat
UZB: вафот

vahdaniyat وحدانيت ARABIC *Theology n.* monotheism; oneness
KAZ: уахданиет
TAJ: ваҳдонияг
TAT: вәхданиятъ
TUR: еке-тәк
UZB: вахданият

vahdat-i vujud وحدت وجوب PERSIAN *Sufism np.* pantheism, conviction that God is in all beings, as well as in oneself

TAJ: вахдат

UZB: вахдади вужуд

Vahhab, al- الوهّاب ARABIC *n.* name of God: the Bestower

BAS: Вahап

KAR: Ўахап

TAJ: Ваҳоб

TAT: Вahап, Вahаб

TUR: ал-Ваххап

UZB: Ал-Ваҳҳоб

Vahhabiya وهّابيه ARABIC *Historical n.* Wahhabism, an ultra conservative Islamic movement from the Arabian peninsula that came into being in the 18th century and is the leading ideology in modern-day Saudi Arabia; it notorious for 1) the takfir of non-Wahhabi Muslims, 2) anti-Sufi polemics, and 3) the seclusion of women; named after Muhammad b. Wahhab (d. 1791). In Central Asia and Russia it is used broadly to refer to any Islamist or even pietist Islamic current

KAR: ўахапизим

KAZ: уаххабит, уаhhабшы

TAJ: ваҳобизм

TAT: вәhhабичылык, ваhhабилар, ваhhабизм

TUR: ваххабийлер

UZB: ваҳобийлик, ваҳобизм

vahi وحى ARABIC *n.* revelation, ideas divulged by God to a prophet

BAS: вәхи

KAZ: уахи

TAJ: вахий

TAT: вәхи

UYG: wähi

UZB: ваҳий, ваҳи

Vahid, al- الواحد ARABIC *n.* name of God: the Unique One

BAS: Вахит, Вәхид, Вәхит

KAR: Ўахит

TAJ: Воҳид

TAT: Вахид, Вәхид

UZB: Ал-Воҳид

vahshat وحشت ARABIC *n.* savagery, barbarity

BAS: вәхшәт

TAJ: ваҳшат

TAT: вәхшәт

UZB: ваҳшат

vahshiyana وحشيانه PERSIAN *n.* barbarous, savage

TAJ: ваҳшиёна

TAT: вахшиянә

UZB: ваҳшиёна

va'iz واعظ ARABIC *n.* preacher, one who admonishes

KAZ: уағыздаушы

TAJ: воиз

TAT: вагыйз

TUR: вагыз

UYG: wayiz, wa'iz

UZB: воиз

vajd وجد ARABIC *Sufism n.* ecstasy

TAJ: ваҷд

UZB: важд

vajh وجه ARABIC *n.* occasion, proof

BAS: вәжhе

KAR: ўаж

TAJ: ваҷ

TAT: вәҗhе

UYG: wäjh

UZB: важ

vajib واجب ARABIC *Law n.* incumbent religious precept, obligation (whether or not it is enjoined in the Qur'an or by any other Islamic source)

BAS: важиб, вәжип

KAR: ўәжип

KAZ: уажіп

KYR: важип, убажип

TAJ: воҷиб

TAT: ваҗиб, вәҗип

TUR: ваҗып

UYG: wajip

UZB: вожиб

vajib al-vujud واجب الوجود ARABIC *Theology np.* the Necessary Being (a formula affirming the necessary existence of God on the basis of the existence of His creation)

TAT: ваҗибәл вуҗуд

UZB: вожибал вужуд

Vajid, al- الواجد ARABIC *n.* name of God: the Finder

KAR: Ўажит

TAJ: Воҷид

TUR: ал-Ваҗыд

UZB: Ал-Вожид

vakalat وكالت ARABIC *n.* divine authorization (e.g. of a prophet)

BAS: вәкәләт
KAR: ўакәләт
TAJ: ваколат
TAT: вәкяләт
UZB: ваколат

vakil وكيل ARABIC *n.* representative, messenger
BAS: вәкил
KAR: ўәкил
KAZ: өкіл
KYR: өкил, өкүл
TAJ: вакил
TAT: вәкил
TUR: векил
UYG: wäkil
UZB: вакил

Vakil, al- الوكيل ARABIC *n.* name of God: the Trustee
BAS: Вәкил
KAZ: Өкіл
KYR: Өкил, Өкүл
TAJ: Вакил
TAT: Вәкил
TUR: ал-Векил
UZB: ал-Вакил

vali ولى ARABIC *Sufism n.* friend (of God), Muslim saint ☞ ***avliya***
BAS: вәли, изге
KAR: ўәлий
KAZ: уәли
TAJ: валӣ
TAT: вәли, изге
TUR: вели
UYG: wäli, äzgü
UZB: вали

vali ahd ولى عهد ARABIC *np.* crown prince, heir to the throne
TAJ: валиаҳд
TAT: вәли гаһед
UYG: wäli'ähd
UZB: валиаҳд

Vali, al- الولى ARABIC *n.* name of God: the Friend
BAS: Вәли
TAJ: Валӣ
TAT: Вәли
TUR: ал-Вали
UZB: ал-Валий

vali ni'mat ولى نعمت ARABIC *np.* benefactor, patron
TAJ: валинеъмат
TAT: вәли нигъмәт
UZB: валинеъмат

vallahu a'lam والله اعلم ARABIC *intj.* God knows
TAJ: валлоҳи аълам
TAT: валлаһе әгъләм
UZB: валлоҳи аъламҳ, валлоҳу аълам

vallahu a'lam bil-savab و الله اعلم بالصواب ARABIC *intj.* only God knows for certain, God knows better (than men)
TAJ: валлоҳи аълам
TAT: валлаһе әгъләм биссәваб
UZB: валлоҳи аълам, валлоҳи аълам билсавоб

vaqf وقف ARABIC *n.* pious foundation; property set aside for religious purposes
BAS: вағыф
KAR: ўақыф
KAZ: уақиф
KYR: вакуп, увакып, вакф
TAJ: вақф
TAT: вәкыф
TUR: вакф, вакыф
UYG: waqp
UZB: вақф

vaqfa وقفه ARABIC *Hajj n.* standing in place for approximately a minute at Arafat between the 9th of Zu'l-hijja and Qurban Bayram (as a requirement in performing the hajj)
TAJ: вақфа
UYG: wakhpä
UZB: вақфа

Vaqi'a واقعه ARABIC *Qur'an pn.* the 56th sura of the Qur'an
KAR: Ўақыя сүўреси
KAZ: Уақиға сүресі
TAJ: сураи Воқеъа
TAT: Вакыйга сүрәсе
UYG: sürä Waqi'ä
UZB: Воқеа сураси

vaqif [1] واقف ARABIC *adj.* informed; aware (esp. of religious knowledge acquired by the Prophet Muhammad)
BAS: вәкиф
TAJ: воқиф
TAT: вакыйф
UZB: воқиф

vaqif [2] واقف ARABIC *Law n.* person who wills property to a pious foundation

TAJ: воқиф
TAT: вакыйф
UZB: воқиф

vara'[1] ورع ARABIC *adj.* pious, godly
TAJ: вараъ
TAT: вәрәгъ
UZB: вараъ

vara'[2] ورع ARABIC *Sufism n.* piety, godliness; a state or precondition on the Sufi path
KAZ: уара
UZB: вараъ

varaqa ورقه ARABIC *n.* leaflet
TAJ: варақа
TAT: вәрәка
UYG: wäräqä
UZB: варақа

varasat وراثت ARABIC *Law n.* the right to inherit; inheritance
TAJ: варасат
TAT: вирасәт, вәрасәт
UZB: вараса

varis وارث ARABIC *Law n.* heir
BAS: вариҫ
TAJ: ворис
TAT: варис
TUR: варыс
UYG: waris, wärisa
UZB: вараса, ворис

Varis, al- الوارث ARABIC *pn.* name of God: the Inheritor
BAS: Варис
TAJ: Ворис
TAT: Варис
TUR: ал-Варис
UZB: Ал-Ворис

vasan وثن ARABIC *n.* idol; cross (Christian)
TAJ: васан
TAT: вәсән ① *cross (of Christians)* ② *idol, illicitly venerated object icon*
UZB: васан

vasani وثنى ARABIC *n.* idolater, pagan
TAJ: васанӣ
TAT: вәсәни
UZB: васаний

Vasi', al- الواسع ARABIC *pn.* name of God: the Englober
TAJ: Восӣ
TUR: ал-Васи
UZB: Ал-Воси

vasiqa وثيقه ARABIC *Law n.* title or deed to property
TAJ: васиқа
TAT: вәсика
UZB: васиқа

vasiyat وصيت ARABIC *Law n.* will, testament (oral or written)
BAS: васыят, васият
KAR: ўәсият
KAZ: өсиет
KYR: осуят
TAJ: васият
TAT: васыять
TUR: весъет, весиет
UYG: wäsiyat
UZB: васият

vasiyatnama وصيتنامه PERSIAN *Law n.* will, testament (written)
BAS: васыятнамә
KAZ: өсиет-нама
TAJ: васиятнома
TAT: васыятьнамә
UYG: wäsiyätnamä
UZB: васиятнома

vasl وصل ARABIC *Sufism n.* meeting, union (as a stage of the Sufi path)
BAS: васил
TAJ: восил, васл
TAT: васыл
UZB: восил, васл

vasvas وسواس ARABIC *n.* a person's fear at the point of death
TAJ: васвос
UZB: вос-вос

vasvasa وسوسه ARABIC *n.* temptation
BAS: вәсүәсә
KAZ: уәсуәсә
TAJ: васаваса
TAT: вәсвәсә
UYG: wäswäsä
UZB: васваса

vatan وطن ARABIC *n.* homeland, native land (in contrast to the umma)
BAS: ватан
KAR: ўатан
KAZ: отан

KYR: отан
TAJ: ватан
TAT: ватан
TUR: ватан
UYG: wätän
UZB: ватан

Vays al-Qarani ويس القرانى ARABIC *pn.* name of a companion of the prophet Muhammad
KYR: Ойсул Ата, Султан Вайис Гарани *companion of the prophet Muhammad and patron saint of camels*
TAJ: Увайс ал-Қаранӣ
TAT: Вәйселкарани
UZB: Увайс ал-Қараний

va'z وعظ ARABIC *n.* sermon, admonition, advice
BAS: вәғәз
KAR: ўәғз, ўаз
KAZ: уағыз
TAJ: ваъз
TAT: вәгазь
TUR: вагыз
UYG: wäz
UZB: ваз

vazifa وظيفه ARABIC *n.* duty, obligation
BAS: вазифа
TAJ: вазифа
TAT: вазыйфә
UZB: вазифа

vazir وزير ARABIC *n.* minister (esp. in an Islamic state)
BAS: вәзир
TAJ: вазир
TAT: вәзир
UZB: вазир

vijdan وجدان ARABIC *n.* conscience, responsibility
☞ ***wujdan***
BAS: выждан
KAZ: ұждан
KYR: уждан
TAJ: виҷдон
TAT: виждан, вөждан
TUR: выждан
UYG: wijdan
UZB: виждон

vildan ولدان ARABIC *n.* servants in Paradise
BAS: вилдан
TAJ: вилдан
TAT: вилдан
UZB: вилдон

viqar وقار ARABIC *n.* giant
TAJ: виқор
UZB: виқор
virasat ☞ ***varasat***

vird [1] ورد ARABIC *Ritual n.* short prayer, consisting of part of the Qur'an, performed at night
BAS: вирд
KAZ: уерд
TAJ: вирд
TAT: вирд
UZB: вирд

vird [2] ورد ARABIC *Sufism n.* type of daily prayer of litany specific to individual Sufi orders that consist of ayats, hadiths, or words of saints, or simply of repeated appeals to God
BAS: вирд
KAZ: уерд
TAJ: вирд
TAT: вирд
UZB: вирд

virsa ورثه ARABIC *Law n.* property that is inherited
TAJ: вирса
TAT: вирсә
UZB: вирса

vitr وتر ARABIC *Ritual n.* a supplemental prayer performed after the obligatory night prayer
☞ ***salat al-vitr***
KAZ: уітір
TAJ: витр
TAT: витер
TUR: вүтир, витир
UZB: витр

vujud وجود ARABIC *n.* existence, being
☞ ***vajib al-vujub***
BAS: вөжуд
KAR: вүжүт
KAZ: ұжуд
TAJ: вуҷуд
UYG: wujut
UZB: вужуд

vuquf وقوف ARABIC *Hajj n.* standing; the name of a ceremony during the pilgrimage to Mecca performed on Mount 'Arafat
TAJ: вуқу
TAT: вөкуф
TUR: вукуф

UZB: вуқуф

vuquf-i 'adadi وقوف عددی PERSIAN *Sufism np.* awareness of counting, (i.e. remaining aware of counting in dhikr)

TAT: вукуфи адәди

UZB: вуқуфи адади

vuquf-i qalbi وقوف قلبی PERSIAN *Sufism np.* awareness of God in one's heart

TAT: вукуфи кальби

UZB: вуқуфи қалбий

vuquf-i zaman وقوف زمان PERSIAN *Sufism np.* awareness of time (during the performance of dhikr)

TAT: вукуфи заман

UZB: вуқуфи замон

vuzu' وضوء ARABIC *n.* ablution, ritual of canonical purification

TAJ: вузу

TAT: вөзуэ

UZB: вузу

Y

ya allah يا الله ARABIC *intj.* Oh God!

BAS: йә аллам

KYR: жаа алда

TAJ: ё Оллоҳ!

UYG: ya Alla!

UZB: ё Аллоҳ!

ya pirim يا پيرم *intj.* Oh Pir, Oh God

KYR: жа пирим

TAJ: ё пирим

UYG: yä pirim

UZB: ёппирим, ё Пирим

ya rabbi يا ربّى ARABIC *intj.* Oh God

BAS: йә рабби, я рабби, ярабби, ярабым

TAJ: ё Рабби!

TAT: ярабби, йа рабби

UYG: ya räbbim

UZB: ё Рабб !, ё Раббим!

ya ramazan يا رمضان ARABIC *Ritual n.* songs sung in the evening during the month or Ramazan ☞ ***shahr-i ramazan***

KAR: жарамазан, ярамазан

KAZ: жарапазан, жарамазан

KYR: жарамазан

TAJ: ё Рамазон

TUR: ярамазан

UYG: yä Ramazan

UZB: ё Рамазон

Ya Sin يسين ARABIC *Qur'an pn.* the 36th sura of the Qur'an

BAS: Ясин

KAR: Ясин суўреси

KAZ: Ясін сүресі, Жасын, Йа син

KYR: Жаасын

TAJ: сураи Ёсин

TAT: Ясин, Йасин

TUR: Ясын

UYG: Yasin

UZB: Ёсин сураси

yad dasht ياد داشت PERSIAN *Sufism np.* concentration upon God (one of the eight principles of the Naqshbandi Sufi order)

TAJ: ёддошт

TAT: йад дәшт

UZB: ёддошт

yad kard ياد كرد PERSIAN *Sufism np.* remembrance of God by performing dhikr (one of the eight principles of the Naqshbandi Sufi order)

TAJ: ёд қард

TAT: йад кәрд

UZB: ёд кард

Yafis يافث ARABIC *pn.* Japhet, one of the sons of the prophet Noah, from whom the Turkic peoples are believed to be descended

KYR: Жапес, Жапас, Жафет, Жапет

TAT: Яфес

TUR: Яфет, Яфес

UZB: Яфас

yahu ياهو ARABIC *intj.* Oh God! ☞ ,

TAJ: Ёҳу

TAT: Яһу, Йаһу

UYG: Yahu

UZB: Ёҳу

yahud يهود ARABIC *n.* Jew

BAS: йәһүд

KAR: жөхит

KAZ: жақүт, яһуд

KYR: жөөт, жүүт

TAJ: яхуд

TAT: яһүд

TUR: яхуди

UYG: yähudi
UZB: яҳуд

yahudi يهودى ARABIC *adj.* Jewish
BAS: йәһүди
KAZ: яһуди, яһудилік
TAJ: яҳудӣ
TAT: яһүди
TUR: яхуди, ехуды
UYG: yähudi
UZB: яҳудий

Yahya يحى ARABIC *pn.* the prophet John the Baptist
BAS: Яхыя
KAZ: Жақия, Яхя
TAJ: Яҳё
TAT: Яхъя
TUR: Яхя
UYG: Yähya
UZB: Яҳё

Ya'juj va Ma'juj يأجوج و مأجوج ARABIC *pn.* the name of a barbarous tribe mentioned in the Qur'an that Zu'l-Qarnayn kept at bay by building a wall, but whose reappearance will signal the approach of the apocalypse
BAS: Йәьжүж-Мәьжүж, Йәьжүж вә Мәьжүж, ① *the name of a barbarous tribe mentioned in the Qur'an* ② *pagan, idolater (Ya'juj only)*
KAZ: Яжүж-Мажүж, Яжуж-Мажуж
KYR: Жажуш-мажуш
TAJ: Яъҷуҷу Маъҷуҷ
TAT: Яэҗүҗ вә Мәэҗүҗ
TUR: Әҗит-Мәҗит
UYG: Yäjäj-Mäjäj
UZB: Яъжуж-Маъжуж

Ya'qub يعقوب ARABIC *pn.* the prophet Jacob
BAS: Яҡуп
KAR: Жақып, Яқып
KAZ: Жақып, Яғқұп
KYR: Жакып
TAJ: Ёқуб
TAT: Якуп
TUR: Якуп
UYG: Yäqüb, Yä'qub
UZB: Ёқуб

yar يار PERSIAN *Sufism n.* friend, companion (esp. signifying God)
BAS: йәр
KAR: яр
KYR: жар
TAJ: ёр
TAT: яр
TUR: яр
UYG: yar
UZB: ёр

Yaratqan ياراتقان TURKIC *pn.* God, the Creator
KAR: Жаратқан, Яратқан
KAZ: Жаратушы
KYR: Жараткан
UZB: Яратган

yarhamukallah يرحمك الله ARABIC *intj.* pious phrase spoken after committing an inadvertence, esp. sneezing
TAJ: ярҳамукалло
TAT: йәрхәмүкә
TUR: ерхемукаллах
UZB: ярҳамукалло, ярҳамукаллоҳ

Yar-i Ghar يارغار PERSIAN *pn.* "Friend of the Cave" (epithet of the caliph Abu Bakr, who, together with the prophet Muhammad, hid in a cave from the inhabitants of Mecca
TAT: Яргар
UYG: Yari ghar

yarullah يارالله PERSIAN *n.* Friend of God, honorific typically preceding the name of a prophet
BAS: ярулла
TAJ: ёриаллоҳ
UZB: ёриоллоҳ, ёрулло

Yasu' يسوع ARABIC *pn.* the Prophet Jesus
TAT: Йасуг

yatim يتيم ARABIC *Law n.* orphan
BAS: йәтим
KAR: жетим
KAZ: жетім
KYR: жетим
TAJ: етим, ятим
TAT: ятим
TUR: етим
UYG: yitim
UZB: етим

Yazdan يزدان PERSIAN *pn.* God
TAJ: Яздон
TAT: Йәздан, Язьдан
UZB: Яздон

yighi ييغى TURKIC *Ritual n.* weeping ceremony

(during mourning)
TAJ: гиръя
UZB: йиғи

Yunus [1] يونس ARABIC *pn.* the prophet Jonah
KAR: Жүнис
KAZ: Жүніс, Юныс, Жунус
KYR: Жунус
TAJ: Юнус
TAT: Юныс
TUR: Юнус
UYG: Yunus
UZB: Юнус

Yunus [2] يونس ARABIC *Qur'an n.* the 10th sura of the Qur'an
KAR: Жүнис сүўреси
KAZ: Юныс сүресі
TAJ: сураи Юнус
TAT: Юныс сүрәсе
UYG: sürä Yunus
UZB: Юнус сураси

Yusha' يوشع ARABIC *pn.* the prophet Joshua
TAJ: Юшо
TUR: Юшаг
UZB: Юшо

Yusuf [1] يوسف ARABIC *pn.* the prophet Joseph
BAS: Йософ, Йосоп
KAR: Жүсип, Юсүп, Юсип
KAZ: Жүсіп, Юсып, Юсыф
KYR: Жусуп, Азирети Жусуп
TAJ: Юсуф
TAT: Йосыф
TUR: Юсуп
UYG: Yüsüf
UZB: Юсуф

Yusuf [2] يوسف ARABIC *Qur'an n.* the 12th sura of the Qur'an
KAR: Жүсип сүўреси
KAZ: Юсып сүресі
TAJ: сураи Юсуф
TAT: Йосыф сүрәсе
UYG: sürä Yüsüf
UZB: Юсуф сураси

Z

zabiha ذبيحه ARABIC *Ritual n.* sacrificial animal
TAJ: забиха
TAT: зәбихә
TUR: зебаих
UZB: забиҳа

zabt ضبط ARABIC *n.* conquering, capturing
TAJ: забт
TAT: забыт
UZB: забт

Zabur زبور ARABIC *pn.* the Psalms of the Prophet David
BAS: Зәбур
KAZ: Забур
KYR: Забур
TAJ: Забур
TAT: Зәбур
TUR: Зебур
UZB: Забур

zafar ظفر ARABIC *n.* victory, triumph
TAJ: заъфар
TAT: зафәр
UYG: zäpär
UZB: зафар

zahadat زهادت ARABIC *n.* asceticism, monasticism
TAJ: заҳадат
TAT: зәһадәт
UZB: заҳодат

zahid زاهد ARABIC *n.* hermit, ascetic; Sufi
KAZ: захид, заһид
TAJ: зоҳид
TAT: заһид
TUR: захид
UYG: zahit
UZB: зоҳид *ascetic*

zahir ظاهر ARABIC *adj.* exoteric (as a category of sciences)
BAS: заһир
KYR: зайыр
TAJ: зоҳир
TAT: заһир
UYG: zahir
UZB: зоҳир

za'if ضعيف ARABIC *Hadith adj.* weak (as a category of

hadith, where the tradition is of questionable authority)
TAT: зәгыйф
UZB: заиф, заъиф

za'ifa ضعيفه ARABIC *n.* woman, female believer
KAR: зайып *wife*
TAJ: заифа
TAT: зәгыйфә
UYG: zä'ipä
UZB: заифа

Zakariya زكريا ARABIC *pn.* the prophet Zachariah
KAZ: Зәкәрия
TAJ: Закариё
TAT: Зәкәрия
TUR: Зекеря
UYG: Zäkäriya
UZB: Закариё

zakat [1] زكات ARABIC *Taxation n.* obligatory tax incumbent upon all Muslims and equivalent to one-fortieth of a household's income
BAS: закат, зәкат
KAR: зәкәт, закат, зәкат
KAZ: зекет
KYR: зекет, закет, секет
TAJ: закот
TAT: зәкят
TUR: зекат
UYG: zäkat, zakat
UZB: закот

zakat [2] زكات ARABIC *Ritual n.* slaughtering an animal in a canonical manner
TUR: зекат

zakat al-fitr زكات الفطر ARABIC *Ritual np.* offerings given in honor of breaking the fast ☞ ***fitr***
KAR: рамазан пытыри
KAZ: оразаның бітірі
TAJ: закотал фитр, фитри закот
TUR: зекат ал-питре
UYG: pitir sadiqisi
UZB: закотал фитр, фитр закоти

zalalat ذلالت ARABIC *n.* straying from the Islamic path, erring
KAZ: залалат
TAJ: залолат
TAT: зәляләт, заләләт
UYG: zalalät
UZB: залолат

zalim ظالم ARABIC *n.* tyrant, oppressor
BAS: залим
KAR: залым
KAZ: залым, зәлім
KYR: залим
TAJ: золим
TAT: залим
TUR: залым
UYG: zalim
UZB: золим

Zamzam زمزم ARABIC *Hajj pn.* the sacred well located by the Ka'ba in Mecca ☞ ***ab-i zamzam***
BAS: зәмзәм
KAR: Зәмзәм
KAZ: Зәмзем, Зәмзәм
KYR: Абу Замзам, Замзам
TAJ: Замзам
TAT: Зәмзәм
TUR: Абу земзем, Зем-Зем, Земзем чешмеси
UYG: Zämzäm, Zämzäm quduqi
UZB: Замзам

zamzami زمزمى ARABIC *Hajj n.* water-carrier in Mecca
TAJ: замзамӣ
TAT: зәмзәми
UZB: замзамий

zanb ذنب ARABIC *n.* sin, transgression
TAJ: занб
TAT: зәнб
UZB: занб

zanni ☞ ***haram zanni***

Zaqqum زقّوم ARABIC *pn.* The Tree of Hell (The fruits of which sinners are compelled to eat)
BAS: Зәккум, Зәкым
KAZ: Заққұм
TAJ: Заққум
TAT: Зәкъкум, Заккум
UZB: Заққум

zar zaman زار زمان PERSIAN *np.* time of sorrow, era of lamentation
KAZ: зар заман
KYR: зар заман
TAJ: зарзамон
UYG: zarzamän
UZB: зарзамон

Zariyat ذريت ARABIC *Qur'an pn.* the 51st sura of the

Qur'an
KAR: Ўаз-зәрият суўреси
KAZ: Зәрят сүресі
TAJ: сираи Зориёт
UYG: sürä Zariyat
UZB: Ва-з-зориёт сураси

Zarr, al- الضارّ ARABIC *n.* name of God: the Distresser
KAR: Әд-Дар
TAJ: Ад-Дорр
TUR: ад-Дарр
UYG: Darr
UZB: Ад-Дорр

zarurat ضرورت ARABIC *n.* moral requirement, moral necessity
BAS: зарурат
KAR: зәрурият
TAJ: зарурият
TAT: зарурәт
UZB: зарурат, зарурият

Zat-i kibriya ذات کبریا PERSIAN *np.* name of God: the Great Being
UZB: Зоти кибриё

Zat-i pak ذات پاك PERSIAN *n.* name of God: the Pure Being
TAJ: Зотӣ пок
TAT: зате пакь
UZB: Зоти пок

zaval زوال ARABIC *n.* death
BAS: зәуал
KAR: зәўәл
TAJ: завол
TAT: зәвал
UZB: завол

zaviya زاويه ARABIC *n.* small mosque where daily prayers can be performed
KAZ: завия
TAJ: завия
TAT: завия ① *small mosque where daily prayers can be performed* ② *Sufi lodge*
TUR: завия
UZB: зовия, завия

zidd ضدّ ARABIC *adj.* contradictory, opposite, detestable; enemy
KAR: зыт
TAJ: зидд
TAT: зыйдд
UZB: зид

zifaf زفاف ARABIC *Ritual n.* wedding party
BAS: зифаф
TAJ: зуфаф
TAT: зөфаф, зифаф
UZB: зуфоф, зифоф

zikr ذکر ARABIC *Sufism n.* dhikr, Sufi prayer or litany during which the name of God or the shahada is constantly repeated until an emotional state is reached
BAS: зекер
KAR: зикир
KAZ: зікір
KYR: зикир
TAJ: зикр
TAT: зикер, зикр
TUR: зәкир, зыкыр
UYG: zikir
UZB: зикр

zikrchi ذکرچی TURKIC *Sufism n.* one who performs dhikr
KAR: зикирши, зикирбант
UZB: зикрчи

zikr-i jahr ذکر جهر PERSIAN *Sufism np.* the vocal dhikr (historically associated with the Yasaviya Sufi order)
TAJ: зикри чаҳр
TAT: зикре җәһри
TUR: җәхер, җәр
UZB: зикри жохр

zikr-i khafi ذکر خفی PERSIAN *Sufism np.* silent devotion, silent dhikr (typically performed in the Naqshbandi Sufi order)
KAR: зикри хупи
TAJ: зикри хуфӣ
TAT: зикре һафи, зикре хәфи
UYG: zikri khup
UZB: зикри хуфи

zikrkhana ذکرخانه PERSIAN *n.* place for performing dhikr
KAR: зикирхана
TAJ: зикрхона
UYG: zikirkhana
UZB: зикрхона

zillat ☞ *zalalat*

Zilzal زلزال ARABIC *Qur'an n.* 99th sura of the Qur'an
KAR: Зәлзәла суўреси

KAZ: Зілзал сүресі
TAJ: сураи Зилзол
TAT: зулзилə сүрəсе
UYG: sürä Zälzälä
UZB: Залзала сураси

zimmi ذمّی ARABIC *n.* non-Muslim residents of a Muslim state who are under special protection
KAZ: зимдер
TAJ: зиммӣ
TAT: зимми
TUR: зүмми
UZB: зимми

zina زنا ARABIC *Law n.* fornication
BAS: зина ① *fornication* ② *prostitution*
KAR: зина
KAZ: зина, зинақорлық
KYR: зына, зина
TAJ: зино
TAT: зина ① *fornication* ② *prostitution*
TUR: зына
UYG: zina
UZB: зино

zinakar زناکار PERSIAN *Law n.* fornicator
KAR: зинакор, зинахор
KAZ: зинақор
TAJ: зинокор
TAT: зинакяр ① *fornicator* ② *prostitute*
TUR: зынахор
UYG: zinakar
UZB: зинокор

zindan زندان PERSIAN *n.* prison, dungeon
BAS: зиндан
KAR: зиндан
KYR: зындан
TAJ: зиндон
TAT: зиндан
UYG: zindan
UZB: зиндон

zindiq زندیق ARABIC *n.* unbeliever, atheist, heretic
BAS: зиндиҡ
TAJ: зиндиқ
TAT: зиндикъ
UZB: зиндиқ

ziya' ضیاء ARABIC *n.* divine light ☞ ***nur***
BAS: зыя
TAJ: зиё
TAT: зыя
UYG: ziya
UZB: зиё

ziyarat زیارت ARABIC *n.* pilgrimage (e.g. to a holy place)
BAS: зыярат ① *pilgrimage* ② *cemetery*
KAR: зыярат
KAZ: зират, зиярат ① *pilgrimage* ② *cemetery*
KYR: зыярат, зиярат *pilgrimage to a shrine (but excluding the pilgrimage to Mecca)*
TAJ: зиёрат
TAT: зиярəт, зират ① *pilgrimage* ② *cemetery*
TUR: зыярат
UYG: ziyarät
UZB: зиёрат

ziyaratchi زیارتچی TURKIC *Ritual n.* pilgrim (esp. to a Muslim saint's tomb, rather than to Mecca)
KAR: зыяратшы
KAZ: зиратшы
KYR: зыяратчы
TUR: зыяратчы
UYG: ziyarätchi
UZB: зиёратчи

ziyaratgah زیارتگاه PERSIAN *n.* Muslim shrine; Muslim saint's tomb
TAJ: зиёратгоҳ
TAT: зиярəтгяһ
UYG: zaratka, ziyarätga
UZB: зиёратгоҳ

ziyaratkhana زیارتخانه PERSIAN *n.* Muslim shrine; Muslim saint's tomb
KAR: зыяратхана
TAJ: зиёратхона
UZB: зиёратхона

zubani زبانی ARABIC *n.* the fiends of Hell
BAS: зобаный
TAT: зобани

Zuha ضحی ARABIC *Qur'an n.* the 93rd sura of the Qur'an
KAR: Ўаз-зуха суўреси
KAZ: Зұха сүресі
TAJ: сураи Зуҳо
TAT: Зоха сүрəсе, Вəддухə сүрəсе, Дохə
UYG: sürä Zuha
UZB: Ваз-зуҳа сураси

zuhd [1] زهد ARABIC *n.* asceticism
KAZ: зухд
TAJ: зӯҳд

TAT: зөhд, зөhед, зөхед ① *asceticism* ② *piety, godliness*
TUR: зухт
UZB: зуҳд *abstinence*

zuhd [2] زهد ARABIC *Sufism n.* asceticism (as a stage on the Sufi path)
KAZ: зухд
TAT: зөhд, зөhед, зөхед
UYG: zühd
UZB: зуҳд

zuhr ظهر ARABIC *n.* the obligatory prayer noon prayer ☞ ***salat al-zuhr***
TAJ: зуҳр
TAT: зоhер
UZB: зуҳр

Zukhruf زخرف ARABIC *Qur'an n.* the 43rd sura of the Qur'an
KAR: Зухруф суўреси
KAZ: Зұхрұф сүресі
TAJ: сураи Зухруф
TAT: Зәхрәф сүрәсе
UYG: sürä Zukhruf
UZB: Зухруф сураси

Zu'l-fiqar ذوالفقار ARABIC *pn.* the name of the Caliph Ali's sword
BAS: Зөлфәкәр
KAR: Зулпықар
KAZ: Зұлпықар
KYR: Зулпукор
TAJ: зулфиқор
TAT: Зөлфөкар, Зөлфикар
TUR: Зүлпикәр
UYG: Zulpiqar
UZB: зулфиқор

Zu'l-hijja ذوالحجّه ARABIC *n.* the twelfth month of the Islamic lunar calendar
BAS: Зөлхизә
KAR: зүлхиже
KAZ: Зу-л-хиджжа, Зілхажжа
TAJ: Зулҳаччa, Зулҳиччa
TAT: Зөлхиҗҗә, Зилхиҗҗә
TUR: Зульхичҗе, Зүлхичҗе, Гурбан
UYG: Zulhijjä, Zulhäjjä
UZB: Зул-ҳижжа

Zu'l-ihsan ذو الاحسان ARABIC *n.* name of God: the Lord of Grace
TAJ: Зулиҳсон
UZB: Зулиҳсон

Zu'l-jalal va'l-ikram ذو الجلال و الاكرام ARABIC *n.* Possessor of Majesty and Generosity (epithet of God)
BAS: Зөлйәләл
KYR: Зулжалал
TAJ: Зилчалол
TAT: Зөлҗәлал
TUR: Зул җалал ва-л-Икрам
UYG: Zul-jalälu valikräm
UZB: Зул-Жалолу вал -Икром

zu'l-janahayn ذوالجناحين ARABIC *Sufism n.* possessor of two wings (a Sufi term denoting a student who has mastered both the esoteric and exoteric sciences, i.e. the two "wings" of knowledge)
TAJ: зулчанаҳайн
TAT: зөлҗәнахәен
UZB: зулжанаҳайн

Zu'l-Kifl ذو الكفل ARABIC *pn.* the prophet Zu'l-Kifl
KAZ: Зу-л-кифл, Зүлкәфил
TAJ: Зул Қуфл
UYG: Zulkifl
UZB: Зул Қифл

zulm ظلم ARABIC *n.* oppression, tyranny, despotism
BAS: золом
KAR: зулым
KAZ: зұлымдық, зұлым
KYR: зулум
TAJ: зулм
TAT: золым
TUR: зулум
UYG: zulm, zulum
UZB: зулм

zulmat [1] ظلمت ARABIC *n.* darkness; the pre-Islamic period
BAS: золмәт, зөлмәт
KAR: зулмат
TAJ: зулмат
TAT: золмәт, зольмәт
UYG: zulmät
UZB: зулмат

zulmat [2] ظلمت ARABIC *n.* the land of eternal darkness, where, according to Islamic legend, Iskander Zu'l-Qarnayn obtained the Water of Eternal Life
TAT: дияри золмәт
UYG: zulmät
UZB: зулмат

Zu'l-qa'da ذوالقعده ARABIC *n.* the eleventh month of the Islamic lunar calendar

BAS: Зөлкәғиҙә
KAR: зулқәдә
TAJ: Зулқаъда, Зилқаъда
TAT: Зөлкагдә, Зилкагдә
TUR: Зулькаъда, Зүлкаада
UYG: Zulqä'dä, Zulqä'idä
UZB: Зуул-қаъда

Zu'l-Qarnayn ذوالقرنين ARABIC *pn.* Possessor of the Two Horns (Quranic epithet of Alexander the Great)

BAS: Зөлкарнай, Зөлкәрнай
KAZ: Зұлқарнайын
KYR: Зулкарнайн
TAJ: Зулқарнайн
TAT: Зөлкарнәен
UYG: Zulqarnayn, Zulqärnäyn
UZB: Зулқарнайн

zulum ظلوم ARABIC *n.* tyrant, oppressor

KAZ: зұлым
KYR: зулум
TAJ: зулм
UYG: zulum
UZB: зулм, зулум

Zumar زمر ARABIC *Qur'an n.* the 39th sura of the Qur'an

KAR: Зумәр суўреси
KAZ: Зүмәр сүресі
TAJ: сураи Зумар
TAT: Зумр сүрәсе
UYG: sürä Zumär
UZB: Зумар сураси

zunnar زنّار ARABIC *n.* object worn outside of the clothing to identify the wearer as a non-Muslim

TAJ: зуннор
TAT: зөннар
UZB: зуннор